NAZI
TERROR

The Civilization of Crime: Violence in Town and Country Since
    the Middle Ages (1996)
Urbanization and Crime: Germany, 1871–1914 (1995)

NAZI TERROR

THE GESTAPO, JEWS, AND ORDINARY GERMANS

ERIC A. JOHNSON

JOHN MURRAY
Albemarle Street, London

First published by Basic Books in the United States of America in 1999

First published in Great Britain in 2000
by John Murray (Publishers) Ltd,
50 Albemarle Street, London W1X 4BD

A catalogue record for this book is available from the British Library

ISBN 0–7195–5581 7

Printed and bound in Great Britain by
The University Press, Cambridge

FOR MARY ORR JOHNSON

AND

OUR SONS BENJAMIN ERIC JOHNSON AND
JONATHAN ORR JOHNSON

CONTENTS

LIST OF TABLES

PREFACE

Researching and writing this book have consumed nearly a decade of my life. It has been a momentous time for me and my family. During this period my father died, my wife's father died, and both our children were born. It has also been a momentous time in German and European history. The Berlin Wall and Communist regimes in eastern Europe fell; Germany became a nation again; western and central Europe joined closer together in a monetary union; and racial hatred reappeared on the European continent and took the lives of thousands in the Balkans. Although I am happy to be back home once again in the United States, I feel fortunate that I have had the opportunity to spend much of the last decade living in Germany and elsewhere in Europe where I conducted almost all of the research and did much of the writing of this book.

I began working on it in the fall of 1989 when a Fulbright Fellowship brought me to the University of Cologne as a visiting professor to research what I then expected to be a moderate-sized book on the topic of "ordinary justice in Nazi Germany." Soon I discovered that there was very little that was "ordinary" about Nazi justice and that there was no way that I could complete the research on my subject within the year of my fellowship. Luckily I managed to persuade other fellowship-granting organizations—most notably the National Endowment for the Humanities, the National Science Foundation, and the Alexander von Humboldt Foundation—that they too should support my research on a topic and a book that had rapidly become much larger than I had originally planned. Hence one year of research in Germany mushroomed into six, and it was not until the summer of 1995 that my wife and I and our two young sons finally returned from Cologne to the United States, where I was to begin writing this book. As was the case with the research on my book, I greatly underestimated how long it would take for me to write it, and the year that I originally thought it would take became four.

Just before our family flew home, our colleagues and friends at the Central Archive for Empirical Social Research at the University of Cologne, which had hosted my project and provided me with an office, threw a going-away party for us. In addition to the usual well-wishing, eating, drinking, and reminiscing that take place at such affairs, I was asked to sit for an hour or so in "the hot-seat" at the front of a large seminar table. According to German custom, each of my friends and colleagues was then to be given the opportunity to ask one question that person had always wanted to ask, and I would be obliged to answer. Perhaps the most important question I was asked was to sum up in a nutshell what my experience in Germany over the last several years had meant to me. This was impossible to answer adequately at the time, and I still find it impossible to answer adequately now. My time in Germany had meant too much to me for any facile words. Still, I did give something of a response.

I began saying that I had benefited enormously both personally and professionally from my nearly six years in Cologne and would always treasure the time I had spent with German colleagues who became close friends over the years and who made both me and my family feel at home. I then explained that I was grateful to all of these people because they had been so gracious and kind to someone who was working on a subject that had caused intense pain and difficulty for their country and sometimes for them personally. After this I apologized for the difficulties and discomfort I may have caused them, for I knew that their phones had rung off the hook from angry callers during the surveys I had conducted, that I had burdened them with scores of embarrassing questions, and that I had probably made them squirm in their seats at times during formal lectures I had delivered and in the course of private conversations with them. Finally, I said that I could only hope that my German friends and colleagues could conduct research on one of my own country's most disturbing and traumatic historical problems and receive such decent treatment as I had received in their country.

Another question I have often been asked and will probably be asked in the future is why I would spend so much time and energy on such a depressing topic as Nazi terror, especially when I seem to be neither Jewish nor German. Occasionally I have bristled when answering this question, as I did when a young assistant editor at a respected publishing house in New

York, which is not the publisher of this book, asked me over the phone: "Why should anyone care about a book on Nazi terror written by someone named Eric Johnson who is obviously neither Jewish nor German?" Still, it is a fair question. My answer to her, though somewhat defensive in nature, is still the best answer I have.

When I spoke with her, I wondered how she could have determined simply from my name that I was neither Jewish nor German, and I asked her if this really mattered anyway. I then said to her that Nazi terror is a subject that touches all of humanity, and I insisted that what is important is not the identity of the author but the quality of the author's research, writing, and thinking. Nevertheless, I also told her that this topic has indeed touched me and my family personally. As I explained to her, even though she was probably correct in assuming that I am neither Jewish nor German, this still may not be a correct assumption. Although I was raised in a more or less average New England Protestant family, I found out a few years ago while reading through assorted letters and other material stuffed into an old family Bible that my father's mother had been brought up by a woman named Schnitzler who was her maternal grandmother. Therefore this may mean that I am in part either Jewish or German or both. But this has had little to do with my motivation for writing this book.

In some ways I have been plagued by this subject my entire life, and some of the earliest dreams I remember from my childhood in the 1950s involve my trying to escape from a Nazi prison or concentration camp. I do not know why I had these dreams. But I do know that my father was an American pilot of a P-38 fighter-bomber in the Second World War who was shot down in the fall of 1944 on his way back to his base in southern Italy from one of his missions. When his parachute landed he was quickly taken prisoner by the local militia and brought to a jail in a small town not far from the Austrian city of Salzburg. My father never told me much about what happened to him after that time, even though I asked him about it on several occasions. Sometimes what is left unsaid haunts someone more than what has been said. It is clear, however, that it was always a painful subject for him and for some unknown reason he felt a terrible sense of guilt about it. He did tell me, though, that he was strapped to a chair in the little jail in the small town in Austria and that he had feared for his life as various townspeople beat him and yelled at him, one of whom was an older woman who pounded him with a metal plate. Also he told me he hadn't blamed the woman because he suspected that she had probably lost a son or a husband in the war. After spending some period of time in that jail he was transported by train to Germany, possibly to Frankfurt, where he was interrogated rigorously for a period of days. Not long before he died he once indicated to me, though somewhat cryptically, that he may have divulged more than his name, rank, and serial number. Maybe this is why he had felt such guilt. After his interrogation he was sent to a prisoner-of-war camp called Stalag Luft I on the Baltic Sea between Rostock and Stralsund where he remained until he was liberated by the Russian army in May 1945. My mother has told me that when he returned home he was a changed man. I was born three years later.

I wish that my father were still alive. He would have enjoyed suggesting ways in which I could have improved the manuscript of this book, and we might have had the opportunity to talk finally and at length about his past. I would like to have had the chance to tell him that I have read the Gestapo case files of hundreds of people from all kinds of backgrounds and nearly all of them divulged a lot more than their name, occupation, and address.

Even though I cannot talk with my father any longer, I still want to thank him for guiding me in the path I have taken in my life. I hope with this book I have done justice to and cast some new light on some issues that were very important to him.

There are many more people and some institutions as well that I want to thank. At the top of my list are two women, Christiane Wever and Ana Perez Belmonte, who were my research assistants in Germany for several years and who have continued to help me in the years I have spent writing this book elsewhere. In many ways they have been my eyes and ears and, sometimes, brain. They helped bring my fledgling German to a competent level as we talked endlessly about Nazi terror and all manner of subjects. They helped me understand the Gestapo records. They helped me conduct interviews with perpetrators, victims, and bystanders. They increased my sensitivity a hundredfold. And they made it a joy to go to work day after day even though the work we were doing sometimes brought tears to our eyes.

This book could not have been written without the friendship and collaboration of Karl-Heinz Reuband, now a professor of sociology at the University of Düsseldorf. Karl-Heinz is perhaps the only person I know who has the courage, tenacity, and flexibility necessary to work closely and for years with a foreign scholar such as myself on such a sensitive topic as Nazi terror. Our collaboration has now lasted for eight years, and soon we will write a book together based on the thousands of surveys and hundreds of interviews we have conducted with elderly German citizens and Jewish Holocaust survivors spread out all over the world.

At the Central Archive for Empirical Social Research at the University of Cologne I also especially want to thank my former colleagues and co-workers—Erwin Scheuch, Ekkehard Mochmann, Willi Schröder, Maria Rohlinger, Ralph Ponemereo, Stefan Lampe, Franz Bauske, Rainer Metz, Rainer Hinterberg, and Willi Weege—my two other former research assistants—Christian Knopp and Michael Riesenkönig—and the secretary at the Center for Historical Social Research, Lilo Montez. Also my friend Helmut Thome, now a professor of sociology at the University of Halle-Wittenberg, and his wife, Lucia, receive my gratitude for sharing their warm hospitality and keen minds with us in the years we lived in Cologne.

There are several other German friends and colleagues I want to thank as well. Among these are our closest German friends for more than twenty years, Rolf and Asja Hamacher, as well as Margaret and Peter Schuster, and the entire Antoine family of Cologne.

A special word of gratitude also goes to the many German archivists in Cologne, Krefeld, Düsseldorf, and other cities who gave greatly of their time and shared their knowledge with me about my topic. In particular I would like to thank Peter Reuter, Thomas Becker, Annette Gebauer-Berlinghof, and Rainer Stahlschmidt who assisted me at the justice archive in Düsseldorf-Kaiserswerth; Peter Klefisch and Horst Romeyk at the Mauerstrasse archive in Düsseldorf; Dieter Hangebruch, Joachim Lilla, and Paul-Günter Schulte at the Krefeld Stadtarchiv; Werner Jung and Horst Matzerath at the NS-Dokumentationszentrum in Cologne; and Willi Dre-

sen at the Zentrale Stelle für Landesjustizverwaltungen in Ludwigsburg.

I have many people to thank in America and in other countries as well.
Mel Richter became my friend and mentor when I began writing this book
at the Institute for Advanced Study in Princeton. His encouragement and
his guidance are greatly appreciated. So too do I appreciate the other friendships I made and the scholarly exchange I profited from at the Institute with
other cofellows such as Steve Aschheim, Joseph Blasi, Johannes Fried, Sally
Nalle, Klaus Schreiner, and Allen Wells. Thanks also go to the permanent
faculty of the Institute's School of Social Science for giving me the opportunity to spend a year with them—Clifford Geertz, Albert Hirschman, Joan
Scott, and Michael Walzer—and to Linda Garrett, who helped me prepare
my survey of Krefeld Holocaust survivors, and Rose Marie Malarkey who
gave me much important advice and support.

I began writing this book in Princeton, and I finished writing it at its
sister institution in Holland, the Netherlands Institute for Advanced Study
(NIAS). As in Princeton, I made many lasting friendships there, and I
gained greatly from the lively intellectual atmosphere that NIAS provided.
Among those who have discussed my work with me at length and provided
me with many insights are Joost van Baak, Graeme Barker, Arif Dirlik, Rog-
ers Hollingsworth, Reinhart Koselleck, Wolfgang Mommsen, Xavier
Rousseaux, David Schoenbaum, Ola Svenson, and rector and fellow historian Henk Wesseling. My wife and I additionally want to thank the entire
NIAS staff for making our year so pleasurable and profitable, especially
Ruud Nolte, who came to our rescue during many family crises and always
kept a smile on his face; Yves de Roo, who brilliantly solved many technical
problems for me; Saskia Lapelaar, who helped me prepare my manuscripts;
and Sven Aalten, Rita Buis, Jos Hooghuis and Wouter Hugenholtz. Finally,
in Holland I want to thank Peter Spierenburg of the University of Rotterdam and his wife Astrid Ikelaar. We would not have gone to Holland had
Peter not recommended me to NIAS in the first place, and our time there
was made all the more enjoyable because of their hospitality and friendship.

This book was also written in part at Central Michigan University
where I have been employed for more than two decades. My colleagues in
the history department have been extremely supportive, and I thank them

for putting up with my long absences researching and writing this book. Also, many colleagues and former colleagues in the department have provided me with excellent criticism, intellectual stimulation, and warm friendship. Here especially I would like to mention Tom Benjamin, George Blackburn, Claudia Clark, Charles Ebel, John Haeger, David Macleod, Patricia Ranft, David Rutherford, Steve Scherer, Jim Schmiechen, Dennis Thavenet, and our present chair John Robertson. I would also like to thank my two student assistants, Andrea Dykstra and Dave Stockton, and Carole Beere, JoAnn Gust, and Doug Spathelf of the College of Graduate Studies.

Other institutions and their staff members that I also want to thank for their help and support are the United States Holocaust Memorial Museum, the National Registry of Jewish Holocaust Survivors, and the Lucius N. Littauer Foundation. The first two of these institutions placed us in contact with nearly one thousand German-Jewish Holocaust survivors, and the Littauer Foundation provided a needed infusion of funds at a crucial time to add to the generous support my project had received from the National Endowment for the Humanities, the National Science Foundation, and the Alexander von Humboldt Foundation.

Although I cannot state their names because of promises I have made about preserving their anonymity, I particularly want to thank all of the people who shared their experiences with me and my coresearchers about their lives in Nazi Germany in interviews that at times must have been excruciating. Although he was not interviewed directly, John Rosing should be thanked in this regard for providing me with an accurate list of the names and addresses of former Krefeld Jews such as himself so that I could contact them and who also shared with me other important information that I have found helpful in writing this book.

There remain a few individuals who should receive some of my sincerest thanks. Jim Schmiechen read every word of my manuscript and offered unending encouragement while providing needed but ever constructive criticism. George Mosse read and commented expertly on nearly my entire manuscript, but could not read the final chapters because he fell ill and died just before I could send them to him. His former student and his and my old friend Steve Aschheim filled in brilliantly for him, however, and read and commented on the chapters that George never had a chance to see. Joseph

Blasi read many of the chapters of the book and gave me sound advice. Additionally, I received valuable suggestions, criticisms, and support from several others, especially from old colleagues and friends such as Richard Evans, Bob Gellately, and Konrad Jarausch, from Father John O'Malley, S. J., and from a number of people who have played key roles in the development and production of my book. Georges Borchardt receives my gratitude for being an insightful critic and considerate adviser as well as a superb literary agent. I thank Don Fehr and Grant McIntyre for being supportive, patient, and talented editors. Thanks also go to John Bergez, who has a keen eye for spotting weaknesses in a manuscript's style and presentation, and to Tony DiIorio, who can detect factual errors in a text as can almost nobody else.

Near the very last moment in the long process of researching and writing this book, my college roommate and friend of more than thirty years Steve Hochstadt was literally there for me when I needed him most, as he has been so many times in the past. Now the chairman of the history department at Bates College in Lewiston, Maine, and a respected historian of Germany and the Holocaust, Steve dropped all that he was doing although I had given him next to no warning and spent a very hot and long summer day with me in his office printing out my book manuscript.

Final and most profound thanks go to my immediate family. My mother's strong backbone, prodigious energy, sound common sense, and loving nature have always provided a model for how I should lead my life, and, as she somehow manages to grow younger with each new year, she continues to guide me and fill my life with sunshine. My sons Benjamin and Jonathan have lived their entire lives with what they call "daddy's Nazi book," yet seem never to radiate anything other than ebullient cheerfulness and optimism. They, their love, and their smiles are precious to me. For my gracious wife Mary—with whom I share the welcome responsibility of raising children as well as my days and nights, my hopes and fears, and my heart and soul—I hope my dedication of this book to her and our sons brings joy.

Harpswell, Maine
AUGUST 7, 1999

PART ONE

NAZI TERROR AND THE GESTAPO

The Gestapo in Cologne was exceptionally weak. The calm, elderly officers let things come to them and did not undertake any of their own initiatives.

—Dr. Emanuel Schäfer,
former head of the Cologne Gestapo

In the handling of individual cases . . . we indeed had a free hand.

—Richard Schulenburg,
former head of the Krefeld Gestapo's Jewish desk

CHAPTER ONE

LOCATING NAZI TERROR: SETTING,
INTERPRETATIONS, EVIDENCE

T

he Gestapo in Cologne was exceptionally weak. The calm, elderly officers let things come to them and did not undertake any of their own initiatives," testified Dr. Emanuel Schäfer on Tuesday, July 6, 1954, the first day of his trial before a Cologne jury court for assisting in the deportation of the Cologne Jews to the death factories in the east in 1941 and 1942.[1] Tried along with Schäfer were two other former leaders of the Cologne Gestapo, Franz Sprinz and Kurt Matschke. In the course of the previous several years, the state prosecuting attorney's office had investigated more than one hundred former Cologne Gestapo officers for their part in the mass murder. But in the end only these three men were put on trial, and their sentences would be light. The scenario would prove to be similar in the rest of Germany.

The courtroom was quiet. Only seven people sat in the audience as the trial began. The most prominent of these people was Moritz Goldschmidt, the presiding head of the Cologne Jewish community as well as the representative of the Central Committee of Jews in Germany and its delegate to the Jewish World Congress. After the first day's session was over, Goldschmidt told the court reporters that of the 13,500 deported Cologne Jews, only 600 survived.[2] Despite the appalling proportions of this mass murder, few Germans appeared to have been particularly interested. Maybe they were afraid or ashamed to show interest. The newspaper headlines on the following day seemed almost tired and apologetic for having to report on such commonplace events. "Again a Gestapo-Case in Cologne," read the headline in the Cologne newspaper *Kölnische Rundschau*. In the beginning of its coverage of the case, the paper noted matter-of-factly, but with a touch of sarcasm as well, that there had been none of the emotional atmosphere and popular appeal of a trial held in the same courtroom only a week before. That case, which had filled the courtroom to overflowing, involved a twenty-three-year-old mother from the neighboring town of Brühl who had been charged with hanging her illegitimate two-year-old daughter on a window-fastener.[3]

The trial was over in four days. Schäfer, the fifty-three-year-old former head of the Cologne Gestapo from October 1940 to January 1942, during which time the Jewish "evacuation" to the east was organized and set in motion, maintained that he had only adhered to the existing laws, that the Jews had been well treated, and that he had no personal responsibility because he was only following orders from higher party and SS officials. In his words:

> The Nuremberg Laws were well known at that time to all judges and attorneys. Today they are thought of as criminal. The Jews were placed outside of the German community because of the laws. This was indeed wrong, as I now know, but at the time it was the law of the land. In an official discussion with the Gauleiter Grohé after a bombing attack, I learned that the Jews were to move out of their homes to make space for people who had been bombed out of theirs. The Jews were then given lodgings in the fortress in Müngersdorf. After this time, an order came from Heydrich that they were to be evacuated.[4]

Although Schäfer had presided over the planned and well-orchestrated murder of thousands of Cologne Jews, the wrongful arrest and incarceration of thousands of other Cologne citizens, and many other misdeeds of the rankest order both in Germany and abroad during his prolific career, the court was partially persuaded by his defense. Many other countries, like Yugoslavia, Poland, and the Soviet Union, demanded that he be deported to stand trial for his leadership role in the deaths of thousands of their citizens during the Third Reich. But he was not deported. Instead, the Cologne court convicted him of *schwere Freiheitsberaubung* (aggravated deprivation of liberty), a crime of much less gravity than abetting mass murder, the prosecution's original charge against him in the official indictment.[5] For his crimes he was to serve six years and nine months in prison, minus the time he had already spent in jail awaiting trial. In addition, he would have to forgo his civilian rights for an extra three years after he was let out of prison.[6]

The fifty-year-old Sprinz and the forty-six-year-old Matschke got off even easier. Their defense was similar to Schäfer's. After Schäfer had been sent to Belgrade in the winter of 1942 to preside over the elimination of the Serbian Jews, Sprinz replaced him. Sprinz then oversaw the remaining "evacuations" of the Cologne Jews and stayed in his post in Cologne until February 1944. In trying to justify his actions, he asserted that he had never been anti-Semitic and that "the 'Jewish parasitism' was only one of the problems to be solved." He had "never thought that a 'biological solution' [which he called the annihilation of the deported Jews in gas chambers] would be used." Furthermore, he testified, he was "personally of the opinion" that he "had really nothing at all to do with the Jewish transports." As he put it, "I did not wish to intercede in the already well organized process. Once I did observe the preparations for a transport of 800 Jews, which took place in the Cologne trade center. Nurses were on hand and a doctor. Of course I did not notice any enthusiasm."[7] As Schäfer had done, therefore, he defended himself by claiming that he was not involved in the physical aspects of the deportations themselves, that the Jews were well treated as long as they were in Cologne, and that he did not and could not have known what was to become of them after they had been deported. And most important, he had only passed along orders from those above him to those below him in the chain of command. Convicted of the same minor offense that Schäfer was convicted of, Sprinz was given a three-year prison sentence minus the time he had already served awaiting trial.[8]

Matschke was also convicted of the same offense but received only a two-year sentence. Although he admitted to having been the head of the section of the Cologne Gestapo dealing with Jewish affairs from 1943 on, he had only been involved, he said, in the transport of the small number of Jews who were still residing in Cologne after the main deportations had been completed in late summer 1942. From all that he had heard about the transports, everything had proceeded smoothly, he explained, and he had acted in an official capacity only and thus bore no personal responsibility. "There had been no protests or complaints and everything had taken place without a hitch. In my department, everything proceeded along purely official lines."[9]

In the typewritten summary of the final judgment in the case, the court made it clear that it did not believe that these men held more than marginal responsibility for what finally happened to the Cologne Jews. Compared with the guilt of the people who were truly responsible—who remained unnamed but whom the court referred to as the "leading perpetrators"—the responsibility of these men was deemed only modest. The "leading perpetrators," on the other hand, bore such "unending guilt that their deeds could not be punished adequately by any earthly court."[10] The court pointed to several factors that served to reduce even further the share in the guilt attributable to Schäfer, Sprinz, and Matschke. All of these men had led supposedly "unobjectionable lives," and each of them had made some effort to ease the hardships faced by the unfortunate Jews. Their guilt lay mainly in their foolish, but understandable, adherence to an ideology and a leadership that had led them astray. It is left for the reader of this document to assume that the court believed these men's alibis that they had not known that the Jews were to be murdered after they were deported. (It is important to point out here that this document has never been made public and that this particular reader is one of the first to gain access to it.) The court ruled that these men were not the truly guilty culprits because each had merely followed orders from his superiors; Schäfer and Sprinz had served at such a high level of command that they had little to nothing to do with the actual deportations; and Matschke came so late to the Cologne Gestapo as to have been involved in only a limited number of deportations. The identities of the truly guilty culprits remained unspecified.

This verdict settled the case at the time. It also set a precedent for the trials and investigations in other German localities that came several years later. It made clear that the new German state was not about to exact heavy penalties from a large number of past wrongdoers. The cases against former Gestapo and SS men and Nazi Party officials would, with few exceptions,[11] be confined to handing out mild sentences in individual cases of wrongdoing in relatively minor but highly specific matters, as opposed to heavy sentences for the many people involved in more momentous, though less well defined, acts of inhumanity.[12] The verdict in this Cologne case and those that followed it elsewhere may have helped the new German nation get on with the pressing business of its present and future by covering over some gaping sores from its past. But such verdicts did not resolve many important questions about the nature of the Nazi terror and the murder of the Jews of Cologne and the rest of Germany. Many of these questions continue to burn painfully today. To what degree were rank-and-file Gestapo officers below the leadership level culpable for the murder of the German Jews? How were the deportations organized locally, and who specifically carried out the deportation orders? To what extent were local party officials and average citizens aware of and involved in the deportations and mass murder? And more broadly, how pervasive was the Nazi terror for average citizens, and how much freedom of action did they have? How did the terror work on an everyday basis?

The Cologne prosecutor's office chose to put only three top Gestapo leaders, all comfortable targets, on trial. This decision came after an extensive investigation of all identifiable Cologne Gestapo officers, an investigation that took the Cologne prosecutor's office and the police several years to conclude.[13] One does not have to have read the long documentary trial evidence generated by this investigation to wonder why only these three officers were chosen. These documents do reveal, however, ample grounds to incriminate many more people than were finally put on trial. One cannot avoid coming to the cynical conclusion that these three people were chosen as particularly malevolent fall guys with whom the Cologne population and the Federal Republic could easily dispense, thereby putting the matter to rest. In so doing, many other Gestapo officers, party officials, and individual citizens who also took part in, facilitated, or profited from the deportation and murder of the Cologne Jews would not have to atone for their actions. In Cologne as elsewhere in Germany, "normal" Gestapo officers and other former Nazis and Nazi sympathizers would never have to face justice for putting the most stupendous crime of the century into motion.[14]

For example, Karl Löffler, the head of the "Jewish desk" of the Cologne Gestapo during the deportations of 1941 and 1942, and his counterparts in other German cities, such as Richard Schulenburg of the Krefeld Gestapo, were spared by this precedent. Whereas local Gestapo chiefs like Schäfer and Sprinz were sometimes punished, local Eichmanns like Löffler and Schulenburg almost never were. Löffler's activities were examined in the investigation preceding the trial, but he served only as a witness in the trial itself. It will be illuminating to explore why Moritz Goldschmidt, one of the seven people in the audience for the Schäfer trial and a man who served as the first and probably most important witness in the entire investigation and trial itself, chose to deflect the finger of blame away from Löffler. In his testimony he asserted that Löffler had been reassigned to the Gestapo in Brussels in the fall of 1941, before the deportations took place. In reality, Löffler first went to Brussels in the fall of 1942, after the main waves of deported Cologne Jews had ridden off to their deaths in train cars.[15]

The precedent set by the Cologne case may have allowed Löffler and other responsible people to get off scot-free, but the careers, actions, and mentalities of individuals like Löffler and other Gestapo officers and policemen bear closer examination if we are to understand how the crime of the century was perpetrated in the Nazi years and how it was dealt with in the first decades of the Federal Republic. In seeking an understanding of this crime in particular, and of Nazi terror in general, it will be necessary to compare it with the myriad crimes of the Gestapo officers, German justice and lay officials, and common citizens who helped ensure the success of dictatorial terror and pave the way for mass murder in the Third Reich.

This book focuses therefore on both the role of individuals, such as Gestapo officers and ordinary citizens, and the role of the society in making terror work. While stressing the centrality of Jewish persecution in the Nazi example of terror, it also examines more than one thousand individual cases of persecution, and sometimes protest, pertaining to the entire spectrum of people who suffered from Nazi terror or acted to make it possible. It deals in flesh-and-blood narratives—sometimes quite graphically, to convey a true sense of how the terror operated—as well as in facts and statistics to tell the story and to provide an explanation of the terror that was perhaps the defining characteristic of the Nazi dictatorship.

Many of the central questions this book confronts have already been mentioned or alluded to in the discussion above. A fuller list includes the following: How did the terror affect the everyday lives of German citizens, Jewish and non-Jewish alike, in average German communities? What was the progression of the terror over time? Who suffered the most from it, and who suffered the least?

How did the central instrument of the terror, the Gestapo, function? How powerful and how pervasive was it? How did other "justice" organs work, such as the prosecutors' offices and the "Special Courts" (*Sondergerichte*) set up to try political offenses in the Third Reich? What biases did they display?

Who carried out the terror, and how responsible and culpable were they individually? What kinds of backgrounds did Gestapo officers, for example, come from? What was their mentality? Were they, as they claimed after the war, simply "normal" police officers who only followed orders and did their duty with regard to the existing laws and without any particular malice on their part?

How did individual German citizens respond to the Nazi terror? What differentiates the people who protested against it from those who acted to support it? How involved were common German citizens in the policing and control of their fellow citizens? What motivated citizens to denounce their neighbors, work colleagues, and relatives? How often did such denunciations occur?

How did the degradation, expropriation, and mass murder of the Jews play out in individual German communities? How much were common citizens involved? What did they and the local Nazi officials know about the fate of the Jews?

What happened to the perpetrators in the Federal Republic after the war? How did they seek to avoid prosecution, resume their careers, and reclaim their pensions? Who helped them achieve these goals?

THE EVOLVING INTERPRETATION OF THE TERROR

The last half-century has witnessed an enormous outpouring of books and articles on nearly all aspects of Nazi society, and many people have made

excellent contributions to the understanding of the terror that reigned in
Germany for the twelve and a half years of that society's existence. As German society has shown an ever greater willingness to open its archives and
to confront squarely the most painful chapter in its recent history, German
scholars have joined forces with scholars from several other countries in
what is now an international and cooperative effort that has exploded many
of the old myths about Nazi terror. The following discussion acquaints the
reader with some of the exemplary work done on the topic and concludes
with a statement about the overarching interpretation that this book
provides.

The scholarship on Nazi terror has progressed through at least three
distinct stages.[16] The first two stages each lasted for about two decades, and
the third stage has gained momentum throughout the 1990s. Several vari-
ables distinguish these stages and their differing versions of what the terror
was, how it operated, and who bears responsibility for it: the centrality or
marginality of the Holocaust; the centrality or marginality of Hitler personally; the power and pervasiveness of the Gestapo; the focus of the investigation of the terror (on the highest echelons of German society, where the
terror was centrally ordered and organized by the Berlin leadership, or on
individual localities, where it was carried out); the nature of the Nazi state's
ruling apparatus; the nature and extent of protest and dissidence; the role
played by common citizens in their own policing; and the people who have
conducted the most influential research on the subject.

The first stage began at the end of the Second World War and lasted
until the late 1960s. At the beginning of this period the world was reeling
from revelations about the concentration camps and the Holocaust. Enriched by the many eyewitness accounts that soon appeared—published by
former concentration camp inmates and some of Hitler's former henchmen[17]—formal scholarship on the terror focused on the role of Hitler and
the central organs of the terror apparatus in Berlin and on the disastrous
fate of the Jews. German scholars were largely discredited at this time for
having either supported or gone along with Hitler, so the bulk of the significant work on the subject came from the pens of foreigners and German
emigré scholars living abroad.[18] The archival sources for much of this work
were limited. Even though Raul Hilberg and some others did make solid use

of the voluminous Nuremberg trial records, most researchers believed that nearly all useful local archival sources were either lost during the bombings or destroyed by the Gestapo and other Nazi Party officials at the end of the war.[19]

The guiding assumptions of this primarily top-down history were that a maniacal Hitler was firmly in command of a smoothly functioning, monolithic state and party apparatus that controlled the German population by means of unrestricted terror. At the center of this terror stood a supposedly all-powerful, all-knowing, and omnipresent secret police empire spearheaded by the Gestapo. First appearing in Berlin in April 1933, when Hitler had been in power for only three months, the Gestapo shortly thereafter established large central posts in Germany's major cities and smaller outposts in the rest of Germany's communities. Allegedly endowed with a huge army of specially trained agents and spies and employing advanced technical means of surveillance, the Gestapo, like the "thought police" of George Orwell's terrifying postwar novel 1984, had more than sufficient means to keep close tabs at all times on all citizens—from Jews, Communists, and other "enemies" of the regime to the most insignificant members of German society.[20]

Emphasizing the historic roots of anti-Semitism and racism in her famous study of the origins of totalitarianism published six years after the end of the war, Hannah Arendt was one of the first to examine the nature and implementation of the terror in Nazi (and to a lesser extent Soviet) society. Totalitarianism, she argued, threatens nearly all citizens. Totalitarian societies like Nazi Germany employ "a system of ubiquitous spying, where everybody may be a police agent and each individual feels himself under constant surveillance." Secrecy and the secret police prevail to such an extent that victims disappear without leaving a trace. "The secret police . . . sees to it that the victim never existed at all."[21]

Many scholars soon elaborated on Arendt's Orwellian argument. The French author of one of the earliest books on the Gestapo explained in a chapter he entitled "The Gestapo Is Everywhere" that

> the Gestapo acted on its own account by secretly installing microphones and tape recorders in the homes of suspects. In the absence of

the victim, or on the pretext of making repairs or of checking the telephone or the electric installations, a few microphones were discreetly installed, allowing the individual to be spied upon even in the bosom of his family. No one was safe from this type of practice. . . . Spying became so universal that nobody could feel safe.[22]

The second stage in the evolving interpretation of the Nazi terror began in the mid-1960s and lasted until the end of the 1980s. During this stage German scholars started to come to grips with their own recent history. This effort would cause considerable pain and controversy. So much so, that by the mid-1980s nearly the entire German intellectual establishment had become embroiled in an acrimonious debate (*Historikerstreit*) played out in leading newspapers and national media about the uniqueness of the Holocaust and how it and Germany's Nazi past should be properly studied and understood.[23] Its early phases, however, started out more tamely. It was heralded in the mid to late 1960s by the appearance of seminal works by, among others, the sociologist Ralf Dahrendorf on the endemic weakness of democracy in German society, the historian Martin Broszat on the nature and structure of the German dictatorship, and the former Nazi architect and armament minister Albert Speer on Hitler's character and daily routine.[24] The initial effect of these works was to recast the view of the German dictatorship and the German people in a more nuanced and also somewhat more favorable light.

Guilt continued to be heaped onto the person of Adolf Hitler, but his hold, and that of his regime, over the society was now seen as having been more tenuous than previously believed. Instead of running a tight ship of state over a willing and united population, Hitler's top brass were now portrayed as having been rent by internal divisions, overlapping jurisdictions, and conflicting goals. The population was also seen as having been more diverse. If not always on the brink of full-scale resistance and outright revolution, the German citizenry had been made up of a wide variety of individuals, many of whom were seething with discontent and searching for ways to express their disagreements with the leadership through minor but nonetheless significant expressions of their unhappiness.

In this new wave of more German-dominated scholarship, the persecution of the Jews and the Holocaust moved from the center to the periphery of the debate. Perhaps unintentionally, but nonetheless noticeably, the pioneering works of Broszat and Dahrendorf and the revelations of the former Nazi Speer hardly touched on the Jews and the Holocaust.[25] In the second wave of scholarship in this stage, in the mid-1970s to the mid-1980s, following the lead of Broszat and company, a new consensus began to emerge that the German population was less anti-Semitic, and the plight of the Jews less important to their support for the Nazi dictatorship, than was previously thought. Many Germans, it was shown, had been appalled by the barbarous *Kristallnacht* pogroms of November 9 and 10, 1938; that reaction forced the Nazi leadership to put pressure on and later murder the Jews in greater secrecy. Only a few dyed-in-the-wool Nazis, it was now believed, had been animated by the Jews' misfortunes. Most Germans seemed to have cared little about the issue. As the British historian Ian Kershaw explained in one of his two influential books published in the early 1980s treating the mood and morale of the German citizenry, "the road to Auschwitz was built by hate, but paved with indifference."[26]

Although Kershaw's evaluation of the extent of the German population's anti-Semitism is important in itself, his careful study of local opinion formation in the Third Reich focuses even more on the issues of day-to-day compliance and noncompliance by average German citizens. Kershaw was involved in a large project on this theme, entitled "Bavaria in the NS Period," that was led by Broszat and published in six influential volumes between 1977 and 1983.[27] He and others working on this and on other projects of the time helped move the focus of the study of the Nazi terror away from the top leadership in Berlin to the plight of the average German citizen living in the provinces of the Third Reich.[28] This new emphasis on the history of everyday life, though adding needed texture and lifeblood to Broszat's and the other pioneers' scholarship of the period, basically confirmed the arguments originally laid out in a more macro fashion by their senior colleagues. The analysis carried on in this period of Gestapo and Social Democratic Party in exile (SOPADE) mood and morale reports and of local court documents and other local records buttressed the arguments of Broszat and others that there was considerable disharmony and disunity at all levels in Nazi society.

These new studies also helped to illustrate Broszat's argument that Hitler was crucial to the Nazi movement. Without his guiding hand, Broszat argued, the Third Reich would simply have crumbled into disarray and discord. A veritable cottage industry of studies on the subjects of resistance and persecution developed at this time, suggesting at least implicitly that the Third Reich could not possibly have survived Hitler's death.[29] As Edelweiss Pirates, swing youth, and other youngsters refused to conform to Nazi dictates and struggled with increasing vehemence against Hitler Youth and local Nazi Party leaders, their parents grumbled constantly about lower wages, harsher conditions, and the Nazi leadership.[30] Additionally, a barrage of studies pointed to the sufferings and discontent of Communists, clergymen, religious sects, women, and others who may not always have expressed their dissatisfaction in openly rebellious ways but were nevertheless longing for a way out of the Nazi straitjacket.[31] According to Kershaw, Broszat, and several others, only Hitler continued to be held in esteem; only Hitler could have kept this turbulent society intact.

The high degree of discord these studies uncovered and their new focus on the daily lives and aspirations of common Germans prepared the way for the third and currently reigning perspective on the Nazi terror. Impressed by the demonstration that many Germans found ways of disobeying Nazi dictates in their everyday lives, a new wave of scholars began questioning how this could have been possible if the Gestapo and the other organs of the terror were as powerful and pervasive as previously thought. A wholesale reevaluation of the Nazi terror apparatus and of the role of ordinary Germans in the terror and the Holocaust has resulted.

The second stage of the scholarly research on and interpretation of the Nazi terror often highlighted the resistance to the terror and the victims of the terror, while at the same time continuing to assume that the terror was total even if the organs of the Nazi power structure were structurally polycratic instead of monolithic. In contrast, the newest perspective on the terror rejects outright the notion that the terror was total and has a far more negative view of the role played by common German citizens. Beginning as the *Historikerstreit* began to cool down in the late 1980s and gaining momentum throughout the 1990s, a number of important studies have scrutinized the powers and activities of local police and judicial organizations,

stressing the role that common citizens played in the execution of Nazi justice and social control. Using records either believed to have been destroyed
or not previously accessible to scholarly investigation, like local Gestapo
and Special Court case files, these studies have produced some provocative
findings.[32] They have shown that the Gestapo often had less manpower,
fewer spies, and less means at its disposal to control the population than had
been assumed by nearly everyone since the Nazi period came to an end.[33]
With its limited resources, the Gestapo had to rely heavily on the civilian
population as a source of information. This information seldom came from
paid informants; rather it was usually supplied by plain citizens acting out
of a wide variety of motivations. Angry neighbors, bitter in-laws, and dis-
gruntled work colleagues frequently used the state's secret police apparatus
to settle their personal and often petty scores. By means of political denunciations, common citizens frequently served as the eyes and ears of the Gestapo.[34] As former head of the Cologne Gestapo Dr. Schäfer had testified in
his trial, the "officers let things come to them."

According to the new argument, then, the population largely controlled itself. Collaboration and collusion characterize the activities of the
German people much more than meaningful resistance and true dissent. In
the words of the German scholars Klaus-Michael Mallmann and Gerhard
Paul, who in 1991 published an exemplary study of the everyday activities
of the terror apparatus in the Saarland:

> Our study shows over and over again that what in other places has
> been celebrated as resistance, was merely a mixture of unintentional
> polycratic conflicts, normal social conflict behavior and pious wishes
> of exiles. . . . Neither the propaganda nor the terror were totally effec-
> tive. There were many niches left over in which the people could con-
> duct themselves quite normally. Their behavior inside of these not
> completely "coordinated" spaces or inside of the polycratic power
> structure had nothing to do with resistance and opposition.[35]

The opening up of previously inaccessible records and the intense interest in local resistance activity and deviant behavior in the Third Reich that
was generated in the 1970s and 1980s have also led to a reappraisal of the

functioning of German courts and other justice organs in Nazi society. Several works have appeared in recent years that investigate the role played by judges, prosecuting attorneys, and the courts in helping to keep the population in line.[36] The effect of these studies is to demonstrate that the more "normal" legal officials of the Third Reich certainly did not impart "positivistic" impartial justice, as many justice personnel claimed after the war. Prosecuting attorneys and judges, just like Gestapo officers, acting at both the local and national level, dispensed arbitrary and biased justice. Whereas some used their authority almost benignly, others eagerly pushed for maximum penalties for minor misbehavior. On the one hand, a mild political offense like listening to BBC during the war years could have resulted in a dismissal before going to trial at a local court, an acquittal, or a minor sentence, all depending on the recommendation and judgment of the police, prosecutors, and judges. On the other hand, it could have led in extreme cases to a referral to Roland Freisler's feared People's Court (*Volksgerichtshof*) in Berlin, where the death sentence was the expected outcome.[37]

The reevaluation of the Gestapo and the justice system, and of the people's role in helping them operate, has done much to demystify the Nazi terror apparatus. Detailed archival evidence laying bare the actual workings of the Nazi terror at the grassroots level has been amassed and analyzed by resourceful scholars. No longer can we believe that the Gestapo itself was everywhere and that the power of the state over the individual was total. Nor can we continue to sort the German people into one of two polar opposite camps, with one camp consisting of blind followers of the Führer and the other camp of guiltless victims and resistance fighters. Although the sufferings of large numbers of Germans and many Germans' discontent with various aspects of the Nazi dictatorship have been well documented, the evidence suggests that a great majority of the German population found ways to accommodate the Nazi regime, despite whatever inner reservations they might have had. It also suggests that considerable numbers of ordinary citizens used the repressive political means afforded them by the Nazi dictatorship, especially through the vehicle of political denunciations, to their own advantage.

Echoing these disturbing revelations about the participation of ordinary German citizens in Nazi terror, landmark books published in the early and mid-1990s by the American scholars Christopher R. Browning and Daniel Jonah Goldhagen have demonstrated chillingly that ordinary Germans were also more active than previously believed in the perpetration of the Holocaust. A fierce scholarly debate, reminiscent of the German *Historikerstreit* of the 1980s, has ensued, but this time the controversy began in the United States before it spread to Germany and then around the world.[38] There are many layers to the debate, but its epicenter is clearly Goldhagen's best-seller *Hitler's Willing Executioners: Ordinary Germans and the Holocaust,* and especially his contention that common German citizens willingly killed Jews during the Holocaust because they were motivated by what he claims was a historic and uniquely German "eliminationist anti-Semitism." One of Goldhagen's foremost critics is Christopher Browning, who argues in *Ordinary Men: Reserve Police Battalion 101 and the Final Solution in Poland* that Germans acted no differently than people from any country might have acted in their extreme situation. Nevertheless, though he comes to different conclusions, much of the empirical evidence he employs in his equally graphic portrait of the murderous activities of reserve German policemen during the Holocaust differs in only minor ways from the evidence Goldhagen presents. Thus, both Browning and Goldhagen relate essentially the same scenario: sizable numbers of ordinary, often middle-aged German civilians, with little to no ideological indoctrination or training, were called up for brief periods during the war as reserve policemen all over eastern Europe to shoot thousands of defenseless Jews at point-blank range and then allowed to return to their normal civilian lives and families in Germany.

Further casting a pall on the ordinary German population's involvement in Nazi crimes has been a haunting exhibition attended by large audiences in many of Germany's leading cities in the last few years. Organized by the Hamburger Institute for Social Research and entitled "Vernichtungskrieg: Verbrechen der Wehrmacht 1941 bis 1944" (War of Annihilation: The Crimes of the German Army, 1941 to 1944),[39] this exhibition displays scores of photographs and other visual materials to document the regular German army's direct involvement in the criminal atrocities perpetrated against Jewish and other eastern European civilians during the Second World War.[40] Combining these materials with the evidence provided by

Browning and Goldhagen, it is no longer possible to maintain that the Holocaust was perpetrated exclusively, or even especially it seems, by elite Nazi
special-forces units, for average German citizens formed the core of both
the reserve police battalions and the German army.

As Daniel Goldhagen's best-seller and the well-attended exhibition on
the crimes of the German army demonstrate, the subject of Nazi terror and
Nazi crimes has riveted popular audiences and fueled scholarly controver-
sies around the world in ways that would have seemed unimaginable not
long after the Second World War ended over a half-century ago. In the immediate postwar decades people everywhere wanted to lay to rest the
trauma of the war and the Holocaust so that they could move forward to
rebuild their societies and their lives, but today the world's thirst for new
knowledge about the leading example of terror and inhumanity in the
twentieth century seems unquenchable. Given that there remains much to
be discovered and understood about how the Nazi terror operated, whom it
affected most, and who was most culpable for perpetrating its crimes against
humanity, and given that terror, mass murder, and crimes against humanity
continue to threaten citizens in many countries long after Hitler's death, it
is likely that the study of Nazi terror will continue to flourish well into the
twenty-first century.

To help ensure that the future study of the Nazi terror rests on a secure
foundation, this book aims to provide an assessment that both places the
burgeoning literature on the terror in a proper and clear perspective and
casts new light on how it operated. Over the past fifty years, as already
mentioned, knowledge about the terror has expanded enormously and the
dominant interpretation of the terror today rests on far better and more
plentiful evidence than the interpretations of several decades ago. There are
signs, however, that in the scholarly zeal to uncover more and more new
information about the terror and to unmask ever wider groups of people
who were involved in perpetrating it, the interpretation of the terror is
starting to get out of balance.

Fifty years ago, when the first stage in the scholarship on the terror
began, it was assumed that the leading organ of the terror, the Gestapo, was
all-powerful and all-knowing. Today scholars argue that the Gestapo was
relatively weak. With few officers and few spies, the Gestapo, they argue,

was almost completely dependent on civilian denunciations as its source of information. Fifty years ago scholars assumed that nearly the entire German population was terrorized by the Gestapo and the other organs of Nazi repression. Today the ordinary German population is under indictment for having played a leading role in the terror itself, charged with voluntarily providing the Gestapo with information about fellow citizens and willingly participating in the mass murder of the Jews. At the Nuremberg Trials more than fifty years ago, the Gestapo was branded a criminal organization. Today books and articles portray Gestapo officers as more or less "normal" police officers, if overly career-minded and eager.[41]

Many ordinary Germans certainly did participate in the Nazi terror and the Holocaust. The Gestapo clearly had limited manpower and resources. Indeed, the Nazi terror never became fully total, and ordinary Germans enjoyed considerable space to vent their everyday frustrations with Nazi policies and leaders without inordinate fear of arrest and prosecution. These are by now uncontestable facts for which this book will provide much fresh evidence. But the newest perspective on the terror, although it is to be credited for helping to bring these facts to light, needs to be revised, for several important reasons.

The newest perspective on the Nazi terror has begun to stress the importance of the role played by the ordinary German population to such an extent that it is beginning to lose sight of the fact that the terror would not have existed at all had it not been put into motion by the Nazi leadership and led by the Gestapo. This shift in focus has also begun to underestimate the ruthless effectiveness of the Gestapo; indeed, the newest perspective is nearly at the point of excusing Gestapo officers for their overwhelming culpability. Finally, the newest perspective on the terror needs revision because, in its determination to debunk what some of its leaders refer to as "the myth of 'popular opposition' and '*Resistenz*,'"[42] it undervalues the resistance activity that did take place. It is undoubtedly true that, as Mallmann and Paul note, "the greatest amount of dissent did not develop into opposition and resistance activity . . . that the basic support of the Third Reich functioned until the bitter end."[43] But it is also true that many people —among them Communists, Socialists, Jehovah's Witnesses, clergymen, and others—acted consciously and bravely at various times during the

Third Reich to try to undermine the Nazi regime. Even though they were unsuccessful, they, their efforts, and their suffering should not be forgotten.

As this book demonstrates, the key to understanding the sometimes brutal, sometimes quasi-legalistic, but always effective Nazi terror lies in its selective nature. Never implemented in a blanket or indiscriminate fashion, it specifically targeted and ruthlessly moved against the Nazi regime's racial, political, and social enemies; at the same time it often ignored or dismissed expressions of nonconformity and mild disobedience on the part of other German citizens. This dualistic treatment of different sectors of the German population helped the Nazi regime garner legitimacy and support among the populace. Indeed, many Germans perceived the terror not as a personal threat to them but as something that served their interests by removing threats to their material well-being and to their sense of community and propriety. This acceptance helped guarantee that the leading organs of the terror, like the Gestapo, would not be hampered by limitations to their manpower and means.

Jews were ultimately the foremost targets of the terror. But in the early years of Nazi rule the terror was applied with equal, and sometimes even greater, force against Communist and other leftist functionaries and activists. Once the threat from the political left was eliminated (by the mid-1930s), the terror began to concentrate on silencing potential sources of opposition in religious circles and on removing from society what the Nazi regime deemed social outsiders, such as homosexuals, career criminals, and the physically and mentally disabled. During the war the terror reached its most drastic phase, with the mass murder of the Jews serving as the most ominous example of its fury.

Although many German citizens belonged to one or more of the targeted groups, most did not, and consequently most Germans suffered not at all from the terror. There was no need to target them because most Germans remained loyal to the Nazi leadership and supported it voluntarily from the beginning to the end of the Third Reich, if to varying degrees. Although some Germans strongly agreed with the regime's anti-Semitic and antihumanitarian policies, many did not. In the same vein, some Germans voluntarily spied on and denounced their neighbors and coworkers to the Nazi authorities, but the overwhelming majority of German citizens did not. Furthermore, civilian denunciations were typically made for personal and petty reasons against normally law-abiding citizens whom the Gestapo seldom chose to punish severely, if at all. It remains true, however, that the civilian German population figured heavily in its own control, and its collusion and accommodation with the Nazi regime made the Nazis' crimes against humanity possible.

It is necessary not to overlook the ordinary German population's complicity in Nazi crimes. It is also necessary to realize that most Germans were motivated not by a willful intent to harm others but by a mixture of cowardice, apathy, and a slavish obedience to authority. After the war Gestapo officers and other Nazi authorities tried to justify their participation in Nazi crimes by arguing that they had been similarly motivated. Although these excuses are not to be dismissed out of hand, especially since they were frequently accepted by prosecuting bodies as well as by influential members of the local communities of these officers, the analysis in this book of the backgrounds, motivations, and actions of Gestapo officers who cruelly, efficiently, and willfully implemented the Nazi terror uncovers the hollowness of their alibis. These not so "normal" men, though enjoying considerable support from many in the German population both during the Nazi years and afterward in the Federal Republic of Germany, need to be seen as the arch perpetrators they most certainly were. If they are not to be held accountable in historical memory, then almost nobody can be.

THE SETTING AND THE EVIDENCE

This book is set primarily in three Rhineland communities, Cologne, Krefeld, and Bergheim, and their outlying villages. Although they differed in size and spirit, all three communities had a strong industrial base, a predominantly Catholic majority, a moderate-sized Protestant minority, and a small but, for Germany at the time, average-sized Jewish population. All of these communities were hit hard by the depression of the 1930s, but none of them were particular wellsprings of Nazi support. In the last democratic elections of the Weimar Republic, the population in all three communities voted less frequently for the National Socialist Party than was the average for the rest of Germany.

Cologne, straddling the Rhine River about fifty miles to the east of the Dutch and Belgian border outside of Aachen, lies on the southwestern outskirts of Germany's most industrialized heartland in the Ruhr Valley. With nearly one million inhabitants today and about three-quarters of a million inhabitants in the Nazi years, Cologne is Germany's fourth-largest city and oldest big city.[44] It is home to Germany's most famous cathedral and numerous other churches of great architectural and religious significance, a six-hundred-year-old university, and a variety of large and small industries. Its inhabitants gave the Catholic, Communist, and Socialist parties opposed to Hitler nearly two-thirds of their votes in the last three Weimar elections and Hitler's National Socialist Party (NSDAP) the lowest percentage of votes that it received in any large German city.[45] Once Hitler came to power, however, most of Cologne's population, with some important exceptions, quickly fell in line, just as others did elsewhere in Germany. In the war years Cologne suffered perhaps more heavily from the constant bombing attacks than any other German city.[46] In the ashes and the rubble of the almost completely destroyed city, some of Germany's most famous—some would say infamous—resistance activity came to the surface.[47] Its Jewish minority of about 16,000 people, or about two and a half percent of the total population of the city, was slightly larger than average for the rest of Germany in 1933, but smaller than the Jewish population in several other large German cities.[48]

Krefeld and Bergheim were less remarkable communities that could have been anywhere in Germany. About forty miles north of Cologne on the Rhine River and twenty-five miles east of the Dutch border town of Venlo, the medium-sized city of Krefeld was by far the larger of the two, with a population of roughly 170,000.[49] It was known for silk manufacturing but contained many miners, some farmers, and a considerable mix of shopkeepers, tradespeople, professional people, and industrial workers. Its Jewish population of about 1,600, or 1 percent of the total population, was very close to the average size of Jewish populations in the rest of Germany's cities and towns.[50] The support its population gave to the Nazi Party in the

Weimar years was at an average level for a community of its type. The support it gave to the Nazi movement later on was typical as well.[51]

Bergheim, lying about fifteen miles to the west of Cologne and the
Rhine River on an old trade route between Cologne and the Dutch border,
was a small town in the Third Reich. Today it is much larger. On the eve of
the war in 1939 it consisted of a small town center and several tiny outlying
villages, and it totaled 18,173 inhabitants.[52] It was not remarkable in any
particular way except that many of its residents saw themselves as fervently
devout Catholics. Miners, farmers, and tradespeople formed the bulk of its
population. Although its citizens gave Hitler only a relatively modest number of its votes in Weimar elections, and many of its devout residents resented Nazi encroachments on their religious practices, Bergheim certainly
never became a hotbed of Nazi resistance. It had only a few Jewish families.

Although Cologne, Krefeld, and Bergheim were more Catholic and
more industrial, and somewhat less likely to have voted for Hitler's Nazi
Party in Weimar elections than some communities,[53] the Nazi terror operated in these communities more or less in the way it operated elsewhere
in Germany. They were selected for in-depth study for reasons of size and
typicality, logistics, and the availability of data. Together with the primarily
farming villages surrounding them, the large city of Cologne, the medium-
sized city of Krefeld, and the small town of Bergheim represent the spectrum of communities of different sizes, degrees of urbanization, and socioeconomic makeup found elsewhere in Germany during the Nazi period.

When I began this study, I thought that focusing solely on the investigations and judgments contained in the voluminous case files of the Special
Courts established in Cologne and other cities to try political offenders in
Nazi Germany would provide sufficient archival evidence to understand
how the Nazi terror worked. After some time I learned otherwise. The case
files of the Cologne Special Court are the most plentiful in all of Germany.
They involve cases of political dissidence and resistance brought to the attention of the Cologne state prosecuting attorney's office from early 1933
to early 1945. These mostly minor cases run the gamut from libeling Hitler
and other Nazi Party authorities and listening to foreign radio broadcasts
to outlawed sexual relations between Jews and Gentiles. There are nearly
20,000 of these cases involving almost 30,000 alleged wrongdoers. They are

well cataloged, and they are often very detailed, sometimes running to several hundred pages in length. They contain the original records, or at least
copies, of the investigations of the Gestapo and other police agencies. (Because small towns in the Cologne area and elsewhere in Nazi Germany typically had no Gestapo headquarters or officers, ordinary police had to handle
the original investigations.) The case files also include the prosecutors' investigations and, if the case went to trial (only some of them did), the trial
records and judgments.

As plentiful and rich as these records are, they still have deficiencies.
Most important, they do not treat all of the cases of political disobedience
in the Third Reich. The Gestapo and other police authorities handled many
cases on their own. This was the norm in fact in many cases of a minor
nature. Often the Gestapo chose to conclude its investigation of a case with
a summary dismissal or a mere warning if its officials did not think the case
was significant enough to burden the court's caseloads. Other times, most
commonly in cases involving Communists or Jews, the Gestapo chose to
send the accused person directly to a concentration camp without involving
the higher judicial bodies. The Special Court case files are also deficient in
cases of serious political resistance. Since cases that involved high treason,
spreading defeatist ideas, or otherwise damaging Germany's military effort
during the war were passed along from the police authorities to higher regional or national courts, no record of the people involved in such severe
cases is usually to be found in the Special Court case files.

Hence, the Special Court records need to be augmented by the original
Gestapo case files. These files not only contain information about the original Gestapo investigations but usually contain information about what
happened in the case later on, gleaned from copies of court verdicts, concentration camp referrals, and sometimes even death notices. But there are
problems with the Gestapo case files too. First of all, they did not survive
the war in Cologne, Bergheim, or most other communities in the Third
Reich. (A large number, about 3,000, are available, however, for the city of
Krefeld.) Even where they are available, as in Krefeld, they are not as well
cataloged as the Special Court records; some types of issues are thus more
difficult to study. More troublesome is that they are often not complete. A
large number of the files appear to be missing even in places like Krefeld

where the archivists believe that they are more than 70 percent intact.[54] Especially in cases involving upstanding Germans who had been accused of making libelous statements against the authorities, the Gestapo apparently often sent most of its case file, and sometimes all of it, to the state prosecuting attorney's office and kept only a small dossier or card file on the case for its own records. It could requisition the larger case file from the state prosecuting attorney's office if that became necessary in the future.

For all these reasons, I decided that the best strategy was to analyze and compare the records of both the Special Courts, which were available for Cologne and Bergheim, and the Gestapo, which were available for Krefeld. Although these records often overlap and contain basically the same information, this is not always the case. Thus, both need to be studied carefully. The problem of incomplete and fragmentary records is a common one for all historians, not just for those who study the Nazi experience. But on the whole, the police and court records for Cologne, Krefeld, and Bergheim are among the best that exist anywhere in Germany, and they provide an excellent basis for studying the operation of the Nazi terror in fine detail.

These records form the core of the materials analyzed in this book. In total, I have systematically read and analyzed, both quantitatively and qualitatively, more than 1,100 Gestapo and Special Court case files. These include every available Special Court case file for the town of Bergheim (nearly 100 cases), every available Gestapo case file involving political infractions by Jews for the city of Krefeld (more than 100 cases), and a random sample of more than 900 Gestapo and Special Court case files (dealing with all segments of the German population) for the cities of Cologne and Krefeld. I have carefully recorded, placed in machine-readable form, and analyzed statistically the information in each case pertaining to the nature of the offense; the background of the offender; the means by which the offender came to the attention of the police authorities (for example, whether through the Gestapo's own information network or through denunciations from the civilian population); the background and motivation of the denouncers and their relationship to the people they denounced; and the final result of the case (whether it led to a mere warning from the Gestapo, a dismissal from the prosecuting attorney, a court conviction or acquittal, or a referral to a concentration camp).

The resulting analyses make possible a number of important observations about how the Nazi terror operated on a daily basis. Among other things, they help distinguish between the large volume of minor acts of nonconformist behavior that were never intended to help bring about the fall of the Nazi dictatorship and the modest number of real acts of resistance that did aim at bringing down the Nazis. They help to reveal how the terror functioned differently for different groups of people at different times—for example, how the terror could have appeared to be, and often was, omnipresent and constant for some (such as Jews, Communists, and Jehovah's Witnesses), partial and intermittent for others (clergymen, other religious faithful, malcontents), and almost nonexistent for a large proportion of the population. They help to show which kinds of average citizens were willing to assist the Gestapo in its spying and on whom and why they spied. These analyses also make it possible to put some old myths about the Gestapo and the nature of the Nazi terror to rest—for example, that the Gestapo was omniscient and all-powerful and that the terror was so pervasive and so insidious that children often denounced their parents and wives their husbands. And finally, they help put into better balance the assertions of some revisionists who currently place too much emphasis on civilian denunciations and portray the Gestapo as less powerful and capable than it really was.

I have augmented the information in the Gestapo and Special Court case files with many other types of records and evidence. Especially important are the written surveys and in-depth interviews conducted especially for this study with German citizens and Jewish Holocaust survivors who experienced the Nazi terror and the Third Reich firsthand and the detailed records pertaining to the careers of Gestapo and other police officials (police personnel files, Nazi Party and SS files, denazification records, Interior Ministry records, and trial records for "crimes against humanity" lodged against Gestapo and police officers after the war). To gain a greater understanding of the mentalities, backgrounds, and activities of the police officials who served as the most significant enforcers of the Nazi terror in the city and the countryside, I have followed the lives of several Gestapo and other police officers from cradle to grave. Included among these are the heads of the Gestapo (Emanuel Schäfer and Franz Sprinz in Cologne and Ludwig Jung in Krefeld), the heads of the "Jewish desks" of the Gestapo (Karl Löffler in Cologne and Richard Schulenburg in Krefeld), the rest of the relatively small contingent of ordinary Gestapo officers in Krefeld, and the two policemen responsible for political cases in the small town of Bergheim (Gottfried Schleiden and Wilhelm Servos).

The book begins with a discussion of these men and of the structure, nature, and functioning of the Gestapo and the political police. The book also ends with these men, detailing their postwar attempts to return to police service, to retain their pensions, and to avoid justice at all costs. In the beginning and final chapters of the book, Richard Schulenburg of Krefeld and Karl Löffler of Cologne receive special consideration because, as the Gestapo's "specialists" for "Jewish affairs," they were the men in their local communities who coordinated the Nazi terror's most heinous undertaking, the systematic persecution and ultimate mass murder of the Jewish population. The middle of the book analyzes the Nazi terror as it unfolded chronologically and as it affected different groups of people at different times. The chapters in this part begin by examining the persecution of the Jews in the 1930s and the recollections of Jewish survivors about their treatment by their fellow German citizens and by the Nazi authorities. The next chapters treat the pressure imposed on leftist and religious opponents and organizations after Hitler's takeover in the early and mid-1930s and then consider the rest of the "ordinary" German population's encounter with Nazi terror in first the prewar and later the wartime years. The last chapters of the book focus on the deportation and destruction of the Jews and examine the participation in and awareness of the Holocaust on the part of the Gestapo and the domestic German population.

Throughout this book, I stress the role of individuals in creating and maintaining the Nazi terror. Although the Nazi Party leadership in Berlin set the terror in motion and determined its broad contours, its implementation and effectiveness depended on the voluntary choices and local actions of individual German citizens.

CHAPTER TWO

INSIDE GESTAPO HEADQUARTERS:
THE AGENTS OF THE TERROR

G estapo officers were an unrepentant lot. After the war some went into hiding under false identities, but in the western parts of Germany at least, most stayed at home. Staying at home usually required facing some period of internment under the American, British, or French occupational forces. Those who wanted to return to government service (if they were younger men) or receive their pensions (if they were older) also had to face denazification and other hearings and investigations evaluating their past activities.[1] Most who underwent this process did so confidently, even indignantly. Few admitted any guilt, and many may even have believed that they bore no guilt.

How could this have been possible? What kinds of people were these Gestapo officers? How had they acted in the Third Reich, and what became of them afterward? How was the Gestapo organized, and how did it function in Nazi Germany? A way to begin answering these questions is to consider some of the evidence provided in the postwar denazification records of Richard Schulenburg, the former head of the Krefeld Gestapo's "Jewish desk," and the postwar trial records of Alfred Effenberg, one of the Krefeld Gestapo's average officers.

RICHARD SCHULENBURG'S DENAZIFICATION

After the war ended Richard Schulenburg spent four months in a British internment camp and then returned to his home in Krefeld. Haggard (he

listed his height as six feet and his weight as 153 pounds in his first denazification questionnaire), already in his late sixties, and suffering from rheumatism, he was too old to try to return to government service or find other
meaningful employment. The only work he was able to find was with the
local Protestant church distributing its Sunday newspaper. He wanted his
state pension. To get it, he had to go through denazification proceedings.[2]
This entailed convincing the "denazification committee"—a panel of five
fellow Krefelders—that he was not a Nazi criminal. They would base their
judgment on letters he submitted in his own behalf, a detailed twelve-page
questionnaire about his personal background and involvement in National
Socialist activities, and other information they had about him, the Krefeld
Gestapo, and the local Nazi Party. The denazification committee held its deliberations in the large Hansa-Haus office building in downtown Krefeld.
Facing a large, open square, and just across the street from the main train
station, the Hansa-Haus also housed the Krefeld police and, until 1940, the
Krefeld Gestapo.[3]

Schulenburg opened his case on July 1, 1947, with a letter to the committee summarizing his background and professing his innocence. He began the letter with a plea to the committee members' sympathy, stating that
he was no longer able to work because of his age and his rheumatism. He
then continued matter-of-factly: "I have been employed in state and community service for forty-eight years. On May 1, 1907, the Krefeld police
authorities hired me at the rank of police sergeant. In November 1919 I was
detached to the criminal police and remained there until 1938. From 1934
to 1938 I served in department I Ad [political police]. In 1938 this department came under the state authorities and thereby, without any initiative
on my part, I became part of the Krefeld Gestapo outpost where I remained
until March 31, 1945." He concluded: "I hereby declare under oath that in
my long years of service I never committed any crime or misdemeanor. I
always treated each person, independent of their political views or racial
background, correctly and humanely."[4]

In the follow-up documentation, which started to emerge even before
Schulenburg wrote his own original letter to the denazification committee
and stretched out over more than a decade, Schulenburg supported his

claims with several letters from prominent Krefelders, including the heads
of the Catholic and the Protestant churches, the former mayor, the leader
of the local Christian Democratic Party, and even some Jewish victims still
residing in the city. These people attested to his upright manner, respected
standing in Krefeld society, and many good deeds. Many recounted individual episodes when Schulenburg had interceded on their behalf or on the
behalf of other potential victims of the Nazi terror apparatus. One of these
letters was submitted on February 27, 1947, in both German and English
translation, by the leader of the Krefeld Catholic Church, Dr. Schwamborn,
prelate, canon, and dean of the main parish church of the Holy Dionysius:

> Mr. Richard Schulenburg was head criminal secretary in the political
> section of the police force. When the police force was nationalised it
> was compulsory for him to remain with the state police. Here he was
> exceedingly humane and just in carrying out his duties. As an almost
> "permanent guest" of the Gestapo, I heard this repeatedly from vari-
> ous sides. I was told the same especially by many persecuted Jews who
> came to me in great numbers as I was entrusted with the care of Jewish
> religious relics. Schulenburg was in charge of the "Jewish Depart-
> ment" and as the Jews told me, he always treated them decently and,
> as far as he was able, offered them many possibilities. Any injustice,
> hardness and ill-treatment was incompatible with the decency of his
> character. I am glad to be able to issue this evidence for a gentleman
> who belongs to the Protestant community.[5]

As impressive as this and many of the other letters were, Schulenburg
failed, at least initially, to convince the denazification committee members
of his innocence. Furthermore, their original judgment in his case in 1947
was confirmed by higher denazification authorities in the state capital of
Düsseldorf on August 31, 1949. Of the five possible categories one could
receive from the denazification committee—from being considered a major
Nazi leader guilty of serious crimes (category I) to a person who had no guilt
whatsoever (category V)—Schulenburg was put in category III (minor perpetrators).[6] As such, he could not return to public service and he could re-

ceive only 50 percent of his pension; moreover, his years in the Gestapo and his promotions during those years could not be included in calculating his pension. The grounds for the committee's decision were that Schulenburg had, as one of the earliest Krefelders to join the Nazi Party in 1927, helped pave the way for the Nazi dictatorship.[7] The committee also noted that he had remained in the party for the rest of the Weimar years even though he had to break his oath of fidelity to the Weimar constitution as a state official in 1930 when it became illegal for police officers to be members of the Nazi Party. In that he had served "clearly to the satisfaction of his superiors" as an "executive officer of the Gestapo, which was the severest terror instrument of the Nazi dictatorship that used *every* means to promote the dictatorship's success, for more than ten years [even though he said he had served for only seven years]," there were "no convincing grounds for his exoneration even if he had acted humanely in some individual cases." Schulenburg "admits that he had *not* offered any resistance, for he says that [if he had resisted] he would have been threatened with being put in a concentration camp and [furthermore] he believed that he had to do his duty as an officer. Important to note, however, is that in 1930 he had another conception of what his duty was."

Schulenburg was not happy with this judgment. Although it is impossible to know for certain what was in his mind, his persistent attempts for more than a decade to change his denazification status and reclaim his full pension suggest that he truly believed that he had been unfairly judged and had done no wrong. On July 26, 1949, Schulenburg's lawyer began his process of appeal. In a letter to the higher denazification authorities in nearby Düsseldorf, his lawyer wrote that even "the occupational forces in no way viewed Herr Schulenburg as the kind of Gestapo officer which one commonly imagines. When one considers that not even the most limited complaint has emerged against Herr Schulenburg from any quarter of the population, it is certainly correct to say that it is not right to be holier than the pope [in judging him]."[8]

In Schulenburg's view, he too was a victim of the Nazi regime. He had been forced to join the Gestapo in the first place and had not been allowed to retire when he first asked to in 1939 at the age of sixty.[9] He had been left with no other choice but to do his duty in what he saw was the correct and honorable manner and to try to help worthy individuals avoid horrible fates when possible. As described by Dieter Hangebruch, the author of a study of Krefeld Jewry under National Socialism, Schulenburg was "an old-style policeman, moderate and sober in manner, without malice or ambiguity. . . . The head of the Jewish desk of the Gestapo outpost in Krefeld was a typical *Schreibtischtäter* [desk perpetrator], a man, who through his proper treatment of victims sought to block out any personal responsibility."[10]

Despite Schulenburg's dissatisfaction with his denazification status, he was far from destitute. His two daughters had already grown up, leaving only himself, his wife, and his teenage son to care for. His income was not limited to his reduced pension, for left intact was his ownership of a rent-drawing, medium-sized apartment house on a quiet street on the south side of the city that he had acquired in 1937. From the many letters of support he received from well-positioned Krefelders over the next several years, it appears that his standing in Krefeld society was left intact as well. The only significant punishment he received for his Gestapo activities was a temporary blow to his pride. Eventually he would even manage to reclaim his full pension. His weight and health soon returned to normal, and he would live several more years, dying at the age of eighty-three in 1962.[11]

ALFRED EFFENBERG'S TRIAL
AND THE KREFELD GESTAPO

In the midst of his denazification proceedings, Schulenburg was called to the Krefeld county court on June 14, 1949, to testify in a case of "crimes against humanity" lodged against a forty-seven-year-old former Gestapo colleague in Krefeld named Alfred Effenberg.[12] Effenberg, who had been interned by the occupational forces for nearly three years between April 17, 1945, and March 8, 1948, had fallen on hard times after his release.[13] A robust and athletic man in his youth, he held several decorations for his sporting accomplishments.[14] A former career police officer of limited formal education who had served in the Krefeld police since 1926, he was now struggling to feed his wife and six children (four from an earlier marriage with a woman who had died in 1936) with a job as a dye-worker at the local Bayer factory in Krefeld-Ürdingen. His hope was to be able to return to police work, but his category III denazification status (received on July 5, 1948) made this impossible at the time.[15] Given his aspirations and familial responsibilities, he could ill afford a conviction in this trial. His trial testimony makes clear that he was defensive about his past and worried about his future.

Effenberg was accused by two Krefeld natives of being responsible for sending their spouses to concentration camps, one in 1939 and the other in 1944, where they later died. One of the deceased was a man named Toni M.; the other was a woman named Sybilla C. Both had been sent to a concentration camp after being denounced to the Krefeld Gestapo by fellow Krefeld residents for having made libelous statements against the regime. Each surviving spouse claimed that Effenberg had personally made the decision to resolve the case by committing the accused to a concentration camp. In both cases, Effenberg, they charged, had been fully unsympathetic to their spouses and themselves, barred their way to having an audience with the head of the Krefeld Gestapo, Kommissar Jung, and threatened them with being sent to concentration camp themselves if they persisted in their demands for such an audience.

In the case of Sybilla C., which had its origin in a dispute over a half-pound of butter stolen from her cellar, Effenberg sent the woman to Ravensbrück concentration camp after her case had been dismissed by the prosecuting attorney attached to the Düsseldorf Special Court. Her husband now charged that

> Effenberg was completely and totally responsible for the death of my wife. Effenberg could have prevented this if he had wanted to. Despite all of my pleas, he remained hard and inflexible. He displayed absolutely no human sympathy. . . . In my numerous visits to the Gestapo headquarters and discussions with Effenberg about my wife's case, I came to learn that he alone is to be made responsible for my wife's fate and her committal to the concentration camp. . . . Effenberg's superior Kommissar Ludwig Jung, head of the Krefeld Gestapo, testified previ-

ously before the *Spruchkammer* [a kind of trial held in internment camps] in Darmstadt-Lager, where I appeared as a prosecution witness, that his *Sachbearbeiter* [desk heads] had each worked independently for themselves. . . . Jung said that he as the head of the Gestapo indeed signed the reports which were sent to him by the individual desk heads, but he made no changes in the reports that were submitted to him and simply signed them without commentary.

Herr C. then concluded his charges against Effenberg by repeating that "Effenberg is fully responsible for the death of my wife. . . . He wrote his report in the case in such a way that the *Reichssicherheitshauptamt* in Berlin could do nothing else but confirm his recommendation to send my wife to concentration camp."[16]

Schulenburg was one of several former Gestapo officers and former employees of the Krefeld Gestapo called to testify about Effenberg's character and responsibilities as a Gestapo officer in particular, and about the way in which the Gestapo in Krefeld had functioned in general. At issue was the question of whether individual officers had any personal decisionmaking authority, and hence culpability for the fates of individuals persecuted by the Gestapo and the rest of the Nazi justice machinery. Effenberg argued that they had none.

Effenberg's main line of defense was that he had merely followed standard procedure in handling the cases and that only his superiors had held the authority to send anyone to a concentration camp. He also argued the standard line used by Gestapo officers in postwar trials and denazification proceedings: he had always been privately "anti-Nazi" in his political views and he was merely an ordinary career police officer who had been forced "against [his] will" to join both the Gestapo and the Nazi Party. (He did not mention that he had been a member of the ultra-nationalist paramilitary Freikorps organization between 1919 and 1920 and later had joined two of the most notorious Nazi surveillance and strong-arm organizations, the SD [Sicherheitsdienst] and the SS [Schutzstaffel].)[17] His hostility to the Gestapo had been so extreme from the very beginning, he claimed, that he had been called several times in 1933 to the *Säuberungskommission* (a commis-

sion for weeding out unreliable police officers) that met at the time in the
Hansa-Haus and threatened with dismissal. Later, during the war years, his
opposition had become so bitter that his superior, Kommissar Ludwig Jung,
had, he said, "reproached me several times for holding Communist views
and threatened me with arrest." Moreover, he asserted, he had done everything he could to protect people from persecution throughout the Nazi
years. "Indeed I can supply proof that I often took measures against denouncers and that every month I destroyed between ten and fifteen denunciations that had been made by party authorities or by individual
persons."

To support his claims and assertions, Effenberg named eleven people
who could testify on his behalf, including two of the people who also provided Schulenburg with supporting letters taken under oath, the Catholic
prelate Dr. Schwamborn and the former mayor and city councillor Dr.
Hürter. Among the others Effenberg listed as potential supportive witnesses were several people he claimed to have helped to escape from a severe
fate during the Nazi years.

The presiding mayor of Mönchengladbach, Wilhelm Elfes, was the first
person on Effenberg's list of character witnesses. Elfes was supposed to have
been arrested after the July 20, 1944, assassination plot against Hitler, but
Effenberg had tipped him off ahead of time so that he could successfully
flee and escape arrest. The second man on Effenberg's list was Adolf M. of
Krefeld, who was slated for arrest and concentration camp after he had completed an eight-year prison sentence. Instead, Effenberg had recruited him
as a *Vertrauensmann* (Gestapo spy) and had found him a job, the same job
at which M. was still working after the war. Effenberg claimed to have saved
the third man on his list, Emil M. of nearby Süchteln, from being sent to a
mental hospital after he had been accused of high treason. A fourth person
was Fritz K. of Krefeld, whom Effenberg said he had saved from being sent
to a concentration camp in 1934 for making a derogatory statement against
the regime. He had done this, he explained, by persuading the medical examiner in Krefeld, Medizinrat Dr. Klaholt, to declare officially that K. was
not well enough to be sent to concentration camp. Effenberg's fifth support
witness was Dr. Klaholt himself, from whom Effenberg expected documentation that he had frequently saved people from being sent to concentration

camps in this way. The last person on Effenberg's list was a Gestapo colleague named Gustav Burkert, who could prove, Effenberg said, that the two of them had, in the fall of 1944, prevented a large roundup of hostages ordered and planned by the local Nazi Party leadership.

Schulenburg began his testimony in the Effenberg case in his usual calm and unflappable manner. At the top of his one-page typewritten testimony, he listed his age, residence, and occupation as seventy years old, resident of Krefeld living at am Königshof. 47, and *Kriminalobersekretär a.D.* (senior criminal secretary, out of service). Schulenburg then stated openly what his position had been in the Krefeld Gestapo: "I was the head of the desk for Jewish affairs from the time that the Krefeld Gestapo outpost was established until the final collapse." Then he explained carefully how ordinary Gestapo officers had operated: "In the handling of individual cases, which were always presented to us from the head of the Gestapo outpost, we indeed had a free hand." But, he clarified,

> the decision whether a person was to be put into protective custody
> [and thus into concentration camp] lay without exception with [our
> superiors in] the regional head Gestapo office in Düsseldorf or indeed
> with the Reich Security Main Office in Berlin. . . . The desk officer
> could make recommendations about the disposition of a case . . . but
> he had absolutely no final decisionmaking authority.

After completing his testimony, Schulenburg signed his long name carefully, slowly, and clearly, just as he had thousands of times before while processing the myriad forms and affidavits pertaining to the emigration, regulation, and "evacuation" of the Krefeld Jews. Just as he now appeared to demonstrate that he had nothing to hide by his opening statement that he was the head of the Krefeld Jewish desk from beginning to end, he also apparently saw no reason to rush. Schulenburg was a patient man.

Schulenburg's intent in his testimony was obviously to deflect blame away from Effenberg. He also wanted to deflect whatever possible blame he himself, as the Gestapo officer who oversaw the deportations of the Krefeld Jews, might someday be called to account for in sending a far larger number of people to their deaths in concentration camps. By pointing to the higher

Gestapo authorities in Düsseldorf and Berlin, he also helped to excuse his own former immediate superior at the Krefeld Gestapo outpost, Ludwig Jung, from having had any authority and culpability in this and other crimes. This was a shrewd tactic on his part, for there had as yet been no trial in Krefeld that had taken up the matter of local Gestapo officers' responsibility for the deportations and mass murder of the Jews. Furthermore, Jung was not a man whom he would want as an enemy.

Jung was twice summoned to testify in Effenberg's trial, once in April and a second time in October. Both times he failed to appear, sending instead only written depositions from his residence in Darmstadt. These letters give the impression that he was impatient with and irritated by the entire matter. Still a young man of only thirty-nine years, prematurely bald, rather short for a former SS man (five feet seven inches), and having failed to complete his university education, Jung always seemed to be perturbed and in a hurry.[18] As the head of the Krefeld Gestapo outpost from 1939 to 1945, he, unlike the cool-headed Schulenburg, had always signed his short name quickly and impatiently, sometimes with a mere "J.," on the numerous forms he had processed daily. Now he communicated to the court that pressing business commitments did not give him the time to come to Krefeld. He was, so he claimed, constantly on the road in his job as a car accident claims' inspector for an insurance firm in Darmstadt, the town of his birth, to which he had returned at the end of the war.

Jung mailed off his first deposition on April 9, 1949, while the trial was still in the preliminary investigation phase. This document is typed (single-spaced) and two and a half pages long. In it his argument is somewhat different from what Sybilla C.'s husband had reported about his previous testimony in the Darmstadt internment camp hearing. Once again Jung denied any personal guilt in the matter. He stated that since he had become personally involved in only particularly sensitive cases, and since this had been a rather trivial case, he had never known anything about it in the first place. Nevertheless, he was careful to formulate his written testimony in such a way as to deflect the blame away from Effenberg in this case and away from all of the former desk heads who had served under him in the Krefeld Gestapo in other cases. His argument was that the Gestapo outpost in Krefeld

was at the bottom of a fully legal and highly regulated decisionmaking ladder and that only those at the top of the ladder in the Düsseldorf *Staatspol-
izeileitstelle* (the superior Gestapo post in the area to which the Krefeld Gestapo outpost reported) and in the central headquarters of the secret police
(RSHA) in Berlin had made final decisions.

Jung put it this way:

> In my oral *Spruchkammer* hearing of June 12, 1949 [1948?], C. testi-
> fied that his wife had been denounced by a person from her same apart-
> ment building to the Krefeld Gestapo outpost in February 1944. His
> wife was then sent to Ravensbrück concentration camp in August
> 1944. From there she never returned. C. does not know me, but he
> assumes that I am guilty for all of these events. I have already replied
> in this same case that I personally was not involved in the handling of
> Frau C.'s case and that the entire facts of the case are still unknown to
> me. In any case it is correct that the Krefeld outpost in no way held
> the authority to, or can be made responsible for, sending Frau C. to
> concentration camp. One can also not make the Krefeld outpost or any
> of its officers responsible for the death of Frau C. in the concentration
> camp. In my opinion, the *Staatspolizeileitstelle* in Düsseldorf acting
> on orders from the RSHA in Berlin had to have reported, after consul-
> tation with the head prosecuting attorney attached to the Düsseldorf
> Special Court, that Frau C. was to be transferred [sent to concentration
> camp]. This process was a unified one throughout the entire Reich on
> the basis of an agreement between the Reich Justice Ministry and the
> RSHA in Berlin and the individual justice authorities throughout the
> Reich.[19]

Like Effenberg, Jung was noticably defensive in the matter. He appeared to believe that he was still being accused in the case even though the
effect of the most recent testimony of Sybilla C.'s husband had been to put
the entire blame for her death on Effenberg's shoulders, probably because
he had been unsuccessful in getting Jung convicted in the previous hearing
held in the internment camp in Darmstadt. Had Jung chosen to come to

Krefeld, he might have known this. But he realized that showing up in Krefeld might have been dangerous for him, and he therefore chose not to come. It has been difficult to find out exactly what Jung did or what happened to him after the Effenberg trial since many of his records and those of his wife (who had also been employed by the Gestapo, in the Düsseldorf headquarters) appear to have been purged sometime after Effenberg's trial ended.[20] What is clear, however, is that Jung refused to come to Krefeld a second time in October 1949. Although he had received a mailed summons well in advance that he was to appear on October 6 to testify at Effenberg's jury trial, he had his wife telegram to the Krefeld court—at the last moment before he was scheduled to appear—that he was out of town on a business trip and could not possibly testify in person at the trial. He followed this up after he returned home with a brief letter saying that he had already communicated all that he knew about the case in his previous letter of April 9.

Of the other people called to testify in the Effenberg case, the most significant testimonies were provided by another former Krefeld Gestapo officer and by three women who had worked as secretaries for the Krefeld Gestapo between 1937 and 1944. All of these people testified in June 1949, around the time when Schulenburg gave his testimony. The effect of their testimony, though they had mixed views of Effenberg, was to muddy the waters further by casting more of the blame back onto Jung's shoulders.

Gustav Burkert, Effenberg's former colleague and friend whom he had named as one of his original defense witnesses, provided Effenberg with his strongest support. Burkert's background was almost identical to Effenberg's. At the time of the trial he was a forty-six-year-old, former career policeman working as a low-level businessman. Like Effenberg, Schulenburg, and most of the rank-and-file Gestapo officers in Krefeld, he had a limited formal education, only eight years in the primary school. Also like his friend and former colleague Effenberg, he was a family man with an athletic build and several athletic medals to his credit that he had proudly referred to in his application to join the SS in 1939. Although he had first joined the Nazi Party in 1937 along with Effenberg and many other Gestapo officers in Krefeld and elsewhere throughout Germany, he had already been a block warden for a Nazi Party branch organization, the NSV (National Socialist People's Welfare Organization). He also, like Effenberg, had joined the SD sometime before he applied to join the SS in 1939. His highest rank in both the SS and the Gestapo was identical to Effenberg's (SS *Sturmschar-führer* and *Kriminalsekretär*), as documented by an organizational plan of the Krefeld Gestapo of April 23, 1944, and he had performed much the same duties in the Krefeld Gestapo. The organizational plan of 1944 lists them as having the same areas of jurisdiction within the Krefeld Gestapo outpost: left-wing movements, illegal opinion statements, and opposition. Prior to the late war years, however, Burkert and Effenberg had also worked in other areas. From reading a great number of the existing Krefeld Gestapo files, it is possible to determine that Effenberg had previously been involved in homosexual cases and Burkert had often seconded Schulenburg in Jewish cases. Burkert first joined the police the same year Effenberg did (1923), came from the eastern part of Germany, and, again like Effenberg, was transferred to the Krefeld police in 1926.[21]

In his testimony, delivered a week after Schulenburg's on June 21, 1949, Burkert echoed Schulenburg's assertion that individual desk heads had enjoyed a relatively free hand in treating individual cases. He then qualified this statement, however, in a way that Schulenburg had not done—by explaining that the desk heads frequently consulted with Jung or his deputy on how best to proceed during the course of an investigation and on the final course of action to be recommended at the conclusion of an investigation. Most important, he stated that "without exception, the final decisionmaking authority as to the appropriate measures to take lay with the commanding officer [Jung] or with his deputy [when Jung was away]." Burkert then went on to explain that Jung's and his deputy's final decisions had determined whether the cases led "to a state police warning, to arrest for a period of up to twenty-one days, to being handed over to the court authorities, or to being sent on to [higher Gestapo authorites in] Düsseldorf for final determination."[22]

Burkert's statements about how decisions were made in the Krefeld Gestapo were all the more persuasive to the court because they largely corroborated the testimony of three women who had served as secretaries in the

Krefeld outpost but apparently were not friendly with Effenberg and did not hold him in such high esteem. The first of these women, called on June 8, was a married, twenty-nine-year-old bookkeeper named Frau T. who had worked with another secretary (a certain Frau B., who did not appear in the case) between 1942 and 1944 in an office that was in an anteroom to Jung's office. From this vantage point she had clearly had an excellent opportunity to observe how the entire operation functioned, and she provided several important details about how individual cases were handled by the Krefeld Gestapo outpost.

When a case was opened, she explained, Jung would first determine which officer was to take over the investigation. This officer would then gather information, call witnesses, and conduct interrogations as he saw fit, though often he would consult with Jung on how to proceed. After he was finished with his investigation, he would file a report on the case with a recommendation as to its disposal, which she or Frau B. would type up. Jung would then read this report, sometimes amend it heavily, and sign it. When Jung was not there, his deputy Karl Schmitz took over for him and made whatever changes were necessary in the final report and then signed it. (Schmitz, like Schulenburg, was an older officer, born in Krefeld in 1887, who had also attained the rank of *Kriminalobersekretär* by the later war years. Like Schulenburg and many of the other officers, he had also been a career policeman. In addition to being Jung's second-in-command, he had led the ominous "Special Treatment Department" of the Krefeld Gestapo outpost.)[23] Although Frau T. was not on good terms with Effenberg and described him in unflattering terms—she said he had the reputation of being "rather harsh"—and although she claimed that she herself had been arrested in 1944 for sympathizing with a French prisoner to whom she had given an apple, she did Effenberg a major service when she concluded her testimony by pointing to Jung as always having had the final say: "In every case the final decision about what measures were to be taken lay with the head of the Gestapo outpost."[24]

The other two secretaries were called in just prior to Schulenburg on June 14. The first of them, Frau L., said she had been the Krefeld Gestapo outpost's only secretary for nearly four years between the time it formally came into being on August 1, 1937, and the middle of 1941.[25] At this time she was a thirty-five-year-old housewife. She explained that there were only seven officers at the Krefeld outpost when she worked for it, and then she named them: Jung, Schulenburg, Schmitz, Effenberg, Burkert, Herbert Braun, and Kurt Joost. (For unknown reasons, she left out at least six Gestapo officers—Otto Dihr, Albert Fleischer, Jakob Schmitz, Theodor Schommer, Wilhelm Weber, and Kommissar Bolle—who also worked for the Krefeld Gestapo during the time when she was a secretary.)[26] Nevertheless, her testimony helps demonstrate that the Krefeld Gestapo outpost grew in size sometime after mid-1941: the organizational plan of 1944 lists fourteen officers on active duty. After this she described the functioning of the outpost in much the same way that Frau T. had described it. Written letters of denunciation or other information leading to the opening of individual investigations arrived in the morning mail. Jung read the post over and decided which cases were to be investigated. He then handed over the information he had at that point to the individual officers he selected to handle the cases. These officers completed the investigations and usually typed up the reports themselves. (Note how this compares with the previous secretary's testimony that she had typed up the reports in the later years.) Jung then read the reports, amended them as he felt necessary, and signed them. Only a few of the cases, she said, were passed on to higher authorities in Düsseldorf. Finally she stated that, although Jung most often accepted what the individual officers had recommended, "the individual officer had absolutely no independent authority, only the Kommissar [Jung] or his deputy [Schmitz] had this." She made no comment at all about Effenberg.

The last secretary to testify was a thirty-year-old housewife named Frau H. She stated that she had worked for the Krefeld outpost for a brief period of two weeks in October 1942 and later for a more extended period between September 1944 and the end of the war. Between these two periods she had worked for the central Gestapo headquarters in Düsseldorf. Among other things, her testimony demonstrated that the secretarial support staff in Krefeld had grown significantly in the later war years: she had worked as a personal typist for Effenberg and Burkert in her second period of employment with the Krefeld Gestapo. In testimony more directly relevant to the

Effenberg case, she claimed that all of the important decisions were made by the head of the outpost (Jung), but that even he could not order someone to be placed in "protective custody" (the first step toward being sent to a concentration camp); this step had to be ordered by, as she put it, "Düsseldorf or indeed by Berlin." She finished by saying that, although Jung had made the final decisions, the many conversations he had with the officers under him had certainly been an important influence on his final decisions.

Several other witnesses also testified in Effenberg's case (which had begun in January and was not completed until October 1949). Most were mere character witnesses suggested by Effenberg to support his claims that he had been an honorable police officer who performed many good deeds during his many years in service. Several of these people were older policemen who had served with him in Krefeld before the Gestapo came into existence. Others were common citizens for whom he had done favors during his years with the Krefeld Gestapo.

In the end the court had to make its decision based primarily on the conflicting testimony of the plaintiffs, the defendant Effenberg, the Gestapo officers Schulenburg and Burkert, and the three secretaries. This was not an easy task. The plaintiffs had charged that Effenberg alone was to be held responsible for the incarceration and subsequent deaths of their spouses. Effenberg, Burkert, and two of the secretaries alleged that Jung or perhaps his deputy Schmitz (they could not apparently remember which) was the real person to be held responsible. Jung, Schulenburg, and the third secretary pointed to the higher authorities in Düsseldorf and Berlin as the responsible parties. Since the original Gestapo case files were never brought into evidence (probably because they were presumed to have been destroyed, just as most other records of the Gestapo's activity were), it was impossible to determine whether Jung or Schmitz had signed off in these particular cases or whether either of them had amended Effenberg's reports. Indeed, it was impossible to know exactly what the reports had contained. Additionally, the neighbors, who had made the original denunciations to the Gestapo that had served to open the cases in the first place, were not charged or even called to testify.

The case was decided on October 6, 1949. In its decision, the court acquitted Effenberg of any responsibility for the murder of the two spouses and of crimes against humanity generally. Still, Effenberg did not quite get off unscathed. The court convicted him of a lesser charge—*Beihilfe zur schweren Freiheitsberaubung* (acting as an accomplice in an aggravated case of deprivation of liberty)—and sentenced him to a three-month jail term. This was, considering the fate of the two people who had lost their lives, a comparatively light sentence. In Effenberg's opinion, however, it was unfairly harsh. Worst of all to him was that it severely damaged his chances of repealing his category III denazification status, which he needed to do to be able to return to police service.

The Effenberg case, though unspectacular, is revealing. It provides a window through which one can begin to view how the machinery and agents of terror operated on a day-to-day basis in the Third Reich. In identifying several of the officers who worked in an average Gestapo outpost like Krefeld, it helps to open a discussion of the mentality and backgrounds of such officers. Finally, it introduces the thorny problem of apportioning individual blame for the persecution under which many people had suffered in Nazi society. As we see in Effenberg's trial, Gestapo officers after the war had little trouble in coming up with excuses, and people who would help to excuse them, for their behavior in the Third Reich: they claimed that they had not wanted to be in the Gestapo in the first place; that they had always held anti-Nazi views; that they personally had interceded on behalf of many people who would otherwise have been persecuted or persecuted more harshly; that they had worked in a highly regimented chain of command where final decisions were always made by people above them; and that they had simply followed orders and regulations. Finally, the Gestapo officers could often make a reasonable claim that they had not acted alone in initiating, carrying out, and legitimizing the pervasive terror in Nazi society.

Whereas the Effenberg trial focuses on the central role of Gestapo officers in individual cases of persecution, it also suggests that many other people played significant roles as well. Neither Toni M. nor Sybilla C., for example, would have been brought to the attention of the Gestapo in the first place had their neighbors not denounced them. We will come to observe that such denunciations, often motivated by personal jealousy and petty grievances, frequently led to the persecution and sometimes to the death of large numbers of people like Toni M. and Sybilla C. Nazi court officials, like prosecutors and judges, though mentioned only in passing in the Effenberg trial, also deserve a not inconsiderable share of the blame. Not only did their indictments and verdicts lead to enormous pain and misery, but the veneer of "legality" and "normality" that they helped to provide to a criminal regime made its persecution all the more effective and terrifying. Additionally, other Nazi Party, police, and governmental officials were often instrumental in making the terror work.

The roles of all of these people will not be overlooked. But as in the Effenberg trial and in the deportation of the Cologne Jews trial introduced in the previous chapter, it was most often the Gestapo officers who were the leading perpetrators deserving of indictment. The remainder of this chapter delves more deeply into the backgrounds, mentality, and careers of Cologne and Krefeld Gestapo officers and the police officers who did the political policing in the absence of a formal Gestapo outpost in the small town of Bergheim.

GESTAPO OFFICERS

In the testimony of the former secretaries in Effenberg's trial, one learns that the Krefeld Gestapo outpost had only a small staff of officers and office employees. According to Frau L. and what can be ascertained from other documentation about the Krefeld Gestapo, between 1937 and 1941 it had at most twelve or thirteen officers and she was the only secretary. From an organizational plan of the Krefeld Gestapo of April 1944 and from the testimony of the other two former secretaries in Effenberg's trial, one observes that the Krefeld outpost grew to fourteen officers and at least two secretaries sometime after 1941 and remained at or about this level thereafter.[27]

Given that Krefeld had a population of about 170,000 inhabitants during the Nazi years, simple arithmetic can be employed to arrive at a ratio of about one Gestapo officer for every 10,000 to 15,000 citizens. This ratio appears to hold for other cities too. Cologne, a city of approximately three-quarters of a million inhabitants in the same period, had 99 Gestapo officers in 1939 and only 69 officers in 1942.[28] Scholars who have studied the Gestapo organizations that operated in other German cities, such as Saarbrücken, Würzburg, Potsdam, Hannover, and Leipzig, arrive at similar estimations of the ratio of the Gestapo to the general population.[29] One would arrive at an even higher ratio by factoring in the thousands of foreign laborers who were not counted in the population censuses but who came under the control of the Gestapo in Krefeld, Cologne, and other cities. And this applies only to urban communities. As I learned from studying the small town of Bergheim and from interviews I conducted with former residents of small towns from various parts of Germany (such as a former policeman from the small city of Eberswalde to the northeast of Berlin, and a former railroad official and Nazi Party functionary from a small village outside of Saarbrücken),[30] there were typically no Gestapo officers operating in the German countryside at all. In rural localities, the local gendarmerie or *Schutzpolizei* (regular police), working under the authority of the local mayor's office, performed the police work that the Gestapo performed in the cities. Only in the most serious cases did the local police feel a need to call in urban-based Gestapo officers for expert advice and assistance.

If there were such a limited number of Gestapo officers in the city and if the bulk of political policing in rural towns and villages was carried out by the regular police, could it be that the Gestapo officers were just ordinary police officers, albeit with a scary title ("secret state police") and some especially nasty business to attend to? This is what most former Gestapo officers said about themselves in their hearings and trials after the war. Elderly officers like Richard Schulenburg of Krefeld and Karl Löffler of Cologne, men already in their declining years by the war's end, pointed frequently to their long policing careers beginning before the First World War to back up their claims that they were only policemen of "the old school" who, even in the opinion of the Allied occupation forces, did not fit the popular view of secret policemen. Rather, these men seemed to fit the mold of "calm, elderly officers [who] let things come to them and did not undertake any of their own initiatives," as they and other Gestapo officers were characterized in 1954 by the former Cologne Gestapo chief Dr. Emanuel Schäfer in his testimony

when he and other Cologne Gestapo officers were on trial for the deportation and destruction of the Cologne Jews.[31] And as we have seen in the
Effenberg trial, even comparatively younger officers like Alfred Effenberg
and Gustav Burkert could and did make similar claims about being ordinary
policemen of long standing.

Indeed, some of the best-informed recent research on the Gestapo argues a similar line: Gestapo officers were simply "ordinary men," largely
indistinguishable in background and nature from other German police officers.[32] Although, as mentioned in the previous chapter, there is some danger that this line of argumentation might have an exculpatory effect, it does
not consciously attempt to excuse Gestapo officers for their evil deeds, nor
does it deny that evil deeds were committed. Rather, it tries to spread the
blame to a wider spectrum of average German citizens for having provided
the Gestapo and the other police organs with their main sources of information on political suspects. Because average citizens were so often willing to
keep watch over and denounce fellow citizens whenever they stepped out of
line, and many times even when they had not stepped out of line, relatively
few secret police officers were needed to control a German population that
was quite ready and able to control itself.[33]

The subsequent chapters treating resistance activity, nonconformity,
and persecution in Cologne, Krefeld, and Bergheim will provide numerous
examples that support this hypothesis. They will also provide many coun-
terexamples, particularly in cases of the persecution of Jews, Communists,
Jehovah's Witnesses, recalcitrant clergy, and other groups of people whom
the Gestapo wanted out of the way. The Gestapo may have been somewhat
complacent about the surveillance of average German citizens who sometimes listened to BBC, criticized Hitler, or involved themselves in other minor unlawful activities. Denunciations were common enough to keep such
people in line. But in truly important cases—and the Gestapo was expert at
distinguishing between the important and the non-important—the Gestapo acted with conviction and might.

The Gestapo may not have been "all-knowing, all-powerful, and omnipresent," as many people previously thought it was, but it was not incapable
either. Denunciations were important sources of the Gestapo's information.
Individual citizens had much to do with the success of the Nazis' "social

control," just as individual citizens play an important role with respect to social control in other types of society. But the Gestapo was still the leading instrument of the Nazis' control, and the culpability of Gestapo officers was not the same as the culpability of average citizens.

All men are ordinary to some degree or another, and on several dimensions most Gestapo officers were quite plain people. But they were not "ordinary men" in the sense used by both Christopher Browning and Daniel Goldhagen to describe middle-aged reserve police officers from Hamburg and other cities who were called up for short periods of active service to shoot Jews in Poland and the former Soviet Union before returning home, as if nothing had happened, to their normal lives as workers, businessmen, and professionals.[34] To be sure, not all Gestapo officers were highly trained scientific experts, hand-selected by the SS to terrorize the German citizenry because of their supposedly superior racial, intellectual, and physical characteristics, as some people's preconceptions would lead them to expect. But some were, especially many of the heads of local Gestapo posts and outposts. Most of the rank-and-file officers had limited formal education and police training, had served in other police branches before joining the Gestapo, were physically indistinguishable from other policemen, and were not even members of the SS or the Nazi Party until after they became Gestapo officers. Nevertheless, these men were after all German policemen, and the German police force of Imperial Germany and the Weimar Republic certainly did not enjoy a democratic or moderate reputation.[35] Also, most of the older officers among them were former members of the Weimar political police who had survived an ideological purge shortly after Hitler's takeover that had claimed about two-thirds of the former political policemen.[36] They were able to do this because most could point to a background in the Freikorps, SA (brown-shirted Nazi stormtroopers), or other Nazi or proto-Nazi organizations. Some, like Richard Schulenburg, had been long-standing members of the Nazi Party, even when it was in violation of their oath as Weimar police officers. In short, most of the men who joined the Gestapo could prove that they would be reliable and even zealous upholders of the Nazi ideology.[37] Most ordinary Germans could not do this so easily.

Through intensive study of the existing records of all Krefeld Gestapo officers and several representative Cologne Gestapo officers, one can identify at least three distinct types of officers who operated in local Gestapo posts and outposts across Nazi Germany—commanding officers, rank-and-file officers, and officers who presided over the Jewish desks. After discussing the backgrounds, careers, and mentalities of these officers in this chapter, it will be illuminating to follow their activities in subsequent chapters when they can be observed enforcing Nazi ideological and racial doctrine between 1933 and 1945 and struggling to demonstrate their innocence thereafter.

COMMANDING OFFICERS
OF LOCAL GESTAPO POSTS AND OUTPOSTS

The commanding officers of local Gestapo posts and outposts probably come closest to fitting the stereotype of what a Gestapo officer was supposed to be like. These were intrepid, career-oriented men without compassion. Like their chief in Berlin, Reinhard Heydrich, they were young, middle-class, highly educated—typically holding a degree in law (often a doctor's degree)—and early converts to the National Socialist movement.[38] Also like Heydrich, many were scarred individuals with insecure identities. Heydrich notoriously suffered from self-doubt and self-hatred over his father's possible Jewish ancestry.[39] National Socialism gave these men a career and an identity, however false and flawed. They thrust themselves zealously into the movement, joined the SA, SS, and Nazi Party as soon as they could, and rose quickly through the ranks. Along the way, they were selected, or they volunteered, for special training and special assignments. Many visited a special leadership school for the security police in Berlin-Charlottenburg before they were commissioned to head a particular Gestapo post or outpost. Most did not originate from the community whose Gestapo headquarters they led, and they seldom stayed for more than a few years in any particular community.[40]

As heads of urban Gestapo headquarters, they mediated between the rank-and-file Gestapo officers under them and the Gestapo authorities in Berlin above them. As described by the secretaries of the Krefeld outpost in the Effenberg trial, they had a considerable amount of control over the entire local operation and had a hand in almost every investigation in one way or another. They determined which cases were to be investigated and which Gestapo officers were to lead the investigations. And even if they seldom were physically involved in dragnets, shakedowns, and individual interrogations, they would intercede as they felt necessary to guide the course of investigations. Sometimes they would disagree with the investigating officer's recommendation as to the outcome of a case, write up their own position statement on the case, and make a different recommendation. In most cases they simply accepted the recommendation of the investigating officer, amended the final report for content and grammar, and passed it on to the RSHA in Berlin for a final official determination of how the case was to be resolved. The heads of the secret police in Berlin (Heydrich and later Ernst Kaltenbrunner or one of their deputies), in all but rare cases, rubberstamped their recommendation and telegrammed back their reply within a few days.

Although there was a highly routinized procedure and chain of command that they were to respect, the local Gestapo heads had considerable decisionmaking power. Not only did they guide the course of the investigations and make the final recommendations as to their outcome (that is, whether the accused person was to be finally let go, with or without a warning, passed on to the prosecuting attorney and court authorities, or taken into protective custody en route to being sent to a concentration camp), but they also could hold the accused prisoner for more or less as long as they thought necessary to complete their investigation (most often a matter of hours or days, but sometimes a matter of years),[41] and they could order that the accused be put into protective custody for as long as three weeks without the approval of any higher authority. Finally, they also had the responsibility of overseeing reports on the progress of concentration camp prisoners and could order that the prisoners be kept in the camps for extended periods even if the local camp authorities recommended otherwise.

These were certainly not "ordinary men." And they were not simply *Schreibtischtäter* pushing papers around either. These were enthusiastic Nazis who took an active role in persecution and murder. Many, like the wartime heads of the Cologne Gestapo, Dr. Erich Isselhorst, Dr. Emanuel Schäfer, and Franz Sprinz, took time out from their normal Gestapo jobs to lead some of the Third Reich's most notorious and heinous operations, including heading up SS *Einsatzkommando* units that gunned down hundreds of thousands of defenseless Jews in Poland and the former Soviet Union. Others, like the chief of the Krefeld Gestapo, Ludwig Jung, helped the Nazi murder machine in smaller ways.

Unlike the situation in Cologne, where seven different men headed the local secret police headquarters at one time or another, the Krefeld Gestapo outpost had only one commanding officer for nearly its entire duration.[42] Ludwig Jung came to head the Krefeld Gestapo at the beginning of 1939 after completing the special course of study for future Gestapo leaders in Berlin-Charlottenburg. Born the son of a master butcher in Darmstadt in 1910, Jung never quite measured up to the standard of Gestapo heads in larger localities. Short in stature and with thinning hair already in his twenties, he failed to complete his legal studies at the University of Giessen, where he studied between 1928 and 1932, and this was probably a particularly sore point with him and a roadblock to his achieving higher rank and status in the Gestapo. Nevertheless, he was the only university-trained Gestapo officer in the small Krefeld outpost and the only one to reach a police rank (*Kriminal Kommissar*) commensurate with that of a military officer.

From Jung's handwritten curriculum vitae that he submitted as part of a standard SS questionnaire on December 1, 1938, we learn that he had been an active member of the Nazi German Students' Union while attending university and had joined the Nazi Party at the young age of twenty in October 1930. After leaving the university without finishing his degree in 1932, allegedly because of his "parents' economic distress," he soon entered on a career in the police. He took his first post in March 1933 as a nonpaid honorary member of the Hessian state police (*Landespolizei*) shortly after Hitler came to power. He then rose quickly through the ranks of the Hessian police, along the way joining the SA in March 1934 and later leaving it in May 1935; he also attended several police training courses lasting for periods of up to ten months. After finishing the longest of these training courses at the end of December 1936, he was promoted to the rank of *Kriminal Kommissar* and transferred at the beginning of 1937 from his native Darmstadt to the SD office of the Düsseldorf Gestapo. Within a few months he became engaged to his future wife, Elisabeth S., a secretary at the Düsseldorf Gestapo headquarters. He joined the SS almost a year later in March 1938 and in November of that year was summoned to attend the three-month leadership training course in Berlin-Charlottenburg.[43] After completion of the course, he was made head of the Krefeld Gestapo outpost, where he remained until the end of the war. In later chapters, we will have opportunity to note that he served faithfully in that capacity and that his reputation for "political fanaticism" and "hatred of Jews" was well deserved.[44] Despite his ideological zeal, however, he was never promoted beyond the rank he had achieved in 1937. After the war he returned to his native Darmstadt as a relatively small-time, former Nazi policeman looking for a job.

Men who successfully completed their university studies, like the commanding officers of the much larger Cologne Gestapo post, were able to climb higher in the secret police. Ascent in rank often demanded a descent into greater acts of inhumanity, as the grotesque career of one of the Cologne Gestapo's wartime commanding officers, Dr. Emanuel Schäfer, demonstrates.

Born on Adolf Hitler's eleventh birthday on April 20, 1900, Emanuel Schäfer was a heavy-set, ambitious, ruthless, and somewhat rootless man with an insatiable appetite for violence and adventure. Like many other uprooted young men of his generation—perhaps especially men who came from territories taken away from Germany after the First World War—Schäfer found an ideological home and a chance to prove his Germanness in the Nazi movement. It also provided him with an outlet for his violent yearnings. The son of a hotel owner, Schäfer moved as a young boy with his family to the town of Rybnik in Upper Silesia where he was brought up. At this time Rybnik was part of the German Reich. But after the First World War, Rybnik became part of Poland, making Schäfer a Polish citizen until he was naturalized as a German citizen in February 1925.[45] Schäfer attended primary school in Rybnik and later a humanistic gymnasium. In June 1918, before completing his gymnasium studies, he was called up to serve in the army. Although he claimed in 1937 in an SS questionnaire that he had been a "participant in the war," in fact he never served at the front.[46] This may have come as a disappointment to him: he soon embarked on a long career of extremist right-wing activities centered on violence.

At one time or another, Schäfer would become a member of almost every single Nazi and proto-Nazi strong-arm organization. He also would stand at the center or near the center of several of the Nazis' most heinous operations. After returning home to Rybnik for a couple of months at the end of World War I, he joined the German border patrol (*Grenzschutz*) along Germany's eastern border in Upper Silesia in January 1919. He remained with the border patrol for most of the next two and a half years and several times saw action with the Freikorps paramilitary organization.[47] Because of his border patrol service, his gymnasium granted him a diploma at the end of 1919 without requiring that he pass examinations, and he enrolled as a law student at the University of Breslau in the fall of 1920. With the exception of a two-month break in his studies when he joined a student company to fight in the third Polish uprising in mid-1921, he studied continuously for the next five years. In August 1925 he received his doctorate degree with a dissertation on civil law.

Just before he graduated, Schäfer joined the nationalist Stahlhelm organization (in which he remained from March 1925 until March 1928).[48] After graduation he entered into a career with the German police, a career that was ended only by the downfall of the Third Reich. His first appointment came in April 1926 with the Potsdam criminal police. A year later he spent several months at the special school in Berlin-Charlottenburg for the training of higher secret police officers and on graduation found a position in March 1928 with the Breslau police headquarters, where he was soon promoted to senior police officer rank with a lifetime commission. Shortly thereafter, in 1928, and probably for careerist reasons, Schäfer converted from the Catholic faith of his parents to the dominant Protestant faith of the rest of Germany's citizens. (In 1936 he renounced Protestantism and became *gottgläubig* [a kind of agnostic], as was the fashion in Nazi circles; after 1945 he reconverted to Protestantism.) At the end of 1928 he became the head of the Breslau police's homicide department. He retained this position until late February 1933, shortly after Hitler seized power.

Schäfer moved quickly to identify himself with the Nazi movement, and his star rose quickly with the Nazis' success. Although Weimar police officers could not legally join the Nazi Party, Schäfer had made his Nazi colors evident early on, sometime in 1930 or 1931, by joining the SS as a sponsoring member. Within months of Hitler's takeover, Schäfer joined the SA (on his and Hitler's birthday on April 20, 1933) and applied to join the

Nazi Party (on May 1, 1933).[49] He also soon joined other Nazi organizations, such as Heydrich's spy network, the SD, and the Reich Association of State Officials—where, as he openly stated in his SS records of 1937, he served as a *Vertrauensmann* spying on other members.

Schäfer's readiness to partake in the Nazis' dirty work, particularly in spying and undercover operations, brought him quick promotions in his policing career. He also rose quickly through the ranks of the Nazi spying and stormtrooper organizations, taking on ever more momentous assignments. On February 26, 1933, he left his "ordinary" policing career for good when he became the head of the political police in Breslau. In May 1934 he became the head of the Gestapo in the city of Oppeln, where he remained until the war broke out in September 1939.

Schäfer was given even higher assignments in the war years. He was considered by the SS to possess an "unobjectionable character, strong and energetic will, healthy human understanding, excellent intelligence and perception, sound educational background, and solid National-Socialist worldview," and to be "faultless in his manner and conduct both in and out of service";[50] with these qualities, as well as his background in policing and spying, Schäfer could be counted on when Hitler had a truly special task to perform, like starting the Second World War. After the war was over, while Schäfer was in hiding at the home of one of his former secretaries and her husband, Marianne and Friedrich K., he bragged to the husband about how he had personally started the war by leading the infamous attack on the German radio transmitter along the Polish border at Gleiwitz. In Schäfer's subsequent investigation and trial for his activities as head of the Cologne Gestapo, the following details came out in the husband's testimony of January 23, 1951.[51]

In late August 1939, a few days before the war started, Schäfer was ordered by the secret police chiefs Himmler and Heydrich to drive alone to the Oppeln airport to meet their plane coming from Berlin. When they landed, they told him the minute details of a special assignment ordered by Hitler personally. Hitler commanded Schäfer to lead a company of SA stormtroopers dressed covertly in Polish uniforms and attack the German radio transmitter at Gleiwitz, thus making it appear that Poland had started the war against Germany. "Each of the details of this operation was laid out to him, among others the bodies of certain people were to be positioned in such a way that it would appear that these people had fallen in the battle. . . . These people were relatives of leading army officers who Hitler disliked. . . . As Schäfer explained to me ironically, of course none of the members of this SA company survived the war, and only he and one other SS leader are still alive today."

Once the war broke out, Schäfer spent a few weeks as head of an SD special forces unit operating in Poland before he became the head of the newly established Gestapo headquarters in Kattowitz (near to where the Auschwitz concentration camp was established during the period when Schäfer was in Kattowitz).[52] In October 1940 he became the head of the Cologne Gestapo, where he remained until he received yet another murderous assignment as head of the security police and SD in Serbia in early 1942. While in Cologne, Schäfer oversaw the first deportations of the Cologne Jews, beginning in October 1941; at least 3,000 Jews were sent to their eventual deaths before he moved on. He also started an adulterous relationship (Schäfer was married with three children) with a twenty-four-year-old typist working in the Cologne Gestapo headquarters named Marianne K., who later would become his personal secretary in Belgrade and who hid him for several years after the war. Her husband, the same man who provided the details of Schäfer's involvement in the Gleiwitz raid to the Cologne court authorities in 1951, also explained to the court that his wife had told him as early as December 1941, when he had returned to his native Cologne for a brief vacation from the front, that Schäfer had forced her to have sexual relations with him. Although he said that he had tried to stop his wife from continuing her relationship with Schäfer, he did not confront Schäfer himself for fear that Schäfer would have him sent to a concentration camp.[53]

This was not an irrational fear on his part, for Schäfer was known to be a severe man who did not hesitate to punish his own subordinates. One of the men who worked under him at his next post in Belgrade, where he went after leaving the Cologne Gestapo in 1942, testified at the Cologne deportation trial in 1952 that "Schäfer was rumored to have said that for him the human being begins with the *Hauptsturmführer* (captain in the SS). He was extremely harsh. Whenever anyone at our post committed even the smallest infraction, like, for example, overstepping the curfew, Schäfer punished him immediately and severely. . . . Schäfer was not loved by the people who worked under him. He wanted things done chop-chop and he demanded iron discipline."[54]

Schäfer spent most of the rest of the war in Belgrade. Under his command, several thousand Yugoslavian Jews met their deaths either by deportation or by being gassed in local camps like the one at Semlin. In January 1945 he was transferred one last time to become the head of the security police and SD in Trieste. At the end of the war he traveled across the Austrian border to Klagenfurt and joined a regular army unit. There he was able to obtain false papers giving him the fictitious name of "Dr. Schneider." Later he secured another set of papers under the name of "Dr. Schleiffer." After spending a brief period in an American prisoner-of-war camp, he was released by the Americans in the summer of 1945. Sought by the Yugoslavian, Soviet, and Polish governments, he went into hiding, still under the name of Dr. Schleiffer, and spent most of his time in the next several years in the Cologne apartment of his former secretary and her husband before being arrested in April 1951.[55]

The other former commanding officers of the Cologne Gestapo did not quite have the whirlwind career of Emanuel Schäfer, but they too were no ordinary men, as the following brief descriptions of the careers of Dr. Erich Isselhorst and Franz Sprinz make clear. Even though their tenure in Cologne was relatively brief, Isselhorst, who led the Cologne Gestapo from February 1936 to the middle of 1940, and Sprinz, who took over for Emanuel Schäfer in February 1942 and remained as head of the Cologne Gestapo until February 1944, were the two longest-serving heads of the Cologne Gestapo.[56] A comparison of their backgrounds with those of Emanuel Schäfer and Ludwig Jung demonstrates that they all had much in common.

Like Schäfer, Jung, and the commanding officers of Gestapo posts elsewhere in Germany, Isselhorst and Sprinz were young, university-educated, zealous Nazis from lower-middle to middle-class backgrounds.[57] Isselhorst, born in St. Avold in Lorraine on February 5, 1906, was the son of a military sergeant who later had a career as a justice inspector. Sprinz was born on February 9, 1904, in Friedrichshafen on Lake Constance, and was the son of

a druggist. Both had university degrees in law, both joined the Nazi Party
in 1932, well before Hitler came to power, and both were members of the
SA, the SS, and the SD before becoming Gestapo officers.

After Isselhorst completed his university studies with a doctorate in
law in 1931 from the University of Cologne, and before he took his first
Gestapo post in February 1935 with the Berlin Gestapo, he became a practicing attorney specializing in defending Nazi Party members. Two months
later he moved to Erfurt as the head of its Gestapo, and less than a year later,
just before his thirtieth birthday, he was made head of the Cologne Gestapo.
After four years in Cologne, he became head of the Gestapo in Klagenfurt
and later in Munich. Between the fall of 1942 and the summer of 1943, he
led *Einsatzkommando* detachments that mowed down Jews and other civilians behind the lines of the German army along the eastern front. On June
30, 1943, he was made head of the security police and the SD for the district
of White Ruthenia in Minsk. In December 1943 he moved to his final post
as the head of the security police and the SD in Strasbourg. After the war,
he was accused by the British of having given orders to murder British paratroopers in Alsace in August 1944. He disputed this charge, arguing that
"despite the Führer's orders to kill all captured paratroopers, he only carried
out this order when members of the underground were involved."[58]

Sprinz came to the Gestapo relatively late in comparison with Isselhorst and many other local Gestapo commanding officers—in part because
he did not finish his university legal studies until 1935. Before taking his
first Gestapo post in Koblenz in 1939, he had spent four years with the SD
in Stuttgart, Allenstein, and Koblenz. In 1941 he became deputy head of the
Dortmund Gestapo, and just prior to his thirty-eighth birthday in 1942, he
became head of the Gestapo in Cologne. After two years as the head of the
Cologne Gestapo, during which time the majority of the Cologne-area Jews
were deported, he was made the head of a special forces unit operating in
Hungary and Croatia. At the end of the war, he, like Schäfer, also made his
way to Klagenfurt in southern Austria. With the aid of false identity papers
listing him as "SS corporal Prinz, civilian occupation: businessman," he was
able to escape from a Russian prisoner-of-war camp and to be subsequently
released from an American prisoner-of-war camp in June 1946. Fearing deportation to either Hungary or Yugoslavia, he spent the next six years in

hiding, mostly in Dortmund. On November 22, 1952, a warrant from a local Cologne court was put out for his arrest. Six days later, he was taken into custody to stand trial for the deportation of the Cologne Jews.[59]

RANK-AND-FILE GESTAPO OFFICERS
AND POLITICAL POLICEMEN IN THE COUNTRYSIDE

Under the commanding officers of Gestapo posts and outposts served a corps of hardened Gestapo officers with less impressive credentials. Although their lack of formal education barred them from rising to the highest levels of authority in the Gestapo organization—those positions were reserved for men with university training—it did not stop them from playing active and sometimes leading roles in some of the Third Reich's most barbarous operations. Many answered the call during the war years to take time out from their daily routine of extracting confessions through beatings, threats, and other forms of intimidation to participate directly in murder by resolving cases through "special treatment" or by serving in death squads in occupied territories. Often used in cases involving illegal sexual relations between foreign prisoners and German women, "special treatment," explained a former Düsseldorf Gestapo officer named Erich Preckel at the trial of a former Wuppertal Gestapo officer in 1959, invariably meant "execution by hanging without a legal process of any sort. I believe that I can say with a good measure of assurance that a decree existed already in 1940 and 1941 demanding that special treatment be used in all cases of sexual relations between German women and Polish prisoners of war."[60] A famous example of such "special treatment" in Cologne took place on October 25, 1944, when eleven foreign workers were hanged in public outside of the local train station in the working-class section of Ehrenfeld. This was followed two weeks later on November 10, 1944, by an even more controversial case of "special treatment": thirteen Germans, including five teenage youths, were hanged at the same place for being associated with the Edelweiss Pirates movement in Cologne. Both sets of hangings were carried out by the Cologne Gestapo without the involvement of any judicial bodies.[61]

Such public demonstrations of the Gestapo's barbarism were the exception, however; most instances of "special treatment" were carried out away

from the public eye. Unfortunately, because of a lack of surviving documentation, it is difficult to determine exactly how often "special treatment" was
employed and which officers carried out the "special treatment" assignments.[62] The Gestapo often did not keep case files on foreign workers; the
records they did keep on these people were most typically in the form of a
mere note card, sometimes containing the letter L (for "liquidation") or S
(for "special treatment") if they were killed. These card files appear to have
been destroyed in Cologne, Krefeld, and other cities at the end of the war or
shortly thereafter.[63] Nevertheless, it is clear from a postwar crimes-against-
humanity investigation that large numbers, perhaps thousands, of foreign
workers in the city of Cologne, for example, were given "special treatment"
in the last weeks of the war alone. The evidence points to two former Cologne Gestapo officers, Kriminalsekretär Josef Dahmen (born in 1895) and
Kriminalsekretär Winand Weitz (born in 1906), as having organized these
operations, but they were never convicted, and the case against them and
various others was finally dismissed on April 19, 1968, because of "lack of
evidence."[64]

Somewhat more is known about Gestapo officers who took part in death
squad operations on foreign soil. As Gerhard Paul has shown, at least one-
quarter of all Gestapo officers from the city of Würzburg took time out from
their normal responsibilities during the war years to participate in mass
executions (or in Nazi parlance, *Partisanbekämpfung*, "combating partisans") in Poland and the Soviet Union.[65] In Cologne and Krefeld the situation was no different. Two examples of ordinary Gestapo officers who periodically served in *Einsatzgruppen* death squads are Wilhelm Weber of the
Krefeld Gestapo and Kurt Matschke of the Cologne Gestapo. Weber, who
served in the Krefeld Gestapo until sometime after 1941 (mainly handling
cases involving left-wing movements and Jewish affairs), led a *Sonderkommando* and appears to have personally shot at least fourteen Dutch prisoners in Assen, Holland, on April 10, 1945, just before the Allied troops
took over the town.[66] Kurt Matschke, already mentioned in the previous
chapter in the discussion of the trial for the deportation of the Cologne Jews,
received a promotion in 1943 for his leadership of a particularly bloody *Einsatzgruppen* detachment in the Soviet Union from December 1941 to February 1942. He returned to Germany in late 1942 and was transferred to the

Cologne Gestapo, where he headed department IIb dealing with churches, religious sects, freemasonry, and Jewish affairs.[67]

If willingness to partake in murder did not clearly separate the Gestapo's rank and file from its commanding officers, what, other than their lower levels of academic achievement, did? One of the most obvious factors, as shown in table 2.1, was their date of entry into the Nazi Party, which may or may not have been an indicator of commitment to the Nazi movement. As demonstrated in the table,[68] which lists information about the backgrounds of nineteen men who served in the Krefeld Gestapo from 1937 to 1945 (organized in descending order of rank), the only man other than Kommissar Jung to be a member of the Nazi Party before Hitler's takeover was the head of the Jewish desk, Richard Schulenburg. Most rank-and-file Gestapo officers joined the party sometime after the Nazis were in power; most of the Krefeld officers did so in 1937. The reason for most officers' relatively late date of entry into the Nazi Party was not, however, a lack of sympathy for the Nazi movement. Rather, most were late to join because they had been police officers in the Weimar Republic and in 1930 it had been made illegal for Weimar police officers to join the Nazi Party. Nevertheless, many rank-and-file officers had been members of extremist right-wing organizations like the Freikorps at the beginning of the Weimar Republic or had joined Nazi affiliates like the SA in the later Weimar years.[69] And even if many still did not join the Nazi Party until the mid-1930s, most signaled their allegiance to Nazism at an early date by joining Nazi branch organizations and stormtrooper units shortly after Hitler's takeover in 1933.[70]

When a state police outpost in Krefeld was first established shortly after the Gestapo was created in Prussia by a law of April 26, 1933, most of the officers were former members of the old political-police force of the Krefeld criminal police department. Several of these men were already middle-aged, career police officers, like Richard Schulenburg, Karl Schmitz, and Theodor Schommer, and would remain with the Krefeld Gestapo until 1945. Four or five others, like Johann Krülls, who led much of the crackdown on Krefeld Communists and Socialists in 1933 and early 1934, were transferred in March 1934 to the Düsseldorf Gestapo headquarters, under which the Krefeld Gestapo was posted.[71] Later in 1934, a few younger officers, like Alfred Effenberg, Gustav Burkert, and probably Otto Dihr, were

TABLE 2.1 *Krefeld Gestapo Officers, 1937–1945*

NAME[a]	POSITION/DESK	POLICE RANK[b]	SS RANK[c]	BIRTH	BIRTHPLACE	FATHER'S OCCUPATION	PARTY MEMBER SINCE	EDUCATIONAL LEVEL	RELIGION[d]
Ludwig Jung	Head	KK	HSF	1910	Darmstadt	master butcher	1930	university	gg.
Karl Schmitz	Deputy Head/Special Treatment	KOS	none	1887	Krefeld	?	1937	primary	gg.
Richard Schulenburg	Jewish Affairs/Churches, Emigration	KOS	none	1879	Wiepke/Gardelegen	?	1927	primary	Protestant
Otto Dihr	Religious Sects/Left-Wing Movements	KOS	?	1902	Kalzig/Brandenburg	farmer	1937	primary	?
Herbert Braun	Churches/Religious Sects	KS	none	1900	Königsberg	?	1933	?	gg.
Gustav Burkert	Left-Wing Movements/Opposition	KS	SSF	1903	Neustadt/Upper Silesia	factory worker	1937	primary	gg.
Alfred Effenberg	Left-Wing Movements/Homosexuals	KS	SSF	1901	Hernsdorf/Silesia	farmer	1937	primary	Protestant
Kurt Joost	Abwehr Spying/Physical Evidence	KS	SSF	1902	Elbing	master butcher	1933	primary	Catholic
Theodor Schommer	Statistics/Protective Custody	KS	none	1893	Hinsbeck	?	?	?	?
Wilhelm Weber[e]	Left-Wing Movements/Jewish Affairs	KS	none	1900	Luisenhof	?	?	?	?

Name	Department	Police rank	SS rank	Birth year	Birthplace	Occupation	Year	Education	
Jakob Schmitz[f]	?	KS	?	1891	?	?	?	?	?
Alfred Fleischer[g]	?	KOA	joined 1943	1906	Remscheid	Filtermeister	1937	Handelsschule	gg.
BECAME MEMBERS AFTER 1941									
Friedrich Fürschbach	Foreign Workers	KS	SSF	1899	Mettmann	master baker	1937	primary	gg.
Karl Homberg	Abwehr Spying/News Service	KS	SSF	1906	Gelsenkirchen	miner	1937	primary	gg.
W. Homberg	Foreign Workers	KS	none	?	?	?		?	?
Heinrich Humburg	?	KS	?	1913	Kassel	train engineer	1933	gymnasium	gg.
Fritz Steglich	Foreign Workers	none	OSF	1908	?	?	?	?	?
Hubertus Terpoorten	Foreign Workers	none	SF	1915	?	?	?	?	?
? Nelles	Organizational Matters	PS	SSF	?	?	?	?	?	?

SOURCE: Information about the backgrounds of these men comes primarily from Berlin Document Center SS and Nazi Party records and, especially in regard to the men who never joined the SS, from denazification and Interior Ministry records.

a. Omitted from the table is Kommissar Bolle, who served as head of the Krefeld Gestapo for only a short period in 1937 and 1938 before Ludwig Jung took over for him; no other information on him has been found. The men listed in the table were identified by means of organizational plans of the Krefeld Gestapo for 1940 and 1944 and by a reading of the Krefeld Gestapo case files.

b. Highest police rank achieved, in descending order of rank: KK = *Kriminal Kommissar*, KOS = *Kriminalobersekretär*, KS = *Kriminalsekretär*, KOA = *Kriminaloberassistent*, PS = *Polizeisekretär*.

c. Highest SS rank achieved, in descending order of rank: HSF = *Hauptsturmführer* (captain), SSF = *Sturmscharführer* (master sergeant), OSF = *Oberscharführer* (sergeant), SF = *Scharführer* (corporal).

d. gg. = *Gottgläubig*.

e. Weber left the Krefeld Gestapo after 1941.

f. Schmitz left the Krefeld Gestapo in 1942.

g. Fleischer left the Krefeld Gestapo sometime before 1944.

transferred from the Krefeld criminal police to the Krefeld Gestapo as replacements.[72]

For reasons that are unclear, the Krefeld Gestapo outpost reverted back to the control of the local Krefeld criminal police on December 1, 1934, and its name was changed back to its former title of "political police." The change was mainly cosmetic, however, so that when the Krefeld Gestapo outpost was again officially constituted on August 1, 1937, there were no significant changes in how political policing was carried out in the city. Already by this time, or just after it, Herbert Braun, Kurt Joost, and Alfred Fleischer (also former *Schutzpolizei* officers in their thirties) had also joined the Krefeld outpost.[73] When Ludwig Jung was transferred from the Düsseldorf Gestapo headquarters at the beginning of 1939 to replace Kommissar Bolle as the head, the staff and leadership of the Krefeld Gestapo outpost was set for the next several years. The last major changes that took place in the staff of the Krefeld outpost came during the middle of the war years when three officers—Weber, Jacob Schmitz, and Fleischer—were assigned elsewhere and replaced by seven new officers. As table 2.1 shows, most of these were younger men from police departments in other cities who were needed in Krefeld to handle problems with foreign workers.[74]

After the war many Krefeld and Cologne Gestapo officers, both commanding officers and members of the rank and file, made the claim in their denazification hearings and in their attempts to secure their full police pensions that they had been forced to join the Gestapo in the first place and that they had been members of the Gestapo only since the time when there was an official Gestapo organization in place in their city; some claimed that had not happened until April 1937 in Cologne, and not until August 1937 in Krefeld.[75] The denazification authorities recognized that these claims were false.[76] Gestapo officers had joined the organization of their own free will and had done so in the hope of furthering their careers.[77] Whether or not the police of a particular city at a particular time called itself the political department of the criminal police, the state police, or the secret state police was unimportant. The name was only a bureaucratic issue: each of these policing organizations performed the same duties and reported to the secret police headquarters in Berlin. As Inge Marssolek and Rene Ott explain in regard to the city of Bremen but with application to the rest of Germany:

The Gestapo, as the political police of the Third Reich and therefore as the most important institution of repression of political opposition, has repeatedly and falsely been seen as a totally new and specific institution of the National-Socialist regime. . . . [When the Gestapo came into being in a particular locality, this was] in fact only a renaming of a long-existing and, in the months after [Hitler's] take-over of power, an already fully coordinated police force.[78]

In rural towns and villages across Nazi Germany, as in the small town of Bergheim, political policing was carried out under the control of the regular police department, which in turn was under the control of the local mayor's office. But even though there was no official Gestapo organization in place, Communists were tracked down, religious leaders and practices were kept in line, Jews were deported, and nonconformists were punished with scarcely less efficiency. Only in unusual cases were Gestapo agents from nearby Cologne called in for assistance. In Bergheim two police officers, Gottfried Schleiden and Wilhelm Servos, carried out the bulk of the political-police work for the entire Nazi period. Schleiden, who had the higher rank, eventually reached the level of senior criminal secretary in the war years (the highest rank that a man of little formal education could normally expect to reach in the police) and was the man in charge. Born in the village of Waat in 1890 near the Dutch border, Schleiden was a career police officer of moderate height and somewhat heavy build. His only education consisted of eight years in a primary school and the typical three-month police training course, which he attended in the city of Düsseldorf in 1921. Like most German police officers, he had no troubles whatsoever in the denazification process. Even though his personnel records could not be found, and even though by his own admission on the mandatory questionnaire that he filled out on June 29, 1946, he had been a member of the Nazi Party since May 1, 1933, and a Nazi Party block warden as well, the denazification committee quickly (on August 6, 1946) decided to put him in category V, thus clearing the way for his return to active police work. The committee justified this classification by accepting his argument that he had been forced into the Nazi Party in the first place, had never been a member of the SS or Gestapo, and had been "no activist" in the Nazi movement. In addition, the committee noted that he had the reputation of being "much loved" by the citizens of Bergheim; it needs to be said, however, that not all Bergheimers have remembered him this way.[79]

Servos had more trouble with the denazification committee. Gray, bald, and diminutive (five foot six and 128 pounds) when he came before the committee on August 21, 1946, Servos, born in Kirchtroisdorf in 1892, was two years younger than Schleiden and held a lower police rank (*Polizei Meister*). Like Schleiden, he had only a primary school education, and he had attended the same police training course in Düsseldorf, albeit a year later, in 1922. At first the committee gave him a category IV denazification status, which barred his way to returning to police service and reduced his pension rights. The committee members considered him a "brutal Nazi" who had been known to blackmail local youth into joining the SS and to torture downed Canadian pilots near the end of the war. But with letters of support from several prominent Bergheimers, including the leading Catholic priest in the town, Servos was able to overturn this decision several months later and go back to his career in the German police.[80]

The rural policemen Schleiden and Servos, therefore, had backgrounds not unlike those of the older Gestapo officers in Krefeld. They were career police officers of limited education and limited formal police training. They were neither born nor raised in the community they policed during the Third Reich. (Of the Krefeld officers, only Karl Schmitz appears to have been born in Krefeld.) They never became members of the SS. Only some, such as Schleiden or Schulenburg, joined the Nazi Party at the earliest possible date, but most remained loyal Nazis to the end.

The profile of most of the other Krefeld Gestapo officers is not much different from that of the older officers, except that most did become members of the SS eventually (though most did not join until the mid to late 1930s) and they were younger. Like the older officers, most of the younger officers were career policemen (in Krefeld only Heinrich Humburg and Hubertus Terpoorten seem to have been exceptions), had limited formal police training, and were posted to the Krefeld Gestapo after having been brought up elsewhere and serving some years in the *Schutzpolizei*.[81] As table 2.1 shows, the average Gestapo officer in Krefeld was born sometime around the turn of the century, had only a primary school education, came from a working-class or lower-middle-class family background, joined the Nazi Party in the mid-1930s, and changed his religious status during the Nazi years to *gottgläubig*. Recent research on other localities paints a similar picture of the Gestapo rank and file.[82]

Before turning to a discussion of the Jewish desk heads, a few remarks need to be made about the mentality of these men. These remarks can only be speculative since they are based on limited sources. Nevertheless, some clues to the personalities of these officers can be obtained by a reading of their SS and Nazi Party files, which contain photographs for which they posed, lengthy handwritten curriculum vitae they personally composed in the late 1930s, their reports and position statements in cases they investigated during the Nazi years, and their denazification, Interior Ministry, and trial records after the war. In some ways, Gestapo officers seemed like rather typical Germans one might have met anywhere between 1933 and 1945. Most were athletic men (almost all had attained one kind of athletic medal or another) of average size and build and with regular features. Although they were of only average intellectual attainment (the vast majority of Germans at this time had only a primary school education, like most of these men), they may have possessed somewhat higher than average intelligence. (They had to be reasonably good at grammar and spelling; they made few mistakes in their résumés and position statements.) Since most were German policmen with lengthy police careers that had begun sometime in the Weimar Republic, these were men who may have been attracted to violence but believed in law and order. The problem was that they were willing to enforce and carry out whatever laws and orders they were given, no matter how criminal.

They were also career-minded opportunists who wanted to be Gestapo officers and were willing to do whatever it took to be successful in their Gestapo careers, including joining the Nazi Party and other Nazi organizations, leaving the church (most rejoined immediately after the war), and taking part in "special treatment" and *Einsatzgruppen* operations when given those assignments. They enjoyed the power they held over people (handing out blows or mercy depending on their inclination) and benefited from the promotions and prestige the Gestapo gave them. Many seemed defensive about their schooling, their parentage, or their family,[83] and many suffered from the early loss of an important female figure, whether a wife, a mother, or even a grandmother.[84] On the whole, they were hard and sometimes brutal German policemen who probably would have served any regime independent of ideology, though their preference most certainly was for the political right.

THE HEADS OF THE GESTAPO'S JEWISH DESKS

When one considers the men who headed the Jewish desks in Cologne and Krefeld, one is reminded of Hannah Arendt's famous portrait of Adolf Eichmann at his 1961 trial in Jerusalem District Court, which was serialized in the *New Yorker* and later published in her famous and much-disputed book *Eichmann in Jerusalem: A Report on the Banality of Evil.*[85] Arrested in Buenos Aires on May 11, 1960, flown to Israel nine days later, and put on trial on April 11, 1961, this man who from his desk at the RSHA in Berlin organized and coordinated the extermination of the European Jews came as a great disappointment to many. One expected to encounter a demon sitting in the dock, but one found instead a somewhat pitiful, prevaricating, middle-aged man.

Pronounced to be "normal" by half a dozen psychiatrists— "more normal, at any rate, than I am after having examined him,"[86] one of them was said to have exclaimed—Eichmann did not even have a sense of his own enormous guilt. He continued to profess his innocence throughout the trial: "With the killing of the Jews I had nothing to do. I never killed a Jew, or a non-Jew, for that matter." Not only was he innocent, he claimed, but he had no hatred for Jews; he had once had a Jewish mistress, even though this could have led to his severe punishment under the *Rassenschande* laws against intercourse with Jews, and he had even helped many individual Jews escape death. "I myself had no hatred for Jews, for my whole education through my mother and my father had been strictly Christian; my mother, because of her Jewish relatives, held different opinions from those current in SS circles. . . . I explained this to Dr. Löwenherz [the head of the Jewish community in Vienna] as I explained it to Dr. Kastner [the vice president of the Zionist organization in Budapest]; I think I told it to everybody."[87] Hitler's order for the physical extermination of the Jews came to him com-

pletely as a surprise. He testified that he himself had "never thought of . . .
such a solution through violence. . . . I now lost everything, all joy in my
work, all initiative, all interest; I was, so to speak, blown out."[88]

Eichmann may or may not have had such feelings at that moment; nevertheless, he diligently carried out what he saw as his duty. "As for his motives," Arendt explains, "he was perfectly sure that he was not what he
called an *innerer Schweinehund*, a dirty bastard in the depths of his heart;
and as for his conscience, he remembered perfectly well that he would have
had a bad conscience only if he had not done what he had been ordered to
do—to ship millions of men, women, and children to their death with great
zeal and the most meticulous care." "The trouble with Eichmann," Arendt
concludes

> was precisely that so many were like him, and that the many were
> neither perverted nor sadistic, that they were, and still are, terribly
> and terrifyingly normal. From the viewpoint of our legal institutions
> and of our moral standards of judgment, this normality was much
> more terrifying than all the atrocities put together, for it implied . . .
> that this new type of criminal, who is in actual fact *hostis generis hu-
> mani*, commits his crimes under circumstances that make it well-nigh
> impossible for him to know or feel that he is doing wrong.[89]

Two days before the death sentence was delivered at nine o'clock on the
morning of Friday, December 15, 1961, Eichmann gave his last statement.
He told the court once again that, as Arendt relates it, "he had never been a
Jew-hater, and he had never willed the murder of human beings. His guilt
came from his obedience, and obedience is praised as a virtue. His virtue had
been abused by the Nazi leaders. But he was not one of the ruling clique, he
was a victim, and only the leaders deserved punishment."[90] The Israeli court
did not accept these arguments, nor did it accept his appeals that followed in
the next months. Just before midnight, on Thursday, May 31, 1962, Eichmann was hanged.

Richard Schulenburg of the Krefeld Gestapo and Karl Löffler of the Cologne Gestapo, the officers in charge of "Jewish affairs" in their respective
cities, would have a much different fate. One might argue that their guilt

was greater than Eichmann's even if the number of victims they were responsible for was smaller. Eichmann had carried out his orders at a great
remove from the annihilation process. As a true "desk perpetrator," he seldom came into contact with his victims. But Schulenburg, Löffler, and the
other Gestapo officers who served as heads of Jewish affairs throughout
Germany had daily contact with the people they eventually deported to
their death. As Dieter Hangebruch explains, for example, "Schulenburg
was the representative of the National-Socialist state for the Krefeld Jews.
All organizational matters, orders, and decrees were communicated by
Schulenburg to the Jewish community or to the affected persons through
invitations to his office or by telephone."[91]

In the prewar years, Schulenburg and Löffler met daily with individual
Jews to arrange for their emigration or to process complaints about them.
In the war years, they were in constant contact with the heads of the Jewish
community to make the selections and work out the details of the "evacuations." As the son of the former head of the Nuremberg Jewish community
related to me in a recent interview, the heads of the Jewish communities
were even allowed to keep their personal telephones, which had been taken
away from all other Jews, because they often needed to speak several times
a day with the head of the Gestapo Jewish desk.[92] Schulenburg and Löffler
also continued to meet with ordinary Jewish people during this time, especially between October 1941 and July 1942, when the major waves of deportations of the Rhineland Jews took place. They met with the head of each
Jewish family shortly before they were "evacuated" to make sure that they
had not held back any property, making them sign an affidavit to that effect,
and warning them that they would have to "reckon with the harshest state-
police measures" if they had.[93] Schulenburg and Löffler also had occasion
to get their hands even dirtier. They were on hand at the collection points
and the train stations when the Jews were carted off.[94] Sometimes they even
went to the homes of Jews to fetch them and personally escort them to the
trains. The surviving daughter of a middle-aged Krefeld Jewish woman described for me how Schulenburg, at the age of sixty-five, rode her mother
in September 1944 on the handlebars of his bicycle from the village of Anrath to the collection point in Krefeld before both she and her mother were
deported to Theresienstadt concentration camp.[95] On another occasion, in

June 1942, the athletic Schulenburg jumped out of a streetcar to chase after a forty-one-year-old Jewish man through the streets of Krefeld. The man, who ironically was born in Auschwitz, had learned that he was to be deported from his home in Berlin (probably to Auschwitz) and had fled to Krefeld en route to the nearby Dutch border. Schulenburg helped him return to his original home.[96]

Despite their greater proximity to the Jewish victims, Schulenburg and Löffler share many similarities with Eichmann. I will discuss the similarities of their rationalizations in more detail in a later chapter; here I will concentrate on the similarities in their backgrounds and mentalities. Were they "normal" men, as Arendt termed Eichmann? Indeed, was Eichmann "normal"?

Certainly Adolf Eichmann was quite ordinary in many ways. He was born in Solingen, Germany (not far from Cologne), on March 19, 1906, to a middle-class family of five children in which he was the eldest. At the time of his birth, his father was an accountant for the Tramway and Electricity Company in Solingen. In 1913, when Adolf was seven, his father was transferred to Linz, Austria, and made an official of the company's Austrian branch. When Adolf was ten years old, his mother died. He did poorly in school and left gymnasium without a diploma. Later he also left an engineering vocational school, again without a diploma. Eventually Eichmann's father left the Tramway and Electricity Company and went into business for himself, buying a small mining enterprise in which he gave his eldest son his first job. Soon Eichmann's father helped him get a better position in the sales department of an electrical company, where he stayed for two years. In 1927 Eichmann left the electrical company and took a job as a traveling salesman for the Vacuum Oil Company of Vienna. He then spent five and a half years with this company until he was fired on Pentecost in 1933. One year before that he had joined the Austrian Nazi Party, and with the encouragement of a family friend named Ernst Kaltenbrunner from Linz (later the head of the RSHA after Heydrich was assassinated), he entered the SS as well. After he lost his job in 1933, he moved back to Germany and served for fourteen months in two Bavarian SS camps. At this time he was only an SS corporal. When he joined the SD and moved to the Berlin RSHA in the fall of 1934, his career finally started to take off. After four or five months of work in a department dealing with freemasonry, he moved to a newly constituted department dealing with Jews. Eventually he became its head. Along the way he received several promotions in the SS ranks. In October 1941, when the Jewish deportations began, he received his biggest and final promotion, attaining the rank of SS lieutenant colonel.[97]

Arendt depicts Eichmann as a "joiner." As a youth, he was a member of the YMCA, the German youth organization *Wandervögel,* and the youth section of the German-Austrian war veterans organization (which was "violently pro-German and anti-republican"). When Kaltenbrunner introduced him to the SS, Eichmann was on the verge of joining the freemasons. When the war came to an end and Germany was defeated, he was bewildered. In Eichmann's own words, "I sensed I would have to live a leaderless and difficult individual life, I would receive no directives from anybody, no orders and commands would any longer be issued to me, no pertinent ordinances would be there for me to consult—in brief, a life never known before lay before me."[98]

In many ways, Schulenburg, Löffler, and other Gestapo officers in comparable positions in other German cities were more "normal" than Eichmann. But again one must ask: What does "normal" mean? If normal means not being psychotic and being capable of holding a job and interacting with other human beings, then they were indeed very normal. Social skills were extremely important for these men. Had they not been career policemen, they might have been more successful salesmen than Eichmann, and in fact Löffler spent the last several years of his working career as a sales representative for a Cologne brewery.[99] They had to sell the Nazi expropriation and extermination program to the local German community and, in a sense, to the Jewish community as well, keeping both sides cool and calm as the Nazi murder machine heated up. A Jewish woman who had been personally interrogated by Schulenburg in January 1940 after she was denounced by a former classmate for having had sexual relations with a soldier, and whose mother was the woman Schulenburg escorted to the trains in September 1944 and eventually to her death, described him as a "jovial" type of person, "one you could easily imagine sitting at the *Stammtisch*"—a local pub—with his cronies.[100] The son of the former Jewish community leader in Nuremberg during the Nazi period likewise described Schulenburg's counterpart in his former city as cordial and friendly.[101]

But these men were not "normal" if normal refers to typical men in the German population. In some ways they were not even normal Gestapo officers. They were particular types of people—elderly, calm, and outwardly friendly, yet loyal Nazis and ardent anti-Semites—whom the Nazi authorities cynically selected for their most important project.

Schulenburg and Löffler played the role of "good cops" in the Gestapo's persecution of the Jews. The Gestapo needed reliable, patient officers, with strong ties to the local communities in which they served, to coordinate the Nazis' program of expropriating and annihilating the Jews. Endless forms needed to be filled out. Secrecy had to be maintained. Both Germans and Jews had to be assured that the best was being done, under the circumstances, that the laws were being scrupulously adhered to as the Jews' rights, property, and finally lives were taken away from them. This was no job for young hotheads, though such men were needed on occasion to play the role of "bad cop" when the "good cop" needed a display of force.[102] Whenever possible, however, the Gestapo preferred to persecute the Jews with calmness. As described to me by one Cologne Jewish man—who himself was deported from Cologne to Poland in the fall of 1938 and lost nearly his entire family in the Holocaust—the Gestapo came to take him and his father away "on tiptoes."[103]

Schulenburg, born on April 3, 1879, and Löffler, born on January 8, 1888, were much older than most Gestapo officers. Both were born and raised in eastern parts of Germany (Schulenburg in a small town near the city of Magdeburg, and Löffler in the city of Erfurt) and had only a primary school education. Schulenburg was raised Protestant, and Löffler's upbringing was Catholic. Neither left the church in the early or mid-1930s, as many other Gestapo officers had done, though Löffler eventually did leave the church in September 1941; Schulenburg's religious convictions were also questionable, as evidenced by his membership in the Nazi-based German Christian Movement. Both probably kept up their formal church membership as long as they did primarily to keep up appearances, especially because their areas of jurisdiction included the churches as well as the Jews until 1941.[104]

Other than information on his birth, religion, and schooling, nothing is known about Schulenburg before he joined the Krefeld *Schutzpolizei* at the rank of police sergeant in 1907 (though, according to police regulations in Imperial Germany, he had to have been in the military for at least five years and to have attained the rank of sergeant before he joined the police).[105] One might speculate, however, that he was not particularly proud of his upbringing, for unlike most other officers, he never mentioned his parents in the detailed documentation about him that has survived. Löffler clearly did have problems as a youth. When he was ten, his mother died. Three years later, in 1901, his father, a cabinetmaker by profession, died as well. He then entered a Catholic orphans' home, finished his schooling at a Catholic primary school a year later, and spent the following several years as a cabinetmaker's apprentice. Beginning in 1908, he spent five years in the military, leaving in 1913 at the rank of sergeant. Immediately thereafter he joined the Cologne police force. In 1918 he was promoted to the Cologne criminal police force, where he remained until the Nazis took over power in 1933. Schulenburg's records show that he too was promoted to the criminal police force at the beginning of the Weimar Republic (in 1919). By 1933 both men had become members of the political police, which at the time was still considered part of the criminal police. As soon as a Gestapo post was formed to replace the old political-police department in their cities, they became Gestapo officers.

Like Eichmann, both Schulenburg and Löffler were inveterate "joiners," and both demonstrated their allegiance to the Nazi movement at an early date. In his denazification questionnaire, Schulenburg proudly listed June 1, 1922, as the date when he first joined the prestigious Garde Verein 1861 Krefeld, a war veterans' organization that boasted many of Krefeld's leading citizens as members. Also in the Weimar years, Schulenburg is known to have been a member of the Anti-Semitic Party, though in his denazification records he mentioned only having been a member of the German Democratic Party between 1919 and 1923 before he became a member of the Nazi Party in 1927. He did not note there that he was the twentieth person to become a member of the Nazi Party from the city of Krefeld.[106] Schulenburg also became a member of the Association for Saxony-Thuringia in 1912 (and treasurer of that group in 1926), began sitting on the

Kreisparteigericht (local district court of the Nazi Party) at the beginning of 1934,[107] and belonged to the Reich Colonial Association, the Reich Association of State Officials (RddB), the National Socialist People's Welfare Association (NSV), and the German Christian Movement.

Not as much is known about Löffler's affiliations, but his surviving records show that he was also a member of a host of Nazi associations, including the RddB, the NSV, and the Reich Teachers' Association (RLB). He did not join the Nazi Party until 1937, when doing so became comparatively easy and a large number of Gestapo officers signed up,[108] but his strong commitment to the Nazi cause was evident by at least 1935, when he became a "sponsoring member" of the SS. Neither he nor Schulenburg, however, ever attained SS rank, and Löffler allowed his SS "sponsorship" to lapse in 1938. Although several older officers in Cologne, Krefeld, and elsewhere also never joined the SS,[109] it may have been a conscious policy on the part of the Gestapo to keep its Jewish desk heads out of SS uniform. No official documentation on this policy is known, but it also applied in other cities—such as Nuremberg, Mönchengladbach, and Dresden—where elderly, non-SS officers, fitting the Schulenburg and Löffler mold, also served as the heads of the Jewish desks.[110] Interviews with Jewish survivors from Krefeld make it clear that, unlike most of the Gestapo officers, who went to work in black SS uniforms, Schulenburg carried out his interrogations in civilian clothes.[111]

Unlike Schulenburg, who remained steadfast as the head of Jewish affairs in the Krefeld Gestapo until the war was over, Löffler may have suffered some pangs of conscience over his work. A letter of June 1948 in his denazification file from his doctor attests that Löffler had suffered from heart problems caused by a nervous disorder and was in his care for eight weeks prior to late September 1942, when Löffler was transferred to the security police headquarters in Brussels. Although his health problems occurred just after the main waves of Cologne Jews had been deported to the east, Löffler did not attribute them to specific concern over the fate of the Jews:

> I always hated the work I had to do in the political area. I tried therefore
> from the beginning to compensate for it, especially when the heart

beat too heavily. Measures that were ordered to be taken against those who did not hold to Nazi views, in most cases I did not carry out, or I made out my reports in such a way that the people were left untouched. Over time I tried again and again in vain to be sent back to the political police. . . . Even though I was not successful in that attempt, I nevertheless have the satisfaction today that through my passive behavior many people had an easier fate, indeed in many cases lives were saved. . . . I also tried to escape from my office through repeated sick-leaves, the last in 1942, when I spent almost eight weeks under a doctor's care. Despite this I was commanded to go to Brussels.[112]

Löffler returned to business as usual when he went back to the Cologne Gestapo in July 1944 and, like Schulenburg, served the Nazi regime faithfully until the war's end. After the war Löffler, Schulenburg, and other Gestapo officers held to the fiction that they had no knowledge of what finally happened to the Jews they had deported. Löffler's testimony at a hearing held in Bielefeld on August 18, 1948, is a good example:

After the [Nazis'] takeover of power, the Jews over the years became more and more constricted by National Socialism in their rights and their freedom of movement. . . . In the end the Jews were forcibly deported by the Gestapo to the east. As I have heard, from the district of Cologne they were sent to Litzmannstadt (Lodz). What happened with the Jews after that, is outside of my knowledge. I came to know about that only after the end of the war.[113]

In his denazification proceedings in December 1948, Schulenburg made similar claims. Although the Krefeld denazification committee found these to be "untrustworthy,"[114] Schulenburg, like Löffler, was never brought to task for his part in the Holocaust. Only in 1965, after Schulenburg had been dead for three years, did it come to light that indeed he had known what the true fate of the Jews was. According to the testimony of a Jewish survivor whom Schulenburg had personally escorted to the deportation trains in Düsseldorf on January 13, 1944, Schulenburg fleeced the man of the money he had brought for the trip and said to him in a resigned fashion: "In this life you don't need money anymore."[115]

Despite their appearance and demeanor, the heads of the Gestapo's Jewish desks, like Richard Schulenburg of Krefeld and Karl Löffler of Cologne, were hardly nicer than the younger, more obviously brutal officers they worked with and the highly trained Nazi zealots they worked for. They may not always have enjoyed their work, but they faithfully carried it out until the bitter end. Eichmann had done the same. But he was called to pay for it.

CONCLUSION

Although recent scholarship has done much to demythologize the Nazi secret police,[116] especially by stressing the limits of its manpower and resources and its need to rely on reports from the civilian population for much of its information, comparatively little is known about the secret policemen themselves. The few studies that have treated Gestapo officers directly either concentrate on the top leadership in Berlin or provide only limited, mainly statistical, information on the backgrounds of individual officers in other localities.[117]

I have argued in this chapter that there were at least three different types of secret policemen in local Gestapo organizations: commanding officers, rank-and-file Gestapo officers (the term "Gestapo agents" has largely been avoided because it would imply more cloak-and-dagger-type activity than Gestapo officers actually performed), and the officers who headed the Jewish desks in individual Gestapo posts and outposts. The commanding officers were young and highly educated. All attended university and many held a doctorate degree in law. Most were career Nazis first (having been early joiners of the Nazi Party and its various strong-arm organizations) and policemen second, and most had attended advanced secret police and SS training institutes before becoming commanding officers of local Gestapo posts. They usually spent only a few years in any particular locality before being sent elsewhere (Ludwig Jung from Krefeld appears to be an exception in this regard). During the war years, many spent some period of time heading moderate- to large-scale murder operations on the eastern front.

Like the commanding officers, most of the rank-and-file officers were

young men born sometime after the turn of the century, though each Gestapo organization had several older officers on hand as well. With few exceptions, these men were career police officers before they joined either the
Nazi Party or the SS, and some never joined the SS at all. After a primary
school education and some military or paramilitary experience, most embarked on a career with either the regular police or the criminal police,
either in Imperial Germany or in the Weimar Republic, before they joined
the Gestapo (which most considered a promotion) in the Third Reich. Few
had much in the way of secret police training.

Of the three types of Gestapo officers discussed in this chapter, the information provided on the heads of the Jewish desks may come as the biggest surprise, since these men have not previously been studied in any detail
at all.[118] Because their profile is likely to be the most controversial, I have
tried to demonstrate that the Gestapo's Jewish desk heads in Cologne and
Krefeld, Karl Löffler and Richard Schulenburg, were by no means atypical
of the Gestapo's Jewish desk heads in other cities. In the three other localities I have examined for comparative purposes, the small city of Mönchengladbach and the larger cities of Nuremberg and Dresden, the same type of
individual seems to have been in charge of "Jewish affairs." In what must
have been a conscious strategy on the part of the Gestapo, at least in these
cities, the men selected to head the Jewish desks had to appear to be highly
respectable and nonthreatening because the task of expropriating and eventually exterminating the Jews required calmness and trust in both Gentiles
and Jews. Older men with long careers in the local police, the Jewish desk
heads had much deeper roots in the communities they served than either
the commanding officers or the other rank-and-file officers. As activists in
local reservist and other organizations, they enjoyed close contacts with local political and religious leaders. They conducted their investigations in
civilian clothes, having never joined the SS, and they even seemed "jovial"
to some of the Jews with whom they dealt. But this appearance was a cynical
ploy on the part of the Gestapo: these men were every bit as anti-Semitic
and committed to the Nazi cause as the commanding officers and the rank
and file. Schulenburg of the Krefeld Gestapo is known to have supported
the Anti-Semitic Party before he joined the Nazi Party in Krefeld as one of
its first members in 1927, when anti-Semitism was a cornerstone of the

Nazi Party platform. Löffler was described by one of his fellow Cologne officers in the postwar trial treating the deportation of the Cologne Jews as "commonly known as a huge Jew-hater."[119]

Condemning Gestapo officers has gone out of fashion in recent years. In a vein similar to Hannah Arendt's portrait of Eichmann stressing the "banality of evil," some scholars now argue that Gestapo officers were merely "ordinary" men thrust into an abnormal situation who, under the conditions and pressures they faced, did simply what other normal individuals would have done. The rank-and-file officers are viewed, therefore, as plain German policemen with a rightist political bias (nothing out of the ordinary for German policemen) who, seeing the Gestapo as a way of furthering their careers, simply followed the orders they were given. The commanding officers are portrayed as "a new variant of the authoritarian personality type, who, corrupted by a cold objectivity and emotional distance and fixated in an undoctrinaire fashion on the goals of the state, led security police operations without giving them much thought."[120]

There is something wrong in this. Just as we can typologize an "authoritarian personality," we can typologize a schizoid personality or an asocial personality. But that does not make a person who falls into one of these personality types "normal." The fact that psychological theory can help us understand why a person committed a murder does not make that person normal. Such reasoning would be music to the ears of the Cologne and Krefeld Gestapo officers who argued almost to a man after the war that they had only been ordinary policemen who were "commanded against their will" to join the Gestapo in the first place and forced to remain in the Gestapo for fear of being sent to a concentration camp. Furthermore, they argued, they were in their souls "private enemies" (innere Gegner) of National Socialism who did everything they could, in a nearly impossible situation, to help the victims of the regime. These men may have seemed banal after the war when they were sitting humbly in the dock trying to wriggle out of being sent to prison for their crimes. Social psychology can perhaps be used to explain why they had acted as they did and perhaps why so many of them may not even have understood the gravity of their misdeeds. But this does not make them ordinary men.

PART TWO

NAZI TERROR AND THE JEWS, 1933–1939

We had Angst, Angst, Angst!

—Lore M.,
a Krefeld survivor

Nobody knew about the impending doom. . . . The Jews didn't have to fear unless they had done something illegal. They were beyond the pale.

—Karl Muschkattblatt,
a Cologne survivor

CHAPTER THREE

W e had *Angst, Angst, Angst,"* whispered Lore M. as we discussed the plight of Krefeld Jews in Nazi Germany in a mid-
town Krefeld café on January 31, 1995.[1] Karl Muschkattblatt,
formerly of Cologne and living under another name in Chicago, expressed
very different sentiments in a telephone interview of April 16, 1996:

> The climate in Cologne was different from other parts of Germany. . . .
> There never was this anti-Semitism in Cologne, because it was a Cath-
> olic city. The archbishop was not a friend of the Nazis. They were more
> liberal in Cologne. . . . I can remember a man asking me why I didn't
> salute the flag when the Nazis marched by in the street [sometime in
> 1934 or 1935]. I said, "I'm a Jew." He said, "Excuse me," and went
> away. . . . No, I had no fear until I was arrested. I walked around freely.
> Nobody knew about the impending doom. Some of my friends had
> been arrested. Some were in concentration camps. Some were able to
> emigrate. . . . When you are young, you think nothing will happen to
> you.[2]

Lore M. and Karl Muschkattblatt were young people during the Third
Reich; she was born in 1921, and he in 1915. Both suffered heavily in the
Holocaust: her mother died in Theresienstadt concentration camp; his
mother died in Auschwitz. Both had run-ins with the Gestapo for alleged
criminal activities. In November 1939 a former schoolmate denounced Lore

M. to the Gestapo for violating the Nuremberg Laws by carrying on an illicit relationship with a German soldier. Although her interrogation, conducted by Richard Schulenburg at the Krefeld Gestapo headquarters on January 14, 1940, led only to a severe warning at the time, Schulenburg saw to
it that she was "observed" continually thereafter.[3]

Muschkattblatt was arrested by an officer named Büthe of the Cologne
Gestapo in August 1938 and accused of high treason. He had been denounced to the Gestapo by a fellow Communist sympathizer who had previously lived for a time in Muschkattblatt's home. (Muschkattblatt and his
denouncer were members of a leftist organization called the Rote Hilfe,
which provided assistance to Communists and Socialists trying to escape
the Nazis' clamp-down in the early years of Hitler's reign.) After he had
withstood several interrogations and three months in jail, of which "six to
eight weeks were in solitary confinement" in Cologne's notorious Klingelpütz prison, his case was somewhat miraculously dismissed by the Cologne
prosecuting attorney on October 26. The Gestapo released him with the
understanding that he would emigrate immediately.[4] In early November,
just a few days before the barbarous anti-Jewish pogrom of November 9–
10, 1938, known as *Reichkristallnacht*, he left Germany and made his way
to Genoa, Italy, where he boarded a ship sailing to Shanghai.

Karl Muschkattblatt counts himself as one of the lucky ones. He says
that, at the time, he perceived his narrow escape from death "as an adventure." In his youthful optimism, love of Cologne, and trust in his fellow
Germans, he had not been particularly worried about what could have happened to him. Despite his harrowing experiences and despite losing his
mother (his father had already died before Hitler came to power) and all
of his family's possessions in the Holocaust, he still retains much of that
optimism today. He feels that many ordinary Germans treated him with
compassion, and he returns that compassion when discussing Germany and
the German people. Based on his five years under Nazi rule, he believes that
it was the Germans, and not necessarily the Jews, who had "a fear that was
amazing." "A lot of normal Germans had fear," he said, "Communists, trade
unionists, Social Democrats. . . . The Jews didn't have to fear unless they
had done something illegal. They were outside the pale."

Lore M.'s *Angst* was well grounded. The daughter of a Catholic father and a Jewish mother, she was a *Mischling*, according to the Nuremberg Laws passed in the fall of 1935. Throughout the Third Reich she experienced pressure and harassment of both herself and her family. In school she was singled out and ostracized by the teachers and students; eventually she was forced to sit at a front-row desk with empty desks all around her so as to quarantine her from the other students.[5] In September 1935 her electrician father spent a week in protective custody for displaying friendship toward Jews. After this time his main customer, the city of Krefeld, canceled its contracts with him, and only Jews gave him any business thereafter.[6]

Unlike Karl Muschkattblatt, Lore M. did not emigrate. Hence, she was in Krefeld during the anti-Semitic pogrom of November 9–10, 1938, the constant Allied bombing attacks of the war years, and, most terrifying of all, the Holocaust. Although her mixed parentage ultimately proved instrumental in her survival, she did not know at the time that she would survive, and she lived during the war years in constant dread of being placed on one of the transports to the east like the other German Jews who had not emigrated. On September 17, 1944, in what would be the last of the Jewish transports to leave Krefeld, her worst fears were realized: she, her sister, and her mother were all carted off to Theresienstadt concentration camp.

Like all Jews who lived in Nazi Germany, both Lore M. and Karl Muschkattblatt suffered under Nazi terror. Both lost close relatives, both suffered economic distress, both were denounced to the Gestapo by civilians from their own community for having allegedly broken the law, and both were taken from their home and forced out of the country. Still, it is remarkable how differently these two people portray the relative level of fear they remember having and the amount of popular anti-Semitism they remember experiencing in their daily lives in Nazi Germany. How do we account for such different recollections? How typical were their experiences? How constant and how pervasive were the terror and the anti-Semitism that Jews experienced in Nazi Germany? Were Jews constantly spied on? How common was it for German civilians to denounce Jews to the Gestapo? What kinds of people denounced Jews? How was the terror that Jews experienced in the 1930s different from that of the war years? Finally, how did the terror that Jews experienced in Nazi Germany compare with the terror that other groups in the German population experienced?

To begin to answer these questions, we start by tracing the evolution of Jewish persecution in the peacetime years of Nazi Germany as it intensified over time from discriminatory measures that undermined the Jews' economic and social standing in German society to acts of violence that endangered their physical existence. After this historical background has been laid in this chapter, the following chapter will examine the persecution, anti-Semitism, and terror that afflicted Jews in the 1930s in finer detail by discussing the varied results of a survey conducted with Jewish survivors who had resided in the city of Krefeld during the Third Reich and by examining in detail the prewar Jewish case files of the Krefeld Gestapo and the Cologne Special Court.

THE PERSECUTION BEGINS: 1933–1935

The Nazi terror began in earnest before Hitler's regime was one month old. On the wintry night of February 27, 1933, just one week before parliamentary elections were to be held on March 5, the Reichstag building in Berlin burned to the ground. When the police got to the scene, they found a demented, twenty-four-year-old Dutch Communist named Marinus van der Lubbe inside the burning building and charged him with setting the fire. To this day the question of whether van der Lubbe was working on his own or as a kind of Nazi stooge remains unresolved.[7] In a trial held in Leipzig between September 21 and December 23, 1933, the German Supreme Court found only van der Lubbe guilty of the crime and acquitted four other Communists who had been indicted along with him. On January 10, 1934, van der Lubbe was executed by guillotine.

Hitler, however, believed that the fire was part of a larger Communist plot and that the fire was intended to act as a beacon for a Communist revolution in Germany. Recognizing that this presented him with an opportunity as well as a challenge, he reacted immediately to use the fire to his advantage. On the following day, February 28, 1933, he had President Paul von Hindenburg declare a state of emergency under article 48 of the Weimar constitution and issue a decree "for the protection of people and state"; that decree led to the mass arrests of thousands of Communists, Socialists, and trade unionists in the next weeks and months and also provided the original pseudo-legal basis for the terror that plagued German citizens for the rest of the Third Reich's existence.

In its first section, the "Reichstag Fire Decree," as it came to be known, set aside "until further notice" the basic rights of German citizens provided by the Weimar constitution. The decree empowered the government to take "all necessary measures to restore order and public security." It placed severe limitations on personal freedom, the right of free expression, the freedom of the press, and the freedom of assembly; it permitted the authorities to spy on people's private communications through the post, telegraph, and telephone; it allowed the police to conduct search and seizure operations in private homes; and it enabled the police to arrest people and put them in protective custody without charging them with a specific offense.[8] From that point on, therefore, the Nazi police enjoyed extraordinary and largely unlimited powers. Over time the Gestapo emerged as the most important instrument of Nazi terror and its powers became ever greater. A circular of the *Reichssicherheitshauptamt* of 1940, for example, declared that "the legal validity of the state police's dictates are not dependent on the decree 'for the protection of people and state' of 28 February 1933, which authorized the Gestapo to utilize all measures necessary to carry out its duties ... rather they are derived from the general mandate that the German police and the Gestapo have been given in regard to the construction of the National-Socialist state."[9]

Although Jews were not explicitly singled out for repression by the Reichstag Fire Decree, they were to suffer more than any other group in German society under the police state it unleashed. Well before Hitler took power, it was already clear that the Nazi regime would reckon harshly with the Jews as soon as it had the chance. The original Nazi Party program of 1920, for example, made anti-Semitism a cornerstone of its twenty-five-point wish list. Point 4 of the program declared that only people with German blood could be *Volksgenossen*, and only *Volksgenossen* could be citizens; thus, Jews were to be excluded from citizenship. Point 6 demanded the exclusion of Jews from all public offices in the Reich at the state and local levels. Point 7 called for deporting members of foreign nations (which many German Jews were considered to be). Point 23 called for barring Jews from journalism.[10]

With these and other anti-Semitic goals in mind, Nazi Party extremists took the lead over the official organs of state-sponsored terror like the Gestapo in reckoning with the Jews in the first few months of the Nazi regime. The goal at this time, however, was more to destroy the Jews' economic livelihood than to satisfy the bloodlust of SA and SS thugs. As Avraham Barkai explains in the preface to his study of the Jews' economic woes in Nazi Germany:

> When Hitler came to power in January 1933, this Old Guard looked forward impatiently to the immediate ousting of Jews from the economy and their expropriation, as proclaimed in the NSDAP party program, hoping to gain individual lucrative benefits in the process. For this reason, and because more drastic methods were not yet feasible, the place of German Jews in the economy was the main target of the discriminatory policies by the Nazi regime in its early years. The aim of this policy was to undermine and destroy the material basis of existence of the Jews, thus compelling them to emigrate.[11]

SA and SS stormtroopers did not wait very long to exact their pound of flesh. The month of March 1933 witnessed a great outpouring of anti-Semitic violence. Violent demonstrations took place against Jewish businesses; Jewish doctors and lawyers were harassed; individual Jews were beaten up in the streets. Only a few days after the March 5 parliamentary election, the first wave of Jewish arrests in Berlin began when brown-shirted SA stormtroopers marched into one of the city's largest Jewish quarters, the Scheunenviertel, and seized dozens of East European Jews.[12] In Cologne, in the late morning hours of March 31, armed SA and SS troops stormed into the huge courtroom building in the Reichensbergerplatz on the city's north side. Loudly breaking up the legal proceedings, the Nazi stormtroopers searched the courtrooms and judges' chambers for Jewish judges and attorneys. Jewish and sometimes merely "Jewish-looking" jurists were roughed up, rounded up, and placed on an open garbage truck and driven to police headquarters, passing lines of gaping and hooting crowds in the streets on the way.[13]

A day later Jewish stores and businesses in Cologne, Berlin, and other cities across Germany were subjected to a forcible boycott that represented the first centrally organized, nationwide attack on the Jews. Ordered four days earlier, on March 28, by the Nazi Party leadership in Berlin in an effort to manage the anti-Semitic onslaught, the boycott was to replace spontaneous attacks on the Jews. Ostensibly the boycott was ordered to make Jews atone for the "atrocity propaganda" campaign carried out abroad by "international Jewry" in the previous weeks that was damaging German trade and business and threatening German jobs. In reality, "this was a threadbare pretext."[14] Recognizing full well that German Jews could be made to suffer as a consequence of agitation on their part, foreign Jewish organizations and press organs had been cautious and moderate in their coverage of and commentary on events in Germany. The real purpose of the boycott, therefore, was to harass the Jews and ruin their businesses and economic chances of survival.

The boycott began in Cologne and elsewhere at ten o'clock on Saturday morning, April 1. Squads of SA and SS stormtroopers smeared the display windows of Jewish shops and department stores with dreck and Nazi insignia and pasted anti-Semitic placards on them with phrases like "Germans, defend yourselves, don't buy from Jews!" "The Jew is our misfortune!" "Whoever eats Jewish products will die from them!" and "In Answer to the[ir] malicious propaganda, no German buys any more from Jews!" While typically two SA or SS men stood menacingly in front of the entryway of each Jewish store warning the citizenry not to enter and observing who did, the streets were filled with loudspeaker wagons, choruses of shouting Nazis, and Hitler Youth and other Nazi faithful handing out fliers and newspapers—all admonishing the Cologne population to stay united in the government's campaign against the Jews.[15]

Despite the stormtroopers' threats, and even though it was considered a punishable offense for Nazi Party members to shop at Jewish stores and members of the civil service and their families could no longer do so without peril, many civilians in Cologne, Krefeld, and other communities bravely crossed the picket lines to do their normal Saturday shopping. Some Jewish stores even had a banner day. The Krefeld survivor Otto B. reports, for example, that "the Nazis tried to prevent customers to enter our store, but 80 percent came in anyway and bought [2,000 marks worth of goods] on a Saturday."[16] But in most localities, "the great mass of people remained indifferent or even expressed their elation."[17] In contrast to Otto B.'s experiences, the son of the Cologne Jewish department-store owner Julius Bluhm witnessed the smashing of the windows of several Jewish neighbors in the Venloerstrasse and the looting of goods from his father's store after some of the display windows had been broken. "Some onlookers shook their heads [in disgust]; others cursed the Jews," he explained.[18]

Planned originally for only one day, the boycott was called off throughout Germany two days later, on April 4, with the Nazi Party gloating that it had served its purpose as a "weapon for the systematic humiliation of Jewry."[19] Even if the boycott was more of a mixed success in many localities, such as Cologne and Krefeld, in the main the boycott was indeed nearly as effective as the Nazis proclaimed it to have been. It may not have demonstrated "a widespread aggressive antipathy to Jews at the time,"[20] as some have argued. But it was a harbinger of much worse to come. It demonstrated that centrally planned assaults against Jews could be carried out methodically and without protest in every German city and town. Signs in mock-Hebrew letters declaring "Jews not wanted" and other anti-Semitic slogans became ubiquitous features of shopping streets throughout Germany. The radio and the press continued to spread anti-Semitic hate propaganda. The Gentile population became more and more inured to the dehumanization of the Jews. And the anti-Semitic campaign continued.

Between the Jewish boycott of April 1933 and the passage of the infamous Nuremberg Laws of September 1935, a large body of anti-Semitic legislation was passed that served to destroy further the Jews' economic chances of survival, to exclude them from the German community as a whole, and to persuade them to leave the country. Perhaps the most significant such legislation was the Civil Service Law of April 7, 1933. Aimed at removing actual and suspected political opponents of the regime from the civil service, it also encompassed Jewish civil servants who had not served at the front in World War I. The "Aryan clause" of the law called for the "retirement" of Jewish judges, lawyers, teachers, and officials and supplied "a pseudo-legal justification for the exclusion of Jews from other professions"; for instance, Jewish physicians could be barred from practicing medicine because they were now forbidden to work for public-insurance health plans. Other laws passed in the late spring and summer of 1933 reduced the number of Jews who could study at universities to a maximum of 1.5 percent of the total student enrollment, made it impossible for Jews to work as university teaching assistants, and dismissed all "non-Aryan" public-sector employees who did not have tenured civil servant rank.[21]

The anti-Semitic "legal" and extralegal measures of Hitler's first months in power convinced many Jews that they had to leave, but most Jews still found the stakes too high to make such a decision. Nearly 40,000 of Germany's 537,000 Jews left the country in 1933, making it the largest wave of Jewish emigration until after the *Kristallnacht* pogrom of November 1938.[22] Most who left were young and single, but many were either wealthy, well-established Jews who managed to sell their property quickly or politically active Jews threatened with being sent to a concentration camp. Thousands more left between 1934 and 1938, but most stayed behind. As Avraham Barkai explains, "Whoever had a family and children of school age, a shop or some other business, a house or other property found himself unable—unless he was immediately threatened—to arrive so easily at a decision to take leave of his homeland. After the first shock waves of the Nazi takeover and April boycott had passed, people began to get used to the situation."[23]

Those who refused to put up with the situation could usually count on leaving the country empty-handed, or nearly so. In interviews with Jews from Krefeld and other cities, I heard again and again that they had no other choice but to leave the country "pfennig-less," as one man put it.[24] Forced destitution, in fact, became official Nazi policy. A circular from Hitler's foreign office in January 1939 stated that "it is in [the] German interest to force the Jews over the border as beggars, because the poorer the immigrants [become], the greater the burden that the host country [faces]."[25]

In Krefeld slightly over 700 of the city's 1,500 Jews left Germany between the onset of Hitler's regime in 1933 and the fall of 1941, when the doors slammed shut on Jewish emigration. Figures provided by Dieter Hangebruch in his careful study of Krefeld Jews under Hitler's regime show that only 18 Jews left the city in 1934, and that between 1935 and November 1938 only an additional 177 made the decision to leave and were able to carry it out. The vast majority of Krefeld Jews who managed to leave the country left in the year following the violent pogrom of November 9–10, 1938. Getting out during the war years of 1940 and 1941 was exceedingly difficult; only 36 people left at that time.[26] The emigration trend of Jews from other German cities was similar.[27]

The pressure on Jews to emigrate was enormous. Curiously, however, the police organs and the justice officials at first exerted comparatively little direct pressure on the Jews. Although they increased their pressure over time, there were many instances in which their treatment of the Jews seemed mild in comparison with the extreme anti-Semitic behavior of SA and SS stormtroopers, Nazi Party officials, and many civilians. The record of police and justice officials in the Third Reich is a sorry one, especially in relation to the persecution of Jews.[28] But as ruthless, arbitrary, and perverse as these officials could be and often were, they also tried to keep up a facade of legality. Steering a middle course between the goals and aspirations of, on the one hand, fanatic Nazis and anti-Semites and, on the other, those who preferred the traditions of German legal positivism (*Rechtstaatlichkeit*), they channeled the Nazi terror in a way that legitimized it for both sides, thereby upholding the dictates of a criminal regime.

Before the passage of the Nuremberg Laws in September 1935 significantly escalated the Nazis' legal assault on the Jews, relatively few Jews came face to face with the police and the courts in a criminal proceeding. Even after 1935 the majority of German Jews were never accused of having acted illegally. In the city of Krefeld, where the Gestapo's case files are better preserved and more complete than in Cologne, Bergheim, and most other German cities and towns, at least one member of each Jewish family had a police file, and nearly all of these files still exist.[29] Of the approximately 750 of these files in Krefeld, slightly more than 100 involve accusations of having committed an illegal offense; the rest pertain largely to issues of emigration or deportation. This suggests that "only" one out of fifteen Jewish persons had been investigated for charges of illegal activity of any kind. But such an estimate, even though it is several times greater than that of non-Jews, still undercounts the real amount of persecution and terror the Jews experienced at the hands of the "legal" authorities and greatly undercounts the persecution and terror they experienced in general. Some Gestapo files are missing, and many Jews were persecuted by other police agencies that are not contained in these Gestapo files. Nevertheless, most Jewish Krefelders who were eventually sent to a concentration camp— either after the *Kristallnacht* pogrom, when most Jewish men in the city were sent off to Dachau for a period of some weeks at least, or during the deportations of the war years, when nearly all remaining Jews in the city were "evacuated"—were never investigated for or charged with having committed a crime and are therefore not counted in this estimate.

No matter how one calculates, a Jew's chances of being accused of committing a punishable offense in the Third Reich were many times higher than those of a non-Jew; in Krefeld only about one non-Jewish person in sixty had a Gestapo case file.[30] This indicates that Jews were at least four times more likely to have a case lodged against them than non-Jews. But this ratio only begins to demonstrate the differences between the "legal" repression of Jews and non-Jews in Nazi Germany. Far more decisive in separating the repression of Jews from that of non-Jews is the outcome of the cases lodged against them. For a Jew, an insignificant charge, based on a dubious and unsubstantiated denunciation, could lead to a severe sentence or to a committal to a concentration camp. For a German *Volksgenosse*, such a punishment was almost unthinkable.

All of this said, the Nazi secret police had relatively little interest in persecuting Jews at the beginning of the Third Reich. At this time they focused their efforts almost exclusively on destroying real and potential left-wing opponents of the Nazi regime, especially Communists. Although this campaign left most Jews unaffected—most German Jews were solid democrats—the Jews in Krefeld and other German cities who did have Communist affiliations were hunted down just like their non-Jewish party comrades.

Kurt E. was the first Jew to be arrested in Krefeld, and also the first Jew in Krefeld to be put in protective custody.[31] Arrested on February 28, 1933, and placed in protective custody along with several other leading Communist functionaries in the police jail in Krefeld's Weststrasse immediately after the Reichstag fire, this university-educated, twenty-three-year-old businessman was considered a "fanatic Communist and revolutionary" by the Krefeld political police. He remained in custody for four months, the first two weeks in the local Krefeld jail and the remaining three and a half months in a larger jail in the nearby town of Anrath. According to one of the many letters he wrote to the police authorities while in confinement, two weeks elapsed from the time of his arrest before he was even informed why he had been put in jail (the Reichstag Fire Decree of February 28, 1933).

These letters give the impression that he was a bold and brazen young man who at first had little idea of the seriousness of his predicament. Over time the tone of the letters changed markedly. He wrote the first letter on March 7 after only one week in protective custody. Addressed "To the police president Herr Elfes or his deputy," this document was more of a set of demands than a letter. Signed "on behalf of 18 inmates, Kurt E.," the letter contained a numbered list of demands, beginning with "We, the undersigned inmates of police jail Weststr. demand our immediate release." The prisoners also demanded to be told why they had been arrested, why their wives and mothers were not allowed to visit them, why they could not write letters to their wives and mothers even though they were "merely in protective custody," and why they were not allowed to receive "cigarettes, foodstuffs, or even clean clothes."

Kurt E. wrote his next letter a month later, on April 10. This letter was far more polite and written in much neater handwriting. Signed with the respectful salutation *"Hochachtungsvoll* (With great respect), Kurt E.," it was written solely on his own behalf. He explained that he hoped he was not writing in vain, for he had already been confined for six weeks and he needed to be released to care for his wife, who had fallen ill. He had indeed written in vain, however. The response to his letter came a month later, on May 8, when Kriminalsekretär Hoener wrote that he did not think that Kurt E. had changed and, since Hoener considered him to be the "spiritual leader of the KPD [Communist Party]," E. would have to remain in protective custody.

Kurt E.'s wife and family then got into the act and eventually proved more successful at securing his release. Already a few days before Hoener's letter, his wife Marianne wrote a long letter to Kriminalkommissar Adams pleading for her husband to be let go. She began by stating that he had sat "innocently for nine weeks already in the jail in Anrath with no charge against him." Then she explained that he had always been a hard worker and that he was now about to lose his job because he had been away so long.

She also wrote that his parents were suffering greatly. Most significantly, she wrote: "My husband will promise to refrain from all political activities after his release from protective custody." At least she got a reasonably prompt response to her letter, but not the response she wanted. Ten days later, on May 12, the police president of Krefeld wrote back to her saying that "your request can at this time not be granted."

The police then checked his family background and found out that his father, Dr. Hans E., was a physician in Berlin who had served on the front for several years in World War I and been decorated with the Iron Cross. After another polite letter from Kurt E. himself, written on June 7 (again to little effect), his father wrote a long letter to the interior minister three days later on June 10. His father too pleaded for Kurt E.'s release, explaining that he had brought his son up well, that he himself was a patriotic German who had served four years on the front in battle for the Fatherland, but that his son had moved to Krefeld in 1929, lost the influence of his paternal home, and unfortunately fallen in with the wrong circle of people and become a Communist. Dr. E. wrote that he would guarantee that if his son were let out of protective custody, he would see to it that his son refrained from any political activity in the future.

His father's letter had the desired effect. Three days later, on June 30, Kurt E. was let go. The Krefeld political police released him, however, with serious reservations. A report in his file written two days before his release made it clear that the police still considered Kurt E. a "fanatic Communist and revolutionary" who was unlikely to reform and would probably continue his Communist activities after he was sent to his father in Berlin. To make matters worse, the report explained, in Berlin he would be associated with the "entire top functionaries of the Communist Party, right up to the central committee," whom "he already knew because of his activities" as a leader of the local Communist Party in Krefeld and as the leading speaker at Communist meetings. The report concluded that Berlin was a place "especially where he can and also will work for the KPD."

The fact that Kurt E. was a Jew is mentioned only parenthetically near the end of his case file. The policeman who filed this report explained that his reservations about letting the prisoner go included the fact that Kurt E. was the Krefeld leader of the Association of Friends of the Soviet Union

(Bund der Freunde der Sowjetunion), a group that was known to be made up mostly of "highly educated people." Next to "highly educated" the policeman wrote the word *Jew* in parentheses. It can almost be read as a compliment. But this was certainly not the intent.

Just as Kurt E.'s Communist background had more to do with his case than his Jewish background, political affiliation was often the decisive factor in the cases of other Jews in 1933. Six of the seven other Jewish case files in the city of Krefeld in that year also involved people who either were Communist or were accused of having Communist sympathies.

As far as one can tell from the case files, the first Jewish person in Krefeld to be put in a concentration camp was a twenty-two-year-old university student named Erich L.[32] Erich L.'s case is similar in several respects to that of Kurt E. but came later in 1933. Unlike Kurt E., Erich L. was not arrested in the first round-up of local Communist leaders. Until he was denounced to the Krefeld police by an anonymous communication, they did not know that he was part of a Communist student group at the Technical University in Aachen that, among other illegal activities, passed out anti-Nazi fliers and other propaganda literature. When this came to the attention of the police, Erich L. was immediately arrested and placed in protective custody on September 30.

On October 4, his father, as Kurt E.'s father had done, wrote to the police asking for his son's release. His father, a local businessman, explained that two of his sons had fought at the front in the First World War and that he had always raised his children in a patriotic atmosphere dominated by an "irreproachable faithful-to-the-fatherland conviction." In the future, he promised, he would protect his son "from all influences which could impair this conviction in any way."

This letter did not achieve its desired effect immediately, but it probably did have a bearing on the case. On October 23, Erich L. was sent to a concentration camp along with eight others from Oberhausen, Duisburg, Düsseldorf, and Krefeld. Their committal had been ordered by the head regional state official in Düsseldorf (the *Regierungspräsident*), who had written to the Krefeld police on October 18 that, "according to a telegram from the interior minister, all prominent and Jewish protective-custody inmates from the Rhine province are to be immediately transferred to the concen-

tration camp Lichtenburg in the district of Merseburg." Nevertheless, Erich
L. was not interned for long: he was let out of the camp five days later on
October 28 after he signed an official document promising to refrain from
all illegal activity in the future and to commit himself "once again voluntarily to protective custody if the need arises."

Erich L. did not have much time to avail himself of this opportunity: on
December 8 the police came to his parents' apartment in the Krefeld Neus-
serstrasse to arrest him once again. After a month in local custody, he was
then sent, on January 2, 1934, to Aachen, where a case had been opened
against him for the charge of conspiring to commit high treason. Eventually
he was tried before the Superior Court (*Oberlandesgericht*) in the West-
phalian city of Hamm; this court, which handled severe cases of political
disobedience in the Rhine-Ruhr area, sentenced him to a term of several
months in the Siegburg prison near Bonn. After serving his sentence, Erich
L. emigrated to Mexico on October 24, 1934.

The remaining six cases involving Krefeld Jews in 1933 were less dramatic than the Kurt E. and Erich L. cases, but not necessarily less tragic in
their final outcome. The first involved a young Jewish doctor with Communist leanings who was accused of performing illegal abortions. In the midst
of a large street demonstration against him on April 4, he was arrested in his
apartment by several SA stormtroopers and placed in protective custody,
supposedly "to protect him from further excesses." He emigrated to Holland immediately upon his release.[33] Another case involved a young Jewish
teacher who had already fled to Paris by April 11, when the school council
(*Schulrat*) notified the Krefeld police that he should be checked out as a potential Communist.[34] In June the wife of a wealthy Jewish business owner
was arrested when she and her husband were denounced by their chauffeur
for bringing illegal written materials into the country after a business trip
to Holland. Her husband had already fled before the police came to arrest
her, and she too emigrated to Holland as soon as she got out of jail.[35] In mid-
October a twenty-nine-year-old Jewish house-painter was denounced by a
neighboring housewife for libeling Hitler and for harboring Communists
in his apartment. The state prosecuting attorney's office dismissed the case
after it determined that the denunciation had resulted from a neighborhood
quarrel and that the painter had a better reputation among his neighbors

than the denouncer did. But this fortunate outcome in 1933 did not protect him in the end. In mid-December 1941, Kriminalobersekretär Richard Schulenburg wrote the final note in the brief file on the case stating that he had been "evacuated to Riga," along with his family, on December 11, 1941. The final Jewish case in the Krefeld Gestapo files in 1933 was the only Jewish case in that year that did not mention communism in any way. In other respects, it was similar to the case of the house-painter. It involved a wealthy Jewish housewife in a mixed marriage who was denounced by her brother-in-law for libeling the national government. Although her case was also dismissed at the time, her file too had an ominous note at the end: Kriminalsekretär Braun noted that she had been "evacuated to the east" on July 25, 1942.[36]

After most known or suspected Jewish Communists had been arrested or left the country in 1933, the following two years were relatively quiet in regard to the secret police's persecution of the Jews. In 1934 cases were started against only four Jews in Krefeld, marking the lowest number of Jewish cases in any year until 1944, when almost all Krefeld Jews had either already emigrated of their own accord or been carted away to the east during the Holocaust. In 1935 there were only five cases against Krefeld Jews before the passage of the Nuremberg Laws in September. Most of the cases were minor and involved only modest periods of confinement. Communism figured in only one case. In most respects, the cases in both 1934 and 1935 were not very different from the run of cases lodged against non-Jews in the city, though the anti-Semitism factor did mark a noticeable difference.

As in the cases of non-Jews, most of these cases began with an allegation by a neighbor or coworker that the Jew in question had made libelous statements about Hitler or other Nazi Party leaders or violated the laws against freedom of expression in one way or another.[37] One example is the case of a severely wounded Jewish war veteran and businessman who was denounced by a business acquaintance in February 1934 for making statements such as "Heal Hitler," "Shit is also brown," and "One will soon be required to prove his Aryan background back to the apes." Although it was not until November 1935 that the Jewish businessman was called to atone for these statements—by paying a fine of fifty Reichmarks—the Nazis got even with him in the end. Under near constant pressure for years from the Gestapo to leave the country, he made plans to emigrate with his family to Chile but unfortunately never did, and this proved fatal. In June 1942 he and his wife and son were deported to the east.[38]

Spying in a direct sense was seldom used to bring about arrests in cases like these, when communism or other kinds of oppositional political activity did not figure in the case. But Jews who emigrated abroad were sometimes tailed by specially appointed agents who reported back to the Gestapo in Germany on their activities. One twenty-seven-year-old man, for example, emigrated to New York in April 1934 and took a job writing for the *New York Post* and other American newspapers. Soon he incurred the wrath of the Berlin Gestapo headquarters for publishing a book under the alias of Johannes Steel entitled *Hitler aus Frankenstein* (Hitler out of Frankenstein). Since the Gestapo could not arrest him abroad, they put pressure on his family members back in Krefeld. For the next several years his parents' mail was surreptitiously intercepted and read. But knowing that this could happen, Steel wisely never wrote anything of a politically sensitive nature to his parents. Eventually the Gestapo became frustrated and decided to call off the surveillance.[39] Another case involved a Jewish sales representative who fled across the nearby Dutch border at Kaldenkirchen to the town of Venlo in late August 1935 after a local woman had accused him of wearing a Nazi Party pin on his suitcoat and representing himself as a Nazi Party member. Evidence in his file shows that he and other German Jews who also fled to Venlo, which lay only twenty miles from Krefeld, continued to be watched over while they were in exile.[40] Of the other cases during this period, only one contained clear evidence of spying activity on German soil. It involved a traveling Jewish salesman who was rumored to be in league with Communists in the city of Saarbrücken. But no incriminating evidence was turned up, even though the man was spied on for several years, and no arrest was made in the case.[41]

Popular anti-Semitism played a role in at least two cases that took place in Krefeld in the summer of 1935. Both involved alleged violations of the *Heimtücke* law of December 20, 1934, which outlawed political libel and slander,[42] and both were investigated by Theodor Schommer, who held the rank of *Kriminalassistent* at the time but who later rose a notch to the rank of *Kriminalsekretär* in the Krefeld Gestapo during the war years. Neither case was very severe, and each was brought on by an obvious personal feud. Even though the defendants were Jewish, Schommer dismissed both cases himself without passing them on to a higher authority.

In the first case, a single, fifty-five-year-old Jewish woman was accused in late June 1935 by a dentist who rented rooms from her of making derogatory remarks about Hitler and other Nazi Party members.[43] Trying to make his accusation as effective as possible, the dentist had his attorney file the letter of denunciation with the police. In it he and his attorney cited the woman for making seditious remarks and reminded the police that "Fräulein D. is a Jewess and it appears to us to be called for that she be appropriately apprised of her responsibilities as a guest in Germany." Schommer dismissed the case almost immediately, however, with the justification that the accusation had been made out of malice and that the woman's alleged remarks had taken place more than a year earlier and therefore did not fall under the *Heimtücke* law.

The other case began a month later on July 29. A forty-seven-year-old SA member denounced a sixty-five-year-old Jewish egg dealer and stated that he wanted "the Jew put in the cooler for a while."[44] The SA man made his denunciation in the form of a letter to his local SA base, which then passed it along to the Krefeld police. A week later, on August 6, the denouncer, the accused, and a witness (who was also an SA member) were summoned to the Krefeld police headquarters to present their versions of events.

At approximately 5:30 P.M. on Sunday, July 28, the Jewish man had entered a large *Biergarten* inside of the Krefeld Stadtgarten. Soon he walked by a table where two SA men were sitting (denouncer and witness), and one of them yelled out to him, "What do you want here? You look like a nice German all right." To this the Jewish man retorted, "What are you then? You eight-mark [a week] welfare recipient."

After recording this testimony, Kriminalassistent Schommer determined that no punishable offense had been committed. Nonetheless, he gave the Jewish man a serious warning not to get himself in trouble again and told him that the next time he could count on being punished. The Jewish man promised never to set foot in the Stadtgarten again, and Schommer closed the case.

Jews in Cologne, Bergheim, and other cities also had to contend routinely with anti-Semitic indignities and Jew-baiting tactics on the part of Nazi extremists as well as regular citizens, many of them often mere children. But in the early years of the Third Reich at least, the legal authorities often did not pay them much heed. An example from the Cologne Special Court files took place a week after the Krefeld case, involving the Stadtgarten encounter.[45] On the afternoon of August 17, a wealthy, fifty-five-year-old Jewish woman was shopping in the Cologne main shopping street, the Hohestrasse, where she encountered two Hitler Youth selling the Hitler Youth newspaper, *Fanfare*. Noticing that the headline of the paper read "Whoever Is Involved with Jews Pollutes the Nation," she took offense and admonished the youths, telling them, "It is disgusting for you to sell that newspaper, it would be better if red were voted in once again." The boys (aged twelve and thirteen) ran over immediately to an SS man in the street and told him what the Jewish woman had said. He then spotted a nearby policeman, who took her under arrest.

After spending a night in jail while her sixteen-year-old son waited for her in the fashionable Domhotel next to the imposing Cologne cathedral (the woman and her son resided in Leipzig and were on the last day of a Rhine trip when the woman was arrested), she was given a chance to respond to the charges against her. (The elder of the two Hitler Youth had given his version of the affair to the police just before the woman was called in.) She confessed without hesitation to having made the statements but asked to be forgiven for making them. She had made them, she said, in a state of extreme agitation, but in no way did she have "the intention of acting in a hostile manner to the government or the current form of state." As she explained to the police, "I suddenly had the desire to defend my previous way of life and religion." As proof of her support for the present government, she added that her own son had spent three months in the Hitler Youth before being forced to quit on account of his Jewish background.

The officer in charge of the case passed it on to the state prosecuting attorney's office but let the woman go for the time being after making a note

that she had a clean record and a permanent residence in Leipzig where she could be reached. Four days later, on August 22, 1934, the state prosecuting attorney officially dismissed the case with the justification that libel charges had not been made against her by the operational head of *Fanfare* and that no such charges were expected.

Cases such as this one, in which zealous Nazi Youth brought charges against Jews, were by no means uncommon in other German cities. But during the prewar years, the police and justice officials did not seem to encourage them particularly. (During the war years, however, the situation would change: teenagers would often be encouraged to spy on neighboring Jews.) In Krefeld, for example, two mentally impaired, unemployed, middle-aged Jewish brothers named Arthur and Moritz S. were constantly ridiculed by local youth in the streets of Krefeld in the 1930s. Branded by the children with the name "Lullo" (also spelled "Lullu" in one of the police files in the case), Arthur and Moritz were reported several times to the police by the children for returning their sadistic name-calling with epithets of their own. In March 1936, Arthur was accused by a thirteen-year-old schoolgirl of yelling out to her and several other girls even younger than herself, "Heil, Moscow, you pigs." In September 1937, his brother Moritz, after being called Lullo to his face by two Hitler Youth who were selling Nazi Winter Relief Fund pins, was denounced to the police by the eleven- and twelve-year-old boys for telling them to "stick the WHW pin up your rear end." And finally, in September 1938, Arthur was once again brought to Gestapo headquarters after a Hitler Youth accused him of yelling out, "Nazi children, drop dead." The authorities did not press charges against the "Lullo" brothers in any of these cases, but the brothers were interrogated in the state police headquarters each time. The severe warning they received in the last of these recorded cases made it clear that if they were reported again they would have "to reckon with the severest state-police measures."[46]

The first recorded case in the Cologne Special Court files involving people from the town of Bergheim's tiny Jewish community also dealt with alleged seditious statements brought on by anti-Semitic ridicule. (Because it lay just outside the city of Cologne, Bergheim fell under the jurisdiction of the Cologne court.)[47] Two unmarried Jewish sisters, Selma and Berta S., aged thirty-one and twenty, were denounced to the local Nazi Party headquarters in December 1935 by a neighboring housewife after the elder Jewish sister supposedly told her and some other neighbors that "you can lick my ass with the *Kreisleitung* [local Nazi Party leadership]."

After being informed of this episode, the deputy head of the local Nazi Party filed a complaint with the Bergheim police department, which assigned the case to Kriminalbezirkssekretär Gottfried Schleiden, who handled the majority of political cases involving both Jews and non-Jews in Bergheim during the entire Nazi period. Schleiden soon called in the accused Jewish women, the housewife, and several neighbors to provide their observations on the affair. Although some of the witnesses supported the sisters and others supported their accuser, what became clear in the investigation was that the Jewish women had been constantly taunted and threatened over the previous weeks and months by SA bullies and by the denouncing housewife and her husband, whom the sisters claimed had put the SA ruffians up to taunting them. Over and over again the Jewish women had been called offensive names like "pigs." On several occasions, they had also been threatened with physical harm. Once they were told that their house would be burned to the ground. Another time their tormentors said they would slice them into pieces.

Schleiden decided that the case was serious enough to pass on to the state prosecuting attorney's office in Cologne, which in turn filed an official indictment and brought the case to trial. M. Weinberg (a leading Jewish attorney in Cologne) served as the Jewish women's defense counsel and wrote up a fifteen-page defense brief that proved convincing to the Cologne court that tried the case. In the end, the court agreed with Weinberg that there was "a lack of evidence" to convict the sisters, and it acquitted them on April 1, 1936. Nevertheless, this humane decision of the court had come only after the two sisters suffered a long and frightening ordeal, and no action at all was ever taken against their tormentors.

THE NUREMBERG LAWS AND THE PERSECUTION OF THE JEWS, SEPTEMBER 1935 TO NOVEMBER 1938

Nazi Party leaders in Berlin were worried about instances in which the police and justice authorities had to rebuff the anti-Semitic urges of Nazi Party

activists and other Nazi extremists. In 1935 they took important strides to
calm the rank and file and to take control of the situation. On April 11, 1935,
Nazi Party Secretary Hess issued the following order to members of the
party:

> While I can understand that all decent National Socialists oppose these
> new attempts by Jewry with utter indignation, I must warn them most
> urgently not to vent their feelings by acts of terror against individual
> Jews, as this can only result in bringing party members into conflict
> with the political police, who consist largely of party members, and
> this will be welcomed by Jewry. The political police can in such cases
> only follow the strict instructions of the Führer in carrying out all
> measures for maintaining peace and order, so making it possible for
> the Führer to rebuke at any time allegations of atrocities and boycotts
> made by Jews abroad.[48]

In addition to Hess's warning, the Nazi Party leadership also took bold
steps soon thereafter to put additional pressure on the Jews and to clarify
their legal status. The most significant of these was the passage of the Law
for the Protection of German Blood and Honor and the Reich Citizenship
Law on September 15, 1935, which marked a watershed in the "legal" persecution of the Jews and escalated the police role in that persecution.[49] Enacted
on the last day of the annual Nuremberg Party Rally and on the heels of yet
another wave of popular outrages and anti-Semitic boycotts throughout
Germany in the spring and summer months of 1935 (which some former
Krefeld Jews remember as more pernicious than those of 1933),[50] the "Nuremberg Laws" provided the police and legal authorities with powerful new
weapons to be used in persecuting the Jews. The new laws excluded Jews
from citizenship rights, provided a legal definition of a Jew, and proscribed
physical relations between Jews and non-Jews. With this kind of help in
routinizing the state-sanctioned ostracism of the Jews, it was not long before the secret police regularized its own handling of Jewish matters
through the establishment of special departments for Jewish affairs at the
center of the terror apparatus in Berlin and in local Gestapo headquarters
across the country.

By outlawing marriage and sexual contact between Jews and Aryans, forbidding Jews to hire German women under the age of forty-five as domestic help, and making it illegal for them to raise the German flag or display the Reich's colors, the Law for the Protection of German Blood and Honor greatly increased the Jews' legal vulnerability and social isolation. Because Hitler—who took an active role in the formulation of these laws—believed that men are always the initiators of sexual contact, only men were made subject to criminal prosecution for violations of the sexual prohibitions called for in the laws.[51] In theory, both Jewish and "German-blooded" men were to be punished (with prison terms of up to fifteen years) for committing the new crime of *Rassenschande* (often translated as "race defilement") created by the Law for the Protection of German Blood and Honor. In practice, Jewish men were punished far more regularly than Aryan men, and Jewish women were sometimes punished as well, although women were handled by the Gestapo directly, not by the courts.

Given the new strictures against interracial mixing and the tide of new legal measures against the Jews, it became necessary to define who was or was not to be considered a "Jew." This was no easy matter: before the Nuremberg Laws were passed, there had been no agreement over the definition of a Jewish person. Not only were party and state officials divided over the issue, but Jews were themselves. Many Jews had become Christianized long before the Nazis came to power, and many other Jews followed no religion at all. Additionally, a large number of Jews were in mixed marriages or were the product of mixed marriages. In 1931 and 1932 roughly 36 percent of all new Jewish marriages were mixed; in 1933 the number rose to 44 percent. Of these mixed marriages, only about one-fourth of the children were brought up in the Jewish faith.[52]

As a general rule, party officials preferred a more extensive definition of a Jewish person than did members of the civil service. For most party members and officials, anyone with a drop of Jewish blood was a Jew and deserving of being persecuted to the hilt. Many state and justice officials, on the other hand, thought it necessary to distinguish between so-called *Volljuden* (pure Jews) and *Mischlinge* (people who were the offspring of mixed marriages between Jews and non-Jews). As Raul Hilberg explains: "The party 'combatted' the part-Jew as a carrier of the 'Jewish influence';

the civil service wanted to protect in the part-Jew 'that part which is German.'"[53] In the end, the definition was written in the Interior Ministry and the party view lost out.

The First Regulation to the Reich Citizenship Law, passed on November 14, 1935, spelled out the definition. Whereas the Citizenship Law of September 15, 1935, had deprived Jews of citizenship rights by limiting such rights to people of "German blood," it had not defined exactly who a Jew was. According to the new legislation of November, a Jew was anyone with three or more Jewish grandparents. Under a variety of special conditions, however, people with only two Jewish grandparents could also be defined as Jews: if, before September 15, 1935, they were married to a Jew or were a member of the Jewish religious community themselves; if they were the offspring of an extramarital affair between a Jew and a non-Jew and were born after July 31, 1936; or if they were the offspring of a marriage between a Jew and a non-Jew that took place after September 15, 1935. Persons who did not qualify as a Jew under these conditions but who had at least one Jewish grandparent were defined as *Mischlinge*. In subsequent legislation, these people were further subdivided into *Mischlinge* of either the first degree (those with two Jewish grandparents) or the second degree (those with only one Jewish grandparent). As discussed in detail in a later chapter, the *Mischlinge* were not considered Aryans and would remain in a precarious position in Nazi Germany. Despite their difficulties, however, most *Mischlinge* were far better off than "pure Jews," and most survived the Holocaust.[54]

Once Jews had been defined, their persecution could proceed along more technical lines. To carry this out, the center of the terror apparatus in Berlin soon created a special department headed by "Jewish experts" to preside over Jewish matters. In the fall of 1936, a new section of the SD for Jewish affairs was formed, with Adolf Eichmann as its deputy head. Acting to centralize "the entire work on the Jewish question in the hands of the SD and Gestapo," it declared on December 18, 1936, that the primary aims of Jewish policy would be "the pushing back of Jewish influence in all spheres of public life (including the economy); [and] the encouragement of Jewish emigration."[55]

Around this same time, the local secret police headquarters in cities like

Krefeld and Cologne also rationalized their handling of Jewish affairs by creating specialized Jewish desks (*Judenreferate*) under the leadership of "official specialists for Jewish affairs" (*Sachbearbeiter für Judenangelegenheiten*) like Richard Schulenburg of the Krefeld Gestapo. Although Schulenburg testified in the 1949 trial of his former colleague Alfred Effenberg that he had been the head of the Krefeld Jewish desk "since the establishment of the Gestapo outpost in Krefeld" (by which he meant August 1937), evidence from the Krefeld Gestapo case files shows that he started to take a leading role in Jewish affairs in 1936.[56] Before 1936 investigations of Jewish cases in Krefeld were carried out most frequently by other officers, such as Theodor Schommer and Karl Schmitz. After this time, Schulenburg headed most Jewish investigations, though Schommer, Schmitz, Gustav Burkert, Herbert Braun, and other officers continued to oversee some of them or to assist Schulenburg in others, especially when the cases overlapped with their own areas of specialization.[57]

The increased bureaucratization of Jewish affairs enabled the Nazi regime to press ahead with the persecution of the Jews with more discretion as well as with more precision. Fearing a foreign boycott that could damage his rearmament plans, Hitler was intent on presenting a positive face to the outside world during the Berlin Olympic Games in 1936 and in the succeeding years. This effort mandated that public anti-Semitic spectacles be kept to a minimum. To most observers, this policy appeared successful, and 1936 and 1937 have been thought of as "quiet years," or years that presented "the illusion of a 'grace period'" in Jewish persecution.[58]

Many Americans and other foreigners came to Germany to attend the Olympics in the summer of 1936 expecting the worst. To their astonishment, they encountered a bustling and optimistic society with nary a trace of anti-Semitic activity. Julius Streicher's obscene newspaper *Der Stürmer* was no longer placed in prominent view on the walls of major buildings in Berlin and other cities, the boycotting of Jewish stores had ceased, and even some Jewish athletes were allowed to try out for the German team. As Deborah E. Lipstadt explains, "Tourists and visiting reporters—there were over 1,500 of the latter at the Games—were so impressed by what they saw that many dismissed the stories of brutalities as exaggerated."[59] The Nazis were so successful in their charade that one American reporter feared that visitors would be "inclined to dismiss all anti-German thought and action abroad as insipid and unjust. [The visitor] sees no Jewish heads being chopped off. . . . The people smile, are polite and sing with gusto in beer gardens. . . . Everything is terrifyingly clean and the visitor likes it all."[60]

Even many Jews were taken in. When the Gestapo "exhaustively searched" the apartment of the former Jewish Communist Karl Muschkatt-blatt in the Bayenthal section of Cologne on August 24, 1938, Kriminal-assistent Büthe found two large folders of correspondence between Musch-kattblatt and several Jews who had already emigrated. A copy of one of these letters, written to a former German Jew in Belgium and dated February 28, 1938, was particularly incriminating: it indicated that Muschkattblatt was involved in illegal activity at home and was spreading anti-German infor-mation abroad. In the letter, Muschkattblatt stated that he continued to lis-ten to Radio Moscow and that he hated the lack of freedom of speech and opinion in Hitler's Germany. He also wrote, however, that anti-Semitism was not particularly rife in the Cologne area and that much of the local pop-ulation resented the Nazis.

To support his point about anti-Nazi sentiment in Cologne, Musch-kattblatt provided a long description of the 1936 Cologne carnival. After explaining that the local Nazi organization had wanted to have three floats in the *Rosenmontag* procession but was granted only one by the carnival organizers, Muschkattblatt detailed how one of the traditional carnival ora-tors had made a mockery of the Nazis before a huge crowd. Before he began to speak, the man had risen slowly out of a large beer barrel with his right arm outstretched, as if to greet the celebrants with the Hitler salute. This display left the crowd nearly speechless, because carnival in Cologne was not usually the place for displays of Nazi affinity. But with a large SA and SS presence in the crowd, the people had to return the salute and raise their own arms. In Muschkattblatt's words, "The crowd looked dumbfoundedly at him at first, but then it slowly gathered itself and did the same. But then the man merely turned his hand over and said, 'It is raining, isn't it?!!!'" The man then regaled the crowd with a series of anti-Nazi jokes, told in the local low-German Kölsch dialect, about the lack of freedom of expression. For instance: "Yesterday I went to have three teeth pulled out, and wow was that painful! The dentist wanted to pull them out of my nose! [I yelled to him,] 'What the heck is that all about?' [He replied,] 'Oh ja, because the mouth isn't allowed to do anything anymore!'"[61]

If there was something of a lull in outwardly extremist acts against the Jews after the passage of the Nuremberg Laws in the fall of 1935, it did not mean that Germany had returned to its senses, as people like Muschkatt-blatt hoped. The persecution of the Jews was merely carried on more quietly for the next few years. Evidence from the Krefeld Gestapo case files, in fact, suggests that the pace of persecution picked up. With a surge in *Rassenschande* cases—which usually came to the Gestapo's attention through denunciations from the civilian population[62]—leading the way, the Krefeld Gestapo opened more new investigations against Jews in 1936 than in any other year in the Third Reich. The three remaining peacetime years were by no means slack years either.

The cases in this period differed in a number of ways from the cases lodged against Jews in the first years of Hitler's rule. The civilian population became more active in their initiation, perhaps suggesting that there was no real decline in popular anti-Semitic sentiment, as some have maintained. Fewer cases involved allegations of Communist or other left-wing activities (in the Krefeld Gestapo cases files, there were no cases of this type involving Jews after 1934), demonstrating that the regime had already successfully routed any potential left-wing resistance. And relatively fewer cases involved libelous or slanderous statements on the part of Jews, suggesting that the Jews had become increasingly cautious in their public utterances and behavior, now recognizing what might happen to them if they dropped their guard. Indeed, most cases were of a nonpolitical nature and had nothing to do with antiregime statements or activities. Typically they involved punishment for activities that had only recently become criminalized, like violating the new race defilement laws or trying to get money and property out of the country, or for activities that the Jews did not even know were illegal—or that were not in fact illegal, like using the Hitler greeting or salute, or being sent to a concentration camp for an "education" (*Schulung*) after returning to the country from abroad.[63]

Minor as these cases were, their punishment was often severe, especially when compared with the leniency so common in the resolution of non-Jewish cases. The discriminatory justice meted out in race defilement cases provides the best example. German courts were relatively reserved in their punishment of such cases at first. Up until October 1936, there were only 266 cases of race defilement registered with the Reich Justice Ministry in which a verdict was rendered. Of these, 223 ended with a jail sentence of one year or less, and only 43 ended with a prison sentence for a longer period. Although in theory both Jewish and non-Jewish men were subject to the same punishment, in practice this did not take place. Not only were many more Jewish men convicted than non-Jews (206 to 60), but lengthy sentences were reserved almost exclusively for Jews (39 of the 43 prison sentences).

Discriminatory as this justice was, it failed to satisfy either local Nazi Party officials or the central Gestapo office in Berlin (*Gestapa*), which on March 21, 1936, registered a complaint about the courts' leniency in sentencing.[64] After the *Gestapa*'s complaint, the number of cases increased and the sentencing stiffened. A judgment rendered by the Reich Supreme Court of December 9, 1936, ruled that outlawed sexual relations included not just sleeping together but "all sexual activity which served to satisfy the sexual longings of at least one of the partners."[65] With this broader definition in place, the number of prosecutions for race defilement reached a peak in 1937. Then the number gradually tapered off in the following years as ever fewer Jews remained in Germany.[66]

The relative harshness of the punishment that Jews received from the courts masked even harsher treatment at the hands of the Gestapo. A secret decree by Reinhard Heydrich of June 12, 1937, stipulated that persons who had been sentenced for the crime of race defilement were to be sent by the Gestapo to a concentration camp after serving out their jail or prison sentences. The authors of a recent book on Nazi racial practices argue that "in practice, this meant that persons guilty of 'miscegenation' . . . were sentenced to death."[67] But a close examination of Gestapo case files for the city of Krefeld shows that while such sentences were often meted out to Jews, they seldom were applied to Gentiles.[68]

Even more illustrative of the discriminatory treatment of the Jews was the manner in which the female partners were handled in these cases. When an "Aryan" woman was involved, the Gestapo officers usually carried out

their interrogation in a polite manner, warned the woman not to get involved in such a relationship again, and sent her home.[69] Jewish women, on
the other hand, had a different experience. They too were not handed over
to the prosecuting attorney for trial, since the law stipulated that only men
were to be tried by the courts in race defilement cases. But typically they
were not sent back home either; the Gestapo sidestepped the law by sending
Jewish women directly to concentration camp without any legal recourse.

In some ways worse than a concentration camp sentence was the humiliating ordeal that Jewish women underwent in Gestapo headquarters. Several of the Krefeld cases indicate that Jewish women were sometimes used
to satisfy perverse voyeuristic urges of some of the Gestapo officers who
delved into sexual cases at far greater length than was needed for a mere
conviction. They would often carry out their prurient interrogations over
several days—a practice that also frequently obtained in the Gestapo's interrogation of homosexuals. The case of Ruth W. provides a particularly
egregious example.[70]

Ruth W. was a sixteen-year-old housemaid and the daughter of a vege-
table dealer when the Krefeld Gestapo received an anonymous communication in late January 1939 that she and a twenty-year-old Aryan worker
named Josef S. had been carrying on an illicit relationship. She and Josef S.
were immediately arrested and brought to Gestapo headquarters for interrogation. The interrogation of the young man was written up in greater
detail in the case file, but because both the young woman and the young
man were forced to relate their stories in extremely graphic detail, it is likely
that the affair titillated the officer handling the case (a Düsseldorf officer
named Schneider).

Josef S. began his testimony by explaining:

I had been already seduced by the time I reached fourteen, and this was
by the seventeen-year-old-daughter of my teacher H. She led me, as
we were alone at the time, to her bedroom and then told me in detail
about making love. At first she asked me to play with her sexual organs
with my finger, and then she led my member into her. We had several
sexual encounters of this sort in the course of the next three months.

At every available opportunity she opened my pants and satisfied herself with my member. Occasionally this took place six times in a day.

After establishing his sexual background, he went on to discuss his relations with Ruth W. He said that they first had sex in early 1937, when she was fifteen years old and he was eighteen. At the beginning, he said, she was reticent, but eventually she became the one pushing the relations, which happened often: "She invited me to her apartment on one Sunday in the summer of 1937, because her parents and everyone else were away. After a short time she undressed to her underpants and blouse, and then we had sex about three or four times on the sofa. From this time onward we had sex regularly, usually on Sundays when I returned from Düsseldorf to Krefeld, and mostly in the out-of-doors." He then described several meetings in small hotels: one time, after going to bed at 9:00 P.M., they had sex once with their clothes still on, and "then we took all of our clothes off and had sex a total of seven times. On the next morning she grabbed my penis and wanted to have sex once again. [But] I was not up to it anymore." "We also had sex from time to time on the Rhine in Kaiserswerth. At these occasions she often satisfied me with her hand, and she also took my penis in her mouth." Finally, he gave details about their sexual encounters twice on a war memorial, once on Christmas Day, and sometimes while he was in uniform. (He was a member of the *Reichsarbeitsdienst*.) He ended his testimony by saying that it was really all her fault and that he had tried to break off relations with her several times, but each time she had written or spoken to him promising that she "would assume all of the consequences."

Before Ruth W. testified three days later on February 2, the Gestapo officer Schneider wrote in a report: "W. appears to be ethically and morally on a very low level. She creates a great danger for the folk-community, and therefore the application of educational measures appears to be absolutely necessary." He said nothing of the ethical and moral level of the young man who had been having sex with women since he was fourteen and who very likely was at least as avid in pressing the relationship with Ruth W. as she was with him.

In her first interrogation, Ruth W. did not admit to having had sex with

Josef S., but she did provide details about a sexual relationship she had already had with a non-Aryan photographer after a photo session. After another night in jail, during which she may have been tortured (although just being in the Gestapo jail overnight may have been torture enough), she was called in the next morning for a second interrogation. This time she began with the fateful words, "I now wish to tell the whole truth." She then confessed to having carried on the relationship with Josef S. since the beginning of 1938 and described it in detail.

After her interrogation, she was put in "protective custody." Shortly thereafter, she was sent to the Lichtenburg concentration camp, where she remained for nearly three months before emigrating to Holland at the end of March.[71] Josef S. was apparently let go from Gestapo headquarters but forced to stand trial before the county court in Kleve on May 12, 1939. He received a one-year jail sentence for his crime. The judges justified their lenient verdict by noting that he was very young and inexperienced and that he had been seduced by the "Jewess."

That this case was not unusual for the Gestapo in other localities is demonstrated by several cases that were handled by Gestapo officers in Krefeld (the previous one had been handled by an officer from the Düsseldorf Gestapo), like Wilhelm Weber and Gustav Burkert, at around the same time. It suffices to touch on just a few of the details of one of those cases.[72] It began with a denunciation stemming from a business quarrel: two Aryan businessmen and two Jewish sisters were accused of carrying on a sexual relationship between October 1938 and April 1939. Only one of the sisters could be found to testify, however; the older sister had already emigrated to England.

The younger sister's case began when she was arrested on June 20, 1939, and brought to Gestapo headquarters to give her testimony to Kriminaloberassistent Weber. She was a twenty-year-old housemaid at the time and the daughter of a local Jewish businessman. Her typed testimony filled six long pages (forty-one lines per page, with twelve words per line). The interrogation must have stretched out over several hours, since it was repeatedly broken off in the middle when Weber warned her to tell the truth. She described having had sex many times with two men, one a twenty-two-year-old roofer's apprentice and the other a twenty-nine-year-old master carpenter with a wife and two children. She provided many details about when and where she did it (at home while her parents were sleeping, in the front seat of a car while her sister was having sex with the other man in the back seat) and how she did it (always with a condom, she said, which she carried with her in her purse because she feared contracting a sexual disease). She insisted that the men had instigated the sex and that she had warned them several times about the Nuremberg Laws.

Gustav Burkert carried out the men's interrogation, which took place on June 23 and 24. Their typed affidavits are shorter than the woman's (three pages for each man), and if less pornographic, they are nonetheless filled with many graphic details. They claimed that it was the women who had seduced them, and they concurred in their statements that the women had liked to perform oral sex on them as well as normal fornication. In the end, the two men were sentenced to brief jail terms by the court while the woman was forced to spend nearly two months in protective custody in the police jail in Krefeld before she followed in her sister's footsteps and emigrated to England on August 12, 1939.

Whereas, despite many important exceptions, German women were much less likely than German men to have run-ins with the Gestapo and were much less frequently sent to concentration camps or punished severely if they did have such a run-in,[73] being a female offered only limited advantages for Jewish women. Relevant in this context are the cases of the young Jews who, in what would become normal procedure after 1935, were sent to a concentration camp for an "education" after they had returned to Germany from abroad. These cases show that even though Jewish women were nearly as likely to be sent to a concentration camp as Jewish men, some Gestapo officers, like Richard Schulenburg of the Krefeld Gestapo, often preferred (especially if they were attractive) to treat them with some measure of understanding and compassion.

One of the best examples of Schulenburg's occasionally chivalrous treatment of young Jewish women is found in the case of a tall and slender twenty-three-year-old Jewish woman named Rosemarie G., who returned to Krefeld in mid-January 1936 after spending nearly three years studying abroad in France and England.[74] She returned to Krefeld on January 18 and took up residence with her older sister, Cäcilie H., and her sister's husband.

Three weeks later, on February 10, she was arrested and taken for questioning to police headquarters in the Hansa-Haus building across from the main Krefeld train station. Schulenburg handled the case and decided that she was to be placed in protective custody and sent as soon as possible to a concentration camp for "an education." A day after her arrest, Rosemarie G.'s sister wrote a long letter to the Düsseldorf Gestapo headquarters pleading for her release and begging them not to send her to a concentration camp (*Schulungslager*). In her letter Cäcilie H. explained that her two brothers had fought heroically at the front in the First World War (one had been wounded and had also earned the Iron Cross) and that she herself had been decorated with a medal for her wartime service as a nurse.

Cäcilie H.'s letter did not prevent her sister from being sent to the camp, but it did have a positive effect on Schulenburg. When Rosemarie G. was transported to Moringen concentration camp a week after her original arrest, she was not taken, as was the usual practice, by truck or train in a "group transport" with several other prisoners. Instead, Schulenburg mandated that she be driven to the camp by "single transport" in a private car, chauffeured by a young policeman named Josef Peters, with several of her family members accompanying her, presumably to make the journey less terrifying. This so incensed the three SA men to whom she was handed over at the entrance of the camp that they made out a formal complaint to the Düsseldorf Gestapo and to the Krefeld police against Peters, who was later disciplined for his impropriety. In his defense, Peters said that he had certainly not wanted to do a Jew any favors, but he had only been following the orders of his superior officer Schulenburg, who was the acting head of the Krefeld state police outpost on the day when Peters had driven his Jewish prisoner and her family members to the camp.

Rosemarie G. spent nearly four months in Moringen concentration camp before being released on June 10 after the head of the camp wrote to the Düsseldorf Gestapo headquarters that he thought that her "education" had been successful and after her sister had paid for her return passage to Krefeld. Another condition of her release was her signature on a form promising that she would never involve herself with Communist or Socialist supporters or activity that was hostile to the state in any way (which she had never done in the first place). At the same time, she also had to attest that she would never raise an objection against the authorities for the police measures that had been taken against her. She married shortly after her release and emigrated a year and a half later with her husband to London.

KRISTALLNACHT AND BEYOND

Any semblance of moderation in the Nazis' treatment of the Jews came to an end in November 1938 with the unleashing of the *Kristallnacht* pogrom. Evidence suggests, however, that the Nazis' temporary slowdown in their anti-Semitic policy—necessitated in part by Hitler's desire to put up a good front to foreign visitors during the 1936 Olympic Games and to the outside world in general during his rebuilding of the German economy and rearmament campaign—had ended at least a year earlier and that they had entered a new radical phase in anti-Semitic activity.[75]

On November 27, 1937, the Reich Minister of Economics, Hjalmar Schacht, who had overseen the economic revival program but also had opposed radical anti-Semitism in economic matters, was dismissed.[76] With Schacht out of the way, and his former ministry placed under Hermann Göring's Four-Year Plan organization, Jewish businesses were increasingly pressured to sell out to Aryan firms at prices far below market value, and more and more Jews were forced to accept economic circumstances that were less viable than ever. Decrees by Göring, on December 15, 1937, reduced foreign-exchange and raw-material quotas for Jewish businesses and, on March 1, 1938, took away the Jews' right to receive public contracts. To facilitate the "Aryanization" of the economy and to make it difficult for Jews to safeguard their holdings, Göring decreed, on April 26, 1938, that all Jewish property worth more than 5,000 marks was to be registered with the authorities. Between June and July additional measures were passed to ban Jewish doctors, dentists, and veterinarians from treating Aryan patients or their animals, to ban Jewish lawyers from representing non-Jews, and to cause the dismissal of an estimated 30,000 Jewish traveling salesmen.[77]

The harassment and humiliation of the Jews was further exacerbated in several other ways in this period as the regime increased its efforts to force the Jews to emigrate. Anti-Semitic propaganda became more virulent, many communities increased their restrictions on Jewish movement, and signs with "only for Germans" became common on park benches. In June 1938, male Jewish "career criminals" (defined as those who had at least one prior prison sentence) were sent to concentration camps along with other "asocials" such as beggars, gypsies, and vagabonds and were not let out until they had made firm plans to leave the country.[78] Finally, a decree issued on August 17, 1938, regulating Jewish first names, began the process of marking Jews. (This process was completed in September 1941 when Jews over the age of six were required to don a large yellow Star of David with the word *Jew* in the middle of it whenever they went out in public.) According to this measure, which came into effect on January 1, 1939, Jews had to make themselves easily identifiable by naming their newborn children from a prescribed list of "Jewish names"—like Abimelech, Hennoch, or Zedek for males, or Breine, Cheiche, or Jezebel for females. If their own names were not on the list, they were required to take a second first name— Israel for men and Sara for women.[79] A Jew who failed to use this new name in all official interactions, even if he or she simply forgot to use it, was punished severely.[80] For the average German Jewish man or woman at the time— who typically had common German first names like Karl, Hans, or Fritz, and Anna, Ilse, or Gertrude—this was a painful degradation.

Despite the accelerated pace of Jewish persecution, many Jews continued to hold on to the increasingly slim hope that the situation would change for the better—or at least not get any worse. Jewish emigration figures showed only a modest increase over the previous years in the first ten months of 1938.[81] Literally overnight the Jews were brought to their senses. "*Kristallnacht* came in November 1938 and everything was changed," explained Max Rein in a letter he wrote on April 1, 1988, to the organizers of an exchange between former Krefeld Jews and schoolchildren of the city on the eve of the fiftieth anniversary of the pogrom.[82] His sentiments echo those of many other survivors. In a tape-recorded talk, another former Krefeld Jewish man named Kurt Gimson told students at the Berufschule I in Krefeld a year earlier: "I have often made the statement that the Krefelders stood to a certain degree above the level of the rest of Germany, and they probably really did, because, as well as I know, we Krefelders had few National Socialist fanatics. That all came to an end, however, with the *Kristallnacht*."[83]

On the night of November 9–10, 1938, and for several days thereafter, the Jews of Krefeld, Cologne, Bergheim, and the rest of Germany experienced a firestorm of anti-Semitic violence of unparalleled dimensions in all the years of the Third Reich. Within a couple of days, nearly all Jewish synagogues and places of worship had been violated and burned to the ground, thousands of Jewish businesses and private apartments had been ransacked and destroyed, 91 people had been murdered, about 26,000 Jewish men had been sent to concentration camps, and thousands of other Jews had been temporarily placed in protective custody or otherwise detained by the authorities. These outrages were carried out in the open for all to see. As Robert Gellately has explained: "It was virtually impossible to avoid bearing witness. . . . Almost overnight, many small Jewish communities came to an end."[84]

Not only Germans and German Jews witnessed the pogrom. Hundreds of foreign journalists were on hand to provide accurate reports that were published immediately afterward as front-page news all over the world.[85] In the more than sixty years that have now passed, the events of this time in Germany as a whole and in many individual German communities like the city of Krefeld have been well chronicled by historians, journalists, and Jewish victims.[86] Given their horror and significance, however, they bear some further elaboration.

On November 7, 1938, Hershel Grynszpan, a seventeen-year-old Jewish youth brought up in Hannover, shot a young German diplomat named Ernst vom Rath in the German embassy in Paris. Grynszpan's act came in retaliation for the news he had recently received from his sister about his parents being deported to Poland at the end of October, along with about 17,000 other German Jews who held Polish passports. Rath died two days later in the late afternoon of November 9. On that same evening, Hitler, Joseph Goebbels, and other Nazi Party leaders were meeting in Munich's old city hall in celebration of Hitler's attempted putsch of fifteen years earlier. When news of Rath's death arrived at about 8:30 P.M., Goebbels seized the opportunity to take the lead in Jewish persecution. After he made a rousing anti-Semitic speech, in which he demanded that Jews collectively should be made to pay for the assassination of Rath, telephone calls were made to party leaders, SA men, and Gestapo offices across Germany to take immediate action against the Jews.

The task of setting the pogrom in action was made easier by the fact that similar celebrations with Nazi Party faithful were being held on that same evening in cities throughout Germany. The Krefeld festivities, organized by Kreisleiter Diestelkamp, were held in the Krefeld city tavern (*Stadtschenke*) and attended by a large number of local party leaders and *alte Kämpfer*. (So-called old fighters, these were Nazi Party members who had joined the Nazi Party before 1933.) At about 10:30 P.M., the Krefeld Nazi Party regional headquarters (*Kreisleitung*) received a telephone call from Munich with Goebbels's directive to commence actions against the Jews. This directive was then relayed to Diestelkamp, who set the pogrom in motion, assigning mostly young SA and SS men in civilian clothes to carry it out.

The Gestapo's involvement in the activities began somewhat later. At 2:00 A.M. the Krefeld Gestapo outpost received a call from the Düsseldorf Gestapo headquarters instructing them to assemble all of their officers and to await further orders. These came at about 4:00 P.M., by which time the Krefeld synagogue was already in flames. According to these orders— which clearly were sent out to Gestapo posts and outposts around the country as they came from SS and Police Chief Heinrich Himmler, were entitled "measures against the Jews" and addressed "to everyone!"—the Gestapo was not to intervene except to guarantee that certain "guidelines" for the "demonstrations" were upheld. These guidelines included not setting fire to synagogues situated where flames might threaten neighboring buildings; destroying but not plundering Jewish stores and homes; not damaging non-Jewish businesses; and not molesting foreigners, even foreign Jews. As soon as individual Gestapo officers could be freed up from their monitoring responsibilities, they were to arrest as many Jewish men as the local jails could hold, especially Jewish men who were wealthy and not extremely old.[87]

On the morning of November 10 and continuing throughout that day and into the next, the Krefeld Gestapo proceeded to arrest sixty-three Jewish men between the ages of nineteen and sixty-eight.[88] After spending several days in the local Krefeld jail, these men were sent with several hundred other Jews from the Rhine-Ruhr region by a special train from the main train station in nearby Duisburg to Dachau concentration camp outside Munich. In Dachau the men were given a foretaste of what lay in store for Jews who remained in Germany. As Dieter Hangebruch explains: "Dachau meant a turning point in most Krefeld Jews' lives. . . . Even those that previously did not want to think about emigrating recognized that after their legal and economic elimination they were also threatened by their physical annihilation."[89]

Most of the Jewish men were let out in three to four weeks after their family members had paid for their return passage and after they had provided proof that either they had taken steps to emigrate or their businesses had been "Aryanized."[90] In the months following their return to Krefeld, more than three-fourths of the Krefeld Jews who had been in Dachau emigrated, and 1939 became the year of the greatest wave of German-Jewish emigration in the entire Nazi period.[91] After the war broke out in September, the numbers of emigrating Jews slowed to a trickle. The German invasion of the Soviet Union in June 1941 brought the emigration to an end.

The experience of Jews who had not been sent to Dachau was hardly any less frightening. Although most individual Germans only witnessed the pogrom and did not take part in it, many were embarrassed by it, and some even helped Jews during it.[92] But the violence and terror that it unleashed left no Jews untouched. The experiences of Kurt Frank and his family are perhaps typical of those who were not sent to concentration camp:

We lived at the time in a house on Malmedystrasse 21 (today Leverentzstr.) on the corner of Gerberstrasse. It was an old Krefelder building that had been in the possession of my family for a couple of generations. It was destroyed during the war by a bombing attack, and rebuilt after the war, but it does not belong to us any longer. Our business was on the bottom floor, our apartment was on the upper floor, above which was only the attic.

In the night of November 9 we were all in the apartment: my father, 58 years old at the time, my mother 50, brother Herbert 24, sister Edith 26, sister Ruth, only 5 at the time, I 29, and additionally, Edith's fiance, Hans Ruthmann from Bochum, who was by chance on a visit.

At this time Hans and I and my brothers and sisters were about to emigrate. We wanted to go to Kenya, as that was one of the few countries which still took immigrants. From the English consulate in Cologne we had already received a visa stamped in our passports. . . .

At about 11 P.M., it must have been, the door to our house rang and was forcefully pounded upon. My brother went down to open the door and while being belted on the head was forced up the stairs by five or six SS men. We then had to line up in the kitchen where we were watched by two SS men with drawn pistols. My mother was already in bed with little Ruth and was not, as well as I know, bothered. While we were held in the kitchen, the other SS men searched the apartment. What they in fact wanted, I don't know. There was not much to take from us in any case, there was no jewelry and no cash. They only took a few small items like fountain-pen stands and the like. However, an Iron Cross from the First World War and a medallion bestowed by Hitler for four years of service on the front also disappeared.

We then had to put our coats on and we were taken under armed escort to the next police precinct, which at that time was in the Kanalstrasse, only a few hundred meters from our home.

The SS escort then gave us over to the police and went away. The police at first did not know what they were to do with us as we had not committed any crime or done anything else that would justify us being taken to the police precinct. Our particulars were then noted down and we then stood around until apparently about 2 o'clock in the morning a new order had arrived. My father was sent home. The rest of us had to step into a transport wagon which took off over the Malmedystrasse at first in an easterly direction. As we went by our house, we could see that the bottom floor had been destroyed and that an SA man was about to enter the front door. The journey then continued over the Hubertusstrasse to the courthouse. There we were put in the police jail, and after the normal formalities—emptying our pockets, handing over our identification and other papers—we were put in a large cell, in which there were already about twenty other imprisoned Jews. Edith was put in a women's cell.

I can hardly describe our emotions at the time. We were totally defenseless and there was nothing left for us to do but await our fate. We could suspect what might happen to us, as we had already heard about concentration camps and mistreatment. Thank God nothing more had happened to us than the boxing about the ears that Herbert had gotten at the beginning of the evening. I do not remember anymore if I went to sleep that night, and for everyone else in the cell the situation was much the same. Everything was gloomy despair. There were no beds in the cell, only a ten square meter wooden platform, on which one could sit. So there we awaited, fully at a loss and confused, what would happen to us.

About two the next afternoon Herbert and I were taken out of the cell and our effects were handed back to us after we signed for them, as were our precious passports with the big, red "J" and the stamp from the English consulate in Cologne. We were probably let go because we were obviously about to leave Germany. My sister had been let go a bit earlier, but Hans, for whatever reasons, was brought to the police jail in Bochum and had to remain there for fourteen days, causing us all kinds of fears and worries, until he was let go.

When we returned home it was of course a great relief to us and our parents, but the uncertainty remained that at any moment for whatever arbitrary reason everything could go downhill again.

On the journey to the courthouse we had already seen how the bottom floor of our house was totally devastated. All the windows were smashed in, the furniture was hacked up, office cabinets knocked over, typewriters tossed against the wall, and the contents of all of the cabinets and drawers were spread around the rooms in a total chaos.[93]

These events shocked the world and much of German society as well. Even many leading Nazi officials condemned the uncontrolled rowdyism and the damage to German foreign relations that Goebbels had unleashed with the *Kristallnacht* pogrom. Göring, who was riding a train when the actions against the Jews commenced, was incensed when he heard about them upon his arrival at the Berlin train station. Wasting no time to react, he quickly complained to Hitler on November 10 and took steps to gain control of the situation.[94] On the next day, word was sent out that the pogrom was to cease. In an official announcement of November 11 published the following day in the local newspaper, Krefeld's Nazi Party leader, Erich Diestelkamp, proclaimed: "The actions are terminated. Anyone that allows himself to take part in further activities is to be warned that he will be struck by the same severity that has hit the Jews."[95]

On November 12, Göring summoned a conference in Berlin attended by top state, party, and police officials as well as by representatives of German insurance companies. He opened the meeting by stating that he had had enough of such outrages and that once and for all he was going to take steps to solve the Jewish question:

> Today's meeting is of a decisive character. I have received a letter written on the Führer's orders . . . requesting that the Jewish question be now, once and for all, coordinated and solved one way or another . . . this time something decisive must be done! Because, gentlemen, I have had enough of these demonstrations! It is not the Jew they harm but myself, as the final authority for coordinating the German economy. If today a Jewish shop is destroyed and goods are thrown into the street, the insurance company will pay for the damage, which does not even touch the Jew; and furthermore, the goods destroyed come from the consumer goods belonging to the people. . . . I would not wish there to remain any doubt, gentlemen, as to the purpose of today's meeting. We have not come together simply for more talk, but to make decisions, and I implore the competent agencies to take all measures to eliminate the Jew from the German economy.[96]

At the conclusion of the conference, Göring exclaimed: "Once and for all I want to eliminate individual acts [against the Jews]." From this time on, the persecution of the Jews was to be carried out in methodical German fashion, not in uncontrolled popular outbursts and rioting. As Raul Hilberg explains: "The November pogrom was the last occasion for violence against Jews in German streets. . . . From now on the Jews were going to be dealt with in a 'legal' fashion—that is to say, in an orderly way that would allow for proper and thorough planning of each measure."[97]

The rioting had calmed down in most localities by November 11, but there were aftershocks that lasted for several more weeks. The administrative building next to the main Krefeld synagogue was set on fire in the early morning hours of November 12, and the homes of other Jews were broken into and demolished on November 17.[98] In a letter written on April 1, 1988, as part of the exchange between Krefeld schoolchildren and former Jewish Krefelders, Ernst Hirsch (who had been eighteen at the time) provides an account of how his family was first victimized in early December and of the police and the Gestapo actually coming to their defense and punishing their tormentors.

It was one of the first weeks in December. . . . I don't recall the exact date, but it was early on a Monday morning. We lived at the time in the first floor of the Malmedystrasse 34. On the ground floor lived an old Jewish couple named Simons. As I walked down the steps on my way to the train that morning, I was confronted by an SA man coming out of the Simons's apartment who threatened me with a pistol and ordered me to go back upstairs.

I went back and I can remember the words I used to inform my parents about the situation exactly. I said simply, "They are here," and my parents understood immediately. After a few minutes they also came to us, the SA man who I had already encountered and another man dressed in civilian clothes. Both smelled heavily of alcohol, which somewhat impaired the official appearance that they tried to convey.

The official business began with me being forced to stand with my back to the wall and they then threw my breakfast rolls which they took out of my briefcase at me. They claimed that they were searching for foreign currency but they seemed to have an equally zealous interest [in] other valuables. After some time, they momentarily had their attention diverted from me and I dashed out of the apartment seeking help.

I ran to the police headquarters in the Hansa-Haus, where on the ground floor I came upon an elderly patrolman in his office. He was obviously an officer from the good old Weimar years, no Nazi, but also no hero who wanted to get mixed up in Jewish matters. He told me that he could not leave his post and suggested that I should go out into the street and once I had spotted the men I should then yell out and he would come and arrest them.

I turned to go but in the doorway I ran into my father who told me that after I had left both of the visitors had become nervous and bolted. The SA man had found a dozen eggs in the kitchen cabinet, however, and bombarded my parents with them on his way out. They had tyrannized the Simons for half of the night and also had stolen some things from them. When he heard about their stealing, the patrolman then exclaimed that this was out of his area of competence and told us to go to the criminal police on the floor above.

The criminal policeman was obviously not sure whether the whole matter concerned a legal or an illegal action against Jews. He then called up the Gestapo and his beginning words are still in my memory: "I have here two Jews, who say the following things. . . ." This brought the matter into the proper perspective.

After a few hours the Gestapo appeared. Against our expectations they were completely matter of fact. We told them about the particulars of what had happened, and among other things about the formation number on the uniform collar of the SA man that I had noticed. It turned out to be a certain Herr Willi, who was employed by the city of Krefeld and was an *Oberscharführer* in the SA and one of his civilian colleagues and a third man, whom we had not known about as he had stood outside. All three had a case lodged against them.

I believe it was in May 1939 when my father sent a clipping to me in London from the *Westdeutsche Zeitung* with a report on the case.[99] In the weekend before they had visited us, the trio had made a protracted tour of Krefeld guest houses and had attempted to improve their weakened economic situation by a private action against Jews.

They were sentenced to lengthy jail sentences. Unofficial crimes were forbidden in the Third Reich.[100]

This account is not intended to convey the impression that the regime's pressure against the Jews abated in any way after *Kristallnacht*. On the contrary, it stepped up dramatically.

Already on November 12, Göring had issued decrees holding Jews col-

lectively responsible for Rath's murder—for which they would have to pay
a fine of one billion marks and cover the costs of the damage done—and
excluding Jews from German economic life. According to the latter decree,
by January 1, 1939, Jews were forbidden to run retail shops or mail-order
houses or to work as independent tradesmen, and they could no longer offer
goods or services in markets, fairs, or exhibitions. Furthermore, Jews could
be fired with only six weeks' notice from any business concern, and they
would have no claim on retirement funds or unemployment pay.[101] In the
following months, subsequent decrees sped up the "Aryanization" of the
economy and made the situation for the Jews even more untenable. Among
the worst of these decrees was one that began their ghettoization by taking
away their rights as tenants. After April 1939, Jews could neither refuse the
offer of worse accommodations for themselves nor refuse to take in whatever Jewish subtenants the regime might force on them.[102]

The Gestapo and Special Court case files of Jews in Krefeld, Cologne,
and Bergheim underscore the precarious situation Jews lived in between
Kristallnacht and the outbreak of war in September 1939. Few Jews who
were accused of infractions of any type now received any measure of leniency from the authorities. Most were either sent directly to a concentration
camp or sentenced by German courts and then sent to a concentration camp
by the Gestapo upon their release. Many never made it out, though most
were still let go if they could prove that they had made final plans to emigrate.[103] The evidence also suggests not only that the Gestapo and the courts
punished Jews more stiffly after *Kristallnacht* but that the Gestapo invested
more of its resources to incriminate the Jews than previously. Prior to November 1938, the Gestapo had usually been content to let the normal civilian population serve as its eyes and ears in Jewish cases, except when it suspected Communist involvement or other activity dangerous to the regime.
After *Kristallnacht*, the Gestapo relied less heavily on reports from the population for damning information about the Jews and more on its own spy
network.[104] By 1939 Communist, Socialist, religious, and other types of potential protest had long been smashed. The Gestapo and the regime now
made forcing the Jews out of the country their highest priority.

Both the state and many individual Germans, especially those who
were Nazi Party members, profited from the Jews' departure. Dr. Karl D.,

for example, who worked for the Krefeld branch of the Deutsche Bank, was accused of committing a currency violation by the Düsseldorf Office of Finance on December 21, 1938. While he sat in Dachau concentration camp along with other Jewish men arrested on *Kristallnacht*, he was forced to pay a fine of 3,000 marks. When he emigrated to Holland shortly after his release, his home and bank accounts, worth more than 100,000 marks (today upward of $1 million), were confiscated by the Gestapo.[105] Another Krefeld Jewish businessman, Jakob D., who also had been taken to Dachau, was forced to sell his large house on the Krefeld Lindenstrasse for a pittance to a long-standing Nazi Party member with a house-painting business. On November 26, 1938, the Nazi house-painter wrote to the Krefeld Gestapo asking that Jakob D. be allowed to return to Krefeld. He explained in his letter that he needed to negotiate with "the Jew" so that he could buy his property, which "would give me the opportunity to enlarge my business accordingly." Jakob D. agreed to the sale, hoping it would help him finance his emigration to Argentina. But he never made it that far. A note signed by Richard Schulenburg at the end of his file stated that "D. and his family, wife and one son, were evacuated to Riga on December 11, 1941." They had, however, managed to sell their property. Well before their "evacuation," they had moved to Krefeld's Stefanstrasse.[106]

CHAPTER FOUR

A CLOSER LOOK:
SURVIVORS' RECOLLECTIONS AND JEWISH CASE FILES

Over time the plight of Jews in Nazi Germany only worsened. As the previous chapter has shown, however, the goal of Nazi policy toward the Jews in the prewar years was not yet to destroy them physically. Rather, the goal of Nazi policy in the 1930s was to make the lives of Jews so unbearable that they would choose to leave the country. To a large extent, this policy was successful: great numbers of Jews did emigrate in the 1930s. Nevertheless, despite the economic, social, and legal discrimination they faced, many Jews chose to remain in Germany, hoping that eventually Hitler and the Nazis would go away and Germany would return to normal.

Even though the hopes of the Jews who chose to remain in Germany proved illusory in the end, they need not be construed as irrational; indeed, these hopes were often based on clearheaded assessments of the intentions and actions of German neighbors, classmates, and colleagues as well as on the treatment Jews received from Nazi state and party officials. Hence, had the Jews perceived that all or most of the Germans around them harbored extreme anti-Semitic prejudices, and had they lived in perpetual fear that they were likely to become victims of civilian denunciations, police spying, and severe police and judicial prosecution, presumably many more would have emigrated when it was still possible to do so. But as we know from the evidence presented in chapter 3, not all Jews in the prewar years of Nazi Germany had the same experiences with popular anti-Semitism or with police and judicial mistreatment.

How much, then, did Jews experience popular anti-Semitism in the

1930s, and how much did they fear becoming victimized? How typical was
a man like Karl Muschkattblatt of Cologne, who says that he did not experience much anti-Semitism and that he was not very afraid of becoming a
victim during the almost six years he spent in Nazi Germany before leaving
the country in the fall of 1938? How commonly were Jews spied on or denounced to the Gestapo in the 1930s? Who were the people who denounced
Jews, and what motivated their denunciations?

A good way to answer these questions is to begin by considering what
Jewish survivors have to say about their lives and their fears in Nazi Germany and to follow this up with an in-depth analysis of the Jewish case files
of the Krefeld Gestapo and the Cologne Special Court.

SURVIVORS' RECOLLECTIONS

Usually the longer Jews remained in Germany the more terror they suffered and the more terror they remember. Those who left the country before the war years and the deportations, like Karl Muschkattblatt, are therefore more apt to remember the terror as less threatening and fear-inducing
than do those who, like Lore M., did not emigrate and consequently became
caught up in the Holocaust. But not always. In the surveys and interviews
I conducted with former Jews from Krefeld, Cologne, and other German
localities, I frequently encountered people whose recollections of Germany
and Germans are filled with dread and who still burn today with hatred for
that society and its people even though they left Germany in the 1930s.
Also, many of the Jewish survivors I met, even those who were deported to
concentration camps in the war years, clearly distinguish between the early
and the later years of the Third Reich, and between anti-Semitic Germans
and Germans who were not prejudiced against Jews.

Although the city of Cologne gave Hitler comparatively weak voting
support in Weimar elections and enjoys a reputation as one of the most liberal of German cities, it is unlikely that Cologne residents, as the former
Cologne Jew Karl Muschkattblatt contends, were any more or less anti-
Semitic than the rest of the German population. When one surveys Jewish
survivors today, one often hears that the city in which they had lived in Nazi
Germany was unlike other German cities at the time. In a letter written to

me in April 1996, for example, a man named Max R., whose family had moved to Krefeld from Hamburg in 1934 and then emigrated to the United States in 1939 when he was eighteen, explained that before the Nazis came to power he and his family were treated in a friendly way by non-Jewish Germans; in fact, even after the Nazis came to power, "some people became hostile and abusive, [but] most did not." In the only personal contact Max R. ever had with the Gestapo—when a Gestapo officer came to arrest his father during the 1938 November pogrom—he was treated, he said, with "civility" by the officer. He then explained at length that anti-Semitism did not characterize most Germans, especially not the citizens of Hamburg:

> While most Germans did support Hitler, there were those in opposi-
> tion and a good many who merely "went along" in order to get along
> in their lives without any special enthusiasm about the Nazi pro-
> grams. Particularly in Hamburg, anti-Semitism was not as pro-
> nounced. People in Hamburg always were more conservative and,
> surprisingly, anglophile. Hamburg's heavy involvement in foreign
> commerce and shipping no doubt contributed to this.[1]

Whereas many Jewish survivors have a more jaundiced view of their former German neighbors, the sentiments of Max R. and Karl Muschkatt-blatt are certainly not unrepresentative of a large strain of German Jewish opinion.[2]

The results of a recent survey of Jewish survivors from Krefeld support this statement. The survey was carried out between April and June 1996.[3] All known and presumably still-living Krefeld survivors were mailed a written questionnaire (ninety-four in all) asking them more than fifty questions about their experiences with anti-Semitism and persecution during the Nazi period. Nearly half of the survivors lived in the United States at the time of the survey. The rest were scattered throughout the world: several still lived in Germany (some in Krefeld itself), and others lived in Israel, Great Britain, Holland, Australia, Argentina, Chile, and several other countries. There was a strong response. Forty-five people returned completed questionnaires. An additional nine people wrote letters in lieu of filling out the questionnaire, and many people appended detailed commen-

taries to the written questionnaires on some of their most salient experiences and observations during the Nazi years.[4]

Nearly all had suffered heavily; some remained so traumatized that
they wrote to apologize for not filling out the questionnaire, saying they
could no longer look back. In one elderly woman's words: "I confirm the
reception of your letter of 12 April of this year and I am very sorry that I do
not wish to answer your questionnaire. I have suffered greatly, was incarcerated and mistreated for three-and-a-half years in the Riga ghetto and in
Stutthof [concentration camp], and have tried unsuccessfully to this day for
fifty years to forget this time. After being questioned by Mr. Spielberg's
staff, I once again had terrible dreams which I am trying to avoid."[5]

The typical respondent left Germany during his or her teenage years in
the late 1930s. (The mean year of birth was 1920; 1938 and 1939 were the
peak years of emigration for the Krefeld Jews.)[6] Some managed to emigrate
with their families or to be reunited with their families later on, but many
never saw their parents, siblings, or other relatives again. Few retained
much of their family's property, most of which had been either confiscated
by the state when they left Krefeld or sold to someone in the local population at a price far below its market value. Some had no recollection of being
directly confronted with popular anti-Semitism, but many had suffered
physical beatings or verbal taunts and threats from German civilians or authorities. Julius Streicher's lurid anti-Semitic newspaper *Der Stürmer*, plas-
tered on walls and billboards throughout Krefeld and other German cities,
remains indelibly etched in most survivors' memories. One of the Krefeld
survivors, Otto B., had even been a prime subject of *Der Stürmer*'s bloodthirsty agitation when he was unjustly accused of raping a sixteen-year-old
German girl in 1934.[7] Even for those few who got out of Germany relatively
unscathed by the Nazi persecution, they often had to contend with the consequences of having had their education disrupted at an early age. Many
had to settle on a career that would not have been their first choice, and
their pursuit of it was made all the more difficult by the need to learn a new
language, forge a new identity, and adapt to a new culture in a new country.

Despite their sorrow, bitterness, and memories of loss and degradation,
a surprising number of the Krefeld survivors display considerable charity in

their estimation of the treatment of their families by non-Jewish Krefelders both before and during the Third Reich. This is evident in the responses they gave in the written survey, summarized in table 4.1.

Their answers demonstrate that Krefeld Jews were well integrated into German society before 1933 and felt themselves to be on cordial terms with their non-Jewish neighbors and fellow pupils. Nearly three-quarters of the respondents reported that they and their families had been treated in a "friendly" or "mostly friendly" fashion by non-Jewish Krefelders before Hitler came to power in 1933. Only one of the respondents—a man named Heinz L. who, on having his medical studies in Bonn terminated in 1933, left Krefeld for Milan, Italy, in 1933 and later migrated to England—said that he had been treated in a "mostly unfriendly" fashion. None reported that they had been treated in a fully "unfriendly" manner.[8] Their evaluation of their treatment in school by fellow pupils is somewhat less positive, but this result may be partly attributable to the wording of the question, which did not differentiate between their school experiences before and after 1933. Nevertheless, a large majority answered that they had been treated in a "friendly," "mostly friendly," or "mixture of friendly and unfriendly" manner by non-Jewish pupils in their class; less than 10 percent characterized their treatment as either "unfriendly" or "mostly unfriendly."

After the Nazi takeover on January 30, 1933, the political, legal, and economic situation became worse for the Krefeld Jews almost overnight, but changes in how they were treated by the Gentile population were perceived by the survey respondents as often less dramatic and more gradual than one might expect. In the survey the survivors had been asked: "After the Nazis came to power in 1933, was there a change in the treatment your family received by most non-Jewish citizens in your town? How would you characterize this change?" One-third responded that there had been a definite change for the worse and characterized the change with descriptions such as "horrible," "definitely worse," "disrupted friendships and disconnected relations," and "most non-Jewish friends would no longer socialize with us." But nearly 50 percent in all, and more than 50 percent of those who answered the question (22 percent left it blank), responded either that

TABLE 4.1 *Survey of Krefeld Jewish Survivors, 1996*

1. HOW WERE YOU TREATED BY NON-JEWISH PUPILS?

Friendly	22%
Mostly friendly	18
Mixture of friendly and unfriendly	22
Mostly unfriendly	2
Unfriendly	7
No relationship with non-Jewish pupils	16
Don't remember	0
Other	2
No answer	11

2. *BEFORE 1933,* HOW WAS YOUR FAMILY TREATED BY NON-JEWISH CITIZENS?

Friendly	47%
Mostly friendly	27
Mixture of friendly and unfriendly	11
Mostly unfriendly	2
Unfriendly	0
No relationship with non-Jews	2
Don't remember	7
Other	0
No answer	4

3. *AFTER 1933,* WAS THERE A CHANGE IN YOUR FAMILY'S TREATMENT BY NON-JEWISH CITIZENS? HOW WOULD YOU CHARACTERIZE THIS CHANGE?

No big change; friendly or mostly friendly	20%
Gradual worsening; mixture	26
Clearly worse; mostly unfriendly	33
No answer	22

4. DID YOU RECEIVE SIGNIFICANT HELP OR SUPPORT FROM NON-JEWISH GERMANS DURING THE THIRD REICH?

No	89%
Yes	9
No answer	2

5. WERE YOU EVER INTERROGATED BY THE GESTAPO OR POLICE?

No	89%
Yes	9
No answer	2

TABLE 4.1 *(continued)*

6. DID YOU PERSONALLY HAVE FEAR OF BEING ARRESTED DURING THE THIRD REICH?	
I had constant fear	20%
I occasionally had fear	42
I had no fear that this would happen	27
No answer	11
7. DID YOU HAVE FEAR THAT SOMEONE IN YOUR FAMILY WOULD BE ARRESTED?	
I had constant fear	47%
I occasionally had fear	24
I had no fear that this would happen	16
No answer	13
8. WHEN DID YOU LEAVE GERMANY?	
1933	11%
1934	2
1935	2
1936	7
1937	7
1938	20
1939	29
1940	4
1941	4
1942	2
1943	0
1944	2
No answer	9

NOTE: These figures are based on the forty-five people (twenty-seven women and eighteen men) who filled out written questionnaires; nine other people also responded in the form of letters in lieu of the filled-out questionnaire. Ninety-four people with apparently valid addresses were mailed questionnaires. The median age of the respondents when the survey was carried out (April to June 1996) was seventy-six. (Slightly more than half were born in 1921 or earlier.)

there had been no significant change and their family continued to be treated in a friendly or mostly friendly fashion or that the change was a gradual worsening and a mixture of friendly and unfriendly treatment became the norm. One woman, who was born the child of a mixed marriage in 1917 and who remained in Krefeld until 1944, wrote, "Da gab es auch noch gute Menschen" (There were still good people there). Another woman, who was born in 1914 and left Krefeld for England in 1939, wrote that her family's treatment remained "mostly reasonably friendly" and that "it seems to me that Krefeld treated its Jews better than most German towns." Still another woman, who was born in 1919 and also emigrated to England in 1939, wrote that there was "not much change at first; later some people tried to distance themselves." Others wrote that there was "no change" at all, or that the change came "only after *Kristallnacht,*" as explained by one man born in 1920 who also emigrated to England in 1939.

It bears repeating that most of these people were in their youth when they left Germany, and that most left before the war years when the Holocaust was set fully in motion. Few were on hand to witness the situation at its worst. Nevertheless, some of the Krefeld survivors who did experience the concentration camps report that they were treated decently by fellow Krefelders well into the war years. Werner H., who has been living as a fruit farmer in Chile since 1947, was born in Krefeld in 1924 and deported to Theresienstadt in June 1943 after being arrested for attempting to flee and for not wearing the Jewish star; he was later sent to Auschwitz. He told me in a telephone interview that he personally experienced little anti-Semitism and that his Gentile coworkers were "all very good" to him.[9]

Others who experienced the camps, like Werner S. and Helma T., have very different opinions of their fellow Krefelders. Werner S. now lives in Australia. Born in Krefeld in 1918, he was sent to Dachau with other Jewish men from Krefeld and other German cities after *Kristallnacht.* In December 1941, he was deported to Riga, where he began a long odyssey that eventually took him to eight different concentration camps before the war's end. Although he responded that both he, as a pupil, and his family were treated by non-Jewish Krefelders in a friendly fashion, he explained that there was a definite change after 1933—a change he characterized as "anti-Semitic."

Helma T., now living in the United States, chose not to fill out the questionnaire because she said that she has been tortured by her memories since
1945. She did write a short letter, however, to describe some of her traumatic
experiences; she closed it with some bitterly sarcastic comments about the
anti-Semitic behavior of her former fellow Krefelders: "Krefelders of my
age deny that they were Nazis and that they were bad to the Jews. I was in
Krefeld after the war and there was not a single Nazi to be found, there were
simply none there."[10]

Although Krefeld Jewish survivors report that the treatment they and
their families received at the hands of the Gentile population was not usually overtly anti-Semitic (with exceptions like those mentioned), only a few
report that they received much significant help or support from the Gentile
population. The 9 percent of the Krefeld Jewish survivors who did report
that they received such help or support still remain greatly appreciative of
it today. In a larger survey of the elderly non-Jewish population in Cologne
that I conducted in 1993 and 1994 with my German colleague Karl-Heinz
Reuband, we also found coincidently that 9 percent of the respondents reported that they had actively helped victims of the Nazi regime.[11] Not all of
these victims were Jewish victims, but many were. Since there were many
more non-Jews than Jews in every German community, it is reasonable to
think that the small but significant percentage of Krefeld Jewish survivors
who received help and support from non-Jews reflects the numbers in other
Nazi German communities as well. "Significant help or support" could
mean many things. Occasionally it meant non-Jews actually hiding Jews
from the German authorities. In most cases the supportive or helpful acts
were more mundane. Nevertheless, given the risks and the pressures involved (eventually, in 1941, it became a punishable offense for German citizens even to demonstrate friendship toward Jews), no humane act, however
small, was insignificant.[12]

Unfortunately, these acts, carried out privately, had little impact on
Nazi policy or on the ultimate fate of Jews in general, even if they did help
a few Jews to survive. Often they were carried out by people who publicly
supported or even enforced Nazi racist ideology. A Krefeld survivor named
Kurt G. provides a good example of this in a brief unpublished autobiogra-

phy he wrote while traveling to the United States in February 1939 on the Dutch liner *Zaandam*, sailing out of Rotterdam. In the summer of 1937, he had been suddenly fired from his job in a Krefeld textile factory:

> The superintendent of the firm informed me that ownership of the concern had gone into "Aryan hands" and that they could not keep me any longer. A few nasty words were thrown at me but I didn't take them very seriously. My superintendent was another well-known type of German. He was, like everybody else of his social class, scared as hell to get in bad with the Nazis. So, in front of other people he would show off and employ the usual Nazi-talk, mixed with plenty of snide remarks of an anti-Semitic character. When he was alone with me, he was friendliness itself, he'd do almost anything for me. This latter attitude seemed more sincere to me and I became convinced that he was not a Nazi at heart. Later on, it became obvious that he just blew "hot air" when playing the Nazi for the public (the Nazi-controlled union) but was actually ashamed for acting this way. The promises he made me during our secluded talks were indeed kept by him and, when I finally left the firm 14 months later, the last impression I took with me was a positive one.[13]

The conclusion that follows from this story and from the survey results among Krefeld survivors strongly contradicts the argument put forth recently by Daniel Goldhagen in *Hitler's Willing Executioners*: he maintains that nearly all Germans were motivated by virulent anti-Semitism.[14] Rather than being uniformly anti-Semitic in outlook, the German population was very much divided over the Nazis' anti-Semitic policies. Some found them distasteful. Others plied them enthusiastically. Most were probably ambivalent or indifferent. Nevertheless, many had sympathy for their Jewish neighbors, classmates, and coworkers. More than a few were capable of expressing this sympathy to the Jews in private, but far too few took public steps that could have altered Nazi policy and significantly eased the Jews' plight.

The other questions in the survey concern the survivors' perceptions of and experiences with the official organs of Nazi persecution. Here the findings are especially interesting compared with the findings that Karl-Heinz Reuband and I obtained in our 1993–94 survey of the elderly German population. Despite the fact that German Jews were known to be extremely law-abiding—with a history of having some of the lowest crime rates of any group of people in German society[15]—and even though they were well aware that they had to make special efforts not to disobey any of the myriad laws and decrees of Nazi society, their chance of avoiding the Gestapo's clutches in "criminal cases" alone was only a small fraction of that of non-Jews in Nazi Germany. They were targeted by Nazi law, Nazi police, and the entire Nazi justice apparatus like no other group in German society.

In the Krefeld survivor survey, 9 percent of the respondents reported that they had been interrogated by the Gestapo or police and accused of committing an "illegal act." In the survey of the non-Jewish population, on the other hand, only about 1 percent of the respondents reported that this had happened to them. Considering that these figures pertain only to supposedly criminal acts and that Jews did not even have to be accused of committing a criminal act to hear the Gestapo knocking on the door, it comes as no surprise that the majority of Jews harbored a great deal of fear that they and their family members might be arrested by the Gestapo or by other police organs. It must be kept in mind, however, that most of the Jewish survey respondents had left Germany by 1939. (Only 10 percent of the respondents remained in Germany after 1939.) Hence, the fear they report was not typically the fear of being deported to a concentration camp associated with the Jewish deportation waves of the war years; rather, it was more or less the same kind of fear of arrest that any person living in Nazi society might have had.

A comparison of the results from the Jewish and the non-Jewish surveys demonstrates that this fear was far greater in the Jewish community than in the non-Jewish community. Among Jews from Krefeld, only 27 percent of those surveyed reported that they had no fear of being arrested at any time during the Third Reich, and only 16 percent reported that they had no fear that this would happen to members of their family. Not all Jews reported that they lived in constant fear of arrest, however, as we know from the testimonies of people like Karl Muschkattblatt, who said he had had no fear "until the time that I was arrested." Still, one-fifth of them did report having had such constant fear for themselves, and nearly half reported having had such constant fear for members of their family. In our survey of non-Jews, on the other hand, almost nobody reported having had constant fear of arrest in Nazi Germany, and more than four-fifths of the respondents reported that they had no fear whatsoever of being arrested at any time.[16] One might quibble that the latter survey does not include many Communists, Jehovah's Witnesses, or other target groups of Nazi oppression, who had more grounds for fear than other Germans, but this must be balanced against the realization that the former survey does not include many Jews who survived the war years, when the Jews were targeted for extinction.

Most Jews clearly had more fear of becoming victimized by the Nazi terror than did most non-Jews, and Jews had more reason to be afraid. Nevertheless, as the previous chapter began to show and the following chapters demonstrate more fully, the Nazi terror was not a blanket phenomenon experienced uniformly by all people, Jewish or non-Jewish, in all situations at all times. The Gestapo and other Third Reich organs focused their limited resources on certain groups of people at certain times. Even Jews experienced periods of relative calm interspersed between periods of torment that seductively lulled many of them into believing that they could ride out the storm and survive. As Karl Muschkattblatt said regarding his experiences in the prewar years: "We were not aware of the impending doom." If German Jews had been aware of the impending doom, fewer would have remained in Germany long enough to be sent to their death. In the end the Jews were finally trapped not only by a terror apparatus that did not always utilize or reveal the full measure of its murderous intent but also in part by the friendliness and civility of well-meaning German friends and neighbors. Had bloodthirsty SA and SS bullies and zealously anti-Semitic Nazi Party members been characteristic of the whole of the German population, more Jews might have made the decision to leave before it was too late.

ASSESSING THE JEWISH CASE FILES

As mentioned earlier, German Jews were exceptionally law-abiding, and in the Third Reich they continued this traditional behavior even though the Nazi regime and its judicial authorities promulgated and prosecuted an expanding and increasingly stringent set of laws, decrees, and ordinances aimed against them. Even as conditions became more impossible every day, most Jews opted to keep their heads down, to make whatever accommodations they could within the confines of the law, and to hope that the society would come to its senses. It could be said that this was the strategy of most of the German population.[17] But in the end only Gentiles could survive with a strategy of compliance. Unlike the Jews, only a small minority of Gentiles—primarily Communist functionaries—would be hounded out of the country, and they were never marked for extinction. Moreover, if non-Jews ran afoul of the regime in one way or another, the Nazis believed that most of them could be "healed," a term the Nazis often used in regard to former Communists and other opponents of the regime so long as they were of "German blood." Jews could not be healed.

As much as it could, the regime preferred to put a legalistic cast on its persecution and to dole out terror selectively. In keeping with the German tradition of strict adherence to the letter of the law, this strategy helped the regime to maintain order and to justify its activities. Although the legal authorities enjoyed wide latitude in how they operated and in how they conducted and settled individual cases—sometimes on the basis of arbitrary whims—they did not want terror employed indiscriminately. Even in the *Kristallnacht*—an event that broke temporarily with the regime's preference for the orderly and selective use of terror—"there remained a certain sense [of] order in all that took place," as one Krefeld Jewish survivor recalled forty years after the pogrom.[18]

The evidence found in the Gestapo and Special Court case files of Krefeld, Cologne, and Bergheim confirms this picture of an orderly and selective policy of persecution and terror employed by the authorities against both Jews and non-Jews. It also highlights the civilian population's important role in that persecution and terror. Before systematically analyzing this evidence as it applied to the Jewish population in the 1930s, I would add to my comments in chapter 1 on such evidence a brief discussion here of its nature and contents.

To begin with, the available case files are so voluminous in number and so detailed in nature that I had to employ sampling techniques. From the case files of the Krefeld Gestapo and the Cologne Special Court in which can be found the police and judicial investigations of about 3,500 individuals in Krefeld and 28,000 people in Cologne and its surrounding area, the dossiers of 1,132 people were selected and analyzed systematically. About one-sixth of these cases involve the persecution of Jews. The rest treat others in the German population—such as Communists, Socialists, Jehovah's Witnesses, homosexuals, career criminals, Catholic priests, Protestant ministers, and various kinds of malcontents—against whom the Nazi police and judicial authorities started cases at one time or another.

Although both the Gestapo and Special Court case files provide a wealth of information about the regime's persecution of Jews as well as non-Jews and about the civilian population's role in that persecution, there are several reasons to focus more closely on the Gestapo case files; as a consequence, relatively larger samples of these were drawn and analyzed. Two separate samples were drawn from the Krefeld Gestapo case files. One is a nonrandom sample comprising every documented investigation of alleged illegal activity on the part of Jews in the city of Krefeld; it provided a total of 105 cases between 1933 and 1945. The other is a random sample of every eighth case file for the entire population (433 cases). For Cologne and its surrounding area, a random sample of only 2 percent of the Cologne Special Court case files was selected; because there are so many of these case files, however, that yielded a total of 594 cases, of which 35 involved Jews.

The most important reason to prefer the Gestapo case files is that they more closely reflect the true nature and amount of terror perpetrated against both the Jewish and non-Jewish population in the Third Reich. In the majority of cases, the Gestapo acted on its own to decide the fate of an accused individual and the court authorities did not figure in the settlement of the case. Additionally, the Gestapo often imposed its own punishments— which ranged from several days in protective custody to several months or possibly even death in a concentration camp—on accused individuals after they had served whatever sentence the courts had inflicted on them. In Krefeld the Gestapo, after its initial investigation, forwarded less than one-third of Jewish cases to the state prosecuting attorney's office in the prewar period, and only one-quarter of the Jewish cases during the war years. (These figures do not include the sixty-three Jewish men whom the Gestapo sent to Dachau after *Kristallnacht* without involving the judicial authori-

TABLE 4.2 *Outcome of Krefeld Gestapo Jewish Cases, 1933–1939*

Decided on by the courts	16%
Sent to concentration camp by Gestapo	24
Protective custody ordered by Gestapo	17
Case ended with a warning by Gestapo	13
Dismissal by Gestapo without a warning	21
Other	3
Unknown	5

ties; only those cases involving alleged illegal behavior on the part of Jews are included here.) The cases that did get passed on to higher judicial bodies, like the state prosecuting attorney's office and the Special Courts,[19] were often of a less serious nature, and the majority of them, for both Jews and Gentiles, were dismissed by the state prosecuting attorney's office before going to court. Hence, as awful as the record of prosecuting attorneys and judges in the Third Reich was, a reliance on court records alone can yield only a limited picture of the Nazi terror.

Table 4.2 details the outcome—or rather, the harshest punishment inflicted—in the sixty-six surviving cases of alleged Jewish wrongdoing investigated by the Krefeld Gestapo between 1933 and 1939. The figures reveal several things. The first is that the Gestapo had many options in addition to passing an investigation forward to the court authorities for final determination, which it did rather infrequently when Jews were involved.[20] It could hold the accused persons in protective custody, remand them to a concentration camp, or dismiss their cases with or without a formal warning. Often a person experienced several of these measures: being first placed in protective custody, later tried by the court authorities, and finally sent to a concentration camp by the Gestapo after completion of a jail or prison term. Although the Gestapo's most common and draconian punishment for accused Jewish people in the prewar period was commitment to a concentration camp (during the war years the Gestapo would sometimes go a step further and execute the prisoner on the spot),[21] "only" a minority of Jewish cases ended in concentration camp referrals at this time (24 percent). Furthermore, all of the Krefeld Jews sent to concentration camp before the war broke out were released after a period of a few weeks or months, though, for many, this proved to be only a short reprieve before their "evacuation to the east" during the war years.

In most cases of alleged Jewish wrongdoing in the 1930s, the Gestapo did not apply its harshest measures (this was even more common in cases involving the Gentile population). In addition to those Jews sent to a concentration camp, "only" an additional 17 percent were detained in protective custody. Most Jewish cases were either dismissed immediately by the Gestapo with at most a warning (34 percent) or passed along to the court authorities (16 percent), who most often dismissed them before they went to trial.[22]

There are several explanations for the legal authorities' relative moderation in this period. One is that the regime's main strategy at this time was to force the Jews to emigrate. It hoped to accomplish this with a minimum of damage to its foreign relations and to its support from followers, many of whom were not ardent anti-Semites. Keeping up an image of legality, even when dealing with Jews, helped to serve these ends. For those Jews who had not yet gotten the message that their existence in Hitler's Germany was untenable, a simple run-in with the police often sufficed to make the message loud and clear. Another explanation is that the regime had other internal enemies to contend with, like Communists, whom it perceived as more immediately threatening and whom it needed to deal with first. Most of the Jewish cases seemed somewhat minor in comparison, typically involving unsubstantiated or weakly supported charges that Jews had verbally criticized the Nazi regime or one of its officials, used the Hitler salute or said "Heil Hitler" upon coming into a shop or governmental office (activities that were proscribed for Jews but mandatory for the rest of the German population), or tried to shield some of their property or assets in preparation for emigration. Only a small minority of the Jewish cases (though not smaller than the percentage of such cases for non-Jews) involved serious protest or oppositional activity against the regime, and these cases pertained overwhelmingly to former Jewish Communists or former Jewish Communist sympathizers at the very beginning of the regime's tenure.

If the terror meted out by the Gestapo and the court authorities had elements of moderation at this time, this does not mean that it was not horrible for the Jews. Most Jews may never have been accused of having broken the law at any time in the Third Reich, but all lived under the constant threat that the Gestapo might come knocking at their door at any time and whisk them away under the slightest pretext. Even though most Jews remained strictly law-abiding, they were many times more likely than non-Jews to have a case started against them,[23] and the punishment they could expect to receive if such a case were started was usually far more severe. With some notable exceptions, like Communist functionaries who were rounded up and placed under arrest in the first months of the regime's existence,[24] detention in protective custody, prison, or concentration camp was an uncommon occurrence for all but the most recalcitrant and incorrigible Germans.[25] Upstanding Jews, on the other hand, often found themselves locked up behind bars or barbed wire for no other reason than their ethnic background. An extreme example of this came in November 1938 when nearly all adult Jewish males were carted off to concentration camps just because they were still in the country. But there were many other examples as well.

What was the social and demographic background of the Jews found in the Gestapo and Special Court case files in the 1930s? What were they accused of? How did the police and judicial authorities get information on them? And how can one evaluate the role that the German civilian population played in the Jewish persecution?

The social background of the Jewish men and women the Krefeld Gestapo investigated for illegal activity in the period before the outbreak of World War II closely resembles that of the rest of the Jewish population in that and other German communities. Although this is unsurprising given that these people were almost all highly respected members of the Krefeld community who had no past criminal record, were usually not involved in any kind of antiregime behavior, had not committed any crime, and were merely the victims of Nazi persecution and sometimes of popular resentment against the Jews, it does differentiate them considerably both from people who normally are accused of illegal behavior in most societies and from most of the rest of the German population who showed up in the Krefeld Gestapo files. Like most of the rest of the Krefeld Jewish population, these people typically were well-educated, stable, and industrious individuals of middle- to upper-middle-class background. They resembled other

Krefelders investigated by the Gestapo perhaps only in that they were disproportionately male (84 percent, although this changed during the war years when many more Jewish females also had cases lodged against them) and that nearly half were born and raised in Krefeld itself.

Most were middle-aged, married men who had either a high school (*Gymnasium*) or university education and were gainfully employed. (More than 75 percent were working at the time a case was started against them.) Only 19 percent held working-class jobs, and most of these people were skilled workers like machinists or pipe fitters. An additional 10 percent were small shopkeepers and salespeople of the lower-middle class. The rest included a smattering of doctors, lawyers, teachers, and students and a large number of moderately well-to-do and some quite prominent businessmen. The youngest was fifteen years of age, and the eldest was seventy-two. Sixty percent were in their thirties, forties, or fifties.

This same profile more or less held true for the Jewish people in the Cologne Special Court files. In the random sample of cases selected for analysis, the only significant difference between the Special Court case files and the Gestapo case files was in the gender background of the accused. Here the gender difference was not so pronounced (57 percent were male and 43 percent were female), perhaps demonstrating that the Nazis were especially intent on preserving an appearance of "legality" when women (including Jewish women) were involved in a case. Otherwise, the ages and social backgrounds of the accused were nearly identical to those of the Krefeld cases. The average age was thirty-seven and a half (the youngest was twenty and the oldest was seventy-eight); most had a solid education; few were unemployed; and the largest occupational grouping was middle-class businessmen.

Based on a random sample of one-eighth of all Krefeld Gestapo case files, table 4.3 charts the yearly percentage of Jewish cases from the beginning of the Third Reich in 1933 to its end in 1945. Table 4.4 is based, on the other hand, on the total volume of Gestapo case files pertaining to alleged illegal activities undertaken by Krefeld Jews and lists the types of offenses for which they were charged in the period between 1933 and 1939. Both tables reveal a noticeable trend toward increased Jewish persecution on the part of the Gestapo during the prewar years that coincided with the ever-

TABLE 4.3 *Cases Involving Jews in a Random Sample of Krefeld Gestapo Case Files, 1933–1945*

YEAR	TOTAL NUMBER OF CASES	NUMBER OF JEWISH CASES	PERCENTAGE OF JEWISH CASES
1933	33	2	6
1934	51	2	4
1935	28	1	4
1936	28	7	25
1937	58	7	12
1938	47	17	36
1939	44	12	27
Prewar total	289	48	17
1940	38	11	29
1941	36	13	36
1942	33	11	33
1943	29	7	24
1944	5	4	80
1945	—	—	—
Wartime total	141	46	33
OVERALL TOTAL	430	94	22

NOTE: Based on a random sample of one-eighth of all Krefeld Gestapo case files. There are three missing cases in which the year of the case was not recorded.

increasing volume of laws and regulations circumscribing Jewish activity and the Nazis' growing desire to force Jews out of the country. The first of the two tables provides the most striking evidence of this trend. Here one observes that Jews figured in only a small minority of the Gestapo's overall caseload in the first three years of Hitler's rule. But after 1935, even though Jews represented less than 1 percent of the citizens of Krefeld, they accounted for an average of about one-quarter of all Krefeld Gestapo cases in each year before the war broke out in the fall of 1939, and for about one-third of all Krefeld Gestapo cases during the war.

A large number of the Jewish cases did not involve wrongdoing of any

TABLE 4.4 *Nature of Gestapo Cases*
Started Against Krefeld Jews, 1933–1939

YEAR	POLITICAL[a]	LIBEL[b]	MORALS[c]	BUSINESS[d]	HITLER SALUTE[e]	OTHER[f]	TOTAL
1933	5	2	—	1	—	—	8
1934	1	2	—	—	—	1	4
1935	1	2	2	1	1	—	7
1936	1	3	6	3	—	4	17
1937	—	2	2	2	—	1	7
1938	—	—	3	3	2	4	12
1939	—	1	4	3	2	1	11
TOTAL	8	12	17	13	5	11	66

a. Political = Communist or other antiregime political activity.
b. Libel = Illegal opinion statements, usually against government leaders and officials.
c. Morals = Primarily race defilement (*Rassenschande*).
d. Business = Illegal business activities of all sorts.
e. Hitler Salute = Illegal use of the Hitler salute or Nazi insignia.
f. Other = Includes three career criminals sent to concentration camp in 1938; three cases of returning Jewish teenagers sent to concentration camp for an "education" (two in 1936 and one in 1938); one case each of listening to a foreign radio broadcast, begging, making unlawful threats, and not paying child support; and one case with no stated charge against the person.

kind. Many pertained solely to issues surrounding Jewish emigration and later deportation, which the Gestapo oversaw. But were one to focus only on cases of alleged Jewish wrongdoing, as is done in table 4.4, the Gestapo's escalating preoccupation with the Jews is also evident. Thus, in table 4.4 one observes that between 1933 and 1935 an average of only 6.3 Gestapo cases per year were started against Krefeld Jews for violations of the law. But in the next four years, between 1936 and 1939, the yearly average almost doubled (11.8) even though there were fewer Jews remaining in the city to be charged with unlawful behavior. Additionally, it needs to be remembered that the figures in table 4.4 include neither the sixty-three Jewish men sent to Dachau after *Kristallnacht* nor the many other instances of the Gestapo's surveillance of Jews through the mail and by other means when not enough damning information could be found to call for an arrest or even to start a formal investigation.

If the evidence points to the Gestapo's increasingly strenuous efforts to persecute the Jews over time, there is no corresponding increase in antiregime political activity on the part of the Jews themselves. Whereas seditious political behavior and expressions of antiregime sentiment were the most common offenses that Jews were charged with in the first few years of the Third Reich, the Jews appear to have become ever more cautious in their political activity and guarded in their public statements over time. The growth in the number of Jewish cases in the mid to late 1930s issued primarily from infractions against newly passed laws regulating Jewish social and economic behavior. After the passage of the Nuremberg Laws in the fall of 1935, race defilement and other morals offenses became the most common grounds for initiating cases against Jews, even though the Gestapo had to dismiss many of them after ascertaining that they were based on fully unsubstantiated allegations. Several, for example, involved Jewish men thought to have been carousing with blond-haired Aryan women who turned out to be Jewish.[26] Most of the other cases lodged against Jews in these years involved an assortment of business and property violations frequently associated with the Jews' attempts to secure some of their assets in preparation for emigration. Added to these were several other largely trivial transgressions (though they were sometimes punished severely)—cases of Jews, trying not to bring scorn on themselves, responding to someone else's "Heil Hitler" by raising their own right arm and repeating the National Socialist mantra,[27] or of Jewish teenagers being sent to a concentration camp for an "education" after naively returning to their families from a period of study abroad.[28]

Try as they might to be law-abiding, the Jews found it increasingly difficult to avoid the Gestapo's clutches. The damning information the Gestapo gathered to open cases against them came from several sources, including paid and unpaid Gestapo spies, postal surveillance, reports on Jewish activities from Nazi Party headquarters and individual party men, and voluntary reports from the civilian population (denunciations) on their alleged illegal activities. Table 4.5 summarizes where the Gestapo got its information in

TABLE 4.5 *Source of Information That Started*
Gestapo Cases Against Krefeld Jews, 1933–1939

Civilian denunciations	41%
Gestapo itself (including spies)	19
Other control organizations	5
Nazi Party and Nazi organizations	8
Unknown	27

the cases started against Krefeld Jews for alleged wrongdoing between 1933 and 1939.

As the table shows, the civilian population played a major role in initiating cases against Jews in the city of Krefeld during the 1930s. This finding largely corroborates the findings of the Canadian scholar Robert Gellately, whose pioneering study of the relationship between the Gestapo and German society was published in 1990.[29] In that work he examined 175 cases of race defilement and friendship displayed toward Jews investigated by the Gestapo in the city of Würzburg and determined that civilian denunciations initiated 57 percent of the cases.[30] In Krefeld only 41 percent of the cases began in this way. But controlling for the cases in which the cause of the initiation was unknown (27 percent of the cases in this study and 11 percent of the cases in Gellately's study), the percentage of Jewish cases initiated by voluntary denunciations from the civilian population in Krefeld during the 1930s becomes almost identical with what Gellately found for Würzburg.

Nevertheless, there are some important differences to consider between Gellately's study and my own, both in the realm of evidence and interpretation. After discovering that only one case in his study was initiated by a report from a Gestapo spy, Gellately concluded that in Würzurg "paid informers or agents are conspicuous by their absence."[31] Spying and surveillance played a considerable role, however, in the Gestapo's persecution and control of the Krefeld Jewish population in the 1930s, and a frequently decisive role in their persecution and control during the war years. The different findings on this issue probably result from the different types of cases analyzed in these two studies. Had Gellately examined the entire range of Jewish cases—as is done here—instead of only two types of cases related to Jews, he presumably would have achieved different results, and these might have led him to different conclusions about the nature of Nazi social control and terror.

In more recent work, Gellately has summarized the work of others who have studied the role of denunciations in the Gestapo's enforcement of non-racial crimes, such as the laws against malicious gossip. He has also gone on himself to study other populations, such as Polish workers, and other offenses, such as listening to outlawed foreign radio broadcasts. Having observed that civilian denunciations led to the opening of an even higher percentage of the Gestapo's investigations in these cases than in the original Jewish cases he studied, Gellately now asserts that the Gestapo was primarily a "reactive" organization, that the German society largely policed itself, and that the notion that the Third Reich was a police state needs to be called into question.[32]

Conceding that denunciations were prevalent in Nazi society, I still believe, for reasons that will become more apparent in the following chapters, that Gellately undercounts the Gestapo's active role in the persecution of Jews and the rest of the German society. In particular, he seems to overlook the fact that the civilian denunciations that the Gestapo received were made possible in the first place by an outrageous body of laws and regulations that only a police state would enact or enforce. Also, one might argue that he does not pay sufficient attention to the Gestapo's selective use of its resources, which made the terror less than blanket perhaps, but all the more efficient.

The Krefeld Gestapo, like the Gestapo in other German communities, had a limited number of spies and informants.[33] The Gestapo used these people and its other limited resources judiciously and selectively, engaging them more often to hunt down Communists and other groups the regime particularly wanted to root out and destroy than to police minor transgressions committed by ordinary members of the German population. That the Gestapo would use every means available to it to undermine the Jews' existence in Nazi Germany is, however, only logical. For by the war years, if not even earlier, the Jews had become the prime group that the Nazi regime wanted to eliminate.

At the beginning of the Nazi years, the Gestapo first sought to contain

potential Communist, Socialist, and religious bases of opposition, and it engaged its spy network and other resources accordingly. Jews represented no
immediate threat to the regime at the time. The Gestapo spied on the few
Jews involved in oppositional activity at the time with more or less the same
intensity it brought to spying on non-Jewish opponents of the regime. Once
the Gestapo had dealt with the immediate threats to the Nazi regime's hege-
mony, it had greater means at its disposal to devote to Jewish persecution.
In the first few years of the Reich, the Gestapo's spy network figured in
only a small, though still not insignificant, number of Jewish cases. In later
years—above all during the war, when the Jews were slated for extinction—
specially appointed spies frequently watched the Jews' every movement.
Their reports on the Jews' activities often resulted in Jews being sent to their
death in concentration camps for minor violations such as not wearing their
Jewish star in public or illegally riding on public transportation.[34] Nevertheless, between 1933 and 1939 spying on the part of paid or unpaid "V-
persons" (the Gestapo's codeword for specially-appointed civilian spies) led
to at least eleven of the sixty-six cases started against the Jews (17 percent)
in the Krefeld Gestapo files. Additionally, postal and other types of surveillance helped to initiate at least six more cases.

In sum, one-quarter of all Jewish cases of alleged illegal behavior before
the war years involved at least some kind of spying or surveillance. Typical
of these cases were those that involved Jewish Communists or other politically active Jews, but these were not the only cases that involved spying.
Also included were cases of race defilement, listening to foreign radio
broadcasts, and violating the currency restrictions—cases that had no direct
political content whatsoever.[35] In 1939 evidence of spying is found in more
than half of the Jewish cases, the beginning of a trend that rose even higher
in the war years.[36]

All of this said, voluntary reports from the civilian population were one
of the most plentiful sources of information the Gestapo had in keeping tabs
on the Jewish population as well as the mass of the non-Jewish population.
Who were these people who turned the Jews in to the authorities? What
motivated them?

We have already encountered several of these individuals in the previous chapter: Hitler Youth teenagers selling an anti-Semitic newspaper in

the main shopping street of Cologne that offended a wealthy Jewish woman from out of town; young boys and girls in Krefeld taunting a mentally deficient Jewish man whom they cruelly referred to as "Lullo"; housewives, dentists, and other average citizens in Bergheim and Krefeld turning in their Jewish neighbors after petty neighborhood quarrels; and SA thugs in Krefeld spouting vitriolic epithets at an elderly Jewish man as he entered a popular *Biergarten.* To this list could be added people of almost any age and social background in the German population. About the only significant group of people who did not denounce Jews were Jews themselves. Not one single case against a Jew, or even against any of the more than one thousand other people whose cases are studied in this book, was started by a Jewish denunciation. Given the infamous case of the young Berlin Jewish woman named Stella, whom the Berlin Gestapo used as a paid informer to gain information on the hideouts of Berlin Jews during the war, it cannot be said that there were no Jewish people who turned on their fellow Jews.[37] But the evidence in this study shows that such persons were very rare exceptions.

It also needs to be pointed out that not all Germans were willing to act as denouncers either. Even if all age and social-class backgrounds were represented to some degree among the denouncers, this does not mean that the average German was likely to become a denouncer, of either Jews or anyone else. But there can be no doubt that a considerable number of German people were fully willing to inform on their fellow citizens, sometimes out of ideological conviction, but often with the goal either of resolving petty personal scores or of enriching themselves through another's misfortune. By the mid to late 1930s, the number of denunciations that regularly poured into the Gestapo became so numerous, in fact, that the authorities eventually felt the need to try to discourage them. As evidence of this, an article in the *Frankfurter Zeitung* of August 18, 1937, called for a reward of up to one hundred marks (the monthly wage of an unskilled worker) for anyone who could provide correct information about false informers.[38]

To the extent that one can speak of a typical denouncer's profile (in cases of Jewish persecution), it goes like this. More often than not the denouncer's age, gender, and occupational background corresponded closely with the Nazis' special appeal to youth and young adults, males, and the middle classes. Of the twenty-six cases between 1933 and 1939 of alleged Jewish

wrongdoing in the Krefeld Gestapo files initiated by a denunciation, 79 percent of the denouncers were male and 21 percent were female.[39] The youngest was twelve, the oldest was forty-seven, and most were in their twenties
or thirties. Of the thirteen Jewish cases started by a denunciation in the
random sample taken of the Cologne Special Court case files during the
same period, females were more highly represented among the denouncers,
but they were still in the minority. (Seven cases were started by denunciations from men, and six from women.) The age profile was similar to that of
the Krefeld denouncers: the youngest denouncer was twelve, the oldest was
fifty-three, and the average age was around forty. Occupationally, almost
all of the denouncers were of middle-class background in both the Krefeld
Gestapo files and the Cologne Special Court files. Of the sixteen cases in
which the occupation of the denouncer was specified in Krefeld, only three
came from the working class (one unskilled worker and two chauffeurs).
Businessmen accounted for eight (50 percent) of the denunciations, and the
rest were made by a dentist, a middle-class housewife, a young unmarried
woman living at home, and two middle-class schoolchildren. In the Cologne
case files, only one of the denouncers came from the working class. The rest
were mainly middle-class businessmen, professionals, and middle-class
housewives.

Adding to the impression that the denouncers came from the ranks of
those German citizens who were particularly susceptible to Nazi ideology is
evidence that many denouncers enjoyed some kind of function in the Nazi
Party or one of its parallel organizations. Although this evidence is limited
(the case files usually do not provide information about a denouncer's
political affiliations), it does show that at least one-third of the denouncers
in both the Krefeld and Cologne files were members of the Nazi Party, SA,
or Hitler Youth. These numbers are higher than was average for the general
population, especially when one considers that the Nazi Party and the SA
had very few female members.[40]

In most cases, the accused Jewish person knew the denouncer personally, though it is often difficult to discern how close they were to one another
or exactly what motivated the denouncer. Table 4.6, which details the relationships between the denouncers and the accused in the Krefeld Gestapo
files and the Cologne Special Court files, reveals that at least 58 percent of

TABLE 4.6 *Relationship of Denouncers to Accused Jews and Motives for Denunciations in Krefeld Gestapo and Cologne Special Court Cases, 1933–1939*

	KREFELD	COLOGNE
RELATIONSHIP		
Neighbor	15%	54%
Former lover	15	—
Acquaintance	8	15
Coworker	4	—
Employee	4	—
In-law	4	—
Stranger	—	15
Other	8	8
Unknown	42	8
MOTIVE		
Neighborhood quarrel	12	38
Lovers' quarrel	8	8
Political conviction	35	23
Economic motives	19	8
Other	4	15
Unknown	23	8

the accused Jewish people in Krefeld and 77 percent of the accused Jewish people in Cologne knew the person who denounced them. The figure for the Cologne Special Court cases is higher largely because these files typically included greater amounts of documentation, which makes for fewer cases in which the relationship between the accused and the accuser was unknown.

In his analysis of the Düsseldorf Gestapo, the most detailed existing study of the motives that led denouncers to inform on others, Reinhard Mann found that private conflicts (most often between neighbors) led to more than one-third of the denunciations, that only 24 percent of the denunciations came from political conviction, and that no discernible reason for the denunciation could be determined in 39 percent of the 213 cases he analyzed.[41] Unfortunately, Mann's findings are somewhat difficult to compare with those here because he did not study cases involving Jews (or Communists). Nevertheless, one can observe from the Krefeld and Cologne cases involving Jews that private conflicts were also often present, but that political motivations may have had more salience than they did in the cases Mann studied. In the cases started against Jews in Krefeld in the 1930s, some form of political motive is suggested in at least 35 percent of the cases. In the other cases, business and economic factors ranked second among the grounds for the denunciations at 19 percent, disputes among neighbors ranked third at 12 percent, and disputes among former lovers ranked fourth at 8 percent.

The evidence from the Cologne Special Court case files shows similar trends, with one major difference. Here Mann's argument about the great significance of neighborhood disputes finds more support than in the Krefeld Gestapo case files. Such disputes provided the leading motive behind 38 percent of the denunciations; denunciations arising out of political conviction accounted for only 23 percent of the cases. These findings are somewhat less reliable than those based on the Gestapo files, however, because of the limited number of cases on which this observation is based and the fact that only a subset of the Gestapo's original cases ever found their way to a Special Court. Nevertheless, a balanced conclusion about the denouncers' motivations in cases lodged against Jews would have to stress the importance of both political and personal motives, which not infrequently overlapped in ways that are not always apparent in the case files of either the Gestapo or the Special Court.

CONCLUSION:
NAZI TERROR AND JEWISH RESPONSE, 1933–1939

On April 29, 1945, the day before he committed suicide in his bunker underneath the Reich Chancellery in Berlin, Hitler married his longtime mistress Eva Braun and dictated his last personal will and political testament. In the final words of his political testament, he made plain that the destruction of the Jews remained his overriding goal to the end: "Above all I charge the leaders of the nation and their followers to meticulously uphold the racial laws and to mercilessly resist the universal poisoner of all peoples, International Jewry."[42]

To what extent Hitler's fanatical anti-Semitism was shared by the broad mass of the German people who followed him during the twelve and a half years of the Third Reich is a matter of considerable debate.[43] Nevertheless, whatever their private feelings, most Germans followed him until the bitter end, and the outcome was the near total destruction of German and European Jewry.

It is important, however, not to view the entire Third Reich and all German people, Gentiles and Jews alike, through the lens of hindsight. At the beginning of the Third Reich, no one, save perhaps Hitler, knew what was ultimately in store for the Jews. As the Cologne survivor Karl Muschkattblatt said, "Nobody knew about the impending doom." Mere words cannot describe the terror that beset the Jewish people who remained in Nazi Germany or in Nazi-occupied lands during the war years, the years when the Jews were physically annihilated. But in the 1930s, the terror was not yet absolute.

In the first six years of Hitler's rule, the terror increased unmistakably, but not always in unilinear fashion. Many of the survivors' memoirs and testimonies and many of the Gestapo and Special Court case files demonstrate that at first many Jews believed that they were still empowered German citizens, that most of their German neighbors were not out to get them, and that they could outlast Hitler. Despite the economic boycotts, the increasingly anti-Semitic legislation, and the racist taunts and threats that the Hitler faithful voiced in public and private spaces, many Jews stood up indignantly to their tormentors and threw back the invective of SA bullies with comments like "Shit is also brown" and "Heal Hitler." Some even issued lists of demands to the Nazi authorities from their jail cells. Most Jews remained scrupulously law-abiding in the face of the Nazis' intolerance and persecution, as was the tradition of people of their cultural and class background, but many resisted the Nazi terror as well. The evidence presented here and other evidence on Jewish resistance presented in later chapters dealing with the war years demonstrate that Jews were just as courageous as their Gentile counterparts in standing up to the Nazis.[44]

But standing up to the Nazis was arguably more difficult for Jews than for non-Jews. Even for minor acts of noncompliance—like criticizing the regime in private conversations—the Jews were many times more likely to have the Gestapo start a case against them than were non-Jews, and when such a case was initiated, they were much more likely to be punished severely. This having been said, the Gestapo and the courts in the prewar years sometimes appeared even more moderate than some elements in the German population in their treatment of the Jews. At this time, the Gestapo committed only a portion of its limited spy and surveillance network to Jewish persecution and relied heavily on reports from common citizens to inform it about Jewish wrongdoing. Furthermore, the Gestapo did not always punish the Jews who did come to its attention with utmost ruthlessness, though this would become the rule later on. Many Jewish cases were dismissed by the Gestapo or the courts with no more than a stern warning. Most Jews who spent time in protective custody, prison, or even a concentration camp were eventually released. But this was all before Germany went to war. The war, which broke out on September 1, 1939, accelerated the pace and harshness of Jewish persecution exponentially. For most Jews who had not recognized by this time that emigration was the only way to survive the Nazi terror, it was now too late. The Nazi terror against the Jews turned from oppressive to lethal.

PART THREE

NAZI TERROR AND POTENTIAL OPPONENTS, 1933–1939

The first requirement [is] the elimination of the Marxist poison from our national body.

—ADOLF HITLER

The Nazi henchmen taunt with their impudent mouths:
"You are a pig! Now, what are you, you sow?"
"Catholic priest as I'll always be,"
He answers back distinct and loud.
"You are a pig, why won't you see?"

So on it goes here and there.
There is no threat the preacher fears.
Let them torment him forever long,
Until their fury wanes and is all gone.

—FATHER JOSEF SPIEKER, S.J., OF COLOGNE,
from "Der Empfang" (The Reception)

CHAPTER FIVE

I f Hitler hated the Jews above all others, he loathed the Communist and Socialist left with scarcely less passion. Long convinced that "Jewish-Marxist" traitors had caused Germany's disgrace in World War I and that only resolute action could counter the threat of a new Bolshevik revolution on German soil, Hitler set the eradication of the Communist and Social Democratic movements as the first task of his regime when he came to power at the end of January 1933. As he had written in *Mein Kampf:* "The first requirement [is] the elimination of the Marxist poison from our national body. . . . It [is] the very first task of a truly national government to seek and find the forces which [are] resolved to declare a war of annihilation on Marxism."[1]

Less than a month after he assumed power, Hitler set this war of annihilation in motion. Standing outside the burning Reichstag building in Berlin on the night of February 27–28, 1933, in the company of Göring, Goebbels, and several other Nazi leaders, and with a "face that was flaming red from agitation and from the heat," Hitler, according to his first Gestapo chief, Rudolf Diels,

> shouted uncontrollably, as I had never seen him do before, as if he was going to burst: "There will be no mercy now. Anyone who stands in our way will be cut down. The German people will not tolerate leniency. Every Communist official will be shot where he is found. The

Communist deputies must be hanged this very night. Everybody in league with the Communists must be arrested. There will no longer be any leniency for Social Democrats either."[2]

Hitler's dictates were followed forthwith. On that very night, thousands of Communist functionaries found themselves under arrest; according to one estimate, 1,500 were arrested in Berlin alone.[3] On the next day, at Hitler's urging, Hindenburg signed the Decree for the Protection of People and State. Providing the original "legal" basis for a brutal wave of terror, the decree would lead to the arrest of more than 60,000 Communist and Social Democratic activists and claim the lives of some 2,000 Communists before the Hitler regime was two years old.[4] Indeed, one can well argue that the destruction of the left, particularly the Communist left, was nearly the sole focus of the Nazi terror in the first year and a half of Hitler's regime.

The Communists did not take the terror unleashed against them lying down. Beginning on the first night of Hitler's takeover and continuing over the next several years, Communists throughout Germany opposed Hitler's rule with all the strength and resources they could muster. They disseminated anti-Nazi flyers pointing to the horrors that Hitler perpetrated and calling for a general strike to bring down his government. They painted the walls of buildings with anti-Nazi symbols and slogans to remind those who opposed Hitler that they were not alone. After their party was outlawed and their main leaders had either been arrested or gone into exile, they organized and reorganized their resistance network on an underground basis. They even waged shoot-outs with Nazi Party members and stormtroopers in many localities.

The Communist Party's first flyer under Hitler's new order, for example, appeared on the day Hitler was named chancellor. Culminating in a call for a nationwide general strike, it decried the "shameless plundering of wages, the unbounded terror of the brown plague of murder, the trampling down of the last remaining rights of the working class! The unrestrained course leading to an imperialistic war—that all stands directly in front [of us]." And it warned prophetically that "the bloody, barbaric terror-regime of fascism is being erected over Germany."[5]

HITLER'S "LEGAL REVOLUTION"

But the Communist Party's clarion call to resistance fell on largely deaf ears among the rest of the population, and the kind of united effort required to bring down Hitler seemed doomed from the start. While the Nazi brown shirts triumphantly seized the opportunity to demonstrate the power and optimism of their movement and Hitler took quick steps to consolidate his power, most of Hitler's opponents reacted with skepticism and resignation. They believed that Hitler's chancellorship, like the preceding Weimar governments of Heinrich Brüning, Franz von Papen, and Kurt von Schleicher, would succumb to the weight of Germany's economic distress and fall after a few months.[6] Furthermore, they hoped that Hitler would act more responsibly now that he had an official governmental role, and they believed that he would not be able to wreak much havoc anyway because he was boxed in by a coalition government with only two National Socialist ministers in the cabinet other than himself.[7] They were wrong.

On January 30, 1933, the radio interrupted its regular programming shortly after noon to break the news that Hindenburg had appointed Hitler chancellor. The local Nazi newspaper in Cologne, the *Westdeutscher Beobachter*, reported on the reception of the news in that city with the following words in the next day's edition:

A few minutes later the first Nazi flags already hung in the streets. People who hardly knew each other embraced and said: "Have you heard about it yet?" Party comrades stood in the doorways of apartment buildings and stores and shook hands. SS-men in uniform and SA-people everywhere in the streets exchanged glances: celebrating the day. The news spread throughout the city like wildfire. . . . Opponents, hardly to be seen, kept silent, overwhelmed by the gravity of what was taking place. The first extra editions of the *Westdeutscher Beobachter* went away as fast as the warm breakfast rolls. Everywhere a dozen hands reached out at the same time for the long-desired news. "Hitler is chancellor." The newspaper vendors have never yelled more happily and loudly.[8]

Within hours a nationwide victory celebration had taken over the streets. Nazi flags popped up everywhere on public and private buildings throughout the country. That same evening the Nazi Party faithful were joined by the right-wing Stahlhelm organization of the Nationalist Party in exultant torchlight parades that wound their way through city centers and provocatively through many working-class districts as well, often stopping to demolish Communist Party installations and to pick fights with onlookers en route. In some localities, such as the small towns of Frechen outside Cologne and Hochheide near Krefeld and Duisburg, the first of many shoot-outs between Communists and Nazis were recorded.[9]

The major demonstration in Cologne proper came on the following day. Cologne's SA, SS, and Stahlhelm marched in orderly fashion into the city's crowded convention hall in Cologne-Deutz on the Rhine's right bank to the accompaniment of military fanfare music played by a band clad in the uniforms of the German army of World War I. After singing the German national anthem ("Deutschland, Deutschland über alles"), they were regaled by a rousing speech from Cologne's Nazi Party chief, Gauleiter Joseph Grohé, who thanked the "venerable Field Marshall von Hindenburg" for naming Adolf Hitler chancellor and who left little doubt that the Führer would never let his newly won power slip out of his hands. The other speakers who followed all spoke in ecstatic tones, assuring the assembly that the "November state" had been destroyed and that the new Third Reich would be indestructible and unconquerable.

When evening came, the SA, SS, and Stahlhelm mounted an enormous torchlight parade from the convention hall, over the Rhine bridge, into the city center on the left side of the Rhine, and then on through the arch at the Rudolfplatz and over the city's main thoroughfare, the Hohenzollernring. Chanting and singing Nazi and nationalistic slogans and songs along the way, the marchers' pitch-burning torches illuminated the wintry darkness, and ominous, swastika-bedecked flags and standards cast an eerie foreshadowing of what was to come. This spectacle was repeated elsewhere in city upon city throughout Germany. To many it seemed to symbolize a new dawn of national reawakening. Only a few recognized at the time that it symbolized the beginning of Germany's longest night of horror.[10]

Germany's Communist Party (KPD) did perceive the threat that was in store, but it stood alone. Had it been able to make common cause with Germany's still-powerful Social Democratic Party (SPD), the horror that soon took root in Germany might have been avoided. Among other things, the SPD had strong ties to the free trade unions and led the disciplined, well-armed, 250,000-man *Reichsbanner* paramilitary organization. Also, as a patriotic party committed to democracy, which the KPD certainly was not, it could have provided a bridge to other parties and organizations, especially the army, for a movement of opposition against Hitler.

But the SPD leadership rejected the KPD's repeated calls for a general strike and a united front to bring Hitler down.[11] On the one hand, they feared that a general strike had a limited chance of success. With six million unemployed workers in Germany, there would be hundreds of workers willing to take the place of every striker. On the other hand, SDP leaders distrusted the Communists' ties to Moscow and their boast that a "Soviet Germany will come after the Fascists." The gulf that separated the two parties during the Weimar years was simply too great to overcome. The Social Democrats had refused to support the Communists' candidate, Ernst Thälmann, in both the 1925 and 1932 presidential elections—a position that arguably made the presidency of the archconservative Paul von Hindenburg possible—and they continued to refuse to make common cause with the Communists, even at this crucial time. For their part, the Communists did not help their plea for unified action by continually referring to the Social Democratic Party as "social fascists" and, not infrequently, as the "leading enemies" of the Communist movement.[12]

To be fair, the SPD did not remain completely inert in the following weeks. On February 7, for example, it held a mass protest demonstration in Berlin's Lustgarten. But this was unusual. In the main, the SPD responded like the other democratic parties and followed a policy of strict adherence to legality, fearing that openly hostile acts against the Nazi government would provide the Nazis with a legal excuse to destroy them. Instead of joining the Communists' resistance to Hitler in the streets, the SPD concentrated its efforts on the upcoming Reichstag elections on March 5, hoping that it could improve on its poor showings in recent Weimar elections and garner enough votes to act as a serious bulwark against the Hitler government.[13]

In the words of one scholar, the Socialist Democrats' strict observance of legality in this extreme situation was in reality a "policy of waiting, doing nothing, and self-deception."[14] Thus, for example, in the city of Moers, only a few miles north of Krefeld, while the local SA and SS were beating the citizens bloody with rubber truncheons during their victory celebrations in the beginning of February 1933, and while the KPD staged protest demonstrations, the city's SPD leadership merely filed an official complaint with the local Landrat demanding the removal of Nazi flags that they felt had been illegally placed on the city hall and police station. But even this was not done. The city's SPD leaders were informed that their request had been lodged with the improper authority and that they needed to appeal instead to the *Regierungspräsident*.[15]

Weak-kneed as the SPD's response to Hitler's regime appears, it had some logic to it given the veneer of legality Hitler applied to the Nazi revolution itself.[16] Although violence and terror were always at the heart of the Nazi movement, Hitler had learned from his failed attempt to overthrow the Weimar government (*Bierhallputsch*) in November 1923 that he had to cloak his takeover in outwardly legal trappings. By doing this, he was able to avoid any threat to his movement from either the army or the SPD, for both were committed to taking forcible action only against illegal threats to the republic.[17] Had he not done this, the army might have acted against him, and the SPD might have overcome its aversion to the Communists and joined in an effective general strike against his movement, a joint action that had brought down the right-wing Kapp Putsch in March 1920. Hitler also would have run the risk of losing President Hindenburg's support, which he could not afford to lose.

It took Hitler less than two months from the time he was named chancellor, a legal act in itself, to accomplish his "legal revolution" and to end parliamentary government in Germany by constitutional means. Hitler began his onslaught immediately with an "appeal to the German people" on January 31 to follow him in a "national revolution" to restore the economy, bring unity to a population rent by class warfare, and save the nation from falling to its archenemies, the Communists. On the next day, February 1, he had the Reichstag dissolved; this move gave him a period of seven weeks to rule by presidential decree under article 48 of the Weimar constitution. Three days later, on February 4, he had the eighty-five-year-old and increasingly senile President Hindenburg sign a decree outlawing public meetings held by groups that posed a threat to the nation and curtailing the freedom of the press. This decree was especially used to suppress the Communist press and disallow future Communist gatherings, but it resulted in a clear change in the editorial policies of most other newspapers as well. Now even muted criticism in the press of Hitler and his movement was dangerous, and this no doubt damaged even the democratic parties' fortunes in the upcoming parliamentary elections called for March 5.

Hitler hoped to record a resounding electoral triumph that would provide him with a popular mandate for his revolution and for future moves he wanted to make. The most important of these was the passage of the Enabling Act, which would legally end parliamentary government and place dictatorial powers in his hands. Having gained the support of only one-third (33.1 percent) of the electorate in the most recent national parliamentary election of November 6, 1932, he needed to make significant gains to pass this act, for a two-thirds majority in the Reichstag was necessary for changes in the Weimar constitution.

The burning of the Reichstag less than a week before the election was probably a stroke of luck. Fortuitous or not, Hitler capitalized on it immediately by proclaiming a state of emergency: bold steps were needed to thwart an incipient Communist revolution. It was at this point that Hindenburg passed the Decree for the Protection of People and State, which provided the initial legal sanction for Hitler's police state and enabled him to have his most serious Communist and Social Democratic adversaries arrested forthwith.

On the following Sunday, a huge turnout of 88 percent of eligible voters participated in the election, in which Hitler's party improved significantly on its previous showing. Nevertheless, it registered only a qualified success: 43.9 percent of the German electorate voted for the Nazi Party, giving Hitler 288 Reichstag seats. The majority of the population voted for the other parties; in particular, the Nazis' left-wing and Catholic Center Party adversaries held up surprisingly well. Even with the support of his Nationalist Party allies, Hitler could count on only 51.7 percent of the Reichstag deputies to pass his Enabling Act. Even if he forbade the Communist Party to take part, which he did, the SPD and the Center Party together held more than one-third of the Reichstag seats and could therefore block its passage if they stood firm against it.

In the end, on March 24, Hitler was able to get the act passed by a 444–94 vote margin with only the SPD deputies voting against it. Before the vote was taken, he managed to secure the Center Party's support by promising to respect the rights of German Catholics, such as freedom of religious practice and continued control over their schools. Furthermore, the Center Party and most other Reichstag deputies were intimidated by threats of what might happen to them and their supporters should they not vote for the act's passage. As described by a Bavarian SPD deputy, the passage of the act was accompanied by a frightening scene:

> The wide square in front of the Kroll Opera House [the new site of the Reichstag after the fire of February 27–28] was crowded with dark masses of people. We were received with wild choruses: "We want the Enabling Act!" Youths with swastikas on their chests eyed us insolently, blocked our way, in fact made us run the gauntlet, calling us names like "Center pig," "Marxist sow." The Kroll Opera House was crawling with armed SA and SS men. . . . When we Social Democrats had taken our seats on the extreme left, SA and SS men lined up at the exits and along the walls behind us in a semicircle. Their expressions boded no good. . . . We tried to dam the flood of Hitler's unjust accusations with interruptions of "No!," "An error!," "False!" But that did us no good. The SA and SS people . . . hissed loudly and murmured: "Shut up!," "Traitors!," "You'll be strung up today."[18]

With the passage of the Enabling Act, parliamentary government came to an end. Hitler's government "legally" gained the right to issue laws without the consent of the Reichstag, and Hitler no longer even needed President Hindenburg's signature to pass laws by decree. The Reichstag went into eclipse, passing only seven more laws during the remaining years of the Third Reich and serving as a mere sounding board for Hitler's major speeches. Hitler's dictatorship now enjoyed full legal sanction, and the only means left to express opposition to his rule were illegal ones.

Hitler did not officially proclaim his "national revolution" over, how-

ever, until he had reorganized state and local government, purged the bu-
reaucracy of Jewish and democratic elements, smashed the trade-union
movement, and abolished all political parties other than his own Nazi Party.
The Nazis termed the process of accomplishing this Nazification of German
society *Gleichschaltung*. It took only three and a half months to complete.
On July 5, 1933, one day after banning the last remaining political party,
the Catholic Center Party, Hitler made a speech to the Reich governors
(*Reichstatthälter*)—mainly Nazi Party functionaries who had been appointed by a law of April 7 to head local state governments—proclaiming
that the Nazi Party had become the state and calling for an end to the national revolution and its replacement by an evolutionary process.

This by no means signaled an end to state-sponsored violence and terror. But it did usher in a period characterized by tactical compromises with
some of the traditional elites and a curbing of and eventual crackdown on
some of the Nazi movement's most radical elements. By signing a Concordat with Hitler on July 20, the Vatican accepted the exclusion of the Catholic
Church from political activities in return for guarantees of religious freedom. This and other compromises Hitler made with traditional institutions
angered the SA leadership, but the power and radicalism of this most revolutionary organ of the Nazi Party was itself becoming a problem that Hitler
would soon want out of the way.

With several million armed men, outposts in cities and towns across
Germany,[19] and thousands of its members having been deputized near the
end of February 1933 as an auxiliary police force,[20] the SA posed a roadblock
to the normalization of Hitler's rule and a threat to both the regular army
and Hitler himself. The jackbooted SA stormtroopers had been useful at
first to demonstrate the power and dynamism of the Nazi movement and to
strike fear in the hearts of any naysayers, but under the leadership of the
fanatical Ernst Röhm they had to be restrained. The SA's indiscriminate
brand of terror—publicly hacking up Jews, Communists, trade unionists,
and any others who came in the way—could no longer be tolerated if Hitler
was to secure the allegiance of the broad reaches of the German population.
A controlled and targeted terror could achieve far better results than a continuous orgy of violence. Besides this, Röhm's open displays of homosexuality, indiscreet criticisms of Hitler, and mounting demands for control over

a new German army were becoming ever more provocative. Hitler would not brook insubordination; nor did he want to run the risk of a military coup. After having "drunk a few glasses of wine in quick succession" while lunching at the popular Berlin restaurant Kempinski, Röhm told Hitler's onetime friend and confidant Hermann Rauschning:

> Adolf is a swine. He will give us away. He only associates with the reactionaries now. . . . Getting matey with the East Prussian generals. . . . Adolf is turning into a gentleman. He's got himself a tailcoat now! . . . Are we revolutionaries or aren't we? . . . We've got to produce something new, don't you see? A new discipline. A new principle of organization. The generals are a lot of old fogeys. They never have a new idea.[21]

The curbing of the SA's power proceeded gradually at first; it continued to play an important role in combating leftist opponents throughout the summer and fall of 1933. Nevertheless, the jails and "wild concentration camps" that the SA employed to torture and beat confessions out of scores of Communists—like the one in a powder factory in the Porz-Hochkreuz section of Cologne—were forced to shut down in Cologne and many other localities between the summer of 1933 and the winter of 1934. These had been places full of starving prisoners, broken body parts, swollen faces, and puss-oozing sores that had even disgusted the likes of the Gestapo chief Rudolf Diels. After visiting an underground SA jail in Wuppertal while on a visit to Cologne and the Rhine-Ruhr area, he reported that "Hieronymus Bosch and Pieter Breughel have never perceived such horror."[22] In addition to having its hideous dungeons closed, the SA's arbitrary and brutal raids on workers' apartments and workplaces were soon replaced by more systematic police searches, its *"wilde Aktionen"* in general were brought to an end, and it was increasingly placed under the direction of the Gestapo and the normal police.[23]

But Hitler waited until the next summer to take more drastic action against the SA. In what has come to be known as "the Night of the Long Knives," Hitler personally led a troop of SS men who took Röhm and other SA chieftains by surprise at their encampment in a Bavarian resort at Bad

Wiessee in the early hours of June 30, 1934. In the next days Hitler ordered a bloody purge that claimed the lives of Röhm and nearly one hundred other recalcitrant SA and Nazi leaders. Although many of these leaders, like Röhm, were killed in Dachau concentration camp or Stadelheim prison, others—such as Herbert von Bose, an adviser to Vice-Chancellor Franz von Papen and the leader of the conservative opposition within the regime, and the former chancellor of the Weimar Republic Kurt von Schleicher and his wife—were shot in their offices or private residences. The purge also claimed the lives of several people from outside the Nazi camp, including some important figures in the Catholic Church: the head of Catholic Action in Berlin, Erich Klausener; the Catholic youth leader Adalpert Probst; the Catholic publicist Fritz Gerlich; and one of the leaders of the Catholic students' organization, Fritz Beck.

Despite loud voices raised abroad to protest these murders, no one in Germany, not even the bishops of the Catholic Church, objected publicly to them, even though the purge was not based on any legal proceedings.[24] The army leadership was pleased. Hindenburg sent Hitler a telegram on July 2 thanking him for his "gallant personal intervention . . . [that] stopped treason in the bud . . . [and] rescued the German people from a great danger."[25] Even Minister of Justice Franz Gürtner defended the murders as necessary acts of self-defense for the state in a time of emergency.[26] When President Hindenburg died a month later on August 2, 1934, Hitler abolished the office of the presidency and subsumed it under a new position he gave to himself as "Führer and Reich Chancellor." Soon thereafter all soldiers and public officials were required to take a personal oath of allegiance to Hitler. On August 19, 85 percent of the German people registered their approval of Hitler in a plebiscite.

The step-by-step constitutional measures Hitler took to provide a semblance of legality to his dictatorial leadership were matched by the establishment of a terror apparatus that also provided a quasi-legal, institutional basis for silencing critics and removing any potential opponents to the Nazi regime. Whereas in the first months of Hitler's rule his opponents—mostly Communists and other leftists—were persecuted with utmost brutality and a large measure of spontaneity and arbitrariness by SA and SS auxiliary policemen who had little respect for laws or legal procedures,[27] it was not long before new police and court institutions were established and laws and legal procedures passed to provide a more legalistic aura to Nazi persecution.

The most important of the new institutions, however, like the Gestapo and the Special Courts, never fully replaced the established police and court authorities, which continued their operations and further served to prop up the Nazis' new order. The Gestapo was set up at the end of April 1933 in Prussia and later took over the prime political policing functions in the rest of Germany as well. It was staffed originally by older policemen from the political wing of the detective force (Kripo) and worked for the duration of the Third Reich in accord with the Kripo and other ordinary police organs to combat opposition and deviance and to impose the will of the Nazi leadership. So too with the Special Courts, which were established by a decree of March 21, 1933, in every Superior Court district as courts of last resort to try political offenders with utmost speed: they were presided over by ordinary German judges who also continued to hear cases in the traditional courts.[28] These traditional courts too could be relied on to pass harsh sentences on political opponents who fell within their jurisdiction.

One example of this was a large show trial held before a Cologne jury court in July 1933 of seventeen Communists accused of killing two SA men and assaulting another during a gunfight on February 24, 1933, in the vicinity of the Eigelsteintor, the medieval north gate into Cologne's ancient inner city and a center of working-class entertainment and living. The trial lasted for six days and was used by the local Nazi Party to intimidate all those who had thoughts of resistance. Expecting death sentences for the accused, the Nazi Party's newspaper wrote on July 24 after the trial's conclusion: "The iron desire for order of the National-Socialist movement lies heavily and powerfully upon our people. There are to be no more half-way measures or sentimentality. Every oppositional act . . . will be nipped in the bud. The huge, recently ended KPD murder trial was a renewed and frightful warning to the entire German people."[29] When the judgment was rendered, six of the accused men were convicted of murder and sentenced to death. The rest of the defendants received lengthy prison or jail terms for aiding and abetting the murderers, violating the weapons laws, and having committing various other offenses. According to the personal instructions of Göring, a

hand-axe was used to carry out the executions of the condemned in Cologne's Klingelpütz prison on November 30, 1933.[30] It was a frightful warning indeed.

NAZI TERROR AND THE LEFT

It was to be Germany's great tragedy that such warnings, coupled with the
outward legality of Hitler's revolution, sufficed to cow and cripple the majority of its population, a majority who had supported the Nazi movement
neither in its infancy nor in its drive toward total power. Over time many
would come to regret having been so intimidated, but most made their peace
with National Socialism and moved on with their lives. Too few had the
conviction to stand up in protest to a regime whose criminal and inhumane
acts often defy description. Among those who did, the Communist Party
towered. Many of its members paid dearly for their courage.

From the very beginning of Hitler's rule, he made good on his promised
war of annihilation against the political left by unleashing a furious Nazi
terror campaign against Communist and other hard-core, left-wing opponents. The means of carrying this out changed somewhat over time as the
more disciplined terror of the Gestapo and the courts eventually replaced
the unbridled excesses of the SA, but there was never any ambiguity in
Hitler's resolve to crush his Marxist adversaries once and for all. If recent
historiography has demonstrated that Hitler's terror apparatus employed a
limited number of agents and spies, had to rely heavily on damning reports
from common citizens for much of its information, and was far from being
"all knowing, all powerful, and omnipresent,"[31] it still had sufficient resources to make it seem truly Orwellian from a Communist perspective.

The evidence from the Krefeld Gestapo and Cologne Special Court case
files shows that the Nazi terror concentrated on two groups above all others,
Jews and Communists. Several other groups and individuals—including
homosexuals, Jehovah's Witnesses, handicapped people, gypsies, foreign
workers, and some clergymen—became targets for Nazi persecution at one
time or another during the Third Reich's almost thirteen-year history, but
Jews and Communists alone accounted for nearly half of the Gestapo's entire caseload.[32] This fact by itself only begins to describe how the machinery

of terror concentrated on them throughout the Third Reich. Whereas Hitler used extreme caution in applying this machinery to most of the German
population—so much so that recent surveys I conducted of the elderly German population with my German colleague Karl-Heinz Reuband demonstrate that less than 2 percent of the respondents ever had a run-in of any
kind with the Gestapo and that only 17 percent said that they even feared
having such a run-in[33]—house searches, protective custody warrants,
torture-extracted confessions, concentration camp referrals, and death sentences became almost *de rigueur* for Jews and Communists.[34]

Comparing the suffering of different groups under the National Socialists is a delicate task; I do not mean to diminish the personal tragedies that
hundreds of thousands of people experienced under Nazi rule. An individual who suffered under the Nazi terror gained no solace from the fact of not
being part of a targeted group. Also, in the end even the Communists did
not fall to any "final solution," as the Jews did. But in the beginning years
of the Third Reich, the Communists even surpassed the Jews as objects of
Nazi persecution and terror on some measures.

In 1933 and 1934 Communists accounted for about 70 percent of the
Gestapo case files in the city of Krefeld; this figure was probably matched or
even exceeded in other cities with a sizable working-class presence. Unfortunately, there are no known statistically based studies of the persecution
of Communists based on Gestapo case files in other communities to compare with Krefeld.[35] But evidence from communities neighboring Krefeld
in the *Landkreis* of Moers, where Communists alone accounted for 132 of
137 people taken into protective custody by March 27, 1933, demonstrates
convincingly that it was almost the Communists alone who felt the full
brunt of Nazi terror at the beginning of Hitler's rule. Indeed, as one scholar
put it, "in the research today it is hardly disputed that the rapidly increasing
terror after the 30th of January 1933 concentrated first and foremost on the
KPD and its supporters," while at the same time "the brown dictatorship
remained very cautious toward bourgeois and conservative as well as religious circles."[36]

Although from the very beginning of the Third Reich Jews suffered
from popular anti-Semitism, anti-Semitic legislation, economic boycotts,
spontaneous attacks from SA thugs, and other measures, it was relatively

uncommon for Jews to be arrested by the Gestapo, or even investigated by it, before the mid-1930s, except for Jews who also happened to be Communists or Communist sympathizers.[37] Of the eighty-five cases in my random sample of the Krefeld Gestapo case files for 1933 and 1934, non-Communist Jews figured in only three cases, and two of them merely involved issues pertaining to emigration. Of the twenty-three other cases that did not involve either Communists or Jews in the sample, one pertained to a leading Social Democratic trade-union organizer, five to members of the Center Party, another five to members of the Nazi Party itself (mainly SA thugs arrested in 1934 for assault and battery or morals offenses as part of the crackdown on that organization), and one to a person charged with practicing homosexuality. Most of the rest were minor cases of people accused by revenge-seeking neighbors or coworkers for having spoken out of turn in violation of the laws against freedom of speech. Nearly all of these cases ended in summary dismissals after brief police investigations. The only case in which a non-Communist was punished severely also pertained to the Nazis' crackdown on the political left. A Social Democratic trade unionist was placed in protective custody "for his own protection" during a book-burning episode outside of the Krefeld trade-union headquarters on May 27, 1933; he was later sent to a concentration camp.[38]

The experience of Communists in Krefeld, Cologne, and other German cities with the Nazi terror apparatus was very different from that of most other Germans in the first years of the Third Reich. The police did not simply sit back and wait for denunciations to come across their desks when Communists were involved, and they did not usually dismiss their cases after brief investigations. Denunciations figured in some Communist cases, but almost all of these were minor cases of Communist sympathizers and fellow travelers, almost never those of hard-core activists.[39] Denunciations from the civilian population started only five of the eighty-five Communist cases in the entire random sample of the Krefeld Gestapo case files between 1933 and 1945, and nearly all of these cases had little or nothing to do with resistance and were dismissed after only a brief investigation.[40] In almost every case involving Communist organizers and activists in the sample, the police got its incriminating information on the accused from preexisting police lists of known Communist leaders, or from spies, house searches, and forced confessions. Once the accused Communists were taken into custody, a charge of "conspiring to commit high treason" typically followed, leading most often to lengthy periods of confinement in either prison or concentration camp or both.[41]

Speaking broadly, one can identify several phases in the Nazis' war of annihilation against the Communists and in the Communists' response to Hitler's dictatorship. The first phase lasted roughly from the day Hitler became chancellor until the summer months of 1933. At the beginning of this period, the Communists often brazenly provoked the Nazis by staging anti-Nazi demonstrations, distributing anti-Nazi leaflets, and engaging SA and SS men in street battles and shoot-outs. Before the Reichstag fire in late February, the Nazis first let the ordinary police make arrests and carry out investigations, as it more or less normally had in the past. After the Reichstag fire, mass arrests of identifiable Communist leaders and functionaries were ordered and thousands were placed in protective custody.[42] In addition to this, spontaneous SA and SS raids on working-class homes and haunts put thousands more behind bars. At this time, however, not all arrested Communists or Communist sympathizers remained in custody for long periods. If they had not committed a verifiable offense and were not important Communist leaders or functionaries, police, prosecuting attorneys, and judges, who still paid some respect to the law, often dismissed the cases against them and set them free after only modest periods in detention.

Although the Gestapo claimed that it had almost totally destroyed the Communist Party by the summer of 1933, Detlev Peukert, the author of several important works on the Communist resistance movement, argues that the Communist Party organization remained relatively intact until that time and that the Gestapo's massive raids against the illegal KPD organization did not begin to succeed until the late summer and fall of 1933.[43] Already by the fall of 1933, however, most leading Communist functionaries had been arrested, fled abroad, or gone into hiding as the Nazis engaged in increasingly systematic police raids and roundups, going "step by step . . . through apartment after apartment, searching the cellars and attics, sheds and garden houses."[44] In place of the old leaders, younger and less experienced Communists came forward and did what they could to reorganize the Communist underground organization, recruit new members, and disseminate reams of anti-Nazi flyers calling for a series of work strikes and massive resistance against their tormentors. But they too were up against impossible odds and eventually had to flee or face years in concentration camp, prison, or worse.

By the beginning of 1935 the Nazis had effectively demolished most of the Communist underground organization. The number of arrested Communists fell off dramatically, and new groups of people replaced the Communists as the prime targets of Nazi persecution in the years following. Of the eighty-five Communist cases in the random sample of Krefeld Gestapo files, only eleven began in 1935, and only fifteen began after that time. Additional evidence that the Third Reich shifted its focus away from the political left after its first years comes from the Cologne Special Court files: the number of cases lodged against Communist and Social Democratic adherents and sympathizers declined sharply after 1934.[45]

Many German Communists kept up the fight against the Nazi dictatorship after 1935 but had to do so mainly from positions located outside the Reich.[46] The Gestapo kept a vigilant eye trained on those it eventually let out of prison or concentration camp to ensure that they did not return to their old ways. For some the only way they could prove they had learned their lesson and could gain their release was to promise to serve as an informer. One example is Johann S., a Krefeld Communist who sat in prison for five years before his release in September 1940. According to a report in his case file written by the Krefeld Gestapo officer Karl Schmitz, the Gestapo opted not to confine Johann S. in protective custody after he got out of prison because he had promised to serve as a Gestapo informer. The Gestapo also rewarded Johann S. by helping him get a job as a carpenter. In Schmitz's words: "He conducted himself well and worked hard during his confinement. Placing him in protective custody after the completion of his term is not considered necessary for it can be assumed that he has changed his political views and further illegal activity on his part can be ruled out. Through arrangements made by the Krefeld employment bureau he will be immediately given a position as a carpenter. He signed a statement at his release promising not to partake in illegal activities in the future. Also he voluntarily committed himself to serving the local Gestapo outpost as an informer."[47]

How many former Communists and Communist sympathizers experienced true conversion is unclear. In the view of some observers like Peukert, "the broad majority of the working-class population, while remaining politically passive out of necessity, did not make its peace with the regime, but kept up an attitude of sullen refusal which on many occasions led on to positive acts of opposition."[48] Others are more cynical. One elderly former Communist from the working-class Vingst section of Cologne told me: "At first we were red. Then we were brown. After the war we became religious."[49]

COMMUNIST CASE FILES

Some representative cases from the Cologne Special Court and Krefeld Gestapo records illustrate how committed the Nazis were to eliminating their Communist adversaries and document the Communists' brave but ultimately futile efforts to mount an effective resistance movement in the first two years of Hitler's rule. The Communists may have lost in the end, but they put up a determined fight.

The first of these cases, which took place in the small town of Frechen on the western outskirts of Cologne,[50] is typical in several ways of many of the cases lodged against Communists. First, like many of the cases involving the political left, it is a large case that started out small. Beginning with only a few arrests of local Communist leaders based on a minor charge, it snowballed over time to include numerous Communist organizers and sympathizers who eventually were forced either to flee or to face harsh punishments for serious charges made against them. Second, it is typical of many of the Communist cases in the first months of Hitler's rule in that it shows how Communists initially acted boldly and openly to confront their Nazi opponents, with little apparent regard for the consequences. And finally, it demonstrates that ordinary police and justice officials often treated the Communists with some measure of fairness and sometimes almost with laxness in the beginning months of Nazi rule but became much harsher in their treatment before much time had elapsed.

The case concerned a shoot-out between local Communists and Nazis in the streets of Frechen shortly before midnight of the day when Hitler took over as Reich chancellor. Prior to the battle, both organizations had called meetings of their party faithful and their paramilitary organizations (the Communist Party's outlawed but still functioning *Rotkämpferbund* and the Nazis' SA) to determine what action to take. Who did the shooting and what actually happened took the police and the judicial authorities a long time to determine (the case would last for one and a half years). But in the end, Frechen's Communist Party organization was destroyed.

The police first took action in the case around midnight when a local Frechen policeman, Hauptwachtmeister L., was awakened from his sleep by the sound of gunfire in the street below his apartment. Jumping to the window to see what was happening, L. made out that a large gunfight was taking place close to a nearby school called the Ringschule. According to his estimate, about forty shots were fired. When it was over, he saw twenty to twenty-five people walking toward his apartment from the direction of the Freiheitsring. He then hurriedly got dressed and ran out into the street to ask questions.

It took L. almost no time to determine that all of these people were Communists. One of them, whom he referred to as "the Communist C." in a report he filed in the case, "refused to stay put" and tried to run away. But L. restrained him physically and searched him and the others for weapons. Finding none, L. decided simply to question the men about what had happened. The men explained to him that they had done nothing illegal and in fact had been shot at themselves by SA troops and Nazi Party members while they were standing in the Hülchnerstrasse outside the town's local Nazi Party headquarters and neighboring SA barracks. Having no grounds to detain them further, L. let the men go.

L. then rushed over to the Hülchnerstrasse, where he encountered approximately twenty-five Nazi Party and SA men—and a different version of the events. The Communists, they said, had fired fifty to sixty shots at Nazi Party headquarters in the course of an unprovoked raid and a local wagon driver and Nazi Party member had been shot in the right foot and taken by ambulance to the local hospital. Also, L. was told by the Nazi Party office-head, Reiner S., and the local SA leader, Truppführer Herman B., that none of the local Nazis or SA men had shot back.

On the next morning, January 31, 1933, several witnesses were called to testify at Frechen police headquarters, and a number of well-known Communist functionaries were arrested on charges of breaking the peace and aggravated assault and battery. Most of the witnesses were Nazi Party members, whose version of the events was already known. But one of the witnesses, who did not belong to the Nazi Party, was a thirty-seven-year-old architect named Heinrich L., who testified that before the shots were fired he had observed at about 11:00 P.M. that several Communists, including Johann C. (the man who had tried to run away from the police officer L. the night before) and Johann B. (another leading local Communist), had been questioned in the streets of Frechen by a police officer named K. After that, he explained, he had seen a group of forty to fifty Communists breaking up into two groups and obviously up to no good. He then called the police department and spoke with an officer named W., who told him that there was no need to worry because precautionary measures had already been taken. So he went to bed and gave the matter no more thought.

All of the arrested Communists were young to middle-aged, unemployed workers with families living on social welfare; at first they denied any wrongdoing on their part. Johann B., for example, was a severely wounded war veteran and forty at the time. Unemployed since 1931, he received the small sum of twelve marks per week to support himself, his wife, and their nine-year-old child. Johann C., aged thirty-two, was a tall and striking man with blond hair and blue eyes, but he too had been unemployed for several years and had an equally difficult time supporting his wife and two young children on his thirteen-mark weekly welfare allotment.

Both Johann B. and Johann C. admitted to holding minor organizational positions with the local Communist Party, but both denied having any leadership role and insisted that they had done nothing at all wrong. They had simply met the previous evening at the Communist Party's assembly hall (*Volkshaus*) to attend evening educational courses along with about forty other people. Johann B. said that he had gone straight home to bed afterward and first heard about the shootings the same morning when he had been arrested.

Johann C., however, provided several details about what had happened after the meeting in the assembly hall broke up at approximately 10:00 P.M. He even admitted that he had witnessed the shootings. As he told it, a certain Max S. came to the *Volkshaus* just as the meeting was adjourning and related that several Nazis told him in Wirtschaft Müller (a local bar) that "he had better go home because something was going to happen that night." Johann C. said that several of the younger people present then decided not to go to bed that night and instead went to the corner of the Antoniterstrasse and the Hauptstrasse to see what would develop. Suddenly, he said, several young Communists came by and told them that they had been shot at by Nazis as they were escorting one of their Party comrades home who happened to live in an apartment next door to Nazi headquarters in the Hülchnerstrasse. The larger group of Communists then decided to provide the man with a more powerful escort, only to be shot at again when they got about fifty meters away from his apartment. Johann C. said that, as soon as the shots were fired, he immediately turned and ran away and therefore did not know whether any of the Communists had returned fire. During his retreat, he ran into the policeman L. in the Ringstrasse, and L. searched him for weapons. Afterward he sought refuge in the apartment of a friend, whose name he would not divulge, and spent the night.

By not telling the police where he had stayed or with whom he had stayed, Johann C. added to the police's suspicions against him. But it was another man who first revealed anything of consequence to the police. In his interrogation, George C., also a KPD functionary in Frechen and an unemployed worker with a family and children on welfare, said that he had not gone to the meeting at the *Volkshaus* because he had felt ill and that he had not met up with his comrades until they were escorting the man who lived near the Nazi headquarters to his apartment. George C. said that he went along only because his comrade had told him he was afraid of what would happen to him if he tried to go home alone "because the Nazis were drunk." Hence, since he had not joined the group until a late hour, he allegedly did not know about any attack the Communists might have planned. Furthermore, he claimed that he too had fled the scene as soon as the shooting started. But he did tell the police that both Communists and Nazis had fired at one another, and even worse, he gave the police the names of an

additional nineteen Communists who had been present. From that time onward, though still slowly at first, the case snowballed, finally leading to the
investigations of sixty-four men and five women.

A total of fifteen Communists gave testimony that same day. Although
most kept their lips sealed, as Johann B. and Johann C. had done, George
C. was not the only one to provide the police with additional names and
information. Later in the day, Josef S., another unemployed worker with a
family and, as the police noted, a criminal record (they also remarked that
he "did not stand in good repute"), gave the police the names of twelve more
people. The police underlined each of these names in red pencil and later
arrested them.

One cannot determine from the case files why George C. and Josef S.
provided this information to the police. Although one can never be certain,
they do not seem to have been tortured or seriously threatened. They divulged the names of the other involved Communists on the first day they
were interrogated, and indeed, in their first interrogation on that day. Also,
their testimony was not broken off and then resumed with statements like
"Now I will tell the pure truth" or "I confess" or "I must correct myself,"
as one sees in cases in which threats or torture were obviously employed.
Nevertheless, their testimony provided the police with enough information
to file official charges against Johann C. and Johann B., whom the police
believed to be the leaders of the Communist raid. Johann C. and Johann B.
were taken to jail in Cologne two days later to await trial.

Several others were arrested and forced to testify in the following week,
and additional witnesses were also called in. On April 11, however, the Cologne state attorney's office dismissed the case on the grounds that there
was not enough convincing evidence to prove that Johann C. or Johann B.
had planned or taken part in the shooting. Furthermore, on January 30,
1933, there was as yet no law prohibiting Communist gatherings.

Johann C. and Johann B. were released, but this was not the end of the
case. Nearly six months later, it was reopened when new information about
the shoot-out was provided by a man named Anton K., who had heard about
it while a prisoner in Siegburg.[51] On July 12, Josef S. was arrested once
again. He had provided the Frechen police with much of the original information they had in the case, and this time he sang even more loudly. Now

he admitted that he had been a KPD functionary in Frechen and that he had personally taken part in the gunfight. He then went on to name those who were with him that evening and gave the police the names of ten men who had done the shooting. Johann B. was not on this list, and Josef S. did not know whether he had taken part in the shoot-out. He did, however, say, "I do know that B. always had a gun with him. He once told that to [Johann] C. in my very presence."

Johann C. was on the list, and he was arrested and interrogated once again that same day. Whatever tactics the police used to make him talk are not evident, but they certainly were effective. Johann C. not only divulged the names of several men who had been involved in the shoot-out but also spilled the beans about a typewriter and a duplicating machine the Communist organization was using to produce anti-Nazi flyers and about the Party's illegal weapons-smuggling operation.

Numerous Frechen Communists were arrested, interrogated, and placed in protective custody in the days and weeks that followed. At the same time, the police carried out systematic searches of all of the suspects' residences and confiscated numerous weapons and other materials, providing them with information leading to even more arrests. On December 11, 1933, a twenty-four-page summary of the case was filed by the head of the Frechen police describing the shoot-out in minute detail, elaborating on the entire underground resistance organization that the Frechen Communists had built, and detailing the guilt of fifty-nine local Communists and Communist sympathizers.[52] Johann C., now named the "leader of the whole affair" and the "leading member of the local KPD organization," was termed "the most unscrupulous Communist that one can imagine." Soon a new case was opened in Cologne against Johann C. and the others, all charged with conspiring to commit high treason. The case was handed over to the Hamm Superior Court for trial on January 19, 1934.[53]

The comparative laxity with which the authorities initially handled cases like this one may have been commonplace in small towns like Frechen where the threat posed by local Communist organizations was not perceived as particularly great. In larger cities like Cologne and Krefeld, the authorities acted more stringently and more swiftly to destroy the threat of left-wing opposition. Even before the immediate arrest of all leading Com-

munists was called for by the Reichstag Fire Decree of February 28, 1933,
large numbers of top Communists throughout Germany went into hiding.[54] Under strict orders from the Communist Party leadership to avoid
arrest at all costs,[55] and soon to be hunted down relentlessly by the police,
they quickly realized that the only possible means of combating their Nazi
adversaries was from the underground.

Although many thus succeeded in avoiding arrest and did what they
could to develop an effective resistance organization in the late winter and
spring months of 1933, they soon tired of sleeping in garden houses and
strangers' cellars and attics. Unable to meet with much success in their resistance work because their pursuers were too hot on their trail, many
hightailed it out of the country while they still could. But even abroad they
were not safe. Taking several years to track them down if necessary, the
Gestapo eventually got its hands on great numbers of Communists in exile.
Once they were finally caught, or turned themselves in, they seldom got
away again. The cases of two of Krefeld's most prominent Communist leaders, Oskar H. and Peter Z., serve as examples.[56]

Oskar H. was a married construction worker in his midthirties and a
Communist Party representative (*Stadtverordneter*) on the Krefeld city
council, as well as the leader of the Party's Krefeld-North district. He and
Peter Z. had both gone underground shortly after Hitler's takeover. Oskar
H. soon contracted pneumonia, however, and entered a Krefeld hospital on
March 3, 1933. As soon as he regained some of his health, and realizing that
his arrest was imminent, he left the hospital without permission on March
22 and went back into hiding. In the next month, he often met with other
submerged Communist comrades in a shed in Krefeld's city forest to plan
the reorganization of the Communist Party, and he took part in distributing
anti-Nazi flyers along with many of his compatriots. By the end of April, he
and Peter Z. decided they had to bolt.

Meeting at six o'clock in the morning near the water tower in Krefeld's
Gladbacherstrasse on the day they left, they took off by foot past the towns
of Viersen and Süchteln to the Dutch border town of Kaldenkirchen. Sleeping in garden houses along the way, they covered this distance of approximately twenty-five miles in three weeks. On May 20, they crossed the
border into Holland secretly, without passports. As Oskar H. would later

explain, "Peter Z. knew the way."[57] From the border they walked the short distance to Venlo and took the train to Utrecht, where members of the Communist aid organization Rote Hilfe gave them lodging. Not long afterward, the Dutch police arrested them for not having passports and pushed them across the Belgian border by the town of Rosental.

From the border they rode by train to Antwerp and made contact when they arrived with the Rote Hilfe organization. Provided with lodging and food, they were advised never to use their real first names and to speak only in high German, since their low-German dialect might betray their Krefeld origins. According to information Oskar H. later provided to the Krefeld Gestapo, over the next several months they did little except play cards and chess with other German expatriates in a pub called Solidarität. They respected their orders to avoid all political activity in this period because it could have made the Belgian police suspicious. The Krefeld Gestapo, however, did not believe that they had stopped their political activities, and a note in Oskar H.'s case file written during this time by Kriminalsekretär Johann Krülls stated: "It is undoubtedly certain that even abroad Oskar H. is busy preparing illegal and inflammatory writings. . . . Oskar H., in his entire being, is an enemy of the people who is not worthy of being called a German."

Despite their attempts to remain inconspicuous, they were not able to conceal their whereabouts from the Belgian police. A letter in Oskar H.'s Gestapo file, dated August 30, 1933, and written by the chief of public security (sûreté publique) in Brussels to the Krefeld Gestapo, stated that Oskar H. had arrived in Belgium on July 16; the sûreté publique wanted to know about his criminal and political background. The Krefeld Gestapo wrote back on September 9 that Oskar H. was a dangerous Communist functionary who represented "a danger not only for his own fatherland but for all countries" and asked whether the Belgian authorities might deport him back to Germany. The sûreté publique soon communicated to the German embassy that the Belgian police were willing to force Oskar H. out of the country, but that he could choose which border he wanted to cross. Before they got to him, Oskar H. decided to leave of his own accord.

In January 1934, Oskar H. received a letter from a Krefeld woman informing him that his wife was severely ill. He then surreptitiously crossed the border back into Germany to see his wife; after a stay of five days in Krefeld, he returned to Antwerp. Oskar H. did not bother to seek permission from the Communist organization to make this trip, and for his insubordination he was treated as a spy when he got back, although he was not a spy. Denied further support by the Rote Hilfe and shunned by his peers, Oskar H. decided that his only recourse was to return to Germany and give himself up. At least that way he could be with his wife before she died. Once again he crossed the border illegally, this time at Morsnet on April 28, 1934, and made his way to Krefeld. Two days later he turned himself in to the Krefeld police.

His wife died less than a year later in February 1935, and Oskar H. was allowed out of jail to attend her funeral. Otherwise, he was given little time to see her. The Krefeld Gestapo started a case against him for conspiring to commit high treason and interrogated him constantly. Oskar H. eventually sang chapter and verse, providing the Gestapo with the names of numerous leading Krefeld Communists who had worked with him in developing the Krefeld resistance movement and with whom he had kept company while abroad. He also told the police about the border crossings used by the Communists and about the operations, meeting places, and leaders' names for the Rote Hilfe organization in Holland and Belgium. After spending the better part of a year in jail awaiting trial, Oskar H. was convicted of conspiring to commit high treason on January 17, 1935, and sentenced to a jail term of one year and three months. Not long after he got out, he died, a broken man, at the age of forty on July 7, 1937.

Peter Z. fared somewhat better. As the former head of the Communist Party's Krefeld-South district and also as a former Communist delegate to the Krefeld city council, Peter Z.'s arrest had been ordered since February 28, 1933, along with the arrests of the city's entire Communist leadership. Born in 1893, married with two children, and a bookbinder by trade, Peter Z. had served patriotically in World War I and campaigned courageously against the Belgian occupation of Germany in the early 1920s.

Peter Z. managed to spend more than seven years in Belgium, Holland, and France after leaving Germany in May 1933 with Oskar H. Not long after the Germans invaded France, however, he was arrested in Bordeaux and brought back to Germany, first to Frankfurt at the end of August 1940 and then to Krefeld in early October. Over the next two months, Peter Z. was repeatedly interrogated by several of the Krefeld Gestapo officers, most often by Kriminaloberassistent Wilhelm Weber, who had a reputation as one of the most brutal of the officers. Peter Z. tried valiantly to withhold information and appeared to give Weber only what was already known. Weber wrote in his file, for example, on November 1, 1940, that what Peter Z. had told him about Oskar H. was useless, for he was already dead and "the other Communist functionaries who had been with him back then continue to sit in prison." Even his own sister, aged forty-six at the time, told the Gestapo that his testimony was false in many ways and had been made mostly to find a way to hide the identity of those who had concealed him while he tried to organize the resistance movement in Krefeld in the spring of 1933. In her words: "I am convinced that Peter Z. made false remarks in his testimony in order to try to protect the persons with whom he had hidden out."

The Gestapo believed that Peter Z. had been a major organizer of the Communist resistance abroad despite his protestations that this was not the case. Even the head of the security police and the SD in Belgium and France wrote to the Krefeld Gestapo in February 1941 that he was telling the truth, according to information they had from their own spies. Nevertheless, he was forced to stand trial for conspiring to commit high treason for his earlier activities, and on April 22, 1941, he was convicted by the Hamm Superior Court and sentenced to a jail term of one year and three months. Peter Z. was let out after completing his sentence, thanks in part to one of the Krefeld Gestapo officers, Karl Schmitz, who argued with Weber about his release. Although Schmitz cruelly recommended a continuation of Peter Z.'s sentence for a year in Dachau concentration camp, he argued in a report of December 2, 1941, that Peter Z. had reformed his ways and should therefore not have to spend much more time in confinement. Other mitigating factors he mentioned were that Peter Z. continued to suffer from severe wounds incurred at the front in the First World War, that his son was about to die from wounds he had received fighting for the Fatherland, and that his wife was suffering from a nervous breakdown. Luckily for Peter Z., the head of the Düsseldorf Gestapo ordered on December 5, 1941, that he be let out of jail with a severe warning and not be sent to concentration camp. The

Düsseldorf Gestapo, however, demanded that he be continually watched in the future and wanted reports at regular intervals about his activities. That Peter Z.'s release was an unusual step for the Gestapo was made clear in a remark at the end of the Düsseldorf Gestapo headquarters' order to the Krefeld Gestapo outpost calling for him to be let out of jail: "An exception has been made from the ordering of protective custody after the completion of the sentence."

For the next year and a half, Peter Z. apparently kept out of trouble. Nonetheless, he was arrested once again near the end of August 1944 as part of the general roundup of former opponents of the regime after the attempt on Hitler's life on July 20 by Claus Schenk Graf von Stauffenberg. After only ten days in jail, he was released once again. This time a local Nazi Party *Ortsgruppenleiter* came to bat for him, attesting that Peter Z. had really reformed and that since all the other Communists had been released, he should be too. Apparently Z. had indeed reformed his ways.

By the late spring of 1933, most of the original leaders of the Communist resistance movement either had been taken into protective custody or had fled the country. The new and often less experienced Communist organizers who came forward to take their places made courageous efforts to set up an anti-Nazi underground movement in many localities, but few eluded arrest for very long. From the summer of 1933 onward, the Gestapo, the SA, and the police tirelessly hunted these people down one by one until the entire Communist underground organization lay in ruins and all the Communist organizers had either been arrested or driven from the country. As the Krefeld and Cologne records demonstrate, the destruction of the Communist underground had a snowballing nature: the arrest of one Communist resistance fighter usually led to the arrests of several more, until there were no more left for the Nazis to worry about. Once caught, very few were able to withhold information from the Nazi authorities for very long. Many Communists did try bravely to withhold information, and some even attempted suicide. But in the end, even they were almost invariably unsuccessful. The information was simply beaten out of them.[58]

In the summer of 1933, Paul Z., an unemployed twenty-six-year-old dockworker, helped lead an attempt to reorganize the Communist opposition in the Krefeld-Mönchengladbach area. According to a report in one of his two large Gestapo files,[59] written by the head of the Krefeld Gestapo outpost, Ludwig Jung, on February 28, 1943, Paul Z. first joined the KPD in 1931 and became the Party's political leader in Ürdingen about the time Hitler was named chancellor. Slated, like other Communist functionaries, for arrest in the early months of 1933, Paul Z. went into hiding and tried valiantly in the following months to rebuild the outlawed Communist Party in and around Krefeld and Mönchengladbach. It did not take long for the authorities to catch up with him. Arrested on August 25, 1933, he was put on trial for conspiring to commit high treason and sentenced by the Hamm Superior Court on March 21, 1934, to one year and nine months in prison.

Paul Z. remained a committed antifascist even after he was let out of prison, but he had to go abroad to continue his anti-fascist agitation. After emigrating in 1936, he worked for the Rote Hilfe organization in Belgium and later fought in the Red Militia against the fascists in the Spanish Civil War. The Germans finally nabbed him in August 1940 in Bordeaux and sent him back to Germany to stand trial once again. Sentenced anew by the Hamm Superior Court—this time to two and a half years—he completed his sentence in February 1943 only to be placed, on his release, in Sachsenhausen concentration camp, where he remained until the end of the war. As the Krefeld Gestapo officer Kurt Joost wrote when he ordered that he be sent to Sachsenhausen: "Paul Z. is a person who has demonstrated through his activities that he remains faithful to his Communist ideas. Even today, after completing his second sentence, he will still not make a clear statement about his political beliefs."

The circumstances of Paul Z.'s original arrest in 1933 are worth considering in some detail for they help illuminate both the Communist Party's determined resolve to establish an effective underground resistance organization and the brutal and effective measures the police employed to destroy that organization in the first year of Nazi Rule. In the early morning hours of July 18, 1933, a force of three Krefeld police officers and six SA men, led by Kriminalsekretär Johann Krülls (a longtime Krefeld policeman who was a central figure in the early crackdown on the Communists in Krefeld before being transferred to the Düsseldorf Gestapo headquarters in March 1934),[60] traveled to nearby Mönchengladbach to raid a Communist hideout, arrest a band of Communist organizers, and seize a store of illegal literature. When the Krefeld authorities arrived, they were met by several policemen from Mönchengladbach. While Krülls and another Krefeld policeman waited in their car outside the hideout—the apartment of one of the men they were planning to arrest—the other police officers and SA men broke into the apartment, arrested the four men they found inside, and seized a cache of Communist-written materials. According to Krülls's report, filed eleven days after the arrests were made, "the accused persons had previously been identified in the course of interrogations carried out by the SA in Düsseldorf of already arrested functionaries." The arrested men were then hauled back to Krefeld, put in the local police jail, and interrogated. Two of the four were released the following day. The remaining two were brought before a local Krefeld court on July 29, the same day Krülls filed his report.

Information supplied by the arrested men in the course of their interrogations led to an even bigger police raid a few days later on August 2. This time several Communists' apartments in Mönchengladbach were searched in the early morning hours by a similar group of police officers and SA troops. Again several Communists were arrested and a large amount of illegal literature was found, including five copies of a Communist pamphlet entitled "Long Live the Unity of the Working Class! Open Letter of the Communist Party Central Committee to the Social-Democratic Workers of Germany."[61]

The inflammatory text of the pamphlet urged the German working class to overthrow Hitler's dictatorship through determined action and a series of massive strikes. It began with the following: "Class comrades! Here, one cannot passively stand aside. Here, whining about the vileness of the fascists does not help. In the *Communist Manifesto* Karl Marx said: 'The liberation of the working class can only be accomplished by the efforts of the working class itself!'" Then it explained that if the German working class, which "suffered the worst under the bloodthirsty fascist dictatorship," did not overthrow him, Hitler would not fall down by himself, and this would lead to a "catastrophe for all German workers and farmers" and a "war against the Soviet Union." Finally, it spelled out some specific steps the Communists needed to take to bring Hitler down, beginning with the declaration of August 1, 1933, as a "proletarian day of battle" marked by large but controlled strikes in all German cities.

Ten men were arrested and taken to police headquarters in Mönchengladbach for questioning. Most of the men were unemployed workers in their twenties, although one was fifty-three and another forty-two. From the written protocols recorded during their interrogations, it is clear that several of these men, and possibly all of them, were put under heavy pressure to divulge the names of other Communists who were still at large. They resisted at first. Although each of the men admitted to having once been a member of the Communist Party, all denied any involvement in the Party's activities after it had been outlawed in March 1933, including the dissemination of the seized pamphlets. Each claimed that he therefore could not identify who remained in the Communist movement locally.

Their defiant posture lasted only for the first round of interrogations. In the second round, which took place after a presumably difficult night in jail on August 3, things started to unravel. George J., an unemployed lathe operator, broke down and gave the police what they wanted. Starting his new testimony with the words, "I confess that in my testimony of August 2, 1933, I did not hold to the truth," George J. told the police about a Communist leader with the code-name "Alex" (whom he later named as Paul Z.), who had stayed with him in his apartment on the night before the police raid on August 2, and about the activities of several of the other already arrested men. One of these men, named Anton M., in whose apartment the Communist literature had been found, was also much more forthcoming in his second interrogation. This time he provided the police with details about how he had come into possession of the pamphlets and about the appearance of the man who had given them to him. (Although he did not name this person, the police already knew he had to be Paul Z.) Also beginning his new testimony with words similar to those used by George J., "I confess . . ." —demonstrating that he too had been tortured or at least seriously threatened—Anton M. revealed that he had received a package containing the Communist pamphlets at the train station a week earlier from a man who seemed to be about twenty-seven years old. Describing this man's clothes and appearance in detail, Anton M. said that he had asked him to distribute the materials. In his own defense, he maintained that he had not known what the pamphlets were about until he opened the package when he got home and that he had only slept with them under his pillow and had not handed them out before the police raided his apartment on August 2.

Over the next few days, several more people were arrested and forced to testify, including the twenty-six-year-old wife of George J., who provided the police with further details about Paul Z. and other Communists involved in revolutionary activities in the area. Eventually the police were able to determine where Paul Z. lived, and on August 25 he was arrested. After repeated interrogations, Paul Z. too finally broke down and provided the police with minute details about the revolutionary activities of the underground resistance organization in the area and with the names of several other coconspirators. Most of these people were arrested over the next weeks, though a few did manage to flee abroad before being taken. Subjected to extreme pressure, they also gave the police more names and details about the Communist underground. Like Paul Z., Anton M., and George J. before them, all succumbed to police intimidation. Some explained that they were confessing out of concern for what might happen to their families. But one even incriminated his own sister and told the police where they could find her.

This case dealt a severe blow to the Communist resistance in and around the cities of Krefeld and Mönchengladbach. Paul Z. and twenty-five other Communist organizers were put on trial and sentenced. According to information in another large trial of Communists in the area, held in March 1935, the police crackdown in the summer and fall of 1933 had met with such success that the Communists' local resistance organization was dissolved before the end of 1933.[62] Nevertheless, the Krefeld Communists still did not give up.

A new effort to rebuild the Communist underground in Krefeld emerged in the winter and spring of 1934. This time it was led by some of Krefeld's most venerable Communist activists, such as Aurel Billstein, who had been held for several months in a concentration camp before being released in the early fall of 1933.[63] From an interview I conducted with him in his home in late January 1995, when he was nearly ninety-four years old—still tall, erect, and engaged—and from information in his Gestapo case file,[64] I learned that Billstein was a recently unemployed mechanic with a wife and a young child when he was arrested and placed in protective custody and later concentration camp along with thousands of easily identifiable Communist functionaries in early March 1933 just after the Reichstag fire. Born in Krefeld-Bockum in 1901, Billstein joined the KPD in 1924, served in many of the Party's organizations, and rose during the late Weimar years to be a Communist city councillor and the leader of the Communist Party's Krefeld-South district. After his release from Sonnenburg concentration camp in late September 1933, Billstein spent a few months quietly enjoying his freedom and his family and then took up the cause once again.

In late February of the next year, Billstein was contacted by a man he did not know from the Düsseldorf Communist organization and urged to lead the rebuilding of the Krefeld underground resistance network. Billstein assented. In the next weeks, he met clandestinely every fourteen days in ever-changing locales with members of the Düsseldorf leadership and recruited several older Communist functionaries who, like himself, had been released from custody the previous fall, as well as many lesser-known Communists and Communist sympathizers who were willing to risk all to continue the struggle against the Nazis. By June Billstein and the others had successfully reestablished a Communist underground network with branches in the city of Krefeld and the surrounding communities of Ürdingen, Fischeln, and Kempen. Once again this revived network printed and distributed anti-Nazi flyers and brochures, worked at recruiting new members, collected funds to help maintain the underground resistance in other localities, and demonstrated that Hitler had still not pacified the region.

Despite their brave efforts, Billstein and his compatriots were soon overpowered by the Gestapo. Already by the end of March, the Gestapo had arrested Communists in Mönchengladbach who divulged information about Billstein's operation in Krefeld. Billstein himself was arrested in mid-June along with several others. Using their brutal tried-and-true methods of extracting information, the Gestapo officers handling the case soon got what they were after, leading to yet more arrests and to the apparent end of the Communist underground in Krefeld. Billstein and twenty-five other men were put on trial before the Hamm Superior Court for conspiring to commit high treason and sentenced to prison terms ranging from two to seven years on March 14, 1935. Billstein, identified as the leading conspirator, received the heaviest sentence.

Released from prison in 1941 on completion of his sentence (he received seven months and twenty-one days' credit for his time in jail awaiting trial), Billstein returned to Krefeld and found work as an auto mechanic. During the war he had to report to the police on a weekly basis about his progress. Later he learned that his boss had reported on him regularly to the Gestapo. In 1944 he was called up to serve in a prisoners' company that fought against the invading Allies on what the Germans call the "Western Wall" (*Westwall*). Near the war's end, he was sent to fight in the east, where he was taken prisoner by the Soviet army. After the war he continued his struggle against the Nazis by devoting the remaining fifty years of his long life to writing a series of books and pamphlets documenting the Nazis' crimes in his home city and to serving in the VVN organization of people persecuted by the National Socialists.

Unfairly perhaps, not all Germans believe that people like Aurel Billstein and his fellow Communists should be honored as courageous resistance fighters who stood up against Nazi oppression. Many still fault them for serving the cause of a foreign enemy. Whatever one's opinion of their motives, one cannot contest that they were singled out as the first major targets of the Nazi terror apparatus, that many suffered indescribable torture, and that they endured enormous hardships in their determined efforts to resist Hitler. Their own limitations contributed to their ultimate lack of success, especially their initial unwillingness to cooperate with Social Democrats and trade unionists. Such a coalition might have created the united effort needed to put a stop to the Nazis at the beginning of Hitler's rule, when it still might have been possible to do so. But their failure was even more a product of the Nazis' resolve to destroy them with utmost ruthlessness.

CHAPTER SIX

Germany has only one Führer. That is Christ!" With these words, the blond, blue-eyed, short, and stocky Jesuit priest Josef Spieker brought his 11:00 A.M. sermon on the theme of "true and false Führers" to a close before a packed and adoring congregation in Cologne's Mariä Himmelfahrt Church on Christ the King Day, October 28, 1934.[1] But as the pink-hued church gradually came out of the shade cast by the immense towers of the nearby Cologne cathedral, not all the parishioners felt they were being enlightened. In one of the pews sat a certain Dr. Mathias K.—a fifty-year-old secondary school teacher and lower-level Nazi Party functionary from the Deutz section of Cologne who was furiously recording Father Spieker's every word.[2] When mass ended, Mathias K. hastened to deliver his notes to the Cologne Gestapo, maintaining adamantly that Spieker's entire sermon was a "monstrosity" and a wretched insult to the Führer, "whose being is holy to millions."

Soon Father Spieker became the first Catholic priest to be sent to a Nazi concentration camp in a case that involved the highest reaches of both the Nazi leadership and the Catholic Church hierarchy. His arrest also marked the commencement of a new wave of Nazi terror: potential religious opponents replaced Communist and other leftist agitators as the Nazis' new targets in the mid-1930s. As the evidence in this chapter demonstrates, however, the Nazis' campaign against the churches and the clergy, though harsh at times, generally proceeded more cautiously than its campaign against the political left. On the one hand, this was necessary because an all-out frontal attack on the Christian Churches could have provoked dangerous opposition in the general population and among important elite groups, for large numbers of Germans in the Third Reich continued to hold their faith dear. On the other hand, caution was made possible because most of the leaders of the established churches quickly demonstrated that they were quite prepared to comply with the Nazi regime in political matters so long as they and their followers were accorded some measure of religious freedom. Although a few individual clergymen and some other deeply religious Germans courageously dared to protest openly against the Nazis' inhumanity and immorality, theirs were isolated voices of conscience that resonated only temporarily and in the end usually had little impact. The case of Cologne's intrepid Father Josef Spieker, in which Hitler and the Nazi regime were briefly placed on trial, provides an excellent example with which to begin the discussion.

THE PERILS OF PREACHING AGAINST HITLER: THE CASE OF FATHER JOSEF SPIEKER OF COLOGNE

Initially the Gestapo preferred to deal with Father Spieker in an outwardly "legal" fashion. Spieker's anti-Nazi leanings and pronouncements were well known and he had become ever more brazen in the months leading up to his provocative sermon on Christ the King Day in late October 1934. But Spieker had already proven himself to be as clever and elusive as he was intrepid: the Nazis' mounting surveillance of his activities had not produced enough evidence to support a charge they felt would hold up against him, even in a Nazi court of law. They could simply have arrested him and sent him directly to a concentration camp, but they were worried that such a step might prove dangerous in the court of public opinion because no Catholic priest had yet been treated this way. Most of the populace had no problem with sending Communist and Socialist rabble-rousers to concentration camps, or Jews either, but priests and ministers were a different matter altogether, especially those as popular as Spieker. If, on the other hand, the normal legal machinery could find Spieker guilty of breaking the law, the Gestapo felt that it could move against him with impunity.

With his provocative sermon, Father Spieker appeared to have crossed the line and thrown caution to the wind. Using Mathias K.'s copious notes, the Gestapo believed it could now prove that Spieker had deliberately slandered the Führer in a way that violated the *Heimtücke* law passed on March 21, 1933, protecting the state from malicious verbal attacks made by the citizenry.[3] Spieker would later insist both during his Gestapo interrogations and in the trial that followed that he had done no such thing. Nevertheless, the Gestapo had strong grounds to believe otherwise. Nearly every sentence of his sermon excoriated Hitler for leading the German people astray and for falsely appropriating the role to himself of the people's one true Führer, Jesus Christ. Over and over again Father Spieker admonished that there was only one true Führer to whom the people owed their allegiance, Christ the King. The following are some of the more inflammatory passages of his sermon:

> A Führer must be selfless. That is no Führer who forces the people to the limit so as to live in debauchery at their expense.
>
> A Führer must have the true love of his people. That is no Führer whom the people celebrate because they have been forcibly organized and led into the streets while they fear for their job[s] and daily bread.
>
> A Führer must be loyal. That is no Führer whose subordinates torment and harass, torture and harm the people.
>
> A Führer must be true. That is no true Führer who invents great deeds so as to secure the allegiance of the masses.
>
> Germany has only one Führer. That is Christ! All worldly Führers and spiritual Führers are subject to this Führer. We recognize the state's authority, but we are only subject to it insofar as its laws do not stand in contradiction with the laws of our one and only Führer.[4]

The Gestapo had good reason to worry about the public's reaction in Father Spieker's case. Born on June 18, 1893, the forty-one-year-old Father Spieker had built a large and devoted following since first being sent to the Cologne area slightly more than a year after his ordination in 1926 to preach at the Mariä Himmelfahrt Church and to be the spiritual adviser to several

Catholic men's groups in the area. Starting out with tiny bands of elderly men over the age of sixty who met one evening a month to discuss their religious concerns, the fiery and energetic Father Spieker worked tirelessly to instill these groups with enthusiasm and to expand the numbers and age profile of the members. His success was so great that when he was called to Berlin in 1931 to revive the Catholic men's organization there, the cardinal in Cologne made such a fuss that Spieker decided he would have to split his time between Cologne and Berlin, spending two weeks of every month in each city. In his autobiography, which Spieker recorded on audiotape at the request of the Jesuit order a year before his death in September 1968, he said that he did not mind the stress this put on him; in fact, he loved the challenge. In Berlin he had the opportunity to minister to a Catholic minority population, and in Cologne to Germany's stronghold of Catholicism: he had, as he called it, "in Berlin the Diaspora and in Cologne the so-called Catholic city."[5] His followers loved him in return. By the time the Nazis came to power in 1933, 23,000 Cologne men of all ages had enrolled in Spieker's men's groups in that city alone; a year later the number had grown to 27,000.[6]

Spieker's first confrontation with National Socialism took place three years before Hitler became chancellor. He claimed to be disinterested politically—in his autobiography he stated that he found even the Catholic-based Center Party too moribund for his taste—but a discussion he had with a man during a counseling session sometime in either 1929 or 1930 moved him out of his political lethargy. The man, who was troubled about a growing conflict he felt between his Catholic beliefs and the awe Hitler inspired in him, came to talk with Father Spieker at the Canisius Haus residence of the Jesuit Order in Cologne's Stolzestrasse. "I am a Catholic, an old Center Party follower," the man told him. "I go to mass and to Holy Communion every day." He then went on with his eyes ablaze to lecture Spieker for an entire hour about the greatness of Adolf Hitler, repeating over and over again: "The Center Party has to go! We all have to join Adolf Hitler!"[7]

Spieker concluded the session by providing the man with a few reassuring words about the Center Party, but he himself was left with an uncomfortable feeling. After thinking the matter over, he decided that if Hitler could have such a powerful influence on ardent Catholics like this man, it was time that the church and he did something. Over the next weeks and months, Spieker learned all he could about the Nazi movement. He read the local Nazi newspaper (the *Westdeutscher Beobachter*) on a daily basis and studied Nazi ideological tracts like Alfred Rosenberg's *The Myth of the Twentieth Century*. Soon he prepared his first talk on the subject and delivered it to one of his evening men's groups. Entitled "The Worldview of National Socialism," Spieker's talk sharply criticized the evil influence that Nazism and Hitler portended. Despite the fact that some young Nazi university students from the National Socialist Students' Organization were in attendance, Spieker did not shy away from warning the crowd that he believed the Nazi worldview was "atheistic and anti-Christian."

The next day a long article appeared in the *Westdeutscher Beobachter*; first praising Spieker for his intelligence as a Jesuit priest, it went on to warn him to recognize that the Center Party, unlike National Socialism, was not necessary in these changing times and therefore needed to be dissolved. Spieker was not impressed. In the month that followed, he delivered the same talk to men's groups in parishes all over the Cologne area, just as he had customarily done with lectures on less politically charged subjects. Before Spieker had a chance to develop a new monthly lecture, a subsequent article, entitled "The Subhuman" (*Der Untermensch*), appeared in Cologne's Nazi newspaper proclaiming that Spieker was the vilest of all creatures whom the Nazis had to fight against with all of their might. Moreover, the newspaper spread the rumor that, "when we take over, Spieker will be [made to be] the first to believe!"[8] All of these reactions served only to increase Spieker's resolve. In the years that followed, all the way up to his sermon on Christ the King Day 1934, Spieker continued to speak out against Hitler and the Nazi movement to all who would come to hear him.

Members of the Gestapo were numbered among his most avid listeners. But they left him alone until the summer of 1934. After delivering his sermon one Sunday morning, Spieker encountered two men who had come into the sacristy of the church asking for the pastor. After Spieker told them that the pastor was not in (another priest besides Spieker was the pastor of the church), one of them responded angrily: "Then who gave the last sermon?" To this Spieker answered, "That was I." The men then identified themselves as Gestapo officers and demanded that Spieker give them his name. Spieker refused to do so, saying, "You will have to take the matter to the vicar or the bishop. They alone have authority over me. I will have nothing at all to do with you." "You have to give us your name," they insisted. Spieker simply responded, "No, I don't have to do that, and I will also not do that," and thereupon turned away and left the men standing where they were.[9]

Although the two men decided to let the matter rest on this occasion, the Gestapo took to harassing Spieker wherever he went. Among other things, the Gestapo made regular telephone calls to him at his residence in the Canisius College in Berlin, where he stayed two weeks of each month while carrying out his pastoral duties there, ordering him to report to Gestapo headquarters. But Spieker steadfastly refused to go, referring the Gestapo officers to his church superiors, just as he had done in Cologne. Before long the constant whirr around the outspoken priest had so unnerved the leaders of the Catholic Church in Berlin that they decided to relieve him of his duties there. From that time on, Father Spieker worked solely in Cologne.

When the Cologne Gestapo finally arrested him on Monday, November 19, 1934, it did so almost at his own behest. After his sermon on Christ the King Day, Gestapo officers made several visits to the Jesuit residence in Cologne's Stolzestrasse during the first two weeks of November, asking to speak with Father Spieker. But each time Spieker asked someone to tell them that he was not in. On Saturday, November 17, they came three or four times. Spieker and everyone else around him now realized that his arrest was imminent. He could have fled, but he chose not to. He also did not want to be arrested during a meeting with his men's groups, which he wanted to prepare for what was now certain to come. After doing this in a meeting with the leaders of these groups from the entire city on Sunday the eighteenth, Spieker received a call from his church superior ordering him to report to the Gestapo the next morning: "The Gestapo has been searching for you. You are to report tomorrow morning at once."[10] Spieker did not believe that his superior should have ordered him to do this at the time, but he complied. The next morning he called the Cologne Gestapo. "Gentlemen, you wanted to speak with me," he asked. "*Jawohl*," an officer replied. "When will you be there?" "I am there now," Spieker responded. "How long will you be staying there?" "That, I don't know. Whatever the case, if you wish to speak with me, you will have to come immediately." "Good, we are on our way."[11] A few minutes later Spieker was under arrest.

The two Gestapo officers who arrested him treated him politely: they addressed him with the formal German *Sie,* let him go back alone into the Jesuit residence to gather his things, and assured him that he would not be harmed. In his autobiography, Spieker contrasts these men (one of whom may have been the later head of the Cologne Gestapo's Jewish desk, Karl Löffler), who came from the "so-called old criminal police,"[12] with the head of the Cologne Gestapo, whose office he was taken to almost immediately. In Spieker's description, this was "a very young man, smart and all dressed up," who also treated Spieker politely but with an obvious measure of sarcastic disdain. After being offered a cigarette, Spieker asked the officer why he had been arrested. The officer responded, "You know that already. We have warned you often enough." Spieker then replied, "You have nothing to warn me about. I have nothing to do with you. I am only subordinate to my [religious] superiors and to the bishop's authorities. What particular charge has been made?" After a few more verbal exchanges, the officer tried to cut the discussion off by telling Spieker, "I am not here to carry on a dialectical debate with you." But Spieker wanted the last word:

> Good, then tell me at least one thing. You have had me taken in protective custody. Then there should be something to be protected. You do not need to protect me. No one has done anything to me and nothing will happen to me in the future. But if you believe that my arrest is necessary for peace and order, you are making a mistake. Until now, nothing I have done has disturbed peace and order. But if you allow me to be arrested, you will soon experience that they will be disturbed indeed because of my arrest.[13]

The police and judicial investigations preparatory to Spieker's trial stretched out for four more months. On orders from Berlin Gestapo headquarters, Spieker spent the first three weeks of this time in protective custody in Cologne's Klingelpütz prison. As the key turned in the lock of his cell on the first day of his arrest, Spieker knelt and prayed a *te deum* and then felt completely at peace. "I was internally happy and content," he later recorded in his autobiography. "Now I had my peace, both internally and externally. I had no more responsibility, at least not for the moment. . . . Jail was for me a real respite."[14]

Before the first day of his confinement was over, Spieker had been visited in his cell by his defense attorney, Dr. Viktor Achter, a highly respected man who had also defended many Communists. Together they planned the main lines of Spieker's defense. Both in his interrogation and at his trial, Spieker would admit of no guilt. Through it all, he would insist that he had never been active politically and that no political connotations should be construed from any of his remarks, whether in his sermons or elsewhere. In regard to the belief of his denouncer and the Gestapo that he had used the word *Führer* during his sermon in the Mariä Himmelfahrt Church to slander Adolf Hitler, Spieker told the Gestapo that he had not been thinking of the present chancellor at all. He had referred to Christ as the "Führer" because that was the best way to describe him given current German usage of the term. He had made a direct mention of Napoleon, whom he considered to have been a false Führer, and he had also made indirect references to other false Führers like Nero. But not once during his entire sermon had he ever mentioned Hitler. In the signed testimony Spieker gave to the Gestapo, he explained:

> As such, Christ has always been referred to by the most diverse titles at the most diverse times, according to the conception of the masses at the time. He himself used the title of master, because that was the highest title used by the Jews at the time. Our forefathers called him king. Since for us Germans there is now no more emperor and no more kings, rather the word *Führer* is the term used for the highest ruler, I have assigned this expression to Christ.[15]

If the Gestapo met with little success in getting Father Spieker to cooperate, it did not fare much better with prosecution witnesses during its investigation. Not one person came forward to say a word against the beloved priest that might have served to corroborate Mathias K.'s accusations. During one of his sessions with the Gestapo on November 22, Mathias K. named

Josef B., a fellow teacher from Krefeld, as a witness. But when the forty-five-year-old Josef B. provided his own testimony on December 14, he remained sketchy on all of the details and said that he could not state with certainty that he had even been present at Father Spieker's sermon on the day in question. As he told the Gestapo:

> I cannot with certainty maintain that I attended the Mariä Himmelfahrt Church in the Marcellenstrasse of Cologne at 11:15 A.M. on Christ the King Day, 28 October 1934. Indeed I was there at the 11:00 A.M. mass perhaps twice in both September and October. In November and December I no longer attended Sunday mass in the Mariä Himmelfahrt Church. In my last three visits, I came considerably late, so that I did not hear very much of the sermons. I can only remember that there were at least two different men who delivered sermons, whose names, however, I cannot provide. In regard to the sermon in the case in front of me, I cannot make any comment. In particular, I can in no way remember that a preacher made derogatory remarks of any nature about the Führer concept. Since I usually came too late, I did not comprehend the fundamental ideas of the sermons in their full context and, therefore, I followed the preachers' words with no great interest.[16]

Even Mathias K.'s own wife, who had probably attended church with her husband on Christ the King Day (she was reputed to be a strong Catholic and supporter of the Center Party), refused to back her husband up. When the state prosecuting attorney Rebmann and his assistant came to Mathias K.'s home on January 11 to hear for themselves what he and his wife had to say about the case (Mathias K. could not go to the prosecutor's office because he was suffering at the time from a severe eye infection), Mrs. K. burst angrily into the room where the men were speaking and exclaimed: "We do not wish under any circumstances to have Father Spieker punished for the contents of his sermon." After she had repeated this several times, her husband grabbed her by the arm and emphatically demanded that she leave the room.[17]

A new warrant for Spieker's arrest was issued on February 15, 1935.

(Spieker later maintained that he had been let out of prison in December because Germany wanted to minimize its bad publicity on the eve of the Saarland plebiscite scheduled for January 15, 1935—when the people of the Saarland would vote on whether to reunite with Germany.[18] They did, overwhelmingly so). Spieker's arrest followed on March 2, and he was put in Klingelpütz prison once again to await his forthcoming trial. The trial opened nine days later on March 11 at 9:15 A.M. before an overflow crowd of his supporters and other onlookers in the courtroom of the Cologne Special Court. Landgerichtsdirektor Franz von Vacano formed a forbidding presence as the presiding judge with his gleaming bald head, pointed white beard, and volatile nature. Previously a mere local court judge who had been called at the end of the past year to head the Cologne Special Court, von Vacano was a "150 percent" Nazi in the opinion of Father Spieker and many others. He was also known to be a fervent Catholic with twelve children and a thirteenth on the way. Some have commented that he had little trouble balancing his Catholic beliefs with his Nazi convictions: "Herr von Vacano went to church at 8 o'clock and began condemning clergymen at 9."[19]

The trial lasted six hours. From beginning to end, Father Spieker refused to make any direct comment about the content of his sermon, maintaining steadfastly that he was responsible only to his religious superiors and not to any worldly court. At several intervals, Judge von Vacano almost became apoplectic at this tactic, screaming in rage at Spieker and the Catholic Church for their audacity. Spieker himself remained calm and answered the judge's demands that he speak to the charges against him with a reasoned argument that the Concordat between Hitler and the Vatican guaranteed the church complete freedom in the exercise of its religious rites, including full freedom of expression in religious sermons.

Spieker's attorney, Dr. Achter, added to his defense by reminding the court that Spieker was highly respected and admired throughout all of Germany, that he had a distinguished war record, and that he was well known for standing up against the Communist threat. As Achter explained, Spieker had heroically volunteered to serve the German nation during the First World War and had almost sacrificed his own life several times. He had contracted typhus while working in frontline military hospitals rife with extremely infectious diseases and had many times given transfusions of his own blood to save the lives of severely wounded soldiers. Furthermore, Spieker had long been noted for his anti-Communist beliefs and activities, on several occasions having led large processions of his men's groups through dangerous working-class sections of Cologne in attempts to change the workers' spiritual and ideological leanings. Finally, Achter brought attention to the fact that the only evidence against Spieker rested on the unsubstantiated testimony of an agitated and highly subjective witness. Given these facts, he argued, Spieker would have to be acquitted.[20]

Father Spieker was then given the final word. In his autobiography, Spieker recalled that he warned the judges to be mindful of their responsibilities, for they too would eventually be called to answer to God for their verdict, and He could not be deceived. In God, Spieker said, he placed his trust. He therefore had no fear of what the verdict in this case might be.[21] The newspaper accounts, which had to be cautious, did not mention these bold final statements. Nevertheless, they did record that Spieker sharply denied that he had ever done anything to harm the German nation, and they stressed Spieker's brave struggle against Communism in the past and against the neopaganism movement that he believed was in the ascendancy at the time. According to the *Westdeutscher Beobachter*, Spieker ended what had almost become another provocative sermon with the following words: "Seldom has Catholicism been so abused as by this movement. I must fight against this as a Catholic priest, and I will continue this fight until the very end, for Christianity is the only foundation upon which a state can grow. He who undermines this foundation transgresses against the German people. My watchword is and remains: Everything for Germany and Christ!"[22]

The judges then retired to their chambers to decide on the verdict. When they returned to the courtroom two hours later, they raised their arms in the Hitler salute and loudly greeted the onlookers with a hardy "Heil Hitler!" Von Vacano then read their verdict: "The accused, because of insufficient evidence, is acquitted."[23] The people in the courtroom responded with what the Cologne Gestapo would later describe in Spieker's case file as "tumultuous ovations,"[24] clapping loudly and cheering "Bravo! Bravo!" as they jubilantly registered their approval that for once in the Third Reich justice had been served.

Sadly, this happy moment in German jurisprudence would be short-lived. While the crowd filtered out of the courtroom building just after three o'clock in the afternoon and proceeded to hold a spontaneous victory celebration in the streets, the Gestapo registered its disapproval by taking Father Spieker into protective custody. It justified this move in a letter to Gestapo headquarters in Berlin's Prinz Albrechtstrasse as necessary to protect "peace and order" and "to protect the endangered personal security of the priest given the excitement of the population."[25] For the next six weeks, Spieker sat once again in Klingelpütz prison, but this time he was kept in solitary confinement. He could neither receive visitors nor attend church services, and he was allowed to take only a thirty-minute daily walk in the prison's courtyard under the guard of a prison official. Each day of his confinement Spieker was pressured by the Gestapo to sign a statement promising that he would stop delivering sermons in the future. Spieker refused to sign. Two days before the end of April, Spieker was informed that he was to be sent to a concentration camp.[26]

One day later, Spieker boarded a special prison car added on to a local passenger train, which took him first to Münster, where he spent a night in jail, and then onward over Meppen, where he met up with other prisoners destined to join him in the concentration camp. Finally, he arrived at Börgermoor concentration camp. Located in the Emsland in Germany's northwestern corner, Börgermoor was sometimes called the "Dachau of the North." When Spieker arrived on May 1, 1935, he found that almost all of the 2,000 other prisoners were Communists. A notable exception was the pacifist author and journalist Carl von Ossietzky, who received the Nobel peace prize in 1935 while sitting in Börgermoor. As the only Catholic priest, Spieker was labeled "the preacher" (Der Pfaff) by the SS guards and was later called this by his fellow prisoners as well, and like Ossietzky, he was frequently singled out for especially harsh treatment.[27]

In his autobiography, Spieker describes the horrors of his concentration camp existence. "At the entrance was the reception. The torture began already from that point on."[28] Ordered to run from one place to the next, they were first tripped and beaten by the guards, then forced to lie down on their bellies and crawl like snakes to the washroom. There the guards took away their clothes, shaved their hair to the scalp, and herded them into a burning-hot shower. They then received concentration camp garb, which for the first fourteen days—the worst period that most prisoners had to endure, according to Spieker—included a yellow armband identifying them to the SS guards as "free game" to prey on sadistically.

The workday began before daybreak. At 3:00 A.M. the prisoners were awakened. After a meager breakfast, they were counted and then marched for roughly half an hour to an area where they were forced to shovel up the sandy soil, load it onto iron wheelbarrows, and transport it at a running pace to another destination, with no apparent rhyme or reason, until six o'clock in the evening. To make sure that the prisoners worked with dispatch, SS men stood behind them with outstretched rifles and bayonets and lightly stabbed them from time to time as they carried out their backbreaking work. Spieker's descriptions of this ordeal match well with those of others who experienced life in Börgermoor concentration camp. As one former prisoner described a typical day:

> Speaking was forbidden. . . . Any violations were punished with the rubber truncheon. Whoever did not fill up his shovel to the satisfaction of the SS guards' taste would get to feel the bayonet once again. We were starved, the sun burned down. We got nothing to drink. By the evening one could pull our burned skin away from our bodies. . . . We thought that we would be given a moment's rest, but no, none at all. We got nothing to eat or drink. But we did get one pause: to sing. . . . At six the work ended. Ten comrades had fallen in the meantime. They had not been able to withstand it. They were simply left there in the red-hot sun.[29]

Spieker was not accustomed to such physical strain, even though he had a sturdy constitution. After a few days, he broke down and fell unconscious while pushing one of the sand-filled wheelbarrows. Unable to revive him, some Communist prisoners were then ordered to bring him to the morgue. But he awoke there the next morning and was sent immediately back to work. After this, his strength gradually returned, and he held up well from that time on.

Emotionally Spieker did not seem to have any particular difficulties: by this time he was used to spending long periods in confinement. Nonetheless, the SS overseers made continued attempts to break him down. Often they called in Spieker and another inmate who was a Protestant minister to discuss the ideals of the Nazi movement. The minister allowed himself to be made a fool of and obsequiously told the SS whatever they wanted to hear, but Spieker held to his personal beliefs and said only what he believed. On one occasion, the SS demanded that he relate what people told him during confessions. When Spieker refused, he was told he would be shot. On another occasion, an SS guard ordered him to walk in the strip known as the "path of death" along the electrified, barbed-wire fence where prisoners would be machine-gunned without warning by the guards in the high watchtowers overhead. Spieker wisely refused to do that as well. What pained Spieker more than the SS's chicanery, which he expected, was a growing feeling that he had been forsaken by his church superiors after his arrest and trial. He was concerned by reports he had received that the church considered both his former anti-Nazi activities and his conduct in the courtroom "very unwise."[30] But what bothered him the most was that he and the other prisoners were so abused and mistreated by their fellow Germans. "Had 'Hottentots' done that, I would have understood it, but that our own countrymen, who believed themselves to be cultivated, had treated us in this manner was inconceivable to me."[31]

After several months had elapsed, probably in November 1935, Father Spieker was brought to a different concentration camp in Berlin near the Tempelhof airport called Columbia-Haus, where many prisoners were brought for questioning by the Berlin Gestapo before being put on trial. Soon Spieker learned that he too would have to stand trial once again and that a new case was being prepared against him in Cologne. As he awaited his new trial, he had an easier time of it, for the most part, in Columbia-Haus than he had had in Börgermoor. Spieker came to believe that somehow he was being protected and that his better treatment had been ordered from above. In that he had not yet been proven guilty of anything and was about to come before the German public once again, perhaps the Nazis wanted to limit the adverse effects that any disclosures about his ill treatment as a Catholic priest might have on German public opinion. Hence, the kind of physical and psychological punishment he had suffered in Börgermoor came to a stop. The only thing that seemed particularly uncomfortable for Spieker at this time was that he had to share a cell with a man charged with illegal homosexual activities who believed that Spieker must have been similarly inclined. This was not an unrealistic assumption on the man's part, even though it was false. A large number of the Columbia-Haus inmates were there for violating the notorious "paragraph 175" against homosexuality of the German criminal code. Alleged violations of paragraph 175 were among the most common charges the Nazis leveled against Catholic priests in their growing campaign to destroy the influence of the church over the German population.

In January 1936, Spieker was brought back to Cologne and placed once again in Klingelpütz prison. His trial took place on January 20 in the same packed courtroom, before the same three judges, and with the same prosecuting attorney who had tried him ten months earlier. But this time his accusers were far better prepared. Spieker was put on trial for abuse of his religious office (*Kanzelmissbrauch*). Seven witnesses testified that he had repeatedly used the pulpits in both Cologne and Berlin to wage an illegal campaign designed to turn the German people against the Nazi government and its leaders. One of the specific charges brought against Spieker was that he had made statements during his sermons and public speeches such as, "God will bring the German people to their knees"; "We have only one Führer, that is the Holy Father in Rome, and otherwise no one"; "We have only one Führer, that is Jesus Christ, there is no other one"; and, "That is not a Führer who is there for a couple of years and then disappears." Additionally, Spieker, after pointing out that Jesus Christ himself was a Jew and not an Aryan, had rhetorically asked in a loud voice during one of his sermons, "Have we sunken to the level of animals?" and then ironically said, "Soon one will come and say that everything that God has wrought is Aryan." Another time, during a dinner prayer he composed before a group of young people, Spieker had reputedly said, "May we give our soul to the devil, our heart to a girl, and our life to Adolf Hitler."[32]

When Spieker took the stand, he defended himself in much the same way he had done in his first trial. As he later recalled his words, he said: "Gentlemen, I stand by the same position today as I stood in the first trial: You are not competent to pass judgment in this case. But at the end of the first trial, you said to me, Herr Chairman [von Vacano], that I was a coward since I did not address the charges against me. To demonstrate to you that that was not cowardice, rather a fundamental belief, I will now address the charges made against me. But I repeat: Not you, rather my superiors alone, are competent to judge if what I have said was correct."[33]

Spieker and his defense attorney, Dr. Achter, refuted the charges made against him as vigorously as they could. But this time the judges were not convinced. Whereas in the previous trial they had almost bent over backward to interpret Spieker's remarks and actions in a light favorable to the priest, even fudging parts of the written judgment to make it seem that his words had not really slandered Hitler, they were in no mood to do this again.[34] They deliberated for only three-quarters of an hour before rendering their verdict. This time Father Spieker was convicted.

Oddly perhaps, Father Spieker's conviction may have been a godsend. By sentencing him to a prison term of fifteen months, the judges may have spared him from a far worse fate. Had the judges not found him guilty this second time, the Gestapo probably would have sent him to a concentration camp for an indeterminate period, and Spieker might not have survived.[35] As Spieker himself explained, "In comparison with concentration camp, prison was a wonderful time, only extremely boring as I did not get a decent book to read."[36] In prison the guards were not from the SS, and Spieker found their methods to be "somewhat more humane," especially since they made no direct use of torture and did not justify the deaths of prisoners by claiming that they had been "shot while trying to escape."[37]

Spieker spent most of this period in a prison in Wittlich along the Mosel River in the part of Germany called the Eifel. He also spent briefer periods at the beginning of his term in jails in Siegburg, near Cologne, and in the Aschendorfermoor, not far from where he had previously been interned in Börgermoor concentration camp in the Emsland.[38] The warden of the Wittlich prison was also a Protestant minister, and he treated Father Spieker with considerable respect and dignity, encouraging him on several occasions by telling him that he had heard rumors that Spieker would soon be set free. But Spieker had learned to be distrustful and worried that the Gestapo might have him "shot while trying to escape" if he left jail as little as one minute before his term expired.

On Friday, February 19, 1937, Spieker's prison term came to an end. (Two months of his time awaiting trial had been subtracted from his sentence.) Officers from the Cologne Gestapo picked him up by car and drove him to the Cologne Gestapo headquarters. There he learned officially what he had already heard informally, namely, that his religious superiors had struck a deal with the Gestapo that guaranteed his safety so long as he promised to leave the country immediately and stop all resistance activities. But Spieker remained suspicious, believing by this time that he could trust neither the Gestapo nor the church. When the Gestapo gave him a grace period of two and a half days to gather his things and visit with his family before leaving the country, Spieker surreptitiously telephoned an old friend from his school days, a woman named Frau Brenninkmeyer, who held Dutch citizenship and whose deceased husband had been the former head of the C&A department store in Cologne. Immediately Father Spieker and Frau Brenninkmeyer made plans to cross the border by car the following Monday. On Monday morning, he had his siblings (two sisters who were nuns and a brother who was also a Jesuit priest) call Gestapo officials and tell them that he was leaving by train at seven o'clock. At noon he went to the train station and called the Gestapo himself to say that he was buying his train ticket. But instead of going by train, Frau Brenninkmeyer drove him during a blinding snowstorm across the Dutch border to the Ignatius College of the Jesuit Order in the town of Valkenburg, Holland, just outside of Aachen. Dressed in civilian clothes, and with his Dutch friend Frau Brenninkmeyer at his side, the border crossing took only a few minutes. This was fortunate. Just as he had expected, the Gestapo had been waiting for him at the train-station crossing at the Dutch border. "The Gestapo had something planned for me. . . . But the 'Bird' had flown away!"[39]

Whether the Gestapo wanted to shoot him as an escapee, send him back to concentration camp, or merely wish him bon voyage will probably never be known. He was now safely out of harm's way. Nevertheless, he was not well received at the Ignatius College in Valkenburg. "As a former concentration camp inmate and as a person persecuted by the Nazis, I was not happily seen; one wished that I would quickly disappear. Over and over again I was asked: 'When are you leaving?'"[40] It was not only his fellow Jesuits in Holland who held this attitude. While awaiting his second trial in Cologne's

Klingelpütz prison at the beginning of 1936, he had asked to speak with the head of the Jesuit Order in Rome to inform him and the Vatican of his experiences as the first Roman Catholic priest in a Nazi concentration camp. But the Jesuit Father General Wlodimir Ledochowski refused Spieker an audience. Now that Spieker had left the country, he once again had the feeling that his church superiors considered him a nuisance. To his mind, he had been given "the boot," not just by the Nazis but by the church as well.[41]

It comes as no surprise to learn, therefore, that Spieker also received no hero's welcome after he had made his way by freighter across the Atlantic Ocean to Santiago, Chile, where he landed on May 1, 1937, after a voyage lasting thirty-three days. Even in Chile, the local leadership of the Catholic Church soon became uncomfortable with him, and General Ledochowski in Rome rebuked him several times by letter for anti-Nazi lectures he had given and saw to it that he was sent to a small village in the Chilean hinterland some 600 miles away from the capital city.[42] In 1950 Father Spieker returned to Germany. He died on September 29, 1968, in Düsseldorf.

THE CAMPAIGN AGAINST THE "LICENTIOUS" CLERGY: THE DEATH IN DACHAU OF FATHER G.

Father Spieker's banishment to Chile most likely saved his life, but it was a great loss to Germany. Thousands of other priests and ministers also came to experience the wrath of the Nazi terror apparatus, and many later died in concentration camps or at the hands of Nazi executioners.[43] Very few German clergymen, however, displayed the moral courage and personal heroism of the unsung Josef Spieker or the better-known heroes of the religious resistance movement, such as the archbishop of Münster, Clemens August Graf von Galen, or the Protestant theologians Martin Niemoeller and Dietrich Bonhoeffer.[44]

Indeed, the majority of Catholic and Protestant clergymen who suffered under Nazi persecution had little to do with outright resistance or protest against the Nazi regime, though this does not mean that their suffering was any less painful. Commencing in 1935 shortly after Father Spieker's original arrest in November 1934 and reaching a peak two years later, the Nazis waged a venomous campaign to weaken what they believed to be the dangerous hold that the Catholic Church had over the hearts and minds of the German Catholic population. SD reports about the mood and morale of the people depicted the Catholic Church as the most fertile hotbed of real and potential resistance against the regime now that the influence of the political left had been eliminated.[45] Placing too much credence perhaps in these reports, the Nazis reversed their original policy of seeking compromise with the Catholic Church to one of promoting confrontation. At the heart of this campaign was a huge propagandistic effort to undermine the church's authority by lambasting it for promoting sexual and moral iniquity, especially by harboring homosexual priests who, the Nazis claimed, used their positions of respect and authority to lead German youths astray. Using as a legal justification the long-standing and notorious paragraph 175, which had outlawed homosexual acts between men since the Kaiserreich, the Nazis initiated a witch-hunt that led to several highly publicized trials in 1936 and 1937 and to the arrest and incarceration of hundreds of Catholic clergymen.[46]

After a temporary pause in the witch-hunt had been mandated and several trials had been suspended for propagandistic purposes during the Olympic Games in the summer of 1936, the witch-hunt and trials resumed in early 1937. On March 14, 1937, Pope Pius XI finally spoke out critically and publicly, though cautiously, against the Nazis' persecution of German Catholics in violation of the terms of the Concordat of July 1933 and their dissemination of neopagan doctrines. His words were issued through an encyclical entitled "With Deep Anxiety" (*Mit brennender Sorge*), which was read from all Catholic pulpits in Germany on Palm Sunday, March 21, 1937. The Nazi government immediately outlawed the publication of the text, the Gestapo confiscated all copies it could lay its hands on, and the mere mention of it was made a criminal offense. Hitler, irate that the Catholic Church had dared to defy his authority in such a public fashion, ordered the resumption of the trials against Catholic clergymen on April 6 and laid plans to have all Catholic youth groups amalgamated into the Hitler Youth.[47] On May 28, 1937, Goebbels brought the reheated propaganda campaign against the Catholic Church to a climax by taking to the airwaves to deliver a speech heard nationwide in which he condemned "the ulcer on the healthy body of Germany." Fulminating that the "sacristy has become a

bordello, while the monasteries are breeding places of vile homosexuality,"
Goebbels charged that the Catholic Church proclaimed ignorance while
knowingly concealing and thereby condoning homosexual activity. He also
condemned the church for spreading atrocity tales abroad while promoting
traitorous activity at home. To curb the church's malevolent influence, he
called for an end to the Catholic education of German youth.[48]

All of this struck a painful nerve in the German Catholic Church hierarchy, especially in the Rhineland, where some of the most publicized trials
against homosexual priests had taken place. In attempts to demonstrate that
the Catholic Church did not in fact condone and promote moral turpitude,
Cologne's Cardinal Karl Joseph Schulte had more than once delivered pastoral messages condemning homosexuality among the clergy while at the
same time deploring the Nazis' unjustified and blanket defamation of the
church. On March 12, 1937, two days before Pius XI delivered his famous
encyclical, Cardinal Schulte spoke out once again. In his new proclamation,
he remonstrated against the sinful activity of several Catholic clergymen
revealed in the morality trials and made it clear that the church would not
tolerate such behavior in the future. At the same time, he also reiterated his
complaint that the reportage on the trials was highly tendentious, egre-
giously exaggerated, and damaging to German youth.[49]

Perhaps to demonstrate that the church wanted to distance itself from
charges that it condoned licentious behavior on the part of its clergymen,
and perhaps for other reasons, the Krefeld Catholic Church made a sacrifi-
cial lamb of one of its young priests at precisely this time. On March 10,
1937, the parish rector of the Catholic church in Krefeld-Ürdingen wrote a
letter to the district leadership of the Nazi Party. It had been called to his
attention, he wrote, that several Catholic youths had been sexually molested between 1931 and 1933 by an assistant priest (*Kaplan*) named Suitbert G., who had served during that period as the local leader of the Catholic
youth organization.[50] Apparently to make certain that the charges against
Father G. were justified, the rector had previously called several youths to
his office to tell him personally about their experiences with the assistant
priest before he informed the Nazi Party leadership. These boys, now sixteen to eighteen years of age, had been between eleven and thirteen when
they were molested.

The experiences the boys related to the rector appeared to be fully believable. Out of their lengthy testimonies, a portion of the account by one
boy, who was thirteen at the time of his association with Father G., suffices
to give an impression of what the rector was told.

> I had the responsibility of handing out the youth association's
> monthly publication. In this capacity I came to him frequently in his
> room in the rectory. Because I always went to him to give my confes-
> sion, he knew all about me. When I was with him in his room, he once
> showed me a book in which there were pictures from artists and naked
> figures. As I sat beside him, he grabbed hold of my hip and fondled
> [me]. Because I always confessed to the same sins, he told me that he
> wanted to see my penis. At first I held back from this request. [But
> then] he protested over and over again and even threatened that he
> wanted to send me to the doctor to investigate the matter. . . . I had to
> lie down on the sofa. Then he opened up my pants and took out my
> penis. He played with it and stimulated it.[51]

Eight days after the rector sent his letter to the Nazi Party leadership in
Krefeld, the Krefeld Gestapo summoned six of the boys and one forty-two-
year-old elementary school teacher, who had been named by the rector as
someone who could provide additional information about the matter, to Gestapo headquarters to provide testimony. Each of the boys told the Gestapo
essentially what they had told the rector. The schoolteacher's testimony
provided a small twist in the case. He did not appear to know much about
the specifics of Father G.'s relations with the boys, but he was able to tell the
Gestapo about a meeting he had with Father G. sometime in 1934. The
priest had told him with tears in his eyes that he was being transferred to
another city because he had been accused of mistreating some of the youths
in the parish. The schoolteacher explained to the Gestapo that he had then
tried to comfort Father G. by telling him that he need not be so upset and
that he should simply go and give his accuser a punch in the nose. But Father
G. replied to him that he could not do this because his accuser was his immediate superior. All of this suggests strongly that the rector had known about

Father G.'s behavior for at least three years before he informed the authorities in March 1937.

Father G. was summoned to testify himself two and a half weeks later, on April 5. At the time, he was serving as an assistant priest and head of the Catholic youth organization in Mönchengladbach-Waldhausen, where he had been since he left Krefeld. The son of a Krefeld book dealer, Father G. was thirty-three years of age. He was a tiny man, five feet four inches tall (1.63 meters), with blond hair, blue eyes, and regular features. He was also well educated. Before he was ordained in 1931 and sent to Krefeld-Ürdingen for his first post, he had attended university in Bonn and a seminary in Bensberg. In his typed testimony, which ran for five single-spaced pages, he first denied the charges against him and asked the Gestapo for its sympathy because he had suffered from heart and nervous problems ever since he had been beaten up by a farmer youth in 1931. He explained that, though he had indeed met with several boys in his chambers, he had done so only to help them overcome the sexual problems they had divulged to him during their confessions. He admitted that he had in fact rubbed some of the boys' penises on occasion, and that sometimes this had caused them to ejaculate, but he said that he had been completely surprised by this response and that he had only been trying to determine how "ripe" they were. After making this limited confession, his testimony was broken off. After being reproached, he continued his testimony, admitting to having had more experiences with the boys than he had originally admitted to. He continued to maintain, however, that he had been primarily concerned with the children's "development."

The Gestapo arrested him immediately upon the conclusion of his interrogation and placed him in investigative detention preparatory to trial. Less than five weeks later, on May 10, 1937, the Krefeld county court convicted him on the charge of molesting children under fourteen years of age and sentenced him to serve one year and nine months in prison. Coming as it did in the middle of the Nazis' propaganda campaign against the priesthood, this case received considerable attention in the local newspapers. Long articles appeared the day after Father G.'s trial in the *Westdeutscher Beobachter*, the *Rheinische Landeszeitung*, and other newspapers with headlines like "A Chaplain from Ürdingen Convicted of Morality Offenses" and texts that explained, "He knew them extremely well from their confessions. He heard about their failings and exploited them to satisfy his lechery."[52]

After serving his sentence in Lüttringhausen penitentiary, Father G. was released on January 8, 1939. Having been suspended from his priestly duties by the church, he went to stay with his brother, who was a school-teacher in a small town not far from Cologne. Five months later, he was arrested once again, this time by the Mönchengladbach Gestapo after it learned that he had continued to molest children while he had served in that city. On June 2, 1939, the now thirty-five-year-old Father G. gave his testimony. After strongly denying "with a plain and simple no" that he had continued to practice homosexuality after he had left Krefeld, he was shown the written testimony, given earlier that day, of a sixteen-year-old appren-tice mechanic who claimed that he had been sexually abused by the priest. After Father G. continued to profess his innocence and had spent the night in jail, the boy was summoned the next day and brought into the room with Father G. for a face-to-face confrontation (a typical Gestapo tactic during interrogations). The boy, for his part, said that he continued to stand by his signed testimony and that he was ready to deliver it under oath before the court. Father G.'s only defense now was that he could not remember what had happened.[53]

As in many Gestapo cases dealing with sexual matters, the boy's writ-ten testimony was long and detailed. In five single-spaced typed pages, the boy began by elaborating for a full page on having first been "led astray morally at the age of nine." Then he revealed some of his sexual activities at the age of eleven. Finally, he led into a discussion of his association with Father G. by explaining that he had first told Father G. during confession of his sexual activities when he was either eleven or twelve. He did not confess, however, to any involvement in homosexual activity. Rather, he explained to the Gestapo that he had merely told Father G. during confession that he had once masturbated with another boy after the two of them had talked about girls. According to the boy's testimony, Father G. summoned him soon after his confession to his chambers, told him to sit on his lap, and discussed his confession with him. Father G. then took the boy's penis and testicles in his hand and began rubbing them. When the boy's penis did not become hard, Father G. sent him home. Not long after this, Father G. called him to his lodgings a second time and asked him whether he had gotten stiff after thinking about their conversation. After the boy said that he had not, Father G. offered him the position of altar boy and told him to go to confession and communion more often. The boy's testimony, which by this time had turned into more of an interrogation, was then broken off, and the Gestapo warned him to tell the truth. He then admitted to having masturbated several times in the company of other boys, to masturbating by himself once every three to four weeks, and to having taken part in a kind of orgy with other boys of his age and several girls aged ten to thirteen, all of which he described in graphic detail, with specific dates and the names of the others involved.

The Mönchengladbach Gestapo officer conducting the interrogations of Father G. and the boy wrote up a final report on the case two days later. He stated that Father G. was not to be believed, but that the boy certainly was, especially since he came from a good family. Father G. was kept in jail for the next six months before he was put on trial once again, this time by the Mönchengladbach county court. During this period, the Mönchengladbach Gestapo carried on a detailed correspondence about the case with the regional headquarters of the Gestapo in Düsseldorf, which in turn corresponded with the nationwide Gestapo headquarters in Berlin. On January 5, 1940, Father G. was convicted for a second time and sentenced to prison for a period of one year and six months, minus the time he had spent awaiting trial. Once again he served his term in Lüttringhausen. But when he was released from prison this time, the Gestapo did not let him go free. The Düsseldorf Gestapo held him for two months in protective custody and then sent him to Dachau concentration camp on April 23, 1941. He did not come out alive. According to a telegram the Düsseldorf Gestapo received from Dachau, Father G.'s brother was to be informed that Father G. had died of pneumonia on January 19, 1943. After nearly six years of misery, his ordeal was over.

NAZI TERROR AND EVERYDAY RELIGIOUS PROTEST

The cases of a near saint like Father Spieker and a tragic sinner like Father G. seem miles apart, but they share significant similarities. Both men served in the priesthood; both were tried before Nazi courts; both spent long periods in protective custody, prison, and concentration camp; and both of their cases were widely discussed in the media.

More important than these similarities is the handling of these cases by the Nazi justice system and the church. In each man's case, the justice system acted cautiously. Father Spieker, despite his repeated attacks on Hitler and the Nazi regime, was acquitted in his first trial by a troika of judges presided over by a judge renowned and rewarded for his fidelity to the Nazi cause. Later, in his second trial, Spieker received only a moderate sentence from the same troika of judges who had let him go the first time. Father G., despite almost incontrovertible evidence that he had repeatedly molested children in more than one community, received only comparatively light sentences in both of his trials. Had he been tried by a court of law in many states of the United States or many other countries, he might have received harsher sentences. Because Nazi judges sometimes proceeded cautiously and sentenced leniently, especially in religious matters, some have argued that Nazi judges—who were usually conservatives, but not necessarily convinced Nazis—did what they could to dispense reasonable justice in an unreasonable and unjust society.[54] This may have been the case as far as their own motivations were concerned. Nevertheless, their moderation in many cases also served the more ignoble purposes of their leaders, perhaps even more remarkably than either they or the Nazi leadership understood. The Nazis were sensitive to the mood and the values of the German population. How better to enlist and hold the people's support than to provide them with the veneer of legality provided by a justice system that seemed to observe faithfully the positivistic traditions of German jurisprudence? When the Nazi regime needed to resort to dirty work, it could always call on the secret police, which it relied on to settle matters discreetly after ostensibly fair judicial rituals had been performed in public. Hence, in the cases of Father Spieker and Father G., what the public observed were fair trials. What it did not observe was that both men were sent to a concentration camp after the court had finished with them.

Also noteworthy is the position taken by the church in both cases. The Catholic Church was ill at ease with each of these men and perhaps did not do all it could to make their plight easier. This is somewhat understandable in that both men had put the church in a compromising position with the authorities, and in Father G.'s case, with the public as well. Nevertheless, in Father Spieker's case, the church demonstrated that it would not risk further difficulties with the Nazi regime by letting him relate the truth of what was happening in Nazi concentration camps. Furthermore, when it learned about Spieker's antiregime activities in Berlin, it sent him back to Cologne. When he continued to agitate against the regime in Cologne, and after he had served out his sentence, the church removed him to Chile. When he continued to speak out in Santiago, it banished him to the Chilean hinterland. In no place did the church honor him as a hero; its authorities continually rebuked him for being "unwise."

One might ask what the Catholic Church should have done differently with a man like Father G. He had offended against all standards of decency. He had brought much dishonor to the church and inflicted much harm on individual people. At first, the church responded as it had done with Spieker. It sent him to another locality. Later it turned him in to the Nazis. Could it not have found another solution? From the Spieker and Father G. cases, one can only conclude that the Catholic Church did not want to risk any confrontations that it could possibly avoid with the Nazis. It spoke out on occasion, as Pius XI did in his famous encyclical, to defend its religious rights. But it often turned a blind eye toward the terrible injustice that was all around it.

At the end of the war, the German Catholic Church felt itself under attack for having complied with the Nazi regime. To counter this criticism, Munich's Cardinal Michael Faulhaber, who only months earlier had characterized the Second World War as an exemplary model of a just war and the attempt on Hitler's life as an abominable criminal act, called in April 1946 for an elaborate study of Bavarian clergymen that would demonstrate once and for all "the powerful and nearly universal resistance of the clergy against Nazi ideology and church policy."[55] In the questionnaires returned over the following months by individual bishops and priests, and in the following years in similar studies carried out in the rest of Germany, nearly every instance of suffering and harassment that the Catholic clergy had endured at the hands of the Nazi regime was conscientiously recorded. Although there can be no doubt that these studies uncovered sobering evidence of the Nazis' persecution of individual Catholic clergymen, not all have been convinced that the evidence reflects a significant amount of resistance and protest on the part of the Catholic Church.

In a recent volume that examines the record of protest and persecution in the Saarland district, Gerhard Paul and Klaus-Michael Mallmann call into question what they call "the myth of the Catholic resistance" that studies of this type helped to create.[56] They argue that these studies have uncritically and apologetically inflated the persecution of individual clergymen—often for acts, like those of Father G., that had nothing to do with antiregime behavior—and the church's occasional attempts to register its displeasure with the Nazis' religious policies into a myth of systematic protest and resistance by the church itself. Thus, they strongly reject the concept of *Resistenz* that the Munich historian Martin Broszat made popular in the early 1980s in his multivolume, edited work on Bavaria during the Nazi period, characterizing it as no more than petty acts of nonconformity and noncompliance that had no larger meaning and, as applied to the Catholic Church, were largely exculpatory.[57] Hence, acts like the Catholic Church's refusal to ring its church bells on Easter Sunday 1937 in response to the closing of church schools did not mean "that the church now had nothing more in common with the government," as some have argued.[58] In Paul and Mallmann's estimation, only direct acts of protest against the Nazi regime were of any real significance, and these were confined to only "a few critical individuals and small groups."[59] In sum, they do not believe that there was much real conflict between the Nazi state and the Catholic Church, and they maintain that the Catholic Church largely cooperated with the Nazi regime. Even for its part, they explain, "the Nazi state in no way intended to liquidate the church, rather [it sought] merely the limitation of the church's influence to religious matters. Not necessarily conflict and struggle, rather coexistence . . . characterized the relations between Catholicism and National Socialism."[60]

The revisionist position taken by Paul and Mallmann strongly contradicts that of many of their countrymen and that of the Catholic Church
itself, but it finds plenty of support in the works of many foreign scholars.
Some American historians, for example, have pointed out that the Catholic
Church largely accepted and even supported National Socialism as a bulwark against communism and liberalism. Just five days after he published
"With Deep Anxiety," Pope Pius XI issued a similar encyclical against the
evils of communism.[61] Throughout the years of the Third Reich, the Catholic Church time and again sought to demonstrate its fidelity to the Nazi state
and its patriotic fervor. From the Concordat with the Nazi government in
July 1933, which gave papal blessing to the ending of democratic government and to the destruction of Catholic political and economic organizations, to the last years of Hitler's reign, when the Catholic Church continued to support the war effort and maintained silence about the slaughter of
European Jewry,[62] the church failed again and again to protest the worst
excesses of National Socialism. Instead of screaming out in shock and re-
pugnance, it held its silence over the "Night of the Long Knives," the concentration camps, the "Night of Broken Glass," and the Holocaust.
Throughout it all, the church's bishops continued to admonish the Catholic
population to render obedience to Hitler. Even the celebrated archbishop
of Münster, Clemens August Graf von Galen, whose open and courageous
sermon in the Lamberti Church in Münster on August 3, 1941, criticized
and helped bring to an end the Nazi euthanasia program that had claimed
the lives of over 70,000 innocent people, did not advocate forceful resistance
against the regime or measures that might have harmed Germany's ability
to carry on the fight against its enemies.[63]

What held true for the Catholic Church held in even greater measure
for the mainstream Protestant churches. Although Protestants were in the
minority in Rhineland cities like Cologne and Krefeld,[64] they were in the
majority in most of the rest of the country. Several small denominations,
such as Jehovah's Witnesses, Seventh-Day Adventists, and Baptists, were
pejoratively referred to by the Nazis as "sects," but in the main most of the
German Protestants were Lutherans and members of the state-sponsored
Evangelical Church. In 1934 the Evangelical Church split into two major
wings, a somewhat larger one known as the "German Christians" and a

smaller one known as the "Confessing Church." Of the two, the German Christians supported Hitler and National Socialism more fervently. But the Confessing Church was not as radical as some would have us believe, and like the German Christians, it never fully severed its ties to the established Evangelical Church.[65]

Even before the Nazis came to power, the Evangelical Church showed a preference for Hitler's movement. In the city of Moers, for example, the church's fellowship hall (*Vereinshaus*) served as early as 1931 as a meeting place for local Nazi gatherings.[66] From the time of its foundation under the ardent Nazi Joachim Hossenfelder in the spring of 1932, the German Christian Church did everything it could to prop up and support the Nazi movement. Proclaiming its followers "the stormtroopers of Jesus Christ,"[67] its ministers preached virulent anti-Semitism, male chauvinism, and a blood-and-soil ideology of extreme nationalism and patriotism. The church's organization mirrored that of the Nazi Party, with Hossenfelder at the top as *Reichsleiter* before he was replaced in November 1933 by another young Nazi pastor in his midthirties named Christian Kinder, and with the descending ranks below the *Reichsleiter* of *Landesleiter, Gauleiter, Kreisleiter,* and *Gemeindegruppenleiter*.[68] Needless to say, no resistance came from this faction of German Protestantism, whose "political theology" promised to set Christianity in a war against Marxism, mammonism, and pacifism, whose children donned the Hitler Youth uniform for confirmation, whose churches hoisted the swastika for their church flag, and whose services routinely featured the singing of the Nazi anthem, the "Horst Wessel Lied."[69]

The Confessing Church, on the other hand, had a more ambiguous relationship with National Socialism. It included famed resistance figures like Martin Niemoeller and Dietrich Bonhoeffer among its members, and many of its disciples did what they could to uphold Christian principles of humanity and decency against the onslaught of National Socialism.[70] Niemoeller was arrested after he delivered a sermon critical of the Nazis before a large congregation in Berlin-Dahlem on June 27, 1937, put on trial before the Berlin Special Court in March of the following year, and sentenced to seven months in prison. After his release, the Gestapo sent him first to Sachsenhausen concentration camp and later to Dachau, where he remained until the Allies liberated him in 1945. Bonhoeffer had an even worse fate. Arrested for his links to the German resistance in April 1943, he remained in custody until a summary court-martial ordered his execution, which was carried out on April 9, 1945, only one month before the war's end. But these men were exceptions, and the Confessing Church was not at all synonymous with Protestant resistance against Hitler. More typical of its members were those who either stayed away from political issues or supported the Nazi regime. Many were Nazi Party members.[71] Although the Nazis remained wary of Confessing Church ministers and many of the Confessing Church ministers had cases started against them, especially after Niemoeller's arrest in 1937, relatively few were sentenced to lengthy prison terms or sent to concentration camps.[72] As was the case with the Catholic clergy, the Gestapo neither wanted nor needed to resort to full-scale repression against them. Most Confessing Church clergy remained loyal to the National Socialist regime and were patriotic Germans to the end. Even Niemoeller, who had been a U-boat commander in World War I, wrote a letter to Hitler from concentration camp offering to serve the Fatherland in World War II.[73]

If there are good reasons to question whether the resistance efforts of the clergy have been exaggerated, it is nonetheless no myth that after the first few years of Hitler's rule the Gestapo and the Nazi Party singled out the clergy for heavy doses of repression to guarantee their silence and their parishioners' obedience. Thousands of clergymen, both Catholic and Protestant, endured house searches, surveillance, Gestapo interrogations, jail and prison terms, fines, and worse. Most of these people were not heroes, and many clergymen undeniably gave support to the Nazi cause. But in a situation where the heads of the Catholic and Protestant churches were unwilling to take a strong stand against a repressive regime, or to offer much encouragement to those of its members who did, and in the face of the near certainty of severe punishment for individual priests and ministers who chose to stand up in protest, how many Spiekers, Galens, Niemoellers, or Bonhoeffers could one expect to find in any population? The efforts of the priests and ministers who did speak up or offer resistance, even if more limited than the efforts of the most celebrated figures of the resistance movement, need also to be respected, and their plight acknowledged.

TABLE 6.1 *Judicial Investigations of Clergy (Cologne Area)*
and Catholic Priests Sent to Concentration Camps for
Nonmorality Offenses (Entire German Reich), 1933–1945

YEAR	INVESTIGATIONS[a]	CONCENTRATION CAMP REFERRALS[b]
1933	12	0
1934	51	3
1935	112	8
1936	104	1
1937	260	8
1938	93	3
1939	71	37
1940	11	69
1941	7	112
1942	3	72
1943	0	43
1944	4	47
1945	0	14
?	0	1
TOTAL	728	418

a. Based on a computer analysis of the entire register of the Cologne Special Court files.
b. Based on surveys of 8,021 Catholic priests analyzed by Ulrich von Hehl in *Priester unter Hitlers Terror: Eine biographische und statistische Erhebung* (Mainz, 1984), lxxxviii.

The evidence from the Cologne Special Court files and from the Krefeld Gestapo files illustrates the intensity, timing, and nature of the Nazi regime's efforts to quiet the clergy. It also reveals that many clergymen and religious Germans did in fact take issue with National Socialism, if mostly in rather minor ways. Some indication of the volume, timing, and severity of the cases lodged against German clergymen is provided in table 6.1.

There are two types of data in table 6.1, from two different sources. The middle column presents yearly figures for the total number of Catholic and Protestant clergymen in the Cologne area who had cases initiated against them by the Cologne Special Court. These figures are based on a computer analysis of the entire register of the Cologne Special Court case files, which has information on the cases of 28,920 people.[74] The column at the far right provides yearly figures on Catholic priests sent to concentration camps for all but moral grounds. They are based on surveys compiled by the German Catholic Church, and analyzed by Ulrich von Hehl, that include information on approximately 42 percent of all German Catholic priests in the Third Reich.[75]

The figures in the table show that cases were started by the Cologne Special Court against a large number of clergymen in the Cologne area. (There were only a small number of cases of clergywomen, all of whom were Catholic nuns.)[76] Although it is impossible to state exactly how many of these were Catholics or Protestants without reading each of the case files, one can safely assert that the vast majority involved Catholic priests who were most typically charged with libeling or slandering the Nazi government or its leaders in the course of one of their sermons. In a random sample of twenty-four of these cases, only two involved Protestant pastors; one started in 1934 on the charge of slandering the Nazi Party, and the other started in 1939 on the charge of a currency violation.[77] Of the twenty-two cases involving Catholic clergymen in the random sample, fourteen were based on grounds of libel or slander, three on failing to hoist the Nazi flag on a holiday, and one each on an assortment of minor charges, from staging illegal church gatherings to fraud. Only one case involved the extremely serious charge of conspiring to commit high treason, but this case was dismissed before going to trial in 1938 after the denouncer took back his accusation against the priest.[78]

The timing of the Special Court cases reinforces the observations already made about the Nazis' crackdown on the clergy between 1935 and 1937. Nearly two-thirds of the cases began in these three years, and 1937 marked the crescendo of the Nazis' campaign against the church: more than twice as many cases were started in that year as in any other year.

The number of judicial investigations started against the clergy declined steadily after 1937 and almost disappeared during the war years. The severity of the punishments meted out to the clergy, however, appeared to follow a different progression, according to Hehl's figures. Cases in which a priest was sent to a concentration camp for a nonmorals offense, like Father Spieker's case, were rare before the war. Between 1933 and 1938, only twenty-three priests about whom Hehl was able to gather information met with such a fate. Thus, according to Hehl's figures, about 89 percent of priests who ended up in a concentration camp were sent there during the war years. Why there were so many concentration camp referrals of Catholic clergymen during the war but so few cases in general lodged against them is uncertain. One possible explanation may stem from the Nazis' concern for public opinion. Open trials of clergymen during the war could have had a damaging effect on public opinion. To counteract such an unwanted development, the Nazis tempered their open campaign of harassment of the clergy after the war broke out. Besides, most priests and ministers had already been silenced by the Nazis' measures against them in the 1930s. For those few who continued to pose a potential threat to the regime during the war years, the Nazis could use their concentration camps to remove that threat, for concentration camp referrals were usually shrouded in secrecy.

Despite the fact that many clergymen were sent to concentration camps during the war, the overwhelming majority of the cases against clergymen did not involve severe punishments. In the random sample of clergymen's cases that I read from both the Cologne Special Court files and the Krefeld Gestapo case files, nearly every case was dismissed before trial. This outcome does not necessarily mean that the ordeal was not harrowing and frightening for the accused clergymen. In several of the cases, the clergymen spent lengthy periods in custody before their cases were dismissed; in two of the cases, the clergymen were so fearful about what might happen to them that they fled the country to escape arrest and punishment. In one of these cases, a forty-year-old Cologne priest had been accused of making seditious statements against the regime to a group of 1,500 young men in a sermon delivered in an open field in the town of Bödingen during a Catholic pilgrimage in June 1937; he spent several months in jail before his case was dismissed in April of the following year. Interestingly, for the present purposes, one of the critical remarks he was accused of making was that, in his opinion, too few priests had spoken out against the Nazis. As he sarcastically told the pilgrims (and to great applause, it was noted in his case file), only 60 of the roughly 25,500 German Catholic priests had cases pending against them at the time, so the rest of the priests, as he ironically put it, were surely "model citizens." In another case, a forty-six-year-old priest from Cologne-Höhenhaus had a nervous breakdown after he fled to Holland in December 1934 to avoid arrest for having made critical statements against the regime during his church sermons.[79] Nevertheless, Father Josef Spieker and Father Suitbert G. were the only clergymen in the sample of more than thirty random cases of persecuted clergymen in Cologne and Krefeld that I read who were sent to concentration camps by the Nazis. In Hehl's analysis, he found that of the 344 Cologne-area priests he was able to gain information about, only 21 were sent to concentration camps, and only 99 received jail or prison sentences. The most common punishment they received was a warning, which was handed out to 126 of the Cologne-area priests. The rest of the cases were resolved without even a warning.[80] Since Hehl's figures are not complete, it may be that there were more priests from the Cologne area who received harsh treatment under the Nazis. But this possibility is rendered somewhat doubtful when one considers that his analysis is based on the Catholic Church's own figures. Moreover, the church took great pains to provide information on every priest whom the Nazis punished, whether they were alive after 1945 and could take part in their surveys themselves or they were dead and information had to be provided about them by other means.

A documentary study undertaken by the former Krefeld Communist activist Aurel Billstein further supports the assertion that relatively few clergymen suffered harsh punishments. In his study, Billstein perused all of the Gestapo case files dealing with Catholic priests and Protestant ministers from the Krefeld area (thus including many neighboring communities, like the nearby city of Moers, as well as the city of Krefeld itself). Of 82 Catholic clergymen found in these files, only two were sent to a concentration camp, and only one had a court conviction.[81] Of 23 ministers from the Evangelical Church with a Krefeld Gestapo case file, none was sent to concentration camp or convicted by a court.[82] Again, it must be remembered that the Gestapo files are not always complete. Some priests and ministers may have been excluded. Father Suitbert G., for example, is not listed in this documentation. But that probably resulted from the fact that Father G.'s case was listed under "homosexuals" in the Gestapo files.

If the Gestapo and the courts dispensed harsh punishments for German clergymen only in exceptional cases, the authorities nonetheless manifestly

targeted Catholic and, to a lesser extent, Protestant clergymen for intimidation, especially during the mid-1930s. Few other groups in Nazi society had
as many cases lodged against their members, and few other groups were put
under such constant surveillance. Theoretically, there were thousands of
potential denouncers observing the activities and statements of clergymen,
since the members of their congregations were privy to their viewpoints
on a weekly and sometimes daily basis. But common citizens almost never
denounced clergymen. To the extent that denunciations played any role in
the initiation of cases against clergymen, they were almost invariably made
by Nazi Party members who held leadership positions in the Nazi movement, such as *Zellenleiter* or *Ortsgruppenleiter*, and sometimes by the
wives of these party members, who tried to camouflage their husbands' and
the Nazi Party's direct involvement.[83] Nevertheless, many clergymen were
spied on constantly. Party functionaries, Hitler Youth, regular police, and
Gestapo spies regularly sat in attendance during their sermons and tagged
along during their pilgrimages. Indeed, a few of the Gestapo's informants
were other clergymen.[84]

In only two of the cases in the random sample of clergymen that I read
was the case started by a denunciation from the general population. One of
these was the Father Suitbert G. case, in which his religious superior
brought him to the attention of the authorities. In the other case, the accusation was made by a young seminary student in Bad Godesberg in July 1934.
Although he had left the seminary in early March 1933, he waited for more
than a year to bring charges against one of his former Jesuit teachers. According to the student's statement of accusation, the priest had attempted
to organize his students into a revolutionary group that would infiltrate the
SA. Also, the priest had never used the Hitler greeting with his students and
instead had greeted them with the words *"Grüss Gott"* (Praise the Lord).
Finally, the former student alleged that the priest had constantly made
statements critical of the Nazi regime that were obviously intended to turn
his students against Hitler and Nazism. Among the statements he claimed
the priest had made were: "Göring set the Reichstag on fire"; "National Socialism is much worse than Bolshevism"; and, "An inflation is soon to come
because the German economy is constantly going backward."[85]

After the student made his accusations, the Cologne Gestapo sent two agents to search the priest's apartment. Although they found nothing of importance, they interrogated the priest on the spot. The priest denied the charges against him and told the Gestapo how painful it was for him to be denounced by a former pupil who was "a young man that I considered to be like my own child and who often called me his father."[86] Soon afterward a warrant was put out for the priest's arrest signed by Franz von Vacano of the Cologne Special Court. The priest then decided to leave the country before he could be taken by the police. Four years later, the case against him was dismissed. This transpired primarily because the denouncer, by then a university student in Munich, wrote to the Cologne Gestapo in March 1937 saying that he wished to take back his denunciation. The reason he gave was that at the time he had made the denunciation he was "fanatical" for the Nazi cause and that he had kept company with anti-Catholic and anti-Jesuit comrades who had made his fanaticism all the greater. The Cologne Gestapo thought this odd on his part and saw to it that he was interrogated by the Munich Gestapo on April 15, 1937. The Munich Gestapo reported back to the Cologne Gestapo soon afterward that he seemed "very unsteady" and that he was "a very strong smoker with fingers that were strongly discolored from nicotine."[87] Nevertheless, he continued to hold to his new story, so the charges against the priest were belatedly dropped.

Although the documentation in this case makes it impossible to know whether the priest had in reality tried to organize a revolutionary conspiracy, or even whether he had made the statements his student originally accused him of making, it does seem logical that he had taken an anti-Nazi position with his students at the beginning of Hitler's regime. Why else would he have decided to flee the country? If he had been supportive of the Nazis or merely neutral toward them, he could presumably have counted on many of his other students to back him up.

Indeed, his case is only one of several cases in the random sample in which a clergyman did appear to make something of a stand against the regime. Few of these cases were as dramatic as this priest's or Spieker's; nevertheless, many individual priests and ministers showed more courage and conviction than some revisionist scholars have given them credit for. In addition to this case and the Spieker case, one could return to the case of the priest on the pilgrimage in Bödingen in June 1937 and to several others for supporting evidence. During the pilgrimage, the priest did more than merely criticize his fellow priests for not standing up to Hitler and the Nazi regime. A policeman who spied on him during the pilgrimage told the Gestapo that he had done things like ask the crowd: "Where is the freedom to express oneself and [where is] the law in Germany?" At another point, he reputedly stated to the pilgrims, "Germany is the most unfree country. What do they say abroad about this? In America one has to be ashamed of himself as a German." Finally, the policeman claimed that the priest had lamented to the pilgrims that he did not care if he died ten years earlier or later because "in Germany there is no life anymore. The truth has to stay the truth."[88]

One could also point to several other examples of clergymen, almost all Catholic in the sample, being turned in to the Gestapo by Nazi Party members or other Nazi authorities for allegedly criticizing Nazi society in their sermons. But the case for clerical protest should not be overstated: most of the priests and ministers found in these case files did little more than stand up for their religion. Nevertheless, even that alone is of some significance.

The fact that ordinary Germans almost never denounced priests and ministers helps to demonstrate that many Germans continued to take their religion seriously during the Nazi years and that Hitler never completely won over the hearts and minds of a considerable percentage of the German population. A large number of the case files illustrate this point even more strongly. In the small town of Bergheim, for example, for which I read every one of the existing Special Court cases, more than 25 percent of the cases involved religious matters in one way or another (twenty-two out of eighty-seven cases). Although a few of these cases involved attempts by the Nazi authorities to intimidate priests and ministers, most of them centered on a struggle between religious and National Socialist symbolism. Two examples serve as illustrations.

In the first case, which began in late May 1934 and continued to be a source of agitation among the religious townsfolk of Bergheim for several months thereafter, the Nazi legal authorities manipulated religious symbolism both to garner the support of the local populace and to carry out a crackdown on the local SA.[89] It started on the night of May 28, 1934, when a local policeman filed a report about the damage done to a small statue of Saint Nepomuk that stood on a bridge over the Erft River located in the center of the town on the main shopping street. No one was mentioned specifically in this report. The policeman noted only that the Nepomuk figure had been beheaded and that Nepomuk's head had been replaced by a turnip wearing a bishop's cap with a swastika on it. Nothing further happened in the case for the following two months except that it led to an outpouring of wild rumors about the Nazis' disrespect for the deep religious beliefs of Bergheim's mostly Catholic population.

Had Hitler not decided to take action against the leadership of the SA in the infamous "Night of the Long Knives" on June 30, 1934, and to carry out a nationwide policy of curbing the SA's power and influence in the months that followed, probably nothing further would have transpired in the case. But in the wake of the extralegal Röhm assassination, it was imperative for the Nazi regime to find ways to demonstrate to the German population that it was on their side and that the repression of the SA was being carried out in their interest. A report filed with the Bergheim police on July 16, 1934, by a sixteen-year-old Hitler Youth who claimed knowledge of the perpetrators in the Nepomuk affair fit neatly with the new Nazi policy. Conveniently, this report named several members of the local SA battalion as the beloved Nepomuk's beheaders.

Over the next few days, nearly twenty additional citizens, including many local SA members, were summoned to police headquarters to provide further details in the case (which was handled by Hauptwachmeister Servos). Four young SA men from Bergheim and one from the neighboring town of Frechen, all of working-class background, were arrested and charged with the crime of aggravated property damage. From the testimonies of the witnesses and the men charged in the case, one learns that the Nepomuk figure had been vandalized in the early morning hours of May 28. Several local SA men, fired up from a night of boozing and dancing at a beer-tent party organized by the local SA, had stumbled home through the streets of town and spontaneously decided to lop off the Nepomuk statue's head for nothing more than a petty thrill.

The arrest of these men seemed to pacify the Bergheim population, but it did not sit well with the local SA troop. Even though little happened to these men and they were released after only a brief period in detention because of a general amnesty for SA men throughout Germany, many members of Bergheim's SA battalion continued to chafe from their newly demoted status in Germany generally and from the shabby treatment they felt some of their members had received locally in the Nepomuk affair. Some of them sought revenge.

One of the ways they did this was by attempting to clean house and taking action against some of the members of their own local battalion who had provided testimony in the Nepomuk case, leading to the five arrests. One of these was a thirty-two-year-old man named Hans W., who was arrested by the local SA leadership and placed in one of the special cells in the local Bergheim jail that the SA had commonly used for its own arrestees in the past. But the SA's right to jail people was taken away by a governmental decree of July 25, 1934. After this decree came into effect in Bergheim two weeks later, on August 13, the Bergheim police ordered that the SA would no longer be able to keep Hans W. in the Bergheim jail. Nevertheless, Hans W. was kept in the Bergheim jail for three more days; he was then moved to the local SA headquarters and held for an additional day before being released. At that time, he filed a complaint with the police that led to the arrest of one of the heads of the Bergheim SA battalion, Obersturmbann-führer Hans S.[90]

A series of charges were quickly filed against Hans S. that would keep him in jail for most of the following year;[91] thus signaled that the SA's old mode of operation would no longer be tolerated, Bergheim's SA battalion became even more intent on seeking revenge. Soon bets were being taken among the SA troopers in Bergheim and neighboring towns as to how fast the Nepomuk statue would lose its head again and be delivered to the SA headquarters in the nearby town of Horrem. After another night of boozing, this time at an SA sports festival in Horrem on October 7, 1934, two men who resided in the Bergheim SA battalion's barracks on Hindenburg-allee 6/8 decided that they would win the bet. One of them, Albert W., had been charged in the original attack on Nepomuk, but the other, Alfred M.,

had previously stayed out of the fray.[92] Wearing civilian clothing and felt
slippers to conceal their deed, the two men beheaded Nepomuk anew at approximately 3:40 A.M. and drove off in the direction of Horrem in a car they
had parked some distance away from the bridge over the Erft. Unfortunately for them, they were not able to get away with the crime. At about
5:00 A.M. they got into a traffic accident, and the attending doctor, himself
an SA man, soon provided details to the Cologne Gestapo, which had taken
over the case from the local police, about their dress and demeanor that jibed
with eyewitness reports of the crime. Both of the men, upon release from
the hospital, were arrested by the Cologne Gestapo and placed in Cologne's
Klingelpütz prison, where they remained for two more months before their
case was dismissed on December 12, 1934. The men were subsequently forbidden to return to Bergheim and transferred to another SA post in Wuppertal. This ended the Nepomuk affair.

    This also ended the Nazis' short-lived policy of taking the side of the
Bergheim townsfolk in religious disputes. By the end of 1934, the Nazis had
successfully destroyed any potential opposition from their most important
enemies both outside their movement (Communists and Socialists) and inside their movement (the SA). Since both the Marxists and the SA had a
reputation for godlessness, it had been expedient for the Nazis to make con-
cessions to religious interests in the first two years of Hitler's rule. By 1935
this no longer seemed necessary, and the Nazis now sought to replace the
people's old religious devotion with devotion to their own secular cause. As
shown in table 6.1, the year 1935 marked the beginning of a great escalation
in the number of cases initiated against clergymen. It also brought a significant escalation in cases involving religious symbolism. From this time
onward, the Nazis no longer sought to protect the sanctity of Christian
symbols and images; rather the Nazis sought to strip them of their power
and influence and to replace the people's devotion to the Christian cross and
the Christian savior with devotion to their own Nazi hooked cross and their
own Nazi savior.

    Sacrilegious attacks by Nazi extremists in the SA, SS, and Hitler Youth
on Christian statues and symbols continued to be a source of antagonism
between the religious faithful and the Nazi state throughout the 1930s and
reached such alarming proportions that even many Nazi Party members

reacted in anger and disgust.[93] Nevertheless, the Nazi regime opted to step up the pressure by clamping down more forcefully on Catholic youth groups,[94] by enforcing more strictly the Reich flagging law of October 24, 1935—which mandated that churches fly the Nazi flag on all state and religious holidays[95]—and by stepping up the campaign to destroy the church's influence in the schools. Increasingly in the mid-1930s, the hostility between Nazis and Christians came to center on the crucifix, especially in the context of education. As Ian Kershaw reports in his study of popular opinion in Bavaria:

> Rumours circulating in and around Munich that all wayside crosses were to be removed and the setting-up of new crosses prohibited were already in 1935 causing alarm in the rural population. According to the report of the Munich police, the peasantry was particularly susceptible to such scare-mongering because of their superstitious worries about the blessing for the harvest. Though the removal of crucifixes or disrespect shown towards the cross was the focus of a number of isolated incidents in the early years of the dictatorship, it was in the context of the fight for the retention of the denominational school that the crucifix came to acquire symbolic significance as the representation of the continued dominance of *Kreuz* over *Hakenkreuz*.[96]

An excellent example of the struggle between the cross and the hooked cross took place in an outlying rural village attached to the town of Bergheim at the beginning of the new school year in April 1937.[97] On April 17, three days before Hitler's forty-eighth birthday, the local school superintendent (*Kreisschulrat*), Bernhard E., paid a visit to the small primary school in the village of Wiedenfeld. Shortly after he entered one of the two classrooms, which were typical of the German *Volksschule* at the time, he noticed that a large crucifix, more than a meter in height, hung on the wall at the front of the classroom in back of the teacher's desk, and that the mandatory picture of Adolf Hitler hung on a side wall in the classroom out of the immediate field of the students' vision. Angered by this violation of Nazi school policy, he demanded that the teacher reverse the positions of the two images. The young teacher, Werner J., felt that he had no choice but to comply with this order. He realized that doing so would not be popular with many of the people in the village, but he had only begun his teaching career a few days earlier and was still untenured. Besides, it would have been dangerous for him to stand up to the school superintendent, who was an influential man in the local Nazi Party, a member of the Nazi Party honor court in Bergheim, and also a member of the SS.[98]

When the children returned home from school, some of them reported to their parents the events that had taken place. Before the day was over, rumors spread outward from the village of Wiedenfeld about attacks made on the image of Christ and on the church generally, and soon the entire town of Bergheim was in an uproar. Among the rumors was that the image of Jesus had been hung upside down and that the local pastor in Wiedenfeld had been arrested and carted off to prison.

Three days later, on Hitler's birthday, the Bergheim population demonstrated their anger against these alleged abominations by refusing to hang Nazi flags from their homes. Even the leading Nazi in the village of Wiedenfeld, a thirty-six-year-old Nazi Party *Zellenleiter* and farmer named Hubert W., took the side of his fellow villagers and did not fly the flag from his residence. Four days later, on April 24, he took an even bolder step to demonstrate his solidarity with his townspeople by ordering the teacher Werner J. to rehang the images of Christ and Hitler in their former positions.

Forthwith a series of accusations streamed into the local police headquarters, one of the first of which was made by the wife of the local mayor against a neighboring housewife. The head police officer in the village of Wiedenfeld, a man named Münch, was then called on to make a full investigation of the matter. In a report filed on April 26, he wrote:

> The population of Wiedenfeld registered their indignation over the rehanging of the crucifix by refusing to put up the Nazi flag from their houses on the birthday of the Führer. Flags were hung from the house of the mayor, the school, the monument, the post office and the restaurant Krosch. [But] even the political leader of the NSDAP Hubert W. from Wiedenfeld had not hung the flag on these grounds.[99]

When Kreisschulrat Bernhard E. got wind of the wild rumors that had been spread throughout the community and the news that the images had been returned to their original positions, he was beside himself. Once again he ordered that the images be reversed, and on April 28 he went to police headquarters in Bergheim and filed his own accusation against "all of the instigators and propagators of these senseless rumors," except for the Nazi Party functionary Hubert W., for whom he planned a separate case with the local Nazi Party honor court. Already by the time he made his accusation, eight of the ten people eventually charged in the case had been interrogated at police headquarters and numerous witnesses had been called. The Bergheim police detective Schleiden and the police officer Servos conducted most of the interrogations with the aid of the Wiedenfeld police officer Münch. Five of the accused came from Wiedenfeld, and the rest came from Bergheim proper. They ranged in age from thirty-three to seventy-two. Four were women, and six were men. Farmers, miners, and housewives, they represented a cross-section of the local population. In the end, only two men were arrested, and only one, a fifty-five-year-old miner from Wiedenfeld with a wife and six children, was made to stand trial on the charge of slandering a government official. He admitted during his interrogation on April 26 that he had told other workers at the nearby mine where he worked about his ten-year-old daughter coming home from school and telling him that the crucifix had been hung upside down on the side wall of her classroom. But why he alone had to face trial is unclear from the documentation in the case. Whatever the reason, the court that tried him on June 12 decided to acquit him, and the case came to an end.

At face value, all of this did not amount to much more than a tempest in a teapot. No one was penalized severely; only two persons spent any time behind bars. Illustrative, at most, of *Resistenz*, this small uprising did not demonstrate anything close to a full-scale rejection of Nazi society by the population of Wiedenfeld and Bergheim, or even by any large sector of that population. But by refusing to fly the Nazi flag on Hitler's birthday, these ordinary Germans did demonstrate that they took their religious beliefs and identity seriously and that they resented those who would try to elevate Hitler above God.

PAYING THE PRICE OF RESISTANCE:
JEHOVAH'S WITNESSES

The leniency with which the police and the courts handled most instances of religious opposition demonstrates once again that the Nazis could distinguish between minor acts of disapproval, registered against some of the regime's policies and leaders, and significant attempts to undermine the authority of the Nazi state. But the strong measures taken against recalcitrant priests like Josef Spieker and the pitiable pastor Suitbert G. remind one that the Nazis could act with utmost ruthlessness when they felt threatened. One group that dared to stand up to the Nazi regime as perhaps no other group did was the Jehovah's Witnesses, a group that encountered the ferocity of Nazi terror like no other except the Jews and the Gypsies.[100]

Founded by the American businessman Charles Russell and based in the United States since 1870, the Jehovah's Witnesses were a comparatively small religious minority in Germany, with about 30,000 members in 1933. Fervently religious, upright, sober, hardworking, this community of "earnest Bible scholars," as they were also known, came mostly from the lower classes, kept to themselves, saw themselves as neutral politically, and refrained from violence. Although some Nazi hard-liners, like the ideologue Alfred Rosenberg, constantly compared and associated Jehovah's Witnesses with Communists, freemasons, and Jews,[101] other Nazi leaders understood more correctly that such comparisons were completely false, for the Witnesses had little sympathy for and usually nothing to do with these groups. Had they been willing to make compromises with the new Nazi order and confined their activities to the religious sphere, as most other religious minorities did, the Nazis might have considered them only a minor nuisance and left them largely alone.[102] But the Witnesses were unbending.

Refusing to make any compromises with a regime that they came to view more and more as the incarnation of the devil on earth, the members of this tiny community did more than merely hold true to their religious beliefs. They courageously, often fanatically, took the offensive. Not only did they continue to meet, organize, and proselytize after they were banned in the spring of 1933, at first in the open and later underground, but they refused to use the "German greeting" of "Heil Hitler," even though it was a criminal offense not to do so. They also refused to take part in political ceremonies or to join Nazi political and economic organizations, even though it often cost them their employment, and they refused to let themselves be called up for military service, even after it became compulsory in the spring of 1935. When all they had to do to get themselves released from concentration camp, avoid being sentenced to long prison terms, or even escape the death sentence was to sign an oath promising to stop their illegal activities and renounce their religious faith, they almost invariably refused to sign. Worst of all from the point of view of the Nazis, the majority of Witnesses brazenly demonstrated their opposition to the Nazi regime by stuffing mailboxes and doorsteps with literature that pointed out specific instances of Nazi atrocities, cited Gestapo, police, and Nazi Party torturers by name, and called on the German people to turn away from the false prophet Hitler and to place their faith in the true savior, Jesus Christ.

The Jehovah's Witnesses paid dearly for their intransigence and courage. The first person to study their persecution in any detail, Friedrich Zipfels, argued in 1965 that Witnesses suffered "almost without exception" from persecution in the Third Reich, that 97 percent of them experienced one or another form of persecution, and that about one in three died as a result of that persecution.[103] Michael H. Kater, who wrote about them four years later, used a somewhat more stringent standard of persecution and placed the figure closer to 50 percent. Agreeing with Zipfels that they were persecuted horribly, Kater calculated that upward of 10,000 Jehovah's Witnesses were arrested and between 4,000 and 5,000 died in jails and concentration camps. Reckoning that one out of every two Witnesses spent some period of time under arrest and that every fourth member of the sect died while being incarcerated, Kater summarized their persecution by stating that "outside of the Jews, no other coherent group was so intensively persecuted in the Hitler period."[104]

Most recently, in 1994, Detlev Garbe, in a well-documented book on the fate of the Witnesses in Nazi Germany, has revised these figures downward once again. According to his careful estimate, about one-third of the 25,000 to 30,000 Witnesses who lived in Nazi Germany suffered imprisonment, perhaps 2,000 of them spent time in concentration camps, and about 1,200 were killed.[105] Whatever the correct estimate might be, such figures only begin to give one a sense of the priority the Nazis placed on cracking down on these people and the brutality they employed in the process. From the time the Nazis made their first arrests of Jehovah's Witnesses shortly after the Reichstag Fire in the late winter of 1933 to the very end of the Third Reich in the spring of 1945, the Nazis used nearly every means they possessed to "exterminate" the Witnesses (a term Hitler himself used in reference to them, just as he had with the Jews).[106] Before the Röhm purge in June 1934, the SA carried out unbridled terroristic attacks against the Witnesses by organizing boycotts of their stores, laying waste to their homes and workplaces during searches, and beating them unmercifully in SA dungeons. After the SA's role waned, Nazi courts and the Gestapo took over where the SA had left off, with no decrease in the level of sadism. If the Special Courts, which tried most of their cases, showed leniency in sentencing, the Gestapo "corrected" the courts' decisions by remanding the Witnesses to concentration camps immediately on their release from jail or prison. Usually each Gestapo post assigned a particularly zealous officer to lead the battle against the Witnesses. This officer would stop at nothing to extract the information he sought, threatening, beating, and sometimes killing the Witness during interrogation.[107]

The Gestapo officer in charge of most cases involving Jehovah's Witnesses in Krefeld was Otto Dihr. From the evidence in a case started against him on January 30, 1948, by a member of the Krefeld Jehovah's Witnesses for crimes against humanity, one gains some appreciation of his brutal tactics and of those employed by many of his Gestapo compatriots.[108] When Dihr testified on his own behalf in the case six months later in July 1948, he denied all charges against him. He was forty-six years old at the time. Although he was unemployed and living on social welfare, he listed his occupation as *Kriminalobersekretär*, the highest rank he had achieved in the Gestapo. He had a wife and a twelve-year-old daughter. Born in Krefeld to a family of small farmers, he was one of nine children. His only education was the primary school. He claimed that he did not have a chance to learn a trade on leaving school because he had to take up work in the fields to help care for his younger siblings. Several years later, in 1922, when he was twenty, he embarked on a police career, starting as a member of the Brandenburg *Schutzpolizei* performing traffic duty in Berlin until 1926. In April of that year, he was transferred to Krefeld, where he soon entered the Kripo. After Hitler came to power, Dihr became a member of the Krefeld Gestapo. In May 1937, he joined the Nazi Party.

Many specific instances of his crimes against humanity were brought out in the case. The twenty-seven-year-old woman who brought the original charges against him was still a member of the Jehovah's Witnesses and working as a clerk in Düsseldorf. After reporting that she had heard from many people that he had abused them and sent them to concentration camps without any legal recourse, she related her own harrowing experiences when she had been interrogated by Dihr in 1943.

> When I did not give him the desired information, he delivered a powerful slap on the face. He then called two other Gestapo officers on the telephone, who led me to the cellar. Soon Dihr showed up there. At the order of Dihr, both of the officers then stretched me out across a table standing nearby. After pulling up [my] dress, both of the officers then beat me on my behind with a stick or something like that. After many blows, the officers stopped for a while and Dihr questioned me again. When I continued not to provide a satisfactory answer, I was beaten anew until I said that I would testify. I was then brought back upstairs, where Dihr continued with my interrogation. I confessed to my crime, which was having worked illegally against the Hitler government, because I preferred to receive a death sentence than to be tortured to death. Because of the abuse [I suffered] I was not able to walk for several days, blood kept oozing out of the places where I had been beaten. . . . For the charge of conspiring to commit high treason, I was sentenced on August 1, 1944, to four years in prison. . . . Because of my beliefs, which rest on biblical teachings, I cannot swear to my testimony.

Other Krefeld Jehovah's Witnesses provided similar details about how Dihr had tortured and tormented them into making confessions. Others who had also been beaten by Dihr but were not Jehovah's Witnesses came forward and gave additional evidence against him, and they did swear under oath. It is an irony that Jehovah's Witnesses would not swear under oath. Although they were sometimes the only ones telling the full truth in such cases, they would not swear to their testimony for it was forbidden by their religion. In the end, the Krefeld Landgericht sentenced Dihr to two years in prison, minus seven months of the period that he had already served in an internment camp immediately after the war.

This evidence demonstrates that despite the Witnesses' ability to withstand brutal torture for considerable periods, the Gestapo almost invariably got the information it sought from them. For this, the members of this brave religious denomination were rewarded with lengthy jail and prison sentences, often followed by a trip to a concentration camp. Upon entering the concentration camps, they had to contend with barbaric initiation ceremonies like being beaten repeatedly with steel whips or having to bend down for hours on end with their hands clenched around their throats. They typically received the worst assignments, being forced not only to work at backbreaking and demeaning work like cleaning out the crematoria but to work seven days a week instead of the usual six.[109] Despite all of this, most Jehovah's Witnesses continued to stand tall and never broke down.[110] In the end, their martyrdom gained them the grudging respect of many of their arch tormentors. Himmler is known to have said in 1944 that he hoped to end their persecution after the war was over and resettle them in the east, where they would serve as a kind of eastern defense wall against Asiatic influence.[111]

A huge leafleting campaign carried out in June 1937 provides one of the best examples of the Jehovah's Witnesses' unwavering devotion to their cause and the Nazis' equally fanatic resolve to root out and destroy their dangerous influence. In this campaign, which commenced at precisely twelve noon on June 20, 1937, Jehovah's Witnesses went door to door throughout Germany to distribute copies of a two-page broadside entitled "Open Letter to the Bible-believing and Christ-loving people of Germany."[112]

The "Open Letter" contained strong language accusing the Nazi leadership of carrying out a brutal policy of persecution against members of their sect. It detailed several specific examples of that persecution, including examples of torture, sometimes leading to death, applied by Gestapo officers whom the letter specifically named. It decried the Nazis' attempts to brand the Jehovah's Witnesses as enemies of the state and as Communists and Jews. It provided an example of the exact language of an oath that the Nazis tried to get the witnesses to sign to denounce their faith. And it boldly proclaimed that Jehovah's Witnesses could neither be broken nor intimidated and that they were even prepared to go to their deaths if necessary to uphold their beliefs. Some representative excerpts from the text of the letter follow:

> For many years we, Jehovah's Witnesses, previously named Bible scholars, have taught our fellow countrymen in Germany about the Bible and its consoling truths and thereby in selfless fashion have given all we could to help alleviate the material and spiritual misery of millions of people.

> As thanks for this, thousands of Jehovah's Witnesses in Germany have been persecuted in the most inhuman manner, abused and incarcerated in jails and concentration camps. Despite the most severe mental pressure and despite sadistic physical abuse, even perpetrated on German women, mothers and children in tender ages, they [the Nazis] have not been able in four years to destroy the Jehovah's Witnesses for they will not allow themselves to be intimidated and rather continue to obey God and not human beings, just as in his time the apostle Christ had also done.

> As the above makes clear, the struggle is about depriving the German people of the Bible and persecuting all of those who are called to defend spiritual freedom and belief in the Bible. With Christian patience and because of modesty, we have held back long enough to bring these misdeeds to the attention of Germany and abroad. We have in our hands overwhelming proof of the gruesome abuse of the Jehovah's Witnesses mentioned above. Of this abuse we have evidence in particular about, among others, the Kriminal-Assistent Thiess from Dortmund, and Tennhoff and Heimann of the Gelsenkirchen and Bochum Gestapo. They have not shied away from torturing women with horsewhips and rubber truncheons. . . . We also have intimate details, com-

plete with names, about circa eighteen cases in which Jehovah's
Witnesses have been brutally murdered. At the beginning of October
1936, for example, the Jehovah's Witness Peter Heinen, who lived in
the Neuhüllerstrasse of Gelsenkirchen, Westphalia, was beaten to
death in the Gelsenkirchen Rathaus by members of the Gestapo. The
details of this tragic case were reported to the Reich chancellor Hitler.
Reich minister Hess and the head of the Gestapo Himmler also received copies.

Although some 100,000 or more copies of the "Open Letter" appear to
have successfully reached the mailboxes and doorways of people throughout Germany, scores of Jehovah's Witnesses who took part in the campaign
eventually had to pay a heavy price for their brave actions. The manner
in which Gestapo officers resolutely hunted down the participants in the
campaign is typical of the way they proceeded against Jehovah's Witnesses
in other cases. Once they got their hands on one of the witnesses, they
would beat him or her unmercifully until he or she divulged names and
details, causing a snowball effect: ultimately a great many Witnesses in several localities would be severely punished. Many of them died as a result.

The first Jehovah's Witness involved in the leafletting campaign to be
apprehended was a fifty-five-year-old Krefeld worker, First World War veteran, and father of six children named Hubert H. who had already served a
six-month jail sentence in the previous year for his activities as a Jehovah's
Witness. Hubert H. was caught red-handed by a Nazi Party *Zellenleiter*
named Ludwig W. while he was distributing the last of his copies of the
"Open Letter" in Krefeld's Prinz Ferdinand Strasse. Ludwig W. arrested
him and escorted him straight away to the Krefeld Gestapo headquarters.
Kriminalassistent Otto Dihr then took over his case. During his interrogation, which stretched out over several days, Hubert H. tried valiantly not to
provide the Gestapo with any information that might incriminate others.
In his first interrogation statement of June 22, he admitted to being a member of the Jehovah's Witnesses and to having taken part in distributing the
letters. Otherwise, he tried to lead Dihr on a false path. In his original version of the events that had taken place, he told Dihr that he had left his
apartment in Krefeld at eleven-thirty on the morning of June 20 to look

for his runaway cat. When he got to the gate of his apartment building, he encountered a young girl who asked him whether he was Hubert H.; he replied that he was. She then gave him a folded, handwritten letter bearing the inscription of the Jehovah's Witnesses; he subsequently read it in the bathroom of his apartment. This letter instructed him to go to Krefeld's main train station by twelve noon. There he would be met by a woman in dark clothing holding a white handkerchief in her left hand. She would recognize him because he would be holding a white handkerchief in his right hand. She would then give him twenty-five copies of a letter that he was to place in the mailboxes of people in Krefeld. The *Zellenleiter* Ludwig W. arrested him when he had only three of these remaining.

Dihr was not at all satisfied with this story and interrogated Hubert H. a second time on the same day. Again Hubert H. told him that he did not know the names or whereabouts of the young girl or the woman he had met. He also said that he could not describe how they looked because his encounters with them had been so brief. He did admit that he knew that handing out the letters was an illegal act, but he said that he "had done it nevertheless to carry out the will of the great creator Jehovah." Other than this, he claimed that he did not know anything more about the Jehovah's Witness movement or about the letter campaign.

Two days later, Dihr interrogated Hubert H. again. This time Hubert H. told Dihr what he wanted to find out and provided information about the case that led to the arrest of eight other people—five men and three women, mostly miners, housewives, and common laborers. Hubert H. started his new testimony by saying that "after I have been thoroughly warned to tell the truth, and the advantages of giving a confession have also been brought before my eyes, I declare hereby that I now wish to tell the truth." Clearly Hubert H. had been severely warned about the consequences for himself and his family of further refusal to divulge information. From what is known about Dihr's methods in this and other cases, it is likely that Hubert H. had also suffered immense physical and mental torture over the previous four days. In Dihr's own write-up of the case, filed nearly a month later on July 16, he explained that his interrogation of Hubert H. had, of necessity, been "exhaustive," and that it "had stretched out over several days chiefly because of Hubert H.'s stubborn denials."

In his new version of the events leading up to his arrest, Hubert H. admitted that he had fabricated his original story. In truth, he had been aware of the impending letter campaign for a long time. After he had been let out of jail in December 1936, he had been contacted by the leader of the sect in nearby Rheinberg and Moers, a forty-six-year-old train engineer named Johann C., who asked him to continue to take part in the Jehovah's Witnesses illegal underground activities. In the spring of 1937, he met another man, a fifty-four-year-old miner named Heinrich T., who gave him specific details about the impending letter campaign, which was to be carried out "across the entire country." Heinrich T. told him that the campaign would commence everywhere at precisely twelve noon and that it would last for exactly one half-hour. The story Hubert H. had related to Dihr originally, he said, was the same story that all Jehovah's Witnesses in the entire country were instructed to tell if they were caught.

Kriminalassistent Dihr then placed Hubert H. in protective custody and proceeded to arrest and interrogate all of the other eight people he had named. According to the report Dihr filed on July 16, all of these people also tried obstinately to withhold information, but all confessed in the end.[113] The first to be interrogated was a twenty-eight-year-old, single machinist named Karl H. of Krefeld. After a long ordeal, Karl H. finally told Dihr that he had been a member of the Jehovah's Witnesses since 1933 and that he had taken part in the campaign on June 20. After naming several people who had also taken part, his interrogation was broken off. Later he started once again by stating that "I have to confess," obviously demonstrating that Dihr had put him under terrible pressure. He then proceeded to provide the names of several more involved people, and he added that Hubert H. had been the local leader of the campaign in Krefeld. Furthermore, he confessed to having himself recruited several people who had taken part. One of the people he implicated was his own mother.

This woman was a forty-eight-year-old widow. She was then arrested and also put under immense pressure. Eventually she explained at length how the entire campaign had functioned, and she even implicated her two sons. She and her son were not the only persons to implicate members of their own families. Before Dihr had completed his questioning of the accused sect members in Krefeld, a husband and wife also implicated one another, and a father provided information that led to the arrest of his son.

Further evidence of the brutality with which these people were treated during these interrogations is provided by a thirty-eight-year-old dyer named Karl W. The father of two children and the holder of the Iron Cross for bravery in battle during World War I, Karl W. was one of several witnesses to testify in the crimes-against-humanity trial of Otto Dihr in 1948.[114] During his first interrogation by Dihr in 1937, he quickly admitted to being a member of the sect and to having taken part in previous leafleting campaigns, but he flatly denied any involvement in the present one.[115] When he was interrogated by Dihr a second time, he continued with his denials and still did not divulge any pertinent information or give the names of anyone else who had been involved. Hubert H. was brought into the room during his third interrogation. In the presence of Karl W., Hubert H. told Dihr that he had personally given Karl W. two packages of the letters, which Karl W. had indeed passed out. Karl W. finally broke down in his fourth interrogation and told Dihr everything that he knew. According to his testimony in the trial against Dihr after the war, Dihr had brutalized him from the very beginning. When he held back information during his first interrogation, Dihr punched him twice in the face "so that his gums bled and teeth hurt." It is a wonder that he held out as long as he did.

The information Dihr amassed from these forced confessions enabled him to arrest twenty-five people in Krefeld, all of whom were sentenced to jail terms lasting from four months to two years by the Düsseldorf Special Court in a trial held on August 6, 1937. The information also made it possible for the Gestapo to make numerous arrests in other localities.

From Otto Dihr's final report on the case, one learns about the origination and progress of the entire letter campaign and about the crucial role that Dihr personally played in the crackdown on the Jehovah's Witnesses in much of central and northern Germany. From his interrogation of the suspects in Krefeld, Dihr learned from Johann C. (who had been named originally by Hubert H.) that he had been the leader of the campaign in the entire region of the lower Rhine. Johann C. and another leader of the Witnesses named Albert W., who had fled by the time of Johann C.'s interrogation and could not be found, had commissioned a farmer and former truck-driver named Peter L. from Moers to make a long journey in his car to pick up and deliver large packages of the letters in various German cities. Peter L.'s journey began on June 9. At eleven in the evening, he met Albert W. in front of Krefeld's main train station. Albert W. gave him half of a ten-mark note and told him to attach an artificial bouquet of flowers to the windshield of his car so that he could be recognized. Albert W. then instructed him to drive to the city of Herfort, where he would be met by a man who would give him the other half of the ten-mark note and further instructions. From there he was to drive to Hannover, where he would meet still another man who would ask him if he could provide change for a ten-mark note. After that he was to drive to several other cities, delivering packages of the letters along the way to contact persons who would identify themselves to him by also asking the same question about changing a ten-mark note.

After Peter L. had met his contact person in Herfort, the man signaled to another man, and both of these people climbed into his car with him. These men then ordered him to drive them through a dark and, to him, completely unknown part of the country. After some time they passed an unlit power station that had to have been about twenty to thirty kilometers outside of Herfort. The only thing he recognized along the way was a street sign with "Lemgo" written on it. After the men had driven for another few kilometers, they turned into an unpaved road and continued along that road for a short distance. Finally, he was told to bring his car to a stop in front of a house where two men were standing. These men then took about ten minutes to load his car full of packages that took up the weight of roughly five people. From that point, he drove on alone to a prearranged destination in Hannover. When he arrived, he met a man who rode in front of him on his bicycle and led him to an empty storage depot, where he unloaded ten to twelve packages of the letters, which he calculated to have contained about 60,000 copies of the letter. Then he drove on to Dortmund and unloaded another six packages, containing 30,000 letters, by his estimate. There he met Albert W., who got into Peter L.'s car and drove with him to Duisburg. In Duisburg, Albert W. filled a large suitcase full of the letters and got out of the car. Peter L. then drove back to Moers, just outside of Krefeld, and delivered the remaining 1,500 letters to his father.

The thirty-two-year-old Peter L. provided most of these details to the Gestapo during his interrogation in Krefeld. Later he drove with two Krefeld Gestapo officers, Dihr and van der Rheydt, and a Düsseldorf Gestapo man named Heinzelmann, to the various places where he had loaded and unloaded the letter-containing packages and pointed out to them exactly where he had been. This led to scores of other arrests in the cities to which he had traveled and in other cities where the letters had been handed out. In the end, the Gestapo was able to arrest almost all of the persons involved. For his services, Otto Dihr recommended that Peter L. be given "an appropriately mild sentence."[116] At his trial, he received a six-month jail sentence. His father, who was a fifty-eight-year-old farmer in Moers, did not come out of it so well. After he served out his sentence of one year and three months, the Gestapo sent him to a concentration camp. He died in the camp.

CONCLUSION

It is important to note that denunciations played almost no role in the persecution of the Jehovah's Witnesses, just as they had played almost no role in the persecution of Catholic and Protestant clergymen who dared to stand up to Hitler's regime or to the destruction of the political left, as demonstrated in the previous chapter. Most of the evidence the Gestapo used to bring the Nazi regime's religious adversaries to justice came either from forced confessions or from information the Gestapo received from its own spy network. Very few of these spies came from the ranks of the clergy itself or were members of religious sects like the Jehovah's Witnesses, though there were some. In cases involving religion, most of the informants appear to have been Nazi Party functionaries like the man who turned in Father Josef Spieker.

Many Germans maintained respect for their religion during the Third Reich. Only Nazi Party die-hards and other Nazi true believers—and not all of them certainly—turned their backs on God and placed their entire faith in Hitler. This can be interpreted as a failure of the Nazi totalitarian movement. It can also be seen as a failure of the religious authorities, who seldom used their pulpits to warn their followers about the evils of Hitler and his regime and usually made the accommodations necessary to be permitted to continue their religious practices. The Nazis were prepared to tolerate a certain level of religious identification on the part of the German people so long as it did not seriously impede the achievement of their major goals. Usually it did not, so the Nazis often averted their gaze when confronted with minor religious protestations. Churches and churchgoers often looked away as well when confronted with Nazi crimes so long as they were not directly threatened. Only a small number of people—some priests and ministers like Josef Spieker and Dietrich Bonhoeffer and some religious zealots like the Jehovah's Witnesses—truly protested strongly. When they did, the Nazis showed no scruples and gave them no quarter. The Nazis were well aware of whom they needed to worry about, and they acted ruthlessly to destroy them. They also were aware that few people wished to become martyrs.

PART FOUR

NAZI TERROR AND "ORDINARY" GERMANS

Everyone listened. My father listened to BBC every night!

—A Cologne housewife

But it was all right, everything was all right, the struggle was over . . .
He loved Big Brother.

—George Orwell

CHAPTER SEVEN

Most Germans were not Nazis. Nor were they Jews, members of the Communist underground, or Jehovah's Witnesses. Most slept soundly at night, worked productively by day, and enjoyed their lives during the peacetime years of National Socialist rule. Why should they not have? The economy was improving, most were finding employment, and their country was regaining its pride and was still at peace. They knew that Jews, Communists, Socialists, and some religious activists suffered persecution. They could read about it in the daily newspapers.[1] They knew that there was a strong police presence, a surfeit of laws placing limitations on personal freedom, and potential danger for those who refused to comply with Hitler's wishes. Many grumbled and complained privately, but most found little difficulty in conforming. Many, probably most, still believed that the police and the laws were there to protect them. Nazi terror posed no real threat to most ordinary Germans.

Many will disagree with this last statement and with many others in the previous paragraph. Even if one accepts the findings of recent scholars who have noted that the Gestapo was not all-knowing, all-powerful, and omnipresent and that it had only limited resources and a limited number of agents and spies,[2] one can point to other recent scholarship that highlights the importance of denunciations from the civilian population in keeping the German population in line.[3] This new research on denunciations can be interpreted to mean that the German population had just as much to fear, or perhaps even more to fear, as it would have had if the secret police were as well endowed as was once thought. Hence, the Gestapo did not have to have a huge army of spies and agents to know of the activities and opinions of normal citizens. Neighbors, coworkers, and family members were always nearby and watching. A neighborly quarrel, a lover's spat, a colleague's jealousy, or a generational conflict could easily lead to an anonymous letter or a formal accusation that would set the Gestapo in motion and lead to one's ruin. Furthermore, other research carried out over the past two decades from the "everyday life" perspective has maintained that even if outright resistance and protest were not common activities, Nazi society still bristled with discontent, resentment, and opposition. High-spirited and refractory youth groups such as the Edelweiss Pirates, Kittelbach Pirates, Navajos, Nerother, Meuten, the swings, and other youth bands, gangs, and cliques refused to conform, waged war on their Hitler Youth adversaries, and jeopardized the Nazis' plans for a Reich that would last for 1,000 years. Many ordinary women detested their subservient role in the oppressive, male-dominated society and expressed their displeasure through gossip, dress, and behavior that endangered the society's moral fabric. Numerous men and women from all social classes and backgrounds told anti-Nazi jokes, spread malicious rumors, obstinately held on to their religious identity, gave succor to victims and opponents of the regime, carried out their work without enthusiasm, and did what they could, short of taking up armed resistance, to undermine the regime's authority.[4]

These new perspectives and the evidence they have uncovered on Nazi terror and everyday opposition are compelling. They threaten to distort, however, the uncomfortable truth that the overwhelming majority of German people complied willingly with Nazi ideology and policy and suffered little if at all as a consequence of their occasional and largely harmless indiscretions, even when the Gestapo learned about them through denunciations from the civilian population or through its other means of gaining information. A wide assortment of evidence put forward in this and the next two chapters demonstrates that this uncomfortable truth prevailed throughout the years of the Third Reich, even during the war, when the Nazi regime threatened to punish all nonconformity and disobedience with utmost severity. Never the focus of the Nazi terror apparatus, most ordinary Germans had an experience during the years of the Third Reich wholly unlike that of the Nazi regime's targeted enemies.

A SURVEY OF "ORDINARY" COLOGNE RESIDENTS

Some of the most revealing evidence pertaining to the experiences that ordinary Germans had with National Socialism comes in the form of a scientific survey that the German sociologist and opinion-research expert Karl-Heinz Reuband and I administered to 300 randomly selected German citizens living in Cologne in the fall of 1993. So that we not only would be able to measure the responses from different age groups but could be sure that all of the respondents were old enough during the Third Reich to have been aware of the events around them, we decided to mail our survey only to people born before 1929. Roughly half of the people we wrote to were aged sixty-five to seventy-four, and the other half were seventy-five or older. Slightly more than half of the respondents had resided in the city of Cologne during the Third Reich. The other half had lived in another community before moving to Cologne sometime after 1945. The survey took between thirty and sixty minutes to fill out. It contained several batteries of questions pertaining to the social and economic backgrounds of the respondents; their experiences with and observations about the Nazi terror apparatus; their involvement in illegal activity during the Third Reich (from minor types of illegal activities common to many citizens like telling illegal jokes or listening to forbidden foreign-radio broadcasts to more serious types of resistance activities like handing out antiregime flyers and brochures); their remembrances about how they had felt about National Socialism and Hitler; and the information they had possessed before the end of the war about the persecution and murder of the Jews and other victims of the Nazi regime.

When we first administered our questionnaire, we were not at all sure that we would receive a positive response. Being asked to remember and to reveal, even if confidentially, details about their lives in the Third Reich put many of these ordinary Germans in an uncomfortable position. We offered them no incentives and no rewards. Several people communicated to us through either a telephone call or a letter that what we were doing was rude and outrageous. It was *eine Frechheit* ("an abomination"), some said with snarls in their voices. Others communicated to us that they were too old or sickly to take part. A few threatened to inform the police if we continued to harass them. (Those who did not answer were sent reminders on two occasions, in compliance with standard survey research practice.)[5] One person mailed back a blank questionnaire with inch-high blue letters written in a felt pen across the first page of it saying *Leck mich am Arsch Kokoshinski* ("Lick my ass, Kokoshinski"). We took this to mean that the person was not happy with our survey. Nevertheless, nearly two-thirds of the people we contacted (63 percent) filled out the questionnaires and mailed them back to us. About one-third of the respondents indicated that they were willing to talk with us personally about their experiences in subsequent face-to-face interviews. Since then, we have talked with a large number of these people. In lengthy, tape-recorded interviews, most of them confirmed the responses they made on the written questionnaires and provided a wealth of other vital information.

The responses surprised us initially, coming as they did before I had completed the archival research for this book. First of all, it was astonishing that 55 percent of the respondents—people living in a city that prided itself on having given the Nazis the lowest level of electoral support of all major German cities—admitted to us that they had believed in National Socialism at the time.[6] They could have lied or remembered what they had previously believed in a self-exculpatory fashion. Hence, had they replied that they had not believed in National Socialism, we could not possibly have known whether this was true or false. Unsurprisingly, given what is known about Cologne's low voter support for the Nazis in Weimar elections, those who had lived in Cologne proper during the Nazi years were somewhat less likely to report that they had believed in National Socialism than were those who had moved to Cologne after the war (52 to 59 percent). Nevertheless, the difference between the two groups was not great enough to suggest that National Socialism had found significantly fewer adherents in Cologne than in other German localities after it rose to power. Indeed, it was sobering to observe from these responses that the Nazis had obviously enjoyed great success in winning over new supporters among the Cologne population, and among the German population generally, after Hitler came to power. Only 33 percent of Cologne citizens, and only 44 percent of all German citizens, had voted for the Nazi Party in the election of March 5, 1933, which had marked Hitler's greatest electoral triumph. One can only speculate about how high the Nazis' approval rating might have soared had the German people been surveyed before they lost the war and before they earned the opprobrium of the world for murdering European Jewry and millions of others. Also, one might fairly expect that the percentage of people who said fifty years afterward that they had believed in National Socialism would have been even higher than 55 percent had we achieved a 100 percent response rate to our survey. One cannot be sure of this, but one would expect that those who did not choose to answer our questions were probably more likely to have been Nazi supporters than enemies of the regime.

The respondents' belief in National Socialism varied considerably along educational, gender, age, and religious lines. Previous scholarship had already established that the Nazis enjoyed somewhat more support from the middle classes than from the working classes, but that National Socialism had significant appeal for people across the social-class spectrum of German society. It therefore did not surprise us to find that people who had attended gymnasium or university registered a moderately higher level of belief in National Socialism (60 percent) than did those who had only an elementary school background (55 percent).[7] More dramatic were the great differences we observed between men and women. Whereas nearly three-fourths of the men in the survey responded that they had believed in National Socialism (71 percent), less than half of the women responded that they had held such a belief (47 percent). Age was also of considerable significance. Although 68 percent of the youngest group of people who took the survey, those between sixty-five and sixty-nine in 1993, reported having believed in National Socialism, only 33 percent of the people over eighty years of age responded that they had been believers. This finding indicates that Nazism may have been far more successful in gaining the allegiance of youth than in winning over the adult population, which had given it only modest electoral support during Hitler's rise to power. Finally, the differences between Catholics and Protestants were not as great as the differences between the genders and the generations, but there was nonetheless a perceptible difference: 65 percent of the Protestants, as against only 51 percent of the Catholics, responded that they had believed in National Socialism. This finding jibes with electoral studies that have shown that more support for Nazism came from Protestant than Catholic quarters, as well as with our previous discussion of the Nazis' confrontation with religious denominations.

In some ways more astonishing than the responses concerning the German people's belief in National Socialism were the responses we received concerning their involvement in illegal activities in Nazi Germany. We provided respondents with a list of possible illegal activities that we believed to have been most common in the Third Reich and asked them to check off which ones applied to them. To our surprise, nearly everyone reported that they had done something illegal, and people who had reported that they had believed in National Socialism were nearly as likely to have been involved in illegal activities as those who reported that they had not believed in National Socialism. Although most of these illegal activities had been of a fairly minor nature, they could have gotten these ordinary Germans in severe trouble. By far the most common type of illegal behavior was listening to foreign-radio broadcasts during the war (usually the BBC), an activity that 53 percent of the respondents reported having done.[8] This was a strictly illegal activity that could (but seldom did) lead to very stiff penalties, even the death sentence.

One day in the summer of 1995, shortly before my family and I returned to the United States from Cologne, where we had lived for nearly five years while I was doing research on this book, I was asked by an elderly neighbor woman what my research in Germany had been all about. For all the time we had been neighbors, I had always been careful not to discuss my work with her and her husband. He had been a member of the Waffen SS and spent several years after the war in a Russian prison camp; she had lost her father and sister on one of the last days of the war during a German artillery attack against the American troops who had occupied Cologne in March 1945. Given their difficult experiences, I had not wanted to disturb these kind and considerate neighbors whom our children referred to as Grandma and Grandpa. I tried to give the wife a true but innocuous answer. I told her that I was studying things like foreign-radio broadcasts during the Third Reich. When her husband heard this, he responded, "Um Gottes Willen!" (For heaven's sake!), made a slicing movement across his neck, and quipped, "Niemand hat das gemacht. Das wäre der Tod!" (Nobody did that. It would have meant death!). He then turned his back and marched hastily into his apartment. His wife followed in his footsteps, but before she entered the door behind him, she turned around and whispered to my wife and me that her husband had not known what really took place for he had been away at the front for most of the war. "Everyone listened," she told us. "My father listened to BBC every night!"

Indeed, in the face-to-face interviews we conducted with respondents to the survey, nearly every one of them told us that they had listened to BBC broadcasts regularly. Some had done this with a blanket over their radio set so that their neighbors could not possibly hear what they were listening to; others had listened to illegal radio broadcasts without worrying about it and had set their radios at normal volume. A former policeman from the city of Eberswalde near Berlin—who as an SS auxiliary policeman had personally taken part in the murder of Russian Jewry during the war and had also been a guard in Dachau concentration camp—told me that he had listened to BBC every night in his apartment with earphones on.[9] Another man, who had been a radio operator in the army and was present at the massacre of the Pinsk Jews, told me that he and some of his fellow soldiers on the eastern front had listened to BBC regularly during the war. He said that they had particularly enjoyed the dirty jokes the British told, but that they also listened regularly to music and news reports.[10]

For a final piece of evidence on this topic (for the moment—we will return to it in the next chapter on the war years), one can cite the archival record. In a report of August 13, 1943, on the popular mood, a forty-seven-year-old Catholic priest from Aachen, who acted as a spy under the code name "Mons" for the Cologne and Aachen Gestapo in the mountainous Eifel region southwest of Cologne, noted: "A considerable part of the population are tuning in more than previously to foreign-radio broadcasts. One priest stated at a clerical conference in the northern Eifel that in his opinion about 90 percent of his parishioners have tuned in to foreign-radio broadcasts."[11]

Listening to illegal foreign-radio broadcasts was a largely passive activity so commonplace that it could have been considered normal had it not been outlawed by the regime. The other kinds of illegal undertakings the respondents admitted to required more active involvement. Also, they were carried out in the company of others and could therefore be considered more dangerous by the authorities. A prime example of such an illegal undertaking was the telling of political jokes that slandered the regime. In the Gestapo and Special Court case files, one finds numerous examples of cases that began with such jokes. Most of these jokes were relatively harmless and not intended to injure the regime seriously. The Gestapo and the court authorities realized this themselves, but over time, and especially during the war years, they tolerated such jokes with decreasing equanimity. In the 1930s a person coming to the authorities' attention for telling a libelous or slanderous political joke could usually count on no more than a few weeks' or months' detention, but Hitler himself demanded during the war that such offenses be prosecuted harshly by the People's Court for the crime of either "defeatism" or "undermining the military effort." Although this was still not done in the average case, it happened frequently enough to put any sane jokester in a foul humor.

In a book on black humor in the Third Reich, Ralph Wiener cites the case of a graphic designer who had recently lost her husband at the front but was nonetheless sentenced to death on June 26, 1943, for telling the following joke to a coworker at the armament industry installation where she worked: "Hitler and Göring are standing atop the Berlin radio tower. Hitler says that he wants to give the Berliners a bit of joy. To this Göring replied to Hitler: 'Then why not jump down off the tower.'"[12] The threat of such draconian punishment did not apparently intimidate large reaches of the Cologne population. Twenty-seven percent of the survey respondents answered that they had told such illegal jokes during the Third Reich, and many of them gleefully regaled us with examples of some of their favorites during subsequent interviews. It appears that the Cologne population's reputation for jocularity is well deserved.

Two additional types of illegal behavior to which respondents admitted were helping victims of the regime (9 percent) and participating in outlawed youth groups (4 percent). These figures are small but not insignificant. Furthermore, they once again indicate that many ordinary Germans took part in at least minor acts of illegality of a political nature at one time or another during the Third Reich. Had we asked the respondents about other types of nonconformist or illegal activity, such as listening and dancing to forbidden swing music or spreading gossip and rumors critical of the regime, almost no one would have been excluded from the list of people who had violated the Nazis' laws. Many people, for example, told us that they had discussed the persecution and murder of the Jews, the murder of the mentally and physically impaired, and the Gestapo's practice of employing physical and mental torture during interrogations. We did not ask them explicitly, however, whether they themselves had spread such information.

One could interpret all of these findings to mean that Nazi society was extremely unpopular. But this would be a false interpretation. Not only did the majority of these same people tell us that they had believed in National Socialism, but they also told us that they did not consider their minor acts of noncompliance to hold much importance. In another question we asked the respondents whether they had participated in "active resistance" against the regime. Only one person, representing only 0.5 percent of all of the respondents, told us that she had done so. A dentist by profession and the daughter of a former Center Party politician who had opposed the Nazis strongly from the beginning, this woman told us that she had been a member of an illegal organization that disseminated anti-Nazi flyers during the war years.

Another indication that the German people realized that taking part in activities like listening to illegal radio broadcasts, telling anti-Nazi jokes, providing aid to victims of the regime, and belonging to outlawed youth groups did not pose a serious threat to the Nazi regime is that 75 percent of the respondents maintained that they had never been afraid that they would be arrested for their behavior during the Nazi years. Nine percent of the respondents did not answer the question about whether they had ever had such fear; when this figure is subtracted from the total number of respondents, the percentage of the respondents answering that they never feared arrest during the Third Reich rises to 82 percent. Among the small number of those who did fear arrest, gender was not much of a factor, but age, religion, educational attainment, belief in National Socialism, and place of residence were important in separating those who were afraid of arrest from those who were not. Those who responded that they had feared arrest were more often people who had been adults for most of the Third Reich, had attended university, were Catholic, had not believed in National Socialism, and had lived in Cologne during the Third Reich. Those who had been youths for most of the Third Reich, had a primary school education, were Protestant, believed in National Socialism, and had lived somewhere besides Cologne were less likely to have been afraid of arrest. Adding to this picture of citizens who believed they had little to fear from Nazi terror are our findings that a strong majority of the respondents did not even know anyone personally who had been arrested or simply accused by the Gestapo or the police during the Third Reich. Moreover, only a tiny minority had any awareness of spying activity that had taken place in their neighborhood or workplace.

The results of our survey do not prove that most Germans agreed with all of the Nazis' policies and initiatives. They also do not prove that most Germans had nothing to fear from Nazi terror. They do suggest strongly, however, that most of the ordinary German population supported the Nazi regime, did not perceive the Gestapo as all-powerful or even as terribly threatening to them personally, and enjoyed considerable room to express frustration and disapproval arising out of minor disagreements with the Nazi state and its leadership. An examination of the actual record of Nazi terror that was applied to different constituencies among the ordinary German population, as revealed by documentary and archival sources, supports these observations.

YOUTH AND NAZI TERROR

Most of the people who participated in the Cologne survey experienced some part of their formative years during the Third Reich. As relatively young people, they represented the future of the Nazi state. "Whoever has the youth, has the future," the Nazis confidently liked to proclaim.[13] From the evidence brought out in the survey, the Nazis had good reason to be confident in using this slogan, for the younger the respondents were during the Nazi years, the more they now say that they had believed in National Socialism. But the fact that so many of the respondents indicated that they had partaken in unlawful activities during the Third Reich suggests that the Nazis also had some grounds for concern about German youth.

Anyone who has read Hitler's *Mein Kampf* or viewed Leni Riefenstahl's propaganda film *The Triumph of the Will* knows that the Nazis' concern for youth was always great. Hitler devoted many pages of *Mein Kampf* to a discussion of the evils facing contemporary German youth during the Weimar Republic and to prescriptions for their indoctrination, training, and comportment in the coming Nazi society. He even wrote about their clothing style.[14] Energetic and enthusiastic youth appear constantly in Riefenstahl's infamous film of 1934: flag-waving, drum-beating, smiling, and swooning in the sunny presence of their Führer. The intended message is obvious. The past was behind them, and the future was theirs. If they stood by the Führer, that future would surely be bright.

Hitler's propagandistic portrayal of his movement as one of youth and regeneration had more than a kernel of truth in it. He himself was only forty-three when he came to power in January 1933. His leading subalterns were even younger. Hermann Göring was forty, Rudolf Hess was thirty-eight, Joseph Goebbels was thirty-five, Heinrich Himmler was thirty-two, and Reinhard Heydrich was only twenty-eight. Michael Kater calculates in his exhaustive study of Nazi Party members that the average age of the Nazi Party's rank and file was younger still.[15] In many localities before the Nazis came to power, the average age of members was in the midtwenties. By the time the party took power in 1933, the average age of its members had risen somewhat, but the party continued to attract a far more youthful following than its competitors. While the Nazi Party optimistically promised national rebirth, reawakening, regeneration, and a break with the bourgeois traditions of the past—all themes that had long been attractive to many in the highly organized German youth movement and to large numbers of German youth in general—most of its adversaries had little more to offer German youth than a call for perseverance.

Despite the attractions of the National Socialist message for German youth, the Nazis' own organized youth movement, the Hitler Youth under Baldur von Schirach, himself just twenty-five in January 1933, had attracted only about 55,000 members by the time of Hitler's seizure of power. At the time, this was only a tiny fraction of the five to six million organized young people in Germany. This situation soon changed as Hitler moved quickly to "coordinate" German youth, just as he did with the rest of the society. Before 1933 was over, nearly all of the political, religious, and other organized youth associations—except the Catholic ones, whose autonomy was guaranteed by the Concordat of July 20, 1933—had either merged voluntarily with the Hitler Youth, as did the 800,000 members of the Protestant youth organizations and most of the independent *bündisch* youth associations, or had been shut down by force, like the Communist Youth Association of Germany, the Social Democratic Socialist Working Youth, and the German Socialist Youth Association.[16]

Although it would take several more years before the Hitler Youth became compulsory for all German boys and girls, it enjoyed a truly meteoric rise in almost all localities. At first serving primarily as a funnel into the Nazi Party and attracting mainly lower-middle-class and working-class adherents, the Hitler Youth was quickly transformed into the world's largest youth organization, with members from nearly all social strata of the German population. Membership figures show that by the end of 1933 more than two million German youth between the ages of ten and eighteen had become members. By the end of the next year about half of all German youth had joined; the Hitler Youth now had more than three and a half million members.[17] In the Cologne area, where the strong influence of Catholicism and a generalized anti-Nazi sentiment had originally diminished Hitler's appeal to youth as well as to adults, the Hitler Youth organization's success in attracting new members was even more pronounced than in the nation as a whole. Whereas at the beginning of 1933 the Hitler Youth could attract 800 members in the district of the middle Rhine, with Cologne as its capital, by the end of 1934 this number had multiplied more than 200 times to 170,000.[18]

The next great increase in membership in the Hitler Youth came as a result of a law passed on December 1, 1936. The Hitler Youth Law called for the incorporation of all German youth between the ages of ten and eighteen into the Hitler Youth organization; as a result, the organization's membership increased to nearly five and a half million by the end of that year. Despite this law, it was not until an amendment to it was passed in March 1939 that the Hitler Youth became compulsory. From that time forward, all children were required to register for admission to the Hitler Youth by March 15 of the year when they became ten years of age. Parents and legal guardians were held responsible for the registration of their children, and it became a criminal offense, punishable by a fine of 150 marks or imprisonment, if their children did not join on time. Between the ages of ten and fourteen, boys were members of an organization called the German Young People (DJ) and girls were organized in the Young Girls League (JM). After this, boys entered the Hitler Youth proper (HJ), where they remained until the age of eighteen, and girls joined a parallel organization known as the League of German Girls (BDM).

Membership in the Hitler Youth may have become an obligation, but it still held undeniable attractions for large numbers of German children and teenagers. Many youths enjoyed the holidays and hiking outings organized by the Hitler Youth and the sporting and leisure-time activities that it sponsored. Also, many youths felt pride in the power and status their uniforms gave them and relished the opportunity they now had, as Detlev Peukert explains, "to engage, sometimes aggressively, in conflict with traditional figures of authority: the teacher, the father, the foreman, the local clergyman."[19] One might expect that the militaristic cast of the Hitler Youth appealed more to boys and young men than to girls and young women. Ute Frevert, however, argues that this was not so. Girls and young women, she explains, may even have enjoyed the military atmosphere more than boys and young men did and may have found it a liberating experience. In the Young Girls League and the League of German Girls, they had "opportunities to escape from the restrictions and duties that typified female socialization; the chance to shake off the bonds of omnipresent maternal authority for a few hours represented a slice of personal freedom not to be scorned, even if this freedom had its limits within a BDM group."[20] In sum, Frevert argues that Nazi girls' and women's organizations provided them with opportunities for participation and promotion, a rise in political status, and the chance to exercise power that they had never before had in German society.[21]

Granting the many advantages offered by membership in the Hitler Youth, its downside became increasingly evident in the mid to late 1930s as the organization became larger. Legions of new members who had joined only out of obligation and many others who had joined voluntarily came to resent the drill, regimentation, political indoctrination, enforced uniformity, and lack of freedom and individual means of expression that Hitler Youth membership mandated. At a time in young people's lives when they most wanted to break with the precepts of their parents' generation and experiment socially and sexually, the Hitler Youth demanded conformity and thereby stifled the natural yearnings of many youths. Smoking, drinking, partying, and sex were frowned on, even criminalized eventually, and the Nazi state depended on Hitler Youth patrols to enforce the puritanical restrictions it placed on youthful behavior. According to the Law for the Protection of Youth of March 9, 1940, young people under eighteen were banned from the streets after dark and could not frequent bars, restaurants, cinemas, or other places of entertainment after nine o'clock in the evening if unaccompanied by an adult. In addition, it made it illegal for youths under sixteen to smoke in public or to be served with spirits.[22] Perhaps worst of all for many German youths was the Hitler Youth's restrictions on sexual experimentation and flirtation. Enforcing a kind of sexual apartheid policy, the Nazi youth organizations kept boys and girls separate except on rare official occasions. To dampen the libido, prudish dress styles were prescribed for both sexes, and girls and young women under the age of twenty-one were especially discouraged from perming their hair or wearing makeup, short dresses, or high-heeled shoes. Young women who broke with this early-nineteenth-century vision of proper grooming by perming their hair instead of wearing it in pigtails or in a "Gretchen-style" wreath of braids sometimes had their hair shaved off in a punishment ceremony.[23]

Although it is essential not to overemphasize the point, for most youth conformed just as willingly or perhaps even more willingly than did the older generation in the Third Reich,[24] there is considerable evidence that a spirit of restiveness grew among large numbers of German youth from the mid-1930s onward. Official crime statistics, for example, show that after an initial decline in youthful criminality at the beginning of Hitler's reign, the rate of juvenile delinquency grew demonstrably from 1937 on into the war years. As the rate of juvenile delinquency as a percentage of all criminal offenses tripled between 1937 and 1943, the number of juvenile property offenses and sexual offenses grew by more than 100 percent and the number of forgeries rose by 250 percent, probably reflecting the desire of many young people to obtain identity documents that would allow them to partake in forbidden pleasures reserved only for adults. Nevertheless, it is important to bear in mind that juvenile delinquency rates during the Third

Reich never rose to levels as high as had been recorded during the First World War.[25]

Other indications of a growing sense of youthful discontent come from mood and morale reports compiled by the Social Democratic Party in exile (SOPADE). One must allow for possible exaggerations in these reports, coming as they do from a source that wished to bolster the morale of opponents to the Nazi regime, but many scholars have used them with profit to gain an understanding of changes in popular attitude.[26] In attempting to show that a crisis had developed in the Hitler Youth by the late 1930s, one that he thought revealed a "radical shift of attitude among the young, from initial attraction to growing rejection," and that grew in the war years into "a massive opposition movement on the part of groups and gangs of young people," Detlev Peukert cites a SOPADE report for 1938:

> In the long run young people too are feeling increasingly irritated by the lack of freedom and the mindless drilling that is customary in the National Socialist organizations. . . . Young people are causing the relevant Party agencies much anxiety. Both boys and girls are trying by every means possible to dodge the year of Land Service. In Greater Berlin in May 1938 a total of 918 boys and 268 girls were reported missing, having secretly run away from home because they did not want to go away on Land Service. Police patrols in the Grunewald, the Tegel Forest and the Wannsee district periodically round up whole lorry-loads of young people, some Berliners, some from the provinces. There is a section of youth that wants the romantic life. Whole bundles of trashy literature have been found in small caves.[27]

The most recent cohort of German scholars who study youth in the Third Reich has begun to turn away from the argumentation of scholars like Detlev Peukert, who may have searched a bit too uncritically for examples of youthful nonconformity and opposition and thus incorrectly elevated the usually spontaneous, unpolitical, and largely innocuous activities of many German youth bands, gangs, and cliques into examples of heroism and martyrdom.[28] There can be no doubt, however, that the Nazi authorities often found these groups troublesome and that many of them frequently waged vicious struggles with the Hitler Youth for the allegiance of young Germans. There were many types of such groups, and they successfully recruited members from nearly all communities and all social backgrounds in German society. Catholic youth organizations proved to be particularly impervious and hostile to Nazi pressure to curb their activities, until they were forcibly shut down in February 1939. Bands of working-class and middle-class youth, however, continued to flourish; known by different names in different localities, they were often referred to generally as *bündisch* or independent youth groups. These groups even seemed to gain in strength and intransigence after a law of February 1936 made them illegal. In addition, many upper-middle-class and aristocratic youth snubbed their noses at Nazi conventions and their social inferiors in the Hitler Youth by joining swing clubs, where they danced frantically and lasciviously to forbidden jazz music and adopted the dress style, language, and international chic of the Nazis' Anglo-American rivals.

When Hitler came to power, Catholic youth organizations were the largest and best organized in Germany. With 1.4 million members organized in 28 separate associations, the Catholic Youth at the beginning of 1933 had more than 20 times as many members as the Hitler Youth. The largest of these associations, the Catholic Young Men's Association (KJMV), had some 400,000 members and was headquartered in Düsseldorf, a short distance from both Krefeld and Cologne.[29] Düsseldorf was the administrative center, but the symbolic heart of Rhineland Catholicism for German youth was in Cologne, with its many age-old churches and its majestic and towering cathedral.

Endowed with a holy aura and the capacity to hold up to 40,000 people at a time, the Cologne cathedral was one of the most preferred meeting grounds for Catholic Youth demonstrations and rallies.[30] Throughout much of the 1930s, typically on Catholic holidays and feast days, Catholic youth frequently met there and in other localities, often in open country-side fields, to profess their faith and thereby to distance themselves spiritually from the Nazi movement and particularly from the Hitler Youth organization. Originally protected by the Concordat, Catholic youth organizations also sponsored sporting, musical, and educational events, marches, trips, and other leisure-time activities that other youth in Germany could enjoy only within the Hitler Youth organization. These were hardly revolutionary activities, but the Nazi authorities tolerated them with increasing displeasure.

The Hitler Youth did not want to tolerate them at all. Starting in early 1933 and continuing for as long as the Catholic youth organizations were allowed to exist, the Hitler Youth constantly complained about Catholic Youth gatherings and used all the means it possessed to interfere with them—chanting Nazi slogans, singing Nazi songs, breaking into the gatherings, and often provoking fights with Catholic Youth members.[31] On occasion Catholic young people fought back. If one were to believe the reports filed by Hitler Youth leaders, it was most often the Hitler Youth who were on the defensive. One such report, filed in the Cologne area in October 1933, contended: "Ever since the Concordat, a spirited agitation against the Hitler Youth has become noticeable. . . . [Even] when there has been no special reason for it, the representatives and leaders of the Catholic organization disparage the Hitler Youth movement as well as National Socialism in a scornful fashion."[32] Another report, filed by the Cologne district leader Wallwey in December 1934, complained that Catholic youth had better leaders, better quarters, and a better propaganda organ than the Hitler Youth possessed.[33]

Catholic youth groups may have tried valiantly to hold their ground against attacks from the Hitler Youth, but they fought a losing battle against National Socialism. Whereas government leaders increasingly felt the need to restrain the Hitler Youth, fearing that their attacks would cause the local population to lose sympathy for the Hitler Youth and National Socialism[34] (the Gestapo sometimes even resorted to placing some Hitler Youth members under arrest), they did not hold back from exerting other kinds of pressures on Catholic youth. The latter efforts ultimately proved more successful. A KJMV report of November 1935 listed the following types of pressure the Nazi regime had placed on Catholic youth organizations: "false press reports, unfair battle tactics, statements by Hitler Youth leaders, pressure in the schools, pressure on officials, economic pressure, criminal punishment and the administration of justice."[35] In addition, the administrative offices of the Catholic youth associations were attacked, homes for Catholic youth were closed, Catholic Youth newspapers and magazines were censored, and many Catholic Youth leaders and priests were arrested.

These pressures led to a significant decline in Catholic youth association membership: by the middle of 1934 the KJMV had shrunk to 100,000 members. They did not, however, break the resolve of these associations, which continued to hold demonstrations, rallies, and marches and to engage in other activities in the face of the growing animosity of the Nazi authorities. As discussed in the previous chapter, the Nazis' campaign against their Catholic adversaries accelerated markedly in 1935. In addition to making a mass wave of arrests of Catholic priests and leaders, the Nazis decided to take much firmer measures against the Catholic youth associations. By a Gestapo decree of July 23, 1935, all Catholic youth associations in the entire state of Prussia were forbidden to participate in any activities that were not of a purely religious nature. In particular, Catholic youth could no longer wear uniforms, or clothes that resembled uniforms in any way; they could not wear pins or medallions in public that would link them with Catholic associations, nor could they publicly display Catholic flags and banners; they were forbidden to go on marches or to go hiking and camping; and they were forbidden to participate in organized sporting activities of all kinds.

Individual decrees in Düsseldorf and Cologne and other localities had already limited such activities of Catholic youth associations more than a year before (in Düsseldorf in February 1934 and in Cologne in March 1934).[36] In some places, the measures taken against the local Catholic youth associations forced them to close down entirely. Nevertheless, many Catholic Youth leaders and Catholic youth themselves refused to comply with these decrees, though they often had to camouflage their activities. A supposed "parents' evening" of the Catholic Youth's "pathfinders' association" (*Pfadfinderschaft*), held on Sunday evening, February 24, 1935, in the town of Marienheide, about twenty miles east of Cologne, provides an example and demonstrates that the Nazis were usually wise to such tactics.[37]

A copy of the broadsheet advertising the parents' evening and inviting them to attend was used as evidence by the Cologne Special Court in a subsequent case started against the organizers and some participants in the event; it is clear from that document that the Nazis had no difficulty in determining where and when the event would be held. It also makes clear that the organizers knew the "evening" would contravene local police ordinances against such assemblages by flaunting Catholic flags and banners, singing songs and holding speeches likely to be critical of the regime, and having the Catholic youth march in and out of the assembly. Additionally, some of the phrases prominently featured in the broadsheet, such as "youth in battle," "on the journey," and "everything for Germany—Germany for Christ," would be sure to alarm Nazi die-hards. Nowhere did the broadsheet mention allegiance to, or support for, Hitler and National Socialism. At the top stood the words "Give Your Praise to God! Dear Parents!" The Nazis would have preferred "Heil Hitler."

Two local policemen dressed in civilian clothing and several uninvited Hitler Youth attended the event. A day later, one of the policemen, Gendarmeriehauptmeister K., filed a formal complaint at Marienheide police headquarters that started a case against the thirty-two-year-old Catholic curate, Father Wilhelm K., who had organized and led the event. The complaint charged that Father K. had violated a state police decree of May 29, 1935. He had led a procession of seventy to eighty youth to a sporting event in which the youth were illegally marched into and away from the premises. They had illegally waved church flags and had illegally worn Catholic Youth uniforms, and during the event they had sung anti-Nazi songs and been treated to public speeches disparaging the National Socialist movement.

> Led by vicar K. from Marienheide . . . the young men were marched up to the stage and indeed in uniform clothing. The youths wore short, dark trousers, dark jackets and white shirts with open collars. Several pennants were also displayed. A chorus urged the youth to fight for christianity and against all enemy attacks. In a speech, vicar K. declared that the Catholic youth followed the path of Christ but not the path of a Rosenberg.[38]

Two days after the policeman had made his complaint, a fifteen-year-old Hitler Youth, who was also an apprentice mechanic, was called into police headquarters in Marienheide to file a written report as a witness of the affair. His report confirmed the accusations made by the policeman. Three days later, the mayor of Marienheide wrote out his own report of the affair and sent it to his superior, the *Landrat* of the Oberbergischen district, asking for advice on how to proceed. The *Landrat* then wrote a week later, on March 8, 1935, to the Cologne Gestapo for its recommendation and asked it to bring the case to the attention of the Cologne state prosecuting attorney's office. On March 25, the state prosecuting attorney Rebmann responded to the Marienheide police, telling them that they should interrogate the entire lot of people involved.

Over the next two weeks, the Marienheide police started proceedings against Father K. and seven young men who had participated in the event, summoning all of them to provide testimony. In his interrogation, which took place on April 9, 1935, Father K. admitted that there had indeed been an event involving seventy to eighty youths on the evening in question. He noted, however, that several of the youths taking part had worn other kinds of clothing, so the procession was not "uniform" in nature. He added that all flags, banners, and pennants had been kept in the Catholic Youth building itself and had not been displayed in public, and he also denied making any attacks on the state. He did admit, however, that "in my speech I showed the path of Christ to the youths and thereby pointed out that our path was, could not, and will not be that of a Rosenberg."[39]

Rebmann, the Cologne state prosecuting attorney, suspended the case against the priest and the youths three weeks later. He justified this decision by noting that the youths had not worn uniform clothing and that the event had not taken place in public, since only the parents of the youths and the youths themselves had been in attendance. He also stated that he could have proceeded with a case against several members of the pathfinders' association, because they had marched into the assembly from the streets, but decided not to do so because it was impossible to determine exactly which youths had taken part in the marching.

This decision demonstrates once again that the Nazi authorities could at times show leniency in dealing with mild religious opposition, even at a time when scores of Catholic priests were being arrested for similar activities in localities throughout Germany. But the threat of punishment was certainly evident in this case, even if it was not meted out, and it helped to stifle further activities of this nature in Marienheide and elsewhere. After this time, such overt demonstrations of anti-Nazi sentiment on the part of

Catholic Youth leaders and members became ever rarer, and the Catholic Youth movement soon turned inward and restricted itself to private protestations of its religious identity. This shift in focus was what the Nazis wanted, but even this change was eventually not enough for them. In the next years, Catholic youth associations in one diocese after another were closed down permanently. The first to be shut down was the diocese of Paderborn, on July 7, 1937. It happened in Cologne on February 1, 1938. A year later, on February 6, 1939, what was left of Catholic youth organizations in the rest of Germany followed suit. From this time onward, Catholic youth were on the same footing as the rest of the German youth. Almost all had already joined the Hitler Youth. Those who still wanted to oppose the Nazis in unison with other youths or who simply wanted to enjoy the camaraderie offered by a non-Nazified youth organization had to take the risk of joining an illegal band, clique, or gang. As the respondents to our survey attested, many did.

An alternative youth culture had a long tradition in Germany, dating back to the Wandervögel of Imperial Germany. During the Third Reich, this tradition continued to thrive. Despite the dangers involved, large numbers of youths in Cologne, Krefeld, Düsseldorf, and nearly every other community of any size formed into *bündisch*, or small, locally based, autonomous associations. After all such associations were outlawed in 1936, their members were sometimes prosecuted for an offense called *bündische Umtriebe* (unlawful agitation perpetrated by outlawed independent youth groups). Nevertheless, with the exception of the Hitler Youth, which frequently exaggerated the harmful nature of *bündisch* youth activities and tried to incriminate their members, most Nazi authorities recognized that this supposed "agitation" was largely harmless youthful folly. Punishment for members of such groups did stiffen somewhat during the war years, but during the 1930s at least most cases that came to the attention of the Gestapo led to nothing more than a brief interrogation followed by a warning and a subsequent dismissal.[40]

This is exactly what happened in a typical example of *bündisch* youth activity in the Krefeld Gestapo files. Over the Pentecost holiday, on June 5–6, 1938, seven working-class youths from Krefeld between the ages of sixteen and twenty set out on a bicycle tour that took them first to Düsseldorf and later to Mönchengladbach. Dressed in clothing typical of such groups—shorts, long stockings hanging out over tall boots, checked shirts, and colored kerchiefs around their necks—they went swimming by day and by night sang songs around a campfire that they made in the woods. The songs were the kind of hiking and wandering songs that youths of past eras had always sung, with unthreatening and slightly kitschy titles like "On the Other Side of the Valley," "When We Are Fighting," "Who Lurks There in the Dark Woods," and "In a Little Polish Town." In the late afternoon of the second day of their tour, they were spotted and picked up by a regular police patrol outside the city of Mönchengladbach and brought to that city's Gestapo headquarters for questioning. While questioning them, the Gestapo ascertained that five of the seven youths were Catholic and the other two were Protestant, that none had a criminal record, and that all had a primary school education and held gainful employment either as an apprentice in a common trade or as a simple worker. The interrogation lasted only a few hours before the Gestapo decided to dismiss the case with a warning to the youths not to take part in such activities again. As evidence that their touring activities reflected nothing more than a desire to visit nearby towns and countryside while enjoying time off from work in the company of friends over the holiday weekend, and that those activities most certainly did not imply any criticism of or agitation against the Nazi state, all but one of the youths (a twenty-year-old worker with Dutch citizenship living in Krefeld) were able to point out that they had long been members of the Hitler Youth organization. One of them had even been a member of the Hitler Youth since 1932, before Hitler came to power, and had recently joined the Nazi Party proper in 1937.[41]

If not all members of *bündisch* youth groups had such solid National Socialist credentials as these youths—and many in fact hated the Hitler Youth as much as the Hitler Youth hated them—the backgrounds, dress, and activities of this small Krefeld group were nevertheless characteristic of most of these small bands in other parts of Germany.[42] When the Gestapo and the court authorities eventually got in the business of actively discouraging membership in these associations in the mid to late 1930s, most of the members of such groups came from working-class backgrounds. Middle-class youths, who had been heavily represented in the independent youth group movement in the Imperial Germany and the Weimar years, had most often found the conservative and patriotic ideas of the Hitler Youth congenial to their ideological tastes and had decided to disband their associations sometime in 1933 or shortly thereafter. Although the remaining independent youth groups had been made illegal after 1936 and were populated by the children of former Socialists and Communists, they did not necessarily espouse political opinions hostile to the Nazi state. Like the Krefeld group cited earlier, most either had no particular political positions at all or were conformist in their political beliefs.

Usually these groups simply wanted to have some fun and some freedom to spend time with their friends away from the regimented routine mandated by the Hitler Youth. They organized into small bands, often on a neighborhood basis, gave their groups names like Navajos, Nerother, Edelweiss Pirates, or Kittelbach Pirates, wore clothing, pins, medals, and other insignia that gave their group a common identity, and participated in group activities like hiking, bicycle touring, swimming, tenting, playing the guitar, and singing. In warm weather they usually met in the evenings, and on weekends in parks or woods. In cold weather they moved indoors to bars and restaurants. On summer vacations they often ventured further afield, touring the Alps or the Black Forest and visiting faraway cities like Berlin, Munich, or Vienna. These groups were also attractive to many German youths as a venue for the kind of activities that teenagers in all countries like to experiment with, but that were forbidden within the confines of the Hitler Youth. On the journeys and outings they often smoked cigarettes, drank alcohol, and caroused with members of the opposite sex. Even the Gestapo and the Hitler Youth recognized correctly that allowing girls to join gave these independent groups special recruitment advantages over the Hitler Youth, which kept the activities of boys and girls strictly separate.[43]

Despite their similarities in style and activities, and despite the similarity of their names, these groups had no organizational ties beyond the local level. Resembling gangs in postwar American and European cities, rival bands from different parts of the same city often fought territorial battles against one another. They also fought frequently with Hitler Youth patrols. The Hitler Youth knew that they were often hated by the *bündisch;* otherwise, even they were divided over what these groups were about. A Hitler

Youth leader in Cologne in September 1936 defined a Navajo simply as "any young person who wears a colorful, checked shirt, very short pants, and boots with overturned stockings." In December 1940, a member of a Hitler Youth patrol in Essen identified Edelweiss Pirates in his city as "youths who no longer go to church." This characterization contrasts with that of a Hitler Youth leader in another city two years later: he defined the Edelweiss Pirates in almost the exact opposite terms, saying that they "are all Catholic."[44]

Whatever they were or were not, the Nazi authorities finally took strong measures against them in the war years. A large dragnet organized by the Düsseldorf Gestapo in December 1942 broke up twenty-eight groups of Edelweiss and Kittelbach Pirates; 739 adolescents were arrested in the cities of Düsseldorf, Duisburg, Essen, Wuppertal, and Cologne.[45] Citing their agitation as illegal youth group members, the Cologne Special Court started a large case in June 1943 against local Edelweiss Pirates who met in the Leipziger Platz in Nippes on the city's north side. According to the specific charges against them, in the fall of 1942 they had painted provocative graffiti on the walls of local buildings and distributed flyers around the city—some of which had even been sent to different local police precinct headquarters—advertising an upcoming "week of accomplishment" to be carried out by the *bündisch* youth. Convinced that the case dealt with "a political and in part criminally contaminated circle," the Gestapo's painstaking investigation led to a total of thirty-eight arrests. On September 15, 1943, the Cologne Special Court convicted twelve of the arrested youths, and on April 9, 1944, an additional nine were convicted. Their sentences ranged from six months in jail to four years and three months in prison.[46]

But this was still not the most draconian example of the punishment of Edelweiss Pirates in the war years. On November 10, 1944, without the judgment of any court, the Cologne Gestapo publicly executed thirteen people in the working-class Ehrenfeld section of the city. Five of them were youths of sixteen or seventeen years of age. Three others were in their early twenties. Most were Edelweiss Pirates, though the rather amorphous group of executed people also included some fleeing eastern workers, deserting German soldiers, and a few outright criminals. The Gestapo believed that this extreme punishment was justified by the Edelweiss Pirates' traitorous and criminal acts and necessary to serve as a warning to the rest of the Cologne population not to fall out of line in the final stages of the war. No one disputes that this was one of the most egregious examples of the Gestapo's ruthlessness. But ever since this event, scholars and the Cologne population have remained divided in their evaluations of the activities of the Ehrenfeld Edelweiss Pirates. Some consider them patriotic heroes. Others see them as traitors and common criminals. Among the many controversial acts of the Edelweiss Pirates were providing shelter for army deserters, prisoners of war, forced laborers, and concentration camp escapees; stockpiling weapons after armed raids on military depots; and carrying out partisan-style attacks on local Nazi leaders, one of which claimed the life of a Cologne Gestapo officer in the fall of 1944.[47]

Although the example of the Edelweiss Pirates of Cologne-Ehrenfeld shows that some independent youth groups eventually became involved in resistance activity in the latter phases of the war, such activities were not typical of the *bündisch* youth for most of the Nazi period, and certainly not in the prewar years. With only a few modest exceptions during the war years, the underground Communist Party's overtures to enlist these youths in resistance activities ended in failure. The age gap between the generations was one reason. Another was that most Navajos, Edelweiss Pirates, and other independent youth group members did not truly hold anti-Nazi views. They should be seen for the most part as somewhat nonconformist youths seeking adventure and romance. As the German scholar Alfons Kenkmann explains, "Youthful Edelweiss Pirates and Kittelbach Pirates in the early phases of the National Socialist regime were by no means born anti-National Socialists."[48] Many voluntarily joined the German army and navy. Still others were drawn to the Waffen SS, finding its elitist and manly consciousness particularly to their liking.

A longing for romance and adventure and a nonconformist inclination also motivated many youths of the higher social classes in Nazi Germany. Probably the best example comes from a somewhat bizarre phenomenon known as the swing movement. Best documented for the city of Hamburg during the 1940s, with its uniquely patrician and English-influenced upper classes, swing dancing and swing clubs arose in the mid-1930s and spread rapidly to nearly every large and mid-sized German city.[49] There was nothing political about this phenomenon. Its members were in fact emphatically apolitical. There was no organization to it whatsoever. Indeed, it is a stretch to even call it a movement. Its teenage and young-adult adherents simply found the stodgy and sentimental Nazi "moon in June" music and Nazi restrictions on youthful comportment and social intercourse boring and tiresome, preferred the popular American swing music enjoyed by their peers across the world at the time, and adopted the casual style of American and British youth.

"Swing Boys" and "Swing Babies," as they called themselves, or "Swing Heinis," as the Nazis often referred to them, were usually well-educated and well-heeled youths of the middle and upper classes who loved to intersperse their speech with English phrases like "Hello, old Swing Boy," which was one of their favorite salutations. They met in wine bars and nightclubs and sometimes held parties in their families' homes. They dressed foppishly and provocatively, flirted lewdly and openly, and danced lasciviously and wildly, sometimes with two cigarettes hanging out of the sides of their mouths. Boys wore custom-tailored suits, sometimes in glen-checked patterns, sported trench coats, Homburg hats, and white silk scarves, carried tightly rolled umbrellas, and let their hair grow long. Girls wore heavy makeup, painted their nails, wore short skirts and sexy blouses, and also let their hair grow long.[50]

The Nazis were both wary and ambivalent about the swing movement and hesitated to pass a national law banning it. They disliked its English and international style, its cult of sexuality and sleaziness, its tolerance for Jews, and its celebration of what the Nazis believed to be Jewish- and Negro-inspired American music. Nevertheless, they were split between their desire to promote a German *völkisch* culture and their fear of deviating too far from public mood and taste. For the most part, they left control of the movement in the hands of local communities and individual party and state organizations. The first-known ordinance prohibiting swing dancing was enacted in the city of Düsseldorf in November 1937, when Bei Toni, a local wine bar, was commanded to stop this style of dancing. Many other communities followed Düsseldorf's lead in the next two years, so that by the summer of 1939 swing had been officially prohibited across much of Germany. During this time, state and party agencies such as the army, the SS, the

German Labor Front, the Reich Labor Service, and the Nazi student organizations also joined in the condemnation of the swing movement.[51]

The restrictions placed on the swing movement notwithstanding, swing music and swing dancing continued to flourish into the war years. It did so, however, in the face of a growing propaganda campaign against it, which sometimes led to the arrest of its adherents.[52] For its part, the Hitler Youth leadership became more and more convinced that swing did indeed have a political component and argued strongly for harsh measures to be taken against the movement. An example of this is a study of illegal bands and cliques that the Hitler Youth completed in September 1942.

> The swing-youth has developed today into a fashion epidemic that has spread over almost all of Europe. . . . It is an alliance of youths who come for the most part from the so-called "upper middle-class," are only interested in enjoying sexual and other debaucheries, who follow almost entirely an "English model," and who are fanatic devotees of the most lurid jazz music (hot and swing music). Because of their fundamental rejection of any limitation on their personal freedom (including the Hitler Youth and work and military service), they have very quickly developed a sharp opposition to the Hitler Youth and to National Socialism. They should, therefore, also be considered political opponents.[53]

The reports on the swing movement by the Hitler Youth and other Nazi bodies condemned the swings for their nonconformity and lack of patriotism and, in accounts teeming with sexual details, alleged that the swings practiced and promoted sexual intercourse among minors, group sex, perversions of various kinds, and homosexuality.[54] A concern of possibly even greater moment developed around the swings' tolerance of Jews and admiration for the American "King of Swing" or the "swing Jew Benny Goodman," as the Nazis called him.[55] Indeed the urbane, tolerant, middle-class, laissez-faire, and international nature of the swing movement captured the fancy of many German Jews, and Jews and "half-Jews" mixed comfortably with other swing enthusiasts in cities throughout Germany. As attested in a recent interview by Helmut Goldschmidt—a Cologne Jew who survived

Buchenwald and Auschwitz and later returned to Germany to rebuild many
of West Germany's synagogues—this was true even after the first waves of
Jewish deportation left for the concentration camps in the east.

Helmut Goldschmidt was not only a talented architect but also an accomplished musician who, as a member of a small musical combo, performed in various nightspots in Cologne in 1941 and early 1942. One of the
members of his group, as strange as it seems, was the son of a Gestapo officer. Goldschmidt said of this period:

> During these months I concentrated mainly on my music. I was al-
> ways interested in music and could really play the piano well. Above
> all, I played jazz music, and I was especially expert at swing. Through
> my music I came in contact with a group of young people, some of
> whom I already knew, and we began to play together. They were all
> swing enthusiasts. . . . Naturally there were no National Socialists in
> the group, but one can also not say that this was a resistance group. It
> was simply a group of young people, mostly university students tem-
> porarily freed from military service, who wanted to play jazz music
> that the regime forbade. Except for me, K. H. Wagener, and Helmut
> Berg, all of the members of our group were not Jewish.
>
> I played in this period with some of my friends . . . even one time
> in a dance bar. But after a few days, it became too hot for me. There
> were constant military controls, and, even though the musicians in the
> bar were never controlled, it was simply too dangerous for me.
>
> Furthermore, one of our group was the son of an important Ge-
> stapo man. The son visited me frequently at home and gave us, for
> example, whole crates of oranges that he brought home from his work
> in the Grossmarkt. He was also a swing enthusiast and attempted to
> persuade me to continue to perform, at that time with my clarinet.[56]

Helmut Goldschmidt's recollections serve as an excellent reminder that
swing enthusiasts should not be glorified as Nazi opponents and help to
demonstrate that the Nazis largely considered the swings rather harmless.
Goldschmidt himself states that his group was not to be considered "a resis-

tance group." Even the son of a Gestapo officer performed along with him and encouraged him to keep playing in the midst of the Holocaust. As was often the case with many minor offenses in the Third Reich, taking part in the swing scene became dangerous only when one had another strike against oneself. But as a Jewish *Mischling,* Helmut Goldschmidt already had one strike too many, and he was arrested in November 1942.

Most young Germans, however, did not have a prior strike against them and did not get into serious trouble with the Nazi authorities for minor non-conformist activities. Even if this discussion indicates that many youths did not conform in all ways at all times to the ideal image of Nazi youth, the police and justice officials seldom became concerned. Another way to demonstrate this is to consider the evidence from the Krefeld Gestapo and Cologne Special Court case files.

Non-Jewish youths under the age of eighteen seldom appeared in these files, and the evidence in them suggests that youthful protest and the persecution of youth neither became very serious nor increased dramatically over time. In a random sample of 339 cases handled by the Krefeld Gestapo between 1933 and 1945 that did not pertain to Jews, only 4.4 percent of the cases involved boys and girls under the age of eighteen. In the prewar years between 1933 and 1939, the percentage was almost identical (4.1 percent). Almost none of these cases had anything to do with serious opposition to or protest against the Nazi regime. Most of the cases involved allegations that the youths had either violated the conventions of the Hitler Youth movement, often through their involvement in a *bündisch* youth group, or committed a sexually based offense against morality, most commonly involving alleged homosexuality.

Boys far outnumbered girls in these cases, thirteen to two. In the prewar period, there were no girls at all in the sample. Of the ten prewar cases, five were initiated against boys for participating in a *bündisch* youth group, and the other five were initiated against boys for practicing homosexuality. All of the boys in these ten cases came from working-class backgrounds and had only a primary school education. Four of the five boys involved in *bündisch* youth activities were also members of the Hitler Youth, and the Gestapo dismissed all of these cases without administering any punish-

ment. The Gestapo also dismissed one of the homosexual cases, but it sent
the other four forward to the state prosecuting attorney's office for further
action.

In the sample coming from the war years, there were two girls and three
boys. None of the cases led to serious punishments, but one case involving
a girl who had fraternized with a French prisoner of war was forwarded to
the court authorities. The Gestapo itself dismissed the rest of the cases,
three of which had been lodged against boys for participating in an illegal
youth group and one of which was brought against a girl for a violation of
her membership in the BDM.

Although it is not always possible to ascertain from the Krefeld Gestapo
case files what finally happened with youths whose cases were sent forward
by the Gestapo to the state prosecuting attorney, the evidence from the Cologne Special Court files demonstrates that usually not much happened at
all. In a random sample of 559 cases handled by the Cologne Special Court
between 1933 and 1945, only 1.9 percent of the cases involved youths under
the age of eighteen. Nine of the cases began in the prewar years, and only
one case started during the war. Boys were involved in nine of the ten cases,
and none of the cases ended with a punishment of any kind.

Even if German youths appeared infrequently in Gestapo and Special
Court case files as alleged lawbreakers, one might expect to encounter them
in these files as people who helped to initiate cases against adults. One of the
most common stereotypes of the Nazi period is of politically indoctrinated
Hitler Youth viciously defending the Nazi state and taking revenge on the
presumably less-Nazified older generation, even their own parents, by
means of political denunciations.[57] But this rarely happened, and with the
important exception of cases involving Jews, the cases started by a young
person's denunciation were most often quite insignificant in nature and did
not lead to severe punishment for the accused. In a random sample of 105
Krefeld Gestapo cases that began with a denunciation from the civilian population, youths under the age of eighteen made the denunciations in only
three of the cases, and none involved the youth's parents. Youthful denunciations were also uncommon in the Cologne Special Court files. Of 346 randomly selected cases prosecuted by the Cologne Special Court that began
with a denunciation, only sixteen of the denouncers were under the age of

eighteen, and once again, not one of them denounced his or her own parents. The people the youths denounced came from a variety of social backgrounds, but Jews and employers appear to have been their most frequent targets. Indeed, the evidence from the Gestapo and Special Court files indicates that the only real validity that the stereotype of youthful denouncers had in the Third Reich obtained in the persecution of Jews. In the Krefeld Gestapo files, for example, young German boys and girls made the denunciations in four of the twenty-one Jewish cases that began with a denunciation, or 19 percent of the total. In at least one of these cases, death for the accused was the result.[58]

It would be wrong to conclude a discussion of youth and Nazi terror on such a dire note, however, for the number of people involved in these cases was very small. A more proper conclusion would be that the overwhelming majority of youths in Nazi Germany displayed little interest in political matters and should be seen neither as young Nazi fanatics nor as youthful opponents of the regime. Most fulfilled their obligations to the Hitler Youth organizations, but many found these obligations burdensome at times. Some became involved in minor acts of insubordination, such as joining a local gang, clique, or club that went on unsanctioned weekend outings or danced to forbidden swing music. Occasionally, and more so in the war years than in the 1930s, the Nazi authorities took repressive measures to curb the activities of such groups. Mostly, however, the Nazis left them alone, realizing full well that the youths mainly sought adventure and romance, not the downfall of Nazi society.

KEEPING "ORDINARY" GERMANS IN LINE

The situation of most adult Germans was not unlike that of German youth. Outside of specially targeted groups like Jews, Communists, and staunch religious opponents, there was a considerable measure of grumbling and nonconformity on the part of the ordinary German population but very little protest or serious opposition. The Gestapo realized this too and committed little of its time, energy, and resources to such trivial matters. Very often it left the control of the everyday lives of ordinary citizens to other official and unofficial bodies or to citizens themselves. Indeed, in most instances involving ordinary Germans, Gestapo officers did sit back, as the former Cologne Gestapo chief Emanuel Schäfer testified in his postwar trial, and "let things come to them and did not undertake any of their own initiatives."[59] Furthermore, when an accusation against an ordinarily trustworthy German did come to its attention, the Gestapo usually remained composed and did not react with brutality or severity. The many-headed hydra that was the Gestapo had many faces.

The Gestapo's overall lack of concern for the day-to-day activities and vicissitudes of most ordinary Germans starts to become evident when one examines the Gestapo's caseload. The figures in table 7.1, which are based on a random sample of every eighth case handled by the Krefeld Gestapo in the prewar years, show that more than half (55 percent) of the Krefeld Gestapo's caseload in this entire period dealt with the persecution and control of three groups—Jews, leftist activists, and clergy and religious sects—that together added up to only a small minority of the German population.

Small as these groups were, they received not only the majority of the Gestapo's attention in the prewar years but the lion's share of its brutality. When members of these groups were involved, the Gestapo did not sit back and "let things come to them." It targeted them pointedly for destruction and aggressively employed the full spate of its terroristic weaponry to achieving that end. As discussed already in previous chapters, denunciations from the civilian population were not much of a factor in the Gestapo's information-gathering efforts toward these targeted groups except in cases involving Jews; it gained most of the information it sought against these groups through spying, house searches, and torture-extracted confessions. Once it had gathered this information, it proceeded ruthlessly against the members of these groups, hounding them out of the country, taking them in protective custody, committing them to concentration camps, or urging the court authorities to punish them severely.

The Gestapo's treatment of the majority of the population stood in stark contrast to its treatment of these targeted groups. Here again, there were some exceptions, most importantly in its often barbarous handling of male homosexuals, who might also be considered a targeted group. But by and large, the Gestapo showed a much kinder face to the "ordinary" German majority population. Taking up only 45 percent of the Gestapo's actual

TABLE 7.1 *The Krefeld Gestapo's Caseload, 1933–1939*

YEAR	TOTAL NUMBER OF CASES	TARGETED GROUPS			HOMOSEXUALS	ORDINARY GERMANS		
		JEWS	KPD/SPD	CLERGY / RELIGIOUS SECTS		REGIME CRITICS	NSDAP	OTHER
1933	33	2	21	—	—	3	1	6
1934	51	2	38	—	—	5	4	2
1935	28	1	9	2	—	4	10	2
1936	28	7	4	1	3	3	8	2
1937	59	7	5	27	1	11	6	2
1938	47	17	2	—	3	4	14	7
1939	44	14	1	—	8	12	5	4
?	1	—	—	—	1	—	—	—
TOTAL	291	50	80	30	16	42	48	25

NOTE: Based on a random sample of every eighth case in the Krefeld Gestapo case files.

caseload if one includes homosexuals, and only 40 percent if one does not, the ordinary German population was not targeted for persecution by the Gestapo. Unlike leftist opponents, whom the Nazi regime cracked down on immediately after it came to power, recalcitrant clergy and religious sects, which it targeted in the mid-1930s after it had eliminated the Communist and Socialist threat, and Jews, who suffered throughout the Third Reich but with increasing intensity after the November pogrom in 1938, there was no significant chronological pattern to the cases started against ordinary Germans. When ordinary Germans were concerned, the Gestapo almost never engaged paid informants or spies to uncover information about them, seldom sent agents to search their homes and workplaces, and very rarely employed torture to extract confessions from them. In marked contrast to the situation with the targeted groups, the information the Gestapo received about these people frequently came from denunciations from the civilian population. But mean-spirited and damning as these denunciations often were, they seldom held much interest for the Gestapo, and either the Gestapo or the court authorities summarily dismissed the vast majority of the cases that resulted from them, without any punishment at all for the accused.

Finally, it needs to be added that only a small number of "ordinary" Germans had cases lodged against them in the first place. Even if one includes homosexual cases in the total number of cases of ordinary Germans that the Krefeld Gestapo handled during the 1930s, the evidence in table 7.1 shows that less than 1 percent of the ordinary Krefeld population had any brush at all with the Gestapo during these years. To calculate this percentage, one merely has to multiply the 131 cases of ordinary Germans enumerated in table 7.1 by eight (as every eighth case was selected for the sample) and divide this number by 170,000 (a reasonable estimate of the Krefeld prewar population). The findings from the survey of Cologne residents strongly suggest that Krefeld was no anomaly in the Third Reich. Even though a majority of the respondents to the survey reported that they had violated one or more of the laws of the Third Reich, less than 1 percent reported that either the Gestapo or some other policing body had ever arrested or interrogated them for illegal activity.

A more detailed discussion of the most common types of cases that were started against ordinary Germans supports these assertions about the Gestapo's relative lack of concern for or persecution of ordinary Germans in the prewar years. (The next chapter, focusing on the war years, demonstrates that these assertions can also be made for the entire Nazi period.) Table 7.1. shows that more than four-fifths of these cases were of one of three types: homosexual cases; cases lodged against people for criticizing the Nazi regime or its leaders in the course of their everyday lives; and cases involving members of the Nazi Party, its SA paramilitary organization, or its youth group organization. The remaining cases, listed under the heading of "other" in the table, are a scattered lot of minor infractions of little consequence.

As seen in the discussion of youth and Nazi terror, the control of sexual deviance and sexual license was of prime concern to the Nazis, but they were often divided over the severity of the measures they should use in sexual matters. On the one hand, many Nazis wanted their movement to stand as a bastion of bourgeois respectability to win popular support; on the other hand, Hitler himself was a bohemian, and many Nazis saw their movement as a revolt against bourgeois values.[60] Although the advocates of bourgeois respectability eventually gained the upper hand, the tension that resulted from this division in the movement was never completely resolved, and a measure of ambivalence in sexual matters continued to manifest itself in Nazi policy throughout the years of the Third Reich.

Nowhere was this ambivalence more evident than in the Nazis' perverse and sadistic treatment of male homosexuals.[61] No laws were passed against lesbianism, and very few female homosexuals suffered persecution for their sexual activities,[62] but the Gestapo's persecution of male homosexuals grew in intensity throughout the 1930s and reached a crescendo on the eve of the Second World War. Although raids on homosexual bars and nightspots became commonplace from 1933 onward, the Röhm affair in the summer of 1934 provided a pretext for the police to compile a formal list of all known homosexuals. The notorious paragraph 175 of the criminal code, which defined homosexual acts as illegal and had been on the books since the late nineteenth century, was widened in 1935 to include behavior that merely aroused homosexual desires.[63]

No one knows exactly how many homosexuals were punished in the

Third Reich, but official figures and unofficial estimates demonstrate that the persecution of gay men clearly escalated after the conclusion of the Röhm affair in 1934 and the commencement of the terroristic campaign against the clergy in 1935. Official statistics from the Reich Ministry of Justice indicate that convictions under paragraph 175 of the criminal code rose from 948 in 1934 to 5,321 in 1936, and to 8,270 in 1937.[64] How high these numbers continued to rise is unclear, but the figure of 50,000 that has often been cited in unofficial estimates for the total number of homosexuals convicted by Nazi courts of law does not seem out of line.[65] Nevertheless, even these high numbers do not adequately convey the suffering of homosexuals under Hitler's rule. After 1937 homosexuals, as we saw in the case of the Krefeld priest Suitbert G., were often sent to concentration camps upon the completion of their court sentences. It is uncertain just how many homosexuals experienced this fate; estimates range from 5,000 to 15,000 for the total number of homosexuals who were interned in concentration camps in the Third Reich. Moreover, there is strong evidence that the concentration camp experience for homosexuals was more horrible and more fatal than for most other groups of people. Some estimate that the death rate of homosexuals in the camps stood at approximately 60 percent, a rate that was almost twice that of Jehovah's Witnesses and 50 percent higher than that of political prisoners.[66]

These horrifying figures notwithstanding, the Nazi regime never intended to exterminate all homosexuals, and not all Nazi leaders regarded homosexuality as dangerous. Hitler himself, as George Mosse has pointed out, had originally supported Ernst Röhm even though he was aware of his homosexuality and had based his attitude toward Röhm on "tactical considerations rather than moral judgments." In 1932, when Röhm had been accused of seducing some of his men, Hitler blamed Röhm's homosexuality on his prior life in the tropics, where he had organized the Bolivian army, and asserted that Röhm's private life should be his own affair.[67]

As the Dutch scholar Harry Oosterhuis recently argues in a provocative essay, "Medicine, Male Bonding, and Homosexuality in Nazi Germany," there was a great deal of ambivalence in the Nazis' treatment of homosexuals. He explains that, "in contrast to the 'Holocaust' of the Jews, the persecution of homosexuals was neither wholesale nor systematic."[68]

Furthermore, Oosterhuis objects to "bracketing homosexuals with Jews, the Sinti and Roma, ethnic minorities, psychiatric patients and hereditarily ill people as principal victims of Nazi terror,"[69] as has commonly been done by those who view the Nazis' persecution of homosexuals as a kind of medically oriented purification policy.[70]

To support his argument, Oosterhuis points out that only a small fraction of Germany's homosexuals ever received punishment in Nazi Germany—in a speech to SS officers on the "question of homosexuality" on February 18, 1937, Heinrich Himmler estimated that two million German men were homosexuals—and the majority of those punished were not sent to concentration camps. One of the major reasons for this, Oosterhuis contends, was that a policy calling for the wholesale extermination of homosexuals would have devastated the entire Nazi movement, including not only the SA of Ernst Röhm but also the SS, the Hitler Youth, and the Nazi Party itself. Although Himmler pushed for extreme punishments for homosexuals and had advocated in his speech of February 1937 that SS men found guilty of homosexuality be sent to a concentration camp and then shot "while attempting to escape," the sometimes wide gap between rhetoric and reality in the Third Reich continued to apply to the persecution of homosexuals both in the society and in the Nazi movement. The SS newspaper *Das schwarze Korps* took issue with the contention of the leaders of the German homosexual emancipation movement under Magnus Hirschfeld that homosexuality was an inborn and immutable trait; it maintained that most men who had practiced homosexuality had not done so because they were born homosexuals but because they had been seduced. Thus, the newspaper advocated that a sharp distinction be made in the prosecution of those who had acted as seducers and those who had merely been seduced and called for the "re-education" of the latter through psychological means.[71]

This is, in fact, what generally transpired. Numerous homosexual Nazis, members of the Hitler Youth, and German soldiers were given treatment and "cured" in places like the Institute for Psychological Research and Psychotherapy in Berlin and then released to resume their normal lives.[72] Numerous others, including many who were and many who were not members of the Nazi movement, were "re-educated" in prisons and concentration camps and also managed to return to society or went on to fight with the German army in the war.[73] The majority of Germany's homosexuals, however, never received any punishment or "therapy" at all. Either their activities were never detected or, if they were, the police determined that they were not true homosexuals, for their homosexual acts were the result of being seduced by others. Typically the police let them off with a warning not to let it happen again.

A closer inspection of the homosexual cases in the random sample of Krefeld Gestapo case files helps to illustrate all of this. As table 7.1 shows, there were sixteen cases (all involving males) in the sample. All took place in the mid to late 1930s, when the persecution of German homosexuals was at its height. Most of the cases involved adolescents and young men: only three of the accused were over thirty, six were in their twenties, and seven were teenagers when their cases began. The Krefeld priest Suitbert G., thirty-three at the time of his first arrest in March 1937, was the oldest of the group. The youngest were three boys of fifteen. The accused came from a broad variety of social backgrounds. In addition to the priest Father G., four were simple workers, nine were skilled laborers or technicians, and two were businessmen. In twelve of the sixteen cases, it is possible to determine whether they were affiliated with the Nazi movement: about half of them were. One of the men, a twenty-five-year-old dental technician when his case began in March 1939, had been a member of both the NSDAP and the SA since 1933. Another man, who was a thirty-year-old traveling salesman in May 1937, was a member of the SA.[74] Five of the seven teenagers in the sample were members of the Hitler Youth.

Denunciations started only four of the cases. The Gestapo gained the information it needed to start most of the cases either through previously compiled police lists of known homosexuals or through brutally forced confessions that had led to further accusations. But even if many of the accused individuals in these case files suffered from beatings and other kinds of torture during their interrogations, only four (25 percent of the total) were later convicted in court. Moreover, it appears that only Father G. was sent to a concentration camp, though one cannot rule out the possibility that this also happened to some of the others, even if there is no evidence of such in their Gestapo files. Prison terms for the four people who were convicted by a court ranged from one and a half to three years.

Although these were the only cases that I read in their entirety, I also analyzed archival index cards concerning the prime suspects named in all of the existing Krefeld Gestapo case files that fell under the heading of "homosexuality." These cards provide only summary information on the cases, but they do provide enough details to give one confidence that the cases in the random sample are representative of the rest of the Krefeld Gestapo cases lodged against purported homosexuals. In all, there are 55 separate cases listed under "homosexuality." Given what we know from the cases in the random sample,[75] there had to be between 100 and 200 people in Krefeld who were involved in these cases. But looking only at the 55 prime suspects in these cases, one observes the following. The majority of the cases took place in the late 1930s. Although a clear date was indicated in only one-third of the cases, none took place during the war years. Sixteen, or over 25 percent, of the 55 suspects were clearly affiliated with the Nazi movement, and many others were probably also affiliated with the movement, even though this was not noted on the index cards. Four clearly held Nazi Party membership, at least four others were members of the SA, and six were listed as members of the Hitler Youth. As in the random sample, most of the accused were quite young. Although a few were either teenage or over forty, people in their twenties or early thirties formed the majority. It is not possible from the limited information on the index cards to determine how the Gestapo obtained its information on these people. It is possible, however, to determine that most of the prime suspects were also like the people in the random sample in that only a minority were ever sentenced to a jail or prison term or sent to a concentration camp. Although the cards show that nine of the defendants were convicted by a Nazi court and sentenced to jail or prison terms ranging from a few months to several years, and that four more were taken into "protective custody" and probably sent to concentration camps, it appears that the cases against thirty-six of the accused, or nearly two-thirds, were dismissed either by the Gestapo or by the court authorities. It is unclear what happened to an additional five, or 9 percent of the rest.

The statistical evidence generated from the random sample and from the index cards, showing that most people charged with practicing homosexuality in Krefeld did not receive maximum punishments for their activi-

ties, supports Oosterhuis's argument that the Nazis did not seek the wholesale extermination of German homosexuals and that the police and court
authorities commonly distinguished between those who had had only a
fleeting sexual encounter with another man and those whose manifest sexual preference was for men. Statistical evidence, however, does not convey
the perverse and brutal means that were employed to make these distinctions and the horror and humiliation that homosexuals experienced when
they came face to face with the Gestapo.

    An examination of the case narratives reveals that Gestapo officers like
Alfred Effenberg and Otto Dihr, who conducted many of the interrogations
in the homosexual cases in Krefeld, forced the accused, even those who were
children, to divulge full details about their sexual experiences dating back
to their earliest childhood, sometimes as far back as to the age of three,[76] and
to betray all those with whom they had had relations. These confessions did
not pour out voluntarily. That they came as the result of beatings, threats,
and other forms of torture becomes obvious when one observes that the
interrogations were broken off time and again and then resumed with by-
now familiar phrases like "I confess," "after having been warned," and "I
must correct myself." Finally, the graphic details of the sexual experiences
that the accused were compelled to provide—how they "sucked," "blew,"
"fingered," and "fondled" until the "discharge of semen" resulted—at
times take on such a pornographic cast that one begins to ponder whether
Effenberg, Dihr, and the other Gestapo officers in charge of these cases were
merely eager to uncover objective facts or whether their penetrating questioning and unrestrained authority had aroused other interests in them.[77]

    Indeed, a pronounced sexual and one might say scatological component
is evident in a huge number of cases handled by the Gestapo. We have already witnessed how significant this component was in cases of Jewish men
and women charged with conducting sexual relations with non-Jews and in
cases involving the control of youthful desires for romance and adventure.
It also figured heavily in the remaining two leading categories of offenses
involving "ordinary" Germans listed in table 7.1: cases against Nazi Party,
SA, and Hitler Youth members, and cases against critics of the regime and
its leaders.

Unlike Jews and homosexuals, the offenders in these categories seldom suffered torture during their interrogations or had to endure long periods of confinement in Nazi prisons and concentration camps. The Gestapo generally wasted little of its resources, time, and energy in dealing with these people. When the Gestapo learned about their alleged infractions, it very often had received its information from voluntary denunciations by neighbors, coworkers, and sometimes family members. These denunciations, however, aroused no more than the Gestapo's passing interest in the vast majority of cases. This will be demonstrated in a later chapter through a detailed analysis of the role that denunciations played in the entire run of cases treated by the Krefeld Gestapo and the Cologne Special Court and of the backgrounds and motivations of the individual denouncers. But first, some discussion of the remaining cases involving "ordinary" and sometimes not so ordinary Germans needs to be made.

Allegations of homosexual leanings were not the only type of sexually based charges that implicated members of the Nazi movement. The random sample of the Krefeld Gestapo files contains several cases that pertain to real perversity practiced and perpetrated by Nazi Party members. Sometimes these cases have a cartoonlike character, but they are often so disgusting that they bring no amusement. Two examples will suffice.

The first example is important for several reasons, one of which is that it is the only case in all the cases analyzed for this study in which a child denounced one of his own parents. But this was no young child; it was a married, twenty-eight-year-old milk dealer and Nazi Party member named Heinrich S. After a quarrel at his parents' home in the farming village of Traar on Krefeld's north side on November 2, 1936, in which his father, Dietrich S., kicked him and his new bride out of the parental home, Heinrich S. and his wife went straight away to the local Nazi Party leadership and filed a formal accusation against his father, charging him with a whole host of improprieties. Among these were that his father—a sixty-two-year-old local farmer and Nazi *"alte Kämpfer"* (old Nazi warrior) who had been a member of the Nazi Party since 1930—had repeatedly criticized Hitler, Göring, and other Nazi leaders in the presence of both themselves and others, and that his father had become a dangerous sexual pervert. A few days later, the local Nazi Party leadership informed the Krefeld Gestapo about the charges.

The Gestapo assigned the case to Otto Dihr. In the following month, Dihr summoned several people to testify, including the son and daughter-in-law, a local farmhand, the accused man himself, and his wife and daughter. All but the accused man and his daughter provided a wealth of details in long, signed statements that supported the original accusation. According to those who testified against him, Dietrich S. had come unglued in recent months and had taken to ranting and raving about the shortcomings of Hitler and other top Nazis while walking around his domicile with his fly unzipped and his penis sticking out. On many occasions, they claimed, he had made specific statements like: "What Hitler wants [to create] is communism, only he makes it more slowly"; "Göring is an old whoremonger"; and "The present government [is made up of] nothing but scoundrels and criminals."[78] Worse than this was his strange sexual behavior, on which all of his accusers commented. A passage in his son's sworn testimony contains the following: "When he has his bad days, he walks around the house and also outside in the yard with an exposed penis. It has often come to pass that he has openly masturbated in the house and also in the yard so that everyone in the family could see. . . . The worst perversions that a person can imagine, and these from a mere insane person . . . he commits with our cow. Twice I have clearly and distinctly observed how my father went into the cowshed, wiped the anus of the cow with a rag, then kissed the [cow's] anus several times, and finally climbed up on the milk stool and stuck his member into the cow's anus. My mother has in fact observed that he has done this with all of the cows."[79]

Indeed, when his mother gave her testimony, she supported all of these charges. As she explained, she and her husband had enjoyed a solid relationship up until about three years previously, when her husband started carrying on sexually with a young servant girl, got her pregnant, and then started to become fully weird in ways she elaborated on in even greater detail than her son had done already. All of this was more than enough for the Krefeld Gestapo. On January 25, 1937, Adolf Riekmann, the presiding head of the Krefeld Gestapo (which was still officially called the Krefeld "state police"), wrote a letter to Dr. Klaholt of the Krefeld health bureau stating that Dietrich S. was "a serious danger to the public" and that state police measures against him needed to be taken.

As often transpired in cases involving party members, little happened to Dietrich S. in the end. After being sent for observation to a local psychiatric clinic, he was given a clean bill of health in a matter of weeks and sent home. A few months later, the Krefeld prosecuting attorney's office dropped all charges against him, and the case was closed. The justification used was that Dietrich S.'s daughter had testified that her brother and her mother had fabricated the charges against her father because they wanted to cover up the fact that they had been sleeping with one another.

An even more unseemly case began on August 21, 1938, when two local Krefeld men brought charges against another long-standing Krefeld Nazi who, like Dietrich S., had also joined the Nazi Party in 1930.[80] According to their accusation, a woman they knew had recently told them that her daughter had revealed to her that a fifty-six-year-old, retired customs inspector named Josef J. was molesting her eleven-year-old friend, who had been a foster child in his home for about a year. On the next day, the police summoned both the woman's daughter and the foster child to testify.

The foster child confirmed that what had been charged was basically true, except that she had willingly taken part. Referring to Josef J. as her "father," she told the police that she had had relations with him several times in the following manner. She, her eight-year-old brother, and her foster father all slept upstairs in the attic of their two-floor apartment while her foster mother slept downstairs. Sometimes before she went off to school in the morning, her father would call her to his bed and ask her to play with his penis. Then, she explained, "I always laid down on top of my father and had to hop up and down. Occasionally my father lay down upon me, stuck his peter inside of me, and also hopped up and down. It did not hurt. When water came out from my father, I cleaned it off with a cloth."[81] She concluded her testimony by revealing that she had also done similar things with her foster father's son, who was in his twenties and away from Krefeld in military service at the time.

When Josef J. testified on that same day, he admitted only that he had indeed had the little girl in bed with him on occasion, but he denied that he had ever molested her. To support his statement, he claimed that he was no longer capable of having sex anymore because, he pointed out, "my sexual organ is only one inch long."[82] This fact, he asserted, would be supported by his wife. In her testimony, given later that same day, his wife backed him up, saying that they most certainly did not have sex together anymore. But that was not enough to save him. After his wife had testified, another eleven-year-old girl came forward and told the authorities that Josef J. had also molested her. Josef J. finally gave in and confessed to nearly everything. Two months later, the Krefeld county court sentenced Josef J. to a jail term of one and a half years, and he was also dismissed from the Nazi Party.

Even if the perverse sexual content in these two cases is extreme, the crude behavior of these two aging Nazi die-hards and their lenient treatment by the police and court authorities were not untypical of other cases involving Nazi Party members and others affiliated with the Nazi movement. As is made clear in the second of the two cases, association with the Nazi movement did not make one fully immune to punishment under all circumstances, but it surely helped if one got into trouble. Not one of the scores of Nazi Party members from Krefeld, Cologne, Bergheim, and other communities whose cases were analyzed for this study was ever placed in a concentration camp, even though many of them were charged with openly criticizing Hitler or other leading Nazi officials, perpetrating sexually based felonies, or committing other criminal acts, whether of a political nature or otherwise. This is not to say that it never happened, but it is to say that it happened only on the rarest of occasions. Even membership in the SA, despite its declining status after the Röhm affair, usually helped to shield one from severe prosecution.

In fact, many of the remaining cases involving people affiliated with the Nazi movement were those of SA members who received light or no punishment at all for brutal and thuggish behavior that both the Nazi regime itself and most any other society would not normally tolerate from its citizens. One such case began in the early morning hours of July 18, 1937, when the wife of a local Krefeld pub owner called the police to lodge a complaint for assault and battery against a twenty-nine-year-old, married businessman and member of the SA named August S.[83] After a bout of heavy drinking with several other SA cronies, August S., dressed in his SA uniform, had gotten into an altercation with another man and demanded that he show him his identity papers. When the man refused, August S. beat him to a pulp, and soon the whole bar was in an uproar. When the bar owner's wife asked him to leave the premises, he pulled out a knife and stabbed her on the hand. She then called the police. After a brief investigation, the police decided to dismiss the case without any further ado. The Gestapo originally had nothing to do with the case against August S., but when he was cited a few months later for a similar encounter in which he beat up a Swiss businessman working in Krefeld, his case this time was referred to the Gestapo and handled by Kriminalassistent Theodor Schommer. After his investigation, Schommer did pass the case on to the state prosecuting attorney's office for further action, but that office also decided to dismiss the case against the SA miscreant. Once again, nothing happened to August S. in the end.

It probably comes as no major surprise that Nazi Party members, SA men, and others affiliated with the Nazi movement often received special consideration from the police and court authorities. More eye-opening, however, is the fact that most ordinary Germans, so long as they were upstanding members of the "folk community," which most were, were also permitted a relatively wide degree of latitude to give vent to their everyday frustrations. Even when these were aired in the form of open criticisms of Hitler and the regime, whether in the form of political jokes or outright statements of disapproval, severe punishment seldom followed as a consequence. The Krefeld Gestapo and Cologne Special Court case files are replete with alleged violations of the *Heimtücke* laws against malicious attacks on the Nazi Party and its leadership. But the vast majority of these cases ended in either outright dismissals or modest punishments at the very most. Hundreds of examples could be called on to demonstrate this, but only a few brief examples will be mentioned before such *Heimtücke* cases and the rest of the cases involving ordinary Germans are analyzed statistically in a later chapter (Chapter 9).

On January 26, 1937, a cranky sixty-two-year-old grandmother named Barbara C. from the village of Quadrath who was "well known for not shying away from any means to bring her fellow citizens in a bad light" filed a formal complaint against a man whom she alleged had called Hitler an *"Arschficker"* (a vulgar characterization of a pederast) and a *"warmer*

Bruder" (a common and pejorative term for homosexual).[84] The man, Josef
P., was a married father of two children and a railroad worker in good standing from the neighboring town of Bergheim. According to her denunciation, she herself had not heard Josef P. make these derogatory statements.
They had been made to her nephew more than two years earlier during a
soccer game in late 1934 when the two of them were discussing the Röhm
purge. After her nephew had told her about these remarks shortly after they
had been made, she had brought them forthwith to the attention of the
mayor of Quadrath, who was also the leading Nazi Party official in her village. As it came out in the investigation in January 1937, which was taken
over by the Bergheim policeman Gottfried Schleiden, the mayor had then
passed the information on to his superiors in the local Nazi Party. They, in
turn, decided that the matter was of little consequence and let the matter
rest without informing the police.[85]

Barbara C.'s renewed attempt to bring down Josef P. took place at a time
when she herself had been charged with making similar utterances about
the Führer to her neighbors in Quadrath. In two separate cases pending
against her in early 1937, one that originated with a denunciation by a Nazi
Party *Blockleiter* and the other with a denunciation by his wife, she was
accused of telling the Nazi Party official's wife on one occasion that "Hitler
is [nothing] but an *Arschficker*," and of exclaiming to the *Blockleiter* himself on another occasion that "the [Nazi] Party can lick my ass."[86] In other
details that came out in the course of these two cases, the *Blockleiter* and his
wife charged that not only Barbara C. but also her daughter had scatologi-
cally impugned the reputation of the Führer. Allegedly, in May of the previous year, her daughter had, in their presence, angrily ripped a picture of
Hitler out of the local newspaper and, as she made a wiping motion with the
picture across her backside while she was en route to the toilet, boasted,
"With Hitler I will now wipe my ass!"

Because of Barbara C.'s tarnished reputation and because of a split in
the testimony of the five witnesses summoned in Josef P.'s case, the Cologne
state prosecuting attorney dismissed the charges against him in a ruling
of May 26, 1937. Barbara C. had already been acquitted by a Cologne lay
assessor's court (*Schöffengericht*) on February 27 because of a similar split
in the testimony of the witnesses in the case started against her by the Nazi

Party official. The other case against her was dismissed on April 16 by the Cologne state prosecuting attorney's office for lack of evidence. No official charges were ever brought to bear against Barbara C.'s daughter.

The decisions made by the Nazi Party, police, state prosecuting attorney, and court demonstrate that they considered the cases of Barbara C. and Josef P. rather trivial even though they involved graphic insults of Hitler and the Nazi Party made in the very presence of local Nazi functionaries. Trivial cases that came to naught like these make up the bulk of the Krefeld Gestapo and Cologne Special Court cases lodged against ordinary German citizens in the prewar years. Only exceptional cases started against ordinary Germans concluded with serious punishments for the accused. As mentioned earlier, one became such an exception only if one already had a strike against oneself stemming from a past association with the Communist movement, a history of prior convictions, a Jewish background, or, in some cases, a demonstrable compassion for or association with Jews or other enemies of the state. The case of Heinrich H. from Bergheim was just such an exception.[87]

When the case against him began, Heinrich H. was a married, fifty-seven-year-old milk dealer who had fought in the German infantry in the First World War but also had a police record owing to a minor conviction for libel in 1931. On the morning of June 18, 1938, Heinrich H. went to deliver milk and butter to a restaurant at the Bergheim railroad station as part of his normal daily rounds. While he was handing over the dairy products to the wife of the restaurant owner, a fifty-three-year-old woman named Frau T. whose husband was a member of the Nazi Party, he struck up a conversation with some of the diners. When the conversation turned to the persecution of some members of Bergheim's tiny Jewish community, like the sisters Selma and Berta S. and the cattle dealer Isador F., and to the persecution of German Jews in general, and when Heinrich H. voiced sympathy for the persecuted Jews, the restaurant owner's wife took exception and an argument ensued. At the conclusion of the argument, Heinrich H. threatened to stop making deliveries to the restaurant, and, in fact, he did not make such deliveries for the next several days.

Five days later, on June 23, Frau T. wrote a letter to the Nazi Party leadership in Bergheim accusing Heinrich H. of having made malicious verbal attacks against Hitler and the state and of having made illegal statements in support of Jews. Among the seditious statements she alleged he had made were the following: "The Jews . . . are but decent people; the party is out to get the poor Jews, but the government works with Jewish money"; "The biggest banks in Germany are in fact owned by the Jews Oppenheim and Goldstein. With this money . . . the big cheeses are working"; "The Jews are excellent soldiers. Now they are out to get them. If there is war once again, however, then they will again have need of the Jews."[88]

A week and a day later, on July 1, the Nazi Party *Kreisleiter* Bergmann passed Frau T.'s letter of denunciation on to the Bergheim police, and four days after that the police arrested Heinrich H. In his interrogation, Heinrich H. refused to confess to the charges against him and asserted that it was Frau T. who had started the conversation about Bergheim's Jews in the first place. He also maintained that Frau T.'s denunciation resulted from a struggle he had been having with her husband over his refusal to pay Heinrich H. for the deliveries of milk and butter to his restaurant. His son Peter, a twenty-nine-year-old factory worker, supported this in testimony to the Bergheim police a month later, on August 9. According to his son, the Nazi restaurant owner had warned Heinrich H.: "If you do not provide me with butter within twenty-four hours, I will put you up on charges upon which you will think about for a lifetime."[89]

This was no idle threat. Although there was not enough evidence against Heinrich H. to keep him in jail permanently for his alleged remarks and the Cologne state prosecuting attorney finally suspended this case against him on November 22, 1938, the authorities did not set him free. While he sat in investigative detention, first in Bergheim and later in Cologne's Klingelpütz prison, a new case was mounted against him for child molestation. For that crime the Cologne *Landgericht* sentenced him to a jail sentence of seven months and one day on October 6, 1938. Unfortunately, the records of that case are not available, so it is not possible to determine whether the charges against him were fabricated. But a report to the Reich Ministry of Justice in Berlin on October 21, 1938, written by the Cologne state prosecuting attorney Reuter, arouses one's suspicion, especially because it suggests that the Nazis considered him to be an "asocial" pervert largely because of his open support of Jews:

Cologne Gestapo
Headquarters
(EL-DE-Haus),
c. 1935–1942.
(Historisches
Archiv fer Stadt
Köln)

Row of cells in
the basement of
the Cologne
Gestapo
Headquarters.
(Rheinisches
Amt für
Denkmalpflege)

Krefeld Police
at Gestapo
Headquarters
(Hansa-
Haus), 1934.
(Stadtarchiv
Krefeld)

Wieder ein Gestapo-Prozeß in Köln

Hohe Gestapo-Beamte vor dem Schwurgericht - Schwere Freiheitsberaubung im Amt mit Todesfolge

Top: July1954 trial of the leaders of the Cologne Gestapo. Emanuel Schäfer is standing; Franz Sprinz is the third man sitting down on Schäfer's right; Kurt Matschke is sitting in the foreground (Kölnische Rundschau).

Left: Ludwig Jung, the head of the Krefeld Gestapo, 1938. (BDC)

Ein Reich Ein Volk Ein Führer

Top: Krefeld Rathaus decked out for Saar Plebiscite, 1935. (Stadtarchiv Krefeld)

Right: Alfred Effenberg, a rank-and-file Krefeld Gestapo officer, 1938. (BDC)

Top: Jewish businessmen march through the streets of Leipzig (the placards exclaim: "Don't Buy from Jews! Shop in German Stores"), date uncertain. (William Blye)

Left: Krefeld Synagogue burns on the Peterstrasse during the "Night of Broken Glass" pogrom, Nov. 9–10, 1938. (Stadtarchiv Krefeld)

Bottom: Nazi takeover of the Cologne Rathaus. (Kölnishes Stadtmuseum)

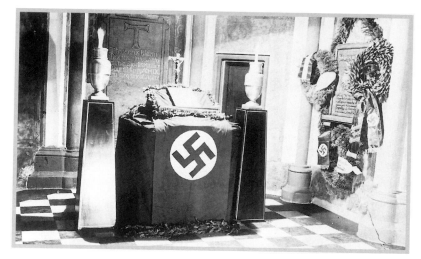

Top: Altar of a Cologne "German Christian" church (Antoniterkirche), 1935. (Evangelisches Gemeindearchiv Köln)

Right: Cologne's Father Josef Spieker. (Norddeutsche Provinz der S. J. Archivin)

Bottom: Cologne carnival float in the Rosenmontag Parade, 1934 (banner reads:"The Last Ones Are Moving Out"). (NS – Dokumentationszentrum *Köln)*

Top: Cologne elementary school (Volksschule) in the Altleinizigenweg, 1937. (Rheinisches Bildarchiv)

Left: League of German Girls (BDM) propaganda placard ("You too belong to the Führer"). (NS - Dokumentationszentrum Köln)

Gestapo mugshots of a Jewish victim from Krefeld, Josef Mahler, 1940. (HStAD)

Top: Hitler salute by
the young "King of the
Schützenfest" in
Krefeld-Fischeln, 1936.
(Stadtarchiv Krefeld)

Right: Krefeld carnival
float in Rosenmontag
Parade, 1939 (The ban-
ner states: "Strength
Through Joy").
(Stadtarchiv Krefeld)

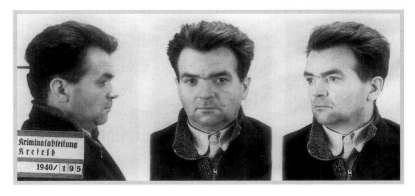

Gestapo mugshots of a leading Krefeld Communist, Peter Z., 1940. (HStAD)

The Cologne
Cathedral and
Rhine Bridge
near the end of
the war.
(Historisches
Archiv der Stadt
Köln)

Head of the
Krefeld Gestapo
Jewish Desk,
Richard
Schulenburg, c.
1936.
(Stadtarchiv
Krefeld)

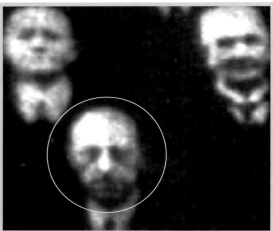

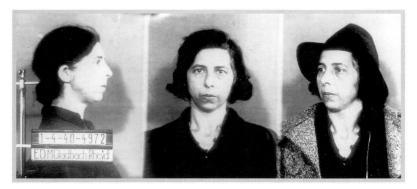

Gestapo mugshots of a Jewish victim, Hedwig Mahler,
from Krefeld, 1940. (HStAD)

The statements of the accused display a strongly adverse attitude toward the National Socialist state and, in particular, to National Socialist racial policy. Since he previously sympathized with leftist parties and cannot integrate himself into the folk community, there are reasons to conclude that what is involved here is a person who is fundamentally hostile to the state. In this regard, one must also add that he has recently been punished as a morals' offender, thereby confirming his asocial nature.[90]

The case of Heinrich H. shows that denunciations from the civilian population could lead to dire consequences. But the prior cases of Josef P. and Barbara C., which were more typical of the run of cases involving ordinary Germans, demonstrate that they usually did not. Josef P. was an upstanding citizen. Barbara C. was an innocuous, if quarrelsome, old woman. But Heinrich H. was tainted because he had a past association with the left and because he had a criminal record. Criticizing the Nazi Party and even Hitler could be tolerated within limits, for it was often understood as rather normal behavior. For the Nazis, however, only a dangerous "asocial" person would openly show compassion for Jews.[91]

CHAPTER EIGHT

On the morning of September 1, 1939, citizens of Cologne, Krefeld, and other German cities turned on their "people's radios" to hear Hitler's Reichstag speech. The Führer informed them that a German broadcasting station one mile from the Polish border at Gleiwitz had been attacked the previous evening by regular Polish troops and that at 5:45 A.M. he had ordered German troops to return fire. They did not know at the time that the alleged Polish attack was a fabrication planned weeks earlier by Heinrich Himmler and Reinhard Heydrich and that it had been carried out by German stormtroopers masquerading in Polish uniforms under the leadership of the notorious SS and SD dirty trickster Alfred Naujocks and the soon-to-be head of the Cologne Gestapo, Dr. Emanuel Schäfer.[1] This nicety aside, the Second World War had begun.

Remembering well what the First World War had meant for Germany, most Germans were apprehensive at first. Soon their fears gave way to cautious optimism as the German military's *Blitzkrieg* tactics easily demolished the Polish army in a matter of weeks. When France capitulated in June 1940, the popular mood became euphoric.[2] This time there was no "miracle of the Marne." Hitler and the German army seemed invincible, and the German population was awash in the spoils of war. Howard K. Smith, the celebrated television anchorman, was an American newspaper reporter stationed in Berlin before America entered the war in December 1941. In a book he published in 1942 on his return to the United States, Smith remembered:

> The conquest of France, for instance, yielded a wide-open treasure chest to the German civil population. . . . Berlin charwomen and housemaids, whose legs had never been caressed by silk, began wearing silk stockings from the Boulevard Haussman as an everyday thing—"from my Hans at the front." Little street corner taverns began displaying rows of Armagnac, Martell and Courvoisier cognac from the cellars of Maxim's and others. Every little bureaucrat in the capital could produce at dinner a fine, fat bottle of the best French champagne. . . . War was almost fun.[3]

The Russian invasion, beginning on June 22, 1941, seemed victorious at first but soon brought worries. In the summer and early fall of 1941, the German army marched quickly through hundreds of miles of eastern European territory, taking eastern Poland, the Baltic states, White Russia, and much of Ukraine. Before winter fell and halted its advance, the German army stood at the gates of Moscow and Leningrad. Nevertheless, the Russian campaign demanded serious sacrifices for the first time on the part of the civilian population, since the needs of the troops—stretched out along a front of hundreds of miles of "scorched earth"—came first. The riches and booty that German civilians had enjoyed in the first two war years came to an abrupt end. War was no longer enjoyable.[4]

German rations had held up well compared with those of other countries for most of the war, and life had continued on an almost normal basis for most Germans in Cologne and other communities well into 1942.[5] But the German people's unshakable belief in the "Hitler myth" started to crumble with the attack on the Soviet Union. Most shed no tears, but not a few became concerned when rumors about mass shootings of Jews and others in the wake of the German army began to seep back home soon after the Russian invasion commenced. Those rumors started to become believable with the first large-scale deportations of German Jews to the east beginning in October 1941.[6] The archbishop of Münster, Clemens August Count von Galen, had already alarmed the German public in a sermon of August 3, 1941, in which he decried the heartless and cold-blooded murder that had already taken place of up to 100,000 mentally and physically ill persons in German extermination centers.[7] His sermon was repeated soon afterward by several clergymen elsewhere and copied, duplicated, and dropped by RAF bombers across Germany. Unlike the easy victories the German army had enjoyed in the west, the war in the east dragged on into the winter of 1941–42 and beyond, and fears began to mount about the length and possible outcome of what now was certain to be a protracted war. And finally, Hitler's reputation also suffered when the German population began to refer cynically to the Luftwaffe leader Hermann Göring as "Marshal Maier" with the escalation in ferocity and intensity of RAF bombing attacks.[8] Before the war began, Göring had boasted that people could call him Maier if a single foreign warplane managed to fly over Germany territory.

According to Ian Kershaw, by the summer of 1942, and especially after the fall of Stalingrad, rumors became widespread that Hitler was mentally and physically ill, that he had "fits and frenzies of rage, [and] that he had to be accompanied everywhere by a doctor specializing in mental illness."[9] When Stalingrad fell in January 1943, Kershaw explains, "the 'Führer myth' was now plainly on the defensive. . . . Deep shock, dismay, and depression were recorded everywhere. It was correctly viewed as the low point of wartime morale on the home front."[10]

Despite the precipitous drop in Hitler's prestige after Stalingrad and a growing sense that the war would be eventually lost, most Germans at the front and at home continued to soldier on to the bitter end, believing that their fate was inexorably tied to that of their Führer. Many were disillusioned and pessimistic, but only a few mounted meaningful resistance efforts against the regime, even in the last years of the war. Needless to say, the Gestapo soon found out about nearly all of those who seriously tried to resist, and many of them had to pay for their attempts with their lives.

One can point, for example, to the courageous resistance efforts of the "White Rose" group led by the Munich University students Hans and Sophie Scholl and Alexander Schmorell. With some contacts at other universities in Berlin, Vienna, and especially Hamburg, they spread anti-Nazi leaflets and tarred university buildings with phrases and slogans calling for passive resistance against the regime from the summer of 1942 to February 1943. Those efforts soon cost them their lives.[11] Of more potential consequence was the attempted assassination of Hitler on July 20, 1944, by Claus Schenk Count von Stauffenberg. That attempt was part of a broader conspiracy against Hitler organized by nationalist conservative leaders of the Kreisau Circle who had important ties to some leading figures in the military, counterintelligence service, and aristocracy, and to some others in the clergy and even in the trade unions.[12] But this attempted coup also failed, and most of the people involved in it were uncovered and put to death, many in show trials presided over by the notorious hanging judge Roland Freisler of the People's Court.[13] One can also mention working-class and Communist resistance efforts such as those of the Edelweiss Pirates, the National Committee "Free Germany," and the "Red Orchestra," which also were brutally dealt with near the end of the war.[14] All of these resistance circles, noble as they were, offered too little too late and probably had little chance for success anyway, especially because they had little support from the broad reaches of the German population. Gerhard Weinberg offers a harsh, though perhaps fitting, summation: "The population, combining fear and apathy with devotion and hope, continued to support the regime until the last days of the war. Only as Allied troops appeared in Germany itself did substantial numbers turn their backs on the system they had served."[15]

The will of the German people to resist the Nazi leadership was far less powerful than their will to resist their foreign enemies. Perhaps the best example of their resolve is the continued high level of productivity of German workers in the face of near-constant aerial bombardment, which brought far more Germans face to face with terror than anything the Gestapo and the other organs of the Nazi terror apparatus had dealt them. Cologne and Krefeld were two of the hardest-hit cities in all of Germany. Between May 1940 and March 1945, the alarm sirens rang out 1,122 times in Cologne, and the city was hit by 262 separate air attacks. Most of these were carried out by the British RAF bombers in the cover of night, but toward the end of the war the U.S. Army/Air Force joined in as well, bombing mostly during daylight hours.[16] The first attacks in 1940 caused little damage, even if they exposed the lie in Göring's earlier boast. But after March 2, 1941, when 100 RAF bombers pounded the city and lines of fire 500 meters long raged through the working-class Kalk section on the east side of the Rhine, the citizens of Cologne could no longer go to bed without suffering constant fear that the next morning they might be found lying dead among the ruins and ashes or that they would no longer have a roof over their heads.

In February 1942, the British war cabinet decided to target the German civilian population as the major focus of RAF air attacks to try to turn them away from Hitler. This policy clearly did not work and may even have had the opposite effect. The most devastating wartime air raid to hit the city of Krefeld was carried out by 705 RAF bombers between one-thirty and two-thirty in the early morning darkness of June 22, 1943; it took the lives of 1,036 Krefeld citizens. In an introductory essay to a book about eyewitness accounts of this air raid, Hans Vogt writes: "The bombing attacks triggered nothing other than horror and swooning rage in the German population that was not directed primarily against the National Socialist state but against the allies and their 'terror bombers.' Despite the air attacks on the cities, the German war economy reached its high point in production in 1943 and 1944."[17]

Similar reactions in other German cities have been recorded.[18] Some Germans go so far as to call the terroristic RAF bombing attacks "war crimes." In his book on Cologne in the Third Reich, the jurist Adolf Klein writes: "This type of carrying on warfare had little to do with humanity; it was a repeated [and] severe war crime."[19] Klein goes on to describe in detail the unnecessary suffering of the Cologne population owing to the RAF's terror tactics. He argues that these had little impact on the city's industrial capacity: almost no damage was done to factories in and around the city until the last year of the war. But they caused an enormous loss of life, particularly of children, women, and elderly people, since young men were away at the front, and a senseless destruction of the city's priceless cultural icons. One of Klein's prime examples is the first of the RAF's 1,000 bomber attacks on Cologne. In this single raid on May 31, 1942, an otherwise "mild spring night," nearly 13,000 houses were damaged and more than 3,000 completely destroyed, making some 45,132 people homeless. Although "only" 496 were killed in this attack, 21 churches were demolished, including some of the oldest and most revered houses of worship in all of Germany, such as Saint Maria im Kapitol, Saint Aposteln, Saint Gereon, and Gross Saint Martin's Church.

Some consider it a miracle that the most prized of all of Cologne's churches, the Cologne cathedral, managed to survive this attack and indeed survived the war largely intact. The tallest structure in northern Europe

until the Eiffel tower in Paris was erected in the late nineteenth century, the
cathedral still stands majestically, and at the time vulnerably, atop a hill only
a short distance from the Rhine River and just adjacent to Cologne's main
train station and one of the most important railroad bridges across the
Rhine in the entire country. In November 1989, I marveled at the beauty
and size of the cathedral in the company of my father, who had been an
American B-24 bomber pilot during the war and was later the pilot of a P-
38 fighter-bomber. He was subsequently shot down and spent the last six
months of the war in a German POW camp, Stalag Luft I in Barth on the
Baltic Sea between Rostock and Stralsund. Although my father had not
taken part in the bombing of Cologne, I figured he could explain why the
cathedral had been spared when every other building in the central city,
including the train station, had been leveled by the end of the war. I suggested that the cathedral must have been left intact because of the precision
bombing and because no Allied pilot wanted to have the destruction of a
cathedral on his conscience. My father replied that my reasoning was false.
"Precision bombing," he explained, "meant within a diameter of about
three miles." Furthermore, he observed, the nighttime carpet bombing used
against Cologne had very little to do with "precision bombing." Later I
learned that the cathedral had in fact been struck fourteen times, mostly
during the later stages of the war. Hence, it was something of a miracle that
the cathedral survived. Well into the mid-1990s, a kind of "wailing wall" in
front of the main entrance of the cathedral confronted visitors with well-
intended messages written piously, if sometimes a bit sanctimoniously, in
several languages. Some were accompanied by eerie photographs of the
proud church looming ominously above the ruins of an obliterated urban
landscape, reminding one and all of the horror that the war and the bombing
wrought upon Cologne and Germany.

A diary entry of September 3, 1944, by a soldier on the eastern front
who was shocked at the sight of the city when he returned home on furlough provides a vivid description of how Cologne looked near the end of
the war. "Cologne offers the picture of a city at the front. The dominant
color: a gloomy gray. The nights of bombing have stamped an impression
of devastation upon the city: the wreckage of houses, the ruins of churches,
mountains of rubble on the streets and sidewalks, bomb craters, weeds, gar-

bage, rubbish. . . . The people in a hurry, constantly on the way to the bunker, always listening for the howling of the sirens."[20] There is no exaggeration in this description. Cologne had been bombed roughly once a week throughout the war. The air-raid sirens sounded more than half the days of the week from May 1940 to March 1945, and nearly nightly for the last three years. The number of people killed in the bombing equaled the number of soldiers who died at the front (about 20,000). Roughly 40,000 more people were wounded. More than 200,000 private dwellings lay in ruins; nary a house still stood in the entire inner city or in the working-class sections like Nippes, Ehrenfeld, Kalk, and Mühlheim. Only about 40,000 people still lived in the soot and ashes when the first American tanks entered the city on March 5, 1945.[21]

The terror that German citizens suffered from Allied bombing attacks, though horrific, cannot be compared with the terror that the Nazi state and many of its citizens perpetrated on the Jews, handicapped, Sinti and Roma, foreign enemies, and a few other groups of people. To their credit, most Germans today realize this, quite unlike, perhaps, the Japanese. The bombings of Hiroshima and Nagasaki, images that emphasize Japanese victimhood, have become the central images of the war that many Japanese choose to remember, overlooking examples of their own hideous cruelty—to the victims of the rape of Nanking, for instance.[22] German society may have done more than Japan to come to grips with its responsibility for what happened during the war, selecting Auschwitz and the Holocaust instead of the bombing of Cologne, Dresden, and other German cities as the prime symbols of German remembrance. But many Germans also find solace in emphasizing the victimhood of common German citizens during the Third Reich, both from Allied bombing attacks and from the supposedly all-knowing and all-powerful Gestapo.

As the previous chapters on the Gestapo and Nazi terror in the 1930s have demonstrated, however, the Gestapo was not all-knowing and all-powerful. It recognized that most German citizens posed no threat to the stability of the Nazi state and leadership, and it devoted most of its resources and energy to the task of combating specifically targeted groups while leaving most of the rest of the society largely untouched. In the main, this was also true during the war. The targeted groups changed somewhat, and the punishments the Gestapo and the courts meted out frequently became harsher, but most ordinary Germans on the homefront suffered far less from Nazi terror than from the terror that came raining down on them from the skies.

The war provided the Nazi leadership with a new set of opportunities and a new set of problems. Under the cover of warfare, the regime took the initiative to realize its most radical racial and social goals, like the murder of the European Jews and the elimination of the Sinti and Roma and the mentally and physically ill from German society. The successful accomplishment of these goals required that the Nazi leadership be particularly sensitive to the popular mood of German citizens; it needed their silence and complicity. Upholding public morale became ever more difficult in the face of the continuous bombing attacks and the increasing privations and hardships that the citizenry had to endure during the course of the war. In addition, the regime had to devote an increasing amount of its resources to the control of the millions of foreign workers it had imported to replace the German workingmen called away to fight at the front.[23] Finally, all of this had to be accomplished with a reduced staff of Gestapo officers and other policemen in many German cities and towns. During the war many of these men were called up for military service, posted to conquered territories outside the Reich, or sent abroad for brief periods to take part in *Einsatzgruppen* murders of Jews and "partisans." The staff of the Cologne Gestapo, for example, declined from ninety-nine officers in 1939 to only sixty-nine officers in 1942.[24]

If it was to accomplish its radicalized racial and social goals, with a reduced number of Gestapo and police officers on hand, while keeping up industrial productivity and popular morale, the Nazi regime could ill afford to police every minor incidence of civilian noncompliance and wrongdoing. Although it issued a series of new laws and decrees calling for the drastic punishment of violators and made a big play in the newspapers and other media of selected show trials followed by summary executions, it often displayed, at the same time, remarkable leniency and understanding in dealing with ordinary Germans. One might say that a tacit Faustian bargain was struck between the regime and the citizenry. In most instances, the regime chose to look the other way when average citizens listened to outlawed radio broadcasts, complained privately about the economy and the war, or committed other minor infractions. In return, the citizenry kept up their productive efforts and looked the other way—or even took part if called on[25]— as the Jews were being butchered.

As applied to most ordinary Germans, therefore, the Nazi terror in wartime had much in common with the Nazi terror in peacetime. Nevertheless, some important differences between the wartime and the peacetime terror need to be considered. Three of the most important relate to the stiffening of the sanctions applied by the Nazi terror apparatus during the war; the policing of new, war-related offenses, such as plundering after bombing attacks, listening to foreign-radio broadcasts, and spreading defeatist sentiments; and finally, the raging insanity that came to characterize Nazi terror at the war's end.

THE INCREASING HARSHNESS OF SANCTIONS IN WARTIME

Three days after Cologne suffered its first 1,000-RAF bomber attack, the major Cologne newspapers featured a shocking story about the beheading of a single, forty-six-year-old seamstress named Paula W. earlier that morning in Cologne's Klingelpütz prison. Reported executions were nothing new to the Cologne citizenry: in addition to being the main prison in the Cologne area, Klingelpütz was the site for carrying out executions ordered by courts from a wide territory in the Rhine-Ruhr region, stretching from Münster in the north to Koblenz in the south, and from Dortmund in the east to Aachen in the west. But this execution, ordered by the Cologne Special Court on the previous day and coming only seventy-two hours after Paula W. had committed her crime, was meant to be special. It would serve as a demonstration of the lightning-quick speed of the wartime justice system and as a severe warning to one and all that they could expect the same thing to happen to them if they attempted to enrich themselves at the expense of others who had suffered from the Allied bombing. It was indeed a severe warning. Paula W., a woman with no previous criminal record, had been denounced anonymously and sentenced summarily to death for committing what most people would consider only a minor criminal act. Returning to the smoking ruins of her bombed-out apartment building in the

downtown Beethovenstrasse on the afternoon following the bombing attack to retrieve what was left of her belongings, she was observed taking, in
addition to her own personal effects, some curtains, a few pairs of men's
underwear, a dress, and three cans of coffee.[26]

Ralph Angermund, the author of an important study of Weimar and
Nazi justice, demonstrates that some people were executed for even less.
The Essen Special Court, for example, sentenced a retired and disabled Lith-
uanian man on March 8, 1943, for pilfering three tin bowls with a total
worth of about three marks from a partially destroyed local store after a
heavy bombing attack on the city of Essen.[27] Similar examples can be found
elsewhere. Nevertheless, we need to ask: How typical were these cases, and
how characteristic of Nazi justice in wartime were they? After all, Paula
W.'s case would not have received such propagandistic play had it not been
unusual.[28] A register of Klingelpütz prisoners shows, in fact, that Paula W.
was only one of five Cologne women, and only one of a total of twenty-two
women from the entire Rhine-Ruhr region (including four foreign workers), who were sentenced to death and executed in Cologne between 1941
and the end of the war.[29]

As Angermund correctly admonishes, it would be incorrect to describe
the administration of justice in wartime Germany in broad brush strokes as
a mere "series of death sentences." When one examines the issue carefully,
one finds a complex picture that varied greatly depending on the particular
judges and prosecuting attorneys involved, the nature of the offense, the
background of the accused, and a variety of other factors.[30] Several other
cases of plundering and other war-related offenses to be discussed shortly
will show that the death sentence was certainly not the typical sanction
handed out by German courts for offenses like plundering after a bombing
attack, or for most other criminal offenses either. Also, it will be demonstrated that the Gestapo did not send most accused Germans to a concentration camp without recourse to a judicial proceeding or after they had served
out their sentences. Finally, one must bear in mind that most criminal and
political offenses went unreported in the Third Reich, perhaps particularly
in the war years. In an official pronouncement of November 30, 1943, the
head of the Cologne Superior Court, Dr. Lawall, stated that "although an
exceptional amount of plundering has taken place in Cologne, only rela-

tively few cases have been attained to pass judgment on." He speculated that "many folk comrades today hold back from making complaints because they do not want to take responsibility for the expected high sentences." Later in the same pronouncement, Dr. Lawall also referred to cases of listening to foreign-radio broadcasts, which he described as "not seldom listened to" and as "talked about much more openly than one commonly would expect given the threat of severe punishment."[31]

Punishment in wartime Germany may not have led to death sentences or concentration camp in most cases, and many offenses certainly went unreported. Nevertheless, Nazi justice became more severe and brutal in the war years. Throughout the war, the Justice Ministry in Berlin constantly urged local prosecutors and judges to speed up their deliberations and rebuked them frequently for rendering verdicts that it considered "too mild."[32] Only a few days after the war began, the Justice Ministry declared that German justice authorities were henceforth to consider themselves "soldiers on the homefront." They were to proceed against Volksschädlinge (a Nazi term meaning "antisocial parasites" but that here referred to criminals of almost any sort who might weaken Germany's ability to wage war) with the "utmost severity" so as to guarantee that the valiant sacrifices of German troops would not once again be sabotaged by a "stab in the back" from the miscreants at home whom Nazis believed caused Germany's defeat in the First World War.[33] With the attack on the Soviet Union, the Justice Ministry's demands for harsher punishment became ever more urgent. Hence, on July 9, 1941, the ministry wrote to all local prosecutors: "While the German soldier places his life out there on the line, the German administration of justice must unconditionally guarantee that undisciplined rabble-rousers cannot endanger the peace, security, and working environment [on the homefront] behind his back."[34] In a subsequent circular letter of October 28, 1941, the ministry's tone became even sterner: "The administration of justice must proceed with the most severe measures against all habitual and professional criminals, all antisocial parasites, and all those who commit crimes damaging the war economy, in sum, all those who weaken, undermine, or endanger the fighting efforts of our people." To accomplish this, the Justice Ministry commanded justice authorities to proceed with "speed and severity even in preliminary proceedings."[35]

Demands made on the justice authorities to deliver harsh and speedy
punishments, such as those already described, often came as echoes of pronouncements made by the Führer himself. In a powerful Reichstag speech
of December 12, 1941, Hitler proclaimed: "In a time when thousands of our
best men, fathers, and sons of our people are dying, no one who dishonors
those who sacrifice their lives on the front deserves to live."[36] Three days
after Hitler's speech, the Justice Ministry once again reminded local justice
officials to prosecute with vigor and dispatch, this time in a letter to the
presidents of all Superior Court districts: "An important factor in maintaining the undiminished ability of the German people on the homefront to
resist [the enemy] is the quick and efficient work of the German administration of justice."[37]

The continual urgings by Hitler and the Justice Ministry to impose
harsher and speedier justice would not have been necessary if local justice
authorities had readily complied with them. Angermund cites many examples of delaying tactics employed by judges in several localities who tried to
maintain some respect for law and decency.[38] An analysis of a large random
sample of cases from the Cologne Special Court files demonstrates in fact
that the wheels of justice for those whose cases were decided by the courts
actually turned more slowly during the war years than in the prewar period.
Between 1940 and 1945, the average time that elapsed from the day an investigation was opened against a defendant to the day a verdict was reached
by the court was approximately six months; in the prewar period, the average case lasted for about half that length of time. And even though there can
be no doubt that the severity of sentences for convicted defendants increased considerably in the war years, many of the judgments eventually
rendered remained relatively mild under the circumstances.[39]

If most defendants managed to escape the executioner's axe, many others did not. Richard Evans, the author of a recent and massive study of capital punishment in German history, calculates that before the outbreak of
the war "only" 644 persons had been sentenced to death in Nazi Germany.[40]
During the war, the number of those condemned to death increased exponentially. Already in the first months of the war, many new offenses came
on the books that were punishable by the death penalty; by the early 1940s,
the death penalty was called for in more than forty separate types of of-

fenses. Examples of offenses for which the death penalty could now be imposed were spreading news obtained from foreign-radio broadcasts in "especially serious cases"; plundering during air raids; attempting to undermine the German military effort (*Wehrkraftzersetzung*); arson; treason; and using guns while committing a robbery, rape, or any other serious crime of violence or in resisting arrest. In February 1941, the criminal code was further amended to make "habitual criminals" and even sexual offenders liable to the death penalty.[41]

Although the Special Courts, which grew in number from 27 in 1938 to 74 by the end of 1942, handled the majority of political and war-related offenses, and their jurisdiction during the war years was extended to cover the majority of criminal offenses, by the mid-1940s the most dreaded tribunal in Nazi Germany was unquestionably the People's Court in Berlin.[42] In existence since July 1934, the People's Court was expected "to exterminate the enemies of the Third Reich, especially Communists and Social Democrats, to the last man."[43] In the 1930s, however, the People's Court did not resort to the death sentence in most of its cases. Between 1934 and 1936, it imposed the death penalty only 23 times, and between 1937 and 1939 only 85 times. In the first two years of the war, these numbers rose substantially, with 53 death sentences imposed in 1940 and 102 in 1941. The major expansion came, however, when the German war effort took a turn for the worse in 1942 and the sadistic Roland Freisler took over as the head of the People's Court. In that year, nearly twelve times more people received the death sentence (1,192) than in the previous year, and from that time on the numbers of condemned continued to grow. It is unknown how many death sentences followed the attempted assassination of Hitler on July 20, 1944, but up until that time the People's Court had sentenced 5,191 persons to death.[44]

Richard Evans, who includes sentences rendered by all German courts in his analysis, uncovers trends in death-sentencing similar to those of the People's Court, with 1942 marking the year of the greatest escalation in judicial murder. According to his estimate, about 16,500 persons were condemned to death by civilian courts in German territory between 1933 and 1944, but these included annexed territories such as Austria, parts of Poland, and Czechoslovakia. Nevertheless, he calculates that more than 11,000 of these death sentences were imposed during the war, and as many as 20,000 additional executions, he says, were also ordered by military courts.[45]

These statistics are sobering. They can also be misleading if not interpreted cautiously. For one thing, many of those who received a harsh sentence in Nazi Germany were not of German background. Realizing this, Evans points out that an enormous number of those who received the death sentence were foreigners and Jews. He explains that in the first half of 1942, for example, 530 out of 1,146 death sentences imposed by German courts were passed against Poles alone.[46] Ralph Angermund estimates that more than 90 percent of life sentences and more than 50 percent of all death sentences in 1941 were handed out by courts in eastern European territories where only 16 percent of the total population of the greater German Reich lived and where the overwhelming majority of the population was of foreign background. In 1942 the percentage of foreigners receiving the death sentence appears to have been even higher than in 1941: according to Angermund's calculations, foreigners accounted for more than 55 percent of all death sentences in that year.[47]

An offense that would have been punished by a limited prison term for a German often led to a sentence of life imprisonment or death for a Pole, Russian, Jew, or Gypsy. But even this level of severity was not enough to satisfy many leading Nazis. Hence, in 1942 the head of the SS, Heinrich Himmler, stated that "doubtlessly the justice system now passes very harsh sentences against such persons, but that is not sufficient. It also makes no sense to conserve such persons for years on end in German jails and prisons." For Himmler, only the systematic extermination of all non-Aryan wrongdoers would be satisfactory, and this, he believed, could be accomplished only by direct police action taken outside the confines of the legal system.[48]

In sharp contrast, the Justice Ministry sent repeated instructions to local justice authorities to make sure that the stiff sentences it had urged them to pass against serious offenders did not come at the expense of the war economy. Thus, in the same letter it sent to Superior Court prosecutors on October 28, 1941, demanding that they proceed quickly and severely against "antisocial parasites" and "habitual and professional criminals," the Justice Ministry also warned the prosecutors to make certain that the war economy was not harmed by false denunciations of important workers, who were accused "not seldom on the basis of envy, ill will, and injudiciousness."[49] Ten months later, on August 7, 1942, the Justice Ministry went even further by urging the prosecutors to distinguish between what they termed "real antisocial parasites" and upstanding citizens who had made only a minor blunder: "The uncompromising hardness of the criminal justice system against real antisocial parasites on the one side must be accompanied by the understanding treatment of those comrades who, while conducting respectable lives in society and carrying out their duty, have made only one insignificant error without any great harm done."[50]

The evidence from the Cologne Special Court and the Krefeld Gestapo case files shows that such distinctions were always made in the Third Reich, but increasingly so in the war years. An analysis of 373 randomly selected prewar cases and 143 randomly selected wartime cases of the Cologne Special Court files shows that Nazi justice was almost always lenient on German citizens who had no prior criminal record so long as they were not members of "targeted" groups like Communists, Jews, or Jehovah's Witnesses. Even if one includes members of these targeted groups in the analysis, however, one finds that the vast majority of cases did not end in convictions for those with no prior criminal record, and that those defendants who were convicted received comparatively light sentences—typically a jail term of a few weeks or months or a fine and only rarely a jail term of more than one year.[51] In the 1930s only 8 percent of first-time defendants' cases ended in a conviction, 4 percent ended with an acquittal, and the remaining 88 percent ended in a dismissal. During the war, there was a marked trend toward more frequent convictions, but still less than one-fifth (18 percent) of the cases of defendants with no prior criminal record ended with a conviction, as against more than four-fifths whose cases ended with either an acquittal (3 percent) or a dismissal (79 percent).

"Habitual and professional criminals" always accounted for a sizable proportion of the Special Court's cases and an even higher proportion of those who suffered punishment. In an average year in both the prewar and wartime periods, Special Court defendants with a prior criminal record made up about one-quarter of all defendants, and about one-half of those who were convicted. As one might expect, the peak years for the prosecution of those with a criminal record came during the last years of the war. Hence, when the Justice Ministry directed local justice officials in 1942 to make extra efforts to distinguish between "real antisocial parasites" and upstanding citizens who had only made a single blunder, the percentage of defendants with a history of past offenses reached its zenith at 38 percent, and in the following year it continued to hold steady at 32 percent. More important, however, was the differential treatment these people received once a case had been started against them. Throughout the years of the Third Reich, they were more than three times as likely to be convicted if a new case was started against them as were those being subjected to a criminal procedure for the first time. It was in the war years, however, that this difference between the two groups became most pronounced. Between 1940 and 1945, defendants with a prior criminal record accounted for more than 50 percent of all convictions, their rate of conviction climbed to 61 percent, and they more often than not received severe sentences if they were convicted.

The case files of the Krefeld Gestapo display similar trends. Over the entire period of the Third Reich, non-Jewish defendants with a criminal record accounted for about one-quarter of all non-Jewish cases, just as they did in the Cologne Special Court case files. Also, as had been the case in the middle war years in Cologne, the percentage of all new investigations accounted for by these defendants rose sharply, reaching over 33 percent in 1941 and 1942. Moreover, they were much more likely to be punished than those with no prior criminal record if an investigation was opened against them, and the punishment they received was usually more severe.[52]

The racial background and past criminal records of defendants are only two of the important factors to consider in comparing the record of Nazi persecution in the war years with that of the prewar period and in assessing to what extent Nazi persecution stiffened during the war for ordinary Germans. An equally important factor is the sheer volume of cases handled by the Gestapo and the Special Courts. Consideration of this factor uncovers the fact that a trend toward harsher punishment was significantly mitigated by an overall decline in the number of cases during the war years. This effect was so pronounced that one could argue that any stiffening of punishment in the war had little to no effect on all but a tiny minority of ordinary German citizens.

TABLE 8.1 *Krefeld Gestapo and Cologne Special Court Cases, 1933–1945*

	KREFELD GESTAPO[a]		COLOGNE SPECIAL COURT[b]	
	NUMBER	PERCENTAGE	NUMBER	PERCENTAGE
1933	33	8	2,574	9
1934	51	12	4,199	15
1935	28	7	4,063	14
1936	28	7	3,606	12
1937	59	14	3,361	12
1938	47	11	2,229	8
1939	44	10	1,889	7
1940	38	8	1,407	5
1941	36	8	1,072	4
1942	33	8	1,445	5
1943	29	7	1,168	4
1944	5	1	1,679	6
1945	—	—	164	1
TOTAL	431		28,856	

[a]Based on a random sample of every eighth Krefeld Gestapo case file.
[b]Based on a computer analysis of the entire register of Cologne Special Court cases.

The figures for yearly trends in the total number of cases handled by the Krefeld Gestapo and the Cologne Special Court displayed in table 8.1 show that both the Gestapo and the courts had their largest caseloads in the 1930s when Nazi terror concentrated on leftist and religious adversaries. By the outbreak of the war, these targeted groups had been largely dealt with and the Nazis could place their focus on other groups that they wished to reckon with, such as habitual and professional criminals, foreign workers, prisoners of war, and Jews. This is demonstrated in table 8.2, which breaks down the Krefeld Gestapo's caseload into separate categories of defendants in the prewar and the war years.

As table 8.2 further indicates, the percentage of "ordinary German" defendants held mostly steady throughout the years of Nazi Germany, though there was a modest decline in the percentage of cases they accounted

TABLE 8.2 *Krefeld Gestapo Caseload,*
by Category of Defendant, 1933–1945

	1933–1939	1940–1945	1933–1945
Jews	20%	35%	25%
KPD / SPD	27	6	20
Religious sects	9	—	6
Foreign workers and prisoners	—	18	6
"Ordinary Germans"	44	41	43
NUMBER OF CASES	291	141	432

NOTE: Based on a random sample of every eighth Krefeld Gestapo case file.

for during the war years. But as shown in table 8.1, the absolute number of all defendants declined in the war years to a level that was only a fraction of what it had been previously. In 1941 and 1943, for example, the number of cases handled by the Cologne Special Court was only about one-fourth the number of cases the court had handled in 1934 and 1935; in war years with a lower volume of cases, like 1940 and 1942, the court handled only one-third to one-half the number of cases it had handled during most of the years of the 1930s. The drop-off in the caseload of the Krefeld Gestapo was less pronounced, but also significant.

What accounts for the decline in the number of cases is a matter of speculation, but it was not caused by more law-abiding behavior on the part of the population. Even if few resisted the Nazis in any meaningful way, SD mood and morale reports show that there was an increase in grumbling about economic hardships, Hitler's mental state, and the progress of the war after 1942. Survey data, memoirs, and other sources demonstrate that a majority of German citizens broke the law by listening to foreign-radio broadcasts. Additionally, official statistics for juvenile and adult property offenses rose during the war.[53] The explanation for the decline in the number of Gestapo and Special Court cases therefore lies elsewhere, since the Nazi police and justice officials were presented with plenty of illegal behavior they could have prosecuted had they chosen to do so. Among the possible explanations are the preoccupation with solving the "Jewish problem" that took pride of place in the Nazi terror generally, and especially in wartime; the desire not to damage the economic productivity of the population by putting able-bodied workers behind bars or barbed wire; the fact that most Communists and other left-wing activists had already left the country or been silenced through the waves of prosecution during the 1930s; the reduced number of young men who had been sent off to fight in the war; and finally, the possibility that fewer people wished to provide incriminating evidence to the authorities, either because they started to have moral qualms or because they began to realize after the invasion of the Soviet Union stalled that they might have to pay a price for it in the future.

Whatever the reason for the overall decline in the number of cases, the data presented above provide evidence that supports some of the most surprising results of the survey of "ordinary" Cologne citizens discussed in the previous chapter. Very few of the respondents reported that they had felt any fear of Gestapo arrest during the Third Reich, and only a very small number of them had indeed ever been investigated for any offense during the Nazi years, even though most of them claimed that they had broken the law in one way or another. Indeed, their perceptions fit quite neatly with the archival record, even during the war years, when the Nazi authorities' pleas for stiffer punishment became most urgent. From the Krefeld Gestapo case files, we know that during all of the years of the Third Reich only about 1 percent of the non-Jewish population was ever investigated by the Gestapo for any reason, and that a large percentage of those prosecuted belonged to one or another targeted group, such as Communists and Jehovah's Witnesses in the 1930s and foreign workers and prisoners of war in the 1940s. Also, we know that most investigations of ordinary Germans by the Gestapo resulted in nothing more than a warning. Only a fraction of such cases were sent on to the courts, and very few cases of ordinary Germans were resolved by internment in concentration camps. From the Cologne Special Court case files, we know that only a small percentage of those who had a case started against them were convicted and that a majority of these people had a prior criminal record.

In sum, the evidence shows that the Nazis, even in the war years, were extremely cautious when dealing with the ordinary German population and always concentrated the bulk of their terror on selected groups of targeted enemies. They did occasionally make victims out of some individuals, like Paula W., who did not come from one of the targeted groups, but only when they believed they could obtain maximum propagandistic value. Nazi terror undeniably intensified in the war years, but relatively few ordinary Germans experienced it.

WARTIME OFFENSES: BRUTAL TERROR OR COMPARATIVE LENIENCY?

Consideration of some of the most typical wartime offenses helps illustrate the comparative leniency the Nazis commonly displayed in treating illegalities committed by ordinary Germans. By far the most frequently committed offense was listening to foreign-radio broadcasts. It was also the least frequently detected and punished offense.[54] Although the law of September 1, 1939, that proscribed this activity carried with it the threat of the death penalty, large numbers of people from all types of social and political backgrounds and from nearly every community in Germany—indeed, possibly from every single community—continued to violate it throughout the war.

With the same affordably priced "people's radio" that provided cheap home entertainment and the opportunity to hear the Führer's speeches to almost every German household by the war years, or with somewhat more expensive and powerful sets (people's radios cost only about half of an average worker's monthly wage for a large set, and about half of that for a small set),[55] nearly every German household could also tune in to German-language broadcasts of the British BBC and, depending on the locality and the stage of the war, to other German-language broadcasts from France, Luxembourg, Switzerland, Poland, and Russia.[56] Despite the risks involved, powerful evidence shows that they did.

Some evidence has already been put forward on this issue, such as a report from a priest working as a Gestapo spy in the mountainous Eifel region, a pronouncement from the head of the Cologne Superior Court, and surveys and interviews conducted in recent years with elderly Cologne citizens. It gains further credibility when one considers memoirs written by important politicians and journalists and the case files of the Cologne Special Court and the Krefeld Gestapo. This new evidence needs to be treated in some detail, for it sheds light on several of the most important aspects of Nazi terror. It demonstrates once again that the Gestapo was far from omniscient and all-powerful. It could not stop Germans from listening regularly to foreign-radio broadcasts, especially because its surveillance system, even with the voluntary support of legions of civilian eavesdroppers and snitches, was neither powerful nor effective enough to ascertain who was actually listening to these broadcasts and when they were listening. The evidence shows that the Gestapo did not attempt to apply its terror evenly to all groups of the society. By and large, only targeted groups of the regime's designated enemies were prosecuted severely if they were caught listening to foreign-radio broadcasts, while others typically suffered no more than a reprimand. Finally, it indicates that the threat of terror was not credible enough to keep ordinary Germans in the dark about the regime's failures and its most guarded secrets. By listening intently and without undue fear to German-language broadcasts from the BBC and other foreign transmitters, many ordinary Germans received a great deal of accurate information about the progression of the war and about the mass murder of the European Jews while it was taking place.

Some of the strongest evidence to demonstrate that the German population was kept well informed by listening to foreign-radio broadcasts comes from the memoirs of one of modern Germany's most respected political leaders, Konrad Adenauer. Near the beginning of his memoirs dealing with the end of the war and the early postwar period, the former mayor of Cologne and Germany's first postwar chancellor explains why he was so well apprised of the location of the Allied armies while he spent the last days of the war with his family at their home in Rhöndorf (a short distance south of Cologne) awaiting liberation:

> It may seem surprising that I was so well informed about the course of the fighting. The reason was that, apart from the time I spent in concentration camp or prison, I did not let a day pass without listening to several foreign broadcasts. The stations I listened to most were the BBC German broadcasts from London and the Swiss transmitter at Beromünster. In addition my friend Herr von Weiss, the Swiss

Consul-General in Cologne, who lived in Godesberg after his house in Cologne had been destroyed, kept me informed by word of mouth and by giving me foreign newspapers.[57]

The American correspondent Howard K. Smith noted in his own memoirs that in October 1941, while he was living in Berlin, the Propaganda Ministry tried harder and harder to impress a German public that was less and less convinced by its propaganda efforts. A common joke that circulated around the city at the time, he said, was: "Why do people want to read only the 'BZ' (the newspaper *Berliner Tageblatt*) anymore?" "Because it lies only from B to Z, while all the others lie from A to Z."[58]

The Berlin population knew that it was being lied to, Smith explained, because there had been a "rapid increase in listening to news broadcasts from foreign capitals—especially London and Moscow." He then elaborated on how he knew this:

> An official of the Propaganda Ministry told me arrests for this "crime" in Germany tripled after the [recent] Dietrich speech. In the newspapers it was announced that two individuals were punished with the extreme penalty, death, for listening to London! . . . In November, every citizen in Germany received, with his ration tickets for the month, a little red card with a hole punched in the middle of it so that it might be hung on the station-dial of a radio set, and on the card was the legend: "Racial Comrades! You are Germans! It is your duty not to listen to foreign stations. Those who do so will be mercilessly punished!" . . . The conclusion to be drawn from this is obvious: there had been a tremendous increase in listening to enemy radio stations; people distrusted their own propaganda. So far as I could discover, the main effect of the new wave of propaganda and threats against listening was to make those who had been afraid to do so curious. After all, it is almost impossible to catch a person actually listening to foreign stations, it is so easy for him to switch back to the *Deutschland Sender* the moment the doorbell rings. Almost all those who have been arrested were apprehended, not while listening but while telling others, in public places, what they had heard.[59]

Smith was certainly correct in his view that alarming reports of draconian punishments in the newspapers and the other efforts of the Propaganda Ministry did not stop a curious German population from listening to foreign-radio broadcasts. Had the punishment for this crime normally been so drastic, the newspaper reports might have achieved their intended effect. As a rule, however, the punishments for this crime were anything but severe. In Cologne, Krefeld, Bergheim, and their surrounding areas, hundreds of thousands of German citizens listened regularly to these foreign broadcasts, just as millions did in the rest of Germany. Party officials, policemen, and common citizens all listened. During the war, the BBC broadcast over thirty hours per week of regularly scheduled news and entertainment programs to its German audience. According to an August 1944 estimate the BBC made based on reports from captured German soldiers and other sources, the BBC concluded that it had good reason to believe that between ten and fifteen million Germans tuned in daily to its broadcasts and that "the listeners came from all strata [of the population]."[60]

The results of the survey of elderly Cologne citizens and of other surveys taken just after the war by the U.S. Army in other areas suggest that the BBC's estimate of its German audience, large as it was, may have been overly conservative.[61] Whatever the true number of listeners may have been, the evidence from the Cologne Special Court and Krefeld Gestapo case files attests that even though millions of Germans listened to these broadcasts, few were caught, even fewer were punished, and severe punishment was truly exceptional. The Special Court records show, for example, that in the town of Bergheim not one single case of listening to foreign-radio broadcasts was forwarded for prosecution to the state prosecuting attorney's office in Cologne, which had the responsibility to investigate and try political offenses committed by people from that community. Similarly, the Cologne Special Court case files contain only one case of an investigation against anyone from the large Bayenthal section of the city for committing this offense.[62] To be sure, many other small towns and parts of big cities under the jurisdiction of the Cologne Special Court did forward cases of listening to foreign-radio broadcasts to Cologne prosecutors, but the number of accused individuals everywhere was small. As table 8.1 shows, the Cologne Special Court handled the cases of at least 7,500 people who were investigated for wrongdoing of one kind or another during the war years in Cologne and scores of other communities in the Cologne Superior Court district, but only around 300 of these cases pertained to foreign-radio broadcasts. The lack of such cases is also noticeable in the Krefeld Gestapo case files. Although the number of Krefeld cases can be estimated only on the basis of a detailed examination of a random sample of Gestapo case files—because no quantifiable general register of specific offenses exists for the Krefeld Gestapo, as it does for the Cologne Special Court—it appears that only about 50 of the 1,200 people investigated by the Krefeld Gestapo during the war were investigated for listening to foreign-radio broadcasts.[63] And more often than not this was only a secondary offense in the case, for the archival card file of the Krefeld Gestapo's cases contains only sixteen cases listed under the heading of *Rundfunkverbrechen* (illegal listening to foreign-radio broadcasts).

To gain a greater understanding of these cases, and especially to determine how these cases came to the Gestapo's attention and how they were resolved, I carefully read and analyzed 32 cases of people accused of listening to foreign-radio broadcasts. These cases include all 16 Krefeld Gestapo cases listed under the heading of *Rundfunkverbrechen* in the archival card file; 4 additional cases that also involved listening to foreign-radio broadcasts that turned up fortuitously in my random sample of every eighth case file of the Krefeld Gestapo but that had not been listed under *Rundfunkverbrechen;* and 12 cases from my random sample of 594 Cologne Special Court case files.

These cases strongly support the BBC's contention that its listeners came from all strata of the German population, with the only exception being Jews. This might seem strange, since Jews had special reasons for wanting to hear truthful appraisals of the wartime situation and the course of their persecution in Germany and in other countries that the BBC reported on frequently and accurately during the war. It can be explained, however, by the fact that the radio sets of German Jews were confiscated shortly after the war broke out. Hence, those Jews who did manage to find a way to listen to foreign-radio broadcasts must have taken extreme precautions to avoid being caught in the act. Ordinary Germans of almost all backgrounds, on the other hand, had much less to worry about unless they came from one of the other groups targeted by the Gestapo for persecution.

Most of the persons accused of this crime were common citizens who came from backgrounds that more or less mirrored the general German population. Their occupations ranged from simple workers and tradesmen to housewives, businessmen, and professional people. Several were members of the Nazi Party; a few had previously been associated with left-wing parties; most were not active politically. Men outnumbered women three to one among the thirty-two cases, but this ratio was almost identical to the gender breakdown for all offenses during the war years.[64] There was also nothing remarkable about their age background: they ranged in age from the twenties to the sixties, as did the vast majority of people accused of any political offense.

Just as the backgrounds of these people did not distinguish them from the rest of the German population during the war years, there was also nothing of special note about the timing of their cases, as they were spread out rather evenly throughout the war years. A computer analysis of the entire register of Cologne Special Court cases shows, however, that the greatest wave of prosecution for this crime came at the beginning of the war. Of the 310 cases the Cologne Special Court handled, 53 came in 1939 and 99 came in 1940. In 1941 the number of cases sank by more than 50 percent to only 43, and it remained at about that level until the end of the war.[65] The Krefeld Gestapo cases, on the other hand, did not display such a downward trend, though the numbers are too small to be significant. It is not clear whether these yearly trends are particularly meaningful. Perhaps what they show best is that the German population continued to listen to foreign-radio broadcasts throughout the war and that the regime mostly paid little heed, except on rare occasions.

The Nazis' lack of concern in this matter comes across even more strongly when one examines how these cases were detected and prosecuted. Almost without exception, each of the defendants came to the attention of the Gestapo by means of a denunciation from a revenge-seeking neighbor, coworker, or family member (typically an in-law). In none of the cases did the Gestapo commit its own agents or spies to nab these people surreptitiously. Also, the Gestapo did not employ any special technical means of surveillance in any of the cases. It should be mentioned, however, that many of the denouncers held positions in either the Nazi Party or the SS, but this was also true of denunciations in general.

The comparatively small numbers of people accused of committing this crime and the fact that the Gestapo relied overwhelmingly on accusations from the civilian population for the initiation of investigations indicate that the Nazi regime did not consider this offense threatening enough to waste the enormous amount of manpower, time, and energy that would have been required to police it effectively. The leniency that the Gestapo and the courts displayed in prosecuting the people who did come to their attention attests further to the Nazis' lack of concern over the issue of the population's listening habits. It also reveals that they wanted neither to condemn vital workers at a time of national distress nor to risk damaging the popular mood by clamping down heavily on ordinary people for what they knew was a common everyday occurrence. After all, policemen, soldiers, and party officials also listened to BBC and other foreign transmitters.[66]

Both the Gestapo and the court authorities showed remarkable restraint in their treatment of all but a few persons accused of listening to foreign-radio broadcasts. None of the thirty-two cases under consideration ended with the accused person being sent to a concentration camp.[67] Only four of the cases even went to trial, and one of these ended in an acquittal. All the rest of the cases ended in dismissals before trial, ordered by either the Gestapo itself or the state prosecuting attorney. The most severe punishment that anyone suffered in these cases was a one-year prison term. This sentence was meted out in December 1943 to a forty-seven-year-old Krefeld lathe hand who was a former member of the Socialist Party and who confessed to listening frequently to BBC broadcasts on his *Deutschen Kleinempfänger* (the smallest and cheapest type of "people's radio") and to relating what he had heard to his colleagues at work. The relatively stiff sentence he received no doubt had something to do with his past leftist associations, as well as with being denounced by his boss for the grave offense of attempting to undermine the German military effort.[68] In each of the other cases that found their way to court, the defendant also had been or still was a member of either the Communist or the Socialist Party.[69]

Nearly all of the thirty-two cases dealt with BBC broadcasts. One of the more illustrative cases, however, involved listening to a French radio transmitter in the first months of the war.[70] The case began in November 1939 in the small town of Burgbrohl—just to the west of the Rhine Valley, about fifteen miles northwest of Koblenz and forty miles south of Cologne. On November 17, a thirty-five-year-old house-painter and minor functionary (*Zellenleiter*) in the local Nazi Party named Gregor K. angrily went to the police station and filed a complaint against his brother-in-law Arnulf V., a fifty-year-old factory worker, for libeling Hitler and listening regularly to foreign-radio broadcasts in his very presence. The obvious source of Gregor K.'s anger lay in a family dispute. Only a few hours before he went to the police station, he had concluded a tumultuous family feud that ended with him, his wife, and his young daughter being tossed out of Arnulf V.'s home, where they had been staying. Without a roof over his family's head, he was seeking revenge.

The Burgbrohl police reacted swiftly and placed a call to the Koblenz Gestapo at 5:45 that evening, informing it of the charges leveled against Arnulf V. The next day, a young Koblenz Gestapo officer named Simmer made his way to the town to carry out the investigation, in which he had the assistance of the Burgbrohl police department. Soon after his arrival, he questioned Gregor K. and his wife about what they had witnessed. Gregor K.'s wife, who was the sister of Arnulf V.'s wife, backed up her husband's allegations by telling Simmer that "Arnulf V. listened regularly to the German-language broadcasts of the Strasbourg radio station at 7:45 in the evening."[71] These assertions made Simmer curious, however; he wondered why a Nazi Party *Zellenleiter* had tolerated this practice for so long without reporting it and why he had also listened to the broadcasts himself. When he was questioned about this, Gregor K. responded that he had feared being made homeless; this answer seemed to satisfy Simmer for the time being. When they returned to their testimony against Arnulf V., Gregor K. also brought out that his brother-in-law had constantly criticized the Führer and the Nazi state with outbursts like "Hitler, that burned-out character. For what reason does that idiot sacrifice so many lives?" and, "What the German news reports is certainly not correct."[72]

This convinced Simmer, and he ordered Arnulf V.'s arrest. The interrogation, which took place the next day in Koblenz, had to have been quite brutal. While attempting to deny the charges against him, Arnulf V. broke off his testimony several times and then resumed with the phrase, "I will now confess," which was followed by a pronounced change in his account of the affair. In the end, Arnulf V. admitted that he had indeed listened to the French transmitter several times in Gregor K.'s presence. But he made an appeal for mercy by pointing out that he was a decorated war veteran and a loyal German citizen who suffered from a nervous condition since being wounded four times at the front in World War I, where he had served coura- geously as a sergeant. The Gestapo officer Simmer, however, seemed more impressed by Arnulf V.'s former role as a local leader in the Social Demo- cratic Party during the Weimar Republic. After the interrogation ended, Simmer ordered that Arnulf V. be kept under arrest while awaiting the re- sults of a further investigation.

Arnulf V. remained in jail for three weeks before being released on De- cember 12. During this time, a Burgbrohl policeman, together with a Ko- blenz Gestapo officer named Didinger, carried out a search of his apartment and made inquiries with the local Nazi Party headquarters about Arnulf V.'s standing in the community. Nothing of substance turned up in his apart- ment, save for the radio he had listened to and some old SPD materials. The Nazi Party gave Arnulf V. a mixed report: he was diligent and hardworking, but he also fought with his wife and, like many of his former ideological comrades, distanced himself from the Nazi movement, attended few Nazi functions, and contributed little to Nazi welfare efforts.

Two months later, on February 23, 1940, the Koblenz Gestapo com- pleted its investigation and sent a report to the state prosecuting attorney's office in Koblenz recommending that Arnulf V. be put on trial. Following protocol, the Koblenz prosecutors then forwarded the case to the Cologne Special Court. Before Arnulf V.'s case came to trial, however, the Koblenz Gestapo also opened an investigation against Gregor K. and his wife for lis- tening to the French broadcasts with Arnulf V. and, on March 9, filed a re- port recommending that they be prosecuted too. But this did not happen. Gregor K. joined the Luftwaffe, and on August 4, the charges against both him and his wife were dropped. Save for the three weeks he had spent in jail earlier, Arnulf V. also came out of the affair relatively unscathed. When his case was finally heard on September 27, 1940, more than ten months after the original charges against him had been made, the judges, taking note of his admirable military and work record and the fact that a motive of revenge had led to his accusation, decided to acquit him of all charges.

Except that Arnulf V.'s case concerned listening to a French station instead of BBC, that he confessed to the charges against him, and that the case took so long to resolve, it was in most ways quite typical. Brief discussions of three additional cases handled by the Cologne Special Court show that, as in Arnulf V.'s case, most other cases involving listening to foreign-radio broadcasts were initiated by civilian denunciations stemming from revenge motives and that they were, as a consequence, usually taken rather lightly by the authorities. They also highlight the fact that people of all types of socioeconomic and political backgrounds and from all types of communities listened to foreign-radio programs during the war.

The first of these cases began only a week and a half after the outbreak of the war in the small town of Bergneustadt in the hilly Sauerland region, about thirty miles east of Cologne.[73] A forty-one-year-old businessman and World War I veteran was denounced, along with his wife and her twin sister, by a thirty-four-year-old master mechanic and member of the SS named Eugen P. On September 11, 1939, Eugen P. brought charges to the local Nazi Party organization, which in turn informed the local police, that his neighbor and former employee, Fritz T., listened every evening with his wife and sister-in-law to news reports about the war broadcast by the BBC and by a Polish radio station as well. Eugen P. knew this because at his urging two of his SS comrades had sneaked onto Fritz T.'s balcony adjacent to his living room for the previous four evenings to overhear what he was listening to while Eugen P. attempted to tune into the same broadcasts so as to know exactly what Fritz T. was hearing and to provide specific information against him. Within a week, the Bergneustadt police turned the case over to the Cologne Gestapo, which then, after a brief investigation, passed along a report to the Cologne state prosecuting attorney's office with the recommendation that no criminal charges be leveled against Fritz T. and his wife and sister-in-law. The Cologne state prosecuting attorney's office followed the Gestapo's advice and wasted no time before it dismissed the case on September 28, the same day it received the Gestapo's report. Although the Gestapo

had determined in the course of its investigation that Fritz T. had once been
a member of the Communist Party, it decided not to press charges against
him because he had been a solid citizen since leaving the party in 1928, the
two SS men who had spied on him were divided in their testimony, and
Eugen P. was motivated by a desire to seek revenge over a business dispute
he had with Fritz T. that was pending at the time in a local court.

Another case that started with a neighbor's quarrel and came to a similar conclusion took place only a few miles south of Bergneustadt in the small
village of Oberdollendorf in the late summer and early fall of 1941.[74] This
case also involved a married couple accused by a neighbor who had spied on
them. But this time the accused couple had no leftist associations; indeed,
the husband, a forty-two-year-old electrical welder named Heinrich G. who
had his own workshop, was a member in good standing of the Nazi Party.
Again the local police carried out the initial investigation before turning
the case over to the Gestapo. In the police investigation, which began on
September 4, 1941, the denouncer, Mathias J., a fifty-four-year-old coal
dealer, explained to a local *Hauptwachtmeister* that he had strolled by his
neighbors' house the previous evening and had overheard them listening to
a foreign-radio broadcast. He also told the policeman that he had noticed
this shortly after he had had a heated altercation with Heinrich G. in which
Heinrich G. called him a "scoundrel, a criminal, and a vagabond" and had
threatened to kill him while holding up a heavy object. This apparently was
enough for the policeman. Although he did take the time to summon the
accused couple to provide their own version of the affair, he filed a report
the same day saying that it was "almost inconceivable" to him that such a
"good German family" could have listened to a foreign-radio broadcast.
This assessment proved persuasive to the Gestapo and the state prosecuting
attorney; neither had any interest in pursuing the case further, though it
took two more months before the case was officially dismissed on November 6, 1941.

The final case to be considered also took place in the summer and early
fall of 1941, but this time in the city of Cologne itself. It also involved a
married couple with Nazi Party affiliations, though in this instance both the
husband, a fifty-three-year-old civil servant, and the wife, a homemaker

ten years younger than her husband, were party members, he since 1937 and she since 1940.[75] Given their social standing and political background and the fact that they were denounced by a person of far inferior position, their seventeen-year-old maid—who gained no support from the other domestic employees summoned to testify in the case—they had little trouble in gaining the sympathy of the Cologne Gestapo, which saw to it that the case was dismissed only six weeks after it began. The maid's denunciation, which she had made originally to the criminal police, nevertheless seemed plausible. According to her testimony, her employers, Thea and Karl B., listened "every evening to BBC." Furthermore, she told the Cologne Gestapo officer Brodesser, who conducted the investigation, Karl B. often made comments in her presence criticizing the Nazi regime. These comments, which she believed to be illegal, were based on what he had heard in the BBC broadcasts and included: "When a military report states that we have shot down so and so many pilots, I do not believe it," and, "Everything that the *Westdeutscher Beobachter* [the local Nazi newspaper] reports is all lies."[76]

Had the backgrounds of the denouncer and the accused been reversed, such comments could have had dire consequences: they might have led to an investigation for the serious charge of *Wehrkraftzersetzung* (public attempts to paralyze or undermine the will of Germany or one of its allies to defend itself). But their backgrounds were what they were, so the maid was not believed and nothing happened to the accused man and his wife. Unlike the relatively inconsequential offense of listening to foreign-radio broadcasts, *Wehrkraftzersetzung* often did result in punishment, not infrequently in the death penalty ordered by the People's Court in Berlin, or, for soldiers, by a military court.[77] This offense was also interpreted broadly. According to a senior official in the Ministry of Justice in 1944, a whole catalog of remarks could constitute the capital crime of *Wehrkraftzersetzung*. Examples he gave were:

"The war is lost"; "Germany or the Führer started the war frivolously or to no purpose, and ought to lose it"; "the Nazi Party should or would resign and clear the way for peace negotiations, as the Italians have done"; . . . "people ought to work more slowly, so as to bring an end to the war"; "the spread of Bolshevism would not be so bad as the propaganda makes out, and would harm only leading Nazis"; . . . saying the Führer is sick, incapable, a butcher of men, and so on.[78]

Precisely how often statements of this nature were punished severely is unclear. Ingo Müller, in his well-regarded book on the courts of the Third Reich, argues that "such remarks were always punishable by death—regardless of whether they were made in public or to family members or close friends."[79] Although Müller buttresses his argument with some alarming case examples, his evidence is largely impressionistic. H. W. Koch, who has examined the judgments of the People's Court in more detail, is more skeptical and explains that the evidence "is scant and sketchy and reliable statistics are difficult to compile."[80] The records of the Cologne Special Court and the Krefeld Gestapo cannot fully answer this question either. They do show, however, that a great many of the people accused of making such remarks during the war, even while in the company of family, friends, and others, were prosecuted for the less severely punished crime of *Heimtücke* instead of for the more harshly punished crime of *Wehrkraftzersetzung*. Also, these records reveal that even those charged with the latter offense were certainly not always punished with a death sentence.

The Krefeld Gestapo and the Cologne Special Court case files do not contain many cases of *Wehrkraftzersetzung*. A random sample of every eighth Krefeld Gestapo case file in fact uncovered only two people charged with this offense, out of 433 people in the sample. Unless the sample is skewed terribly, and there is no reason to believe that it is, this means that the Krefeld Gestapo investigated fewer than twenty offenses of this type during the war years. Such cases were also rare in Cologne and other communities. The Cologne Special Court case files show that only 234 of a total of 28,920 people found in these files had cases started against them for this offense, and only 102 of them came from the city of Cologne proper. The rest came from other communities that fell under the jurisdiction of the Cologne Special Court. Since the population of Cologne was roughly five times that of Krefeld, this means that proportionately there were almost an identical number of these cases in both Cologne and Krefeld.

These figures alone call into question Ingo Müller's argument that, "as the war went on, this decree [concerning *Wehrkraftzersetzung*] gradually came to replace completely the 1934 Law against Treacherous Attacks on the State and Party [*Heimtücke*]."[81] Although his argument is not quite correct, the number of *Wehrkraftzersetzung* cases did increase dramatically in the last phase of the war. Whereas the Cologne Special Court processed fewer than fifteen of these cases per year until after the debacle at Stalingrad in January 1943, the number of cases grew from 37 in 1943 to 127 in 1944. In that year, 63 of the cases involved people from the city of Cologne itself, and the rest came from the many other cities and towns in the large Cologne Special Court district.

Even though the number of these cases grew swiftly in the last two years of the war,[82] they never eclipsed *Heimtücke* offenses of political libel and slander, for which most people who spoke out against Hitler and National Socialism continued to be prosecuted. In the sample of Krefeld Gestapo case files, only two people were investigated between 1940 and 1945 for having committing *Wehrkraftzersetzung;* twenty-eight people were investigated for the lesser charge of violating the *Heimtücke* law in the same period. In the sample of Cologne Special Court case files in this same period, the numbers were thirteen and thirty-one, respectively.

Determining what ultimately happened in *Wehrkraftzersetzung* cases is made difficult because there were so few of these cases in Krefeld and because the Cologne Special Court case files pertaining to the offense almost invariably lack detailed information since the Cologne prosecutors forwarded the information they obtained in their investigations of *Wehrkraftzersetzung* charges to the People's Court in Berlin for prosecution. To help remedy this situation, I combed the Krefeld Gestapo files for additional cases of this offense that did not turn up in the random sample of every eighth case. Whereas no claim can be made that this search located all of the cases of this offense that the Krefeld Gestapo handled, it did provide another four cases to add to the original two in the random sample.

The most significant observation to be made from an analysis of these cases is that they demonstrate conclusively that people charged with committing *Wehrkraftzersetzung* did not always receive the death penalty, or even long prison terms. Most of the cases involved loose talk in someone's home or in a pub by or to a soldier on leave from the front about the war or the economy, and most ended with a jail sentence of a few months to one year. A typical case involved a thirty-eight-year-old bartender.[83] On April 3, 1940, Willy N. met a twenty-five-year-old soldier in a local Krefeld tavern and offered to take the soldier over the border to Holland, where the bartender had lived for many years. After leaving the establishment, the soldier reported Willy N.'s offer to him to his superior officer, who in turn reported the incident to the Krefeld Gestapo a day later. On April 11, Kriminalsekretär Kurt Joost, who investigated most of these cases in Krefeld, summoned the soldier to Gestapo headquarters and ordered him to try to get the bartender to make his offer to him once again. While the soldier searched for Willy N., Joost ordered a postal surveillance of the bartender's incoming and outgoing mail. This, however, turned up nothing damning, and the soldier was unable to locate the bartender. When a military court tried Willy N. on May 2, the court decided that the whole affair was only a matter of drunken pub talk, and it sentenced him to a mere three months in jail.

Far more meaningful than this case was that of Eduard B., for his was one of a very small number of cases of any type found in the Krefeld Gestapo or the Cologne Special Court case files that contained any direct mention of the Holocaust.[84] Because of its singularity and because it sheds light on one of the important ways in which German citizens on the homefront became aware of the murder of the European Jews, it needs to be treated in some detail.

The case began on August 19, 1943, when a fifty-five-year-old truck-driver with no apparent association with the Nazi movement appeared voluntarily at Krefeld Gestapo headquarters to deliver a scorching denunciation of a soldier he had met the previous day. In his accusation, he asserted to Kriminalsekretär Friedrich Furschbach, who initially handled the case, that he was only doing his duty as a German citizen and had no reason to accuse Eduard B. on the grounds of animosity or revenge, for he did not know him personally and had only met him the previous day for the first and only time in his life. He then explained in what became a one-and-a-half-page typed and signed statement that he had gone a day earlier to the apartment of Eduard B.'s mother near the Dionysius Church in downtown Krefeld simply to pay a social call. In the apartment, in addition to Eduard

B., he encountered two other soldiers whom he had never met before. Before long, he and the soldiers got into a heated discussion about the progress of the war. Eduard B. carried on a tirade about the horrible situation that German soldiers faced at the front and about the superior weaponry of the Russians; the German soldiers, he claimed, had only "rifles, hand grenades, and machine guns for defense." These remarks were detailed in two long paragraphs of the truck-driver's statement.

This was sufficient to get Eduard B. into serious trouble, but the truck-driver provided the most incriminating evidence against him toward the end of his testimony: "In this discussion Eduard B. then stated that he did not believe that there would be a German victory without a miracle taking place. We will indeed lose the war, [he said], and if we won, it would not be any better for us; we will still be losers. For then we will get a state in which we will not be able to take a shit without permission." After this the truck-driver alleged that Eduard B. explained how he had tried to sabotage the military effort: as a medical orderly, he always dressed the wounds of the soldiers who came to him with twice the number of bandages that were necessary, "with the intention of bringing the war sooner to an end." Finally, the denouncer came around to Eduard B.'s comments about the mass murder of the Jews: "About the discovery of the mass murder in Katyn [perpetrated by the Russians on the Poles], Eduard B. asserted that we should not make such a big fuss, for he did not believe the reports about the matter and considered them to be unprovable nonsense. [Furthermore, he explained,] we have done exactly the same thing with the Jews in Russia."[85]

Two days after the truck-driver made his original denunciation, the Krefeld Gestapo summoned him again to its headquarters for further questioning. This time Kriminalsekretär Gustav Burkert took over the questioning. Once again the truck-driver provided a long statement about Eduard B.'s remarks that jibed fully with his previous statement. Burkert then asked him several questions about the other people who had been present in the apartment, but the truck-driver said that he could be of no help because he did not know who the others were. Later that day, Burkert summoned Eduard B.'s mother to Gestapo headquarters, but she said that she had heard none of the conversation that night because she had been sitting in another room at the time. She did, however, provide Burkert with the

names of the other two soldiers who had been present, and the name and
address of another woman who had been with her in the apartment and
who might have listened to the discussion. Burkert was unable to locate this
woman, however; she had been bombed out of her apartment, and no one
seemed to have any idea about her present location. Also, he could not arrest
Eduard B., for his furlough had ended and he had returned to the front.

Ludwig Jung, the head of the Krefeld Gestapo, realized this was a very
important case and kept a close watch over it until after it was resolved.
Although Jung had to turn the case over to the military authorities because
Eduard B. had returned to his unit and the case now fell under their jurisdiction, he did so only after carefully reading through all of the written documentation in the case and signing the truck-driver's denunciation statements in his characteristic hurried style. Over the next months, he
continued to inquire with the military authorities as to how the case was
progressing.

The military officials did not take the matter lightly, but Jung ended up
being disappointed with how they handled it. The materials in the case show
that after an initial investigation by the local military post in Krefeld, the
case was handed over to a military field court in Russia.[86] During the initial
military investigation, the two soldiers who had been present in the apartment when Eduard B. carried on his alleged tirade were interrogated and a
renewed attempt was made to locate the fifty-one-year-old woman who had
also been present. But the woman was never found, and the two soldiers
gave full support to Eduard B. and denied that he had said anything
objectionable.

Six months after it had begun, the case came to an end in February 1944
when a military field court in Russia decided to dismiss the charges against
Eduard B. In a letter written on February 13 that arrived eight days later,
the military court informed the Krefeld Gestapo that it had decided on this
course of action because it did not believe it had enough evidence for a conviction and because it had determined that Eduard B. had the reputation of
being an honorable soldier who made "a good impression." Besides, in the
court's estimation, he had not made his remarks in public; he had made
them only in the company of "three acquaintances who were guests in his
home." This decision obviously displeased Jung, and he tried to have it over-

turned. Three days after he had received this letter, the persistent and hard-hearted Jung wrote to the military court to inform it that he would check again in six weeks to see whether Eduard B. had been punished. But this time Jung's efforts were in vain: it appears from the records in his Gestapo file that Eduard B. simply returned to his fighting unit and the case was closed.

Given the Nazis' intense desire to keep news of the Holocaust a secret, Eduard B.'s case was more sensitive than most cases found in the Cologne Special Court and Krefeld Gestapo files. Nevertheless, these files are replete with critical comments that ordinary Germans were accused of making during the war about Hitler, other top Nazi leaders, the economy, the chances for victory and defeat, and a variety of other taboo subjects. Any such remarks could have been treated as an attempt to undermine the military effort. Most of the time, however, the legal authorities did not deal with them as cases of *Wehrkraftzersetzung;* rather, they prosecuted them as cases of political libel or slander that typically ended in only mild penalties and most often did not result in punishment of any kind. Table 8.3 lists the most common types of illegal opinion statements made by German citizens that the Cologne Special Court and the Krefeld Gestapo investigated as *Heimtücke* offenses in both the prewar and the wartime years.

As the table indicates, Eduard B.'s case was indeed an unusual one: not just because he had been accused of spreading news of the Holocaust, but also because he had been accused of making critical comments about the situation of the Jews at all. In both the Cologne Special Court and Krefeld Gestapo records, and in both the prewar and wartime periods, only a tiny fraction of cases dealt with Jews or racial policy, although why this is so is somewhat of a mystery. It does not mean that such issues were not discussed commonly by the ordinary German population; indeed, SD reports make clear that *Kristallnacht* and other outrages against the Jews received the condemnation of legions of German citizens.[87] Furthermore, our survey of elderly Cologne residents indicates that large numbers of ordinary people passed on news to friends and family members about even the most sensitive subject concerning the Jews, namely, their mass murder during the war.[88] One can only opine that the German people knew very well that this was in fact the most sensitive and dangerous of all subjects, so they took

TABLE 8.3 *Illegal Opinion Statements in Cologne Special Court and Krefeld Gestapo Case Files, 1933–1945*

TOPIC OF STATEMENT	COLOGNE SPECIAL COURT		KREFELD GESTAPO	
	1933–1939	1940–1945	1933–1939	1940–1945
Nazi Party	26	2	2	1
Hitler	56	7	14	9
Other Nazi Party leaders	24	2	11	6
National Socialism in general	86	10	8	4
Living standards	15	2	4	2
War	6	15	6	18
Freedom of expression	12	4	1	2
Support for other countries	5	4	2	3
Support for other parties	24	2	3	—
Jews	10	2	2	2
Other	38	1	8	1
TOTAL	302	51	61	48

NOTE: Based on random samples of 594 Cologne Special Court cases and 433 Krefeld Gestapo cases.

extra precautions not to let their remarks fall on the ears of people they could not fully trust.

The figures in the table reveal, on the other hand, that Germans were much less circumspect when commenting on a large range of other topics in such a way that could also have put them in grave danger. During both the prewar and war years, for example, criticisms of Hitler himself were among the most common topics found in cases of political libel and slander. As we know from previously discussed case examples, the Führer frequently was the butt of the most unflattering jokes and vituperative outbursts. Even during the war years, when the risk of severe punishment increased markedly given the wide possible interpretation of the crime of *Wehrkraftzersetzung*, citizens of Krefeld, Cologne, and smaller towns and villages were often accused of blurting out things like "Hitler can lick my ass" or of calling

Hitler "a criminal," "an idiot," "a greasy rag," or an insane person who "goes into fits of frenzy and lies on the floor and bites on the rug" after he has heard about military setbacks.[89]

While the figures in the table indicate that the German people lampooned and demonized Hitler more than any other Nazi leader, Goebbels and Göring came in second as targets of the people's ire. Otherwise, the most common remarks that got ordinary Germans in trouble centered on the Nazi movement itself or the progression of the war. Often these remarks were rather general in nature, but sometimes they could be quite graphic. In one case, for example, three middle-aged women in Krefeld in July 1940 were accused by the husband of one of the women of having made a mockery of the Hitler salute. According to his testimony, after one of the women had lifted a leg and broken wind in the summer heat wave, all three of the women had then stretched out their arms and bellowed "Heil Hitler" in a gesture that one of them proclaimed to be "the new German greeting."[90]

Harrowing as it must have been to deal with the shock of being denounced to the Gestapo and suffering through an interrogation at Gestapo headquarters, nothing more seems to have happened to these women, and the Düsseldorf state prosecuting attorney soon dismissed their case for lack of evidence. This was also what usually transpired in *Heimtücke* cases of all types, even those involving verbal attacks on Hitler, the Nazi Party leadership, the German military effort, and the rest of the subjects included in table 8.3.[91] Indeed, there are indications that the prosecution of cases of political libel and slander even became milder during the war years than they had been in the prewar period. As the table shows, the Cologne Special Court handled far fewer of these cases during the war than prior to it. But the table also shows that there was no commensurate decline in the number of Krefeld Gestapo cases of this offense in the 1940s, suggesting that there were fewer court cases in the wartime period because the Nazi legal authorities simply chose to prosecute fewer people for this offense after the war broke out. During the 1930s the *Heimtücke* law had proved instrumental in the Nazis' campaign to destroy its leftist adversaries, silence the clergy, and force the Jews to emigrate. By the war years, however, these groups either had already been reckoned with or, in the case of the Jews, were being removed from German society by other means, namely, through deportation to the death camps. Hence, in the 1940s the Nazis had much less need to deal severely with the for the most part loyal German population remaining in the society who were accused of speaking out of turn. Also, as discussed already, the regime had to be ever more mindful during the war of the adverse effect that severe punishment of ordinary Germans for minor transgressions might have on public opinion. Other indications that Nazi authorities were in fact mindful of this possibility is that even when the Gestapo did forward cases of political libel and slander to the court authorities, only a small minority of them came to trial, and those defendants who were convicted generally received modest sentences. In a random sample of 249 Cologne Special Court cases of political libel or slander, more than four-fifths of the cases were dismissed before going to trial in both the prewar and the wartime periods, and only 13 percent of the cases in each period ended in convictions. For the unfortunate few who were convicted, the typical sentence was a term of from six months to one year in jail.

To conclude the discussion of the legal authorities' surprisingly mild treatment of ordinary Germans who were accused of verbally attacking the Nazi leadership and society during the war years, I will draw once again on the Cologne Special Court records. Included there is a case that could have cost the lives of three people but ended up quite differently. It began in typical fashion, with a denunciation from a revenge-seeking and opportunistic neighbor. In early September 1943, Gerhard V., a cantankerous, seventy-three-year-old retired master roofer and long-standing Nazi Party member from the town of Porz, which lay on the east bank of the Rhine River just south of Cologne, took out a red-ink pen and wrote a scathing letter denouncing three of his neighbors. He delivered the letter to a local Nazi Party *Zellenleiter*, who passed it on to the local Porz police.[92] The charges Gerhard V. made against his neighbors could not have been more damaging. They included spreading news gained from listening to foreign-radio broadcasts, publicly trying to undermine the German military effort, spreading defeatist sentiments, showing support for the enemy, and making a wide range of slanderous public remarks against the Nazi Party leadership. To make matters worse, Gerhard V. alleged that these remarks had been made repeatedly in a public building to large numbers of people at a time when the eastern front was caving in after the German army's defeat at Orel and when Italy, Germany's ally, had just surrendered.

A Porz police lieutenant named Vohwinckel conducted the initial investigation, which began on September 11 when he summoned the first of an eventual total of sixteen witnesses—fifteen women and one man—to testify about what they had heard and what they knew about the character of the accused persons and the denouncer Gerhard V. Most of these people were housewives who shopped daily in the neighborhood grocery store run by two of the accused, a middle-aged married couple named Margaretha and Clemens R., and frequented also by the third person accused in the case, Anni K., another middle-aged housewife. Before they gave their testimony, Lieutenant Vohwinckel informed the witnesses of the specific remarks that Margaretha and Clemens R. and Anni K. had supposedly made in their presence. The denouncer had attributed most of these remarks to Frau R.; he alleged that she had often blurted them out loudly in the store while laughing boisterously: "Italy has surrendered. What do you say about this now? Have you not heard about it?"; "The heads of the party are a bunch of scoundrels. When rations are handed out, they serve themselves first and leave almost nothing for the rest of us"; "Everything in the newspaper is a lie. Don't believe it. When the Russians invade us, they won't do anything to us"; "Now we know that we are going to lose the war. We are always retreating farther and farther back. I can absolutely not understand how the enemy pilots can blow everything here to bits and we can do absolutely nothing about it"; "When the Nazis lose and come back, then they will all have their throats slit." In addition to alleging that Frau R. had made these outrageous statements, the old Nazi Gerhard V. also accused Herr R. of commenting: "Italy has surrendered. The war will soon come to an end. What has this war done for us? There are many here in Porz who are frightened out of their wits." Finally, Gerhard V. also charged that he had overheard Anni K. saying in the store: "One cannot believe anything anymore. We have nothing more to give."[93]

The witnesses were divided in their testimony. Some of them said that they had not heard these remarks. Others said that they had. Only one of them, a thirty-one-year-old widow who was a neighbor of both the de-

nouncer Gerhard V. and Margaretha and Clemens R., came to the defense
of the accused by reporting that Gerhard V. had threatened to denounce her
as well and that he had conflicts with many people; in her opinion, he was
"an old *Schweinhund.*"

When the police finally got around to interrogating Herr and Frau R.
and Anni K. on September 15, they called them to police headquarters by
means of an official summons. Surprisingly, the police found no need to
arrest any of them. At least not yet. In their interrogation, all three disputed
Gerhard V.'s charges. Furthermore, Margaretha and Clemens R. told the
police that Gerhard V. had denounced them in an attempt to seek revenge
over his dispute with Frau R.'s sister-in-law, who had recently filed a civil
suit to resolve it. Unfortunately for them, their denials and their explanation of Gerhard V.'s vindictive motives did not convince Lieutenant Vohwinckel. On September 17, he took Frau R. under "temporary arrest" and
placed her in the nearby jail in Cologne-Deutz. He also filed a closing report
on his investigation that outlined their guilt in no uncertain terms, and he
handed the case over to the Cologne Gestapo. In this report, he explained
that almost all of the couple's customers had testified to their belief that, in
particular, Frau R. had "to finally have her mouth shut." He also argued that
Frau R. could have made her comments about Italy's surrender only after
hearing about it from the BBC because the German government had not
yet broadcast this news to the German people. He concluded his report by
urging that harsh measures be taken especially against Frau R. because
her comments were an intentional attempt to "considerably weaken our
fighting effort."

Margaretha R. sat in jail for the next three months. During this time,
the Cologne Gestapo proceeded in an orderly fashion. It first put the case
before a local court (*Amtsgericht*), which determined, after a brief hearing
on September 25, that the accused should be charged with violating the
Heimtücke law of December 12, 1934. The accused then hired an attorney,
who wrote a letter on their behalf on September 29 petitioning the Cologne
state prosecuting attorney to set Frau R. free while she was awaiting trial on
the grounds that there was no danger that she would try to flee, for her
husband was severely ill and she needed to care for him and their three chil-

dren. He also reminded the prosecutor that Gerhard V.'s denunciation had arisen from a motive of revenge.

This plea was unsuccessful. Not only did the state prosecuting attorney not order Frau R.'s release, but he forwarded the case to the People's Court in Berlin to determine whether in fact the case should be tried as a case of *Wehrkraftzersetzung*. The People's Court decided that indeed it should be so prosecuted but referred the case on October 18 to the Superior Court in Hamm for trial. Soon after reviewing the case materials, the court in Hamm, however, indicated that it was uncomfortable with the accuser's motives, and also that it found it strange that he had waited an entire month before making his charges to the Nazi Party officials in Porz. Six weeks later, on November 25, after having investigated the affair more fully, the Hamm Superior Court decided to dismiss the charges of *Wehrkraftzersetzung* and referred the case back to the Cologne Special Court for trial as a simple *Heimtücke* case.

While this was taking place, a Nazi Party district leader named Aldinger wrote to the Cologne Gestapo demanding that Margaretha and Clemens R.'s store be taken from them and given to another grocer whose store had recently been destroyed by a bombing attack. Furthermore, the mayor of Porz wrote a damning report to the Gestapo on November 24 about his own findings about the background of the accused. He called Frau R. a "fanatic Catholic" and Herr R. "an enemy of the state" and "a drinker and rabble-rouser" and urged that they be punished severely.

Strong as they were, these pleas did not impress the Cologne Gestapo as much as the decision of the Hamm Superior Court to have the case tried on a lesser charge. Two weeks later, Frau R. was released from jail. Also feeling uncertain that all of the facts in the case had come to light, the Cologne Gestapo officers Trierweiler and Kirschbaum decided to investigate the matter even more fully and called in an additional twelve witnesses to testify on January 7, 1944. From these witnesses, they now heard that the denouncer Gerhard V. was a violent and quarrelsome alcoholic who lived in conflict with all of his neighbors and that his major supporter, Frau H., was also a nasty person who, like Gerhard V., had often threatened to denounce others.

This new testimony carried considerable weight, especially because much of it came from the wife of a trusted *Altekämpfer*. Two months later, on March 24, the Cologne state prosecuting attorney decided to bring the case to an end by dismissing all of the charges against the accused, even though that decision no doubt angered the local Nazi Party and went against the advice of the Porz police and mayor. It is true that Frau R. had been forced to endure three months in jail, that she and her husband had almost lost their store, and that they, Frau K., and their families had all suffered a wrenching ordeal. But theirs was also a case that Nazi justice officials could point to with pride as proof of their commitment to legality. At the very least, it shows that some Nazis could have a heart when they wanted to. More important, the case demonstrates once again that the Nazi terror that ordinary German citizens like Margaretha and Clemens R. and Anni K. experienced was completely different from that experienced by the regime's enemies. Had these people had a Communist background or a record of prior arrests, they might have lost their lives.

THE REIGN OF INSANITY AT THE END

Beneath the veneer of the Gestapo's orderliness, restraint, and concern with procedure, as featured in many of the cases discussed in this chapter, lurked a dark underside of capricious and sadistic brutality. Many Communists, Jews, Jehovah's Witnesses, habitual criminals, and other enemies of the regime came to know this well, but relatively few ordinary Germans experienced it during the Third Reich, even well into the war years. In the last months of the war, however, all pretenses were dropped as Nazi society descended into an abyss of chaos, horror, insanity, and murder. With the Allied armies streaming across its borders, its cities reduced to rubble, its leader Hitler alternating between abject despondency and maniacal lunacy, and the blood of millions of Jews, Poles, Ukrainians, Russians, and others on its hands, Nazi Germany came fully unglued, and the Nazi terror finally became nearly indiscriminate.[94]

Thousands of German citizens were put to death in the madness that reigned in the last months of the war by court decrees related to Stauffenberg's failed attempt on Hitler's life in July 1944 and in death marches, concentration camps, Gestapo headquarters, and even normal jails and prisons. It is impossible to determine exactly how many died at this time, but a look inside the labyrinthine Klingelpütz prison in Cologne in the final months before the U.S. Army conquered the city in early March 1945 provides an impression of the barbarity that prevailed across Germany and of the fate that met thousands of people who were caught in the Gestapo's clutches at the war's end.[95]

Murder and cruelty were not new to Klingelpütz. More than 100,000 people had spent some period of confinement in the prison before the last year of the war, and between 1,000 and 1,500 individuals had been put to death by the guillotine inside its walls.[96] Before the last months of the war, however, most of these executions had followed judicial processes conducted by Special Courts in the Rhineland area or by the People's Court in Berlin, the Reich Supreme Court in Leipzig, or a military court.[97] Space in the prison had always been tight, and the regimen had always been difficult for the prisoners. Nevertheless, from the postwar memoirs of many former inmates, it appears that, under the circumstances, their treatment in the prison itself, if not in Gestapo or Kripo headquarters, had usually been reasonably decent and the space cramped but adequate for most of the Nazi years. In testimony published in 1993 in a book recording the experiences of several Cologne Jews in the Third Reich, Helmut Goldschmidt, then a young half-Jewish man, recounts sitting alone in a cell in Klingelpütz prison for three months before he was deported to Auschwitz in March 1943. This experience compared very favorably, he explains, with the eight days he had spent in one of the cells in the basement of the Cologne Gestapo headquarters in the notorious EL-DE-Haus in the Elisenstrasse. "I believe that I was the only German there, all others were forced laborers, Russians and members of other nations. The rooms were stuffed full of people. One could not even lie down properly, so crammed it was in these narrow cells; and in the night one had to find a way to sleep, covered only by one's coat, in a half-upright position."[98]

In the fall of 1944, conditions in Klingelpütz took a dramatic turn for the worse when the Gestapo decided to take over a wing in the prison's cellar because of the extreme overcrowding in the ten cells of its own "house jail." Before Cologne was liberated by American troops the following March, this "Gestapo wing" in Klingelpütz became the scene of epic horror that included drunken sex orgies between female prisoners and guards, raving mad Gestapo officers running amok, beatings and whippings of naked male and female prisoners while they ran the gauntlet between six to eight Gestapo officers and other assorted guards and overseers, and the violent deaths of hundreds of prisoners through beatings, gassings, poisonings, shootings, hangings, and medical experiments.

The evidence for this comes primarily from numerous eyewitnesses who were incarcerated in Klingelpütz prison in the last months of the war and who provided testimony in a case of crimes against humanity that the Cologne state prosecuting attorney's office investigated after the war ended.[99] This investigation stretched out for nearly a quarter of a century before all charges were dropped and the case was dismissed on April 19, 1968. For somewhat unclear reasons, it took the state prosecuting attorney's office two decades to locate the prime suspects, two former Gestapo officers, Winand Weitz and Josef Dahmen, and two former female prisoners, Anna P. and Hubertine S. By the time it had done so, the two who seemed most guilty, Josef Dahmen and Anna P., had died and the charges against the others had to be dropped because the statute of limitations for their alleged crimes had run out.[100] Nevertheless, the tale told by the eyewitnesses is both believable and shocking.

Two of the most important witnesses were Adam P., an ordinary police watchman who had worked in the prison for years as a guard and a medical orderly, and Otto P., a physician who, after his arrest for a *Heimtücke* offense in September 1944, was forced to spend the last months of the war treating sick inmates. Both of these men agreed that conditions in the Gestapo wing of Klingelpütz had been reasonable until Christmas 1944. It was true that many of the 600 to 800 inmates soon became covered with lice and infected with typhus, that space was so cramped that prisoners had to share their cells with up to thirteen others and had barely enough room to sit and not enough to lie down in, and that when winter came all were freezing cold because the last windows in the prison had long since been blown out by air raids. But these were almost luxurious quarters in comparison with the ghastly situation in the subterranean jail at the EL-DE-Haus Gestapo headquarters where Otto P. had spent nine days crammed in a tiny and nearly airless cell with thirty other prisoners before he was transferred to Klingelpütz. The EL-DE-Haus facility had to be quarantined and closed down completely in February 1945 because of a raging typhus epidemic.

In its first months of existence in the fall of 1944, the Gestapo wing in Klingelpütz was headed by an SS *Sturmführer* named van Knappen who seems to have treated the prisoners fairly and to have "acted in a generally correct" manner. But when he was replaced by the SS *Untersturmführer* and Gestapo *Kriminalsekretär* Winand Weitz in January 1945, "another wind [began] to blow," explained Otto P.[101] Under his tutelage and that of his subaltern, the SS *Unterscharführer* Josef Dahmen, and their female-prisoner assistants, Anna P. and Hubertine S., the Gestapo wing soon became a house of horrors.

In a letter he wrote to the Cologne state prosecuting attorney's office on October 13, 1947, Adam P. pointed to Dahmen as the "leading force behind all of the serious atrocities and murders" and said that he could not personally attest to having witnessed any murders committed by Weitz.[102] Others testified, however, that Weitz was also responsible for the gross mistreatment of numerous prisoners and that he himself had either murdered or ordered the murder of several inmates. As the medical man Otto P. testified on September 9, 1948, the prisoners were "constantly beaten and abused" and robbed of their "food and tobacco rations." Moreover, he had heard from several of the prisoners that on one occasion, when a prisoner was groveling on the ground begging for mercy, the irritated Weitz, whom Otto P. said had become "raving mad" with the onset of typhus and, according to another prisoner, had been "run[ning] about the prison like a crazy man firing aimlessly throughout the area with his machine gun," simply took out his revolver and shot him at point-blank range.[103]

Although the evidence in the case reveals that Weitz was as brutal as he was sick, his sadism seems to have been no match for that of his subordinate Dahmen or Dahmen's lover Anna P., whom some described as a "monster" and others as a "brutal man-woman." In his letter to the state prosecuting attorney, Adam P. explained that he personally had seen Dahmen shoot a Polish or Ukrainian woman in the head when she, so weakened that she could not stand, had begged for his assistance by throwing her arms around his legs. He also related in his letter that Dahmen had bragged to him after a heavy bombing attack on January 14, 1945, that he had ordered the murder of several male prisoners whom Adam P. had found dead in one of the cells with their heads split apart. Dahmen had proudly told Adam P. that he had them killed because they were physically incapable of walking to the train station with 300 other prisoners who were being transferred to Buchenwald concentration camp. Since there was no possibility of having them transported to the train station on the day they were scheduled to leave, he decided that the easiest thing for him to do was to have them bludgeoned to death in Klingelpütz while the others walked to the station.

Finally, Adam P. charged that Anna P. had "made herself guilty of the worst atrocities against her fellow inmates."[104] For example, on a cold day in January 1945, he maintained, she had forced the female prisoners to strip off their clothes and lie naked on the floor, whereupon she walked on top of their exposed bodies and beat on their breasts with a rubber truncheon until many of them bled profusely.

While atrocities like these were being committed on a daily basis inside the Gestapo wing in Klingelpütz prison in the last months of the war, they accounted for only a small fraction of the murders the Cologne Gestapo committed in the final days, weeks, and months of Nazi rule. The former Gestapo officer Kurt Mayer testified on November 20, 1967, that the Cologne Gestapo hanged between 300 and 400 people between October 1944 and February 1945 on the five-meter-long gallows erected in the inner courtyard at Gestapo headquarters.[105] Several other witnesses supported this allegation by describing something that happened two to three times a week. When the prisoners gathered for roll call, the guards yelled out the names of thirty to thirty-five inmates who had been selected for "special treatment." Many of them were foreign workers accused of having sexual relations with German women, but others were ordinary German men and women accused of having committing either political or economic crimes. As the former prisoner Hubertine S., who had served for a time as a guard in the prison and was thought to have had intimate relations with some of the Gestapo officers along with Anna P., stated in her testimony of May 29, 1967, "Officially these inmates were to be transported [elsewhere]. [But] among the prisoners who were not called there was unanimous certainty that the delinquents were taking their last steps."[106] This account jibed fully with testimony provided by Otto P. and Adam P. years earlier. As Otto P. had put it, "Hundreds of prisoners were carted off from Klingelpütz to the Gestapo building where they vanished without a trace."[107] In Adam P.'s words:

> After Christmas 1944 prisoners were taken away daily who never returned. Each time 10 men. In the last execution at the beginning of March 1945, 105 men were taken off. It is obvious to me that they were executed. After the war ended I went with several American officers to the EL-DE-Haus [Gestapo headquarters] and noticed a large number of corpses lying in the inner courtyard. The way the dead had been killed could not be determined. I did not see any bullet holes.[108]

CHAPTER NINE

A Summation:
Defendants, Denouncers, and Nazi Terror

The insanity that reigned in Klingelpütz prison, Cologne Gestapo headquarters, and elsewhere across Germany in the last months of Nazi rule notwithstanding, the great majority of German citizens did not suffer personally from Nazi terror during the Third Reich. The Gestapo and other Nazi officials knew well that millions of common citizens in their everyday lives regularly broke the law by listening to foreign-radio broadcasts, telling political jokes, and criticizing Nazi leaders and Nazi policy in the company of their family, friends, and neighbors. They also realized that such minor acts of insubordination, carried out largely in private by loyal citizens, were largely harmless in nature and seldom constituted the kind of serious protest that might have endangered the regime. Moreover, they understood that policing such acts harshly could have placed the regime at greater risk than generally overlooking them, for to do so not only would have had a negative impact on popular opinion but would have required the utilization of precious resources that were needed to combat real threats to the regime.

If Nazi society afforded German citizens considerable space to grumble, complain, and vent frustration over policies and leaders they sometimes disagreed with, this does not change the fact that Nazi Germany was a police state. Nor does it indicate that the Gestapo was merely a "reactive" organ, as prevaricating and mendacious Gestapo officers like the former Cologne Gestapo chief Emanuel Schäfer liked to testify in their own defense in their postwar trials for crimes against humanity, and as some well-intentioned scholars who stress the role that civilian denunciations played in Nazi terror now suggest.[1] Nazi Germany most certainly was a police state, and the Gestapo did not merely react to information offered to it by eager-to-please and revenge-seeking civilians in the form of voluntary denunciations. Denunciations were indeed plentiful in Nazi Germany, and they did provide the Gestapo with useful sources of information. But their importance should not be overestimated: they were only one of the sources of information the Gestapo had at its disposal, and they figured most often in comparatively minor cases involving ordinary citizens whom the Gestapo did not worry about very much. There were some significant exceptions to this, particularly in the persecution and destruction of the Jewish population. Nevertheless, in the Gestapo's control of groups and individuals who posed serious threats to the Nazi regime's authority, denunciations played at most a secondary role. In these cases, the Gestapo routinely took "proactive" measures and received most of its information through forced confessions, reports from designated informers and paid spies, house searches, police raids, information supplied by Nazi Party officials, SS and SA storm troopers and police auxiliaries, long-existing police registers of political opponents and known criminals, and other official sources.

Even the most brutal police state needs to be able to count on the compliance and complicity of ordinary citizens to destroy its enemies and to accomplish its goals successfully. Through voluntary denunciations and other means, large numbers of ordinary Germans indeed helped to sustain the Nazi police state. But, except on very rare occasions, the Gestapo did not dole terror out indiscriminately against the German population. It wisely concentrated its limited but sufficient resources on selected targets like Jews, Communists, and Jehovah's Witnesses and at times turned its attention to Socialists, homosexuals, clergymen, habitual criminals, and some other groups of people. For the unfortunate minorities, whom the Gestapo persecuted resolutely, there could be no question that they were victims of a police state. But the majority population had a different experience in Nazi Germany. To a large degree, ordinary German citizens controlled themselves.

Before turning to the most murderous project of the Nazi terror apparatus, the Holocaust, I will present some final statistical evidence compiled from systematic analyses of the more than 1,000 randomly selected Gestapo and Special Court case files read for this study. This evidence supports the argument about the targeted and selective nature of Nazi terror, indicates what types of people suffered from that terror, and helps to assess the role that civilian denunciations played in it.

DEFENDANTS

Tables 9.1 and 9.2 show how the Krefeld Gestapo and the Cologne Special Court resolved the cases they handled in both the prewar and wartime periods. Table 9.1 provides evidence that supports the observation that the Gestapo applied radically different sanctions to people it targeted than it did to ordinary German citizens accused of illegal activity. Before one considers the figures in this table, however, one needs to bear in mind that the people in the targeted groups were many times more likely to have had a case started against them in the first place than those in the nontargeted groups. Even though, for example, Communist and Socialist activists and members of the tiny sect of Jehovah's Witnesses represented only a small fraction of the Krefeld population in the 1930s, they accounted for almost as many of the Krefeld Gestapo's cases in the prewar period as did all other non-Jewish Krefelders combined (104 cases versus 137 cases in a random sample of every eighth Gestapo case file).

As table 9.1 makes clear, the stark differences in the number of cases started against these various groups of people only begin to give one an impression of the differential treatment they received at the hands of the Gestapo. In both the prewar and wartime periods, the Gestapo forwarded only about one-third of the cases it investigated to the court authorities, and it made its own determination about what sanctions to apply in the majority of its cases. Having one's case sent to the courts was often a godsend for the accused: in table 9.2, one observes that the prosecuting attorneys associated with the Special Courts, like that in Cologne, dismissed the vast majority of cases they received without sending them to trial. Dismissal usually meant that all charges were dropped against the accused and they were free to resume their normal lives. It is true that the Special Court's conviction rate grew in the war years (from 11 percent of the Cologne Special Court's cases

TABLE 9.1 *Outcome of Krefeld Gestapo Cases, by Category of Defendant, 1933–1945*

	JEWS	KPD / SPD	RELIGIOUS SECTS	FOREIGNERS	OTHERS
1933–1939					
Decided on by the courts	16%	33%	—	—	31%
Concentration camp	24	6	—	—	1
Protective custody	17	33	100	—	9
Gestapo warning	13	5	—	—	18
Dismissed without a warning	21	14	—	—	30
Other	3	—	—	—	3
Unknown	5	9	—	—	9
NUMBER OF CASES	66	79	25	—	137
1940–1945					
Decided on by the courts	12%	45%	—	—	36%
Concentration camp	33	—	—	—	—
Protective custody	8	9	—	50%	12
Gestapo warning	22	—	—	38	26
Dismissed without a warning	15	45	—	12	22
Other	—	—	—	—	3
Unknown	10	—	—	—	1
NUMBER OF CASES	40	11	0	8	74

NOTE: The Jewish cases are based on a complete sample of all existing Krefeld Gestapo cases involving Jews who were accused of illegal behavior. All other information in the table is based on a random sample of every eighth Krefeld Gestapo case file.

TABLE 9.2 *Outcome of Non-Jewish Cologne
Special Court Cases, 1933–1945*

	1933–1939	1940–1945
Conviction	11%	27%
Acquittal	2	3
Dismissal	87	66
Unknown	1	2
Passed on to People's Court	—	3
NUMBER OF CASES	388	155

NOTE: Based on a random sample of 543 Cologne Special Court cases with a non-Jewish
person as the defendant.

in the 1930s to 27 percent in the 1940s), but even during the war roughly
two-thirds of the cases forwarded to the Special Court continued to end in
either dismissals or acquittals.

From the numerous examples of specific cases that have been discussed
in previous chapters, we know that the sentences that the Special Courts
handed out ranged from executions and lengthy prison terms to short periods in jail and modest fines. We also know that ordinary Germans had a
far greater chance of receiving moderate sentences than did those from the
targeted groups, who, on completion of their court-mandated jail or prison
terms, were often sent by the Gestapo to concentration camps for additional
punishment. Ordinary Germans, on the other hand, almost never met such
a fate. Returning to table 9.1, one sees that the Krefeld Gestapo took relatively few ordinary Germans into protective custody—which sometimes,
but not always, was the first step toward being sent to a concentration
camp—and sent almost no ordinary Germans to concentration camps directly in either the prewar or the wartime periods. This contrasts sharply
with the Gestapo's treatment of those in the targeted groups. Whereas, in
the 1930s, 41 percent of the cases in our sample that involved Jews, 39 percent of those involving Communists and Socialists, and 100 percent of those
involving members of religious sects ended with such drastic measures,

only a modest 10 percent of the cases of those in the "others" category ended this way. Most of these people were habitual criminals, homosexuals, or targeted clergymen like the young homosexual priest Suitbert G. of Krefeld or the brave opponent of the regime Father Josef Spieker of Cologne.

By and large, these trends continued to hold during the war years. Once again, the Gestapo rarely ordered protective custody or concentration camp confinement for ordinary Germans; most ordinary Germans continued to have their cases dismissed, either by the Gestapo itself or by the court authorities. For the Jews who remained in Germany, however, the picture darkened ominously. As the figures in table 9.1 reveal, Jews who had a case started against them for disobeying the law during the war years had an even greater chance of being sent directly to a concentration camp than they had had during the 1930s. But figures such as these only start to hint at the horror of the Nazis' persecution of Jews in the war years. Caught as they now were in the midst of the Holocaust, Jews in wartime Germany no longer needed to have violated any law to be sent to a concentration camp and most often death. Just being Jewish was now crime enough to be subject to having their lives snuffed out. Hence, the vast majority of the Jews whose cases the Gestapo resolved by measures short of protective custody or concentration camp received only a brief respite before they too were murdered in the end. Finally, one notes in table 9.1 that the number of cases against leftists and members of religious sects declined precipitously during the war years, since most of their hard-core activists had already been dealt with in the 1930s. Foreign workers and prisoners of war, however, took up some of the resulting slack in the Gestapo's caseload. That they accounted for a disproportionate number of the people who were executed by Nazi courts during the war years was discussed in chapter 8. Table 9.1 provides additional evidence of the brutal treatment they often received if they were charged with disobeying the laws of their captors. Though the numbers here are small, it is significant to note that 50 percent of the Krefeld Gestapo's cases involving these people, who most often had been accused of engaging in an illicit relationship with a German woman, were resolved by protective custody. What the figures in the table do not show, however, is that protective custody for foreign laborers usually was tantamount to a death sentence.

Although political and ethnic considerations took pride of place in determining which types of people became targets of the Nazi terror apparatus, socioeconomic factors also mattered. Among these factors, as demonstrated in table 9.3, gender figured prominently. Although women were by no means spared from Nazi persecution and suffered in sometimes greater numbers than men from Nazi eugenic, family, and racial policy, women were typically more successful than men in steering clear of the Gestapo and Nazi courts.[2] This was especially true in the 1930s, when female defendants accounted for only 10 percent of the Krefeld Gestapo's cases and 15 percent of the Cologne Special Court's cases. But it became less true in the war years, when the percentage of female cases more than tripled with the Gestapo and nearly doubled with the Special Court. This increased female percentage is explained in large part by the fact that so many men were away at the front, but this may not be the only explanation. Our survey of elderly Cologne citizens found that Cologne women today claim to have had far less sympathy for Nazism than did Cologne men. If women elsewhere in Germany also felt this way—as they probably did, for about half of our respondents had lived in communities other than Cologne during the Third Reich—and if female antipathy for National Socialism grew over time, that growth could logically have accounted for at least some of the increase in the percentage of female defendants during the war years.

Unlike their gender, the age, religion, and occupational standing of the defendants varied less dramatically over time in Nazi Germany. Both during the 1930s and later during the war years, defendants were of all ages and religions and came from nearly all ranks of German society, but working-class Catholics in their thirties and forties and Jews of all ages were the most typical defendants. The average age of defendants was higher in the war years than it had been earlier. This change, like the change in the number of cases against women, had much to do with the military having called so many young men away to fight, but the average age of defendants may also have increased over time because Nazism was always a movement that celebrated youth and energy over age and wisdom.

The relative absence of court cases involving Jews, particularly during the war, underscores the obvious fact that the Gestapo preferred to employ extralegal sanctions far more often with Jews than it did with other Ger-

TABLE 9.3 *Characteristics of Defendants in Krefeld Gestapo and Cologne Special Court Cases, 1933–1945*

	KREFELD GESTAPO			COLOGNE SPECIAL COURT		
	1933–1939	1940–1945	1933–1945	1933–1939	1940–1945	1933–1945
GENDER						
Male	90%	63%	81%	85%	73%	82%
Female	10	37	19	15	27	18
NUMBER OF CASES			433[a]			28,920[b]
AGE						
Under 20	8%	6%	7%	4%	3%	4%
20–29	24	13	21	20	12	18
30–39	29	19	26	30	24	28
40–49	21	24	22	22	28	24
50–59	12	19	14	19	23	20
Over 59	6	19	10	5	10	6
NUMBER OF CASES			433[a]			594[a]
RELIGION						
Catholic	35%	46%	39%	61%	65%	61%
Lutheran	9	13	10	16	15	15
Jewish	16	31	20	6	2	5

No confession	14	8	11	7	1	5
Other	9	—	6	4	1	3
Unknown	18	3	13	7	15	11
NUMBER OF CASES			433[a]			594[a]
OCCUPATION						
Unskilled worker	—	—	31%	—	—	27%
Skilled worker	—	—	34	—	—	24
Clerk, shopkeeper, pub owner	—	—	6	—	—	9
Businessman	—	—	11	—	—	9
Professional	—	—	4	—	—	8
Government service/military	—	—	3	—	—	2
Farmer	—	—	1	—	—	4
Retiree	—	—	1	—	—	1
Housewife	—	—	7	—	—	14
Pupil/student	—	—	—	—	—	1
Other	—	—	2	—	—	2
NUMBER OF CASES			321[c]			544[c]

a. Based on a random sample of case files.
b. Based on all existing case files.
c. Jewish cases excluded in the random sample.

mans. It is also noteworthy that the number of Catholic defendants exceeded their proportion in the Krefeld and Cologne populations, suggesting that, in this region at least, Catholics were relatively less enamored of National Socialism than were Protestants and therefore more prone to getting in trouble with the authorities.[3]

Since Communists and Socialists came most often from modest backgrounds and were leading targets of Nazi terror, it is no surprise to find that the majority of both Gestapo and Special Court defendants held working-class occupations. Table 9.3 shows that almost two-thirds of the Krefeld Gestapo's defendants and more than 50 percent of the Cologne Special Court's defendants were either unskilled or skilled laborers; these percentages grow even higher when working-class housewives are included in the calculations. The percentage of working-class defendants would be higher still if Jews were not counted in the figures: a large number of the businessmen in the table were of Jewish background. Among non-Jewish Germans, people of higher social status rarely got into trouble with the Gestapo or the courts. People from such backgrounds did occasionally come into contact with the Nazi legal authorities, but much more often as denouncers than as defendants.

DENOUNCERS

Over the last decade, several scholars, such as Robert Gellately and Gisela Diewald-Kerkmann, have published extremely significant work on the topic of civilian denunciations as a source of the Gestapo's information, and this work has gone a long way toward demystifying the Gestapo and the Nazi dictatorship.[4] There are reasons to think, however, that the current focus on denunciations has overstated their significance, leading to a possible underestimation of the heinous and willful actions of the Gestapo and overestimation of the criminal culpability of the German population. No attempt will be made here to absolve the German population from guilt. On the contrary, a central argument of this book is that the German population was indeed guilty of a great measure of complicity in the murder of the Jews and in many other crimes committed in Nazi society. But it is important not to indict the entire German population for a crime (denunciation) that only a relatively small fraction of the population committed.

In a recent study of political denunciations made to the Nazi Party organization in the small district of Lippe, Diewald-Kerkmann argues that the "records of the justice authorities and of the Gestapo demonstrate that the readiness of the German population to denounce was of unimaginable proportions." She also asserts that the German population's "readiness to denounce" supports the argument made lately by scholars such as Gerhard Paul, Klaus-Michael Mallmann, Robert Gellately, and others that "the Gestapo was not in many ways an active organ itself, rather it only operated reactively."[5] Although denunciations were mean-spirited acts and far from rare, and although denunciations did provide the Gestapo with much information, especially about ordinary German citizens, I cannot agree with these statements.

To begin with, even though one finds many denunciations in Gestapo and Nazi Party records, acts of denunciation were less common than many people think, and the Gestapo did not as a rule, except in its more trivial cases, rely on denunciations for the majority of its information. Those who have placed the most stress on the importance of denunciations would presumably come to realize this were they to extend the scope of their studies beyond the subset of cases they have investigated to include an analysis of the Gestapo's crackdown on Communists and Socialists, religious sects, the clergy, and some other types of the Gestapo's more serious cases, which they have largely ignored.[6]

As tables 9.4 and 9.5 make clear, an analysis of a large random sample of all the Krefeld Gestapo's cases reveals that civilian denunciations initiated only a minority of the cases, both in the prewar and wartime periods. Table 9.4 shows that denunciations did serve to initiate the majority of the cases of the Cologne Special Court, but these were generally not very severe cases, and most ended in dismissals. Likewise, table 9.5 shows that denunciations provided the most common source of the Krefeld Gestapo's information in cases involving "ordinary Germans," but these too were usually trivial cases that ended more often than not without punishment for the accused, or at worst with a brief jail sentence or fine.[7] In stark contrast, de-

nunciations began only a tiny fraction of cases involving Communists, Socialists, and members of religious sects; the great majority of the cases
against these targeted groups were initiated by information the Gestapo
obtained through its own surveillance network or through confessions it
beat out of people during interrogations. Also, as we saw in Chapter 6, the
Gestapo's campaign against the clergy in the mid-1930s relied far less on
denunciations than on information it received from Nazi Party officials
and spies who infiltrated church gatherings and eavesdropped on priests'
sermons.

Of the main targeted groups, Jews were the most affected by civilian
denunciations. During the 1930s, when the Nazis sought to discredit and
demoralize Jewish Germans and to appropriate their property and force
them to leave the country, civilian denunciations initiated the same proportion of Jewish cases as they did of the cases of ordinary Germans. Since
many more Jews proportionately had cases lodged against them, this means
that Jews suffered more frequently from denunciations in this period than
ordinary Germans; since Jews were punished far more rigorously than ordinary Germans, it can be argued that denunciations harmed the Jewish
community more than any other group of people during these years in Nazi
society. Even though in the war years the percentage of the Gestapo's Jewish
cases started by denunciations abated somewhat, denunciations continued
to plague Jews at this time when the stakes involved became much higher.
Chapter 10 will document several cases in which voluntary denunciations
from German citizens cost Jews their lives. Nevertheless, it needs to be recognized that most Jews were never denounced by German citizens; that
during the war most Jewish cases of alleged wrongdoing did not come to the
Gestapo's attention through denunciations (as table 9.5 shows); and that
even had there been no denunciations of Jews at all, most Jews probably still
would have lost their lives.

How many people made denunciations? Table 9.4 shows that 24 percent
(or 105) of the 433 cases in the random sample of every eighth Krefeld Gestapo case file began with a clear denunciation from someone in the civilian
population. Because some people denounced more than one person, only 85
individual denouncers provided the Gestapo with the information it used to
start 24 percent of its cases. If one were to estimate the number of de-

TABLE 9.4 *Source of Information That Started Krefeld Gestapo and Cologne Special Court Cases, 1933–1945*

	KREFELD GESTAPO			COLOGNE SPECIAL COURT		
	1933–1939	1940–1945	1933–1945	1933–1939	1940–1945	1933–1945
Civilian denunciations	21	31	24	60	57	58
Gestapo/police	41	15	32	13	7	12
Information from Nazi Party and other Nazi organizations	6	12	8	18	11	16
Anonymous accusations	1	2	1	6	9	7
Other	6	9	7	—	1	—
Unknown	26	31	28	3	15	8
NUMBER OF CASES	291	141	432	416	162	578

NOTE: Based on random samples of Krefeld Gestapo and Cologne Special Court case files.

TABLE 9.5 *Source of Information That Started Krefeld Gestapo Cases, by Category of Defendant, 1933–1945*

	ORDINARY GERMANS		JEWS		KPD/SPD		RELIGIOUS SECTS	
	1933–1939	1940–1945	1933–1939	1940–1945	1933–1939	1940–1945	1933–1939	1940–1945
Civilian denunciations	41	47	41	29	5	13	4	—
Gestapo/police	24	12	21	39	58	63	96	—
Nazi Party and other								
Nazi organizations	9	24	8	15	1	—	—	—
Anonymous accusations	2	—	3	7	—	—	—	—
Unknown	24	17	27	10	36	24	—	—
NUMBER OF CASES	131	58	63	41	79	8	25	—

NOTE: All figures, except those pertaining to Krefeld Jews, are based on a random sample of every eighth Krefeld Gestapo case file. The Jewish cases are based on a complete sample of every existing Krefeld Gestapo case file that involved a Jewish person who was investigated for alleged illegal behavior.

nouncers in the Krefeld population during the Third Reich, one would need to multiply the 85 denouncers by 8. This yields a figure of 680 denouncers. To this figure one would add many of the anonymous denunciations listed in the table, though not all of them, since some came from Gestapo spies. More important than this (anonymous tips began only 1 percent of the cases), one would need to include many of the 28 percent of the cases started by information from unknown sources. It should be mentioned, however, that a large number of the cases in this category had nothing to do with political wrongdoing; they most often involved matters of emigration or other noncriminal issues that led the Gestapo to open a case file. Nevertheless, for the sake of argument, were one to count all of these cases and all of the cases stemming from anonymous accusations as having been initiated by civilian denunciations, one would increase the number of denouncers in the Krefeld population by 1,005 to a total of 1,685 people. Doubling this figure to include denunciations that never made their way to the Gestapo or that the Gestapo thought were too insignificant to use to open an investigation would raise the total to about 3,000 people who denounced others in Krefeld during the Nazi years. This estimate, although probably high, does point to a large number of denouncers. But does it reveal that the "readiness of the German population to denounce" was of "unimaginable proportions?" I think not. Using a figure of 170,000 for Krefeld's population during these years, this would mean that between 1 and 2 percent of the population acted as denouncers. This estimate is probably high considering that the city's population figure was only a fraction of the total number of people who lived there at one time or another during the twelve and a half years of Nazi rule (many died, others moved away, and so on) and that this figure includes many cases that did not start with a denunciation. Even if one does not consider this a high estimate, however, it indicates that most German people, in fact the overwhelming majority of German people, never denounced anyone.[8] More than this, it suggests that the willingness of German people to inform on others in Nazi Germany may have been considerably less pronounced than in the German Democratic Republic, where 2 percent of the adult population, Timothy Garton Ash estimates, "had a direct connection with the secret police"; others have estimated that the number of informers in the GDR was probably many times that figure.[9]

Who were the denouncers, and what was their relationship to the people they denounced? Denouncers, like the people they denounced, came from nearly all strata of the German population. The most glaring exception to this was the Jews. Although, in their impossible situation, a tiny number of Jews, like the beautiful and young Jewish Berlin woman portrayed in the book *Stella* by her former classmate Peter Wyden, did seek advantage through collaboration with the Gestapo, not a single case of a denunciation by a Jewish person was found in the 1,132 randomly selected Krefeld Gestapo and Cologne Special Court cases analyzed for this study.[10] As table 9.6 shows, a large number of the denouncers were members of the Nazi Party or the SS, SA, Hitler Youth (HJ), or League of German Girls (BDM). Unfortunately, the records do not always reveal the Nazi Party affiliations of the denouncers, but there is clear evidence that the denouncers in a large number of cases had no such affiliations. Also, it is usually impossible to determine the religious background of the denouncers, although it would most likely have been mentioned had they been Jews, which, again, they were not.

One can state with confidence, however, that the typical denouncer was male, middle-aged, and middle-class. Perhaps the biggest surprise is the comparatively low rate of female denunciations. Before denunciations were studied systematically, and this has transpired only recently, it was rather widely assumed that women denounced more readily than men. In one of the earliest treatments of this issue in Nazi Germany, Richard Grunberger, for example, argued in 1971 that women, especially in the war years, took the lead in denouncing their fellow citizens. According to his logic, "Women tended to take the lead both because there were more of them about and because many thought that prying into their neighbours' affairs constituted a female contribution to the war effort while their menfolk were at the front." Grunberger's argument sounds reasonable enough, but his evidence was based on only a few case examples and was thus largely impressionistic and not fully trustworthy.[11] Hence, when scholars like Gisela Diewald-Kerkmann and Klaus Marxen quantitatively examined the role of gender in denunciations in studies they published in the last few years, Grunberger's argument failed to hold water. In Diewald-Kerkmann's 1995 book, which she based on an examination of 292 denunciations made to the Nazi Party in

Lippe, she found that women accounted for only ten denunciations between 1933 and 1941, and for only a total of thirty-two in all of the years of Nazi Germany. Similarly, in the quantitative analysis of People's Court cases that Marxen published in 1994, he found that female denunciations accounted for only 17.5 percent of all denunciations.[12]

Nevertheless, one might question whether Diewald-Kerkmann's and Marxen's studies are truly representative of denunciations in general since the former study is based on mostly minor cases handled by party authorities and the latter on what some might think are equally unrepresentative cases of a far more serious kind. As the figures in table 9.6 demonstrate, however, Diewald-Kerkmann's and Marxen's findings do indeed provide accurate estimates of the role played by gender in denunciations. Independent of which authority handled the cases—the Nazi Party, the Gestapo, the Special Court, or the People's Court—and in both the prewar and the war years, women most certainly denounced far less often than men. Thus, in a random sample of 105 Krefeld Gestapo case files initiated by denunciations, female denunciations began only 17 percent of the cases, almost the exact same figure arrived at by both Diewald-Kerkmann and Marxen. In a random sample of 346 Cologne Special Court case files started by denunciations, women did play a somewhat larger role, accounting for nearly one-third of the denunciations (31 percent), but this was still only a bit part compared with the leading role played by men. Also similar to Diewald-Kerkmann's findings, the ratio between male and female denouncers did narrow somewhat in the war years in both the Gestapo and Special Court case files. But even at this time, when millions of German men had been called away to do battle, male denouncers continued strongly to outnumber female denouncers.

It may also be surprising to note in the cases of denunciation analyzed in table 9.6 that so few young people acted as denouncers even though many have believed that Hitler Youth were strongly urged to denounce adults in general and their parents and teachers in particular and by the late 1930s all German youths had to be members of this organization.[13] To be sure, some youths did make denunciations, but this happened far less often than one might expect. As the table shows, only 6 percent of the denunciations handled by both the Krefeld Gestapo and the Cologne Special Court were made

TABLE 9.6 *Characteristics of Denouncers in Krefeld Gestapo and Cologne Special Court Cases, 1933–1945*

	KREFELD GESTAPO (N = 105)			COLOGNE SPECIAL COURT (N = 346)		
	1933–1939	1940–1945	1933–1945	1933–1939	1940–1945	1933–1945
GENDER						
Male	86%	77%	83%	73%	56%	69%
Female	14	23	17	27	44	31
AGE						
Under 20	—	—	6	—	—	6
20–29	—	—	22	—	—	21
30–39	—	—	19	—	—	30
40–49	—	—	22	—	—	20
50–59	—	—	18	—	—	18
Over 59	—	—	13	—	—	5
OCCUPATION						
Unskilled worker	—	—	6	—	—	14
Skilled worker	—	—	37	—	—	23
Clerk, shopkeeper, pub owner	—	—	13	—	—	11
Businessman	—	—	9	—	—	8
Professional	—	—	9	—	—	8

Government service/military	—	6	—	8
Farmer	—	1	—	3
Retiree	—	5	—	2
Housewife	—	10	—	19
Pupil/student	—	3	—	3
Other	—	—	—	3
NAZI PARTY AFFILIATION				
Nazi Party member	—	15	—	10
Member of SA, SS, or HJ/BDM	—	9	—	8
None	—	20	—	8
Unknown	—	56	—	12
				70

NOTE: All figures are based on random samples of case files. In the random sample of 433 Krefeld Gestapo cases, 105 were initiated by denunciations. In the random sample of 594 Cologne Special Court cases, 346 were initiated by denunciations.

by youths under the age of twenty, and only 3 percent of the total number of denunciations came from youths who were still in school. Of equal importance in this regard is that in the 1,132 randomly selected Gestapo and Special Court cases analyzed for this book, involving people who came from all types of political, socioeconomic, and ethnic backgrounds, not one parent was denounced by his or her underage child, and only one pupil denounced his teacher, and he later recanted his denunciation.[14] Denunciation, therefore, was predominantly an adult as well as a male activity. Among the adult denouncers, however, age seemed to be of relatively little importance: denouncers were rather evenly spread throughout the age groups, and the median age of the denouncers was around forty, similar to that of the people they accused.

The least surprising finding about the denouncers' backgrounds relates to their occupational standing. Studies of the Nazi Party and the Nazi vote have established that Nazi ideology attracted people from all parts of the social spectrum, but debate still rages over whether to characterize the Nazis as a "catchall party," with great numbers of working-class converts, or as a movement that remained above all a lower-middle-class and middle-class phenomenon.[15] The evidence here cannot resolve this debate, but it does provide modest support for the latter position. Whereas almost one-third of all defendants in the Krefeld and Cologne case files came from the ranks of unskilled laborers (see table 9.3), very few denouncers in either the Gestapo or Special Court records held such lower-class occupations. Skilled workers, on the other hand (many of whom were master craftsmen, whom one might consider middle-class, or at least lower-middle-class), made up the largest single group of denouncers, just as they made up the largest single group of defendants. Otherwise, lower-middle- and middle-class people from a large number of occupational backgrounds—professionals, businessmen, shop owners, and so on—made up most of the rest of the denouncers.

Although lower-middle-class and middle-class people denounced more frequently than people from more humble backgrounds, their motivation to denounce did not necessarily stem from political conviction. Most people denounced others because of trivial and personal matters, above all because of quarrels with their neighbors, differences at work, fights in a bar, or just sheer malice. To be sure, many people denounced because they felt it was their duty. Others denounced with the goal of currying favor with the authorities. It is usually very difficult to discern what the denouncers' true motives were. Nevertheless, a reading of hundreds of cases that began with denunciations makes it clear that Gestapo officers and court officials often viewed denunciations as less than honorable acts that provided less than reliable information, and they took pains to devalue denunciations that came from cranky and ingratiating types or from those seeking revenge or possible reward.

The relationship of the denouncers to the people they denounced is easier to assess than their motives. In the 451 cases featured in table 9.7 that started with a denunciation, neighbors, acquaintances, and coworkers account for a majority of the denouncers, in both the Krefeld and Cologne records. Siblings, friends, children, and even former lovers are almost entirely absent. Marital disputes did lead to denunciations somewhat more often, and in-laws as well as spouses made up a small but not insignificant proportion of the denouncers. Nevertheless, it was the rare spouse or former spouse, the rare in-law, and the rare person in general who denounced a person with whom he or she had shared a close relationship. Most Germans remained true to their family and friends, and most realized that denunciations were repugnant acts, even in the Nazi dictatorship.

The fuel that these base and vile acts of denunciation provided for the Nazi terror machinery helped ultimately to incinerate many Jews. Most often, however, denunciations helped the Gestapo keep ordinary Germans in line. They seldom weighed heavily in cases involving serious resisters to and other enemies of the regime. The Gestapo was primarily a "reactive" organ most often in cases of little consequence. When it mattered most, the Gestapo was more proactive than reactive. It could afford to be lenient and less than vigilant with most ordinary Germans, for they did not need to be watched. Even without the threat of denunciations, most Germans probably would have remained loyal to the Nazi leadership. The Cologne survey demonstrates that the overwhelming majority had no fear of arrest and had never been denounced in Nazi Germany. Most of the respondents did not even know anyone personally who had been denounced in the Third Reich.

TABLE 9.7 *Relationship of Denouncers to Accused Persons in Krefeld Gestapo and Cologne Special Court Cases, 1933–1945*

	KREFELD GESTAPO	COLOGNE SPECIAL COURT
Neighbor	22%	26%
Friend	—	1
Spouse	2	4
Child	1	—
Sibling	—	—
Other relative	1	4
Former lover	1	2
Acquaintance	12	19
Coworker	9	8
Employer	3	3
Employee	—	4
Stranger	21	14
Other or unknown	28	16
NUMBER OF CASES	105	346

NOTE: All figures are based on random samples of case files. In the random sample of 433 Krefeld Gestapo cases, 105 were initiated by denunciations. In the random sample of 594 Cologne Special Court cases, 346 were initiated by denunciations.

CONCLUSION

In the fictional police state of Oceania that George Orwell created in his anti-utopian novel *1984*, proles and animals are allowed to roam freely while the thought police closely monitor the activities of the members of the inner party who might be capable of fomenting revolution and Big Brother whips up hatred against alleged Jewish traitors like Emanuel Goldstein and foreign enemies from Eurasia and Eastasia. Similarly, the Nazi police state targeted its real and potential enemies carefully and left most ordinary citizens alone to their own devices. In *1984* everyone is expected to worship Big Brother, and even though some do not, the telescreens and the thought police torment only those few who might have the ability to revolt. By the same token, the masses in Nazi Germany largely celebrated Hitler, and the Gestapo reserved its brutality for Jews, Communists, Jehovah's Witnesses, and other selected groups and individuals whom the Nazi regime despised or felt threatened by. Denunciations provided the Gestapo with useful information. But the Gestapo and the Nazi regime would still have disarmed leftist, religious, and other threats and persecuted and murdered millions of innocent people without them. These horrendous acts would not have been imaginable without the loyalty, complicity, and silence of the German population, of whom only a minority by their own admission were motivated by the fear of being denounced or arrested. Most went along willingly, even if they did not condone all of Hitler's policies.

PART FIVE

THE GESTAPO, "ORDINARY" GERMANS, AND THE MURDER OF THE JEWS

The machinery of destruction included representatives of every occupation and profession.

—Raul Hilberg

Had we known about it, we would have had to kill ourselves.

—a Cologne bystander

CHAPTER TEN

PERSECUTION AND DEPORTATION,
1939–1942

I n the Third Reich, not all Germans were ardent Nazis; nor were all Germans ardent anti-Semites. Some Germans actively opposed Hitler's regime; many privately held anti-Nazi convictions. Not a few offered aid and support, sometimes at their own great peril, to Jews and other victims of Nazi terror. Nevertheless, there is no escaping the fact that Germans mounted next to no meaningful protest against Nazi Germany's greatest criminal endeavor, the mass murder of the German and European Jewish population. Hitler, the Nazi Party, the SS, and the Gestapo did not murder the Jews alone. They led the charge certainly, but it took nearly the entire German population to carry out the Holocaust. Many people from other countries also had Jewish blood on their hands before the killing stopped. One can argue that even people from faraway lands like America or Great Britain, countries that did their utmost to bring about Hitler's defeat, could have done more to save the Jews.[1] So too could the Vatican and those from neutral countries like Switzerland and Sweden. Had it not been for Hitler and the Germans, however, six million Jews would not have lost their lives, and millions of other Jews would not have had their lives shattered.

In the past few years the role that ordinary German citizens played in the Holocaust has become the subject of much attention and heated debate. First Christopher Browning and then Daniel Goldhagen wrote chilling accounts of how ostensibly average German citizens—many of them middle-aged men with no close ties to the Nazi movement—periodically left their homes, families, and civilian careers behind to serve in reserve police battalions that shot thousands of defenseless Jews at point-blank range in the kill-ing fields of Poland and the former Soviet Union, where roughly one-quarter of the Jews who died in the Holocaust were murdered.[2] Both Brow-ning and Goldhagen also make the alarming point that these men fre-quently volunteered to do the shooting and that they did not take part in the murders because they feared severe punishment for refusing to obey orders. Even if some of their officers put them under pressure to shoot, they were nonetheless apprised of their right to stand aside, which some in fact did. As Browning explains, "In the past forty-five years no defense attorney or defendant in any of the hundreds of postwar trials has been able to docu-ment a single case in which refusal to obey an order to kill unarmed civilians resulted in the allegedly inevitable dire punishment."[3]

To be fair to both authors, it must be pointed out that even though Browning and Goldhagen agree that most of the members of the reserve police battalions they studied were quite ordinary German citizens who clearly participated in the massacre of thousands of Jews, they disagree bit-terly over what motivated these people to kill. Their fundamental differ-ences in interpretation become evident as soon as one considers the titles of their books: the title of Browning's book is *Ordinary Men;* the first two words in the subtitle of Goldhagen's book are *Ordinary Germans.* Proceed-ing from the position that the reserve policemen were simply "ordinary men" who acted presumably in the same way that men in other societies in such extreme situations also would have acted, Browning attributes their participation in the Holocaust to group pressure to conform, ideological indoctrination, and essentially human weakness. He stresses that even though "80 to 90 percent of the men proceeded to kill . . . almost all of them—at least initially—were horrified and disgusted by what they were doing."[4] Goldhagen, in sharp contrast, maintains that "ordinary Germans," not "ordinary men," perpetrated the massacres and that these "ordinary Germans" were, with only a few exceptions, not at all upset about the duties they performed. As he argues, "The perpetrators, 'ordinary Germans,' were animated by antisemitism, by a particular *type* of antisemitism that led them to conclude that Jews *ought to die*" and that stemmed from what he claims was a long-standing "eliminationist antisemitic German political culture."[5]

Virulent anti-Semitism was certainly prevalent in Nazi Germany, and many Germans of ordinary backgrounds played a significant role in the murder of the Jews. Nevertheless, some important evidence in this book, particularly that stemming from questionnaires and interviews with Jewish survivors, has already raised strong doubts about Goldhagen's harsh contention that most ordinary Germans were motivated by an "eliminationist antisemitism." Nevertheless, both Goldhagen and Browning deserve credit for bringing attention to some very disturbing facts. As both of these scholars have powerfully demonstrated, the Holocaust was not simply a cold, machinelike example of modern "industrial killing" ordered by men on high and carried out by a small cadre of specialized subalterns with no will or choice of their own. The Holocaust was at times a viciously bloody spectacle perpetrated by both trained specialists and fully ordinary human beings who often had considerable decisionmaking latitude. This is true not only in regard to the fields, trenches, woods, ghettos, concentration camps, and gas chambers (most of which lay outside of Germany) where most of the Jews were put to death. It is also true in regard to the situation inside the Reich itself, where the mass murder of the Jews was initiated.

Although the level of a person's guilt needs to be assigned individually, and some individuals bore much more guilt than others, tens of thousands of ordinary Germans participated in the mass murder of the Jews, many actively, many more passively. While some rounded up Jews, guarded Jews, interrogated Jews, sentenced Jews, or placed Jews on trains, others clamored for their removal, denounced them to the authorities, liquidated their assets, pronounced them medically fit for transport, and arranged for their deportation in myriad ways. Much of this was done in the open, in full view of a German population that came to be well informed about the ultimate fate of European Jewry well before the end of the war. Many Germans had qualms and misgivings. Some deeply deplored what was happening. Nevertheless, although many discussed it privately among family and friends and tuned in to their radio sets to gain more details, almost no one openly broke the silence about the "terrible secret" that was eventually no secret at all to most German people beyond childhood.[6] Had the silence been broken and the pretense of the secret been shattered, millions of Jews might not have died. A Cologne man I interviewed in early 1994 told me that "had we known about it, we would have had to kill ourselves," but he probably had in fact "known about it" and had options other than suicide. In the questionnaire his own wife sent back to us earlier as part of our survey of elderly Cologne residents, she admitted that she had indeed known about it herself.[7]

JEWISH DEGRADATION
AND WARTIME ANTI-SEMITIC LEGISLATION

The sadistic on-again, off-again persecution and discrimination that Jews suffered in the 1930s was only a cruel prelude to the constant and mounting terror they faced after the *Kristallnacht* pogrom of November 1938 and during the war years of Nazi Germany, when the terror lodged against the Jews turned lethal. For most of the 1930s, as Marion Kaplan in her insightful new book on Jewish life in Nazi Germany explains, "Jews experienced mixed signals not only from the government but also from loyal or sympathetic 'Aryans,' giving some Jews a glimmer of hope. The direction and speed of Nazi policies in the 1930s—legal disenfranchisement, social ostracism, economic collapse and forced emigration within a few short years— appeared obvious to those who had suffered it only in retrospect."[8] But even if hope springs eternal, after *Kristallnacht* few German Jews held much of it anymore. In the words of the Cologne jurist Adolf Klein: "After November 9, 1938, even the most optimistic Jews in Cologne lost all hope."[9]

Although a concrete plan for the systematic annihilation of the Jews had not yet been formed in 1938—it would not be set until the time of the invasion of the Soviet Union in mid-1941 and would take final, written form with the Wannsee Conference in Berlin on January 20, 1942—Hitler announced what he had in store for the Jews well before the Second World War broke out.[10] On January 30, 1939, in a Reichstag speech that was shown in the theaters, broadcast on the radio, printed in the newspapers, and cited again and again by many others over the next three years, Hitler declared: "I have often in my life been a prophet, and usually people laughed at me. . . . Let me be a prophet again today: If international financial Jewry, in Europe and beyond, should succeed in plunging the nations into another world war, the result will not be the Bolshevization of the world, and thus the victory of Jewry, but the destruction of the Jewish race in Europe."[11]

Hitler's speech, prophetic as it indeed was, came at a time when new anti-Semitic laws and decrees were being enacted almost daily. Between the November pogrom and the outbreak of war on September 1, 1939—a period of less than one year—more than 200 anti-Jewish measures came into force. After the war started, the pace of the new legislation sped up even faster, and the intensity of the terror that befell the Jews became lethal.[12]

But for the most part the Jews in Germany were trapped. Theoretically it remained possible for German Jews to emigrate until October 1941, when the major waves of deportations to the ghettos and death camps in the east began and the "Final Solution of the Jewish Problem," as the Nazis called it, moved out of its planning stage to become a reality. In practice, few of the Jews who remained in Germany had the means, health, and connections that emigration required at this last possible moment. Whereas Jewish emigration had reached a peak in 1939 when between 75,000 and 80,000 left the country, it fell to 15,000 in 1940 and was reduced to a trickle in 1941, when the last 8,000 German Jews managed to leave the country on their own.[13] Upward of 90 percent of the 163,696 Jews who remained in Germany on October 1, 1941 (the number recorded by official statistics of the Reich Association of German Jews [*Reichsvereinigung der Juden in Deutschland*]) would soon be put to death.[14]

Before Jews were murdered, however, they were degraded so thoroughly that some of them voluntarily boarded the first "transports" to the east, believing that their chances might be better than if they remained in Germany. One of these people, Lore Schlesinger, was a young Cologne woman of twenty-four. Somewhat miraculously, she lived to tell her story:

> For us in Cologne everything became ever worse. . . . In 1941 we were forced out of our apartment and resettled in one of the so-called "Jewish houses." I moved in together with my mother. . . . Helene Lützzeler, the widowed sister of my mother also moved in with us. We then lived in this "Jewish house" for about half a year until deportation. . . . The apartment in which we lived was very tiny. All of us had brought

furniture and house wares, and everything was therefore chock full. . . .

Then the deportations began. Most of our relatives who had lived in Mülheim and Deutz were already deported on the first Cologne transport to Litzmannstadt [Lodz] on October 21, 1941, and we knew that we would also be taken away soon. The three of us, my mother, my aunt, and I, sat down together and thought it over. As it was known that the second transport was also to go to Litzmannstadt, we thought that it would be better for us to volunteer to go on it. Then our family could be together once again in Litzmannstadt. We thought that we could leave my grandmother behind in Cologne. She was already in her late seventies and we hoped that one would leave her in peace.

So we decided to register voluntarily for the next transport. I cannot remember anymore how we did that, but in any case we soon in fact received a summons for the second transport and we were supposed to come to the Messehalle [the Cologne congress center]. I can still remember how we rode on the tram to the Messehalle with backpacks and suitcases, and how some of the people looked at us with sympathy, while others stared at us joyfully, as if they wanted to say: "Uh huh, thank the lord, again a few less [of them]." The Messehalle is still present in my mind. There were letters written on the gates to the building and we had to line up alphabetically. My aunt named Lützeler had to stand by the letter L, my mother named Schottländer and I named Schlesinger were to stand by SCH. The names were then called out and the people went into the hall. About 15 people were still standing by S and SCH, whose names began with these letters, when all at once the gates closed. I still hear the noise today. They banged shut and we were standing outside, but my aunt was inside. An SS man came to us and said, "You can go back home. You will go on the next transport." I then thought to myself: "My God." I felt guilty somehow. I had persuaded my aunt by saying: "Come with us, then we will remain together." I begged the SS man to take out two people and to let my mother and me in. But it could not be done. He said: "Go home. The next transport will also go to Litzmannstadt." So we were consoled somewhat—we had no idea! After eight or ten days we received an order once again to get ourselves ready. But this transport went to Riga. Graphically stated, the dear Lord had already decided for us: My destiny was to remain alive, for no one except, I think, Dr. Lewin, who went on that transport to Litzmannstadt came back.[15]

Lore Schlesinger's decision to volunteer for deportation, though drastic and unusual, was not altogether irrational given the humiliating and tormenting circumstances for German Jews at the time. For years they had been subjected to ubiquitous anti-Semitic invective that labeled Jews as "traitors," "parasites," "rats," and "poison carriers" deserving of absolutely no human sympathy. A commentary in the Moers newspaper on the recent showing of the vile Nazi propaganda film *The Eternal Jew* in early 1941, for example, stated that the film will "clarify to the very last Germans that the Jew as a race is, and will forever remain, beneath human kind, as the rats are beneath the animals: parasites, poison carriers, and subversive scroungers."[16]

Although the pernicious and pervasive Nazi propaganda efforts may never have convinced many Germans that the Jews were subhuman, they certainly contributed to demoralizing further a Jewish population that was nonetheless treated as subhuman. By the time the deportations to the east began in the fall of 1941, the majority of Jews had surrendered most of their property and valuable possessions, given up their homes, and lost their careers. They had to observe a curfew that prohibited them from being out on the street after 8:00 P.M. in winter and 9:00 P.M. in summer. They could shop only at designated hours, and they could no longer purchase lingerie, clothing, or shoes. They had to perform forced labor, but their rations were so reduced that they had to subsist with almost no meat in their diet, and if they still remained in Germany after September 1942, without coffee, fish, milk, eggs, poultry, canned goods, apples, tomatoes, and various other vegetables. Their children were deprived of candy. They were isolated in "Jewish houses" and specially designated Jewish apartments from the rest of the world, and their isolation was made more complete by their being prohibited to own radios or private telephones. (In December 1941, even the use of public telephones was denied them.) The only outside place for their children to play was often in Jewish cemeteries, since Jews could no longer go into the forests or visit public parks and neighbors complained about Jewish children playing outside Jewish day-care centers.[17]

In addition to these tragic realities of Jewish life in wartime Germany, two other discriminatory measures imposed on the Jews merit special comment: one took away their anonymity by requiring that they be physically branded with the yellow Star of David, and the other limited their access to air-raid shelters during bombing attacks. Needless to say, both of these measures made life particularly painful and dangerous for the increasingly downtrodden Jewish population.

On September 19, 1941, Jews over the age of six were required to affix a large, six-pointed Star of David (which the Nazis called the "Jewish Star"), outlined in black against a yellow cloth background, with the word *Jew* written in bold, Hebrew-like letters, on the left breast of their outer clothing and to don the star every time they went out in public. Not wearing the star or attempting to hide it from view by covering it up with a shopping bag or a briefcase or anything else was a punishable offense. For many Jews this was the most painful day of their lives. One sixteen-year-old boy related in his memoir that the star made him feel "naked. . . . The star seemed as big as a plate and to weigh a ton."[18] The evening before the new law came into effect, the Dresden professor Victor Klemperer recorded in his diary that henceforth his Aryan wife would have to do all of the shopping for he would venture out of his apartment only to grab a bit of fresh air under the cover of darkness. The next day, as his wife sewed the star onto his jacket, he was overcome by "a fit of raving despair."[19] From that time on, Jews had no chance of avoiding the stares and epithets of the German population. After March 1942, Jews also had to display the Star of David on the doors of their residences, which made them all the more visible a target for anti-Semitic neighbors, the Gestapo, and other Nazi authorities and enthusiasts.

The "Jewish Star" also served to curb the Jews' chances of surviving the devastating Allied bombing attacks. In October 1940, a decree was passed calling for the strict separation of Jews and Aryans in bomb shelters. At best this meant that from that time onward Jews had to endure the attacks of the bombers, and the verbal attacks of many Germans who blamed the war on them, in cramped, substandard sections of the shelters. Often it meant that

Jews were denied access to the shelters altogether; many shelters provided no space at all for the Jews, who, after September 19, 1941, could be easily recognized and kept out because of the star. As Lore Schlesinger explained: "The war was in full gear and we too experienced all of the bombings until the end of 1941. The residents of the Salierring, where we lived, went into a bomb shelter during the attacks, where we were not allowed to enter. We were indeed allowed to leave our apartment, but, because we were Jews, we could not go into the bomb shelter."[20]

Some Jews who decided to risk entering the shelters later wished they had not. In a postwar crimes-against-humanity case started in November 1948 against a Krefeld policeman, a sixty-six-year-old man named Emil Löwenstern testified that in the three years he had spent in Theresienstadt concentration camp he had suffered nothing comparable with what happened to him "in one night at the Kanalstrasse police station in Krefeld" in 1941.[21] Having recently come to Krefeld, the city of his birth, to spend some time with his siblings and to gain a respite from the persecution he was subjected to in Essen, where he had been living, Löwenstern was out in the street one night when a bombing attack began. Along with many others in the area, he immediately sought refuge in a bomb shelter at the corner of Krefeld's Hochstrasse and Südwall that forbade Jews entry. Before much time had passed, and although he was not wearing a Star of David, someone recognized him and brought him to the attention of two regular policemen in the shelter, who took him under arrest. When the bombing attack ended, the policemen forcibly escorted him to the nearby police station in the Kanalstrasse, giving him repeated kicks along the way. Inside the police station, the real brutality began. After administering a severe beating, one of the policemen ordered him to undress and, when Löwenstern delayed, personally ripped off his coat and his vest. Next the policeman told Löwenstern to stand with his back against the wall while he reached into his desk and pulled out his revolver. He then pointed his revolver at Löwenstern and told him to shut his eyes. After an excruciating pause, the policeman screamed out, "What, you pig, you are not worth the bullet!" He then locked Löwenstern up in one of the cells and commanded him to stand the entire night with his head up against the wall. When Löwenstern later tired and slumped down on the floor, one of his jailers, acting on orders from the policeman, beat his head against the wall. The next day, the Krefeld police handed Löwenstern over to the Gestapo.[22]

The harrowing accounts of people who survived the war and the Holocaust, like Lore Schlesinger and Emil Löwenstern, only begin to convey an impression of the terror that German Jews experienced in wartime Germany. The Krefeld Gestapo case files, the investigatory materials assembled for the July 1954 trial of the heads of the Cologne Gestapo for their part in the deportation and murder of the Cologne Jews, and painstaking efforts by German archivists and historians to reconstruct the deportations of the Jews from Krefeld, Essen, and Düsseldorf in minute detail help to document the tragic experiences of the Jews who did not survive.

WARTIME JEWISH CASE FILES

The Krefeld Gestapo case files demonstrate that the terror that German Jews encountered in the war years bore only a limited resemblance to that of the 1930s. During the peacetime years of Nazi Germany, Jews were only one of several targets of Nazi terror. During the war years, Jews became the prime target. In the 1930s, Jews accounted for only a small fraction of the Gestapo's caseload (20 percent in Krefeld) as the Gestapo and the other Nazi control organs concentrated their resources on rooting out Communists and other immediate political and religious threats to the Nazi regime and relied primarily on voluntary denunciations from the civilian population to keep up the pressure on the Jews. In the war years, as the percentage of the Gestapo's caseload concerning Jews rose dramatically (to 35 percent of all Krefeld Gestapo cases), the Gestapo and the other Nazi control organs jettisoned their former "reactive" posture and sprang into action to facilitate the destruction of the Jewish people. They no longer sat back and waited for denunciations to trickle in for their information.[23] They themselves and others they commissioned constantly spied on the Jews, opened their mail, raided and searched their residences, checked their identification and ration cards, made certain that they complied with every anti-Semitic regulation and decree, and otherwise hounded, tormented, and ultimately took an active part in murdering them.

The change in the Gestapo's tactics became noticeable as soon as the war began. On September 14, 1939, the Krefeld Gestapo arrested a forty-nine-year-old Jewish businessman named Hermann H. and set in motion a train of events that soon took his life.[24] At the time, Hermann H. and his thirty-nine-year-old wife, Gertrud H., were in the process of securing papers from the U.S. consulate in Stuttgart that would enable them to emigrate. They in fact did receive these papers in May 1940. But by that time it was too late to spare Hermann H.'s life, though his wife did manage to emigrate to America on June 10, 1941, less than two weeks before Germany invaded the Soviet Union.

Hermann H. came to the Gestapo's attention through a denunciation made by a twenty-year-old single woman who lived with her parents in a neighboring apartment and who served as an air-raid warden. According to the woman's accusation, on an evening about a week earlier, Hermann H. had left the blinds in one of his apartment windows open about four inches. When she went to his apartment to draw his attention to this, he became angry and told her: "If you want to see something, you need to put on a pair of glasses and then go to the Bismarkstrasse [the seat of the Nazi Party headquarters] to see if they also have observed the blackout!" In the course of the Gestapo's brief investigation of the affair, carried out by the officers Herbert Braun and Wilhelm Weber, it also received damning testimony from a forty-three-year-old shop owner who claimed that shortly before the war started, Hermann H. had said to him: "Whether there will be a war or not, that will be determined by us, you know nothing!"

No one was able to corroborate the accusations made by either the shop owner or the young woman, so after holding Hermann H. for two weeks in protective custody, the Gestapo let him go. By this time, Hermann H., who was already suffering from a nervous disorder, had become extremely "nervous and agitated," according to evidence in his file. Soon he and his wife began making plans to escape over the nearby border to Holland. The Gestapo learned of their plans by an anonymous report filed probably by a spy the Gestapo had commissioned to watch their every move. According to this report, Hermann H. and his wife had plans not only to cross the border illegally but also to smuggle 5,870 marks of their own money out of the country. On September 28, 1939, the Gestapo took them both under arrest and placed them in protective custody. For Gertrud H. this meant spending the next eight months in jail before being set free on May 20, 1940. For Hermann H. protective custody led to his death. After spending two months in Sachsenhausen concentration camp, he spent the following six months in jail in Krefeld, where he became severely ill. In late May he was transferred to a hospital in Bielefeld. A month later, on June 27, 1940, his fiftieth birthday, he died.

Another case that began in the first month of the war also started with a report from a Gestapo spy and contributed to the death of the accused person, even though the offense involved—listening to foreign-radio broadcasts—was not especially severe. Of particular note in this case is that one of Krefeld's own Gestapo officers, Alfred Effenberg, took part in the spying.

The case began on September 18, 1939, when Effenberg received a confidential report that informed the Gestapo that a Jewish woman named Friederike P. frequently listened to foreign-radio broadcasts in the evening in her apartment. Deciding to check out the veracity of the report himself, Effenberg spent the next evening with his ear against a common wall she shared with her next-door neighbor to find out what he might hear. The wall must have been quite thin, and Frau P. must not have taken any special precautions, because Effenberg determined that indeed Frau P. was again listening to foreign broadcasts, at 9:30 P.M. to a "French broadcast and at 10:30 P.M. to the news broadcast in the German language of the English radio."[25]

A day later, Effenberg interrogated Frau P. at Krefeld Gestapo headquarters. She did not deny the accusation made against her. In her defense, she explained that her deceased husband was not Jewish and that, until his death a year previously, he had owned a weaving-mill that made ties and silk fabric. She also testified that she no longer considered herself Jewish and had raised her children outside of the Jewish faith. Finally, she stated that she was listening to the broadcasts merely to try to find out whether her sons, who now ran the weaving-mill, might have to report for military service, and she assured Effenberg that she had not spoken about the broadcasts with anyone, including her three children.

Frau P.'s defense apparently convinced Effenberg, for he decided not to pass the case on to the state prosecuting attorney's office for a possible trial or to recommend punishment of any kind other than a warning and the confiscation of her radio set. He justified this action in the write-up of the case by noting that she had been married "with an Aryan" for more than thirty years, that she had "broken away from the rest of the Jews," and that "her children are married to Aryans and stand, despite their Jewish descent, completely on the ground of the National-Socialist worldview." One can only speculate on what would have happened to Frau P. had she and her children not broken away from the Jewish community. Also, one can only speculate about how difficult this ordeal had been for her. It is known, however, that within a few months this fifty-nine-year-old woman had passed away.[26]

The relatively minor nature of the offenses, the backgrounds of the accused individuals, the tragic final outcome, and the Gestapo's heightened surveillance efforts in these two cases characterize many of the Jewish cases that the Krefeld Gestapo and the Gestapo in other German cities handled during the Second World War. These cases are not typical of the experience of most Jews from Krefeld and other German cities only in that these unfortunate people had a Gestapo case started against them for allegedly illegal behavior in the first place. By the time the war broke out, most Jews were well aware that committing even the most minor infraction against any of the numerous laws and ordinances regulating their lives could easily lead to their demise. Hence, most Jews did everything they could to remain strictly law-abiding so as to try to stay out of harm's way. But this was ultimately impossible for the vast majority of German Jews. Among Jews who remained in Germany after the major waves of deportations began in the fall of 1941, it was mainly only those in mixed marriages and those who were born of a mixed marriage between a Jew and a "German-blooded" parent who had any serious chance of survival.

It must be borne in mind, however, that before the middle of the war years at the earliest, none of the Jews, whatever their status, knew the fate that was planned for them. Almost all Jews believed that the best survival strategy was to adhere scrupulously to the law and to keep their complaints to themselves. As one Jewish Krefeld woman who was charged with voicing an illegal opinion testified to the Gestapo officer Gustav Burkert during her interrogation on July 4, 1941: "As a Jew, I am very careful about making statements of any kind, and I weigh every word in advance. . . . As a Jew, I know exactly how things are and that we no longer have anything to say about it."[27]

No matter how cautious and law-abiding most Jews were, however, many could still not avoid being accused of criminal behavior. Although in raw numerical terms the average yearly total of new Gestapo cases for alleged criminal activity started against Jews held rather constant throughout the Nazi period (in Krefeld at an average of nine per year), this does not indicate that the Jewish "crime rate" held steady during the war years or that the Gestapo's interest in criminalizing the Jewish population had not increased. Because about half of Krefeld's Jews had left the country during the 1930s,[28] the constant yearly total of new cases started against them indicates that the Jews in the war years faced criminal charges at a rate double that of the peacetime years.

Another indication of the Gestapo's zealous persecution of the Jews during the war is the type of offense Jews were accused of committing. Both during the 1930s and during the war years, the Gestapo used all of the Third Reich's laws, ordinances, and decrees to put pressure on the Jewish population. During the war years, however, the number of these laws escalated exponentially for the Jews, and the Gestapo enforced them even more stringently than it had previously. In the 1930s, the pattern of alleged Jewish offenses bore some similarity to the pattern of offenses committed by the non-Jewish population. This was no longer the case during the war years. Before the war, morals offenses (26 percent), economic offenses (20 percent), illegal opinion statements (18 percent), and offenses related to political disobedience (12 percent) accounted for more than three-quarters of the Gestapo cases lodged against Krefeld Jews. During the war, however, the Gestapo had to resort to calling Jews to account for even more trumped-up offenses strictly related to new anti-Semitic legislation, such as not wearing the "Jewish Star," not respecting the Jewish curfew, not having proper Jewish identity papers, or not adhering to Jewish ration requirements. Together, these new types of offenses that applied only to the Jewish population accounted for more than half of all wartime Gestapo cases of alleged

Jewish wrongdoing, with failure to wear or attempts to hide the "Jewish Star" alone accounting for nearly one-fifth of the Gestapo's Jewish cases.

In their vigorous attempt to squeeze the Jewish population beyond the breaking point, the Gestapo also targeted new groups in the Jewish population. Prior to the war years, the gender and age patterns of Jews accused of breaking the law were not unlike those for alleged lawbreakers in the general population. In the 1930s, most putative Jewish offenders had been adult men between the ages of twenty and fifty, and very few Jewish women of any age had Gestapo cases started against them. After the war began, Jewish women, children, and elderly people also became direct targets of the Gestapo's terror. Between January 1933 and August 1939, only 14 percent of the Krefeld Gestapo's Jewish cases involved women, and only 13 percent involved Jews of either sex who were younger than twenty or over sixty years of age. After the war began, these percentages more than tripled for Jewish women, to 40 percent, and more than doubled for children and the elderly, to 28 percent of all new Krefeld Gestapo cases involving alleged criminal activity on the part of Jews.

Two brief examples of the Krefeld Gestapo mercilessly applying maximum sanctions to sick and elderly Jews as punishment for contrived and trivial violations help to illustrate the Gestapo's relentless pursuit of every last Jewish person during the war years. The first involves the oldest Krefeld Jew to have a criminal case started against him in all the years of the Third Reich. On September 14, 1940, the retired Jewish butcher Hermann K. was approaching his eighty-fourth birthday and in ill health when the Gestapo came to his apartment to arrest him.[29] From the evidence in his case file, it is clear that both the Nazi Party district leadership and the Gestapo had long found him a nuisance. In order to find or fabricate a legal pretense for his removal, various neighbors were recruited to spy on his activities. One of these people was a twenty-nine-year-old housewife with whom he frequently argued and with whom he shared the services of a sixty-three-year-old maid who would be called as a witness in the Gestapo's investigation. Although the maid came to Hermann K.'s support by telling the Gestapo that she had repeatedly pleaded with the housewife to respect his advanced age and bad health and to leave him alone, the housewife did not take her advice and turned him in to the Gestapo anyway after he had called her some unflattering names like "dirty cow" and "stupid slut" and had raised his cane in a manner that she took to be threatening. Had he not been Jewish, his behavior would not have concerned the Gestapo in the least. But because he was a Jew, the Gestapo threw the book at him. From the write-up of his case, it is evident that Kommissar Jung wanted to send him forthwith to a concentration camp, but because of Hermann K.'s age, Jung did the most that he could by first holding him for three weeks in protective custody and then sending him to a Jewish asylum in Bendorf/Sayn outside Koblenz. An ominous indication of K.'s fate was entered into his case file more than a year later on January 1, 1942, when Jung closed his file with the words "There is nothing more to do. The [Nazi] district leadership has been apprised of the results of the case. [Further] written communications are to be avoided." It is uncertain whether Hermann K. was still alive when Jung wrote these words. He died either in the Bendorf/Sayn asylum or shortly thereafter when the Jewish asylum was liquidated in June 1942 and the remaining sick and ill inmates were deported to the death camps in the east.[30]

Although Kommissar Jung evidently felt that he had to restrain himself from recommending the final course of action he originally desired in Hermann K.'s case because of K.'s advanced age and physical condition, no such restraint marked his handling of the case of Salomon and Meta G.[31] This difference may have been due in part to the timing of the cases: Jung had opted not to send Hermann K. to a concentration camp before the "Final Solution of the Jewish Problem" had been decided on; the case of Salomon and Meta G. began after the trains had already begun transporting Jews to their deaths. On March 5, 1942, Salomon G., a sixty-year-old former owner of a large silk manufacturing firm in Krefeld with a serious heart condition, and his fifty-year-old wife Meta were summoned to Krefeld Gestapo headquarters. The Gestapo had intercepted a letter they had written that, in the Gestapo's opinion, contained illegal references to the fate of deported Jews. The letter, dated January 18, 1942, had been sent to Salomon G.'s brother in Berlin, who, unknown to them, had already been deported. In the letter, Salomon G. wrote that he had not heard anything from a woman named Lene or from other Krefeld Jews who had been sent off in recent months in the first deportation waves to the east. The important words of this passage were: "From Lene we have not yet heard anything, just like one in general hears almost nothing from those who have been sent away. They will likely not be allowed to write. What a fine state of affairs! Well, I guess that it will all soon be over."

Kommissar Jung made sure that it was indeed soon over for Salomon and Meta G. and their fifteen-year-old son Max. As a temporary solution, Jung first held Salomon hostage in protective custody for several weeks and sent Meta home for the time being with only a severe warning, for she had not written the letter and claimed not to have even read it. Jung's final solution of the case soon followed, however, when he decided to place the couple and their son on the next "evacuation." But before they could be evacuated, Nazi protocol called for them to be examined by the city's medical examiner. In most cases, the medical examiner simply carried out a perfunctory physical examination and then signed a standard form pronouncing that the person examined was "fit for work, concentration camp, and imprisonment and free of noxious insects and infectious diseases."[32] But in a letter written on April 14, 1942, the Krefeld medical examiner noted that Salomon G.'s blood pressure stood at 290/170 (an astronomically high level) and stated directly and succinctly that "Salomon G. is not fit for transport." Nevertheless, and as further evidence of Jung's caprice, heartlessness, and anti-Semitic ardor, Jung simply ignored the medical examiner's recommendation. At the end of Salomon G.'s case file, Jung wrote: "On April 21, 1942, Salomon G. and his wife and his son Max Israel were evacuated to the east." No Krefeld Jew returned alive from that transport, which first went to a transit station in Poland in the Lublin district called Izbica and then on to the gas chambers at Auschwitz, Belzec, and Majdanek.[33]

THE DEPORTATIONS

With the exceptions of those Jews fortunate enough to be sent to the "paradise ghetto" the Nazis erected at Theresienstadt for cosmetic and propaganda purposes and those particularly sturdy and usually youthful Jews who managed somehow to withstand years of backbreaking work and excruciating physical and psychological conditions after being selected for annihilation through labor, most German Jews perished in the concentration camps not long after they had been deported. In Cologne, Krefeld, and other German cities, most of the deportations took place between the fall of 1941 and the summer of 1942. By the end of 1942, most of the deported Jews were already dead, and the only Jews left in these and most other German cities, with few exceptions, were either Jews in mixed marriages or the children of these unions between Jews and Aryans.[34] Although at the end of 1943 more than 18,000 Jews still lived in Berlin (the German city with the highest concentration of Jews and the highest number of deportations), nearly all of these remaining Berlin Jews held special status. Hence, soon afterward, on June 19, 1943, the Nazis officially declared Berlin to be "Jew free."[35]

Eyewitness accounts and other materials assembled for the 1954 trial of the heads of the Cologne Gestapo illuminate how the deportations were carried out.[36] Neither the prosecutors nor the judges at the trial were able to determine the exact number of Cologne Jews who were deported during the Holocaust. Page 16 of the 59-page typewritten judgment, however, documents that about 11,500 Jews from the Cologne area were deported in at least 18 separate transports that began on October 21, 1941, with the transport of 1,000 Jews to the Lodz ghetto, and ended with a transport of an unknown number of Jewish *Mischlinge* and Jews in mixed marriages to Theresienstadt on October 1, 1944.[37] Like the original transport, the second and third contained 1,000 Jews each; they left for Lodz on October 28, 1941, and for Riga on December 6, 1941. The greatest number of transports, carting off the largest number of Jews, departed in 1942. In that year alone, a total of approximately 6,000 Cologne Jews were sent off on one or another of the eight different transports, six of which fell in the three-month period between May and July, to various concentration and death camps in the east. By the end of 1942, therefore, nearly 80 percent of the Jews from Cologne and its surrounding area had already been deported, a figure that only slightly exceeded the average elsewhere in Germany.[38]

The trial documentation described how the Cologne deportations were organized. The Reich Central Security Office in Berlin began the process by sending a written communication, either by letter or by telegram, to the head of the Cologne Gestapo ordering him to assemble a transport of a specific number of Jews of a specific type and age profile, to depart from Cologne on a specific date for a specific destination. Once he had received this communication, the head of the Cologne Gestapo soon shared it with his various department heads so that they could make the necessary preparations for the transport. Soon after this, the head of the Gestapo's Jewish desk, who until the fall of 1942 was Karl Löffler, met with the leader of the local Jewish community and charged him with the responsibility of preparing a list of the Jews who were to be deported and telling them what they needed to know about the impending transport, including when and where to report and what to bring with them. As the written indictment in the trial put it: "The selection and the briefing of the specific Jewish families who were to be deported lay without exception in the hands of the Cologne Jewish community. The Gestapo authorities had next to nothing to do with it."[39]

This statement sounds somewhat suspicious: the Cologne prosecutors seemed to want to blame the victims themselves for organizing their own deportations in order to absolve the head of the Jewish desk of the Cologne Gestapo from charges of criminal guilt. And in fact, not only was Karl Löffler not indicted in the trial, but the prosecutors based many of their statements in their official indictment on Löffler's own self-serving testimony.[40] From Dieter Hangebruch's meticulous examination of the deportations of the Krefeld Jews, we know that the Krefeld Gestapo Jewish desk head, Richard Schulenburg, and other Krefeld Gestapo officers did indeed involve themselves directly in the formulation of the final lists and that there was a great deal of haggling between the Krefeld Jewish community leadership and the Krefeld Gestapo over who should be on those lists.[41] We also know from the Krefeld Gestapo case files that the Gestapo often resolved cases of alleged Jewish wrongdoing by placing the Jewish lawbreaker in question on the next available transport. Finally, one should not forget that the Gestapo ordered the transports in the first place. Hence, it is not at all true that the Gestapo had little to do with the preparation of the lists, though it is also probably true that the Jewish community leadership did take part in what was for them, but not for the Gestapo, the wrenching task of helping prepare the deportation lists.[42]

However the lists were prepared, there can be no question about the sadistic manner in which the Jews were treated while awaiting deportation and about the Gestapo's involvement in the later stages of the deportation process. As the official indictment in the Cologne trial also stated, "When the time drew near that the Jewish victims had to find their way to the Cologne-Deutz congress center [from where the transports left], practically the entire personnel of the Gestapo, up [to] the very last man remaining on duty in the offices of the Cologne Gestapo headquarters, was summoned for the final expedition of the transport."[43] At the congress center itself, which was sealed off with barbed wire and guarded by uniformed policemen and members of the SS, the Jewish victims encountered the most primitive and inhumane conditions imaginable. Inside the gates of the congress center, the Jewish men, women, and children "were herded like animals," as one policeman who had been present at two of the transports recalled, into a large, unheated, and, in winter, freezing cold hall strewn with sawdust, which they were to use for their beds while awaiting the trains.[44] They were then registered and they and their luggage searched for money, jewelry, chocolate, alcohol, medications, and clothing articles that they were prohibited from bringing with them. Usually all that the Jews were allowed to take along on their journey were sixty marks, supposedly to be exchanged for the currency in use at their destination when they arrived; some food, eating utensils and blankets that they would need on their journey; and one suitcase with a maximum weight of fifty kilograms that contained a good pair of shoes, limited clothing articles, two wool blankets, bed linens, and additional food to tide them over for the first two to three weeks after their arrival at their new location. When the trains finally arrived, the Gestapo and the other guards pushed and clubbed the Jews onto the train cars, which in most instances were dilapidated freight cars with no toilet facilities. For their one-way journey, which was guarded by a small staff of policemen led by a Gestapo officer, the Jews themselves had to pay. According to the standard rate for third-class travel, children under ten went free and all others were assessed four pfennigs per kilometer.[45]

Nearly every eyewitness who provided testimony in the investigation preparatory to the 1954 Cologne Gestapo trial related that they had found the whole ordeal far worse than shocking. Many, including several Jewish victims, various lay officials and former policemen, and even a retired former Gestapo officer named Georg Stolze, recalled that the Jewish men, women, and children were physically and psychologically intimidated and beaten, forced to undergo body searches, and robbed of all their cash and valuables, including even the sixty marks in pocket money that the Gestapo had supposedly allowed them to retain. One Jewish man who had the task of helping elderly and sickly Jews with their luggage testified that after one of the transports had been assembled, a group of about 100 Jews was left behind because the Gestapo had already filled its quota. Some of these people had been given various articles for safekeeping by those who were to be deported. Before they were allowed to return to their residences, however, a Gestapo officer took up a megaphone and announced: "It has come to our attention that your racial comrades have illegally handed you money and valuables. I now give you the opportunity to hand over this money and these things, and I bring to your attention that every person I find with money—and after this I will order that body searches be made—will not be arrested, rather they will be put immediately on this transport. I hope that you know what this means!"[46] Several other Jewish victims who had been deported and survived the Holocaust testified that the Gestapo officers made absolutely no effort to register any of the valuables that they took from the Jews during this and other transports. They simply threw everything into a huge heap on the floor, placed it all in large cartons, and often pocketed the best articles for themselves.[47]

Still other eyewitnesses testified that they had observed elderly and handicapped Jews so ill and feeble that they had to be carried to the trains on stretchers, being beaten bloody by the guards with their rifle butts.[48] The onetime police officer Georg Stolze, who had been forced out of retirement during the war years to serve for a time in the Cologne Gestapo, provided a moving summation of the Jews' last moments in Cologne. "The scene that presented itself there aroused one's deep sympathy. Among the Jews were sick people, handicapped people, children, women, men, old and fragile people. The Jews were already in an extremely reduced physical condition from lack of nutrition. Most distressing was the psychological situation of these human beings. The people made such a depressed and fearful impression, [that they looked] like condemned criminals taking their last step."[49]

It would be reassuring to think that most Germans who witnessed events such as these were as deeply touched by them as this retired policemen was, and one wonders what the Gestapo officials, regular police officers, SS stormtroopers, and other German personnel present at places like the

Cologne congress center did after the transports left for their final destinations. When the cries and wails of anguish of the condemned Jews no longer filled the air, were the deportation centers overtaken by a respectful silence? Certainly not in the city of Nuremberg. In that city, as soon as the Jews were gone, the Germans who sent them off threw a party.

On April 26, 1949, Bernard K. wrote a letter from his new residence in Vineland, New Jersey, to the Nuremberg county court in regard to an ongoing trial of former Nuremberg Gestapo officers for their participation in the murder of the Jews of that city. As the head of Nuremberg's Jewish community for many years before he emigrated to the United States after the war, Bernard K. had had "almost daily" contact with the Gestapo during much of the war and gained considerable knowledge about how the deportations of the Nuremberg Jews had been carried out before he himself was deported to Theresienstadt in 1943. He recounted that "the entire staff of the Gestapo" had been mobilized for the transports and had time and again robbed the deported Jews of hundreds of thousands of marks that the Jews were supposedly allowed to bring with them. Some of the officers, he asserted, had stuck the money into "their own pockets" after searching the Jews bodily. Bernard K. then wrote:

> Upon the completion of each transport, a huge party of celebration with women was held in the Langwasser *Lager* with the confiscated food and luxury items, in which, in addition to all of the Gestapo officers, the examiners of the female deportees, cleaning women from the police department, also participated. The jewelry that these women found during their examinations, they took for themselves.[50]

In recent years, the detailed descriptions of the Jewish deportations in other German cities written by German archivists and historians like Dieter Hangebruch and Michael Zimmermann demonstrate that the horror and cruelty witnessed in Cologne and Nuremberg were by no means exceptional.[51] Their work also shows that it was impossible to keep the deportations a secret. Not only were people from nearly all sectors of the German population involved in the deportation process, but the initial stages of the deportations were often carried out in full view of the German citizenry.

Complex undertakings that they were, the deportations would not have been carried out successfully without the efforts of Gestapo, Kripo, SS, and police personnel in rounding up, registering, searching, and escorting the Jews, as well as the efforts of medical examiners, cleaning women, bankers, insurance agents, auctioneers, employers, registration authorities, railroad workers, Nazi Party officials, army officials, and many others. Perhaps relatively few Germans had the opportunity to witness the last stage of the deportation process after the Jews had made their way behind the barbed-wire fences and guarded gateways of the deportation terminals. But before the transports left the terminals, people from all walks of life, going about their normal daily business, often observed the forlorn, soon-to-be-deported Jews with the last of their worldly possessions and the yellow Star of David on their chests being marched under guard through the streets, gathered in train stations, and transported on public streetcars en route to the terminals, usually in the full light of day.

In his exemplary study of Krefeld Jews in Nazi Germany, Dieter Hangebruch has tracked the lives and deaths of each Jewish person who still lived in the city of Krefeld on the eve of the Second World War. Of the 832 Krefeld Jews who had not emigrated, upward of 90 percent died before the Second World War was over. Only eighty-three died of natural causes. Only four survived in hiding in Krefeld. Fifteen committed suicide before being deported. Ten died in a concentration camp or jail while being punished for supposedly illegal activity. Seventy-three moved or were moved to another locality in Germany and then perished, including many who died after being sent to the Jewish hospital in Cologne or the Jewish asylum in Bendorf. The great majority died after being deported to the east on one of the six transports that carted off 599 Krefeld Jews between October 1941 and September 1944. There were only forty Jews whose fate Hangebruch could not account for.[52]

As in Cologne and other Germany cities, most of the Krefeld transports departed in the nine-month period between late October 1941 and late July 1942. Only the sixth and final Krefeld transport left after this date. The first transport contained fifty Krefeld Jews, mostly people between forty and sixty years of age, and left the city on October 25, 1941, with the final destination of Lodz (Litzmannstadt). Since only one of these people survived,

little is known about the deportees' experiences after they left Krefeld.
Much more is known about the second transport, which left Krefeld bound
for Riga on December 11, 1941, because several of the 144 deported Krefeld
Jews on this transport managed to survive to tell about it. They started their
journey at the Krefeld central station, where they were joined by scores of
other Jews from nearby cities in the lower Rhine area. Seventy-one of these
were men, women, and children from Moers who arrived at the Krefeld
train station by streetcar after they had been marched in a long column
shortly after dawn to a local tram stop in Moers from the house of a local
Jewish leader, where most had been forced to spend the previous evening.[53]
From Krefeld, the assembled Jews traveled by train to the Düsseldorf central station, about fifteen miles away. After they arrived, a Gestapo and SS
escort marched them for three-quarters of an hour through the city streets
to a slaughterhouse in Düsseldorf-Derendorf, a fittingly macabre locale for
a deportation terminal but one selected more for its secluded location and
long loading ramps than for its name.[54] A day later, they were put on the
train bound for the Riga ghetto.

Between the second and third transports of Krefeld Jews, the Nazis' annihilation plans took more definite shape at the Wannsee Conference on
January 20, 1942. After that conference, the next deportations went directly
to concentration and death camps. Once again, because there were no survivors, little is known about these third and fourth transports that left Krefeld
on April 22 and May 15, 1942. Other than the number of deported Krefeld
Jews on each transport (133 and 16, respectively), about all that is known
about these transports is that great fear reigned among the Krefeld Jewish
population before they left because nothing had been heard from those on
the first two transports; that they included many prominent Krefeld Jews,
such as the teacher Dannenberg and the medical doctor Adler; and that the
Jews originally left the Derendorf slaughterhouse on freight cars for a transit station called Izbica near Lublin and died not long thereafter in either
Auschwitz, Belzec, or Majdanek concentration camp.[55]

After the fourth transport left, the only Jews remaining in Krefeld were
elderly Jews incapable of working, Jews in mixed marriages, and Jewish
Mischlinge. When the fifth transport left three months later, only the latter
two groups remained. Known as the "elderly transport," it contained 223

Krefeld Jews, of whom 86 were over 60 years of age, 82 over 70, 27 over 80, and one over 90. The oldest person awaiting the train when it departed from Krefeld central station on the late afternoon of July 25 was ninety-four-year-old Josef Gimnicher, who, according to an eyewitness, stood on crutches and proudly and also illegally wore his war decorations on his breast in addition to the required "Jewish Star." The Jews on this transport were to be sent to Theresienstadt, a camp where prominent and elderly Jews were sent and conditions were supposedly so favorable that Nazi propaganda proclaimed it to be the Führer's "gift" to the Jewish people. The Jews recognized correctly, however, that it would be no gift at all to be sent there, and eight elderly Krefeld Jews committed suicide shortly before the deportation. Further evidence that Theresienstadt was no gift is that only 22 of the Krefeld Jews on this transport survived. Since Theresienstadt, like Izbica, was often used as a transit station for large numbers of the deportees, many died in the gas chambers in Auschwitz. Most of the Jews, however, probably succumbed in Theresienstadt itself. Of 68 Krefeld Jews known to have died in Theresienstadt, 46 percent died within the first five months and 33 percent died within ten months. The rest endured the agony awhile longer.[56]

With the "elderly transport" in July 1942, Jewish life in Krefeld came nearly to an end. For the next two years, only handfuls of Jews in mixed marriages and their part-Jewish children remained in the city. On Sunday, September 17, 1944, the sixth and last Krefeld transport removed these people as well. On the morning of that day, the police arrested Krefeld's last 33 Jews and marched them and their families, including many young children, through the middle of the bombed-out city to the Hansa-Haus building in front of the central train station. Along the way, they passed many onlookers coming out of Sunday mass at Krefeld's largest church, Saint Dionysius. In the courtyard of the Hansa-Haus, the Gestapo announced that the Jews were to be deported on a "work transport" and that their non-Jewish partners and young children were to return to their homes. After a heart-wrenching parting, the Gestapo placed the Jews on open trucks and drove them to the Düsseldorf-Derendorf slaughterhouse, which was used for a final time as the deportation terminal of the Rhineland Jews. A day later, the Jews departed for Berlin on a special train with separate cars for men and

women. The journey took several days, and the train made several stops at
various cities to pick up additional Jews along the way. Upon arrival in Berlin, many of the Jews were put to work. Others were placed in overcrowded
jail cells where they nervously awaited their further transport to either
Auschwitz or Theresienstadt. Luckily for the 33 Krefeld Jews, their final
destination turned out to be the latter, and most survived the final months
of the war.[57]

For a final comment on the deportations of the German Jews, one can
turn to an excellent article published in 1995 by the Essen historian Michael
Zimmermann, who carefully examines each stage of the July 1942 deportations of Düsseldorf-area Jews and exposes the involvement of common German citizens from nearly every sector of the population in these deportations and in the deportations in general. In addition to providing a wealth of
evidence to support his charge that "a deportation could not be concealed
from the population," he also exposes as a bald lie the contention made after
the war by Gestapo officers that they had been unaware that the deported
Jews were to be put to death.[58] Arguing powerfully that "the deportation
victims were not 'resettled' [as the Gestapo's euphemisms tried to suggest],
rather they were murdered,"[59] Zimmermann concludes his study by
pointing to the individual culpability of all who participated in carrying out
the deportations:

> Hierarchy and division of labor led to a parcelling out of the responsi-
> bilities and the competencies that at the same time both unburdened
> the participants psychologically and unleashed them. They persuaded
> themselves that other, especially higher authorities, not they them-
> selves, were responsible for the "evacuation" of the Jews. In fact, how-
> ever, those who participated in the deportation undoubtedly had room
> for making decisions or even judgments that extended all the way
> from organizational and financial details to the selection of the
> victims.[60]

CHAPTER ELEVEN

Certainly Michael Zimmermann is correct in arguing that the deportations could not be kept secret from the German population, that large numbers of German citizens participated in them, and that most of the deported Jews were ultimately murdered, not simply "evacuated." Furthermore, although there were machinelike aspects to the deportation process (hierarchy, division of labor, and so on) that helped many of the Germans involved in carrying them out to rationalize their actions and assuage any guilt they might have felt, there was also undoubtedly considerable latitude to make individual decisions that would have made the deportations less bloody and inhumane and that would have resulted in fewer murders. Nevertheless, a question remains as to the individual culpability of the Germans involved. Rumors abounded in the fall of 1941 and the first half of 1942 when the majority of transports left German cities en route to the ghettos and concentration camps in the east, but reliable information about what really awaited the Jews was still not widespread in Germany at the time.[1] Such information did reach large numbers of Germans soon afterward—by Christmas of 1942 at the latest, as will be demonstrated shortly. But before then, even if many Gestapo, police, and SS officials held no illusions about the Jews' final destiny, many and possibly most of the Germans who helped deport the Jews in 1941 and 1942 probably did not fully realize that they were taking part in mass murder. Moreover, their subordinate though not insignificant role in a process that did in fact have industrial or machinelike properties need not be equated with willful murder. As the recent controversy surrounding Daniel Goldhagen's book, *Hitler's Willing Executioners,* has demonstrated, even the intent of those involved directly in murdering Jews at gunpoint remains a matter of heated dispute.[2]

The individual culpability of Gestapo officers and many other German citizens for the murder of the Jews becomes less equivocal, however, when one considers the treatment of the remnants of the Jewish population who remained in Germany in the last years of the war after most of the Jewish transports had departed. After what has been called the "Final Roundup" of Jews employed in war-related industries in late February and early March 1943, those Jews who were living in mixed marriages or were the partially Jewish children of a mixed marriage made up the overwhelming majority of the remaining Jewish population. They had reasonably good chances of surviving the Holocaust. If they were so-called full Jews (*Volljuden*), however, and did not have a non-Jewish partner, their chances were almost non-existent. From whichever group they came, they lived under constant fear and enormous pressure, and their ultimate survival or death often depended on individual choices made by their German captors, their non-Jewish countrymen, or both. Unlike most of Germany's Jews whose collective fate was decided by governmental order and who rode to their deaths on the deportation trains en masse, the fate of these *Restjuden* ("Jewish dregs"), as Nazi discourse labeled them, were often determined one case at a time.

JEWISH RESISTANCE: THE CASE OF JOSEF MAHLER

One of the more tragic, yet somehow inspirational, cases of Jewish persecution in the Krefeld and Düsseldorf Gestapo files concerns the valiant efforts of a middle-aged Krefeld man named Josef Mahler to resist Nazi authority to his last breath even though he had next to no chance of survival once the Holocaust was set in motion.[3] A small (five feet five inches), dark-featured, childless Jewish man of limited education, married to a Jewish woman with an illegitimately born daughter, and an underground Communist organizer and provocateur, Mahler fit the anti-Semitic Nazi stereotype almost to a tee. His Gestapo mug shots, taken after he had not been allowed to shave for several days and after he had probably suffered numerous beatings, were doubtless intended to reinforce that negative image, yet they also reveal a dignified, proud, and defiant individual whom the Nazis could not break. In his refusal to break down and confess, despite long years of incarceration and constant interrogation, Mahler displayed remarkable courage. For more than three years, the Gestapo relentlessly tried to pump him for information about his role in the Communist underground organizations of Germany, Holland, and Belgium. At the least, the Gestapo wanted to use him for a show trial before the People's Court in Berlin. In the end, all the Gestapo could do was kill him.

On March 21, 1940, the Mönchengladbach Gestapo arrested Josef Mahler and his wife Hedwig and placed them in protective custody immediately after the Dutch police had shoved them across the German border at Kaldenkirchen near the small Dutch city of Venlo. Two weeks later, on April 2, the officers Kiefer and Scholten of the Mönchengladbach Gestapo carried out their first interrogation of the couple. It is unclear from the information in Mahler's four large case files with the Krefeld, Düsseldorf, and Mönchengladbach Gestapo how much the Gestapo knew about his activities at this time. It is evident, however, that the Gestapo did know some things about Mahler's background and that it had good reason not to believe his repeated professions of total innocence. Already back in 1937, Mahler had come to the attention of the Krefeld Gestapo after he was fingered by a local Communist organizer who provided details about Mahler's intimate involvement in the organization of an underground resistance organization in Krefeld in March 1933.[4]

Despite their suspicions, all that the two Gestapo officers could get out of Mahler and his wife, who were interrogated one after the other, were basic details about their backgrounds and innocuous descriptions of their lives in exile. In her interrogation, which came first, Hedwig Mahler told the officers the following. She and her husband married at a young age in 1920. Before she was married to Mahler, she had given birth to an illegitimate daughter with whom she no longer had contact and who was now in her midtwenties and presumably living somewhere in Germany. In September 1935, she and her husband emigrated to Holland and settled in Venlo, where he worked as a printer and she assisted him in all aspects of his business. They remained in Venlo for two years. During this time, neither was involved in political activities, but they often received German emigrants as visitors, most of whom, but not all, were Jewish. In 1937 they were forced to move to Belgium after the Dutch police had searched their apartment and found some emigré newspapers, which she believed had been left behind by some of their visitors. In her view, they had been unfairly victimized by some kind of "intrigue" that she could not begin to understand. In Belgium they took up residence in Brussels, where they lived a "withdrawn" life for three years. In March 1940, their residence permit elapsed, leaving them no other choice but to return to Holland, from where they planned to emigrate to Bolivia. But the Dutch authorities would not grant them permission to remain in the country and forced them to return to Germany. Now back in Germany, she still hoped they would be allowed to emigrate to Bolivia.

In his interrogation, which followed immediately after his wife's, Mahler repeated much the same story line to the two Gestapo officers. From the beginning of his testimony—when he told the officers that he had voluntarily joined the German army in early August 1914, that he had served in the army throughout the war, and that he had even been injured and decorated for bravery in service of the Fatherland with the Iron Cross—to the end, Mahler maintained that he was and always had been a loyal German. Moreover, he insisted throughout his lengthy testimony that he had never taken an interest in politics of any kind, that he had never joined any political organization, and that he had never taken part in anti-Nazi activity of any sort, even during his years of exile. In his words: "I state absolutely that in Holland and Belgium I never acted against Germany and that I also did not associate with emigré circles . . . as [I have] already stated, I was completely uninterested politically."

Staunch as the Mahlers were in proclaiming their innocence, the Gestapo did not believe them for a minute. Certain that they had been in the center of dangerous Communist and emigré agitation against the regime and that they had much valuable information to divulge, the Gestapo continued to hold them in protective custody and continuously interrogated them at Gestapo headquarters in Mönchengladbach, and later in Düsseldorf, for over a year. But much to the dismay of the Gestapo, the Mahlers' interrogations yielded nothing of particular interest.

In April 1941, the Düsseldorf Gestapo reached the conclusion that there was nothing more to gain by holding the Mahlers locally and, on April 11, sent the Mahlers to Westerbork concentration camp in Holland. But this did not bring an end to the Mahlers' ordeal. It also did not bring an end to the Gestapo's investigations. Whereas Hedwig Mahler appears to have met her death along with thousands of Dutch Jews deported from Westerbork to the death camps, the Gestapo decided to keep her husband alive for another two years.[5] During this time, it continued to interrogate him periodically while it enlisted the aid of authorities in Holland and Belgium in bringing to light more of his illegal activities.

Some information did indeed come to light, but the Gestapo was still unable to get anything of importance out of Mahler himself. From the Dutch police, the Gestapo learned that a house search conducted in 1937 had uncovered a large cache of Communist printed materials in the Mahlers' former residence in Venlo. Among these materials was a three-page, single-spaced letter that Josef Mahler had written in January 1937 to Soviet radio headquarters (Radio-Centrale der USSR) that displayed deep hostility toward Hitler and Nazi Germany and strong support for the Soviet Union. The Gestapo also ascertained from the German military government in Belgium that Mahler had been a member of the German Communist Party since 1932 and that he had tried unsuccessfully to claim political refugee status in Belgium in 1939. The most important information the Gestapo gained in its three-year investigation of Mahler's activities, however, did not come to light until the spring and summer months of 1943.

On April 19, 1943, the Gestapo finally tracked down and interrogated the illegitimate daughter of Mahler's wife. Having lived in Cologne until sometime after 1940, she now resided in the small Rhine Valley town of Saint Goarshausen, famous to all Germans for the Lorelei myth and song. From the information the Gestapo eventually succeeded in extracting from her, it became apparent that she had served as a conduit of information about conditions in Germany that Mahler had spread abroad among his emigré and Communist contacts. Finally, the Gestapo had assembled almost enough information to put Mahler on trial for high treason. But it still believed it needed to force Mahler into a confession.

In the summer of 1943, the Düsseldorf Gestapo hauled Mahler back to its headquarters for further interrogation. By the end of July, however, Kriminalobersekretär Wagener of the Düsseldorf Gestapo came to doubt that a confession could ever be forced from Mahler's lips. In a report he wrote about the case on July 31, he lamented that "in genuine Jewish fashion, Mahler manages to lie so skillfully that mounting a criminal proceeding against him can meet with no success." Nevertheless, the Düsseldorf Gestapo continued to interrogate him for yet another month until it finally gave up and decided to put the matter and Mahler to rest on September 1, 1943. On that day, the prosecuting attorney's office of the People's Court in Berlin communicated to the Düsseldorf Gestapo that it alone was empowered to make the final resolution of the case because of a decree, enacted on July 1, 1943, that had taken away Jews' rights to court proceedings. On that same day, according to a letter written by the head of the Düsseldorf-Derendorf jail to the People's Court on September 2, 1943, Mahler died. A death certificate appended to the letter listed the cause of his death as a "heart attack."

One cannot know whether Mahler died with a sense of satisfaction that he had not betrayed his compatriots despite the Gestapo's most stringent efforts to force him to talk. One can only hope that he did, because, unless he really had not been involved in resistance activity, as he maintained to the end (a claim that seems highly unlikely), he had shown remarkable strength and fortitude. One cannot imagine a more perfect candidate for a People's Court show trial than this Jewish Communist emigrant. Such a trial could have been of significant propaganda value for the Nazi regime at a time when it was reeling from recent military defeats and when news of the Holocaust was spreading among the German population. A Mahler show trial could have been used to reinforce the oft-repeated propagandistic message that "the Jews are to blame" for the war, and that, as Goebbels proclaimed in his organ *Das Reich* on November 16, 1941, "the treatment we give them does them no wrong. They have more than deserved it."[6]

Perhaps Mahler never broke down because he sensed that withholding information from the Gestapo represented his best survival strategy. For as soon as he talked, the Gestapo would surely have had him killed one way or another. Whatever his motivations may have been, he is one of very few extremely courageous individuals whom the Gestapo's terror tactics could not break. Yet he still died in the end.

Mahler's case, though unusual in some respects, is also a highly instructive one. To begin with, it provides a wartime case to add to several prewar cases of Jewish resistance discussed in previous chapters to demonstrate that German Jews were every bit as likely to resist Nazi terror, and perhaps more so, than non-Jewish Germans. It also helps to point out the dignity with which German Jews conducted themselves in the face of terror and death.

Both before and during the war, most Jewish resistance figures, like Mahler, had associations with Communist and other leftist underground organizations. Some historians now estimate that as many as 2,000 German Jews took part in active resistance at one time or another during the years of Nazi Germany. Small as these numbers still may sound, Arnold Paucker argues that they represent a higher proportion of active resisters among the Jewish population than there were among the general German population: "Measured proportionately against the size of the German population, the Jewish figure would be the equivalent of a mass movement of 600,000 to 700,000 active German antifascists. And [the Germans] certainly can't claim anything like that!"[7]

If, nonetheless, only some German Jews openly resisted the Nazis and most tried outwardly to appear to observe all of the laws, many struggled against the Nazi state and their plight within it in smaller, though not insignificant, ways. Some, like the Dresden professor Victor Klemperer, carried out a kind of quiet resistance against the state by diligently and courageously keeping detailed diaries of their daily lives and their experiences with the Nazi terror apparatus. If uncovered, such diaries could have cost them and possibly their families and friends their lives.[8] Others surreptitiously passed along information about Nazi persecution measures and the Holocaust through what became known as the Jewish "mouth radio." Acting on this information, upward of 10,000 German Jews made the decision to go underground to try to escape the deportations. Although only a fraction survived—in Berlin, for example, it is estimated that of the 5,000 to 7,000 Jews who went underground, only 1,400 survived the war and the Holocaust—the attempts of thousands of Jews to evade deportation often took great courage. Moreover, they provide further evidence that it is both morally dubious and empirically false to claim, as some have, that German Jews simply went off to their deaths like "lambs to the slaughter."[9]

If the Mahler case strongly contradicts the "lambs to the slaughter" image of German Jewry in the Holocaust, it does tell us much about the slaughterers themselves. Slaughtering individuals, not herds of animals, the Gestapo often had to make calculated individual decisions about whom they would slaughter, when they would slaughter them, and how they would slaughter them. One can argue that the ultimate fate of the Mahlers, as Jewish Communists, was never in doubt. Nevertheless, in the end the Gestapo itself made the crucial decisions about when and how the Mahlers died. In making these decisions, the Gestapo made itself culpable for their deaths, all the more so because it did not make these decisions hastily or rashly; it made them consciously and deliberately. For a time, the Gestapo even manifested considerable restraint. Given their backgrounds, the Gestapo could simply have murdered the Mahlers forthwith. But it did not do this. Believing that Josef Mahler had important information to divulge, the Gestapo patiently, as well as resolutely, interrogated him for more than a year and then remanded him to a Dutch concentration camp along with his wife. It did not let him be sent to his death, however, with his wife and other Dutch Jews at Westerbork; it had him kept alive for two years while it searched for more information that it hoped to use to force him to talk. After securing what it believed was enough of this information, the Gestapo brought him back in the summer of 1943 to headquarters in Düsseldorf for several more months of interrogations. But when the Gestapo finally received word from higher authorities that he was in effect useless to their cause and that it alone was to determine his fate, it did not permit him to live a single day longer.

PART-JEWS AND JEWS IN MIXED MARRIAGES

The Gestapo's culpability in the murder of the Jews and its cool efficiency and occasional restraint in managing the Holocaust perhaps come into clearest relief when one examines the treatment of the only sizable group of Jews left in German society after the deportations of 1941 and 1942 and the "Final Roundup" of Jews in war-related industries in early 1943—Jews in mixed marriages and their half-Jewish or partially Jewish children. Not slated at the Wannsee Conference for deportation and death like most Jews, these final traces of Jewish life in the last war years of Nazi Germany were the subject of heated debate and much confusion both in higher Nazi circles and in the population at large.[10] In that they were Jewish or at least part Jewish, many top Nazis strongly advocated that they be treated just like the rest of the Jewish population. Many lower-level Nazis and ordinary German citizens concurred and clamored for, and not infrequently took active part in helping bring about, their death, especially by providing the Gestapo with voluntary denunciations concerning alleged Jewish lawbreaking. But for several reasons, cooler heads prevailed, and most of these Jews were spared.

Whereas humanitarian concerns played some role in this, probably the most salient explanation for the survival of many of these Jews was that their murder would have posed great risks to public opinion and to the Nazis' policy of keeping up the pretense that the Holocaust was a secret. The difficulties the Nazis would have had in trying to keep up this pretense become understandable when one appreciates how numerous they were and how closely interwoven they were into the fabric of mainstream German society. As Marion Kaplan explains: "If the number of half Jews, quarter Jews, intermarried Jews and Christian 'Jews' approached one million, then the number of 'Aryan' relatives who had close or distant contact with them was significant, and the Nuremberg Laws [which began to define them] affected broad kinship networks throughout German society."[11]

Although the figure of one million that Kaplan uses applies only to the mid-1930s, and thus to a time before the largest waves of Jewish emigration had been completed, there were still tens of thousands of these Jews living in Germany in the last years of the war.[12] According to figures compiled by the Reich Association of German Jews before it was dissolved and its last employees were deported in June 1943, there were still more than 18,000 Jews living in Berlin alone at the end of March 1943.[13] Some of these Jews worked in crucial war-related industries, but the great majority lived in the same households with their German family members, either as spouses or children. Hence, murdering these Jews could hardly have been accomplished without embarrassing questions being asked.

Dealing with the remaining Jewish population was a ticklish business. It was also the subject of considerable confusion and irritation, particularly among ardent anti-Semites who could not understand how thousands of Jews continued to remain in German society even after the official end of Jewish life in Germany had been declared on June 10, 1943. A prime source of this confusion related to the definition of these people, for these Jews were not simply divided neatly into the categories of "part-Jews" and "Jews in mixed marriages," but subdivided into a blurry array of subcategories, each with different rights and restrictions.[14] The Nuremberg Laws of 1935 divided Jews into "full Jews" and "part-Jews" (*Mischlinge*) of either the first or second degree. Full Jews were people with at least three Jewish grandparents. First-degree *Mischlinge* were people who did not belong to the Jewish community or practice the Jewish religion, but who had two Jewish grandparents. Second-degree *Mischlinge* were people who also did not belong to the Jewish community or practice the Jewish religion, and who had only one Jewish grandparent. A final category of part-Jews to emerge from the Nuremberg Laws was made up people who had mixed Jewish and non-Jewish parentage but who followed the Jewish religion or were registered in the Jewish community before the Nuremberg Laws came into effect in September 1935. Known as *Geltungsjuden* in Nazi terminology, these people, who accounted for about 11 percent of all part-Jews,[15] were, in theory but not always in reality, to be "considered as Jews" with all of the restrictions that applied to full Jews. Those who fell in one of the two different categories of *Mischlinge*, on the other hand, were at first allowed to retain the status and most of the rights and responsibilities of German citizenship, including serving in the military until April 1940, but over time their rights were seriously eroded and their situation became ever more perilous.

The situation of Jews living in mixed marriages with non-Jews also steadily worsened, particularly in the later war years, and both they and the *Mischlinge* and *Geltungsjuden* lived in constant fear after 1942 that the limited privileges they managed to hold on to would be stripped away and that they too would be deported to the east.[16] Like the *Mischlinge*, they too eventually came to be divided into subcategories, subject to different restrictions. The majority of these people held so-called privileged marriage status, which made them considerably better off than the minority of these people whose marriages were considered "nonprivileged." Those in the former category were either Jewish women married to Aryan men or Jews whose children had been baptized. Those in the latter category were childless couples of Jewish men married to Aryan women or Jews in mixed marriages whose children were *Geltungsjuden*.

With all of these different categories of Jews remaining in German society after 1942, it is small wonder that anti-Semitic Nazi Party members, government officials, and regular citizens were bewildered and frequently complained about the situation. Some (*Geltungsjuden* and Jews in nonprivileged mixed marriages) were obliged to wear the Jewish Star, take on the prescribed Jewish names of either Israel or Sarah, and live in specially designated Jewish houses. Others continued to live, without any visible markings, side by side with ordinary Germans, even if they too were restricted as to whom they could have sexual relations with and what jobs they could work at and the like. Only the Gestapo and the Jews themselves could keep all of this straight.

Indeed, on many occasions, the Gestapo served as a moderating influence in the face of frequent complaints by Nazi officials who wanted to have the Reich once and for all cleared completely of all Jews of all types. Two cases in Krefeld in the summer of 1943 will serve as examples.

In the massive British bombing attack on the city of Krefeld in the night of June 21–22, 1943, a forty-four-year-old Jewish businessman named Bernhard B., who was working at the time as a mechanic in a small firm, was bombed out of the lodgings he shared with his wife. Theirs was a nonprivileged marriage because they had no children. A day later, he and his wife were sent to the small village of Wachtendonk, a few kilometers to the north of Krefeld, where they were to take up temporary lodgings. After only a month had passed, he was denounced to the Krefeld Gestapo by the mayor of the village, who had observed him not wearing a Jewish star and who wanted the Gestapo to inform him whether this was allowed. More than this, the mayor wrote in his letter of denunciation that he found it intolerable that his village, because of this man's presence, was no longer "Jew free" as it had been for centuries. "Since no Jews have resided in my district for centuries, I place value in that it also continues to remain Jew free," he wrote.[17]

Although it took the Krefeld Gestapo an additional month before it summoned Bernhard B. to its headquarters for interrogation, it did not take the matter lightly. In the interim, letters had been exchanged between the Krefeld Gestapo head Ludwig Jung and the Wachtendonk mayor in which Jung affirmed Bernhard B.'s obligation to wear the star and the mayor punctuated his original denunciation with further evidence that Bernhard B. had continued not to wear the star. Immediately after the conclusion of Bernhard B.'s interrogation on August 25, 1943, conducted by the Jewish desk head Richard Schulenburg, he was placed in protective custody while Schulenburg laid plans to have him sent to a concentration camp. Not accepting Bernhard B.'s defense that he had not worn the star he received from the Reich Association of German Jews because it had been destroyed in the bombing attack and he had believed that it would be illegal for him to make his own star now that the association no longer existed, Schulenburg wrote in his case file: "His behavior presents a danger for the public order. It would be appropriate to send Bernhard B. to a concentration camp."

But this did not happen, owing to Schulenburg's and the Gestapo's perverse sense of legality. Schulenburg had clearly wanted to send the man away, and as soon as possible. But a day after his interrogation, the medical examiner had failed Bernhard B. in his requisite physical examination prior to being sent to concentration camp because of a liver condition that might require hospitalization. Hence, Schulenburg backed off and decided to drop the matter after holding Bernhard B. for an additional three weeks in the local court jail. This effectively saved Bernhard B.'s life. Although, along with the last of Krefeld's Jews, he was eventually deported to Theresienstadt in September 1944, he survived the Holocaust. Had he been sent to a concentration camp in 1943, this would hardly have been imaginable.

Schulenburg's curious devotion to the letter of Nazi laws, which had often made him a participant in mass murder, and the Gestapo's sensitivity to popular opinion in the matter of mixed marriages helped to spare the lives of at least two other Krefeld Jews. A zealous, anti-Semitic, Nazi Party functionary named Kreyer had wanted to see them stamped out in the summer of 1943.[18] On July 6, 1943, Ortsgruppenleiter Kreyer wrote a letter to Krefeld police headquarters in the Hansa-Haus building complaining about the activities of a forty-seven-year-old Jewish woman named Klara F., who was separated at the time from her Aryan husband. Using the veiled language of Nazi discourse about the Holocaust, he nonetheless made it clear that he wanted Krefeld's remaining Jews to be put to death; at the very least he sought the removal of Klara F. and a Jewish man named Max S. After detailing some vague misdoings of these two people—he observed that Klara F. was never in her apartment except on Saturdays and spent the rest of the week "carrying on somewhere"—he informed the police that he had decided to hand over her apartment to a young married couple and had ordered her belongings to be sent to the morgue in Krefeld's Jewish cemetery, which he called the "festival hall." Furthermore, he put forward the suggestion that all of Krefeld's remaining Jews, whom he referred to in a hateful manner as the "Jewish Mispoche," should also be sent to the Jewish cemetery's "festival hall," especially Klara F. and Max S.

When Schulenburg received Kreyer's complaint, he reacted in his typically unflappable and legalistic manner. He did open a case file against Klara F., but he recommended that no formal action be taken against either her or Max S. In his notations in her file, he justified his decision not to pay heed to Kreyer's recommendations with words showing that he knew exactly what Kreyer intended: "To think that all remaining Jews could be lodged in the supposed festival hall (morgue) of the Jewish cemetery is not practicable because almost all of them live in mixed marriages and this space is absolutely unsuitable for living quarters." He then indicated that he considered the matter resolved because Klara F. had moved away to Mönchengladbach on July 15. At least in part because of Schulenburg's legalism, both Klara F. and Max S., like Bernhard B., managed to gain a reprieve for another year before they too were sent to Theresienstadt concentration camp in the fall of 1944, from which both returned alive at the end of the war. Had they died there instead, Schulenburg's conscience would not have been troubled. In his way of thinking, he had only done his duty.

Not all Gestapo officers, however, were as dutiful as the imperturbable Schulenburg. And Schulenburg himself, in other cases, often saw his duty in a different light. Hence, evidence of the occasional restraint practiced by the Gestapo should not lead to the false impression that it did not resolutely seek the destruction of Germany's remaining Jewish population. It certainly did seek the destruction of the Jews, and by early 1943 leading officials in the area of Jewish affairs in Berlin, such as Eichmann, were working on plans calling for the systematic elimination of all *Mischlinge* and Jews in mixed marriages.[19] But it was decided that, to the extent possible, the most effective policy would be to employ means that had the appearance of legality. Higher Nazi officials and the Gestapo felt that covering their murderous intentions with a legalistic gloss gave them the best chance of both maintaining order in an increasingly chaotic time and allaying any negative public sentiment that might arise from news of the deaths of intermarried Jews and *Mischlinge*, who had such close ties to the German population.[20]

There were considerable regional variations in the Gestapo's treatment of *Mischlinge* and intermarried Jews. In some localities the Gestapo deported many *Geltungsjuden* and even some Jews in privileged mixed marriages in the later transports of 1942, and in other localities the Gestapo and the police carried out wholesale razzias to round these Jews up and have them deported.[21] For the most part, however, the Gestapo in most localities handled the cases of the last remaining German Jews one at a time. But even in these cases, there were many commonalities in how the Gestapo acted. In cases involving *Mischlinge* and Jews in privileged mixed marriages, the Gestapo sought to have their favored legal status demoted to that of either *Geltungsjuden* or Jews in nonprivileged mixed marriages so that they would have to comply with the much more stringent rules and regulations affecting Jews in those less-favored categories. The Gestapo did this by extensively checking the Jewish ancestry, baptismal records, and prior involvements in the Jewish community of *Mischlinge* and by placing pressure on the "German-blooded" spouses in mixed marriages to seek divorces. This tactic affected only some of Germany's remaining Jews and met with mixed success. Much more successful was the Gestapo's prime strategy for justifying the destruction of intermarried Jews and part-Jews of all types: criminalizing them for real or fabricated violations of the law.

Even if the background checks of *Mischlinge* only sometimes brought the Gestapo's desired result, many Gestapo officers pursued this strategy avidly. The eagerness of Krefeld's Ludwig Jung, for instance, to pull Germany's remaining Jews into the Final Solution is reflected in a case originally involving two partially Jewish Krefeld sisters and later involving their Jewish mother and the partially Jewish husband of one of the sisters.[22] The case also shows that even a minor change in the status of one partially Jewish person, brought about through the persistent interventions of a single Gestapo officer like Jung, could have a domino effect that ultimately threatened the lives of several others. Jung's machinations ultimately succeeded in claiming the life of only one of the four victims in the case, but if not for timing and chance, all four could very easily have died, and nearly did.

We have already encountered one of the sisters in this affair in an earlier chapter: the woman named Lore M. who stated in an interview in her downtown Krefeld apartment and in a nearby café in late January 1995 that throughout the Third Reich she had suffered *"Angst, Angst, Angst!"* She had very good reasons to feel this way. Labeled a "mixed Jew of the first degree" until the fall of 1943, and afterward a person "considered to be a Jewess," she was spied on continually throughout the war years, and her life and the lives of all her family members were seriously jeopardized when she was branded a *Geltungsjüdin* in October 1943. Had it not been for Ludwig Jung's adamant insistence in 1942 and 1943 that she did not deserve to enjoy the status of a "mixed Jew," life for Lore M. and her husband Werner would have been much easier, and she and her sister probably would not have lost their mother in the Holocaust. When the first deportations left Krefeld in the fall of 1941 and the early months of 1942, Lore, her sister Ilse, and their Jewish mother were not included. Because their father was a Gentile and each had been baptized Catholic shortly after her birth, in 1921 and 1925, respectively, they held the status of *Mischlinge* and their parents' marriage was considered privileged. Ludwig Jung did not agree with this classification. He wanted to include the young women on one of the next transports, as he had planned for some other partially Jewish people in the spring and summer of 1942.[23] To do this in compliance with Gestapo protocol, he had to have their status changed to that of *Geltungsjuden*. He tried to do so, but their father, Fritz M., posed strenuous objections in a flurry of letters to Gestapo headquarters in Krefeld and Düsseldorf in April 1942.

Fritz M. insisted that both of his daughters were *Mischlinge* according to German law because both had been raised Catholic and neither had ever been part of the Jewish community. Although these letters did not convince Jung, they were convincing enough to his superiors in Düsseldorf to keep the M. sisters off of the lists for the time being.

On July 2, 1942, the Düsseldorf Gestapo made what it considered to be a final decision about the M. sisters. "According to this henceforth finally determined state of affairs," wrote the Düsseldorf Gestapo officer Breder, the Krefeld Gestapo was to inform the M. sisters' father immediately that the older sister Lore was to retain her status as a *Mischling*, but that her sister Ilse's status was to be changed to that of a *Geltungsjüdin*. Jung was furious with this decision and refused to comply with it. Before the month was over, he composed a long letter to his superiors in Düsseldorf demanding that they reconsider their decision on the basis of new evidence that he believed proved that both of the sisters, not just Ilse, needed to be considered Jewesses. He wrote, "Despite having an Aryan father, there can be no doubt that Lore M. has been raised as a Jew in her parent's home."[24] He bolstered this claim in several ways. Beginning with the assertion that the entire family had always entertained "very close relations to Jewry," he detailed at long length the evidence against the M. family. For many years they had been friendly neighbors with the Jewish Communist Josef Mahler's family, and Fritz M. had been placed in protective custody for a week in 1935 for fostering close business ties with the Krefeld Jewish community, helping many Krefeld Jews find work, and printing the star of David at the top of his stationery. The most damning evidence he produced, however, showed that Ilse had been enrolled in a Jewish school before the date of the passage of the Nuremberg Laws in the fall of 1935 and that Lore, although she had not attended a Jewish school, had been registered as part of the Jewish community for a time in 1937.

Fritz M. was also not happy with the Düsseldorf Gestapo headquarters' "final" decision in his daughters' case, and he was obviously fearful of what Jung's recent interventions might bode for his entire family. Again he wrote a series of letters, this time to Gestapo headquarters in Düsseldorf and Krefeld and to a number of other governmental agencies in these cities as well, pleading his case that both of his daughters should retain their status as *Mischlinge*. Along with these letters he produced declarations from the Catholic Church attesting to his daughters' Christian baptism and rearing and from the Krefeld Jewish community affirming that the local Jewish community did not consider his daughters to be Jewish. He also argued that Lore had been registered with the Jewish community in 1937 owing to a clerical mistake that had been quickly expunged once it was recognized.

Jung could easily have backed off had he wanted to. He even may have run some risk of rebuke for insubordination for his refusal to accept the decisions of his immediate superiors in Düsseldorf. He probably understood, however, that there was little danger of receiving such a rebuke, since a Gestapo officer could be easily forgiven for anti-Semitic zeal. Thus, he continued to press toward his goal. He did not reach it as early as he wanted. It took more than another year before the case came to the conclusion he had sought all along. But finally, on October 5, 1943, Eichmann at the Reich Central Security Office in Berlin personally ruled on the case in Jung's favor. From that time onward, both Ilse and Lore M. were officially "considered as Jewesses"; both were ordered to wear the star of David on their clothing, to adopt the middle name of Sara, and to submit to all the rules and regulations affecting Jews. This ruling also placed their mother and Lore's new husband, Werner G., in grave danger. Their mother immediately lost her privileged marriage status, and Werner G.'s status was demoted from *Mischling* to *Geltungsjude*, like his wife. On October 22, 1943, Werner G. became the last of the four to sign a declaration in the presence of Richard Schulenburg at Krefeld Gestapo headquarters stating that, from then on, "I must submit to all of the proclaimed rules and regulations affecting Jews."

Luckily for these victims of Ludwig Jung's persistence, there were no more deportations of Krefeld Jews until September 1944. Luckier still for them, this last Krefeld transport did not go to Auschwitz, as it could have done, but to Theresienstadt, where they had a much better chance of survival. Technically, all four survived the war. But Frau M. contracted typhus in the Theresienstadt concentration camp and died before she could be brought home.

CHRISTIAN SPOUSES
AND THE ROSENSTRASSE PROTEST

In addition to underscoring the personal culpability of Gestapo officers in the deaths of individual Jews like Frau M., the M. case also provides an important example of how steadfastly most Gentiles with a Jewish spouse held on to their marriages. Throughout the Nazi period, and especially during the war years, the Gestapo and other Nazi authorities placed a strong priority on encouraging the dissolution of such marriages,[25] but their efforts came mostly to nought: some estimate that as many as 93 percent of mixed marriages endured.[26]

There were obvious advantages for Jewish partners in mixed marriages in holding on to their partner. These advantages became most apparent during the war years, when having a non-Jewish spouse often spelled the difference between life and death; by the war's end, intermarried Jews accounted for 98 percent of the surviving Jewish population in Germany.[27] Thus, as long as their marriages remained intact, most intermarried Jews were shielded from deportation and death. But as soon as their marriages dissolved, either through the death of their spouse or through divorce, they usually lost their protection. Evidence from postwar Berlin trials indicates that arrest often followed within twenty-four hours.[28]

Fidelity to their spouse held far fewer advantages for non-Jewish partners in mixed marriages. In that upward of two-thirds of these were women,[29] many had economic incentives to cling to their mate in the early Nazi years, when there was still hope that Hitler might be toppled somehow. But such hopes quickly waned as their husbands lost their jobs and their families came increasingly to rely on them for monetary support. As time wore on, their situation worsened. For both male and female partners of Jews, remaining married eventually came to mean living in poverty and insecurity and being subjected to forced labor, social ostracism, and constant police and governmental pressure. During the war, even their physical safety was threatened as they sat beside their spouses in inadequate and unsafe parts of bomb shelters reserved for Jews, as their rations dwindled to starvation levels, and as their fear increased that they too might someday be included on the deportation lists.[30]

Had the decency and courage that thousands of Gentile partners in mixed marriages displayed during the Holocaust been more widespread among the general German population, many more Jewish lives might have been saved. Although many Germans disagreed with Nazi policy against the Jews, and some provided Jews with aid and compassion,[31] it is telling that the only open demonstration against the deportations of German Jews during the Holocaust was carried out by Aryan wives of Jewish husbands. With some of their friends and relatives, they took to the streets of Berlin in late February and early March 1943 to demand the release of their loved ones.[32] The success of their demonstration is an important reminder of the power that popular sentiment in Nazi Germany sometimes had over the Nazi leadership.

The demonstration began spontaneously on the evening of February 27, 1943, the first day of what Nazi leaders intended to be the "Final Roundup" of the remaining Jews in Germany.[33] Around 200 German women in mixed marriages gathered outside of the administrative offices of Berlin's Jewish community in the Rosenstrasse to inquire about the fate of their husbands, who had been arrested that same day. Soon finding out that their husbands were being held right there in the five-and-a-half-story building and that the Gestapo had plans to deport them to concentration camps, the women began to shout, "Give us back our husbands! Give us back our husbands! Give us back our husbands!"

Over the next week, the demonstration grew in size and intensity. Refusing to pay heed to repeated warnings from the SS and the Gestapo, who brandished their weapons and ordered the crowd to disperse lest they be shot at, the ranks of the demonstrators soon swelled to more than 1,000, and their chants eventually took on a more condemnatory character. To the original refrain of "Give us back our husbands!" some intrepid demonstrators now added screaming choruses of "Murderer, murderer, murderer, murderer!"[34]

The roundup of the Jews also continued apace. Assisted by elite SS *Leibstandarte* Hitler units and by common Berlin policemen, the Berlin Gestapo arrested and carried off truckload after truckload of Jews they apprehended in their workplaces and homes and in the streets of Berlin. Upon their arrest, the Jews were sorted into two groups. The larger of the two came to total over 7,000 Jews who had been shielded from deportation until that point only because they worked in war-related industries. The other and smaller group of around 1,700 Jews consisted of Jewish men and some Jewish women in nonprivileged mixed marriages and *Geltungsjuden* who wore the Star of David. Once the Nazi authorities sorted them out, they took those in the former group to a large Jewish detention center in the Grosse Hamburgerstrasse and all but a few of those in the latter group to the Rosenstrasse office building of the Berlin Jewish community.

On March 6, Goebbels decided that the damage the demonstration posed to public opinion was too great and called for the release of the 1,700 intermarried Jews and *Geltungsjuden* in the Rosenstrasse. Soon thereafter, orders were also given calling for the return of 35 intermarried Jewish men who had been deported to Auschwitz from Grosse Hamburgerstrasse as part of a transport of 7,031 Berlin Jews in the "Final Roundup." Unlike those who had been held in the Rosenstrasse building, however, these men who had experienced Auschwitz firsthand were not allowed to return to their homes and families. The knowledge they now possessed about the Final Solution was simply too dangerous to be allowed to filter back into German society. Once they returned to Berlin, therefore, the Gestapo extracted forced confessions from each of them about supposed crimes they had committed and then sent them all to a labor camp at Grossbeeren three hours outside Berlin. This was not the outcome that they and their wives had hoped for, but their lives had been spared and their wives were informed about their release from Auschwitz. Many wives had the opportunity to visit them at Grossbeeren afterward.

The Rosenstrasse protest thus proved enormously successful. In the end, thousands of Jewish lives were saved because of the actions of hundreds of German women who were willing to risk their lives to save their husbands. Not only did their courageous stance thwart the Nazis' plans to empty Berlin of its last Jews through a bold stroke of will and terror, but it also led to the suspension of the Nazis' plans to deport intermarried Jews and *Mischlinge* from the rest of Germany in the wake of the Berlin deportations.

Propaganda Minister Goebbels, who was also *Gauleiter* of Berlin, had clearly issued the order to release the large group of Jews from the Rosenstrasse building and the smaller group from Auschwitz concentration camp because of his worries about damage to German public opinion. As Nathan Stoltzfus argues convincingly in his gripping account of the Rosenstrasse protest, Goebbels had become especially concerned about the sentiments of German women. After Germany's defeat at Stalingrad and the passage of Hitler's "Total War" decree on January 13, 1943, millions of German women were now expected to enter the workforce while continuing to provide vital emotional support for their menfolk at the battlefront. But foot-dragging on their part, evidenced by legions of complaints about colds and infections that would not go away, painful back flare-ups, severe headaches, and other alleged illnesses, indicated that the morale of German women had reached rock bottom. Goebbels, therefore, gave in to the demands of the women in the Rosenstrasse because he realized that the Rosenstrasse protest, if allowed to continue, could have spread unrest throughout all of Germany. In Stoltzfus's words:

> Goebbels feared that Germans, angered by forced deportations of their partners and children, would begin to question and complain. Unrest about the fate of the Jews could severely hinder the domestic social unity necessary for fighting the war. A parallel development was the increasing need for secrecy around the Final Solution, the revelation of which would have damaged the public morale that the regime strove to nurture, especially during the war. A public discussion about the fate of the deported Jews threatened to disclose the Final Solution and thus endanger that entire effort.[35]

It is unfortunate that the Rosenstrasse protest was not indicative of German sentiment toward the fate of the Jews in general. The German women of the Rosenstrasse had demonstrated exclusively for the release of their husbands and family members, not against Nazi racial and ideological policy in general. No one protested for the 7,000 Jews sent to Auschwitz from the Grosse Hamburgerstrasse who did not have German relatives, and these people were not released. Nevertheless, the Rosenstrasse demonstration's success forced the Nazi leadership to abandon its hopes of making

Germany "Jew free" in one large swoop and made it necessary for the Gestapo to adopt another tactic to deal with Jews with German relatives in the
last two years of the war.

CRIMINALIZING JEWS WITH A VENGEANCE

That new tactic was, essentially, a return to the old policy of criminalizing
the Jewish population. But now the Gestapo did so with added vengeance.
By pressing charges of criminal behavior on the intermarried Jews and the
Mischlinge on a case-by-case basis as a legal pretext for deporting them
instead of merely incarcerating them, as in times past, the Gestapo could
avoid giving rise to any new mass demonstrations by German relatives.
When, for example, on May 22, 1943, the Gestapo informed a "German-
blooded" Krefeld man of an official announcement from Auschwitz Commandant Hoess that his twenty-three-year-old, partially Jewish daughter
had "died from diarrhea at 6:00 A.M. on May 5, 1943, in the local hospital in
Auschwitz," and that "the state has taken over the costs for the cremation
of the corpse and the urn will be laid to rest in the cemetery of the local
crematorium," there was nothing he could do but grieve his daughter's
death quietly and try to accept it.[36] Since the Gestapo commonly provided
surviving German relatives with news of the death of their Jewish family
members, he might have heard through the grapevine that others in Krefeld
and elsewhere had received similar communiqués that their loved ones had
succumbed recently in concentration camp, allegedly because of "an ulcer,"
or "colitis," or "heart and circulatory weakness," or a number of other questionable reasons.[37] But this would have been small consolation to him and
his Jewish wife, who herself was subject to a similar fate if he raised a protest
about their daughter. He and his wife might even have felt guilty and partially responsible for their daughter's death. They may have thought that
they had not warned her strongly enough about the risk she took when
she had not worn her Star of David in public—the "crime" she had been
denounced for by a neighboring fifteen-year-old girl whom the Gestapo had
recruited to spy on her. That this is not just facile conjecture is supported by
the fact that several years after the war, in July 1954, his wife wrote a letter

in support of Richard Schulenburg's attempt to regain his full police pension.[38]

Not only did the Gestapo's policy of criminalizing many of the remaining Jews offer the advantage of keeping to a minimum protest from Germans with Jewish family members and from a German population accustomed to submitting to legal authority, it also helped to channel the support of those anti-Semitic Germans whose support the Gestapo needed to accomplish its racial goals. Whereas it might be somewhat of an exaggeration for Nathan Stoltzfus to state that "a flood of denunciations poured in" against Germany's remaining Jews, he is most certainly correct when he argues that "the deportation of individual intermarried Jews [and *Mischlinge*] as criminals . . . depended on a German public that actively collaborated since charging these Jews required denunciations."[39]

In fairness, one must bear in mind that denouncers constituted only a minority of the German population, even if a large number of Germany's tiny remaining Jewish population suffered from spying and denunciations. Nevertheless, many Germans did make such denunciations, and those who made them came from a wide variety of backgrounds. Some of these denunciations continued to be made by people who were turning to the Gestapo for help in resolving neighborhood, personal, and sometimes even family quarrels, as they had done in the past.[40] But a larger percentage of these denunciations now came from people who voluntarily offered their services to the Gestapo in advance to spy on their Jewish neighbors and acquaintances, even though they had had no obvious quarrels with them.

In any case, the Gestapo, given the willingness of many German civilians to help it incriminate the Jews and the pervasive and onerous nature of the regulations to which the Jews were subject, had little difficulty in conjuring up charges against Jews in mixed marriages and *Mischlinge* in the last two years of the war. And once these charges had been filed, the consequences, as in the case of the young Krefeld woman who died in Auschwitz in May 1943 because she had not worn her Star of David in public, were often devastating for the accused. Her case is only one of several from the case files of the Krefeld Gestapo that show that even unsubstantiated accusations that intermarried or partially Jewish persons had done

something as trivial as not wearing a Star of David, playing a game of poker
in a bar, or breaking any of the hundreds of other Jewish regulations often
landed them in a concentration camp and cost them their lives.[41]

The high point of the campaign to criminalize the last remaining German Jews came in 1943 in the months following the Rosenstrasse demonstration. Since the Nazi leadership now wanted to declare Germany "Jew
free" as soon as possible for ideological purposes, they needed to expunge
all visible signs of Jewry from German society. Hence, the campaign focused
especially on those Jews who were compelled to wear the Star of David, and
thus on Jews in nonprivileged mixed marriages and on the children of mixed
parentage whom the Nazis "considered as Jews." But the Gestapo also put
the squeeze on Jews and part-Jews of all types, even if they were not required to wear the Star of David.

The treatment of the Jews in Krefeld after 1942 provides a good example
of how the campaign worked itself out. By this time, only handfuls of Jews
remained in the city, as was the case in most German communities, and all
were either Jewish partners in mixed marriages or *Mischlinge*. Depending
on how one chooses to count, between 40 and 50 Jews were left out of a
Jewish community that had once numbered 1,500. Most of these remaining
Jews survived the war, but several did not. Had many Gestapo officers, Nazi
officials, and Krefeld civilians had their way, none would have survived.

Between the beginning of 1943 and the fall of 1944, when the final
transport of Krefeld Jews departed to Theresienstadt concentration camp,
about one-third of Krefeld's remaining Jews had criminal cases started
against them, according to surviving Gestapo case files. This percentage
may have been even higher, since one can never be sure of the completeness
of the case files. Numbering fourteen cases in total—twelve of which began
in 1943, and two in 1944—at least five of the cases ended in the death of the
accused person. Four of the recorded deaths (of two men and two women)
occurred in Auschwitz, and a fifth man succumbed in Anrath jail near Krefeld shortly before he was to be sent to Auschwitz.[42] Although all (or almost
all, since it is impossible in every case to be sure) of the other nine defendants managed to survive, most received harsh treatment: at least three
were sent to concentration camps, and two others spent periods of weeks in
protective custody. Charges against only two of the nine were dropped; both

were *Mischlinge* of the more privileged variety who did not have to wear the Star of David. The final two moved to other communities, and it is not known how their cases were finally resolved.

Often the civilian German population played a decisive role in the persecution of these Jews. Typically this role was that of spy, denouncer, or witness for the prosecution. Spying of one type or another was evident in all seven of the cases lodged against intermarried Jews, and it occurred in at least three of the seven cases involving Jewish *Mischlinge*. Sometimes the spying was carried out by special agents, Nazi Party members, or Nazi officials, but often it was carried out by common civilians who volunteered their services to the Gestapo free of charge. Also free of charge were the denunciations from the civilian population that started four of the seven *Mischlinge* cases and two of the cases against intermarried Jews.[43] All of this does not add up to evidence of "a flood of denunciations," but in part only because Krefeld's Jewish community was so small. In a city like Berlin, where the Jewish population still numbered in the thousands instead of in the teens, as in Krefeld, the civilian denunciations that poured in to Gestapo headquarters to incriminate the city's remaining Jews after the Rosenstrasse protest may have approached floodlike proportions.

Although almost no Germans actively resisted the powerful anti-Semitic current of the late war years, there were some who tried to alter it by interceding on the behalf of Jews in individual cases. Sometimes their actions, like those of the women of the Rosenstrasse demonstration, saved the lives of Jews who surely would have died had no one intervened on their behalf. The most significant recorded case of such intercession that took place in Krefeld provides an important reminder that at least some Germans stood up for their Jewish countrymen. But it also demonstrates how relentlessly Gestapo officers and many German civilians continued to push in the very last year of the war for the inclusion of all remaining Jews in the Final Solution. And just as important, it lays bare the perverse, even pathological, blend of ideological conviction and narrow legalistic thinking that motivated Gestapo officers and many in the larger German population while they took an active role in the persecution and murder of the Jewish population even up to the Third Reich's bitter end.

On November 29, 1943, Rudolf Hirschel, a twenty-three-year-old

Krefeld man, was pulled over by the Cologne police for driving a delivery
truck without a license.[44] Hirschel apologized immediately and explained
to the police that he was driving the truck only because the regular driver,
Schmitz, who was sitting in the passenger seat beside him, had been overtaken by a nervous cramp that made it impossible for him to drive any
longer. Schmitz had ordered Hirschel to take over the steering wheel so that
they could make their delivery. When the two were taken to a local police
station, Schmitz supported Hirschel's explanation and further justified his
actions by pointing out that he had been severely wounded in the war and
often suffered such cramps.

Had Hirschel been an ordinary German, this probably would have
ended the matter. At most he would have been fined, and in fact he was (fifty
marks). But he was not an ordinary German for the Nazis. Even though he
professed to be a Catholic, the Nazis labeled him a *Geltungsjude* because he
had a Jewish father and a Christian mother, he had been a member of the
Jewish community until 1938, and he had attended a Jewish school. As a
Geltungsjude, Hirschel was supposed to comply with all of the rules and
regulations affecting all Jews. In particular, he was supposed to wear the
Star of David on his clothing whenever he was in public, and he was to adopt
the additional name of Israel whenever he signed his name or referred to
himself.

When the Krefeld police noticed a month later in the course of their
own investigation of the matter that Hirschel had signed his testimony
without using the prescribed name of Israel, they quickly notified the Krefeld Gestapo. This got him into deep trouble. The Krefeld Gestapo soon
arrested him, placed him in Anrath jail, and carried out a broader investigation of his activities. Nearly three months later, on March 15, 1944, the Gestapo completed its investigation, hauled Hirschel out of jail, and brought
him to Gestapo headquarters for a final interrogation. Richard Schulenburg, who handled the investigation, was unimpressed by Hirschel's contention that he had simply forgotten to sign his name in the correct fashion
because of his distress at the time, not because he was trying to hide his
status as a Jew. In his final report on Hirschel's case, Schulenburg wrote:
"Also, this does not appear to be very believable, rather it is to be surmised
that he had hitherto never used the forename 'Israel.'" Schulenburg then

concluded his report with the following recommendation: "Protective custody with the destination of concentration camp."

For the mere crime of not using the middle name of Israel while signing his name, Hirschel was about to lose his life. Two days later, on March 17, Hirschel had already passed his mandatory medical examination as a last step before deportation. After this he normally would have been deported on the next available transport. But this did not happen. Before a transport could be arranged, his boss at the trucking firm, who obviously had close connections with the police since his office was in the Hansa-Haus building where the police headquarters and previously the Gestapo were located, wrote a long letter on March 22 stating that Hirschel was an excellent and fully law-abiding employee who performed indispensable work for the German army. This letter and whatever behind-the-scenes lobbying took place proved to be a godsend for Hirschel. On April 11, 1944, the Düsseldorf Gestapo ordered that Hirschel be severely warned and then released from protective custody. Although it was against his ideological convictions and his interpretation of the law, Schulenburg had to accede to his superior's orders. So he dutifully administered the warning and released Hirschel six days later.

But Schulenburg was not content to let the matter rest. Two months later, on June 20, an anonymous letter, written by a person Schulenburg had obviously commissioned to spy on Hirschel, reached Gestapo headquarters. Full of anti-Semitic vitriol, the letter accused Hirschel of a series of improprieties, the most damaging of which was that the denouncer had observed Hirschel not wearing his Jewish Star. But the denouncer did not back this up with any specifics about where and when Hirschel had not worn the star, and no witnesses could be found to back up the denouncer's charges. Moreover, Hirschel's boss came forward once again to support his employee with further assurances that Hirschel had always obeyed all of the laws and regulations applying to Jews, including wearing the star. When a new investigation of Hirschel's alleged law-breaking, undertaken this time by both the Cologne Gestapo and the Krefeld Gestapo, uncovered no evidence to support the denouncer's allegations, the matter was finally dropped entirely on July 27, 1944, and Hirschel was released from the Anrath jail for the last time.

The humanitarian interventions of his employer and the support he received from his coworker Schmitz had saved Rudolf Hirschel's life. But his life had also been saved by the Gestapo's desire to have a "legal" justification for deporting him. Had the war not ended only months later, and had it not ended with the defeat of Nazi Germany, such a justification would surely have been found. Schulenburg or another Gestapo officer would have believed that he had only acted within the law when he arranged Hirschel's murder.

CHAPTER TWELVE

I n a lecture he gave at my university in 1985 on the occasion of the fortieth anniversary of the end of the Holocaust, Bruno Bettelheim told the audience: "Above all, it was the silence that condemned the Jews to death." At the time, I did not fully grasp what he meant. Certainly he did not mean to excuse the thousands of perpetrators who had organized and implemented the mass murder of the Jews in their roles as Nazi politicians, Gestapo officers, concentration camp guards, members of firing squads, and others directly involved in the physical killing of the Jews. He also certainly did not intend to excuse those who denounced Jews, helped to deport Jews, or lusted after Jewish property and wealth. What I think he meant was that the Holocaust could not have claimed the lives of six million defenseless Jewish people if protest against the mass murder had risen above the level of whispers. If the necessary secrecy surrounding the implementation of the Holocaust had been destroyed, Hitler would have had to stop the killing.

Although few would dispute that the Holocaust depended on a policy of secrecy and that the Nazis took many precautions to maintain that policy of secrecy, the question of how well the Nazis succeeded in keeping the Holocaust a secret from the German population remains a riddle. For many years after the end of the war, most scholars and laymen alike believed that the Holocaust had in fact been kept a secret to all but a small number of Germans directly involved in carrying it out.[1] In more recent years, however, several studies have been published that challenge this belief. Perhaps the two best known are Walter Laqueur's *The Terrible Secret* and David Bankier's *The Germans and the Final Solution.*[2]

In each of these books, the first published in 1980 and the second twelve years later in 1992, the author puts forward strong, albeit somewhat circumstantial, evidence that leads him to the conclusion that "the terrible secret" had hardly been kept either outside of Germany or in Germany itself. As Bankier sums up his findings: "Large sections of the German population, both Jews and non-Jews, either knew or suspected what was happening in Poland and Russia." Laqueur states the argument even more forcefully: "By the end of 1942, millions in Germany knew that the Jewish question had been radically solved, and that this radical solution did not involve resettlement, in short, that most, or all of those who had been deported were no longer alive."[3] Some of the more significant pieces of evidence that Laqueur and Bankier use to buttress their arguments are summarized in this chapter.

Many German soldiers had heard about, witnessed, or directly participated in the shooting of hundreds of thousands of Jews in eastern Europe and the former Soviet Union, and many of them communicated what they had heard and seen to people back home in Germany.[4] Some did this in letters that managed to escape the censors.[5] Others talked in person about what they had seen when they returned to their hometowns after being wounded or during leaves from the battlefront. Laqueur points out that, until Heydrich ordered the practice to be stopped in November 1941, many German soldiers and members of SD units had even taken private photographs of the massacres that between June and November 1941 had already claimed some 500,000 Jewish lives.[6]

Laqueur and Bankier do not discuss the fact that German soldiers were not the only Germans who took part in or witnessed mass shootings of Jews. As both Christopher Browning and Daniel Goldhagen have demonstrated in their graphic treatments of reserve police battalion 101, numerous ordinary, often middle-aged German civilians spent periods of weeks or months killing Jews as members of reserve police units and then returned to their homes during the war to resume their civilian lives.[7] Many of these "ordinary men" must also have spread information about the mass murders in which they had participated. Additionally, as the German journalist Heiner Lichtenstein documented in a book published in 1990 on the municipal and order police in the Third Reich, thousands of common German policemen also assisted in the mass shootings of Jews in Poland and Russia. Some policemen, he argues, even took part in a kind of Holocaust voyeurism, coming to watch the killings purely to satisfy their curiosity.[8]

Another important source of information about the mass murder in progress emanated from the concentration camps, where millions of Jews were either gassed or worked and starved to death. Many of the camps lay inside of Germany itself. The most notorious concentration and death camp, Auschwitz, had fifty satellite work camps spread out all throughout Silesia and, like other camps, was situated near the German border in close proximity to large German population centers.[9] Laqueur cites the testimony of a former Auschwitz railway employee at the 1964 Auschwitz trial held in Frankfurt; he maintained that it was well known that the five-meter-high flames from the Auschwitz chimneys, which could be seen from a distance of fifteen to twenty kilometers, came from burning human bodies. He also cites the testimony of others at the same trial that the Auschwitz railway station was always full of civilians and soldiers on leave who could not fail to notice the clouds of smoke and the all-pervasive sweet stench of burning flesh.[10] Moreover, thousands of German civilians found employment in and around the concentration camps, where firms from nearly every branch of German industry set up factories and other installations to exploit the slave labor.[11] Many of these German civilians, Laqueur argues, came to know intimate details about the mass murder that was taking place daily in the concentration camps, and presumably many communicated what they knew to their German friends and family members on the outside.

German soldiers and civilians who took part in or had the opportunity to observe the mass murder of the Jews were not the only sources of information on the Holocaust for the German civilian population. Information also rained in on Germans from the skies in the form of BBC and other foreign-radio broadcasts and in leaflets dropped by Allied war planes. Bankier notes that although the high point of the BBC's campaign to inform the German population about the mass murder of the Jews seemed to have been in December 1942, when millions of Germans tuned in to the illegal broadcasts in hopes of learning details about German casualties and other developments in the battle of Stalingrad, the BBC and other foreign radio stations provided accurate information about the Holocaust throughout much of the war.[12] Other accurate information, Bankier also explains, was provided to German civilians by British and American bombers in 1943 and 1944. The millions of leaflets they dropped on cities all over Germany often contained specific references to the systematic murder of European Jewry, the mass shootings, the extermination centers, and the gas chambers, as well as warnings that whoever participated in these atrocities would be held accountable.[13]

Despite the mass of evidence that Laqueur and Bankier marshal to support their argument that the German population had ample sources of credible, specific, and detailed information available to them about the Holocaust while it was taking place, they have very little evidence that most Germans, let alone masses of Germans, in fact received, digested, and passed on this information. Their evidence does not clarify, for example, whether large numbers of Germans or only a few actually tuned in to forbidden BBC and other foreign broadcasts about the murder of the Jews. Also, their evidence provides only a limited number of specific details mentioned in the foreign broadcasts or about the form of the broadcasts themselves. And even if they do have evidence that some soldiers related information about mass shootings of Jews in their letters home, their evidence does not indicate how common and how detailed such letters were.[14] Finally, they present next to no evidence that Germans commonly discussed among themselves what they had seen or heard from others about the mass murder of the Jews.

Since about all they have to go on to prove that Germans knew about the Holocaust comes from a few scattered diaries, memoirs, and isolated SD reports, which do not seem to have been very detailed in nature, in the end all Laqueur and Bankier are able to prove is that some Germans knew about the Holocaust and that many more could have known had they wanted to know. Nevertheless, even if most of their evidence is, as Bankier freely admits, "unquantifiable and impressionistic,"[15] and even if they are not able to prove convincingly that "large sections" or "millions of Germans knew," this does not mean that millions of Germans did not know.

Indeed, as Laqueur and Bankier surmised but perhaps could not quite prove, millions of German citizens did come to know about the mass murder of the Jews before the war was over. Some knew relatively more, and some knew relatively less. Some learned about the mass murder earlier, and some later. Many no doubt tried not to know. But by early 1943 at the latest, the sources of information about the mass murder were so plentiful, so detailed, and so credible that it became difficult for millions of Germans not to know and not to know a lot. To demonstrate this, we will draw on four types of evidence that were unavailable to Laqueur and Bankier when they wrote their books: the copious diaries of the Jewish Dresden professor Victor Klemperer; detailed transcripts of the BBC's German-language broadcasts about the Holocaust to the German people during the war; a 1993 survey of randomly selected, ordinary German citizens who were old enough before the end of the Third Reich to receive information about the Holocaust; and face-to-face interviews with the people who took part in that survey.

A DAILY CHRONICLE OF THE HOLOCAUST: THE DIARIES OF VICTOR KLEMPERER

Victor Klemperer's diaries were first published in 1995.[16] Although many other diaries written by contemporaries in Nazi Germany have become available to researchers, Klemperer's are perhaps unique. In their published form, they provide nearly 1,700 printed pages, filled with exact and often minute details, about the daily existence of Victor Klemperer and his wife in particular and about the persecution and murder of German Jews in general. As a Jew, Klemperer was, of course, not an ordinary German. In some ways, he was no ordinary German Jew either. Born in 1881, and thus in his sixties during the war years, he was a former professor of Romance languages and had been married since 1906 to a Christian woman named Eva, who courageously stood by his side and suffered along with him throughout the years of Hitler's rule. This alone spared his life, though in wartime Nazi Germany he never had the luxury of knowing for certain that ultimately he would survive. It was not only his mixed marriage status, however, that set him apart from most ordinary Germans and most ordinary German Jews. What also made him different from many Germans, Jewish and non-Jewish alike, was that he did not seek to close his eyes and ears to the horrors surrounding him. He dedicated himself to serving as a witness of Nazi oppression and murder "until the very last."

Merely because he had a deep desire to know, and not because he was in a privileged position to find out, Klemperer learned more about the mass murder of the Jews than did most average Germans. Most Germans, had they wanted to know about the Holocaust, would have had more sources of information and more opportunities to acquire it than were available to Klemperer. As a Jew in Nazi Germany during the Holocaust, Klemperer had no radio, was greatly circumscribed in his freedom of movement, was compelled to be guarded at every moment in his conversations with almost everyone, and suffered from greatly reduced physical energy, because of lack of nutrition, and many other disadvantages common only to Jews. Much of the time Klemperer never left his residence. Despite these limitations, Klemperer gained detailed and accurate information from a wide array of sources. Among these were confidential statements from SS concentration camp guards on leave; malicious utterances from Gestapo officers to Dresden Jews as they were about to be deported; BBC and other foreign-radio reports; and above all, conversations he and his wife had with Jewish community officials and trusted friends, who themselves accumulated knowledge about the Holocaust through other conversations and various other sources of information.

What, then, did Klemperer record in his diaries about the Holocaust? We can begin with a brief summary and then move to more specific information. Usually on or about the time they took place, Klemperer faithfully and exhaustively noted down details about the deportations from his own city of Dresden and about those from many other German and foreign cities.[17] These notations often included accurate estimates of the numbers and types of people deported, discussions about how the deportations physically took place, and indications about the final destination of the deportees. He also detailed the mass shootings of Jews at Babi Yar and several other locations in Poland and Russia.[18] On a few occasions, he wrote about how the Jews had to dig their own graves and strip before they were shot. In addition, he recorded what he had learned about conditions in many concentration camps, including Auschwitz, Theresienstadt, Buchenwald, and

Ravensbrück. In regard to the concentration camps, he wrote about Jews dying from a large variety of mysterious illnesses and from being worked to death and gassed.[19] He also described specific examples of the Gestapo's torture tactics that claimed the lives of many Jews. He recorded details of Hitler's speeches and those of other Nazi leaders who promised to annihilate the Jews. He commented again and again on the fact that legions of Jews were being put to death from Germany and all over Europe and that no Jews who were sent off had ever returned.[20] Finally, he provided deeply moving commentary about the reduced conditions for himself and his wife—the burning hunger, omnipresent depression, and constant fear.

This short summary alone indicates that few important details about the Holocaust could remain hidden for long from a man like Victor Klemperer who wanted to find out about them. But to gain an appreciation of the depth as well as the breadth of his knowledge, one must consider some of his specific diary entries. In so doing, one also sometimes finds clues about what others in the German population knew about the mass murder of the Jews.

Several of Klemperer's entries, for instance, reveal that Gestapo officers themselves knew that death awaited the Jews they deported. An example is Klemperer's entry on August 29, 1942. After discussing his fear that his marriage might be dissolved by a decree from the newly named justice minister Thierack, whom he refers to as a "bloodhound," Klemperer writes about the tragic, recent death of a seventeen-year-old Jewish boy in a concentration camp. Noting that the boy had supposedly died from "colitis," he asks himself, "Since when does a vigorous young person die of this?" Then he relates that a nurse from the Dresden Jewish community named Frau Ziegler had told him that the Jews' fear of the Gestapo had become "a general Jewish psychosis." After mentioning several examples of Jews with this psychosis, Klemperer provides the reason this psychosis was well founded: the Nazis intended to exterminate every last Jewish person. To prove this assertion, he again names Frau Ziegler as his source. According to her, the superintendent of his apartment building was interrogated recently at Gestapo headquarters because he had been reported to have friendly relations with Jews. When he defended himself from this allegation by telling the Gestapo officer conducting his interrogation that the Jews he knew were upstanding people, the Gestapo officer replied: "There are no upstanding Jews, and the entire race will be exterminated."[21]

Klemperer writes a week later, on September 8, in a similar vein. That morning Frau Ziegler had come to visit the Klemperers once again. This time she came with news about the terrible night she had just spent assisting in the preparation of a new transport of Dresden Jews. The Jews were herded into the freight cars "like cattle in the dark," she lamented. But the most disturbing scene she had witnessed was an elderly woman's confrontation with a Gestapo *Kommissar*. As the woman had stepped aboard the freight car, she was handed a letter written by her daughter that contained a picture of her granddaughter and the consoling words: "Perhaps, dear mother, we will indeed see each other again. Miracles do happen." The callous Gestapo officer, however, could not abide such solace for Jews. After tearing up the photograph, he read her daughter's sentence aloud and responded: "You [Jews] are not allowed to take along any pictures. . . . For you [Jews] there are no miracles, do not flatter yourselves."[22]

For just one other insight into Klemperer's ever-increasing knowledge about the Holocaust, one might consider what he knew about the final destinations of the transports. At first, when the deportations began in the fall of 1941, he had little definite information to go on, but he did have reason to believe that the end of the journey was a terrible one for the Jews. On November 18, 1941, he records: "The news from various sides about the Jewish evacuations to Poland and Russia sound catastrophic. A letter to us from Lissy Meyerhof, [another] to Kätchen Sara from Voss in Cologne, [many] oral reports. We are hearing many things."[23] Ten days later, on November 28, he writes about the news of large-scale deportations from various German cities, including Dresden, Berlin, Hannover, Munich, and several in the Rhineland: "One knows nothing precisely, not who is to go [on them], not when and not where [they are going]."[24]

Soon, however, Klemperer's information becomes considerably more specific. As this happens, Klemperer carefully records how many people were on the transports, what types of people were selected for them, where they were going, and what the Jews could expect when they got there. By the middle of March 1942, he has even heard about the crown jewel of the Nazi death camps, Auschwitz, which he correctly locates near Königshütte in Upper Silesia. Although at that time he apparently did not yet know about the gassings that took place in the camp, he was aware that Auschwitz had already earned a reputation "as the most dreadful concentration camp. . . . Death after a few days."[25] In the months that follow, the news of new Jewish transports and new Jewish deaths continue to stream in on a nearly daily basis, and Klemperer's understanding of the ultimate fate that awaited the Jews solidifies. On July 4, 1942, he notes sadly: "The one is done away with in three days, the other first in a year—but nobody comes back, literally nobody."[26] Confirmation of this conclusion comes to Klemperer from many sources, even from an SS man who worked in a concentration camp.[27] By mid-January 1943, Klemperer suffers from a "constant, ghastly fear of Auschwitz" that haunts him throughout the day and in his dreams at night.[28] When the "Final Roundup" begins a month and a half later on February 27, Klemperer is certain that "from now on it is no longer to be expected that any Jews will return alive from Poland." "After all," he writes, "it has long been reported that many evacuees do not even arrive in Poland alive. They are gassed in cattle cars during the trip."[29]

EXPOSING THE "TERRIBLE SECRET":
BBC GERMAN-LANGUAGE BROADCASTS

Whereas Victor Klemperer had to piece together fragmentary evidence from a variety of sources to gain a picture of the Final Solution, most Germans only had to turn on their radio sets and listen to the BBC's German-language broadcasts. Somehow this simple point has escaped most researchers. Although some, David Bankier in particular, have stressed the BBC's importance as a source of information about the extermination, no one has investigated very thoroughly what the BBC actually broadcast about the Holocaust or how many people actually listened to the BBC broadcasts about the mass murder of the Jews.[30] Hence, only somewhat sketchy details about the BBC's reporting are known, and these details have been derived primarily from a few diaries and memoirs and from some limited reports of the Nazi government's efforts to monitor foreign-radio broadcasts, which Bankier alone appears to have examined. The lack of interest in this subject is something of a pity, for as we know from the survey of elderly Cologne residents and from many other sources discussed in earlier chapters, millions of German people did in fact listen attentively and regularly to German-language BBC broadcasts even though it was illegal for them to do so. Moreover, the BBC German Service took considerable pains to convey accurate and believable information about the annihilation of the Jews to its German listening audience from the time of the invasion of the Soviet Union onward. These efforts were particularly noteworthy considering that they were frowned on by the British Foreign Office, which did not regard Jewish persecution as an efficacious theme for propagandistic advantage.[31]

The BBC itself also realized that broadcasting to the German population on this most sensitive subject was fraught with dangers. In particular, the BBC feared that its efforts to help the German people cast away their blinders and face up squarely to the horrible truth of the Holocaust might serve to bind them closer to Hitler and the Nazi regime. To avoid this outcome, the BBC carefully tried to present its information in a manner that would persuade the German people that Hitler and his Nazi subalterns alone, not the German people, bore responsibility for the atrocities and that there was no such thing as collective guilt. Nevertheless, the BBC understood that its reporting might blur the sharp distinctions between "Nazi" and "German" that its propaganda had long tried to cultivate and that it ran the risk of uniting Nazis and Germans in a collective fear of Allied and Jewish revenge for the unspeakable crimes their nation had committed against European Jewry. But as documented in several entries under the heading of "The Jews" in the BBC's own internal news guidelines for its European news broadcasts in December 1942, it decided that it had to press on with its reporting whatever the risks.

The longest of these entries came on December 14 in the course of a month-long reporting campaign on the Holocaust that the BBC German Service broadcast to the German population on a daily and sometimes hourly basis. Several excerpts convey a sense of how seriously the BBC took its journalistic responsibilities:

> The Germans may be fairly susceptible to warnings that, with defeat inevitable, some indication that they disapprove of Hitler's maniacal

massacres is desirable. Even if they cannot *do* anything it is good that they should feel uneasy and ashamed. *In any case it is our duty to do what we can to stop the massacres even if our efforts involve a weakening of our distinction between Nazis and Germans.*

We can certainly take the massacres as evidence that Hitler knows the game is up and is either attempting to carry out at least one of his war aims before his defeat or is attempting to blackmail the world into a compromise peace through mass murder of hostages.

The only consequence of this craziness is to render a compromise even more unthinkable, if possible, than ever before and to darken the prospects of the German people after their defeat.

We must make it quite clear, if only by inference, that the massacres of the Jews is nothing to do with the war, is no atrocity story exploited for purposes of propaganda but in fact something which, while not in any way affecting the course of the war, affects solely the fate of Jewry and the fate of the German people.

As the Rabbi Dr. Mattuck said: "War does not supply the shadow of an excuse for the massacres; there is no military value in killing Jewish children."[32]

The BBC's internal European news directives dealing with Jewish persecution and murder that followed on subsequent days in December 1942 were shorter than this entry of December 14. Though they were brief, hardly a day passed without a new directive about how the BBC planned to uphold what it considered its moral duty to report the news of the Holocaust to the German people even if doing so posed propagandistic risks. As a confidential report in the guidelines of December 27 stated: "Our task then tonight and right up to the New Year is to rub the enemy's nose in some nasty facts and nastier interpretations of them."

If the BBC's reporting blitz on the Holocaust in December 1942 most definitely did rub the noses of its German listeners in many nasty facts, the BBC remained careful to present its interpretations of these facts in a manner that eschewed "rhetoric and polemics" and avoided "sweeping indictments of the German people as a whole."[33] This does not mean, however, that the BBC German Service confined itself merely to a broadcasting program of objective news bulletins about confirmed Jewish atrocities. It certainly offered its German listening audience plenty of such factual reports in its fifteen to thirty hours of weekly broadcasting, just as it had done since its first reports on the mass shootings of Polish and Russian Jews in the summer and fall of 1941.[34] But regularly scheduled news broadcasts, which typically lasted from fifteen to thirty minutes and were broadcast twice a day, constituted only part of the BBC German Service's rich and varied broadcasting program. In addition to the straight news reporting that millions of Germans tuned in to hear daily, the BBC's programming captivated wide German audiences with a number of witty comedy series such as *Kurt and Willi, Frau Wernicke,* and *Gong*[35]; with news journal–type programs, such as a show narrated by Lindley Fraser called *What Every German Ought to Know About England*[36]; and with a number of other feature-length programs of varying types and formats.

Especially in December 1942, but also throughout the course of the war, all of these programs, and each in its own ingenious way, took up the theme of Jewish persecution and murder and thereby brought home the reality of the Holocaust to mass German audiences.[37] Sometimes this was done with such subtlety that many German listeners probably did not realize what they were getting into when they turned on their radio sets to hear one of their favorite BBC comedy programs like *Kurt and Willi.* Usually *Kurt and Willi* touched only lightly on serious matters and could thus be counted on to provide fifteen to twenty minutes of harmless escapism to a German public badly in need of comic entertainment. But on December 29, 1942, *Kurt and Willi* had a far more serious theme: "The Persecution of the Jews."[38]

The sketch begins, as it did each week, when the two old friends Kurt Krüger, a teacher, and Willi Schimanski, a bureaucrat in Goebbels's Propaganda Ministry, meet at their regular pub in Berlin's Potsdamer Platz to unwind over a few drinks and some easy conversation. As always, they begin by greeting each other with a perfunctory "Heil Hitler." But noticing that his friend Kurt looks "green in the face" and is obviously bothered about something, Willi suggests that they order a brandy and talk things over. Kurt agrees.

KURT: So, now I feel a bit better.

WILLI: Now tell me what's the matter. You shouldn't work so hard.

KURT: Ach, work. I just experienced something absolutely horrible. Above us, you know, lives a woman, a Jewess, about fifty more or less—and today she turned on the gas valve. We found her an hour ago.

WILLI: Ach.

KURT: They had just informed her that they were going to send her off to the east somewhere.

WILLI: Uh-huh. Oh yeah. I can imagine that that would be upsetting to you.

KURT: And how! We noticed suddenly that the gas was leaking out. So we finally kicked in the door. My wife and I, and then we found her lying there, it was terrible. . . . My wife is completely destroyed. I had to carry her to bed.

WILLI: I am really sorry. What an awful experience!

KURT: Now listen, Willi! We? One has to feel sorry for the poor soul.

WILLI: But I just can't understand why they just now finally got around to deporting her. Why not earlier already?

Kurt explains that the Jewish woman had been spared from deportation until then because she held a job in a war-related industry. But eventually even that had not been enough to save her. As she told him a few days earlier, the Gestapo had come to the laboratory where she worked and torn up her work permit while laughing at her distress. All of this, Kurt says, is "crazy, totally crazy." Although he understands that "war is war," it just does not make sense to him that Germany could waste its best workers at this time of national emergency, even if they are Jewish. Then he elaborates on how he and his wife tried to persuade her not to kill herself. They tried to explain to her that it could not be as bad in the east as she feared, and whatever the case might be, anything was better than killing herself. Willi, though, perhaps because he is employed in the Propaganda Ministry, knows better.

WILLI: No, my dear friend, a quick death from heating gas is much better than starving to death in a cattle wagon or being gassed as a guinea pig.

KURT: What are you saying? Is that really happening?

WILLI: Well . . . it does happen . . .

KURT: Dreadful. But why? Willi, you know that I am no friend of Jews. But I just can't believe that any upstanding German could approve of such a thing.

Willi then explains that as good followers of the party line they should not wallow in liberal thoughts. Kurt responds that he cannot believe that the Führer would approve of such murder. Willi tells him that in fact the Führer expressly gave the order for the "annihilation of the Jews" and that murdering them is, he says, "Adolf Hitler's absolutely personal political line." Kurt is obviously shocked by this revelation about his revered leader. He asks his friend whether it would be possible for someone high up in the Nazi Party, like Göring or Goebbels or somebody who still has some sense, to explain to Hitler that this policy of murdering Jews is just fully unnecessary. In response, Willi once again sets his friend straight about the real state of affairs.

WILLI: No, Kurt—it is necessary.

KURT: It is necessary!

WILLI: I have explained this to you enough times in the past, Kurt, that the war is in such a stage that we have no other way to force our comrades to keep on going except by instilling in them a terrible fear of the consequences of defeat.

KURT: Yes, I know your old theory about "strength through fear." But what has that got to do with the Jews?

WILLI: Mensch, don't you understand? Don't you see that when we commit in the name of the German people the largest mass murder in history . . .

KURT: What, the largest mass murder . . .

WILLI: . . . that thereby we will burden the entire German population with collective guilt and that, as a consequence, if they weaken, they will have to fear collective revenge!

Soon after this, both Kurt and Willi become depressed and vaguely ill and decide to stop talking about such dreadful matters. Quickly they call the waiter over and order another brandy. The sketch ends with both Kurt and Willi in bad spirits.

Many in the German listening audience must also have been in a bad humor by the end of this broadcast, which had discussed Jewish persecution, suicides, deportations, gassings, and the plans of Hitler and the Nazi Party for the annihilation of the Jewish population. Nevertheless, the news of these horrible realities was treated in this supposed comedy program in such a blithe fashion that some Germans may still have believed that the British were simply trying to destroy their morale by muckraking with contrived atrocity stories, not unlike British propaganda in the First World War. But many Germans, given what they already knew from their own experiences or what they had heard through the grapevine or from earlier BBC broadcasts about what was happening to the Jews, had to have realized that what Kurt and Willi said bore close resemblance to the truth, even through the filter of comedy.

Those who remained skeptical about the true fate of the Jews after hearing comedy programs like this one had to have found it extremely difficult to remain skeptical, however, when they listened to the more straightforward accounts of the Holocaust that the BBC also broadcast daily throughout the month of December 1942 and periodically throughout the entire war. The most detailed of these were news feature programs the BBC aired on December 24 and 27, 1942. Entitled "And Peace on Earth" and "The War Against the Jews," respectively, and lasting about forty-five minutes each, these programs broadcast Christmas messages to the German population about the systematic persecution and mass murder of the Jews. These deeply disturbing, unambiguous, and factually based reports left no room for lingering doubt. Surviving transcripts of these broadcasts, which the BBC narrators read aloud word for word in plain German,[39] contain detailed descriptions of the Nazis' murder of millions of European Jews through deportations, mass shootings, gassings, slave labor, and other means; largely accurate estimates of the many hundreds of thousands of Jewish men, women, and children who had already been put to death from Germany, Austria, Poland, and several other countries; and explicit references to several of the most notorious concentration and death camps.

The feature program "And Peace on Earth," which the BBC broadcast at 8:00 P.M. British time on Christmas Eve, was the somewhat milder of the two programs. Blending musical offerings, like Beethoven's Ninth Symphony, that conveyed messages of peace and brotherhood with news from all over Europe about the persecution of people living under Nazi domination, the program reminded listeners that despite the ringing of Christmas bells, this was "no time for celebrations." As the following excerpt from the program demonstrates, the main reason was the fate of the Jews:

Repression, darkness, hatred, extermination, death is the new message of the season. Darkness lies over the concentration camp at Oswiecim [the Polish name for Auschwitz], where thousands upon thousands have had to bear the tortures of the SS. The sadistic desire for extermination has [also] built the death camp at Belzec, where 80,000 victims have been put to death in a scientifically organized manner. 80,000 men, women, and children slaughtered like cattle.

Three days later, on December 27, the BBC reserved its popular 8:00 P.M. time slot to broadcast its feature program "The War Against the Jews." As its title suggests, this program minced no words in making clear to the German population that their government had planned and was actively carrying out the annihilation of millions of defenseless Jews from every country under Nazi control. It began by pointing to a moving and unforgettable scene from ten days earlier, on December 17: for the first time in its long history, the British Parliament had taken time out from its deliberations to stand for a minute of silence to honor the Jewish victims of Nazi terror. This silent tribute had taken place, the program explained at some length, as the foreign ministers of Great Britain, the United States, and the Soviet Union were signing a joint declaration expressing the Allies' disgust over the "ghastly brutality with which Hitler's regime is murdering hundreds of thousands of completely innocent men, women, and children in cold blood only because they are Jews."

After this touching opening, the program devoted the balance of its time to a detailed and graphic description of Nazi Germany's persecution and mass murder of German and European Jewry:

The last act of the Jewish tragedy is beginning. The masses of remaining Jews—old people, women, children—have been freighted off in unheated cattle cars to the Polish ghettos. Uncountable numbers have succumbed underway from exhaustion and hunger; whole transports have been gassed.

From the circa 200,000 Jews that were in Germany in 1939, at least 160,000 have been carted off or have already perished. In Austria at most 15,000 of 75,000 are still alive. . . . In Holland and Belgium only a third of the Jewish population remains. In France nearly 50,000 Jews have been deported to the east. Four thousand children were forcibly taken away from their parents and taken off without identity papers to an unknown destination. . . . In Poland the SS execution squads have killed several hundred thousand. According to an estimate from the Institute for German Labor in the East there were 2,332,000 Jews in the area of the Generalgouvernement at the end of 1940. All of these people are to be "liquidated" by SS annihilation units. These sobering numbers uncover the most ghastly tragedy: millions of people are being exterminated. And why? What stands behind this mass murder?

As it would do two days later in its *Kurt and Willi* comedy sketch of December 29, the BBC answered this question by stressing that Hitler and the Nazi regime realized that the war effort could be maintained only by incriminating the German people in their unparalleled crimes. Pointing out with emphasis that the "Nazi criminals are the guilty ones—they and the German people are not the same"—the BBC maintained that "the Nazis want to remove this distinction by involving the German people in their crimes. Those who are not already guilty are to be made guilty. . . . That is the reason for the mass murder of the Jews. The German people shall become stigmatized for [the cause of] their Führer."

NEW REFRAINS FROM AN AGING POPULATION: SURVEY AND INTERVIEW EVIDENCE

Although the BBC employed propagandistic license in its contention that the mass murder of the Jews resulted from the Nazis' desire to prop up the war effort, it correctly understood that the Holocaust would stigmatize the German population in the future. In a lengthy and perceptive 1991 essay summarizing ordinary German people's knowledge of the Holocaust and their reasons for repressing that knowledge, the German journalist Volker Ullrich points out that the refrain "Wir haben nichts gewusst! Wir haben nichts gewusst!" (We didn't know anything about it! We didn't know anything about it!) was heard so frequently in Germany after the war ended that some observers thought that it sounded like a new German national anthem.[40] Even today, more than fifty years after the war ended, one can still encounter this refrain, for the pall of guilt that the Holocaust cast in the early 1940s still hangs over the new German nation and still clouds the German people's national identity.[41] But one hears it less commonly now that most of the people who once repeated it so often have passed away. In fact, if one listens closely enough, it has even become possible to hear quite different refrains from many of the declining number of Germans who spent their formative years in Hitler's Third Reich.

Indeed, in the survey about the experiences of ordinary people in Nazi Germany that Karl-Heinz Reuband and I administered to a random sample of Cologne residents in 1993, we found that a significant plurality of the aging German citizenry finally are ready to admit that they did become aware of the mass murder of the Jews as it was taking place before the end of the Second World War.[42] In fact, depending on how one chooses to interpret the figures, between slightly under one-quarter and well over one-half of the 188 people who answered the survey divulged that the mass murder of the Jews had not been kept secret from them during Hitler's reign. Some may consider the lower estimate (23 percent) more accurate, for this represents the percentage of people who answered that they had either "known" or "heard" about the mass murder of the Jews before the end of the war. But others may think that the higher estimate is more reliable because only 44 percent of the survey participants responded that they had had no knowledge whatsoever about the mass murder before the war was over. Still others may think that the best estimate falls between these two extremes because, in addition to the 23 percent who said they had either known or heard about the mass murder, another 8 percent responded that they had "surmised" (geahnt) that the mass murder was taking place.

No estimate, of course, can be taken as absolutely correct. One might argue that since 37 percent of the people to whom we mailed the survey to did not fill it out and send it back to us, possibly a much higher or even a somewhat lower number of Cologne residents actually were aware of the Holocaust while it was happening. Others might argue, given the sensitivity of the question and the long time period that had elapsed between the war and the time when the people filled out the questionnaire, that a large

and incalculable percentage of the responses were based on either duplici-
tous statements or faulty memories. Nevertheless, there can be no doubt
that this survey demonstrates conclusively that a very large number of ordinary German citizens, many millions certainly, possessed knowledge
about the Holocaust during the war years.

Before discussing how and when the survey respondents became informed about the mass murder of the Jews, some of the political and demographic considerations that conditioned the participants' responses should
be mentioned. In other parts of the survey, the participants were asked
questions about their support for Hitler and National Socialism and about
their age, gender, religious affiliation, educational level, and place of residence before 1945. Few will find it surprising that the respondents who admitted in the survey that they had "believed in National Socialism" (significantly, a majority of the respondents) were nearly three times less likely
to admit that they had been aware of the Holocaust than were those who
had responded that they had "never believed in National Socialism."[43] Also,
few eyebrows will be raised by the finding that there was a significant correlation between the age of the participants and their awareness of the Holocaust. Older participants in the survey (people who had been adults for all
or most of the Nazi years) displayed a considerably higher level of awareness than did younger participants (people who had only been in their teens
or early twenties at the end of the Third Reich).[44] The final significant background factor that differentiated the people who responded that they were
aware of the Holocaust from those who responded that they were not was
the level of educational attainment. Those who had attended university had
markedly higher levels of awareness than did those with a less advanced
education.[45]

Background considerations of gender, religious affiliation, and place of
residence had much less of an effect on people's awareness of the Holocaust,
or at least on their readiness to admit such an awareness, than political identity, age, and educational attainment. Catholics and women responded more
often than Protestants and men that they had either known or heard about
the mass murder before the end of the war, but Protestants and men responded more often than Catholics and women that they had surmised that

the mass murder was taking place.[46] There may be no special reason to expect either gender or religious background to have had an important effect on individuals' level of awareness about the Holocaust, but some might expect Cologne residents to be more forthcoming about their awareness of the mass murder of the Jews than people from other parts of Germany. The reason for this has nothing to do with geography, for Cologne's location near the Dutch and Belgian borders placed it farther away from the concentration camps and killing fields of eastern Europe than most German cities and towns. It has to do with politics. Since Cologne residents gave Hitler and the Nazi Party very low levels of voter support in Weimar elections and our survey reveals a strong negative correlation between the respondents' belief in National Socialism and their level of awareness about the Holocaust, one might expect Cologne residents to admit to a higher level of awareness than the residents of other German communities. But this did not turn out to be the case: our survey uncovered no meaningful difference in level of awareness between people who had always been Cologne residents and those people who came to Cologne only after 1945.[47] Only slightly more than half (54 percent) of the people who took part in the survey had lived in Cologne during the Nazi years. The rest of the respondents had moved to Cologne after 1945. Before that time, these people had lived in cities and villages spread out all over Germany. Hence, the finding that no difference existed in the level of awareness about the Holocaust between those who had always lived in Cologne and those who had lived in other German communities before 1945 suggests strongly that information about the Holocaust was widespread throughout all of Nazi German society and that the results of our Cologne survey are by no means exceptional.

Some may still question, however, whether these survey results can be trusted. Given the frailties of human memory and the sensitivity of the subject, legitimate doubts can be raised about the accuracy and candor of the respondents' answers. To try to counter these concerns, as well as to find out more about how and when the respondents received information about the mass murder of the Jews, we conducted face-to-face, follow-up interviews with more than twenty participants and with nearly one hundred others who took part in subsequent surveys of a similar nature that we are still analyzing.[48] I conducted about thirty of these interviews myself. The rest were conducted by either my colleague Karl-Heinz Reuband or by one of our research assistants.

The interviews typically took place in the interviewee's home or apartment. Most lasted between one and two hours. All were recorded on audiotape. During the interviews, the participants were asked to talk freely about their personal history and experiences under National Socialism, and they were once again asked whether they had known about the mass murder of the Jews. We did not remind them of what they had answered on the written survey. (About half responded on the written survey that they had been aware of the mass murder of the Jews. The other half said that they had not known anything about it). Like the respondents in the original survey, the interviewees came from a wide mix of age, gender, religious, political, educational, and social backgrounds.

The single most important observation to make about these interviews is that the interviewees remained remarkably consistent in their answers to the question about whether they had known about the mass murder of the Jews before the end of the war. In the interviews I conducted, only one person who had written on the questionnaire that she had heard about the mass murder failed to confirm this in her personal interview. There was a reason for this. Her husband, who said that he was very interested in the subject, insisted on taking part in the interview, which took place in her apartment on the south side of Cologne. Usually we tried to discourage such joint interviews because a spouse's presence often has an inhibiting effect on the interviewee. But there was nothing that could be done in this case. When the question finally arose about what she had known about the Holocaust, he answered for her saying: "Had we known about it, we would have had to kill ourselves."[49] This effectively closed the door on any further questions about the subject.

Fortunately, this did not happen in any of the other interviews I conducted. In fact, there were even a few interviews in which the interviewees revealed that they had indeed heard some things about the mass murder of the Jews before the end of the war even though they had not revealed this in the written survey. One Cologne man in his early seventies, for example, who had responded on the survey that he had known nothing about the mass murder, explained in his interview that he had heard stories about Jews being melted down into bars of soap and that a friend in the SS had once mentioned to him something about mass shootings of Jews. But his rather vague memories were by no means characteristic of most of the interviewees who said that they had either known or heard about the Holocaust while it was happening. Many of these people had vivid memories of exactly when, where, and from whom they had first gained this knowledge.

For example, a former cleaning lady with an eighth-grade education who came from a family with left-wing socialist leanings explained that the first time she heard about the Holocaust was in November 1943 when a half-Jewish friend of the family told her about mass gassings of Jews in concentration camps. The time remains etched in her mind because she had gone to the small town of Beilstein on the Mosel River, where her friend delivered this news to her, to give birth to her son in a peaceful atmosphere far away from the bombings in Cologne. After her child was born and they had returned home to Cologne, she said, she discussed the mass murder of the Jews on several occasions with trusted female friends.[50]

Another Cologne woman I spoke with said that a high-ranking Catholic clergyman informed her and her family about mass shootings of Jews as early as 1940, when she was still living at home with her parents and attending medical school in Frankfurt.[51] Not long afterward, by 1942 at the latest, she became aware of gassings and extermination camps like Auschwitz through subsequent conversations in her family's home with the same prelate and with other high-ranking Catholic clergymen. Her father, who was the head of a local Frankfurt gymnasium, had particularly close ties to the Catholic Church, which was obviously well informed about the Holocaust, because he had been a Catholic Center Party politician before Hitler came to power. She also explained in her interview that a certain Professor Hirt had bragged to her and her classmates in an anatomy class at Frankfurt University about the medical experiments he had been conducting on Jewish brains.[52]

In other interviews with present-day residents of Cologne and Krefeld who had heard about the Holocaust, I heard similar reports. Some of the interviewees related that they had become informed about mass gassings, some about mass shootings, some about both. Many had received their information from their parents. Some had gotten it from other relatives, the BBC, or still other sources. Many had had multiple sources of information. Some could assign an exact date to the first time they had heard about the mass murder. Others had heard about it so often that they could not remember the first time the news had reached them. Some of the people had lived in Cologne during the Nazi years. Others had resided in communities far away from Cologne. Some were well-educated people from middle- and upper-middle-class backgrounds. Others were working-class people with limited formal education. The religious and political backgrounds of the interviewees also varied widely.

Two final examples of the many people who took part in the Cologne survey and subsequent interviews who said they had heard about the Holocaust during the war further illustrate our interviewees' wide diversity of backgrounds, former places of residence, and sources of information. One man with a Ph.D. in agricultural economics related that during the war his father had been a medical doctor in a hospital for handicapped children in the town of Beuthen, not far from Auschwitz. In the fall of 1944, his father, who had also been a Catholic Center Party politician, took him and the rest of his brothers and sisters aside and told them about the gassings of Jews in nearby Auschwitz concentration camp, which he apparently knew all about. He also warned them severely not to repeat to anyone what he had told them for fear that they would all end up in Auschwitz themselves. Another man from a much humbler background—he was a retired worker with a grade-school education whose father had been a Communist—related that before 1943 he had heard about gassings and mass shootings from many sources, including his father, BBC news reports, and his wife's aunt, who came from Strasbourg.[53]

These interviews with people who had only heard about the Holocaust secondhand were often tense and sober discussions over strong cups of coffee. By contrast, the interviews with people who said that they had known about the Holocaust from their own personal observations and sometimes direct participation frequently had an eerie sense of bonhomie. Adding to the high spirits were the wine, beer, and brandy that many of the interviewees served and consumed liberally, even in interviews that took place in the morning and early afternoon. These drinks not only loosened up the lips of the participants but also helped them recapture the actual events they had witnessed or actively taken part in themselves when large quantities of booze had fortified the nerves of execution squad members before they commenced firing.

One elderly man in his mid-eighties, for example, presented me with two bottles of wine from the Saar Valley of the same type that he had drunk in his two-hour interview. He knew a lot about Saar wine, he said, because he came from a small village outside Saarbrücken. During the war, he had been a Nazi Party *Zellenleiter* and had worked as a railroad employee for the Luftwaffe. One of his jobs was to coordinate the passage of trainloads of French Jews, which he met at the French-German border, to the concentration camps in the east. According to his testimony, "everyone" in his small town in the Saarland knew about the mass murder of the Jews.[54]

In other interviews of this type that were accompanied by alcohol, an eighty-eight-year-old man who had been a policeman and a member of the SS in a mid-sized town near Berlin before 1945 related that he had seen Jews killed in Dachau concentration camp, where he served as a guard for a short time during the war. He also told a disgusting story about the shooting deaths of hundreds of Jewish women and children outside a small Russian village, in which he had obviously taken part.[55] Only one interview of this type was more than enough to satisfy the curiosity of this interviewer and to convince him that those who had answered on their questionnaires that they had known about the mass murder of the Jews could back up their answers in spades. Several other interviews disclosed details about the killing that continue to move one to tears long after hearing them.[56]

CONCLUSION

As Volker Ullrich points out in his essay "Wir haben nichts gewusst—Ein deutsches Trauma" (We Didn't Know Anything About It—A German Trauma), "Certainly it was an illusion from the very beginning to think that a crime of the dimension of the Holocaust could be kept secret."[57] Not only were the sources of the information about the mass murder of the Jews—including BBC reports, Allied flyers, soldiers' letters, Hitler's own speeches, foreign newspapers, word of mouth, and personal observation—numerous and widespread, but they were also accessible to almost anyone in the German population who did not have his or her eyes and ears fully closed for several years. Given what we know about human nature and about the Gestapo's generally lax policing of the ordinary German population—who were thus able, among other things, to talk about sensitive matters among themselves—the news of the Holocaust could not have failed to reach millions in the German population. For years after the war ended, especially during the immediate postwar years when crimes-against-humanity trials posed a serious threat to Nazi perpetrators, fearful and guilt-ridden Germans tried to cover up their active participation or silent complicity in the Holocaust with loud choruses of, "We didn't know anything about it! We didn't know anything about it!" But now, more than fifty years after the end of the war and the end of the Holocaust, as many older Germans wrestle with their nation's past and their own past in a way that was perhaps not possible for them some years ago, different refrains are becoming audible. Sometimes these are, "Yes, we knew about it." Other times they are, "Yes, we knew some things about it, but we didn't know everything about it."[58]

Few Germans knew everything about the Holocaust. Maybe even Hitler himself did not know everything. But as our survey demonstrates, millions of ordinary German citizens, coming from every social, political, and religious background and from every corner of German society, certainly were aware that masses of Jews were being murdered. Some Germans did not know this until relatively late in the war. Large numbers of Germans knew much earlier on. Whatever they came to know and whenever they came to know it, almost no Germans raised their voices in protest. The mass of the German population remained silent in public, though not in private. Yet even though it was deplorable as well as ultimately lethal, this silence is in some ways understandable. It did not necessarily result from extreme anti-Semitism. Although it is certainly true that many Germans were anti-Semitic, large numbers of ordinary Germans were either not anti-Semitic or no more anti-Semitic than people from surrounding countries. More than from active anti-Semitism, the silence resulted from a lack of moral concern about the fate of those who were perceived as outsiders and from a tradition of obsequious submission to authority that the Nazis cultivated but did not originate. When their church leaders, military leaders, business leaders, and political leaders did not condemn the persecution and mass murder of the Jews, ordinary German citizens were not prepared or willing to mount a protest on their own.

Nevertheless, one wonders how so many people could find the courage to dance to forbidden swing music, listen to outlawed BBC and other foreign-language broadcasts, spread jokes and epithets about Hitler and other Nazi leaders, and communicate their discontent with their government and society in myriad ways, but could not summon the courage and compassion to register abhorrence and thereby break the silence about the systematic murder of millions of defenseless and innocent men, women, and children.

PART SIX

AFTERMATH AND CONCLUSIONS

If all the Jews had been saved that I was told about in those months, there would have been more Jews alive at the end of the war than there were when it began. . . . A man who had the power to save also had the power to condemn.

—SIMON WIESENTHAL

CHAPTER THIRTEEN

K arl Löffler had little to celebrate as the second postwar Christmas approached in December 1946. Only two months before, the trial of the twenty-two leading German war criminals had ended in Nuremberg. Twelve of the defendants had received the death sentence. Only three—Hjalmar Schacht, Hans Fritzsche, and Franz von Papen— were acquitted. The rest faced lengthy prison terms ranging from ten years to life. Now that the most notorious Nazi war criminals had been dealt with, Löffler and other lesser-known perpetrators had to have been thinking about what the future held in store for them.[1]

The future certainly could not have looked bright to Löffler at that moment. The Allies had long ago promised that all persons who had taken part in the persecution and murder of the Jews would be brought to account for their crimes. The Gestapo, in which Löffler had served as the head of Cologne's Jewish desk for most of the years of the Third Reich, had been branded a criminal organization at the Nuremberg Trials. Since being arrested at his family home in Cologne in October 1945, he had been a prisoner of the British in an internment camp in the Ruhr Valley city of Recklinghausen. He was fifty-eight years old. His life seemed over.

Certainly most people at the time expected that Löffler and all other former Gestapo perpetrators who had played a central role in the Nazi terror's pivotal undertaking—the murder of the Jews—would be punished severely for their past activities. But surprising and shocking as it may seem, this did not happen, and Karl Löffler of Cologne, Richard Schulenburg of Krefeld, and many other former "local Eichmanns" like them in other German communities soon managed to resume their lives as fully rehabilitated

German citizens. An examination of how this came to pass will provide insight into how individual Germans and German society in general dealt with Nazi war criminals and the legacy of Nazi terror after the war. It will also help us to make some final observations on how the Holocaust and Nazi terror were perpetrated and on the nature and character of some of the prime Nazi perpetrators.

In her controversial book about Eichmann and his trial in Jerusalem, Hannah Arendt put forward the idea of "the banality of evil." One might argue that an examination of the cases of Gestapo Jewish affairs specialists like Karl Löffler and Richard Schulenburg—men who had cordial relations with many important people in respectable circles in German society—can provide a key to the understanding of the nature of dictatorial terror as well as of evil itself.

THE EXONERATION AND REHABILITATION
OF KARL LÖFFLER AND RICHARD SCHULENBURG

Karl Löffler's life was neither over nor about to be, even if he did not know that a year and a half after the war ended. The first sign of this outcome was a brief letter Löffler received in December 1946, typed on an official form designed for private communications between German civilians and German prisoners that allowed no more than twenty-five words. Written by a Cologne priest and ostensibly extending Christmas tidings and the promise that a package was on its way, the letter reminded Löffler that he had not been forgotten by his friends and those with whom he had worked in the previous years and offered him hope that he would be able to mount a defense should he be brought to trial. Postmarked in Cologne on November 25, 1946, the text of the letter read:

> *Dear Herr Löffler:*
>
> Am shocked. Package on the way. Do you desire a character reference? Also Dr. Klinkhammer is willing. You were good to us in the Nazi time. Merciful Christmas.
>
> > *Your,*
> > *Pastor Diefenbach*[2]

Unless one knew who Pastor Diefenbach was and understood the importance of Cologne's vaunted network of personal ties and connections, which Cologne residents refer to proudly as *Kölsche Klüngel,* one would not find this letter remarkable. To the British authorities, it probably signified nothing more than that a Cologne clergyman was passing along holiday wishes and mailing a Christmas present to one of his former parishioners. But this letter meant much more than that. As dean of the Catholic Church in Cologne, Diefenbach was the second most powerful Catholic clergyman in Cologne next to the archbishop. Thus, Diefenbach's promise that he was willing to write a character reference and had already arranged for another reference from Dr. Klinkhammer (who was a Catholic priest as well as his cousin)[3] was one of the best Christmas presents Löffler could have received. Even the salutation Diefenbach chose to end his letter with, *Gnadenreiche Weihnachten* (Merciful Christmas), was laden with meaning: the German word *Gnade* also means clemency or pardon in legal as well as religious terminology.

Diefenbach made good on his promise soon after Christmas. On February 11, 1947, he wrote an official letter, stamped with the seal of Cologne's venerable Saint Pantaleon's Church, that tacitly urged the British authorities to take mercy on Löffler.[4] Diefenbach praised Löffler for his correct and tolerant behavior toward Diefenbach and other Cologne Catholic clergymen during the Nazi years, even in the course of official Gestapo investigations and interrogations, which, according to Diefenbach, Löffler's superiors had forced him to carry out. Diefenbach also stressed in his letter that he had come to trust Löffler implicitly, especially because "Löffler had always made it clear in all his dealings [with him] that he had not agreed with the tactics of the Gestapo." Diefenbach's trust had grown so great, in fact, that ever since he had first become acquainted with Löffler in 1937 he had often sought out his confidential advice in difficult situations.

Although Diefenbach's words of support carried special weight in Catholic-dominated Cologne, Löffler's staunch and high-placed supporters were by no means limited to Catholic circles in the city. Even before Diefenbach wrote his letter in February on Löffler's behalf, Löffler had received a similar letter from the head of Cologne's Protestant Church, Superintendent Hans Encke.[5] Stamped with the seal of the Superintendent of the Cologne Protestant Church's district office on January 16, 1947, and written under the underlined superscript of "certificate," Encke's letter had much the same tone and content as Diefenbach's. After indicating that he had known Löffler for many years, Encke began his letter by explaining that Löffler had been a longtime German police officer who joined the Gestapo only because the Cologne police were "taken over" in 1933. He then elaborated on his meetings with Löffler in an official capacity, particularly between 1933 and 1939. Each of these official meetings with Löffler, he explained, had "always been carried out in an absolutely polite manner." Furthermore, in his view, Löffler had always made "earnest efforts to avoid all unnecessary harshness" in the investigations he carried out. Encke had the "strong impression" that Löffler had always done all "that was possible in his position" to protect the people he had been assigned to investigate.

Around the time when Diefenbach and Encke wrote these letters on Löffler's behalf, Löffler also received even more glowing attestations of his good character and anti-Nazi sympathies from a number of private individuals and former colleagues. Although such letters would have been easier for him to obtain and were therefore probably somewhat less influential, they helped him build an outwardly convincing case that he deserved to be spared from prosecution and that he merited every consideration in the denazification process. On June 22, 1947, for example, a high-ranking detective in the Cologne police force who had never been a member of the Nazi Party wrote that Löffler had "rejected National Socialist ideology" and "was an opponent of the Gestapo's persecution of the Jews." Furthermore, he explained, Löffler had thwarted the Gestapo's persecution of the clergy; in particular, Löffler had more than once provided information that protected the Cologne Jesuit priest and radical Nazi opponent Father Josef Spieker.[6] Another man who had never been a party member and who also held Löffler in high esteem was the director of the Dresdner Bank office in Bonn. In his letter of June 11, 1947, to which he applied the heading "Character Reference!," he described himself as a longtime neighbor of the Löffler family. He knew Löffler was strongly opposed to the Nazis, he wrote, because he had never seen Löffler wearing his Nazi Party pin and because he had often had to warn Löffler that his constant anti-Nazi outbursts threatened to get him in deep trouble.[7]

Each of these letters helped to round out the picture of Löffler as an elderly, humane, career police officer with little sympathy for the Gestapo's methods, anti-Semitism, or the Nazi movement in general. Nothing made this favorable image of Löffler quite so believable, however, as the support he received from some members of the tiny remnant of Cologne's Jewish community, especially from the man who had served as its head in the late 1940s and early 1950s, Moritz Goldschmidt. In a series of letters to various authorities about Löffler's case, Goldschmidt seemed to provide unassailable proof that Löffler had enjoyed and deserved a reputation among Cologne Jews as the city's "only upstanding Gestapo officer," as the Cologne chief of police put it in a letter of August 23, 1948, written on Löffler's behalf.[8] A surviving letter written to the Cologne denazification authorities on July 4, 1949, by Goldschmidt himself almost a year later backs up the chief of police's claim that Goldschmidt had provided Löffler with "the absolute best character reference." Since Goldschmidt's letters proved to be of such importance in determining Löffler's fate, it would be instructive to look at the text of that July 1949 letter.

On the sixth of this month the former Gestapo officer Karl Löffler will appear before your chamber. Among other things, Herr Löffler was charged with the responsibility of overseeing religious authorities and their representatives. In this capacity he displayed tolerance in every sense of the word to the Jewish religious community.

He gave us timely information about the orders he received from his superiors so that we could adjust our behavior accordingly. In individual cases, Herr Löffler did not shy away from seeking out, providing information to, and warning accused people about denunciations that had been made against them. Because his superiors had become aware of the decent and humane manner in which Löffler treated the religious communities, they had him transferred to Brussels.

We can provide Herr Löffler with a character reference that attests that, despite his being a member of the Gestapo, he rejected Nazi ideology in religious and racial questions, and that through his decent efforts much harm was avoided. We urge you strongly to take these things into consideration in your judgment.[9]

A letter like this one, coming from such an unimpeachable source, could not be rejected out of hand in postwar Germany. Neither can it be dismissed easily today. Despite all that we know about Nazi terror, the Gestapo's activities, and Karl Löffler himself, could this and the other letters mentioned earlier have been written in earnest? Should they alter one's interpretation of Löffler, Schulenburg, and other Gestapo perpetrators and one's assessment of their guilt? What motivated respected and powerful people like Goldschmidt, Diefenbach, and Encke to write letters like these in the first place? How typical were they? What immediate and long-term effects did they have? How long did it take Karl Löffler and Richard Schulenburg to regain their respectability in German society?

Even though each of Karl Löffler's character references contained some statements that may have been true, Löffler was not the upstanding and humane opponent of Nazism and Jewish persecution that these letters made him out to be. He may not have worn his Nazi Party pin on occasion when he was off duty. He may have performed individual favors for real and potential targets of Nazi terror. He may have disagreed with certain Nazi policies. He may seldom have administered beatings himself or employed physical torture during the interrogations and investigations he conducted. He obviously had a wide circle of contacts in high places in Cologne society, and these contacts may have been sincere in their desire to help him after the war. But none of this lessens his guilt for the enormous crimes against humanity that he and other Gestapo officers like him perpetrated against thousands of defenseless and innocent people. One must remember that most of these letters were written by his friends, neighbors, colleagues, and others with whom he had cordial relations. Few of those who had a more negative impression of him survived to provide their assessment of his nature, behavior, and political attitude. Most of these people died in the Holocaust.

Among those who did not hold a positive impression of Karl Löffler were Friedrich Löwenstein, who immediately after the war had briefly led the Cologne Jewish community and an aid committee for Nazi victims, and his wife Regina.[10] The Cologne branch of the Association of Victims of Nazi Persecution (Vereinigung der Verfolgten des Naziregimes [VVN]) could also be counted among Löffler's detractors. After the war, the Löwensteins held Löffler personally responsible for the death of their son Rudolf in Auschwitz concentration camp, and they, the VVN, and others charged him with having direct knowledge of the death camps to which he had helped deport thousands of Cologne Jews. Additionally, the VVN supported the Löwensteins' contention that Löffler had made himself criminally liable and had even broken the laws obtaining in Nazi Germany when he ordered the deportation of their son in the summer of 1942.[11]

These allegations came to light in the late summer of 1948 while Löffler was still in British custody awaiting a trial that was to determine whether he was guilty of committing war crimes or whether he could move on to the next stage of the denazification process. Several months before this trial was held in the *Spruchgericht* (a kind of denazification court) in Benefeld-Bomlitz on December 9, 1948,[12] the prosecuting attorney commissioned the Cologne VVN to investigate any crimes that Löffler might have committed during his years as the head of Jewish affairs in the Cologne Gestapo. The VVN acted with dispatch to accede to this request. On September 1, it reported its findings to the prosecuting attorney in Benefeld-Bomlitz and attached, along with a sharply worded accusation, copies of the signed testimonies of people who had spoken out against Löffler.

The most accusatory of these testimonies were those of the Löwenstein couple and of a forty-seven-year-old man named Hermann K. who had shared a cell in 1942 with the Löwensteins' son Rudolf in Cologne's Klingel-pütz prison before Rudolf was deported. The anger these people harbored toward Löffler was palpable. This is understandable, for together they made a strong case that Löffler was, as Fritz Löwenstein put it most succinctly, "the murderer of my son."[13] In their view, Löffler was not only a murderer but a premeditated murderer.

As the son of a Jewish father and a Catholic mother, Rudolf Löwenstein had been a *Mischling* and therefore not subject to deportation, as most Jews were. The Löwensteins argued that the Gestapo could deport him, according to Nazi law, only if he had either committed an illegal act or been "legally" classified a *Geltungsjude* (a person of mixed parentage whom the Nazis believed to be more Jewish than Christian and thus "considered a Jew"). In their testimony, the Löwensteins insisted that their son had neither acted unlawfully (there was never a warrant for his arrest, and he was never le-

gally charged with committing a crime) nor been "considered a Jew." To
support this latter contention, they supplied the court with a birth certificate proving that their son had been baptized a Catholic shortly after his
birth in Cologne in July 1916 and other information demonstrating that he
had never been a recognized member of the Cologne Jewish community.
Hence, the Löwensteins argued, when Löffler decided to deport their son in
July 1942, he made himself guilty of intentional murder.

To back up this allegation further, Regina Löwenstein provided detailed
testimony about her regular visits to Löffler, over a period of five full weeks,
during which she pleaded with him to let her son go.[14] Although no legal
charge had been made against her son, she explained, Löffler steadfastly
refused her entreaties "with cynical sneers." The only humaneness he displayed came at the end of these five weeks when he allowed her a brief visit
with her son in Klingelpütz. When she finally encountered her son, she
found him "covered with insects and open sores."

After their son had been in jail for seventy days, the Löwensteins were
notified by the Gestapo through the Jewish community office that their son
had been deported to an unstated destination. Frau Löwenstein and her husband then went to Löffler again and asked him to let them bring clean laun-
dry to their son and to let him out of concentration camp for a day so that he
could be cleaned up. They even offered themselves as hostages to guarantee
that he would not try to escape. But as Regina Löwenstein related angrily,
"Löffler turned this down bluntly . . . with the words: 'so that the young lad
can yet find a way to escape us.' "

After several months had passed, the Löwensteins received mail from
their son from Auschwitz concentration camp. Nearly two years later, in
May 1944, Regina Löwenstein, like the Christian parents of many half-
Jewish children, received an official death notice from Auschwitz notifying
her of the date and cause of her son's death. According to this notice, which
the Löwensteins also produced to the court as documentation to support
their complaint against Löffler, Rudolf Löwenstein had died on March 9,
1944, of "heart failure associated with colitis" and "the body was cremated
in the state crematorium."[15]

This tragic news was not fully to be believed, for the Löwensteins were
in possession of a postcard from their son dated two weeks after the alleged

date of his death. Nevertheless, they were certain that their son Rudolf would not have died had it not been for Löffler's unlawful and ill-intentioned handling of his case. At the end of her long testimony at the Cologne VVN headquarters on September 1, 1948, Frau Löwenstein said: "One thing that is by all means certain is that Löffler knew about the death camps by the way he carried out the arrest and subsequent interrogations of my son."[16]

Corroborative testimony supporting the Löwensteins' allegations was provided by Rudolf Löwenstein's former cellmate, Hermann K.[17] Appearing at the Cologne VVN headquarters on August 28, 1948, Hermann K. explained that Löffler and two other Cologne Gestapo officers had arrested him on May 12 and charged him with holding subversive political views and providing illegal support to Jews. Soon he was placed in a cell in Klingelpütz prison; his cellmate for more than two months was Rudolf Löwenstein. Over this period, he repeatedly warned Löwenstein not to trust Löffler and not to divulge anything to him, because in the course of his own interrogations he had come to recognize that Löffler was a sly character who could be either "cunning or brutal, depending on the circumstances." As further evidence that Löffler had criminal intent when he decided to deport Rudolf Löwenstein, Hermann K. recalled the day when Löwenstein had returned to his cell in tears after an interrogation with Löffler. When he asked Löwenstein what had happened, Löwenstein replied that Löffler had just said to him: "You are a Jew, and you remain a Jew, and I am going to send you where the others also are." Both Hermann K. and Löwenstein clearly understood this to mean a death camp. Soon afterward, Rudolf Löwenstein was deported.

If the charges made against Karl Löffler by Friedrich and Regina Löwenstein, Hermann K., and the VVN raise suspicions about the veracity of the character references Löffler received in his attempt to avoid prosecution and to gain a favorable denazification status after the war, several other reasons to distrust those references should also be mentioned. The first of these is their rather formulaic nature. After the war, there was hardly a former Nazi who could not count on friends and contacts to provide letters of support in times of need, and judicial authorities, denazification committees, and other officials and agencies were almost literally awash in such letters.

Widely referred to as *Persilscheine,* these letters had a cleansing effect that many likened to that of the popular German detergent Persil: they laundered dirty brown shirts and made them turn out white and clean.[18] Those who have studied *Persilscheine* estimate that the average person going through denazification proceedings produced about ten of them, and many people produced twenty or more.[19] The large number of character references written for Löffler, therefore, could hardly be considered unusual. What made them unusual was who wrote them, and why.

Every former Gestapo officer from Cologne and Krefeld whose postwar records I have investigated received a number of *Persilscheine.*[20] Even a proven war criminal of the first rank like the former head of the Cologne Gestapo Emanuel Schäfer received them.[21] None of these former Gestapo officers, however, received quite the kind of letters that Karl Löffler received, except for one man, Richard Schulenburg.

As the head of the Krefeld Gestapo's Jewish desk throughout the years of the Third Reich, Schulenburg had exactly the same job as Karl Löffler. Chapter 2 elaborated on the similarities between Schulenburg and Löffler. Both men were elderly, career policemen of modest formal education and humble social background, known for their calm and orderly manner but also for their disarming jocularity and ability to interact amiably with different types of people, even sometimes including their victims. About the only difference between these two men was that Löffler came from a Catholic background and Schulenburg from a Protestant background. Given the similarities in their jobs, social origins, and personal natures, one might expect them to have had contacts with and success in winning over similar types of people. But could one have expected these two men, who played crucial roles for many years in the local organization and implementation of the worst crimes in Nazi Germany, to have received glowing character references from the leaders of both the Catholic and Protestant churches as well as the leaders of the Jewish communities and other prominent citizens in their local communities?

The *Persilscheine* that Richard Schulenburg obtained and put to good use read almost like carbon copies of Karl Löffler's.[22] The heads of the Catholic and Protestant churches in Krefeld, who held the same positions as those who wrote for Löffler in Cologne, wrote that Schulenburg was "compelled" to join the Gestapo and that they regarded him as an "extremely decent" and "exceedingly humane" man of "upright" character who had warned them frequently about spies and decrees that threatened them. They also attested that Schulenburg had always had an excellent reputation with the Jewish community. From their fulsome praise, one might have thought Schulenburg a more appropriate candidate for sanctification than for denazification. The dean of Krefeld's Catholic Church wrote, on February 27, 1947: "Any injustice, hardness [or] ill treatment was incompatible with his character. I am glad to issue this evidence for a man who belongs to the Protestant community."[23] And on March 24, 1950, the head of Krefeld's Protestant Church concluded a letter he had written in defense of Schulenburg: "Yes, we can attest that if Herr Schulenburg had not held the position he had held that we would have had to face many difficulties from which we remained spared. In those days, we often feared that they would transfer him to another [Gestapo] post because of his conduct."[24]

If these clergymen's letters seem too good to be true, they were nevertheless no more full of praise than the character references that Schulenburg received from other important Krefelders in the late 1940s and early 1950s. In July 1948, for example, the head of Krefeld's Catholic Center Party, who had known Schulenburg for many years as a fellow member of the same veterans' association, wrote that when the Nazis came to power, "Schulenburg had been forced to become a member of the Gestapo." Moreover, he had often heard, "indeed directly from Jewish friends, how humanely and decently Schulenburg had conducted himself" toward them.[25] Similarly, Krefeld's mayor explained, in May 1949, that Schulenburg was a "humane and blameless man" who was also "upstanding and modest", and in May 1953 Krefeld's representative to the federal parliament argued, as did many others, that Schulenburg deserved to receive his full pension.[26]

As in Löffler's case, however, the most astonishing letters Schulenburg received came from Jewish Holocaust survivors. The evidence contained in Schulenburg's copious denazification and Interior Ministry files shows that at least two of the handful of Jewish survivors in Krefeld credited him with saving either their own lives or the lives of one of their children. One of these was a woman whose daughter Änne died in Auschwitz concentration camp in May 1943 after Schulenburg had deported her because of her failure to wear the prescribed Star of David on her outer clothing. In her view, she too would have died in a concentration camp had it not been for Schulenburg's intervention on her behalf. The other was a man who served as the head of Krefeld's Jewish community after the war ended.[27] He was forever thankful to Schulenburg for sparing his daughter Marga's life. According to what he had heard from both Schulenburg himself and from the man who was the head of Krefeld's Jewish community in 1944, Schulenburg had removed his daughter's name from the list of the last Jews who were deported from Krefeld to Theresienstadt concentration camp in September 1944.

It is not clear why Schulenburg had done this. Perhaps in his warped sense of justice he had thought that it would be unfair to deport this young woman, who had been stamped a *Geltungsjüdin* because she once attended a Jewish school, when her sister, who had not attended a Jewish school and was considered only a *Mischling,* had not been scheduled for deportation. If it is true that Schulenburg scratched Marga's name from the list of those to be deported, it demonstrates once again that men who held the position that Schulenburg and Löffler held inside the Gestapo had the power to decide between those who would live and those who would die. This power made them all the more culpable for their decisions and actions.

More often than not, Schulenburg did not take the names of Jews off the deportation lists; instead, he added the names of Jews. One such person is Werner H., who spent nearly two years in Theresienstadt and Auschwitz concentration camps. During the Nazi years, he also was a young man of partial Jewish descent whom the Gestapo had classified as a *Geltungsjude,* and he also had a partially Jewish sister who was not deported.[28] As he stated to me in an interview, however, "this Schulenburg is someone I could strangle." To underscore why he still feels this way, he explained that he was caught near the Dutch border illegally riding the train without his Jewish Star on his clothing in late April 1943 and taken into protective custody in Krefeld. During that time, his mother had gone to Schulenburg several times to beg him to set her son free and to not send him to a concentration camp. As Löffler had done with Regina Löwenstein when she pleaded for the life of her son Rudolf, Schulenburg refused to budge an inch. Worse than this, and possibly because she was a Jew herself, Schulenburg had responded to the pleas of Werner H.'s mother by manhandling her physically and shaking her violently. On June 24, 1943, both Werner H. and his mother were deported to Theresienstadt.

Although Werner H. somehow survived to return to Krefeld after the war before emigrating to Chile, the experiences that he and his mother had with Schulenburg were much like those of Rudolf Löwenstein and his mother with Löffler. Schulenburg and Löffler had had the power to make choices in these cases. They could have chosen to treat these distraught mothers of partially Jewish young men with compassion and decency, but they chose to treat them with derision, and, in the case of Werner H.'s mother, physical violence. They could have chosen to spare lives or to end them. In both cases, they chose to end them.

Given the behavior of Löffler and Schulenburg in these cases and the fact that these men had been central figures in the persecution, deportation, and death of thousands of Cologne and Krefeld Jews, how was it possible that both received such outstanding letters of support from so many of the most respected people in their communities? Some of these letters may have been honestly, if somewhat mistakenly, inspired, especially those written by individuals who had benefited personally from a favor bestowed on them by Löffler and Schulenburg. It is difficult to believe, however, that the heads of both Christian churches and the heads of the Jewish communities in both Cologne and Krefeld could have been so naive as to be taken in completely by these perpetrators that they would have voluntarily written letters to help wipe their Nazi records clean. There must have been something that many of these people either feared or felt guilty about and did not want exposed.

This is precisely the question that surrounded the inflammatory Kastner affair, which rocked Israeli society in the 1950s.[29] Rudolf Kastner had been one of the leaders of the Jewish community in Budapest during the war, and many Jews owed their lives to him for various rescue operations he had helped to organize. After the war, Kastner emigrated to Israel, where by 1952 he was acting as the press spokesman for the Ministry of Commerce and Industry under the Mapai-Party government of David Ben-Gurion. In August of that year, a seventy-two-year-old Israeli man of Hungarian birth and background named Malchiel Gruenwald leveled a series of charges against Kastner that soon led to the first great Holocaust trial in Israeli history, with Gruenwald, somewhat paradoxically, serving as the sole defendant. According to Gruenwald, who printed his charges in a newsletter cum scandal sheet that he self-published entitled *Letters to Friends in the Mizrahi,* Rudolf Kastner had been a treacherous Nazi collaborator who enriched himself and his Nazi friends at the expense of hundreds of thousands of Hungarian Jews whose murder he was at least indirectly responsible for. As clear evidence of Kastner's guilt, in Gruenwald's view, he revealed that Kastner had sneaked off "secretly, like a thief in the night," in 1946 to testify at the Nuremberg Trials in defense of a major Nazi war criminal, SS Obersturmbannführer Kurt Becher, who had been the man most responsible for the deportation and death of the Hungarian Jews.[30]

It took two trials, stretched out over four years between January 1954 and January 1958, to resolve the Kastner affair. Before it was over, Rudolf Kastner had been shot and killed by an assassin's bullets, and he had been stigmatized as a man who "sold his soul to the devil." In the end, the Israeli Supreme Court lifted this stigma, which had been placed on him by the judgment of the Jerusalem district court of June 1955 that had ended his first trial. Indeed, the Supreme Court cleared Kastner of most of the charges that had been lodged against him. Nevertheless, there was one thing that the court could neither understand nor bring itself to forgive, namely, the testimony he had provided after the war for Kurt Becher. As it turned out, Kastner had not given this testimony directly before the Nuremberg Trials, as alleged by Gruenwald, but to a denazification proceeding; it had nonetheless helped Becher escape severe punishment for his crimes. Why Kastner testified on behalf of Becher will probably never be determined, though many will continue to suspect that it had something to do with a deal Kastner had worked out with Becher that enabled a trainload of 600 of Kastner's friends and family members to escape to Switzerland. The Israeli Supreme Court found that, under the circumstances, this had not been wrong for Kastner to do. But the fact that Kastner testified at all for Becher after the war continues to stain his reputation.

Bearing some similarity to the Kastner affair, allegations were also made that the postwar leader of Cologne's Jewish community, Moritz Goldschmidt, had profited from his relationship with Karl Löffler. These allegations emerged during the investigation preparatory to the 1954 trial of the Cologne Gestapo officers Emanuel Schäfer, Franz Sprinz, and Kurt Matschke. Just as he had done in the late 1940s in the form of letters to denazification authorities on Löffler's behalf, Goldschmidt provided Löffler with testimony in this trial investigation that ultimately helped Löffler avoid prosecution and punishment. On May 8, 1952, for example, Goldschmidt testified to the Cologne prosecutors that a Gestapo officer named Kurt Rose, not Karl Löffler, had been responsible for the deportations of the Cologne Jews and that Löffler had been a mere "specialist" (*Sachbearbeiter*) responsible for minor technical details. Furthermore, he claimed, Löffler had been "transferred in 1941 to Brussels because he was considered unfit."[31] This statement may have originated in something Löffler said to him. Whatever its origin, and though it was patently untrue (as was made clear during his denazification procedure, Löffler did not leave Cologne for Brussels until September 1942[32]), Goldschmidt's statement helped absolve Löffler of guilt for all but a supposedly minor role he had played in the first two Cologne deportations in the fall of 1941. Furthermore, it directly backed up the mendacious testimony that Löffler gave to the prosecutors five days later on May 13, 1952: he claimed that he had known nothing about the fate of the deported Jews because he had been transferred to Brussels "at the beginning of 1942."[33]

The evidence indicating that a profit motive may have accounted for Goldschmidt's defense of Löffler came from a former Cologne Gestapo officer from Duisburg who gave his testimony to the prosecutors on October 21, 1952. At first glance, the fact that he had been a Gestapo officer would seem to make him a less than credible witness. But one should also take the following into consideration: he was a former member of the Social Democratic Party; he was released from police service after Hitler took power in 1933 because of his political views, and he was called back into service only because of manpower shortages during the war; he never joined the Nazi Party; unlike most Gestapo officers, he was fully exonerated with a category V rating in his own denazification case; and he was the only Cologne Gestapo officer to admit honestly during the trial investigation that he, like the rest of the members of the Cologne Gestapo, bore responsibility for the deportation of the Jews.

In his testimony, this former Gestapo officer told the prosecutors that he had assisted in the preparation of one of the Cologne Jewish deportations and that he had been well informed generally about what went on in the Jewish affairs department of the Cologne Gestapo. In response to Löffler's claims of innocence and to Goldschmidt's spirited support for Löffler, he made the following statement under oath:

> The leading figure in the Jewish department was Löffler. He was com-
> monly known as a great Jew hater. It may be that he had occasionally
> helped [people out] in individual cases. But such measures were not
> born out of humanitarian compassion; rather, they were tied to advan-
> tages of a material nature. Only in this way can I possibly explain the
> positive testimony that the head of the Cologne Jewish Community
> Goldschmidt has provided.[34]

Moritz Goldschmidt may or may not have had some kind of monetary relationship with Karl Löffler. One can easily sympathize, however, with the other reasons he probably had for being thankful to Löffler. Both he and his family had survived the Holocaust, when most Jews from Cologne and other German cities had not. What Löffler's exact role in this had been will probably remain unknown. Perhaps Goldschmidt simply allowed himself to be deceived by Löffler into thinking that Löffler had spared him and his family when the real reason they had survived was the fact that his wife was a Catholic.

However difficult it is to fathom why Jews like Moritz Goldschmidt and Rudolf Kastner defended Gestapo perpetrators like Löffler and Becher, it is even more difficult to understand the support that the heads of the Cologne and Krefeld Catholic and Protestant churches provided to Löffler and Schu-lenburg. Unlike Kastner and Goldschmidt, these clergymen were not in an extremely perilous predicament during the Nazi years. Some of them may have felt guilty that they did not speak out against the murder of the Jews.[35] One can speculate that they may have had something to hide, and that Löffler and Schulenburg might have threatened to expose their secret if they had refused to provide the letters of support requested of them.[36] All that is certain is that their timely efforts were questioned by neither the

German nor Allied authorities and that they helped shut down the wave of prosecutions that might have followed had men like Löffler and Schulenburg been forced to pay a major price for their crimes against humanity. If the "local Eichmanns" in charge of Jewish affairs in cities like Cologne and Krefeld were not to be held to account, very few others would or could be.[37]

Even before the early 1950s, when the Cold War ended the Allies' interest in continuing their unpopular efforts to make former Nazis atone for their past activities, the Western Allies had already handed over to the Germans themselves the responsibility for carrying out denazification hearings and mounting crimes-against-humanity trials. In the British zone of occupation where Cologne and Krefeld were located, the denazification proceedings, which were already in a chaotic state of disarray, had fallen completely into German hands by the end of 1947. The results were immediate and dramatic. In Cologne between April 1947 and April 1948, for example, denazification proceedings resulted in 10 percent of those tried being put in category III ("minor offenders"), 22 percent in category IV ("fellow travelers"), and 68 percent in category V ("exonerated"). In the following year, the percentages were 2 percent, 24 percent, and 74 percent, respectively.[38] It is unnecessary to discuss the percentages of the more serious offenders placed in categories I and II because in the entire state of North-Rhine Westphalia, only ninety former Nazis were ever put into these two top categories.[39]

Karl Löffler and Richard Schulenburg were both originally classified as category III "minor offenders." This was a somewhat severe classification, though not an unusual one for Gestapo officers in the positions they had held inside the Gestapo. For Löffler and Schulenburg, this classification would prevent them from returning to police service. Worse for them in their minds at the time, since Schulenburg had already reached retirement age and Löffler was nearly that old, they would have to forgo their pensions. Thanks to the loyal support they continued to receive from those who had testified and written letters for them in the past, however, neither Löffler nor Schulenburg suffered for very long. By successfully appealing their denazification status, both men soon managed to be reclassified to a more favorable status that allowed them to receive their police pensions. Löffler received his pension after he rather incredibly joined the ranks of the fully

"exonerated": he was granted category V status from the Cologne denazification committee on the first day of carnival in Cologne on November 11,
1949. Schulenburg was not quite so successful with the denazification authorities, but he too was allowed to claim his police pension when his category III denazification status was improved to category IV in early July
1950.

Despite these favorable developments, neither Löffler nor Schulenburg
was satisfied. Not long after they began to receive their pensions, each man
mounted a campaign to have his years in the Gestapo added to his previous
years in police service. On July 15, 1950, less than two weeks after he started
receiving his pension, Schulenburg wrote a letter to the denazification committee in Düsseldorf protesting the decision to base his pension on only
twenty-eight years in police service. In his view, this decision was unfair
because he had served in the German police for thirty-eight years, even if
ten of those years had been in the Gestapo. Löffler also wanted to receive his
full pension, but he waited a little longer than Schulenburg to begin his
campaign, probably because of the charges that had been made against him
earlier by the Löwenstein couple.

As both men had done in the past, they recruited a number of prominent clergymen, politicians, and police officials to write letters bolstering
the contention that they had reluctantly served in the Gestapo and that they
had always acted in an upstanding manner. Additionally, both men received
new letters of support from some Jewish survivors still residing in their
cities; these letter-writers praised them for treating some of their family
members decently during the Third Reich. Admittedly, it did take the West
German authorities several years to come around to Löffler's and Schulenburg's way of thinking. But eventually they did just that.

In December 1955, the state government of North-Rhine Westphalia
decided to permit Schulenburg's years in the Gestapo to be included in the
calculation of his pension. Löffler's case reached a similar conclusion a few
months later. Nevertheless, the state's generosity failed to meet with the
full approval of the former Gestapo officers: their promotions in Gestapo
service were still being withheld from them. Again Schulenburg and Löffler
took umbrage, and each soon mounted yet another campaign to receive all
that he believed he had rightly earned. This was a ticklish issue, however,

since their most significant and monetarily remunerative promotions had taken effect as they were deporting Jews to the ghettos and concentration camps in the east. Schulenburg's final promotion to the rank of *Oberkriminalsekretär*, for example, had increased his salary by 20 percent, from 3,500 to 4,200 marks, and had transpired on November 1, 1941, only a few days after the first major transport of Krefeld Jews to the east had departed.

But Schulenburg and Löffler, both persistent and resourceful men with excellent connections, prevailed in the end. In late 1956, Löffler received, among others, several new and glowing letters from his staunch supporters Encke and Diefenbach of the Protestant and Catholic churches in Cologne and from an important member of the Cologne police department. Schulenburg lined up similar letters, the last of which was written in March 1958 by Dr. Emil Hürter, a former Krefeld mayor who had headed the Krefeld police department at the beginning of the Third Reich. As Schulenburg's former boss, Hürter maintained that Schulenburg, even if he had never served in the Gestapo, would have been promoted to *Oberkriminalsekretär* by 1943 at the latest, and that he himself had wanted to promote Schulenburg in the 1930s but had not been able to do so because there was not enough money in the Krefeld police department's budget.

A month later, on April 20, 1958 (on what would have been Adolf Hitler's sixty-ninth birthday), the Interior Ministry of the state of North-Rhine Westphalia decided that Richard Schulenburg's pension should be recalculated to include both his years in the Gestapo and all of his promotions. On July 21, 1958, Karl Löffler received the same consideration. Fully rehabilitated and fully compensated, each man lived for several more years to a ripe old age.[40] Their experiences were repeated across Germany.[41]

SOME CONCLUDING THOUGHTS ON GESTAPO PERPETRATORS, ORDINARY GERMANS, AND NAZI TERROR

The wonderful letters of support and strong backing that Karl Löffler and Richard Schulenburg received from leading members of their communities enabled them to avoid punishment, regain their pensions, and be reintegrated into German society soon after the end of the war. Some of the support they received may have been earnestly meant. Some individuals probably offered it, however, because such support helped to shield them from having to face embarrassing questions about their own past activities. For whatever reason it was offered, that support effectively shut down the wave of postwar trials for Nazi crimes that the leaders of postwar German society had been intent on carrying out. When Gestapo officers like Karl Löffler and Richard Schulenburg, who had presided over the systematic destruction of the Jewish population of their communities, were not prosecuted for committing crimes against humanity, then few others could be so prosecuted. Even though they were never adequately punished for what they had done, Karl Löffler, Richard Schulenburg, and other Jewish affairs specialists were nonetheless serious war criminals, no less than, and perhaps even more than, some of the more obviously brutal and fanatical Gestapo colleagues with whom they served.

It is important that these men not be viewed as upstanding, correct, and decent career police officers who were forced against their will to join and remain in the Gestapo, as they presented themselves in their disingenuous postwar self-portraits. Nearly all Gestapo officers created self-serving and deeply false characterizations of themselves as they tried to escape prosecution. Hence, these fabricated images depicted the real nature of the typically older men like Karl Löffler and Richard Schulenburg who had headed the Gestapo's Jewish desks no more accurately than they did the usually younger officers who had been their superiors, or any of the other rank-and-file Gestapo officers with whom they had served. It was true that Löffler and Schulenburg had profiles that were somewhat different from those of most other Gestapo officers, especially in that they were older, calmer, and more patient individuals with closer ties to their local communities. Still, they had chosen to accept their jobs as the heads of the Jewish affairs departments of their cities. They were ardent anti-Semites and convinced Nazis who had believed fully in Nazi ideology. They had used their guile, communications skills, and connections to maximum effect, serving often as important conduits between an otherwise youthful and crass Nazi movement and the established pillars of their local communities. In many ways, their role had been to "sell" as well as to implement the Holocaust.

But these men were not simply salesmen either. They were also not simply paper-shufflers. Hannah Arendt may have been correct in depicting Adolf Eichmann as banal. But she may not have been correct.[42] Some things about Löffler and Schulenburg were, of course, quite commonplace. Individuals like them can be found in almost any society. But this does not make them banal or ordinary. It also does not make the evil they perpetrated banal or ordinary. These "local Eichmanns" may seldom have administered physical force themselves. Nevertheless, they were knee-deep in the blood of their victims. They had met with their victims on a day-to-day basis. Through personal decisions they made, they had determined who should live and who should die. They had spared a few, but they had condemned most to death. They had not been moved by mothers' pleas or young people's tears. They had even escorted their victims to the trains. In sum, the outward appearances of these Gestapo officers, seemingly the most "ordinary" of men, had helped them establish good working relationships with many highly respected leaders in their local communities but were highly deceptive. When one probes more deeply into their mentality and behavior, one learns that they were pitiless Nazi perpetrators of the rankest nature.[43]

A recent trend in historical scholarship places the onus of guilt on ordinary Germans for the perpetration of Nazi crimes. Although two of this trend's pacesetters, Christopher Browning and Daniel Goldhagen, disagree over the depth and uniqueness of German anti-Semitism, they have both demonstrated convincingly that large numbers of ordinary Germans willingly took part in the murder of hundreds of thousands of innocent and defenseless Jewish men, women, and children.[44] In a related vein, Gisela Diewald-Kerkmann, Robert Gellately, Reinhard Mann, and others have stressed the importance of civilian denunciations in the control of the German population, and they have pointed out that the Gestapo had limited resources and manpower.[45] There is much truth in the arguments of all of these scholars. It is certainly correct that the Gestapo was not all-knowing, all-powerful, and omnipresent. It is also correct that Nazi terror relied heavily on the complicity of the ordinary German population. But the recent trend in historical scholarship threatens to underestimate and obscure the enormous culpability and capability of the leading organs of Nazi terror, such as the Gestapo, and to overestimate the culpability of ordinary German citizens. It needs to be remembered that some Germans were far more guilty than others.

This is not to write a *Persilschein* for the German population. Millions of ordinary German people did indeed share in the guilt for Nazi crimes. First of all, the mass of the German population was guilty of making a pact with the devil—in this case, Adolf Hitler. Millions of Germans voted for him, and millions more followed him avidly after he came to power. With the limited exceptions of the Nazis' most strident political enemies on the left in the beginning years of the Third Reich, a few isolated clergymen, some devoted members of tiny religious sects, and a few others, Hitler ruled without serious opposition, and there was hardly any meaningful popular resistance to his rule throughout the years of Nazi Germany. Many ordinary Germans denounced their fellow citizens, Jewish and non-Jewish alike, usually in an attempt to resolve petty personal quarrels, though sometimes to demonstrate their political zeal. Many ordinary Germans took direct part in persecuting and murdering the Jews, as well as other victims of Nazi terror. Millions of Germans looked away as Jewish synagogues were burned, Jewish stores were boycotted, and one law after another made life impossible for Jews in Nazi society. Millions of ordinary Germans knew about the Holocaust as it was taking place and did nothing to try to stop it. But most Germans did not denounce others, few family members and friends denounced one another, and most denunciations did not lead to heavy punishments. Most Germans did not want the Jews to be killed. Many ordinary Germans even provided Jews with understanding and support, as one learns from interviews with Jewish survivors, from questionnaires they completed, and from the diaries and memoirs of Jewish survivors like Victor Klemperer.[46]

The Nazi terror was a selective terror, and Jews were the terror's most important targets. In the early years of the Third Reich, the terror also concentrated on removing other enemies from the society, such as Communists, and on silencing potential opponents of the Nazi regime among the Catholic and Protestant clergy and among the members of tiny religious sects like Jehovah's Witnesses. Over time new groups of people were added to the terror's target list: career criminals, Sinti and Roma, the mentally and physically handicapped, and homosexuals. The overwhelming majority of ordinary German citizens, however, never became targets of the terror and were usually left alone to control their own lives. The terror was therefore not the blanket, indiscriminate terror of popular myth. This helps to explain its success.

The leading organ of the terror was the Gestapo, which admittedly had limited powers but was extremely effective all the same. It was organized intelligently and staffed by capable and cruel officers who did not hesitate to apply barbaric torture tactics to disarm and destroy the Nazi regime's targeted enemies. But many Gestapo officers, as longtime policemen, also understood the need to be sensitive to popular opinion when dealing with ordinary citizens who posed no real threat even if they had been caught committing a minor offense. Hence, by applying leniency or pressure depending on the situation and the offender, the Gestapo officers coated Nazi terror with a legalistic gloss that helped legitimize their activities in the eyes of a largely faithful German populace. The effectiveness of Nazi terror was also enhanced by the support received by the Gestapo from numerous other policing, surveillance, and judicial organs of the state and party, such as the Kripo and regular police, the Special Courts, the People's Court, and regular courts, and the SD, SS, and SA, and the local functionaries of the Nazi Party.

Nazi Germany was therefore a police state, but one that allowed most of its citizens considerable room for their regular activities and for the venting of everyday frustrations. For Jews, Communists, Sinti and Roma, Jehovah's Witnesses, the mentally retarded and handicapped, homosexuals, and some others, Nazi Germany was hell. But most Germans may not even have realized until very late in the war, if ever, that they were living in a vile dictatorship. They knew that there were victims of this dictatorship, but they perceived most of these victims as criminals with whom they had little or nothing in common. By their own admission on our surveys and in our interviews, the great majority of ordinary Germans had believed that they had little reason to fear the Gestapo or the concentration camps. Most ordinary Germans knew that they could usually get away with telling political jokes, complaining about Hitler and other Nazi leaders, listening to illegal BBC broadcasts, and dancing to swing music. They simply had to be careful, as ordinary Germans had always been under previous German governments, when breaking what they perceived to be minor laws and to be contrite if they were caught breaking them.

In recent decades, the German nation has made great strides in its attempt to come to terms with the National Socialist past. In Germany today, one can turn on the television set almost any evening or flip through the newspaper almost any morning and encounter a serious documentary or debate dealing with the Holocaust and other Nazi crimes and criminals. The once loud choruses of "I did not know about it! I did not know about it!" have become faint. But after reading more than 1,000 Gestapo and Special Court case files and speaking with scores of people who spent their younger years in Nazi Germany, it is not clear to me whether many in that older generation feel compassion even now for the victims of the crimes perpetrated by their former country. Most older Germans do regret that these crimes were committed, if only because they placed a heavy and lasting burden on Germans of all ages.[47] Many aging Germans, as they now face their own death, look back at their past not remembering that they were once perpetrators or bystanders but with the sense that they have been the real victims of Nazi terror.

The last interview I conducted in Cologne before returning to the United States after spending most of five years in Germany doing research on this book was on a pleasant June morning with an eighty-eight-year-old man.[48] His wife was dead, and he lived alone in a drab apartment building of many stories. Neatly placed around his living room, where we talked, were many old pictures and mementos of his long life. He was dressed up for the occasion with an ascot around his neck. He was cordial and polite, and he served me red wine in a crystal glass. He drank more than I did, as I recall. We spoke for about two hours. He told me that he had been a policeman in a small town not far from Berlin. He also told me that he had been a concentration camp guard in Dachau for a period of time during the war and that he had known that Dachau had a gas chamber. He also told me that he had been a member of the auxiliary SS. It was hard to imagine how this small, slender old man, who seemed somewhat pathetic, could have been involved in these things. He enjoyed telling me about his past, and he was quite candid. He became animated when he recounted that he had eluded prosecution by the British and American Allies at the end of the war by simply scratching out his occupation on his identity card, which he showed me during our interview. But soon after this, he became somber when he described fighting partisans on the eastern front in the middle of the war years. These "partisans" turned out to be mostly Jewish women and children. I asked him how this had been done. He said that they were shot in the head with revolvers. His most vivid memory was of an afternoon when his detachment (six men in all) shot 300 Jewish women and children. The most horrible part for him was wading among the bodies in the ditch with the other members of his detachment to administer "mercy shots." Three times he stood up from his couch and walked over to me. Each time he bent down to point to the middle of his right calf muscle to demonstrate how deep the blood had been. Over and over again he repeated: "Can you imagine? Can you imagine? Can you imagine?"

NOTES

CHAPTER ONE: LOCATING NAZI TERROR

1. *Kölnische Rundschau*, July 7, 1954.
2. Ibid. These figures have been revised somewhat downward as a result of information that has come to light since the trial. Manfred Huiskes, working in cooperation with the Cologne Stadtarchiv, estimates that between 1941 and 1943 "over 11,500 Jews from Cologne and the Cologne *Regierungsbezirk* were deported in at least 14 transports, leaving from [the train station at] Cologne-Deutz to Litzmannstadt/Lodz, Riga, Theresienstadt, Lublin/Izbica, Minsk, Yugoslavia and Auschwitz. Only about 300 of them came back alive." *Die Wandinschriften des Kölner Gestapo-Gefängnisses im EL-DE-Haus 1943–1945* (Cologne, 1983), 30.
3. *Kölnische Rundschau*, July 7, 1954. Other local newspapers covered the Gestapo trial in much the same spirit as the *Kölnische Rundschau*. See, for example, the coverage of the trial in the *Kölner Stadt-Anzeiger*, July 7–10, 1954, which was even more matter of fact. For clippings from other area newspapers, see Nordrhein-Westfälisches Hauptstaatsarchiv Düsseldorf-Kaiserswerth, Schloss Kalkum (hereafter HStADK), Rep. 231/516II.
4. *Kölnische Rundschau*, July 7, 1954.
5. The indictment (*Anklageschrift*) is a seventy-two-page typewritten document dated December 19, 1952. HStADK, Rep. 231/517, Bl. 31–102.
6. The verdict of July 9, 1954, and the grounds for the verdict are provided in the official judgment (*Urteilsschrift*). This document is fifty-nine typewritten pages long. HStADK, Rep. 231/519, Bl. 4–33. The final verdict in the case revised an earlier verdict of the same court, Landgericht Köln, of June 20, 1953, which gave Schäfer a six-year, six-month sentence for one count of being an accessory to murder (*Beihilfe zum Morde*) and two counts of manslaughter (*Totschlag*), both stemming from Schäfer's later activities as head of the security police in Belgrade. The final verdict of July 9, 1954, in which his actions as head of the Cologne Gestapo during the deportations of the Cologne Jews were

taken into consideration, extended his sentence by a total of only three months. See also Huiskes, *Die Wandinschriften des Kölner Gestapo-Gefängnisses*, 45.

7. *Kölnische Rundschau*, July 7, 1954.

8. HStADK, Rep. 231/519. For newspaper coverage of the verdict, see the *Kölner Stadt-Anzeiger*, July 10, 1954, and *the Kölnische Rundschau*, July 10, 1954.

9. *Kölnische Rundschau*, July 7, 1954.

10. See *Urteilschrift*, 56; HStADK, 231/519, Bl. 31.

11. The major exceptions were trials held in the mid-1960s of those who oversaw the extermination camps such as the famous Auschwitz trial and the Treblinka trial. The Auschwitz trial was held in Frankfurt between December 1963 and August 1965 and led to the conviction of seventeen people, mostly former SS men. Six were imprisoned for life, and the rest were imprisoned for terms ranging from three and a half to fourteen years. For a recent treatment of this case with important comments about the Federal Republic's legal handling of former Nazi perpetrators in general, see Gerhard Werle and Thomas Wandres, *Auschwitz vor Gericht: Völkermord und bundesdeutsche Strafjustiz* (Munich, 1995). The Treblinka trial was held in Düsseldorf between October 1964 and September 1965. Four people were imprisoned for life, five people were given prison terms of between three and twelve years, and one person was acquitted. The written verdict was published in a twenty-two-volume collection of verdicts in cases of Nazi crimes against humanity tried by German courts between 1945 and 1966, Fritz Bauer et al., eds., *Justiz und NS-Verbrechen: Sammlung Deutscher Strafurteile wegen nationalsozialistischer Tötungsverbrechen 1945–1966* (Amsterdam, 1981), vol. 22.

12. Werle and Wandres explain that "the Holocaust first became a matter of concern for the Federal Republic's justice authorities in 1958." In that year a central prosecuting attorney for Nazi war crimes was established in Ludwigsburg (Die Zentrale Stelle der Landesjustizverwaltungen zur Aufklärung von NS-Verbrechen, hereafter ZSL). See *Auschwitz vor Gericht*, 23. Despite the ZSL's diligent efforts, most cases involving Gestapo and other Nazi criminals have been narrowly focused and have led to minor penalities or to no penalties at all. In addition to the recent book by Werle and Wandres, see Adalbert Rückerl, *Die Strafverfolgung von NS-Verbrechen 1945–1978: Eine Dokumentation* (Heidelberg, 1979), and Jörg Friedrich, *Die kalte Amnestie: NS-Täter in der Bundesrepublik* (Frankfurt am Main, 1984).

13. The documentation in the case runs to thousands of pages. HStADK, Rep. 231/447–519.

14. In most places in Germany it was not until the mid-1960s that official investigations similar to the investigation of the Cologne Gestapo for the deportation of the Jews were launched. Still, little is known today about these investigations. Most were dismissed in the late 1960s before going to trial, on grounds of "lack of evidence" that the Gestapo officers knew about the "true fate of the Jews" they deported. Since these cases never came to trial, there was no newspaper or television coverage of them. Furthermore, the documents pertaining to these investigations have never been made public in most localities, and in some places, like Düsseldorf, they have been mysteriously lost. Some information about them, however, can be found at the ZSL. See, for example, ZSL, 415 AR 846/64, and for the Düsseldorf case, ZSL, 414 AR 345/71 (two volumes). For a discussion of how the German public and media have dealt with Nazi crimes, see Peter Steinbach, *Nationalsozialistische Gewaltverbrechen: Die Diskussion in der deutschen Öffentlichkeit nach 1945* (Berlin, 1981).

15. A copy of the Cologne Gestapo's organizational plan (*Geschäftsverteilungsplan*) of April 27, 1942, hangs today in one of the cells of the Cologne Gestapo headquarters and can be viewed by the public free of charge. This document lists Karl Löffler as the head of the Jewish desk at that time—thus during the middle of the deportations. A copy of it can also be found in the Nordrhein-Westfälisches Hauptstaatsarchiv, Düsseldorf-Mauerstrasse (hereafter HStAD), RW34/9. Löffler's personal police dossier provides additional evidence that he in fact remained with the Cologne Gestapo as head of the Jewish desk. Here, for example, one learns that in a hearing of August 18, 1948, in Bielefeld, Löffler explained that he had been "commanded to Brussels at the end of September 1942" after having been ill for the previous eight weeks. (His doctor's letter to this effect is in the file.) This was after most of the Jewish deportations from Cologne had been completed. "Personalakten Sammelbestand," file of Karl Löffler, HStADK, BR PE/49505.

16. For recent discussions of this progression, especially as it applies to the Gestapo, the courts, and the SS, see Robert Gellately, "Situating the 'SS-State' in a Social-Historical Context: Recent Histories of the SS, the Police, and the Courts in the Third Reich," *Journal of Modern History* 64 (1992): 338–65; Klaus-Michael Mallmann and Gerhard Paul, "Allwissend, allmächtig, allgegenwärtig?: Gestapo, Gesellschaft, und Widerstand," *Zeitschrift für Geschichts-*

wissenschaft 41 (1993): 984–99; and Gerhard Paul and Klaus-Michael Mallmann, eds., *Die Gestapo: Mythos und Realität* (Darmstadt, 1995). For
treatments of the research on the terror applied specifically to the Jews and on
the terror itself, see Saul Friedländer, *Nazi Germany and the Jews*, vol. 1, *The
Years of Persecution, 1933–1939* (New York, 1997); Marion A. Kaplan, *Between Dignity and Despair: Jewish Life in the Third Reich* (New York, 1998);
Christopher R. Browning, *The Path to Genocide: Essays on Launching the Final Solution* (Cambridge, 1992); and still important although slightly dated,
Michael R. Marrus, *The Holocaust in History* (London, 1987).

17. See, for example, Eugon Kogon, *Der SS-Staat: Das System der deutschen
Konzentrationslager* (Munich, 1946); and Hans Bernd Gisevius, *To the Bitter
End*, translated by R. and C. Winstone (London, 1948).

18. See, for example, Hannah Arendt, *The Origins of Totalitarianism* (New
York, 1951); Edward Crankshaw, *Gestapo: Instrument of Tyranny* (London,
1956); Jacques Delarue, *The Gestapo: A History of Horror*, translated by Mervyn Savill (1962; New York, 1987); and Gerald Reitlinger, *The SS: Alibi of a
Nation 1922–1945* (1956; Englewood Cliffs, N.J., 1981).

19. Raul Hilberg, *The Destruction of the European Jews* (New York, 1961). See
also Hans-Stephan Brather, "Aktenvernichtungen durch deutsche Dienststellen beim Zusammenbruch des Faschismus," *Archivmitteilungen* 8 (1958):
115–17.

20. See note 18. See also Hans Buchheim, "Die SS—das Herrschaftsinstrument," and Hans Buchheim, "Befehl und Gehorsam," in Hans Buchheim, Martin Broszat, Hans-Adolf Jacobsen, and Helmut Krausnick, *Anatomie des SS-
Staates* (Munich, 1967), 15–212, 216–320.

21. Arendt, *The Origins of Totalitarianism*, 434–35.

22. Delarue, *The Gestapo*, 86.

23. Excellent accounts of the *Historikerstreit* are found in Richard J. Evans, *In
Hitler's Shadow: West German Historians and the Attempt to Escape from the
Nazi Past* (London, 1989); and in Charles S. Maier, *The Unmasterable Past:
History, Holocaust, and German National Identity* (Cambridge, Mass., 1988).

24. Ralf Dahrendorf, *Society and Democracy in Germany* (1965; New York,
1967); Martin Broszat, *The Hitler State: The Foundation and Development of
the Internal Structure of the Third Reich*, translated by John W. Hiden (1969;
New York, 1981); and Albert Speer, *Inside the Third Reich*, translated by Richard and Clara Winston (New York, 1970). See also Karl Dietrich Bracher, *The*

German Dictatorship: The Origins, Structure, and Effects of National Socialism, translated by Jean Steinberg (1969; New York, 1970).

25. Jews are not even mentioned in the index to Broszat, The Hitler State. Speer leaves Jews out of his discussion in Inside the Third Reich. Dahrendorf, Society and Democracy in Germany, spends only a few pages on Jews and anti-Semitism. Bracher, The German Dictatorship, devotes twenty-two pages to Jews and the Holocaust.

26. Ian Kershaw, Popular Opinion and Political Dissent in the Third Reich: Bavaria 1933–1945 (Oxford, 1983), 277; Ian Kershaw, The "Hitler Myth": Image and Reality in the Third Reich (Oxford, 1987). Kershaw's observations have been echoed by many scholars. For example, Detlev Peukert, a leader in resistance studies and the history of everyday life, explained that the "mass of the population . . . was not induced into actively supporting the persecution of the Jews. . . . Hence anti-Semitism was in no sense, as some historians and journalists have supposed, an essential instrument in integrating and mobilising the population in a National Socialist direction." Inside Nazi Germany: Conformity, Opposition, and Racism in Everyday Life, translated by Richard Deveson (London, 1987), 58.

27. Martin Broszat et al., eds., Bayern in der NS-Zeit, 6 vols. (Munich, 1977–83).

28. Lutz Niethammer has been a pioneer both in demonstrating the richness of local archival sources and in broadening the research methodologies with which one can study the Third Reich. See his Entnazifizierung in Bayern: Säuberung und Rehabilitierung unter amerikanischer Besatzung (Frankfurt am Main, 1972), which effectively employs quantitative research methods, and his pioneering oral history study "Die Jahre weiss man nicht, wo man die heute hinsetzen soll": Faschismus-Erfahrungen im Ruhrgebiet (Berlin, 1983).

29. Peter Hoffmann, Detlev Peukert, and Peter Steinbach have been leaders in this research. Whereas Hoffmann has concentrated on the resistance efforts among the military and the elite, Peukert, Steinbach, and others have emphasized working-class, youth, and other resistance movements. See, for example, Peter Hoffmann, The History of the German Resistance (Cambridge, Mass., 1977), and Stauffenberg: A Family History, 1905–1944 (London, 1995); Detlev Peukert, Die KPD im Widerstand: Verfolgung und Untergrundarbeit an Rhein und Ruhr 1933 bis 1945 (Wuppertal, 1980), and Inside Nazi Germany; and Jürgen Schmädeke and Peter Steinbach, eds., Der Widerstand gegen den Na-

tionalsozialismus: Die deutsche Gesellschaft und der Widerstand gegen Hitler (Munich, 1985). Very recently important new compendiums of research on the resistance have been published by leading German- and English-language journals. See, for example, the special issue of the *Zeitschrift für Geschichtswissenschaft* (vol. 42 [1994]) published on the occasion of the fiftieth anniversary of the assassination attempt on Hitler carried out on July 20, 1944. See also the 1992 special supplementary volume of the *Journal of Modern History* entitled "Resistance Against the Third Reich." Two recent studies of resistance in communities in the Rhein-Ruhr area that are particularly rich in detail are Rudolf Tappe and Manfred Tietz, eds., *Tatort Duisburg 1933–1945: Widerstand und Verfolgung im Nationalsozialismus,* 2 vols. (Essen, 1989, 1993), and Bernhard Schmidt and Fritz Burger, *Tatort Moers: Widerstand und Nationalsozialismus im südlichen Altkreis Moers* (Moers, 1995).

30. The literature on the Edelweiss Pirates and other anti-Nazi youth groups has proliferated in recent years. For an excellent collection of essays on the topic, see Wilfried Breyvogel, ed., *Piraten, Swings, und Junge Garde: Jugendwiderstand im Nationalsozialismus* (Bonn, 1991). The extent to which these groups were really "resistance fighters" has been the subject of considerable debate. For a critical study of the Cologne Edelweiss Pirates, see Bernd-A. Rusinek, *Gesellschaft in der Katastrophe: Terror, Illegalität, Widerstand—Köln 1944–1945* (Essen, 1989). Everyday grumbling on the part of adults was no doubt common and was punished, sometimes severely, under Germany's already broad libel laws. Important discussions of the extent and bases of this grumbling are found, for example, in Kershaw, *Popular Opinion and Political Dissent in the Third Reich;* Peukert, *Inside Nazi Germany;* and Marlis G. Steinert, *Hitler's War and the Germans: Public Mood and Attitude During the Second World War,* translated by T. E. J. de Witt (Athens, Ohio, 1977). Many people have studied the Nazi judicial system's prosecution of political libel and slander cases (*Heimtückeverfahren*). The pioneering study is Peter Hüttenberger, "Heimtückefälle vor dem Sondergericht München 1933–1939," in Broszat et al., *Bayern in der NS-Zeit,* 4:435–526. The Düsseldorf Gestapo's treatment of such cases is analyzed in detail and with methodological sophistication in Reinhard Mann, *Protest und Kontrolle im Dritten Reich: Nationalsozialistische Herrschaft im Alltag einer rheinischen Grossstadt* (Frankfurt, 1987).

31. The literature on clergymen, religious groups, and Communists in the Third Reich is too extensive to cover in a footnote. References to much of the literature published before the mid-1980s are found in Schmädeke and

Steinbach, *Der Widerstand gegen den Nationalsozialismus.* Studies on the sufferings of women in the Nazi years have proliferated as well and include: Gisela Bock, *Zwangsterilisation im Nationalsozialismus: Studien zur Rassenpolitik und Frauenpolitik* (Opladen, 1986); Claudia Koonz, *Mothers in the Fatherland: Women, the Family, and Nazi Politics* (London, 1988); Jill Stephenson, *Women in Nazi Society* (London, 1975), and *The Nazi Organisation of Women* (London, 1981); Vera Laska, ed., *Women in the Resistance and in the Holocaust: The Voices of Eyewitnesses* (Westport, Conn., 1983); and Gerda Szepansky, *Frauen leisten Widerstand 1933–1945. Lebensgeschichten nach Interviews und Dokumenten* (Frankfurt am Main, 1983). For a treatment of the persecution of German women by the Gestapo and the courts, see Eric A. Johnson, "German Women and Nazi Justice: Their Role in the Process from Denunciation to Death," *Historical Social Research/Historische Sozialforschung* 20 (1995): 33–69, and "Gender, Race, and the Gestapo," *Historical Social Research/Historische Sozialforschung* 22 (1997): 240–53.

32. A relatively intact set of Gestapo records exists for only a few cities of Germany. The case files of the former Gestapoleitstelle Düsseldorf are the most plentiful of these records. The pathbreaking study using local Gestapo records is Reinhard Mann's posthumously published *Protest und Kontrolle im Dritten Reich* (1987). More recently, Robert Gellately has investigated the records of the Würzburg Gestapo in his *The Gestapo and German Society: Enforcing Racial Policy 1933–1945* (Oxford, 1990). It is also reported that large sets of Gestapo case files for some former East German cities, like Weimar and Erfurt, can be found in Moscow. See *Der Archivar* 45 (1992): 457ff. The Special Court case files are relatively well preserved in many German cities; the largest reserve is found in Cologne. Many recent studies employ Special Court records. Exemplary is Ralph Angermund's *Deutsche Richterschaft 1919–1945: Krisenerfahrung, Illusion, politische Rechtsprechung* (Frankfurt am Main, 1990).

33. Gellately, *The Gestapo and German Society;* Klaus-Michael Mallmann and Gerhard Paul, *Herrschaft und Alltag: Ein Industrierevier im Dritten Reich* (Bonn, 1991); Paul and Mallmann, *Die Gestapo.*

34. The Canadian historian Robert Gellately has brought the issue of political denunciation in Nazi society to the forefront of the debate, even though Reinhard Mann and some others studied the issue before him. See his *The Gestapo and German Society,* and his recent summary of his own and others' research on denunciations in a special issue of the *Journal of Modern History* treating the topic of political denunciations in several countries, "Denunciations in

Twentieth-Century Germany: Aspects of Self-Policing in the Third Reich and the German Democratic Republic," *Journal of Modern History* 68 (1996): 931–67. Several other scholars have followed Gellately's lead in the last few years. For example, see Gisela Diewald-Kerkmann's study of political denunciations made to local Nazi Party authorities, *Politische Denunziation im NS-Regime oder die kleine Macht der "Volksgenossen"* (Bonn, 1995).

35. Mallmann and Paul, *Herrschaft und Alltag,* 414–15.

36. Gellately's recent review essay, "Situating the 'SS-State' in a Social-Historical Context," discusses much of this literature. Other important studies not discussed in Gellately's essay are Lothar Gruchmann, *Justiz im Dritten Reich: Anpassung und Unterwerfung in der ära Gürtner* (Munich, 1988); Angermund, *Deutsche Richterschaft;* and Ingo Müller, *Hitler's Justice: The Courts of the Third Reich,* translated by Deborah Lucas Schneider (1987; Cambridge, Mass., 1991).

37. Most of the literature on the *Volksgerichtshof* is in German. For an English-language treatment, see H. W. Koch, *In the Name of the Volk: Political Justice in Hitler's Germany* (London, 1989). Two German-language studies coming out of a large project that quantitatively analyzes the verdicts of the People's Court are Klaus Marxen, *Das Volk und sein Gerichtshof: Eine Studie zum nationalsozialistischen Volksgerichtshof* (Frankfurt am Main, 1994); and Edmund Lauf, *Der Volksgerichtshof und sein Beobachter: Bedingungen und Funktionen der Gerichtsberichterstattung im Nationalsozialismus* (Opladen, 1994).

38. Christopher R. Browning, *Ordinary Men: Reserve Police Battalion 101 and the Final Solution in Poland* (New York, 1992); Daniel J. Goldhagen, *Hitler's Willing Executioners: Ordinary Germans and the Holocaust* (New York, 1996). For an example of this heated debate, see the angry exchange of letters between Goldhagen and the respected Holocaust scholars Omer Bartov and Christopher Browning in the *New Republic,* February 10, 1997. For other examples, see Norman G. Finkelstein and Ruth Bettina Birn, *A Nation on Trial: The Goldhagen Thesis and Historical Truth* (New York, 1998); and Johannes Heil and Rainer Erb, eds., *Geschichtswissenschaft und Öffentlichkeit: Der Streit um Daniel J. Goldhagen* (Frankfurt am Main, 1998). For examples of the German public's reaction to Goldhagen's book, see Siedler Verlag, *Briefe an Goldhagen* (Berlin, 1998).

39. A catalog of the exhibition containing all of the exhibition's photographs was first published in Hamburg in 1996 and has since gone through several

printings. Hamburger Institut für Sozialforschung, ed., *Vernichtungskrieg: Verbrechen der Wehrmacht 1941 bis 1944* (Hamburg, 1996).

40. On the German army's involvement in crimes against humanity, see, for example, Omer Bartov, *Hitler's Army: Soldiers, Nazis, and War in the Third Reich* (New York, 1992); and Helmut Krausnick, *Hitlers Einsatzgruppen: Die Truppe des Weltanschauungskrieges 1938–1942* (1981; Frankfurt am Main, 1998).

41. See, for example, George C. Browder, *Hitler's Enforcers: The Gestapo and the SS Security Service in the Nazi Revolution* (New York, 1996); and Gerhard Paul, "Ganz normale Akademiker: Eine Fallstudie zur regionalen staatspolizei-lichen Funktionselite," in Paul and Mallmann, *Die Gestapo*, 236–54.

42. This is the title of the concluding section of Mallmann and Paul's book on everyday terror in the Saarland, *Herrschaft und Alltag*, 414. It should be noted that the German term *Resistenz* is not the same as "resistance," which in German is *Widerstand*. *Resistenz* is a neologism for minor acts of nonconformity and noncompliance with the Nazi authorities (resistance with a very small *r*). The term has become popular in Germany in the last two decades among the many scholars who use the everyday-life perspective (*Alltagsgeschichte*) in the study of the Third Reich. Mallmann and Paul are certainly not alone in their reevaluation of the significance of the German resistance. In the important collection of resistance research published on the fiftieth anniversary of the Hitler assassination plot of July 20, 1944, Frank Stern asks, "Is the resistance a German alibi?" "Wolfsschanze versus Auschwitz: Widerstand als deutsches Alibi?" *Zeitschrift für Geschichtswissenschaft* 42 (1994): 645–50.

43. Mallmann and Paul, *Herrschaft und Alltag*, 416.

44. The population of Cologne in 1933 was 756,605. According to official statistics, Cologne had a population of 767,222 inhabitants in January 1940. HStADK, Rep. 23/272. By 1970 the population had risen to 809,247. Today Cologne has nearly one million inhabitants. Reinhold Billstein, ed., *Das andere Köln: Demokratische Tradition seit der Französischen Revolution* (Cologne, 1979), 492.

45. In the last Weimar election of November 6, 1932, before Hitler came to power on January 30, 1933, the Nazi Party received a total of 33.1 percent of all votes cast, but only 20.4 percent of the votes cast in Cologne. In the election of March 5, 1933, the Nazi Party received 43.9 percent of all votes cast, but only 33.1 percent of the Cologne votes. In these two elections the Catholic Center Party received 27.3 and 25.6 percent of the votes cast in Cologne, the Commu-

nist Party received 24.5 and 18.1 percent, and the Social Democratic Party received 17.4 and 14.9 percent. Historisches Archiv der Stadt Köln, *Widerstand und Verfolgung in Köln 1933–1945* (Cologne, 1974), 24.

46. Cologne suffered the first "thousand-bomber" attack of the British Royal Air Force on May 31, 1942. During the war Cologne was hit by more than 200 separate bombing attacks. Air-raid alarms were sounded more than 1,000 times. At the end of the war the entire inner city was destroyed, and only about 42,000 residents remained. Robert Frohn, *Köln 1945–1981: Vom Trümmerhaufen zur Millionenstadt* (Cologne, 1982), 17–22; Gerhard Braun, "Köln in den Jahren 1945 und 1946: Die Rahmenbedingungen des gesellschaftlichen Lebens," in Otto Dann, ed., *Köln nach dem Nationalsozialismus: Der Beginn des gesellschaftlichen und politischen Lebens in den Jahren 1945–1946* (Wuppertal, 1981), 35–72; Adolf Klein, *Köln im Dritten Reich: Stadtgeschichte der Jahre 1933–1945* (Cologne, 1983), 252–56.

47. The most controversial group was the Edelweiss Pirates. For a discussion of this controversy and a detailed discussion of the last war year in Cologne, see Rusinek, *Gesellschaft in der Katastrophe*. For an earlier study offering a more positive view of the Edelweiss Pirates, see Matthias von Hellfeld, *Edelweisspiraten in Köln: Jugendrebellion gegen das 3. Reich: Das Beispiel Köln-Ehrenfeld* (Köln, 1981).

48. Barbara Becker-Jákli, ed., *Ich habe Köln doch so geliebt: Lebensgeschichten jüdischer Kölnerinnen und Kölner* (Cologne, 1983), 324.

49. According to the *Statistisches Jahrbuch Deutscher Gemeinden* (vol. 59 [1972]), the population of Krefeld in 1939 was 171,553, with 31.7 percent listed as Protestant, 61.6 percent as Catholic, and 5.5 percent as foreign.

50. Dieter Hangebruch, "Emigriert—Deportiert: Das Schicksal der Juden in Krefeld zwischen 1933 und 1945," *Krefelder Studien* 2 (1980): 139.

51. Like Cologne, Krefeld was hit hard by bombing attacks during the war. On the bombing of Krefeld, see Hans Vogt and Herbert Brenne, *Krefeld im Luftkrieg 1939–1945* (Bonn, 1986). Although there is no full-scale work on resistance activity in Krefeld, Aurel Billstein, a former Communist leader in the Weimar Republic who spent years in Nazi prisons and concentration camps, published several books and brochures on resistance and persecution in Krefeld during the Third Reich before he died in the mid-1990s. See, for example, his *Fremdarbeiter in unserer Stadt 1939–1945: Kriegsgefangene und deportierte "fremdvölkische Arbeitskräfte" am Beispiel Krefelds* (Frankfurt am Main,

1980), and *Christliche Gegnerschaft am Niederrhein 1933–1945 im Bereich der ehemaligen Gestapo-Aussendienststelle Krefeld* (Viersen, 1987).

52. This population figure is based on the territorial boundaries of present-day Bergheim. In 1990 the population stood at 57,278. Stadt Bergheim, *Kreisstadt Bergheim: Zahlen, Daten, Fakten* (Bergheim, n.d.).

53. All of the leading studies of the Nazi vote in Weimar elections point out that industrial workers and Catholics were less supportive of Hitler than others. Jürgen W. Falter, *Hitlers Wähler* (Munich, 1991); Thomas Childers, *The Nazi Voter: The Social Foundations of Fascism in Germany, 1919–1933* (Chapel Hill, N. C., 1983); Richard Hamilton, *Who Voted for Hitler?* (Princeton, N.J., 1982).

54. It is impossible to know exactly how intact the records are. Reinard Mann reports that the entire collection of case files of the Düsseldorf Gestapo head-quarters, which includes the Gestapo outpost in Krefeld as well as several other neighboring cities, represents about "70 percent of the original amount." *Protest und Kontrolle*, 66. Based on my evaluation of the number of Jewish case files in Krefeld compared with the number of Jewish case files in Düsseldorf itself and several other cities, such as Wuppertal and München-Gladbach, it appears that the Krefeld files may be more complete than in other cities. In Krefeld there is a case file on nearly every Jewish family-head who lived in the city during the Nazi period.

CHAPTER TWO: INSIDE GESTAPO HEADQUARTERS

1. On the denazification process, see, for example, Lutz Niethammer, *Entnazifizierung in Bayern: Säuberung und Rehabilitierung unter amerikanischer Besatzung* (Frankfurt am Main, 1972); and James F. Tent, *Mission on the Rhine: Reeducation and Denazification in American-Occupied Germany* (Chicago, 1982). Also of interest is Ernst von Salomon's satirical and contemporary discussion of the process and the questionnaire (*Fragebogen*) that Germans had to fill out about their past, *Der Fragebogen* (Hamburg, 1951).

2. Schulenburg's two denazification files are HStAD, NW1037-BI 18164 and NW1023–6433.

3. Between 1940 and 1942 the seat of the Krefeld Gestapo was Goethestrasse 108. On June 17, 1942, it was moved to Uerdingerstrasse 62. At the end of 1944 it was moved once again to the town of Opladen. For other details, see Dieter Hangebruch, "Emigriert—Deportiert: Das Schicksal der Juden in Krefeld

zwischen 1933 und 1945," *Krefelder Studien* 2 (1980): 137–412, esp. 186. After December 1, 1935, the seat of the Cologne Gestapo was in the El-DE-Haus on the corner of Appellhofplatz and Elisenstrasse. Before then the Cologne *Staats-polizeistelle* was located in the Krebsgasse 1–3 and for a time in the Zeughauss-trasse 8. On the Cologne Gestapo's location, see Manfred Huiskes, "Die Staats-polizeistelle Köln im El-DE-Haus," in *Die Wandinschriften des Kölner Gestapo-Gefängnisses im EL-DE-Haus 1943–1945* (Cologne, 1983), 9–69, esp. 10–15.

4. This letter is found in the larger of Schulenburg's two denazification files, HStAD, NW1023–6433. This file is seventy-eight pages long and also contains his twelve-page denazification questionnaire.

5. Ibid., Bl. 30.

6. Ibid., Bl. 13.

7. Schulenburg was the twentieth person in Krefeld to become a member of the NSDAP. StAKr, Film B58, "Mitglieder-Liste der NSDAP in Krefeld."

8. HStAD, NW1023–6433, Bl. 55.

9. Schulenburg's lawyer wrote to the denazification committee in Düsseldorf on July 26, 1949, that Schulenburg's attempt to retire at age sixty in 1939 was "not granted because of the outbreak of the war." Ibid., Bl. 55.

10. Hangebruch, "Emigriert—Deportiert," 187.

11. These details come from Schulenburg's two denazification files. The details about his home and weight are found in his second denazification question-naire, NW1023–6433, Bl. 61. His weight had already increased by six kilo-grams (about thirteen pounds) by the time he filled out his second denazifica-tion questionnaire on June 10, 1948, only a year after he filled out his first one. The letters people wrote about him are found in both of his denazification files as well as in his *Innenministerium* file, HStAD, NW130–310.

12. HStADK, Rep. 8/6. For local newspaper coverage of Effenberg's trial, see the articles in the *Rheinische Post* and the *Westdeutsche Zeitung* of October 7, 1948. Both newspapers can be found in the Krefeld Stadtarchiv.

13. The dates of his internment are in Effenberg's *Innenministerium* file, HStAD, NW130–82.

14. In Effenberg's Rasse- und Siedlungs-Hauptamt-SS file at the Berlin Docu-ment Center (hereafter BDC-RuSHA), for example, he notes that he held the silver *Reichssportabzeichen* and had also earned a *Wehrsportabzeichen* in pri-mary school.

15. Effenberg's attempts to return to police service and his denazification classification are discussd in his *Innenministerium* file, HStAD, NW130–82.

16. HStADK, Rep. 8/6, Bl. 12.

17. BDC-RuSHA (Alfred Effenberg).

18. For details on Jung's background and for a photo taken when he was twenty-eight years old, see his BDC-RuSHA file.

19. HStADK, Rep. 8/6, Bl. 22.

20. For documentation on Jung's wife, see BDC-RuSHA, Elisabeth Solbach. She and Jung were already engaged when she filled out her *Rasse- und Siedlungs-Hauptamt-SS* questionnaire on December 30, 1938. It is not clear why she filled out this form and what her role in the Düsseldorf Gestapo was. One has to suspect, however, that like her husband, who had filled out the same form a month earlier on December 1, 1938, she was applying to join the *Allgemeine SS,* since the form was normally part of an application for the SS. On the form she said that she was twenty-five years old, living in Düsseldorf, of Catholic religion, the daughter of a government official (*Regierungs-Inspektor*), and working as an "employee of the Düsseldorf Gestapo" (*Angestellte bei Staatspolizeistelle Düsseldorf*). In the handwritten curriculum vitae that was part of the document, she explained that she had studied until the age of sixteen at the Ursula Lyzeum in Düsseldorf. After that she began working in January 1930 as a secretary (*Stenotypistin*) for the regional government in Düsseldorf and sometime thereafter went to work for the Düsseldorf Landespolizei in the same capacity. In June 1935, however, she changed jobs, she explained, and became an *Angestellte* for the Düsseldorf *Staatspolizei* (Gestapo), where she was still working in December 1938 when she filled out the form. She also said that she was a member of two Nazi organizations, the DAF (German Workers' Association) and the *NS Frauenwerks* (National Socialist Women's Association). It is unclear what she did as an *Angestellte* for the Düsseldorf Gestapo, since the term can mean many things, including a common secretary. It is unlikely, however, that she was only a secretary, since she distinguished her position after 1935 as an *Angestellte* from her earlier jobs as a *Stenotypistin*. In his recent examination of the Würzburg Gestapo, Gerhard Paul explains that there were at least twenty women, most of them young, working for the Gestapo in Würzburg and that many had significant functions far beyond those of typists and secretaries, including taking part in body searches of accused Jewish women about to be deported, acting as translators,

and, after 1944, leading the administrative section of the Gestapo headquarters. "Kontinuität und Radikalisierung: Die Staatspolizeistelle Würzburg," in Gerhard Paul and Klaus-Michael Mallmann, eds., *Die Gestapo: Mythos und Realität* (Darmstadt, 1995), 161–77, esp. 167. I had little luck in searching for more documentation on her subsequent activities and those of Ludwig Jung even though I made a comprehensive search in archives where one might expect such documentation to be found (for example, Zentrale Stelle für Landesjustizverwaltungen in Ludwigsburg, the Hessisches Hauptstaatsarchiv in Wiesbaden, the Stadtsarchiv in Krefeld, and the HStAD and HStADK. An archivist in Wiesbaden explained that there is evidence there that Jung's and his wife's records may have been mysteriously purged sometime in the 1950s, for there had been requests for them at that time. It also appears that Jung never showed up for his own trial in Krefeld, which is mentioned in the Effenberg case. It is possible that denazification records for him cannot be found because he may have decided not to go through the denazification process. Knowing that he probably would have received a bad denazification rating, he could have chosen to avoid the process and continue working in the private sector. It is also possible that he found employment in a secret policing organization in the Federal Republic or elsewhere.

21. The details above come from BDC-RuSHA (Gustav Burkert) and from an organizational plan (*Geschäftsverteilungsplan*) of the Krefeld Gestapo of April 23, 1944, found in HStAD, Rep. 36/45. I know about Burkert's previous involvement in Jewish cases and Effenberg's in cases dealing with homosexuality from reading the individual Krefeld Gestapo case files, HStAD, RW58.

22. HStADK, Rep. 8/6, Bl. 39–40.

23. The documentation on Schmitz's career is fairly extensive in his denazification file, HStAD, NW1010/12909, and his *Innenministerium* file, HStAD, NW130/302. Schmitz filed his denazification questionnaire on April 28, 1948. On May 10, 1948, the Krefeld denazification authorities placed him in category III. The only officer of the Krefeld Gestapo to be born in Krefeld, Schmitz listed himself in 1948 as unemployed (*gottgläubig* and *religionslos*) and still living in Krefeld. His only formal education consisted of the primary school in Krefeld and a brief police training course. After leaving school, he worked until age twenty as a dye-worker in Krefeld. He then spent two years in military service, reaching the rank of corporal, before returning to his job as a dye-worker. In 1923, at the age of thirty-six, he joined the Krefeld *Schutzpolizei*. In his denazification form he claimed that he was "transferred" (*versetzt*) to the Gestapo

in Krefeld in 1934. It is evident in his *Innenministerium* file that this was not believed by the denazification authorities; they wrote that he could not prove that he was "officially transferred" (*von Amts wegen versetzt*) to the Gestapo. The Krefeld Gestapo case files (Gestapo *Personalakten*, HStAD, RW58) demonstrate that Schmitz was already active in political policework in Krefeld by 1933. Although Schmitz had been a member of many Nazi organizations and in 1937, like many other Krefeld Gestapo officers, joined the NSDAP, he never joined the SS. He died in Krefeld in 1956 without receiving his full pension. In 1958 his wife, however, did start to receive his full pension, which included both his years and his promotions in the Krefeld Gestapo.

24. HStADK, Rep. 8/6, Bl. 36.

25. The Gestapo in Krefeld actually was in existence for a short time also in 1933 and 1934.

26. Fleischer and Schommer are identifiable as members of the Krefeld Gestapo from an organizational plan of September 1, 1940, of Abteilung III of the Krefeld Gestapo, HStAD, RW36/45, "Stärkemeldung nach dem Stand von 1.9.1940, Abt. III." The others are identifiable from the Krefeld Gestapo *Personalakten*, HStAD, RW58, and from information provided in Hangebruch, "Emigriert—Deportiert," 185–88.

27. HStAD, RW36/45, "Geschäftsverteilungsplan der Aussendienststelle Krefeld mit Wirkung vom 23.4.1944."

28. Huiskes, "Die Staatspolizeistelle Köln im EL-DE-Haus," 26.

29. Klaus-Michael Mallmann and Gerhard Paul report in their *Herrschaft und Alltag: Eine Industrierevier im Dritten Reich* (Bonn, 1991), 199–200, that Saarbrücken had a rather large Gestapo organization in comparison with other cities. In 1935 Saarbrücken's *Stapo-Stelle* had a staff of 113 people to oversee a local Saarland population of about 780,000 inhabitants. This they contrasted with the *Stapo-Stelle* in Hannover, which had only 42 officers to oversee a population of about 1.5 million people in the cities of Hannover and Hildesheim and their surrounding areas, and those of Stettin with 41 officers, Köslin with 29, Frankfurt am Main with 41, Braunschweig with 26, and Bremen with 44. As in Cologne, the Saarbrücken Gestapo declined in size after the fall of 1939, so that by the fall of 1941 it had only 71 officers. For detailed discussions of the Gestapo in Hannover, Potsdam, and Würzburg, see the relevant chapters in Paul and Mallmann, *Die Gestapo: Mythos und Realität:* Hans-Dieter Schmid, "'Anständige Beamte' und 'üble Schläger': Die Staatspolizeistelle Hannover," 133–60; Sibylle Hinze, "Vom Schutzmann zum Schreibtischmörder: Die Staat-

spolizeistelle Potsdam," 118–32; and Gerhard Paul, "Kontinuität und Radikalisierung: Die Staatspolizeistelle Würzburg," 161–77. See also Hans-Dieter
Schmid's recent study of the Leipzig Gestapo in which he determines that Leipzig's Gestapo had a maximum strength of about 100 officers and that the entire
German state of Saxony had less than 500 officers, making a ratio of about
10,500 citizens per Gestapo officer. *Gestapo Leipzig: Politische Abteilung des
Polizeipräsidiums und Staatspolizeistelle Leipzig 1933–1945* (Leipzig, 1997),
18–22.

30. Interview with Alfred E., Cologne, June 17, 1995; interview with E. W., Cologne, October 13, 1994. Gerhard Paul explains in his new study of the Würzburg Gestapo: "A Gestapo officer never appeared in most communities in Un-
terfranken. . . . Policing under the new system presented itself locally as it
always had, though at the same time it had thousands of new eyes and ears
[through denunciations presumably]." "Kontinuität und Radikalisierung,"
172.

31. *Kölnische Rundschau,* July 7, 1954.

32. See, for example, Gerhard Paul's essay on the leaders of Gestapo posts in
many localities, "Ganz normaler Akademiker: Eine Fallstudie zur regionalen
staatspolizeilichen Funktionselite," in Paul and Mallmann, *Die Gestapo: Mythos und Realität,* 236–54.

33. The leading work on the importance of political denunciations in the Nazi
terror system is Robert Gellately, *The Gestapo and German Society: Enforcing
Racial Policy 1933–1945* (Oxford, 1990). See also his "Allwissend und allgegenwärtig?: Enstehung, Funktion, und Wandel des Gestapo-Mythos," in Paul
and Mallmann, *Die Gestapo: Mythos und Realität,* 47–70.

34. Christopher R. Browning, *Ordinary Men: Reserve Police Battalion 101
and the Final Solution in Poland* (New York, 1992); and Daniel Jonah Goldhagen, *Hitler's Willing Executioners: Ordinary Germans and the Holocaust*
(New York, 1996). Whereas both Browning's and Goldhagen's alarming arguments about the ordinariness of the members of reserve police battalions seem
well supported by the documentary evidence they provide, it is possible that
the men they wrote about were not so "ordinary" as the postwar trial evidence
they rely on seems to show. In an interview I conducted in Cologne on June 17,
1995, with an eighty-eight-year-old former *Hilfspolizist* named Alfred E., who
had been called up during the war for brief periods of *Partisanbekämpfung* in
the former Soviet Union, I learned that E. was not such an "ordinary man."
Before his involvement in brief episodes of shooting Jews, mostly women and

children in groups of a few hundred at a time, he had fairly extensive SS training and had also served for a time as a concentration camp guard in Dachau.

35. On the reputation of German policeman in Imperial Germany, see, for example, Eric A. Johnson, *Urbanization and Crime: Germany 1871–1914* (New
York, 1995), 30–39. See also Albrecht Funk, *Polizei und Rechtsstaat: Die Entwicklung des staatlichen Gewaltmonopols in Preussen, 1848–1914* (Frankfurt
am Main, 1986), and Herbert Reinke, ed., *"Nur für die Sicherheit da?": Zur
Geschichte der Polizei im 19. und 20. Jahrhundert* (Frankfurt am Main, 1993).

36. Huiskes, "Die Staatspolizeistelle Köln im EL-DE-Haus," 16. In a study of
the transition of the Berlin headquarters of the political police from the last
years of the Weimar Republic to the first years of the Third Reich, Christoph
Graf argues that the core of the political policemen who remained in office in
the first months after the Nazis took over, in Berlin at least, were ardent Nazi
supporters: "Indeed only a relatively small part of the higher administrative-
and criminal-police officers were true 'Nazis' in that they had an obvious connection with the Nazi party before 1933, but this made up nevertheless a hard
core." Furthermore, he argues, most officers who were not fully sympathetic to
the Nazi cause left office within a few months, leaving behind mostly "reliable
National Socialists." *Politische Polizei zwischen Demokratie und Diktatur: Die
Entwicklung der preussischen Politischen Polizei vom Staatsschutzorgan der
Weimarer Republik zum Geheimen Staatspolizeiamt des Dritten Reiches*
(Berlin, 1983), 173. On the purge of police officers at the beginning of the Third
Reich, see also Johannes Tuchel and Reinold Schattenfroh, *Zentrale des Ter-
rors: Prinz-Albrecht-Strasse 8; Das Hauptquartier der Gestapo* (Berlin, 1987),
63–66.

37. In Sibylle Hinze's careful study of the Potsdam Gestapo, for example, she
finds that by the end of 1933, "with only one or two exceptions, all [of the offi-
cers] had already long before 1933 been members of the NSDAP, SA or SS."
"Vom Schutzmann zum Schreibtischmörder," 123.

38. Gerhard Paul has shown that most commanding officers of regional Gestapo posts were born in 1905 or later, came from middle-class to upper-middle-
class backgrounds, and were highly educated. "Ganz normale Akademiker."

39. Tall, blond, and athletic, Heydrich was typically "Aryan" in appearance.
Born in Halle on March 7, 1904, he was the son of Bruno Heydrich, a gifted
musician and founder of the Halle Conservatory for music, theater, and teaching. His father's original name was rumored to be Süss, and Heydrich did
everything he could to destroy all documents that might uncover his Jewish

ancestry. Nevertheless, the rumors persisted, and up to 1940 Heydrich repeatedly brought legal action for racial slander against those who spread them. For these and other details about Heydrich's background and personality, see Joachim C. Fest, *The Face of the Third Reich: Portraits of the Nazi Leadership*, translated by Michael Bullock (New York, 1970), 100–101; Edouard Calic, *Reinhard Heydrich: The Chilling Story of the Man Who Masterminded the Nazi Death Camps*, translated by Lowell Bair (New York, 1982), 21–22; and Schlomo Aronson, *Reinhard Heydrich und die Frühgeschichte von Gestapo und SD* (Stuttgart, 1971).

40. The Bremen Gestapo post, for example, had a total of five different leaders between 1933 and 1945, and the Potsdam Gestapo post had four. See Inge Marssolek and Rene Ott, *Bremen im Dritten Reich: Anpassung-Widerstand-Verfolgung* (Bremen, 1986), 179; and Hinze, "Vom Schutzmann zum Schreibtischmörder," 120ff. See also Gerhard Paul's discussion of regional Gestapo heads in general, "Ganz normaler Akademiker."

41. A former Jewish printer and leftist organizer named Josef Mahler from Krefeld was continuously interrogated by the Düsseldorf Gestapo headquarters for over three years before he died on September 1, 1943, ostensibly because of a heart attack but most likely because he was given "special treatment" after the Gestapo decided they could not get any more information out of him. HStAD, RW58/7869, RW58/53199, RW58/34515, RW58/46518.

42. For Cologne's other leaders, see Huiskes, "Die Staatspolizeistelle Köln im EL-DE-Haus," 21–26. Kommissar Bolle headed the Krefeld Gestapo until Jung took over in early 1939.

43. Ludwig Jung's curriculum vitae is in his BDC-RuSHA file.

44. Hangebruch cites the testimonies of several former officers in the late 1960s who described him in this way. "Emigriert—Deportiert," 186.

45. This information is from Schäfer's Berlin Document Center records, which are included as part of his *Innenministerium* file, HStAD, NW130/293. The other details of his life, unless otherwise noted, come from the *Anklageschrift* or the *Urteilsschrift* in his 1954 trial with the *Landgericht* in Köln. HStADK, Rep. 231/517 and Rep. 231/519.

46. See Schäfer's Berlin Document Center records in his *Innenministerium* file, HStAD, NW130/293.

47. Ibid.

48. Ibid.

49. Ibid. For unknown reasons, however, Schäfer dropped out of the party soon thereafter and did not join it again until May 1, 1937.

50. Ibid.

51. HStADK, Rep. 231/447, Bl. 14–15.

52. On the establishment of Auschwitz, see Yisrael Gutman and Michael Berenbaum, eds., *Anatomy of the Auschwitz Death Camp* (Bloomington, Ind., 1994); and Debórah Dwork and Robert Jan van Pelt, *Auschwitz: 1270 to the Present* (New York, 1996).

53. HStADK, Rep. 231/447, Bl. 14.

54. HStADK, Rep. 231/513, Bl. 349.

55. This information is from Schäfer's court testimony of January 19, 1952, HStADK, Rep. 231/448, Bl. 218.

56. Only Dr. Nockemann, who headed the Cologne *Stapostelle* from July 1933 to February 1936, served as long, but Cologne did not officially have a Gestapo headquarters during this entire period. See Huiskes, "Die Staatspolizeistelle Köln im EL-DE-Haus," 23. On Isselhorst, see his *Innenministerium* file, HStAD, NW130/220, which also contains a copy of his Berlin Document Center file. On Sprinz, see ZL, 415 AR846/64, vol. 1, "Evakuierung von Juden," 57–60; HStADK, Rep. 231/517 and Rep. 231/519.

57. The age, social background, and educational patterns hold for leaders of other Gestapo posts as well. Of the heads of fifteen regional Gestapo posts named in a letter signed by Reinhard Heydrich on April 22, 1942, as responsible for carrying out the "final solution," at least seven held doctorate degrees. Their median year of birth was 1905; only three were born before 1903, and the oldest was born in 1892 (making him still only fifty years old in 1942). The youngest of the men was born in 1909, making him only thirty-three in 1942. ZL, 415 AR846/64, vol. 1, Bl. 4–5, 19–21. Gerhard Paul arrives at similar findings in his collective biography of the heads of sixty Gestapo posts and outposts in 1938–39. He found that 78 percent were born after the turn of the century; 47.5 percent were born after 1905; almost all had completed a university degree; and "the large majority of the Gestapo leaders came from well-situated and sometimes upper-middle-class families, none came from the working-class." See "Ganz normaler Akademiker," 238–39.

58. Most of these details are found in Isselhorst's *Innenministerium* file, HStAD, NW130/220. Some details of his activities as an *Einsatzkommando* leader are found in Helmut Krausnick, *Hitlers Einsatzgruppen: Die Truppe des*

Weltanschauungskrieges 1938–1942 (1981; Frankfurt am Main, 1998), 361–62.

59. See the written judgment in the Cologne deportation trial, HStADK, NW231/519, Bl. 8.

60. ZL, AR575/60, Bl. 149. Preckel gave this testimony on October 23, 1959, in a case involving a former Wuppertal Gestapo officer charged with being involved in *Sonderbehandlung* (Special treatment).

61. A great deal of controversy surrounds the Edelweiss Pirates. Some see them as heroic anti-Hitler youth; others see them as common criminals. Evidence that this controversy continues to simmer today is the graffiti one can still see on the walls of the train underpass in Cologne-Ehrenfeld, near where the thirteen were hanged in 1944, saying, "Edelweiss Pirates are faithful" (*Edelweisspiraten sind treu*).

62. The organizational plan of the Krefeld Gestapo of April 23, 1944, lists Karl Schmitz as the head of "special cases" (*Sonderfälle*), but it is not certain that this designation means that he was responsible for "special treatment" cases. HStAD, RW36/45.

63. See, for example, the case entitled *Gestapoflügel in Klingelpütz* (Gestapo-wing in Klingelpütz) and *Rechtswidrige Tötung von Stapo Häftlingen in Klingelpütz* (unlawful killing of Gestapo prisoners in Klingelpütz); lodged against two former Cologne Gestapo officers and others, this case of "crimes against humanity" mentions a missing Gestapo *Kartei* (card file) on foreign workers that was taken out of the main Gestapo prison in Cologne after the war by a common policeman and given to the Allies. The card file reputedly contained information on the "special treatment" of scores of foreign workers. HStADK, Rep. 231/95, Bl. 67 and Rep. 248/265–266. For a discussion of "special treatment" cases in Cologne, see Bernd-A. Rusinek, "'Wat denkste, wat mir objerümt han': Massenmord und Spurenbeseitigung am Beispiel der Staatspolizeistelle Köln 1944–1945," in Paul and Mallmann, *Die Gestapo: Mythos und Realität*, 402–16. For Dortmund, see Gerhard Paul and Alexander Primavesi, "Die Verfolgung der 'Fremdvölkischen': Das Beispiel der Staatspolizeistelle Dortmund," in ibid., 388–401.

64. HStADK, Rep. 248/265–266.

65. Paul, "Kontinuität und Radikalisierung," 176.

66. ZL, 107 AR-Z 571/67, vol. V. This was part of a case started in 1967 and dismissed on January 17, 1972, in Munich against thirty-two Germans for murdering prisoners during the war in Holland. After ordering the shooting of

a group of fourteen prisoners on April 10, 1945, Weber reportedly "gave the motionless people lying on the ground shots in the back of the neck to make sure that they were dead." The charge against Weber by several of the accused was made easier in that he had died a decade earlier on January 16, 1958.

67. Attached to *Einsatzgruppe B,* he was head of its *Sonderkommando 7a.* Mallmann and Paul, *Herrschaft und Alltag,* 204. More details can be found in the written judgment in the Cologne deportation trial, HStADK, Rep. 231/519, Bl. 9.

68. These are the only men I was able to identify as having clearly served in the Krefeld Gestapo between 1937 and the end of the war.

69. The BDC-RuSHA files for Alfred Effenberg and Friedrich Fürschbach, for example, show that both had served in the *Freikorps* between 1919 and 1920. In his detailed study of the Hannover Gestapo, Hans-Dieter Schmid argues that Hannover Gestapo officers were "conspicuously often" former Freikorps members. "'Anständige Beamte' und 'üble Schläger,'" 143.

70. According to their BDC-RuSHA files, Ludwig Jung, for example, was a member of the SA from March 1934 to May 1935, and Heinrich Humburg was in the SA from 1933 to 1935. Many other Krefeld Gestapo officers listed in their BDC-RuSHA files that they had won medals from the SA. Sibylle Hinze finds that nearly all of the early members of the Potsdam Gestapo had already been members of the SA, SS, or NSDAP before joining the Gestapo. Hinze, "Vom Schutzmann zum Schreibtischmörder," 123–24. Hans-Dieter Schmid explains that roughly half of the original members of the Hannover Gestapo had been in the party before 1933 and that many of the members who joined in 1935 or thereafter had been members of the SS. "'Anständige Beamte' und 'üble Schläger,'" 140, 145.

71. This information is from the *Innenministerium* file of Johann Krülls, HStAD, NW130/243. Born in Krefeld on October 31, 1892, Krülls was a long-time police officer in the city with a profile similar to those of several of the older officers. After serving in the military from 1912 to 1918, he joined the Krefeld *Schutzpolizei* in 1919 and later joined the political-police department of the Krefeld *Kriminalpolizei.* On March 14, 1934, he was transferred to the Düsseldorf Gestapo headquarters. Like many Gestapo officers, he first joined the NSDAP on May 1, 1937. In 1940 he was promoted to the rank of *Kriminalobersekretär* in the Düsseldorf Gestapo. Letters in his file marked "confidential" (*vertraulich*) and "constitutional protection" (*Verfassungsschutz*) suggest that he probably became a member of the *Bundesamt für Verfassungsschutz*

(an organization that was something like the secret police force of the Federal Republic, although officially the Federal Republic has no secret police force) after serving a period in internment after the war. Various letters of support in his file claim that he was, like Schulenburg and several others, a policeman of "the old school" who was "tranferred" (*versetzt*) from the criminal police to the Gestapo and who always acted as a decent policeman.

72. The evidence for this comes from the testimony of a former political-police officer in Krefeld named Albert Adams who testified on behalf of Karl Schmitz during his 1948 denazification proceedings. HStAD, NW1010/12909. Adams explained that in 1934 the criminal police in Krefeld had fifty-eight members, and that sometime in 1934 or 1935 many "younger officers and those who were best at writing were transferred to the Gestapo." Both Effenberg and Burkert, in their BDC-RuSHA files, state that they were transferred from the *Schutzpolizei* to the *Kriminalpolizei* in Krefeld in April 1934, but the latter could in fact have been the "Gestapo" even though they did not technically consider themselves part of the Krefeld Gestapo until August 1937, when the Krefeld Gestapo outpost was officially formed. Otto Dihr claimed in a case of crimes against humanity lodged against him after the war for "assault and battery while in office" (*Körperverletzung im Amt*) that he was a member of the criminal police working in the area "of vice and theft" until being "transferred" to the Gestapo in 1937. HStADK, Rep. 10/8.

73. Fleischer claims in his BDC-RuSHA records that he was transferred from the Düsseldorf *Schutzpolizei* to the Krefeld criminal police in June 1936, and from there to the Krefeld Gestapo on October 26, 1937. Joost's BDC-RuSHA records show that he was transferred from the *Schutzpolizei* in Rheydt to the criminal police in Krefeld in November 1936. He became a member of the Krefeld Gestapo outpost when it officially formed on August 1, 1937. Braun appears not to have joined the SS, and only very limited information could be found about him in the Berlin Document Center. BDC, *Partei Kanzlei Korrespondenz*, Herbert Braun. It is unknown when he first joined the Krefeld Gestapo, but from cases he is known to have covered, it is possible to affix the date as before August 1937.

74. All of these men were listed on the organizational plan of April 1944 of the Krefeld Gestapo. But this plan provides very few details about their backgrounds. Although I have been able to obtain detailed information about only three of these men (Friedrich Fürschbach, Karl Homberg, and Heinrich Humburg), through their BDC-RuSHA records, it appears that most of them were

quite young in comparison with the rest of the officers in Krefeld, and that all of them were probably members of the SS and had long been committed Nazis. For example, according to Heinrich Humburg's BDC-RuSHA file (which he filled out in July 1939 when he was applying to join the SS), he was born in 1913 in Kassel and became a member of the SA at the age of twenty in 1933. In 1935 he left the SA and sometime shortly thereafter joined the SD in Reichenberg. He apparently had never served in the police force before he became a Gestapo officer in Krefeld during the war years. Hubertus Terpoorten and Fritz Steglich were also younger officers: Terpoorten was born in 1915, and Steglich in 1908.

75. Huiskes says that it was not until April 22, 1937, that the Cologne Gestapo actually used stationery designating it as "Geheime Staatspolizei: Staatspolizeistelle Köln." "Die Staatspolizeistelle Köln im EL-DE-Haus," 23.

76. In Schulenburg's denazification hearings, he tried at first to claim that he had been in the Gestapo only since 1938. The denazification authorities, however, rejected his claims and wrote that he had been "an executive officer of the Krefeld Gestapo from 1934 to 1945." HStAD, NW1037-BI 18164, Bl. 13.

77. Graf, *Politische Polizei zwischen Demokratie und Diktatur*, 171.

78. Marssolek and Ott, *Bremen im Dritten Reich*, 176.

79. HStAD, NW1049–74433. A former Bergheim resident related to me through a local archivist in May 1995 that he had the reputation in Bergheim of being "very nasty" (*sehr böse*).

80. HStAD, NW1049–73469.

81. BDC-RuSHA (Heinrich Humburg). The information on Terpoorten comes from the National Archives in Washington, D.C. (NARA, RG242, A3343-RS-C5218).

82. See, for example, Mallmann and Paul's discussion of the Saarbrücken Gestapo in *Herrschaft und Alltag*, 203–7; and the chapters on the Gestapo in Potsdam, Hannover, and Würzburg in Paul and Mallmann, *Die Gestapo: Mythos und Realität*.

83. See, for example, the BDC-RuSHA files of Gustav Burkert and Karl Homberg. Burkert never finished primary school and went on at great length in his curriculum vitae about all of the training courses he had attended. Homberg was defensive about his Slavic origins (he had changed his name from Przygodda) and his sister's mental health background.

84. This could be said of at least four of the nine Krefeld officers whose BDC-RuSHA files I have located. Effenberg's first wife died in 1936, leaving him with

four children, and his mother had died before he entered the SS. Fürschbach's mother died when he was ten years old. Fleischer's father's mother died in childbirth at age thirty-five. Heinrich Humburg's father's mother died at age forty-eight. Additionally, Karl Löffler of Cologne was brought up an orphan, and Richard Schulenburg, somewhat curiously, never mentioned his family in any of his extensive denazification and Interior Ministry documentation. There is not enough evidence here on which to build a theory, though one would suspect that the early loss of an important female figure harms an individual's emotional development. And being brought up by parents who lost their own mothers in their youth could have an effect on an individual.

85. Hannah Arendt, *Eichmann in Jerusalem: A Report on the Banality of Evil* (1963; New York, 1994).

86. Ibid., 25. The famous Nazi hunter Simon Wiesenthal also accepts that Eichmann was more or less normal, except that he believes that Eichmann had no human feeling. In his memoirs, Wiesenthal wrote: "Nearly everything about Eichmann remains incomprehensible. I spent years searching his personal history to find something that might explain why he became what he was. . . . He was not jilted by a Jewish girl or swindled by a Jewish merchant. He was probably honest when he said, at the trial, that he'd only done his job. He said he wouldn't have hesitated to send his own father into a gas chamber if he'd been ordered to do so. Eichmann's great strength was that he treated the Jewish problem unemotionally. He was the most dangerous man of all—a man with no human feeling. He once said he was not an anti-Semite. But he certainly was antihuman." Joseph Wechsberg, ed., *The Murderers Among Us: The Simon Wiesenthal Memoirs* (New York, 1967), 98–99. For a discussion of Eichmann's Rorschach inkblot test by experts in psychology and psychiatry, which supports Arendt's portrait of Eichmann as rather normal and even "banal," see Eric A. Zillmer et al., *The Quest for the Nazi Personality: A Psychological Investigation of Nazi War Criminals* (Hillsdale, N.J., 1995), 8–11. It should be noted, however, that the authors of this study find that many other Nazi criminals were not at all "normal" or "banal" psychologically.

87. Ibid., 22, 30.

88. Ibid., 29.

89. Ibid., 25, 276.

90. Ibid., 245.

91. Hangebruch, "Emigriert—Deportiert," 187.

92. Interview with Herbert K., Saddlebrook, New Jersey, July 28, 1995.

93. A man named Berger, for instance, met with Schulenburg to sign a form containing these words on November 26, 1941, two weeks before he and his entire family were deported to Riga (on December 12, 1941). The justification used by the Gestapo for taking his property away was the Reichstag Fire Decree of February 28, 1933. HStAD, RW58/64964.

94. See the testimony given on September 25, 1952, by a former secretary in the Cologne Gestapo who worked in the department of "Jewish affairs," in the investigation leading up to the Cologne deportation trial. HStADK, Rep. 231/512, Bl. 51.

95. Interview with Lore M., Krefeld, January 31, 1995.

96. HStAD, RW58/66125.

97. Arendt, *Eichmann in Jerusalem*, 29–65.

98. Ibid., 32.

99. HStADK, *Personalakten Sammelbestand*, Karl Löffler, BR PE/49505.

100. Interview with Lore M., Krefeld, January 31, 1995. For her Gestapo file, see HStAD, RW58/58239.

101. Interview with Herbert K., Saddlebrook, New Jersey, July 28, 1995.

102. There were no doubt many "bad cops." A reading of the Krefeld Gestapo case files reveals that Herbert Braun often seemed to play this role in the Krefeld Gestapo. Unfortunately, all I know about him is that he was born in 1900 in Königsberg, joined the Nazi Party in 1933, seemed never to have joined the SS (there is no BDC-RuSHA or BDC-SSO [SS Officers' Service Records] record on him), looked to be powerfully built from his photograph, and was clearly hostile toward Jews, as evidenced in several of the write-ups of the cases in which he was involved. In Cologne, however, somewhat more is known about a young man named Engels (born in Cologne on August 14, 1910), whom a fellow officer during the Cologne deportation trial called a "brutal swine" (HStADK, Rep. 231/512). In a case of crimes against humanity lodged against him after the war, he was called the "scourge of the Krefeld Jews." Jewish survivors at his trial charged him with pistol-whipping Jewish men in their cells, beating and kicking Jewish women as they were deported to Theresienstadt, and stealing money from Jews as they were about to be deported. He also had the reputation, they testified, of being extremely "bribable." HStADK, Rep. 231/217.

103. Interview with Max S., Cologne, March 1995. This man's experience was apparently not atypical. In his recently published diaries, Victor Klemperer, a Dresden Jew, reports that he was treated politely by a Gestapo officer during a

house search in June 1942. The Gestapo officer even addressed Klemperer by the formal German *Sie* instead of the informal *Du*, which Nazi officials typically used in addressing the Jews to put them down (the informal *Du* is otherwise used only for close friends, children, and animals). This made Klemperer at the time believe that "only the lower organs are so really nasty. If an officer is present, one has some protection." Klemperer's later encounters with the Gestapo, however, like those of other German Jews, were usually worse experiences. See *Ich will Zeugnis ablegen bis zum letzten: Tagebücher 1942–1945* (Berlin, 1995), 134.

104. Unless otherwise noted, the information on Löffler is from his personnel records, HStADK, BR PE/49505, and from his *Innenministerium* file, HStAD, NW130/252; the information on Schulenburg is from his two denazification files, HStAD, NW1037/BI 18164 and NW1023/6433.

105. See the discussion of police training in the Kaiserreich in Johnson, *Urbanization and Crime,* 34.

106. StAKr, Film B58, "Mitglieder-Liste der NSDAP in Krefeld." I learned about Schulenburg's association with the Anti-Semitic Party from Dieter Hangebruch, an archivist at the city archive in Krefeld and the author of "Emigriert—Deportiert."

107. Schulenburg's role with the local Nazi Party court further proves that he was an ardent Nazi and anti-Semite, even one of the leading Nazis in the Krefeld area. The judges on a Nazi Party court were most often leading members of the local Nazi Party who decided on admission and expulsion from the party and prosecuted offenses by party members. On the jurisdiction and functioning of these courts, see Donald M. McKale, *The Nazi Party Courts: Hitler's Management of Conflict in His Movement, 1921–1945* (Lawrence, Kan., 1974), esp. 121ff.

108. On the rise in Nazi Party membership in 1937, see Michael Kater, *The Nazi Party: A Social Profile of Members and Leaders, 1919–1945* (Oxford, 1983), esp. 91–93.

109. On the attempted and failed merger of SS and the Gestapo, see Mallmann and Paul, *Herrschaft und Alltag,* 195–97.

110. Herbert K., the son of the head of the Nuremberg Jewish community during the war, related that the head of the Nuremberg Gestapo desk had acted kindly toward his father, did not wear an SS uniform, and was an older man probably born in the 1880s. Interview, Saddlebrook, N.J., July 28, 1995. In Mönchengladbach the head of the Jewish desk appears to have been Gerhard

Dahmen. He was born in 1892, never joined the SS, was a member of the German Christian Movement, like Schulenburg, and also like Schulenburg, reached his highest rank of *Kriminalobersekretär* in 1941. The information on Dahmen comes from his denazification records, HStAD, NW1000–22547 and NW1037–A–13529. In Dresden, according to information provided by the keen observer Victor Klemperer, the head of the Jewish desk appears to have been Rudolf Müller, who also fits the profile of Schulenburg and Löffler. By 1943 Müller also held the rank of *Obersekretär*, dressed in civilian clothing, and often treated the Dresden Jews in a much more civil fashion than did the other Gestapo officers Klemperer encountered, two of whom Klemperer described as the *Spucker* (the spitter) and the *Schläger* (the beater). In his diary entry of August 2, 1943, Klemperer describes Müller and another officer he met in Dresden Gestapo headquarters. Dressed in civilian clothing, Müller was a "tall, middle-grade officer sitting at the desk, rather matter of fact, not aggressive." Next to him was "a small man in the doorway, sneering and crude." At first Klemperer seems to have been taken in by Müller, but he eventually caught on to Müller's deceitful guise. In his diary entry of February 28, 1945, Klemperer refers to Müller as "insidious." See *Ich will Zeugnis ablegen bis zum letzten*, 2:414, 688.

111. Interview with Lore M., Krefeld, January 31, 1995.

112. HstADK, BR PE/49505, *Personalakten Sammelbestand*. His doctor wrote that Löffler suffered from a "serious nervous disturbance culminating in heart problems." It is unclear what Löffler did in Belgium, though one suspects that he was involved in the deportation of the Belgian Jews, many of whom were from Germany. Löffler himself claimed at his denazification hearing that he was involved only in "bureaucratic matters."

113. Ibid.

114. HStAD, NW1023/6433.

115. Hangebruch, "Emigriert—Deportiert," 187.

116. See especially Robert Gellately, "Allwissend und allgegenwärtig?: Entstehung, Funktion, und Wandel des Gestapo-Mythos," in Paul and Mallmann, *Die Gestapo: Mythos und Realität*, 47–70; Klaus-Michael Mallmann and Gerhard Paul, "Allwissend, allmächtig, allgegenwärtig?: Gestapo, Gesellschaft, und Widerstand," *Zeitschrift für Geschichtswissenschaft* 41 (1993): 984–99.

117. Gerhard Paul and Klaus-Michael Mallmann's excellent work on the Gestapo in their study of resistance and persecution in the Saarland, *Herrschaft und Alltag*, and in their recent edited volume on the Gestapo in many localities,

Die Gestapo: Mythos und Realität, is somewhat of an exception. Still, most of the information on the backgrounds of Gestapo officers that they and the contributors to their volume provide is of a statistical nature, with relatively little emphasis placed on individual Gestapo officers.

118. The only mention of any of these men that I know of is a one-page treatment of Schulenburg in Hangebruch's "Emigriert—Deportiert," 187.

119. HStADK, Rep. 231/513, Bl. 208ff.

120. Paul, "Ganz normale Akademiker," 250. Paul buttresses his arguments by citing the social-pychological experimentation of Stanley Milgram, who supposedly showed that nearly any normal individual under the right conditions can be made into a murderer.

Chapter Three: The Course of Jewish Persecution in the Prewar Years

1. Interview with Lore M., Krefeld, January 31, 1995.

2. Telephone interview with Karl Muschkattblatt (now Charles T.), April 12, 1996.

3. HStAD, RW58/58239.

4. HStADK, Rep. 112/13237; interview with Muschkattblatt, April 12, 1996.

5. Interview with Lore M., January 31, 1995.

6. HStAD, RW58/30180 and RW58/37672.

7. Richard J. Evans argues in his authoritative study of capital punishment in Germany since 1600 that van der Lubbe set the fire on his own as "a dramatic protest against the recently appointed Nazi-conservative coalition government, and against the failure of the German Social Democrats and Communists to rise up in arms to overthrow it." *Rituals of Retribution: Capital Punishment in Germany 1600–1987* (Oxford, 1996), 619. Lothar Gruchmann, a leading expert on the history of Nazi justice, on the other hand, argued only a decade ago that the "issue is still disputed today." *Justiz im Dritten Reich: Anpassung und Unterwerfung in der ära Gürtner* (Munich, 1988), 535.

8. Gruchmann, *Justiz im Dritten Reich,* 535–37. On the police practice of using "protective custody" against enemies of the Nazi regime, see Klaus Drobisch and Günther Wieland, *System der NS-Konzentrationslager 1933–1939* (Berlin, 1993), 25–36.

9. Cited in Gruchmann, *Justiz im Dritten Reich,* 536–37.

10. Avraham Barkai, *From Boycott to Annihilation: The Economic Struggle*

of German Jews, 1933–1943, translated by William Templer (1987; Hanover, N. H., 1989), 9–12.

11. Ibid., xi.

12. Saul Friedländer, *Nazi Germany and the Jews,* vol. 1, *The Years of Persecution, 1933–1939* (New York, 1997), 18.

13. Adolf Klein, *Köln im Dritten Reich: Stadtgeschichte der Jahre 1933–1945* (Cologne, 1983), 94.

14. Barkai, *From Boycott to Annihilation,* 17.

15. Klein, *Köln im Dritten Reich,* 95–98.

16. Otto B.'s comments were sent to me along with a questionnaire he filled out and mailed on April 11, 1996.

17. Barkai, *From Boycott to Annihilation,* 19.

18. Barbara Becker-Jákli, ed., *Ich habe Köln doch so geliebt: Lebensgeschichten jüdischer Kölnerinnen und Kölner* (Cologne, 1993), 35.

19. Klein, *Köln im Dritten Reich,* 98.

20. Michael Burleigh and Wolfgang Wippermann, *The Racial State: Germany 1933–1945* (Cambridge, 1991), 78. Saul Friedländer, in his important study of Jews in Nazi Germany during the 1930s, rates the April boycott as a failure. *Nazi Germany and the Jews,* 26. David Bankier, in his study of German public opinion toward the Jews, argues on the basis of various governmental and non-governmental mood and morale reports that "although in general the public recognized the necessity for some solution to the Jewish problem, large sectors found the form of persecution abhorrent. The impression these accounts give is that the boycott failed to achieve its objective and that there were misgivings about the brutal methods employed." *The Germans and the Final Solution: Public Opinion Under Nazism* (Oxford, 1992), 68. In his highly respected study of Nazi popular opinion in Bavaria, Ian Kershaw says: "If it [the boycott] met with no opposition to speak of, the response of the public had been markedly cool." *Popular Opinion and Political Dissent in the Third Reich: Bavaria 1933–1945* (Oxford, 1983), 232.

21. Burleigh and Wippermann, *The Racial State,* 78–80.

22. The estimate of total Jewish population at the beginning of 1933 comes from Wolfgang Benz, ed., *Die Juden in Deutschland 1933–1945* (Munich, 1988), 733. The figure of 40,000 leaving the country in 1933 is from Barkai, *From Boycott to Annihilation,* 37. According to Benz's calculations, most of those who left in 1933 had done so already by mid-June 1933, when his figures show that less than 500,000 Jews remained in Germany.

23. Barkai, *From Boycott to Annihilation*, 37. See also Juliane Wetzel, "Auswanderung aus Deutschland," in Benz, *Die Juden in Deutschland 1933–1945*, 413–98.

24. The texts of many of these interviews are to be published in Eric A. Johnson and Karl-Heinz Reuband, *Life and Death in the Third Reich: Germans and Jews Remember* (New York, forthcoming).

25. Wetzel, "Auswanderung aus Deutschland," 426.

26. Dieter Hangebruch, "Emigriert—Deportiert: Das Schicksal der Juden in Krefeld zwischen 1933 und 1945," *Krefelder Studien* 2 (1980): 197–98.

27. Konrad Kwiet and Helmut Eschwege, *Selbstbehauptung und Widerstand: Deutsche Juden im Kampf um Existenz und Menschenwürde 1933–1945* (Hamburg, 1984), 53; Wetzel, "Auswanderung aus Deutschland."

28. See, for example, Ingo Müller, *Hitler's Justice: The Courts of the Third Reich*, translated by Deborah Lucas Schneider (Cambridge, Mass., 1991), 90–119; and Ralph Angermund, *Deutsche Richterschaft 1919–1945* (Frankfurt am Main, 1990), 104–32.

29. In a random sample of the Krefeld Gestapo case files, I read every eighth file. This produced a total of 433 case files, of which 96 were the files of Krefeld Jews. There are therefore approximately 768 Jewish case files for the city of Krefeld, which had only about 1,500 Jewish citizens in 1933.

30. Based on my random sample of Gestapo case files, there were an estimated 2,500 cases lodged against non-Jewish Krefelders. Dividing this figure by 150,000 (total Krefeld population), one arrives at the ratio of one in sixty.

31. HStAD, RW58/19359. For a discussion of the Jews involved in Communist Party resistance activities, see Kwiet and Eschwege, *Selbstbehauptung und Widerstand*, 76–80, 92–101.

32. HStAD, RW58/62732.

33. HStAD, RW58/24266 and RW58/28745.

34. HStAD, RW58/54083.

35. HStAD, RW58/52226.

36. HStAD, RW58/29471. Another case, involving a minor transgression of the foreign currency laws, was lodged against her in 1937 but later dismissed.

37. On the importance of denunciations in starting Gestapo cases, see Robert Gellately, *The Gestapo and German Society: Enforcing Racial Policy 1933–1945* (Oxford, 1990), 130–58; and Reinhard Mann, *Protest und Kontrolle im Dritten Reich: Nationalsozialistische Herrschaft im Alltag einer rheinischen Grossstadt* (Frankfurt am Main, 1987), 287–301.

38. HStAD, RW58/57857 and RW58/58210.

39. HStAD, RW58/29369 and RW58/11560.

40. HStAD, RW58/32825.

41. HStAD, RW58/32821. This case once again illustrates the importance of the Gestapo's spy and surveillance network in cases involving alleged Communist activity on the part of Jews. The case began in August 1934 when an SD *Vertrauensmann* (spy) from the Saar district noticed a car with a Krefeld license plate parked outside a building where Communist sympathizers were thought to congregate. In November the car was tracked to a thirty-year-old Jewish traveling salesman from Krefeld named Georg G. The salesman was watched for the next two and a half years, but nothing of a damning nature could be found against him. In March 1937 the Krefeld political police (they would not be officially called the Gestapo until a few months later) ordered that mail for both Georg G. and his father be intercepted for one month. When this also provided nothing of importance, the postal surveillance was lifted. Georg G. continued to be watched over, however, for at least another year. A note in his file shows that in March 1938 the Düsseldorf Gestapo headquarters contacted the Krefeld Gestapo about the owner of a car with a Krefeld license plate that was observed in Saarbrücken "parked in front of an apartment of a Jew." The Krefeld Gestapo then wrote back that the car was owned by Georg G., who was a Jew himself but had a clean record. In February 1939, Georg G. emigrated to Shanghai.

42. Its official name was the "law against malicious attacks (*heimtückische Angriffe*) on the state and party and for the protection of party uniforms." An earlier version was passed by decree on March 21, 1933. On the law and its application, see Angermund, *Deutsche Richterschaft*, 133–57; and Peter Hüttenberger, "Heimtückefälle vor dem Sondergericht München 1933–1939," in Martin Broszat et al., eds., *Bayern in der NS-Zeit: Herrschaft und Gesellschaft im Konflikt*, vol. 4 (Munich, 1981), 435–526.

43. HStAD, RW58/22706.

44. HStAD, RW58/21382.

45. HStADK, Rep. 112/1013.

46. HStAD, RW58/24267 and RW58/24268.

47. HStADK, Rep. 112/2737.

48. Cited in J. Noakes and G. Pridham, eds., *Nazism 1919–1945: A Documentary Reader*, vol. 2, *State, Economy, and Society 1933–1939* (Exeter, U.K., 1984), 530.

49. On these laws and the events surrounding them, see Uwe Adam, *Judenpol-itik im Dritten Reich* (Düsseldorf, 1972), esp. 125–44.

50. In an unpublished autobiography, Kurt Gimnicher (now living under an-other name) writes: "The boycott of Jewish stores had a slow start in Kref-eld. . . . In August [1935] Nazi SA troopers posted watches in front of every Jewish-owned store in the city, trying to prevent customers from going in. If customers still wanted to enter the store, the storm troopers did not hold them back by force, but took their pictures in order to blackmail them. The whole thing got out of hand and the situation finally died down to almost normal. Many Jewish storekeepers started to sell out, though, and the percentage of Jewish enterprises went lower and lower." "Prelude to Freedom: An Autobiog-raphy" (unpublished manuscript, n.d.), 7. Avraham Barkai discusses how these boycotts throughout Germany in the summer of 1935 led to such a stir in the foreign press that the regime decided it had to end them to ensure the success of the upcoming Berlin Olympic games. *From Boycott to Annihilation*, 56–57.

51. Angermund, *Deutsche Richterschaft*, 125. For a description of the events surrounding the formulation of the Nuremberg Laws, see Raul Hilberg, *The Destruction of the European Jews* (New York, 1961), 46–53. For the text of the laws themselves, see Brita Eckert, *Die jüdische Emigration aus Deutschland 1933–1941: Die Geschichte einer Austreibung* (Frankfurt am Main, 1995), 76–77.

52. Angermund, *Deutsche Richterschaft*, 110–11. According to Angermund, the number of mixed marriages finally receded in 1934 to 15 percent.

53. Hilberg, *The Destruction of the European Jews*, 47.

54. For a more detailed discussion of the definition of Jews and *Mischlinge*, and for the subsequent treatment of the *Mischlinge*, see ibid., 48, 268–77; and H. G. Adler, *Der Verwaltete Mensch: Studien zur Deportation der Juden aus Deutschland* (Tübingen, 1974), 278–322.

55. Noakes and Pridham, *Nazism 1919–1945*, 548.

56. HStADK, Rep. 8/6.

57. It is not always possible to determine which officer handled a particular case, though of the more than one hundred investigations lodged against Kref-eld Jews and investigated by the Krefeld Gestapo (or "political police," as it was called until August 1937), Schulenburg handled at least twenty-nine, Burkert eleven, Braun ten, Schommer nine, and Schmitz six. Additionally, the names of sixteen other officers appear in at least one case. These figures underestimate

Schulenburg's role, however, because they pertain only to cases involving an alleged offense. Schulenburg's role was even greater in the hundreds of other Gestapo case files involving the emigration, regulation, and deportation of the Krefeld Jews.

58. Noakes and Pridham, *Nazism 1919–1945*, 547; Barkai, *From Boycott to Annihilation*, 54.

59. Deborah E. Lipstadt, *Beyond Belief: The American Press and the Coming of the Holocaust 1933–1945* (New York, 1986), 63.

60. Cited in ibid., 80.

61. HStADK, Rep. 112/13237.

62. The active role of the Krefeld population in initiating *Rassenschande* cases was no anomaly. Robert Gellately analyzed eighty-four *Rassenschande* cases in the city of Würzburg and found that the majority were begun by reports from the population and that none were brought to the Gestapo's attention by paid informers or agents. *The Gestapo and German Society*, 162. See also Hans Robinsohn, *Justiz als politische Verfolgung: Die Rechtssprechung in "Rassenschandefällen" beim Landgericht Hamburg 1936–1943* (Stuttgart, 1977); and Hans-Christian Lassen, "Der Kampf gegen Homosexualität, Abtreibung, und 'Rassenschande': Sexualdelikte vor Gericht in Hamburg 1933–1939," in Klaus Bästlein, Helge Grabitz, and Wolfgang Scheffler, eds., *"Für Führer, Volk, und Vaterland . . . ": Hamburger Justiz im Nationalsozialismus* (Hamburg, 1992), 281–87.

63. Eighty-three percent of the Krefeld Gestapo case files in 1933 and 1934 in which a Jew was investigated for alleged illegal activity had a directly political nature; cases of "Communist activity" (*Kommunistische Betätigung*) were the most common. In 1936 and 1937 only 24 percent of the cases started against Jews were of a political nature, and there were no registered cases of "Communist activity." In this later period, the most common offense for which a Jew was charged was *Rassenschande*, followed closely by violations of the currency and financial regulations (*Devisenvergehen*).

64. Angermund, *Deutsche Richterschaft*, 125–29.

65. Ibid., 128–29.

66. Noakes and Pridham, *Nazism 1919–1945*, 540.

67. Burleigh and Wippermann, *The Racial State*, 84.

68. See, for example, HStAD, RW58/54900.

69. This is, of course, a broad generalization that is not meant to undercount

either the barbarous treatment that many German women received at the
hands of the Gestapo or the real suffering that many German women experienced in Nazi Germany. For a treatment of the Nazis' forced sterilization policy,
for example, see Gisela Bock, *Zwangsterilisation im Nationalsozialismus:
Studien zur Rassenpolitik und Frauenpolitik* (Opladen, 1986). For some case
histories of German women who stood up to the Nazi dictatorship, see Gerda
Szepansky, *Frauen leisten Widerstand: 1933–1945: Lebensgeschichten nach
Interviews und Dokumenten* (Frankfurt am Main, 1983). For general assessments of women under Nazi rule, see Claudia Koonz, *Mothers in the Fatherland: Women, the Family, and Nazi Politics* (London, 1987); and Ute Frevert,
*Women in German History: From Bourgeois Emancipation to Sexual Libera-
tion,* translated by Stuart McKinnon-Evans (New York, 1988), 207–52.
70. HStAD, RW58/60839 and RW58/45957.
71. The date of her emigration is provided in the listing of the fate of Krefeld
Jews provided in Hangebruch, "Emigriert—Deportiert," but the page reference
is held back to protect her anonymity.
72. HStAD, RW58/28780 and RW58/62659.
73. For detailed analyses of gender differences in Nazi prosecution practices,
see my "German Women and Nazi Justice: Their Role in the Process from Denunciation to Death," *Historical Social Research (Historische Sozialforschung)* 20 (1995): 33–69; and "Gender, Race, and the Gestapo," *Historical
Social Research (Historische Sozialforschung)* 22 (1997): 240–53.
74. She was listed as 1.73 meters tall (about five foot eight) and "slender" in
her Gestapo case files. The photographs taken of her for these files show her to
have been a strikingly attractive woman. In addition to the case of Rosemarie
G., see also those of returning Krefeld Jews like Paul M. (HStAD, RW58/
30187), who was sent to Esterwegen concentration camp in January 1936, and
Julius S., who spent several months in Dachau in late 1938 and early 1939
(HStAD, RW58/3210). Additional evidence of Schulenburg's solicitude in
cases involving attractive women is provided in the interview I conducted with
Lore M., a woman of mixed Jewish and non-Jewish parentage, in Krefeld on
January 31, 1995. Lore was a very attractive young woman at the time of her
first interrogation with Schulenburg in 1940. Denounced for carrying on illegal
affairs with German soldiers in violation of the racial laws, she might have expected to suffer a horrible ordeal in Gestapo headquarters. But Schulenburg
received her in an almost friendly fashion and treated her with considerable
respect. He even arranged to have her interrogation take place on a Sunday

when the other officers were not present so as to make the experience less frightening. HStAD, RW58/30456 and RW58/24100.

75. Anselm Faust, *Die "Kristallnacht" im Rheinland: Dokumente zum Juden-pogrom im November 1838* (Düsseldorf, 1987), 29; Noakes and Pridham, *Na-zism 1919–1945*, 551.

76. Schacht believed that open anti-Semitism could harm German business in-terests. Although he was acquitted in the Nuremberg Trials and protested vocif-erously during the trial against any suggestion that he was an anti-Semite, his codefendants and the American psychologist ministering to his mental health during the trial were less convinced of this. In the lunchroom during a pause in Schacht's defense testimony, Baldur von Schirach was overheard by the psy-chologist as saying to several of the other defendants: "As for his pretending that he was a democrat and not an anti-Semite—the less said about that the better." G. M. Gilbert, *Nuremberg Diary* (1947; New York, 1995), 316ff.

77. Noakes and Pridham, *Nazism 1919–1945*, 551–52.

78. Faust, *Die 'Kristallnacht' im Rheinland*, 29. Wetzel calculates that about "1,500 Jews, so-called asocial elements, were arrested." "Auswanderung aus Deutschland," 427. In Krefeld, for example, three Jewish men with prior crimi-nal records were arrested in August 1938 and sent to Sachsenhausen concentra-tion camp. They were let out in October after having made firm plans to emi-grate, and their property was confiscated when they left. The value of the property of one of these men was the considerable sum of 35,500 Reichmarks. HStAD, RW58/55365 and RW58/42080. On the persecution of the "asocials" in general, see Buleigh and Wipperman, *The Racial State*, 167–97.

79. Joachim Remak, ed., *The Nazi Years: A Documentary History* (Englewood Cliffs, N.J., 1969), 150–51.

80. See, for example, HStADK, Rep. 112/3538, Rep. 112/3559, and Rep. 112/8353.

81. Hangebruch, "Emigriert—Deportiert," 198.

82. Rein's letter is reprinted in the third volume (pp. 65–67) of a four-volume collection published in a limited edition by the Krefeld Stadt Archiv for the city of Krefeld consisting of letter exchanges between former Krefeld Jews and Krefeld schoolchildren and talks delivered during visits by former Krefeld Jews to Krefeld schools in the 1980s; see Stadt Krefeld, *Krefelder Juden in Amerika: Dokumentation eines Briefwechsels*, vol. 1 (Krefeld, 1984); *Vor dem Besuch in Krefeld—29. Juni bis 7. Juli 1987: Briefe ehemaliger Krefelder Juden an Schüler des Gymnasiums am Moltkeplatz*, vol. 2 (Krefeld, n.d.); *Ehemalige Krefelder*

Juden berichten über ihre Erlebnisse in der sogenannten Reichskristallnacht, vol. 3 (Krefeld, 1988); and *Ehemalige Krefelder Juden im Gespräch mit Krefelder Schülern 1987,* vol. 4 (Krefeld, 1988).

83. Reprinted in Stadt Krefeld, *Ehemalige Krefelder Juden im Gespräch mit Krefelder Schülern 1987* (vol. 4), 31.

84. Gellately, *The Gestapo and German Society,* 114.

85. Lipstadt, *Beyond Belief,* 98ff.

86. For Germany in general, see Rita Thalmann and Emmanuel Feinermann, *Die Kristallnacht* (Frankfurt am Main, 1988; originally published in 1974 in French as *Le nuit de cristal*); and Anthony Read and David Fischer, *Kristallnacht: The Nazi Night of Terror* (New York, 1989). For a documentary history of the pogrom in the Rhineland, see Faust, *Die 'Kristallnacht' im Rheinland.* For the reminiscences of many Cologne Jews, see Becker-Jákli, *Ich habe Köln doch so geliebt.* For the city of Krefeld, see Dieter Hangebruch's extensive discussion in "Emigriert—Deportiert," 201–27; and the Krefeld Stadt Archiv series on the experiences of Krefeld Jews, especially *Ehemalige Krefelder Juden berichten über ihre Erlebnisse in der sogenannten Reichskristallnacht,* vol. 3.

87. HStAD, RW36/9. A text of this order to the Gestapo and a valuable discussion of how the Krefeld Gestapo implemented it is provided by Hangebruch, "Emigriert—Deportiert," 203ff.

88. Ibid.

89. Ibid., 227.

90. For examples, see HStAD, RW58/33980, RW58/26105, RW58/6416, and RW58/26145.

91. Hangebruch, "Emigriert—Deportiert," 198, 227.

92. Ian Kershaw argues in his study of popular attitudes in Nazi Germany that the German populace reacted to the pogrom with "a broad swell of disapproval. . . . Goebbels's claim that the pogrom had been the 'spontaneous answer' of the German people to the murder of vom Rath was universally recognized as ludicrous." *Popular Opinion and Political Dissent in the Third Reich,* 262–63.

93. Kurt Frank, letter to Krefeld schoolchildren, June 4, 1988, reprinted in Stadt Krefeld, *Ehemalige Krefelder Juden berichten über ihre Erlebnisse in der sogenannten Reichskristallnacht,* 3:11–12.

94. Hilberg, *The Destruction of the European Jews,* 24.

95. Hangebruch, "Emigriert—Deportiert," 223.

96. Noakes and Pridham, *Nazism 1919–1945,* 558–59.

97. Hilberg, *The Destruction of the European Jews*, 29.

98. Hangebruch, "Emigriert—Deportiert," 224. In the small town of Bergheim, the home of a single, seventy-six-year-old Jewish man was broken into on November 12 and further devastated even though the furniture in his apartment had already been destroyed on November 10 and he was lying in the hospital from the beating he had taken. HStADK, Rep. 112/3749.

99. The newspaper report was actually published on April 22, 1939, in the *Westdeutsche Zeitung*. The man who stood outside was only given a fine, but the other two men received jail sentences of several months.

100. Ernst Hirsch, letter to Krefeld schoolchildren, April 1, 1988, reprinted in Stadt Krefeld, *Ehemalige Krefelder Juden berichten über ihre Erlebnisse in der sogenannten Reichskristallnacht*, 3:61–64.

101. Noakes and Pridham, *Nazism 1919–1945*, 560–61. For these and other measures taken against the Jews in November 1938, see Friedländer, *Nazi Germany and the Jews*, 284ff.

102. Burleigh and Wippermann, *The Racial State*, 93.

103. In February 1939, an eighteen-year-old Jewish boy from Krefeld was sent to Dachau. He had been arrested by the Aachen Gestapo at the end of January while he was trying to cross the border into Belgium. After three months in Dachau and after his father provided proof that he had paid for his son's passage to England, he was released. HStAD, RW58/61485 and RW58/45959.

104. Sixty-three percent of Jewish cases with the Krefeld Gestapo involving alleged illegal activities on the part of Krefeld Jews in 1936 and 1937 were started by reports from the civilian population, but only 31 percent of the cases began this way in 1939.

105. HStAD, RW58/33980.

106. HStAD, RW58/26105 and RW58/6416. Dieter Hangebruch, in an appendix to his "Emigriert—Deportiert," has made a painstaking effort to determine what eventually happened to each Jewish Krefelder. Jakob D. died in 1943 in Theresienstadt concentration camp. His wife Luise and son Hans also died somewhere in the east.

CHAPTER FOUR: A CLOSER LOOK

1. The prevalence of anti-Semitism in Germany is the subject of enormous controversy, especially since the publication of Daniel Jonah Goldhagen's highly-controversial work *Hitler's Willing Executioners: Ordinary Germans*

and the Holocaust (New York, 1996). Goldhagen argues that the Holocaust was made possible by an "eliminationist antisemitic German political culture" that had characterized German society long before Hitler came to power and only became more virulent during the Nazi period. Others who have studied German public opinion hold different views of the prevalence and virulence of anti-Semitism even in the Third Reich. The British scholar Ian Kershaw, for example, argues that "much points towards the conclusion that, despite its centrality to Hitler's own thinking, anti-Semitism was for the most part of no more than secondary importance as a factor shaping popular opinion in the Third Reich." *The Hitler Myth: Image and Reality in the Third Reich* (Oxford, 1987), 230. See also his *Popular Opinion and Political Dissent in the Third Reich: Bavaria 1933–1945* (Oxford, 1983). For the historical background of German anti-Semitism, see James F. Harris, *The People Speak!: Anti-Semitism and Emancipation in Nineteenth-Century Bavaria* (Ann Arbor, Mich., 1994); and Jacob Katz, *From Prejudice to Destruction: Anti-Semitism, 1700–1933* (Cambridge, Mass., 1980). For a balanced treatment of the historiography on the subject, see Michael R. Marrus, *The Holocaust in History* (London, 1987), 85–94.

2. For the published sentiments of some Cologne and Krefeld survivors, see Barbara Becker-Jákli, *Ich habe Köln doch so geliebt: Lebensgeschichten jüdischer Kölnerinnen und Kölner* (Cologne, 1983), and the four-volume collection of letters between surviving Krefeld Jews and Krefeld schoolchildren, published by the Krefeld Stadt Archiv (see ch. 3, n. 82). For the sentiments of some prominent Hamburg Jews, compare the different viewpoints of members of the famous Hamburg banking family, the Warburgs, in Ron Chernow's *The Warburgs* (New York, 1993).

3. The survey that the Krefeld survivors answered is similar to a larger survey developed by Karl-Heinz Reuband, a German sociologist and expert in opinion research, and myself in 1994. With the help of the research staff of the U.S. Holocaust Memorial Museum and the National Registry of Jewish Holocaust Survivors, we mailed this survey in late 1994 and early 1995 to about 1,500 Jewish survivors who now live all over the globe but previously lived in cities throughout Germany. Reuband and I will be publishing the results of this earlier survey (not yet fully analyzed) in a forthcoming book. I alone administered the present survey of surviving Krefeld Jews while I was a member of the School of Social Science at the Institute for Advanced Study in Princeton in 1996. The names and addresses were provided to me by one of the Krefeld survivors, John Rosing, to whom I am extremely grateful.

4. In conducting the survey, I followed a modified version of the design developed by Don Dillman, published in his *Mail and Telephone Surveys: The Total Design Method* (New York, 1978). The most significant difference between my survey and Dillman's suggested method for receiving an optimal response rate is that I sent out only one reminder instead of two, as Dillman suggests. Because of the extremely sensitive nature of the questions in the survey, I decided it was sufficient to send one reminder thanking the respondents for answering if they had done so already but also asking them to consider answering if they had not. An additional reminder might have resulted in a few more responses, but the psychological cost would have been high for those people who were not answering because they did not want to be bothered by such an unpleasant subject.

5. Letter of Helma T., May 4, 1996. She went on to relate that her mother had died young and her father had been gassed in Stutthof concentration camp shortly before the end of the war. A foundation created by the noted filmmaker Stephen Spielberg—Survivors of the Shoah, Visual History Foundation—is taping interviews with thousands of Jewish Holocaust survivors around the world.

6. Figures on the emigration of Krefeld Jews are provided in Dieter Hangebruch, "Emigriert—Deportiert: Das Schicksal der Juden in Krefeld zwischen 1933 und 1945," *Krefelder Studien* 2 (1980): 198. The years 1938 and 1939 were also the peak time for Jewish emigration in Germany in general. See Herbert A. Strauss, "Jewish Emigration from Germany: Nazi Policies and Jewish Responses," *Yearbook of the Leo Baeck Institute* 25 and 26 (1980 and 1981): 313–61, 343–409.

7. Otto B. explained in his letter to me that the young girl recanted her testimony when the case went to court, thus, in his opinion, saving his life. In a letter of February 4, 1983, to a Krefeld schoolgirl, Otto B. elaborates on the case as an example of the basic decency of many Krefeld citizens. "There was a trend toward hating Jews long before Hitler appeared. But there were also many Krefelders who stood by us, and me in particular, precisely in the time of dire distress. I was the head clerk of my parents' business (Lebensmittel-Feinkost-Rheinstrasse)—two houses next to us was the *Nationalsozialistische Deutsche Arbeiterzeitung.* One day an article appeared in this National Socialist newspaper and in *Stürmer* that I "Jude B.," had raped a sixteen-year-old girl in the basement of our building. She had testified under oath that this was the truth. I was not aware that I had done anything wrong and I tried to hire a defense attorney, but no one defended a Jew. So on the day of the trial I prepared myself

for the worst and carried a suitcase along with me to the court. When the judge questioned "Lucia B." if she confirmed her sworn testimony, she replied: "*No, I was forced to make and sign the false report. I have spoken with my parents and our minister, and I will take the consequences, but I cannot live with a lie.*" Otto B.'s letter is published in Stadt Krefeld, *Krefelder Juden in Amerika: Dokumentation eines Briefwechsels,* 1:21.

8. In Heinz L.'s words, after 1933 his family was "shunned completely and the citizens loved the Nazis."

9. Telephone interview with Werner H., June 5, 1996. Although Werner H. did not fill out the questionnaire, he provided a wealth of important information in his interview. For his case files with the Gestapo, see HStAD, RW58/55235 and RW58/53602.

10. Letter of Helma T., May 4, 1996.

11. Eric A. Johnson and Karl-Heinz Reuband, "Die populäre Einschätzung der Gestapo: Wie allgegenwärtig war sie wirklich?," in Gerhard Paul and Klaus-Michael Mallmann, eds., *Die Gestapo: Mythos und Realität* (Darmstadt, 1995), 432.

12. For analyses of Gestapo cases involving friendship between Jews and non-Jews, see Robert Gellately, *The Gestapo and German Society: Enforcing Racial Policy 1933–1945* (Oxford, 1990), esp. 160–65; and Sarah Gordon, *Hitler, Germans, and the "Jewish Question"* (Princeton, N.J., 1984).

13. Kurt Gimnicher, "Prelude to Freedom: An Autobiography" (unpublished manuscript, n.d.), 8.

14. Daniel Jonah Goldhagen, *Hitler's Willing Executioners: Ordinary Germans and the Holocaust* (New York, 1996).

15. For Jewish crime rates in Imperial Germany, see Eric A. Johnson, *Urbanization and Crime: Germany 1871–1914* (New York, 1995), 201–5.

16. Johnson and Reuband, "Die populäre Einschätzung der Gestapo," 434.

17. The similarities between Germans and Jews have been noted by many. See, for example, Gordon Craig's essay "Germans and Jews" in his book *The Germans* (New York, 1982), 126–46; Erich Kahler, "The Jews and the Germans," in Max Kreutzberger, ed., *Studies of the Leo Baeck Institute* (New York, 1967), 19–43; and George L. Mosse, *Germans and Jews: The Right, the Left, and the Search for a "Third Force" in Pre-Nazi Germany* (New York, 1970).

18. Letter of E. H. Hirsch, April 1, 1988, reprinted in Stadt Krefeld, *Ehemalige Krefelder Juden berichten über ihre Erlebnisse in der sogenannten Reichskristallnacht,* 3:62.

19. On the establishment and jurisdiction of the Special Courts in the Third Reich, see Hans Wüllenweber, *Sondergerichte im Dritten Reich: Vergessene Verbrechen der Justiz* (Frankfurt am Main, 1990); Ingo Müller, *Hitler's Justice: The Courts of the Third Reich*, translated by Deborah Lucas Schneider (Cambridge, Mass., 1991), 153–73; and Ralph Angermund, *Deutsche Richterschaft 1919–1945: Krisenerfahrung, Illusion, politische Rechtsprechung* (Frankfurt am Main, 1990), 137–40.

20. The Krefeld Gestapo passed on to the courts only 32 percent of the Jewish cases it investigated between 1933 and 1939 involving alleged illegal behavior on the part of Jews. But often, as argued later, this was not the "harshest outcome": though the courts would frequently dismiss these cases, the Gestapo would then sometimes either place the Jews in protective custody or send them to a concentration camp.

21. A Jewish Krefeld printer named Josef M., for example, was quite clearly put to death on September 1, 1943, by the Düsseldorf Gestapo immediately after it received word from higher authorities in Berlin that Jews no longer had the right to be tried in court and that it was to decide the outcome of the case by itself. The official cause of Josef M.'s death, however, was a "heart attack." HStAD, RW58/869, Bl. 118.

22. In the random sample of Cologne Special Court cases between 1933 and 1939, 64 percent of Jewish cases were dismissed before going to trial, and an additional 14 percent involved investigations that involved Jews who were never even charged with any wrongdoing and that also did not go to trial. An additional 7 percent of the cases led to acquittals after a trial, and only 11 percent led to convictions (it was not possible to determine the end result in 4 percent of the cases). It must be stressed here, however, that these figures are not out of line with the results in non-Jewish cases. An even higher percentage of these cases were dismissed (83 percent) and the percentage of cases leading to convictions or acquittals after a court trial were 11 percent and 2 percent, respectively.

23. In a random sample of 290 individuals investigated by the Krefeld Gestapo between 1933 and 1939, Jews comprised 17.2 percent of the total. In that Jews represented less than 1 percent of the Krefeld population in 1933, and even less than this with each passing year, it is clear that Jews were many times more likely than non-Jews to have a Gestapo case of one type or another lodged against them. In a random sample of 416 case files of the Cologne Special Court between 1933 and 1939, Jews comprised 6.7 percent of the total. Since the proportion of Jewish to non-Jewish residents in the Cologne area was roughly the

same as in Krefeld, it is apparent that Jews there were also far more likely than non-Jews to have a court case lodged against them.

24. On the massive arrests of German Communists after the Reichstag Fire, see Detlev Peukert, *Die KPD im Widerstand: Verfolgung und Untergrundarbeit an Rhein und Ruhr 1933–1945* (Wuppertal, 1980), 71–97.

25. On detention in protective custody and concentration camps generally in this period, see Klaus Drobisch and Günther Wieland, *System der NS-Konzentrationslager 1933–1939* (Berlin, 1993).

26. In one case, a thirty-five-year-old Jewish businessman was reported to the Krefeld police for riding around the city with two "Aryan" women in his car on the evening of March 19, 1936. When the police called the man in to testify, they found out that one of the women indeed had a "very Aryan appearance [with] light blond hair." But they also found out that both she and the other woman in the car were Jewish. So they dismissed the case. HStAD, RW58/58989. In another case involving the suspicion that race defilement was being committed, a twenty-nine-year-old Jewish dentist was denounced by a man living in his apartment house for frequently having sex with a German woman in his apartment. On August 3, 1936, the denouncer called the Krefeld *Staatspolizei* and reported that "a blond female person is in his [the Jewish dentist's] apartment" and that "this female person is scantily clad." Kriminalassistent Schommer, who investigated both this and the other case involving a blond woman, let the dentist go after determining that his companion, although she had "light blond hair," was "in fact a Jewess." HStAD, RW58/24301.

27. Sometimes the Gestapo and the court authorities seemed to understand the difficult predicament Jews were in regarding the Hitler greeting and let them go. Other times Jews were punished severely. In one case, a fifty-six-year-old Jewish salesman was denounced in August 1938 for having said "Heil Hitler" after entering the mayor's office in the small village of Linnich outside Krefeld. After he explained to Kriminalsekretär Schulenburg of the Krefeld Gestapo that he had done so only after noticing a sign in the office reminding everyone to use the Hitler greeting upon entering, and that he had "really not known that the greeting 'Heil Hitler' was forbidden for Jews," Schulenburg dismissed the case after administering a severe warning. HStAD, RW58/66987 and RW58/40887. In another case, a forty-three-year-old Jewish traveling salesman was denounced in January 1939 to the Gestapo by a pawn-shop owner for using the Hitler greeting upon entering his shop. In his defense, the Jewish man testified to the Gestapo that he had gone into the shop to sell off some of

his possessions in preparation for emigration and that he had used the greeting so as not to compromise the pawn-shop owner in public for dealing with Jews. The case was soon dismissed by the state prosecuting attorney. HStAD, RW58/ 33930 and RW58/65184. But in another case, which took place in July 1938, a twenty-nine-year-old Jewish clothing-store owner was put in protective custody and later sent to Dachau concentration camp after he had said "Heil Hitler" to the head of a health insurance office. What probably made things worse for him was that, as the son of Polish Jews, he had been declared "stateless." HStAD, RW58/23939.

28. An analysis of the Cologne Special Court data largely confirms the trends noted for Krefeld. Of the 28 cases lodged against Jews in the random sample taken between 1933 and 1939, there were an average of 3.3 cases per year between 1933 and 1935 and 4.5 cases per year between 1936 and 1939. Most of the cases in the first three-year period involved political libel or slander (8 out 10 cases). But, after 1935, there were only two more cases of this type. After 1935, most of the cases involved accusations that Jews had committed morals offenses like race defilement (5 cases), had illegally displayed Nazi insignia, or had failed to refer to themselves by the mandated "Jewish" names of Israel or Sara.

29. Robert Gellately's *The Gestapo and German Society* has served as the catalyst for formal studies of political denunciation in both Nazi Germany and many other lands. Most recently, Gellately has expanded his original study of political denunciations in Jewish cases in the city of Würzburg to an analysis of political denunciations in other cities and milieus, including political denunciations in postwar East Germany. Of special importance is a recent special issue of the *Journal of Modern History*, introduced by Gellately and Sheila Fitzpatrick, that contains studies of political denunciations in several countries and an excellent overview article by Gellately summarizing some of his most recent research findings and those of other scholars working on Nazi Germany and the German Democratic Republic. Gellately, "Denunciations in Twentieth-Century Germany: Aspects of Self-Policing in the Third Reich and the German Democratic Republic," *Journal of Modern History* 68 (1996): 931–67. For another important summary article on recent research on this theme, see Gisela Diewald-Kerkmann, "Denunziantentum und Gestapo: Die freiwilligen 'Helfer' aus der Bevölkerung," in Gerhard Paul and Klaus-Michael Mallmann, eds., *Die Gestapo: Mythos und Realität* (Darmstadt, 1995), 288–305.

30. Gellately, *The Gestapo and German Society*, 162ff. Displays of friendship between Jews and non-Jews were outlawed on November 24, 1941.

31. Ibid., 163.

32. Gellately, "Denunciations in Twentieth-Century Germany," 938, 966, and passim. Among the studies of political denunciation he cites to make his argument are some of my own, especially my essay "Gender, Race, and the Gestapo," *Historical Social Research/Historische Sozialforschung* 22 (1997): 240–53.

33. Unfortunately, little of a systematic nature is known about Gestapo spies, and there is only one monograph on the subject, which itself is controversial and probably unreliable because of its speculative and unscientific nature. Walter Otto Weyrauch, *Gestapo V-Leute: Tatsachen und Theorie des Geheimdienstes* (Frankfurt am Main, 1989). For a trustworthy discussion of what has been established by reliable scholars on the subject, see Klaus-Michael Mallmann, "Die V-Leute der Gestapo: Umrisse einer kollektiven Biographie," in Paul and Mallmann, *Die Gestapo: Mythos und Realität*, 268–87.

34. See, for example, HStAD, RS58/21813 and RW58/29393, for the case of a young Krefeld woman of mixed parentage who was sent to Auschwitz for not wearing her Jewish star in public in August 1942. She had been turned in by a fifteen-year-old neighbor girl appointed by the Gestapo to spy on her.

35. For examples, see HStAD, RW58/32823, RW58/28010, RW58/49628, and RW58/49628.

36. In 1940, for example, at least some form of spying or surveillance was involved in all of the cases that the Krefeld Gestapo initiated against Jews and part-Jews.

37. Peter Wyden, *Stella* (New York, 1992).

38. Richard Grunberger, *A Social History of the Third Reich* (New York, 1974), 147. On the prosecution of false informers, see my paper "German Women and Nazi Justice: Their Role in the Process from Denunciation to Death," *Historical Social Research/Historische Sozialforschung* 20 (1995): 33–69.

39. Not all will agree with my assessment of the typical nature of denouncers. Gisela Diewald-Kerkmann, for example, argues in an essay based on her doctoral dissertation, published as *Politische Denunziation im NS-Regime oder die kleine Macht der "Volksgenossen"* (Bonn, 1995), that "if one analyzes denouncers, it is clear that there was no prototype of denouncers in National Socialism. The majority of these people were unremarkable normal citizens, that can neither be characterized as especially malevolent nor as 'monsters.' Con-

vinced National Socialists or ideologically possessed people appear to be in the minority." "Denunziantentum und Gestapo," 301. Although I can agree that these people were unremarkable, normal citizens in many ways, I cannot agree with her that they were not malevolent. If it was so normal to denounce one another, then Jews also would have acted as denouncers, which they very seldom did, if at all. Perhaps the reason she reaches a conclusion so different from mine is that we use different kinds of evidence. Whereas my conclusions are based on the evidence in Gestapo and Special Court case files in various localities, her conclusions are based on letters to the Nazi Party in Lippe. I can also agree, however, with her argument against the once-prevailing notion that "denunciation is a typical feminine phenomenon."

40. The classic work on Nazi Party membership is Michael Kater's *The Nazi Party: A Social Profile of Members and Leaders, 1919–1945* (Oxford, 1983). For studies of SA members, see Richard Bessel, *Political Violence and the Rise of Nazism: The Stormtroopers in Eastern Germany, 1925–1934* (New Haven, Conn., 1984); Peter Merkl, *The Making of a Stormtrooper* (Princeton, N.J., 1980); and Conan Fischer, *Stormtroopers: A Social, Economic, and Ideological Analysis, 1929–1935* (London, 1983).

41. Reinhard Mann, *Protest und Kontrolle im Dritten Reich: Nationalsozialistische Herrschaft im Alltag einer rheinischen Grossstadt* (Frankfurt am Main, 1987), 295–96.

42. Rolf-Dieter Müller and Gerd R. Ueberschär, *Kriegsende 1945: Die Zerstörung des Deutschen Reiches* (Frankfurt am Main, 1994), 176.

43. Most recently this debate has centered on Daniel Jonah Goldhagen's controversial book *Hitler's Willing Executioners.* See ch. 1, n. 38.

44. On Jewish resistance to National Socialism, see Konrad Kwiet and Helmut Eschwege, *Selbstbehauptung und Widerstand: Deutsche Juden im Kampf um Existenz und Menschenwürde 1933–1945* (Hamburg, 1984). Of the Gestapo cases started against Krefeld Jews in the period 1933–39, 5 percent involved serious protest or resistance against the Nazi regime, 13 percent minor but still direct protest or resistance, and 8 percent indirect or inadvertent protest or resistance. There was no evidence of resistance or protest in 65 percent of the cases, and it is impossible to determine whether protest or resistance was involved in a further 10 percent of the cases. Comparing these figures to the non-Jewish population in the same city and period, one finds that the differences between the two groups were not substantial even if the Gentile population was

slightly more likely to be involved in serious protest and resistance, mainly carried out by Communists and Jehovah's Witnesses. Of 339 cases started against non-Jewish Germans in the random sample of the Krefeld Gestapo files, 19 percent involved serious protest or resistance, 7 percent minor protest or resistance, 13 percent inadvertent or indirect protest or resistance, 38 percent no protest or resistance, and 23 percent unknown.

CHAPTER FIVE: DESTROYING THE LEFT

1. Adolf Hitler, *Mein Kampf,* translated by Ralph Mannheim (1927; Boston, 1971), 680.

2. Rudolf Diels, *Lucifer ante portas* (Stuttgart, 1950), 143.

3. Hermann Weber, "Die Ambivalenz der kommunistischen Widerstandsstrategie bis zur 'Brüsseler' Parteikonferenz," in Jürgen Schmädeke and Peter Steinbach, eds., *Der Widerstand gegen den Nationalsozialismus: Die deutsche Gesellschaft und der Widerstand gegen Hitler* (Munich, 1985), 76.

4. Ibid., 79. These estimates are considerably lower than those of East German Communists, who, after the war, set the number of arrests at around 150,000. In their careful study of Nazi concentration camps in the 1930s, Klaus Drobisch and Günther Wieland argue that by April 1933 between 46,500 and 48,500 antifascists had already been arrested. *System der NS-Konzentrationslager 1933–1939* (Berlin, 1993), 38. Before the Third Reich ended, according to Horst Duhnke, some 20,000 German Communists were killed at the hands of the Nazis. *Die KPD von 1933 bis 1945* (Cologne, 1972), 525.

5. Weber, "Die Ambivalenz der kommunistischen Widerstandsstrategie," 73.

6. Brüning was chancellor from March 28, 1930, to May 30, 1932; von Papen from June 1, 1932, to December 3, 1932; and von Schleicher from December 3, 1932, until Hitler replaced him on January 30, 1933.

7. Other than Hitler, the only Nazis in the cabinet were Wilhelm Frick as minister of the interior and Hermann Göring as minister without portfolio. Former Chancellor Franz von Papen, who helped persuade Hindenburg to appoint Hitler chancellor in a coalition cabinet and who served himself as Hitler's vice chancellor, maintained: "Within two months, we will have pushed Hitler so far into a corner that he will squeak." Quoted in Ewald von Kleist-Schmenzin, "Die letzte Möglichkeit," *Politische Studien* 10 (1959): 92. The translation is found in Jackson Spielvogel, *Hitler and Nazi Germany: A History.* 2d ed. (Englewood Cliffs, N.J., 1992), 67.

8. Quoted in Adolf Klein, *Köln im Dritten Reich: Stadtgeschichte der Jahre 1933–1945* (Cologne, 1983), 53.

9. For Frechen, see HStADK, Rep. 112/14749–51. For the events in communities around Krefeld, see Bernhard Schmidt and Fritz Burger, *Tatort Moers: Widerstand und Nationalsozialismus im südlichen Altkreis Moers* (Moers, 1995), 111–12.

10. For a fuller description of the events in Cologne, see Klein, *Köln im Dritten Reich*, 55–57.

11. See Schmidt and Burger, *Tatort Moers*, 191–92; and Detlev Peukert, *Ruhrarbeiter gegen den Faschismus: Dokumentation über den Widerstand im Ruhrgebiet 1933–1945* (Frankfurt am Main, 1976), 48.

12. Weber, "Die Ambivalenz der kommunistischen Widerstandsstrategie," 74–75.

13. Patrik von zur Mühlen, "Die SPD zwischen Anpassung und Widerstand," in Schmädeke and Steinbach, eds., *Der Widerstand gegen den Nationalsozialismus*, 86–88.

14. Ibid., 86.

15. Schmidt and Burger, *Tatort Moers*, 113.

16. On the paradoxical nature of Hitler's "legal revolution," see Karl Dietrich Bracher, *The German Dictatorship: The Origins, Structure, and Effects of National Socialism*, translated by Jean Steinberg (New York, 1970), 191–98.

17. Mühlen, "Die SPD zwischen Anpassung und Widerstand," 89–91.

18. Wilhelm Hoegner, *Der Schwierige Aussenseiter* (Munich 1963), 92–93. Translation provided in J. Noakes and G. Pridam, *Nazism 1919–1945*, vol. 1, *The Rise to Power 1919–1934* (Exeter, U.K., 1983), 159–60.

19. There is no agreement as to the exact size of the SA. Richard J. Evans says that by 1934 the SA was "some three million strong." *Rituals of Retribution: Capital Punishment in Germany 1600–1987* (Oxford, 1996), 637. Other estimates are slightly lower. Jackson Spielvogel estimates that the SA "numbered 2.5 million men" at the beginning of 1934. *Hitler and Nazi Germany*, 78. On the SA in general, see Richard Bessel, *Political Violence and the Rise of Nazism: The Storm Troopers in Eastern Germany, 1925–1934* (New Haven, Conn., 1984); Conan Fischer, *Stormtroopers: A Social, Economic, and Ideological Analysis, 1919–1925* (London, 1983); and Peter Merkl, *The Making of a Stormtrooper* (Princeton, N.J., 1980).

20. A decree of February 22, 1933, issued by Hermann Göring in his capacity as Prussian interior minister, deputized 50,000 SA, SS, and Stahlhelm mem-

bers as an auxiliary police force (*Hilfspolizei*). According to Adolf Klein, they wore white armbands and carried police pistols and rubber truncheons. *Köln im Dritten Reich*, 64.

21. Quoted in Hermann Rauschning, *The Voices of Destruction* (New York, 1940), 152–53.

22. Quoted in Klein, *Köln im Dritten Reich*, 150.

23. Detlev Peukert, *Die KPD in Widerstand: Verfolgung und Untergrundarbeit an Rhein und Ruhr 1933 bis 1945* (Wuppertal, 1980), 89–90; Klaus Tenfelde, "Proletarische Provinz: Radikalisierung und Widerstand in Perzberg/ Oberbayern 1900 bis 1945," in Martin Broszat et al., eds., *Bayern in der NS-Zeit*, vol. 4, *Herrschaft und Gesellschaft im Konflikt* (Munich, 1981), 235ff.

24. Guenter Lewy, *The Catholic Church and Nazi Germany* (New York, 1964), 169–71. As Lewy explains, Bishop Bares of Berlin did address a letter privately to Hitler denying the possibility that Klausener could have been engaged in subversive activity and urging Hitler to explain why he had been killed. Only six days before his murder, Klausener had addressed a large rally of Berlin Catholics urging them to remain faithful to the Fatherland. On orders of Heydrich, Klausener was shot dead in his office on June 30, 1934. Hitler did not deem it necessary to react to the bishop's letter.

25. *Völkische Beobachter*, July 2, 1934. Translation provided by Louis L. Snyder in *Hitler's Third Reich: A Documentary History* (Chicago, 1981), 192.

26. Evans, *Rituals of Retribution*, 637–38.

27. See, for example, Peukert, *Die KPD im Widerstand*, 87–89.

28. On the setup and jurisdiction of the Special Courts, see Lothar Gruchmann, *Justiz im Dritten Reich 1933–1940: Anpassung und Unterwerfung in der ära Gürtner* (München, 1988), 944–56; Ingo Müller, *Hitler's Justice: The Courts of the Third Reich*, translated by Deborah Lucas Schneider (Cambridge, Mass., 1991), 153–73; and Ralph Angermund, *Deutsche Richterschaft 1919–1945: Krisenerfahrung, Illusion, politische Rechtsprechung* (Frankfurt am Main, 1990), 137–39. Originally the Special Courts were established in twenty-six *Oberlandesgerichtsbezirken* and were concerned primarily with violations of the Reichstag Fire Decree and with treacherous attacks against the regime. These were usually made in the form of libelous or slanderous statements of opinion and were considered of less significance than truly treasonous activities. Over time the numbers and jurisdiction of the Special Courts widened. By the war years they handled most forms of ordinary criminality and

not infrequently passed death sentences for looting after bombing attacks or black-marketeering.

29. *Westdeutscher Beobachter*, July 24, 1933, quoted in Klein, *Köln im Dritten Reich*, 136.

30. Ibid., 136. According to Klein, the usual method of execution in the Rhineland since the French Revolution had been the guillotine, so Göring's instruction to use the hand- axe was intended to make the execution particularly bloody and gruesome. Richard Evans explains, however, that the hand-axe, though frequently condemned abroad as barbaric, was still used in most of Germany when the Nazis came to power. After a long debate about which method of execution was most appropriate for general Nazi practice, Hitler himself decided on the guillotine on October 14, 1936. On this debate, see Evans, *Rituals of Retribution*, 651–59.

31. See, for example, Klaus-Michael Mallmann and Gerhard Paul, "Allwissend, allmächtig, allgegenwärtig?: Gestapo, Gesellschaft, und Widerstand," *Zeitschrift für Geschichtswissenschaft* 41 (1993): 984–99; and Robert Gellately, "Denunciations in Twentieth-Century Germany: Aspects of Self-Policing in the Third Reich and the German Democratic Republic," *Journal of Modern History* 68 (1996): 931–67.

32. In a randomly selected, one-eighth sample of the Krefeld Gestapo's case files, Jews and Communists together accounted for 192 out of 433 cases, or 44.3 percent of the total. Of these, 83 involved Communists and 109 involved Jews. Whereas a large majority of the Jewish cases pertained to emigration and other bureaucratic issues, and therefore were not always directly related to the application of terror, the vast majority of the Communist cases involved the arrest and punishment of people charged with treason. Additionally, the true proportion of Communist cases is underrepresented in this sample, because I decided not to code at least an additional 21 Communists in the sample who would normally be coded in cases involving non-Communists (see note 35 for an explanation). If these had been added in, then 213 out of 454 cases (46.9 percent of the total) would have been those of either Jews or Communists.

33. Eric A. Johnson and Karl-Heinz Reuband, "Die populäre Einschätzung der Gestapo: Wie allgegenwärtig war sie wirklich?," in Gerhard Paul and Klaus-Michael Mallmann, eds., *Die Gestapo: Mythos und Realität* (Darmstadt, 1995), 421–22. While these figures are based on a limited sample of 188 people living in the city of Cologne who were born in 1928 or earlier, they are con-

firmed by a larger study of several thousand people from the cities of Cologne, Krefeld, and Dresden that Reuband and I will soon publish entitled *Life and Death in the Third Reich: Germans and Jews Remember* (New York, forthcoming).

34. For a detailed, day-by-day account of the tragic experiences of German Jews under National Socialism, see Victor Klemperer, *Ich will Zeugnis ablegen bis zum letzten: Tagebücher 1933–1941* (Berlin, 1995), and Klemperer, *Ich will Zeugnis ablegen bis zum letzten: Tagebücher 1942–1945* (Berlin, 1995).

35. Of the eighty-five cases in my random sample of Krefeld Gestapo case files for the years 1933 and 1934, fifty-nine (69.4 percent) were lodged against Communists. But this undercounts the actual number of Communist cases in the period, since I decided for the purposes of my sample to code only the cases of Communists from the city of Krefeld itself. In the Paul Z. case (HStAD, RW58/ 21099 and RW58/26636), for example, I coded only five people in the case although there were twenty-six people I could have coded. Unfortunately, little empirical work on Gestapo case files dealing with Communists has been undertaken. In the most extensive statistical examination of Gestapo files to this point, Reinhard Mann decided to leave both Communist and Jewish cases out of his analysis. *Protest und Kontrolle im Dritten Reich: Nationalsozialistische Herrschaft im Alltag einer rheinischen Grossstadt* (Frankfurt, 1987). Communist cases are also not considered in the recent major volume on the Gestapo's activities edited by Paul and Mallmann, *Die Gestapo: Mythos und Realität*. Paul and Mallmann have, however, placed considerable emphasis on the persecution of Communists in the third volume of their huge study of Nazi rule and resistance in the Saarland, *Milieus und Widerstand: Eine Verhaltensgeschichte der Gesellschaft im Nationalsozialismus* (Bonn, 1995).

36. The figures for *Landkreis* Moers are from Schmidt and Burger, *Tatort Moers*, 143. Of the other five people in protective custody, two were from the SPD, one was from the Center Party, one was from the German People's Party (DVP), and one was not affiliated with any party. For the quotation, see Weber, "Die Ambivalenz der kommunistischen Widerstandsstrategie," 76.

37. For a discussion of the Jews persecuted in the first years of the Third Reich for their role in the Communist resistance organization, see Konrad Kwiet and Helmut Eschwege, *Selbstbehauptung und Widerstand: Deutsche Juden im Kampf um Existenz und Menschenwürde 1933–1945* (Hamburg, 1984), 92–101. On the first waves of anti-Jewish violence and economic boycotts, see Saul

Friedländer, *Nazi Germany and the Jews*, vol. 1, *The Years of Persecution, 1933–1939* (New York, 1997), 18ff.

38. According to the Gestapo case files of Heinrich M. (HStAD, RW58/53197 and RW58/54601), a great crowd of people dressed in civilian clothing assembled outside of the Krefeld trade-union headquarters on the morning of May 27, 1933, pushed their way into the building, beat up the people they found inside, and threw a great abundance of Marxist books and other literature they discovered out the window, where it was set on fire in the middle of Krefeld's Steinstrasse. When Krefeld Gestapo officers Krülls and Schmitz arrived at the scene, they arrested Heinrich M. and two other trade-union leaders (Peter B. and Stefan M.) and placed them in protective custody "for their own protection." Krülls and Schmitz made no further arrests, claiming that they could not identify any of the people who had forced their way into the building. After M. and the others were arrested, the Gestapo officers pressed them about any trade-union funds they might have hidden in the building and then went back inside and confiscated some 350 Reichmarks they found in an unclosed safe. According to a report that Krülls wrote nearly a month later on June 22, Heinrich M., aged forty-six in 1933, had been the head of several SPD and trade-union organizations in Krefeld such as the SPD paramilitary organization Reichsbanner Schwarz-Rot-Gold, the railroad workers' union, and the general German trade-union association. Other evidence in Heinrich M.'s two lengthy case files demonstrate that the Gestapo considered him a very dangerous man and spied on him constantly. The Gestapo believed that after he was let out of concentration camp Heinrich M. had worked in the resistance both in Germany and in Holland as the head of the SPD in the Krefeld region, and they saw to it that he sat in either jail or concentration camp throughout most of the Third Reich. After his first arrest, Heinrich M. spent ten weeks in protective custody, only to be rearrested in October 1933 and sent for an additional brief period to Kemna concentration camp outside Barmen. After his release, Heinrich M. could not find work in Germany and apparently emigrated to nearby Venlo, Holland. In 1936 he returned to Krefeld and soon was arrested once again and put on trial for treason. Although Heinrich M. continually professed his innocence and promised that "in the future I will commit myself in every way for the development [of the state] and for the community of the Volk in a National-Socialist manner," he was given a five-year prison sentence. After serving out his sentence, the Krefeld Gestapo took him in protective custody and held him

in a jail in nearby Anrath before sending him to Sachsenhausen concentration camp on July 14, 1942, where he seems to have remained until the end of the war. Already back in April 1942, Schmitz of the Krefeld Gestapo filed a report stating that in his estimation Heinrich M. continued to hold to "fanatical Marxist views" and therefore should be kept "for the rest of the war in a concentration camp." When his sons came home from the front with the hope of visiting their father on May 4, 1944, Heinrich M. was still in concentration camp.

39. Gerhard Paul notes that in his examination of a random sample of 118 cases started by denunciations in the city of Würzburg, most of the cases involved mere "grumblers and grousers." There was not a single case of what he calls a "big fish" in his sample. "Kontinuität und Radikalisierung: Die Staatspolizeistelle Würzburg," in Paul and Mallmann, *Die Gestapo: Mythos und Realität*, 173.

40. The most important exception was the case of Magdelena L., HStAD, RW58/28851 and RW58/71566. She was a twenty-one-year-old, single woman and the daughter of a Communist resistance figure in Krefeld who was serving time in prison for treason. After she had been denounced for unknown reasons by a former housemaid, the Gestapo searched her apartment and found pictures of Lenin and Stalin. Also, the Gestapo determined that she had been involved in the distribution of Communist literature and had listened to Radio Moscow. Magdelena L. was tried by the Hamm Superior Court in 1935 and given a two-year sentence for conspiring to commit high treason. After she was released from prison in 1937, a Gestapo *V-Mann* was assigned to spy on her for at least the next year.

41. "Conspiring to commit high treason" was the charge leveled against the accused Communists in at least fifty-two of the cases in the sample. The specific charge is not always listed in the Gestapo files, nor is the punishment, though in most cases both the charge and the punishment are indicated. Surprisingly perhaps, not one of the Krefeld Communists in the sample appears to have received the death sentence, even if death sentences were relatively rare during the 1930s (when most of the Krefeld Communists were punished). Evidence in the case files shows, however, that about half of the Communists in the sample spent time in protective custody or concentration camp or both, and that most received a prison sentence from one to several years' duration.

42. Most of the arrests took place in the first half of the month of March 1933. In the Cologne *Regierungsbezirk*, for example, there were 982 arrests in the

first half of March, 117 arrests in the second half of March, 157 arrests in the first half of April, and 141 arrests in the second half of April. See Drobisch and Wieland, *System der NS-Konzentrationslager,* 37.

43. Peukert, *Die KPD in Widerstand,* 97.

44. Ibid., 91.

45. Most often these cases involved only minor infractions; the major cases against Communist and Socialist organizers in the Cologne area were either handled by the Gestapo itself or remanded to the Hamm Superior Court for trial. Nevertheless, in my random sample of Cologne Special Court cases the number of cases against people with clearly identifiable Communist or Socialist backgrounds dropped by two-thirds in 1935, and cases started on the grounds of alleged Communist activity by either former Communist Party members or alleged Communist sympathizers dropped almost out of sight after 1934. Peter Hüttenberger found similar trends in his study of the Munich Special Court. See "Heimtückefälle vor dem Sondergericht München 1933–1939," in Martin Broszat et al., eds., *Bayern in der NS-Zeit: Herrschaft und Gesellschaft im Konflikt* (Munich, 1981), 4:448. See also Angermund, *Deutsche Richterschaft,* 140.

46. On the Communists' continued resistance efforts in the mid and late 1930s, see Peukert, *Die KPD in Widerstand,* 251–87.

47. HStAD, RW58/1680.

48. Detlev Peukert, *Inside Nazi Germany: Conformity, Opposition, and Racism in Everyday Life,* translated by Richard Deveson.(London, 1989), 117–18.

49. Interview with Artur V., Cologne, January 20, 1994.

50. HStADK, Rep. 112/14749–14751II.

51. Siegburg prison, about twenty miles southeast of Cologne, was one of the main prisons used by the Cologne courts.

52. HStADK, Rep. 112/14749, Bl. 177–89.

53. *Oberlandesgericht* Hamm handled most of the cases of high treason lodged against Communists and Socialists in the Rhine-Ruhr area in the 1930s. See Angermund, *Deutsche Richterschaft,* 134.

54. When Peter Z., one of Krefeld's leading Communists (see the discussion of his case later in the chapter), was interrogated on October 8, 1940, by Wilhelm Weber of the Krefeld Gestapo, he told Weber that he first went into hiding in February 1933 in his sister's apartment and later hid out in various garden houses before deciding to flee abroad. HStAD, RW58/2610.

55. The Krefeld Communist Oskar H. told the Krefeld Gestapo in his interro-

gation of July 13, 1934, that it had already been decided by the KPD leadership
in 1932 that Party functionaries were to do everything they could to avoid being arrested if Hitler came to power. HStAD, RW58/58325.

56. For Oskar H.'s case, see HStAD, RW58/58325 and RW58/62562. For Peter
Z.'s case, see HStAD, RW58/2610.

57. This account of how Oskar H. and Peter Z. left Germany is a composite
sketch of the details the two men provided to the Krefeld Gestapo in their individual interrogations in their separate cases. These details diverged slightly. On
a few minor points, I have favored Oskar H.'s testimony because he was more
cooperative. Also, he gave his testimony six years before Peter Z. did and may
have remembered what they had done more accurately.

58. For example, in a case in the Cologne Special Court case files that took place
in the Dellbrück section of Cologne, Peter K. was arrested in the village of Ode-
nthal during a house search conducted at four in the morning on July 3, 1933.
He was brought back to Cologne and put under enormous pressure by Kriminalassistent Bartel of the Cologne political police department IA to provide information about the Communist resistance organization in Dellbrück, which he
was said to have headed. Instead of providing the police with what they wanted,
Peter K. tried to commit suicide by slashing his aorta. The police got others
to talk, however, and the Communist underground in Cologne-Dellbrück was
destroyed. See HStADK, Rep. 112/15662.

59. HStAD, RW58/21099 and RW58/26636. Jung's report is in the second file.

60. Details about Krülls's background and career are found in his *Innenministerium* file, HStAD, NW130/243.

61. The text of the pamphlet was printed out in two single-spaced pages in the
written indictment in the subsequent trial of Paul Z. and the other Communist
organizers. HStAD, RW58/21099, Bl. 75–77.

62. HStAD, RW58/10111, Bl. 156. Here we find that a related trial had led to
the arrest and sentencing of an additional sixty-one Communists in the area.

63. I have chosen to use Aurel Billstein's full name for several reasons. The first
is that doing so does not violate the stringent data protection laws in Germany,
because it can be proven that he has died. Second, Billstein is a well-known
figure in Krefeld who spent much of his life fighting against the Nazis and their
legacy both during the Third Reich and after. After the war he was a leader of
the local VVN organization of people persecuted by the National Socialists and
wrote several books and pamphlets on the persecution of Krefelders during the
Third Reich. Some of his works include: *Fremdarbeiter in unserer Stadt 1939–*

1945: Kriegsgefangene und deportierte "fremdvölkische Arbeitskräfte" am Beispiel Krefeld (Frankfurt am Main, 1980); *Christliche Gegnerschaft am Niederrhein 1933–1945 im Bereich der ehemaligen Gestapo-Aussendienststelle Krefeld* (Viersen, 1987); and *Geheime Staatspolizei Aussendienststelle Krefeld: Alltägliche Wirklichkeit im Nationalsozialismus* (Krefeld, n.d.).

64. Interview with Aurel Billstein, Krefeld, January 30, 1995. Billstein's Gestapo file is found in HStAD, RW58/10111.

CHAPTER SIX: THE CROSS AND THE SWASTIKA

1. In his records from Siegburg prison, in February 1936 Spieker is described as 1.68 meters tall (about 5 feet 6 inches), with a powerful build, a broad chin, light blue eyes, blond hair, and about eight missing teeth. HStADK, Rep. 112/16096.

2. Dr. Mathias K. held the position of *Zellenleiter* in the Nazi Party. There are two Cologne Special Court files on the Spieker case, HStADK, Rep. 112/16574 and Rep. 112/16096. Although the Spieker case is not well known outside of Cologne, some of its details are discussed in Adolf Klein, *Köln im Dritten Reich: Stadtgeschichte der Jahre 1933–1945* (Cologne, 1983), 103–4; and in Klein, "Hundert Jahre Akten—hundert Jahre Fakten: Das Landgericht Köln ab 1879," in Adolf Klein and Günter Rennen, eds., *Justitia Coloniensis: Amtsgericht und Landgericht Köln erzählen ihre Geschichte(n)* (Cologne, 1981), 150–51. Otherwise, Spieker has received almost no attention from scholars. His case receives only a few short sentences in Ulrich von Hehl's study of the Catholic Church in Cologne during the Nazi period, *Katholische Kirche und Nationalsozialismus im Erzbistum Köln 1933–1945* (Mainz, 1977), 77, 114; and merits only a footnote in Vincent A. Lapomardo's *The Jesuits and the Third Reich* (Lewiston, N.Y., 1989), 55. In Ulrich Herbert's recent biography of Werner Best, Spieker receives one sentence. *Best: Biographische Studien über Radikalismus, Weltanschauung, und Vernunft 1903–1989* (Bonn, 1996), 157.

3. The Decree for the Protection of the Nationalist Movement against Malicious Attacks upon the Government of March 21, 1933, called for the imprisonment for up to two years of anyone who "purposely makes or circulates a statement of a factual nature which is untrue or grossly exaggerated or which may seriously harm the welfare of the Reich or of a state, or the reputation of the National Government or of a state government or of the parties or organizations supporting these governments." On December 20, 1934, this decree was

replaced and added on to by the Law Against Malicious Attacks on State and Party and for the Protection of Party Uniforms (often called the *Heimtückegesetz*). In particular, the new law extended the provisions of the earlier law to include "malicious, rabble-rousing remarks or those indicating a base mentality" made against the Nazi Party or any of its leaders. In practice, even minor criticisms of the regime or its leadership were now punishable by jail or prison terms. See J. Noakes and G. Pridham, *Nazism 1919–1945*, vol. 2, *State, Economy, and Society 1933–1939: A Documentary Reader* (Exeter, U.K., 1984), 478–79.

4. These passages of Spieker's sermon are quoted verbatim in both Mathias K.'s written testimony and in the written judgment in Spieker's court case. HStADK, Rep. 112/16574, Bl. 7–8, 38–39.

5. Josef Spieker, *Mein Kampf gegen Unrecht in Staat und Gesellschaft: Erinnerungern eines Kölner Jesuiten* (Cologne, 1971), 13.

6. Ibid., 20.

7. Ibid.

8. Ibid., 23.

9. Ibid., 25.

10. Ibid., 30.

11. Ibid.

12. Ibid. Spieker made a point of distinguishing between these policemen and more typical Gestapo officers and of crediting them with treating him decently in the past. In an earlier passage in Spieker's autobiography, he relates that he had been warned by older police officers in the service of the Gestapo not to give a talk at the Saint Kunibert Church in Cologne's Altstadt. As he put it, "The Gestapo now came for the first time, or better put: it was the old criminal police, who had to perform Gestapo service." Ibid., 27. Karl Löffler claimed after the war that he had often "protected" Spieker and had warned him and several other Cologne priests on many occasions when the Gestapo was planting informers during their sermons. HStADK, BR PE/49505, *Personalakten Sammelbestand*.

13. Ibid., 31–32.

14. Ibid., 32–33.

15. HStADK, Rep. 112/16574, Bl. 8–9.

16. Ibid., Bl. 10f.

17. Ibid.

18. Spieker, *Mein Kampf gegen Unrecht in Staat und Gesellschaft*, 36.

19. Klein, "Hundert Jahre Akten," 149; Spieker, *Mein Kampf gegen Unrecht in Staat und Gesellschaft*, 39.

20. *Westdeutscher Beobachter*, March 12, 1935.

21. Spieker, *Mein Kampf gegen Unrecht in Staat und Gesellschaft*, 40.

22. *Westdeutscher Beobachter*, March 12, 1935. The *Kölnische Volkszeitung* on the same day reported similar comments by Father Spieker. His final words were recorded in the latter newspaper as "Everything for Germany; Germany for Christ."

23. Spieker, *Mein Kampf gegen Unrecht in Staat und Gesellschaft*, 40–41.

24. HStADK, Rep. 112/16096, Bl. 78.

25. Ibid.

26. Spieker, *Mein Kampf gegen Unrecht in Staat und Gesellschaft*, 41.

27. Ibid., 43–44.

28. Ibid., 43ff.

29. Cited in Klaus Drobisch and Günther Wieland, *System der NS-Konzentrationslager 1933–1939* (Berlin, 1993), 120.

30. Spieker, *Mein Kampf gegen Unrecht in Staat und Gesellschaft*, 46.

31. Ibid., 47.

32. These statements come from reporting on the trial by two local Cologne newspapers: *Westdeutscher Beobachter*, January 21, 1936, and *Kölnische Volkszeitung*, January 21, 1936.

33. Spieker, *Mein Kampf gegen Unrecht in Staat und Gesellschaft*, 51.

34. HStADK, Rep. 112/16574. Klein also notes that the judges did what they could to provide a "harmless interpretation" (*harmlose Deutung*) of Spieker's sermon. "Hundert Jahre Akten," 150. Comparing the judgment statement (Bl. 39) with the original notes on Spieker's sermon provided by the denouncer Mathias K. (Bl. 7–8), one notes that the judges changed phrases like *stattliche Autorität* ("imposing authority") to *staatliche Autorität* ("civil authority") and took out the word *wahrer* ("true") in the phrase *wahrer Führer* to make Spieker's sermon seem less caustic.

35. This is the position argued by Adolf Klein in *Köln im Dritten Reich*, 104.

36. Spieker, *Mein Kampf gegen Unrecht in Staat und Gesellschaft*, 54.

37. Ibid., 52.

38. Spieker was in jail in Siegburg from February 21 to March 30, 1936; in Strafgefangenlager II at Aschendorfermoor near Papenberg until May 26, 1936; and in Wittlich until his release on February 19, 1937. HStADK, Rep. 112/16096.

39. Spieker, *Mein Kampf gegen Unrecht in Staat und Gesellschaft*, 64.

40. Ibid.

41. Ibid. There is some evidence to support Spieker's contention that the Jesuit Order was uncomfortable with his activities and sought to silence his protests against Nazi injustice. Volume 1 of his two-volume literary estate, found at the Norddeutsche Provinz SJ Archiv in Cologne, contains a letter (Bl. 21), written by Ledochowski on November 7, 1935, which beseeched the Nazi government to let Spieker out of concentration camp. In return for his release, Ledochowski promised that "the heads of the [Jesuit] Order would take pains to ensure that Father Spieker, once he is let go, would be sent out of the country and that outside of Germany he would not involve himself in anti-German activities." It should also be mentioned in this context that Ledochowski's letter makes clear that the Vatican itself had already been informed about this proposal several months earlier in April 1935.

42. Ibid., 70–71.

43. Some have estimated that more than 4,000 clerics died in Nazi concentration camps. See Richard Plant, *The Pink Triangle: The Nazi War Against Homosexuals* (New York, 1986), 136; Benedicta Maria Kempner, *Priester vor Hitlers Tribunalen* (Munich, 1966), 160; and Raimund Schnabel, *Die Frommen in der Hölle: Geistliche in Dachau* (Frankfurt am Main, 1966), 29–178.

44. After noting that perhaps as many as one-third of the lower Catholic clergy were "subjected to some form of political retribution in the Third Reich," Ian Kershaw explains that "few of these cases, however, involved outright or even camouflaged criticism of Hitler, and, whatever their real feelings, most priests were ready to behave in public in politically conformist fashion." Ian Kershaw, *The Hitler Myth: Image and Reality in the Third Reich* (Oxford, 1987), 115.

45. Gerhard Paul and Klaus-Michael Mallmann, *Milieus und Widerstand: Eine Verhaltensgeschichte der Gesellschaft im Nationalsozialismus* (Bonn, 1995), 89.

46. H. G. Hockerts, *Die Sittlichkeitsprozesse gegen katholische Ordensangehörige und Priester 1936–1937* (Mainz, 1971).

47. The encyclical and Hitler's reactions to it have been widely discussed in the scholarly literature. See, for example, Guenter Lewy, *The Catholic Church and Nazi Germany* (New York, 1964), 156–59; J. S. Conway, *The Nazi Persecution of the Churches 1933–1945* (New York, 1968), 165–67; and Ernst Christian Helmreich, *The German Churches Under Hitler: Background, Struggle, and Epilogue* (Detroit, 1979), 279–83.

48. The quotations are from Plant, *The Pink Triangle*, 135.

49. Klein, *Köln im Dritten Reich*, 186.

50. HStAD, RW58/32839 and RW58/2753.

51. HStAD, RW58/32839.

52. This is the title of the article in the morning edition of the *Westdeutscher Beobachter* of May 11, 1933, which is found in HStAD, RW58/32389, Bl. 18.

53. HStAD, RW58/2753.

54. Adolf Klein, for example, credits Dr. Loevenich, who headed the Cologne Special Court between June 1937 and the beginning of 1940, as a man "who indeed used the existing laws, but to the advantage of the accused and without respect to the intentions of the party." *Köln im Dritten Reich*, 103. Elsewhere Klein calls Loevenich "an independent thinking judge." "Hundert Jahre Akten," 151. Others portray German judges in the Third Reich more harshly. See, for example, Ingo Müller, *Hitler's Justice: The Courts of the Third Reich*, translated by Deborah Lucas Schneider (1987; Cambridge, Mass., 1991).

55. Quoted in Paul and Mallmann, *Milieus und Widerstand*, 89.

56. Ibid. The studies they are particularly critical of are Ulrich von Hehl, *Priester unter Hitlers Terror: Eine biographische und statistische Erhebung* (Mainz, 1984), and Heinz Hürten, *Deutsche Katholiken 1918–1945* (Paderborn, 1992). For other assessments of Catholic resistance, see Georg Danzler, *Widerstand oder Anpassung?: Katholische Kirche und Drittes Reich* (Munich, 1984), and Günter van Norden, "Zwischen Kooperation und Teilwiderstand: Die Rolle der Kirchen und Konfessionen—Ein Überblick über Forschungspositionen," in Jürgen Schmädeke and Peter Steinbach, eds., *Der Widerstand gegen den Nationalsozialismus: Die deutsche Gesellschaft und der Widerstand gegen Hitler* (Munich, 1986), 227–326.

57. Martin Broszat, "Resistenz und Widerstand: Eine Zwischenbilanz des Forschungsprojektes," in Broszat et al., *Bayern in der NS-Zeit*, vol. 4 (Munich, 1981), 697–99.

58. Paul and Mallmann, *Milieus und Widerstand*, 90–91.

59. Ibid., 144.

60. Ibid., 141–42.

61. See, for example, Lewy, *The Catholic Church and Nazi Germany*, 159.

62. See Lewy's important discussion of this in ibid., 169–73. In Cologne only one priest, Archbishop Josef Frings, is known to have protested openly against the murder of the Jews. See Klein, *Köln im Dritten Reich*, 191.

63. Lewy, *The Catholic Church and Nazi Germany*, 265, 311. On the Nazi eu-

thanasia program, see Henry Friedlander, *The Origins of Nazi Genocide: From Euthanasia to the Final Solution* (Chapel Hill, N.C., 1993).

64. Hehl, *Priester unter Hitlers Terror*, lxxiv.

65. Doris L. Bergen, *Twisted Cross: The German Christian Movement in the Third Reich* (Chapel Hill, N.C., 1996), 12; Kurt Meier, *Kreuz und Hakenkreuz: Die evangelische Kirche im Dritten Reich* (Munich, 1992), 37–49.

66. Bernhard Schmidt and Fritz Burger, *Tatort Moers: Widerstand und Nationalsozialismus im südlichen Altkreis Moers* (Moers, 1995), 286.

67. See Ernst Klee, *"Die SA Jesu Christi": Die Kirche im Banne Hitlers* (Frankfurt am Main, 1989).

68. On Hossenfelder's replacement by Kinder, see Bergen, *Twisted Cross*, 18. On the descending ranks in the church's hierarchy, see Klein, *Köln im Dritten Reich*, 194.

69. Klein, *Köln im Dritten Reich*, 194; and Schmidt and Burger, *Tatort Moers*, 287.

70. See, for example, the assessments of the Confessing Church by Gerhard Besier, "Ansätze zum politischen Widerstand in der Bekennenden Kirche: Zur gegenwärtigen Forschungslage"; Eberhard Bethge, "Zwischen Bekenntnis und Widerstand: Erfahrungen in der Altpreussischen Union"; and Christoph Strohm, "Der Widerstandskreis um Dietrich Bonhoeffer und Hans von Dohnanyi: Seine Voraussetzungen zur Zeit der Machtergreifung"; in Schmädeke and Steinbach, *Der Widerstand gegen den Nationalsozialismus*, 254–64, 265–80, and 281–313, respectively.

71. Bergen, *Twisted Cross*, 12.

72. J. S. Conway explains: "Of the 17,000 pastors of the Evangelical Church, the number of those sentenced to lengthy terms of imprisonment was never at any one time more than fifty." *The Nazi Persecution of the Churches*, 175. See also Schmidt and Burger, *Tatort Moers*, 288–92.

73. Klein, *Köln im Dritten Reich*, 192.

74. The files themselves are found in HStADK, Rep. 112. The computer file of these cases that I created is archived in the Zentrum für historische Sozialforschung/Zentralarchiv für empirische Sozialforschung of the University of Cologne.

75. According to Hehl, there were 19,068 Catholic priests registered by the Catholic Church in 1937. In his study, Hehl provides statistical and biographical information on 8,021 priests, or something less than 42 percent of all members of the priesthood in the Third Reich given that some people first joined the

priesthood in Nazi Germany after 1937. See *Priester unter Hitlers Terror,* lxxiv. Although Hehl attempts to exclude cases, like Father Suitbert G.'s, that were based on morality offenses, Father G. is nevertheless included in his study. The biographical statement on Suitbert G., found on page 10, says that the priest was arrested on April 5, 1937, for "an unstated reason."

76. See, for example, HStADK, Rep. 112/6880. In this case, two Catholic nuns teaching in a kindergarten in the Bayenthal section of Cologne were denounced by a Nazi Party *Zellenleiter* for encouraging children to rip up voting-propaganda posters on March 3, 1936. Since there were no witnesses, the case against them was dismissed. On the Nazis' relations with and persecution of the Catholic Church in Cologne generally, see Hehl, *Katholische Kirche und Nationalsozialismus im Erzbistum Köln 1933–1945.*

77. In the first of these cases (HStADK, Rep. 112/8809), a young minister named Friedrich H. was denounced by a Nazi Party *Ortsgruppenleiter* in Cologne-Bayenthal for comparing Nazis and Communists in a sermon delivered on December 31, 1933, in the Mehlemerstrasse, and for stating in his sermon that "I am convinced that all of these are nothing other than marionettes in the hand of the devil." When the minister promised in his interrogation, which was led by Karl Löffler of the Cologne Gestapo, not to make such statements in the future, the case against him was dropped. The other case (HStADK, Rep. 112/11724) involved a fifty-six-year-old minister from Cologne-Merheim named Friedrich G., whom the Gestapo itself apparently accused of having paid back a loan without informing the proper authorities of the transaction. His case was dropped on the grounds of an amnesty of September 9, 1939, which called for dismissing cases for which less than a three-month jail sentence could be expected.

78. HStADK, Rep. 112/11381.

79. HStADK, Rep. 112/25040 and Rep. 112/15914.

80. Hehl, *Priester unter Hitlers Terror,* lxxxix.

81. Aurel Billstein, *Christliche Gegnerschaft am Niederrhein 1933–1945* (Viersen, 1987), 22–30.

82. Ibid., 79–81.

83. See, for example, HStADK, Rep. 112/15914.

84. For reports made by Catholic clergymen who served as Gestapo spies in the Cologne and Aachen areas, see HStAD, RW34/3 and RW35/8.

85. HStADK, Rep. 112/11381.

86. Ibid.

87. Ibid.

88. HStADK, Rep. 112/25040.

89. HStADK, Rep. 112/5169.

90. HStADK, Rep. 112/5632.

91. HStADK, Rep. 112/15969.

92. HStADK, Rep. 112/5574.

93. Ian Kershaw, *Popular Opinion and Political Dissent in the Third Reich: Bavaria 1933–1945* (Oxford, 1983), 205ff.

94. A Gestapo decree of June 23, 1935, curtailed all activities of Catholic youth groups in Prussia that were not of a purely religious nature. Barbara Schellenberger, "Katholischer Jugendwiderstand," in Schmädeke and Steinbach, *Der Widerstand gegen den Nationalsozialismus,* 322. For a case example of the Nazis' crackdown on Catholic youth groups in the Cologne area even prior to this, in March 1935, see HStADK, Rep. 112/9225.

95. The Cologne Special Court files contain more than one hundred cases started against local clergymen for not flying the Nazi flag on the required holidays. For a Bergheim case example, see HStADK, Rep. 112/2147. In this case, a young priest in the village of Thorr was cited by a local policeman for failure to hang the Nazi flag on the local Catholic Church and the rectory on New Year's Day 1936. In his accusation, the policeman noted that the priest was "not supportive of the National Socialist government." In his defense, the priest explained that the man he had hired to hang the flags had completely forgotten about it. When he called to ask the man to fulfill his duty in the late afternoon of New Year's Day, the man said that it was already too dark to hang them. Although this sounded like a flimsy excuse to the policeman, the state prosecuting attorney's office in Cologne soon opted to dismiss the case.

96. Kershaw, *Popular Opinion and Political Dissent in the Third Reich,* 206.

97. HStADK, Rep. 112/16219.

98. Details about the background of Kreisschulrat Bernhard E. are found in a subsequent case involving a challenge to take part in an illegal duel in December 1938. See HStADK, Rep. 112/8205.

99. See the file of Margareta D., HStADK, Rep. 112/16219.

100. Detlev Garbe's large and well-researched book on the resistance and persecution of Jehovah's Witnesses in the Third Reich, published in 1994, must now be considered the standard work on the subject. See *Zwischen Widerstand und Martyrium: Die Zeugen Jehovahs im "Dritten Reich"* (Munich, 1994). Before the appearance of his book, the Witnesses had been largely overlooked. In

addition to some brief comments about their suffering and heroism by former inmates of Nazi concentration camps, like Eugon Kogon and Bruno Bettelheim, and some brief treatments in general studies of the persecution of religious groups in Nazi Germany, there are only a handful of detailed studies of their persecution. See Eugon Kogon, *Das System der deutschen Konzentration-slager* (Frankfurt am Main, 1959), 49, 264ff; Bruno Bettelheim, *The Informed Heart: Autonomy in a Mass Age* (New York, 1960), 122–23, 182, 190; Friedrich Zipfels, *Kirchenkampf in Deutschland* (Berlin, 1965), 174–203; Michael H. Kater, "Die Ernsten Bibelforscher im Dritten Reich," *Vierteljahrshefte für Zeitgeschichte* 17 (1969): 181–218; Gerhard Hetzer, "Ernste Bibelforscher in Augsburg," in Martin Broszat et al., eds., *Bayern in der NS-Zeit*, vol. 4, *Herrschaft und Gesellschaft im Konflikt* (Munich, 1981), 621–43; Christine Elizabeth King, *The Nazi State and the New Religions: Five Case Studies in Non-Conformity* (New York, 1982); Conway, *The Nazi Persecution of the Churches*, 195–99; and Helmreich, *The German Churches Under Hitler*, 392–97.

101. In Rosenberg's notorious *Protocols of the Elders of Zion*, published in 1923, he claimed that the Jehovah's Witnesses prepared the way "spiritually for religious-political Jewish world domination." Cited in Kater, "Die Ernsten Bibelforscher im Dritten Reich," 185.

102. See, for example, Conway, *The Nazi Persecution of the Churches*, 199–200; and Kater, "Die Ernsten Bibelforscher im Dritten Reich," 184. The brunt of Nazi terror was also felt by the Seventh-Day Adventists more than most other religious sects. Although they were less intransigent than the Jehovah's Witnesses and usually came from more prosperous socioeconomic backgrounds, many of them were also punished severely for their religious beliefs in the Third Reich. Like the Jehovah's Witnesses, they often refused to perform military service, refused to use the Hitler greeting, and continued with their religious services after they were banned in April 1936. A letter written by Heydrich on April 29, 1936, found in the file of a case lodged against several Seventh-Day Adventists in the Cologne area that began in November of that year (HStADK, Rep. 112/13060), laid out the Nazis' objections to them. Part of the letter reads: "The Seventh Day Adventists' reform movement follows goals under the cover of religious activity that run contrary to the world view of National Socialism. The members of this sect refuse to perform military service and refuse to use the German greeting. They state openly that they do not recognize any fatherland, rather they are international in their leanings and con-

sider all people their brothers. In that the behavior of this sect arouses disorder amongst the population, their dissolution was necessary for the protection of the German people and state." In another letter in this case file, which came from Berlin Gestapo headquarters in November 1936, all Gestapo posts were instructed to search the apartments of Seventh-Day Adventists and to take their leaders into protective custody or start legal proceedings against them if there was enough evidence to guarantee a conviction. In this particular case, which involved the leader of the Seventh-Day Adventists in the district of the Rhineland and over a dozen other Adventists from Bad Godesberg and Remagen, at least two people were tried and sentenced, two others spent periods of time in custody, and the leader of the sect, a sixty-one-year-old salesman named Otto W., fled to Holland.

103. Zipfels, *Kirchenkampf in Deutschland*, 176.
104. Kater, "Die Ernsten Bibelforscher im Dritten Reich," 181.
105. Garbe, *Zwischen Widerstand und Martyrium*, 500.
106. Hitler is known to have told Interior Minister Wilhelm Frick in October 1934, that the Jehovah's Witnesses had to be "exterminated." Ibid., 189.
107. Ibid., 204.
108. HStADK, Rep.8/10.
109. Kater, "Die Ernsten Bibelforscher im Dritten Reich," 208–11; and Zipfels, *Kirchenkampf in Deutschland*, 195.
110. Bettelheim, *The Informed Heart*, 122–23.
111. Garbe, *Zwischen Widerstand und Martyrium*, 457–58; and Kater, "Die Ernsten Bibelforscher im Dritten Reich," 190–91.
112. HStAD, RW58/3863 and RW58/4502. The letter is found in the latter file, Bl. 151–52.
113. HStAD, RW58/4502, Bl. 120.
114. HStADK, Rep. 8/10.
115. HStAD, RW58/3863.
116. HStAD, RW58/4502, Bl. 131.

CHAPTER SEVEN:
NAZI TERROR AND "ORDINARY" GERMANS: 1933–1939

1. Throughout the years of the Third Reich, the heavily censored German newspapers regularly featured lengthy articles on law-breakers, which they carefully selected for maximum propagandistic value. Not infrequently, these

articles even discussed cases of people who had been sent to concentration camps, though they never mentioned, of course, the Jews who were sent to death camps during the war years. On newspaper reporting generally, see Oran J. Hale, *The Captive Press in the Third Reich* (Princeton, N.J., 1964); K. D. Abel, *Die Presselenkung im NS-Staat* (Munich, 1968); and David Welch, *The Third Reich: Politics and Propaganda* (London, 1993), 34–39.

2. See, for example, Klaus-Michael Mallmann and Gerhard Paul, "Allwissend, allmächtig, allgegenwärtig?: Gestapo, Gesellschaft, und Widerstand," *Zeitschrift für Geschichtswissenschaft* 41 (1993): 984–99; Gerhard Paul and Klaus-Michael Mallmann, eds., *Die Gestapo: Mythos und Realität* (Darmstadt, 1995); and Robert Gellately, "Allwissend und allgegenwärtig?: Enstehung, Funktion, und Wandel des Gestapo-Mythos," in Paul and Mallmann, *Die Gestapo: Mythos und Realität*, 47–70.

3. As asserted in a recent article by Robert Gellately, a leading figure in the study of political denunciations in Nazi Germany: "Certainly, the key factor in the routine operation of the Gestapo was the provision of information from the general population by way of denunciations." "Denunciations and Nazi Germany: New Insights and Methodological Problems," *Historical Social Research/Historische Sozialforschung* 22 (1997): 229. For other recent work stressing the importance of denunciations in Nazi Germany, see Sheila Fitzpatrick and Robert Gellately, eds., *Accusatory Practices: Denunciation in Modern European History, 1789–1989* (Chicago, 1997); and Gisela Diewald-Kerkmann, *Politische Denunziation im NS-Regime oder die kleine Macht der "Volksgenossen"* (Bonn, 1995).

4. See, for example, Detlev J. K. Peukert, *Inside Nazi Germany: Conformity, Opposition, and Racism in Everyday Life,* translated by Richard Deveson (London, 1987).

5. Don Dillman, *Mail and Telephone Surveys: The Total Design Method* (New York, 1978); Karl-Heinz Reuband, "Survey Methods as a Monitoring Instrument," in H. S. L. Garritsen et al., eds., *Illegal Drug Use: Research Methods for Hidden Populations* (Utrecht, 1993), 22–27.

6. This and other percentage figures are calculated by first excluding the respondents who gave no answer to this question from the total number of respondents to the survey. Hence, of the 188 people who answered the survey completely or in part, 82 people answered that they had believed in National Socialism, 66 answered that they had not believed in National Socialism, and 40 did not answer the question. To this point, we have presented our findings at

several scholarly conferences and symposia, but we have chosen to publish only
some of the findings of this survey in an essay entitled "Die populäre Einschätzung der Gestapo: Wie allgegenwärtig war sie wirklich?," in Paul and Mallmann, *Die Gestapo: Mythos und Realität*, 417–36. A full report of our survey
and oral-history findings will be published by Basic Books in Eric A. Johnson
and Karl-Heinz Reuband, *Life and Death in the Third Reich: Germans and
Jews Remember*.

7. As was characteristic of the Third Reich generally, most people who took
part in the survey had only an elementary school education (66 percent),
though 17 percent had attended gymnasium or university and the rest had finished their educations in either a *Mittelschule* or a *Realschule*. On education
and National Socialism, see, for example, Geoffrey J. Giles, *Students and National Socialism in Germany* (Princeton, N.J., 1985); and Richard Grunberger,
A Social History of the Third Reich (1971; New York, 1987), 362–85.

8. This finding corresponds almost exactly with that of a survey taken by the
U.S. Army shortly after the end of the war. Between April and May 1945, the
U.S. Army questioned some 666 persons in the cities of Marburg, Hersfeld, and
Eschwege between the ages of eighteen and fifty-five about whether they had
listened to foreign-radio broadcasts during the Nazi period. Fifty-one percent
said that they had listened to these broadcasts; only 37 percent said that they
had listened only to German broadcasts. Most respondents to the U.S. Army
survey said that they listened to these broadcasts only at home, although
many did so in the company of close friends, either in their own homes or in
the homes of their friends. Nearly half of the respondents who said that they
had listened to these foreign broadcasts also admitted that they had talked
about what they heard or had spoken with others who related news they had
heard from these broadcasts. See Reinhard Mann, *Protest und Kontrolle im
Dritten Reich: Nationalsozialistische Herrschaft im Alltag einer rheinischen
Grossstadt* (Frankfurt am Main, 1987), 262–63.

9. Interview with Alfred E., Cologne, June 17, 1995. Unfortunately, the tape to
this interview has been lost. Nevertheless, Michael Riesenkönig, an assistant
in our project at the time who recently received his Ph.D. in psychology from
the University of Cologne, heard much the same things when he reinterviewed
Alfred E. on January 8, 1996.

10. Interview with Adam G., Krefeld, June 14, 1995.

11. HStAD, RW34/3, Bl. 27. The priest joined the Nazi Party in 1933 and had
served as a Gestapo *V-Mann* since January 1943.

12. Ralph Wiener, *Gefährliches Lachen: Schwarzer Humor im Dritten Reich* (Hamburg, 1994), 9.

13. Arno Klönne, "Bündische Jugend, Nationalsozialismus, und NS-Staat," in Jürgen Schmädeke and Peter Steinbach, eds., *Der Widerstand gegen den Nationalsozialismus: Die Deutsche Gesellschaft und der Widerstand gegen Hitler* (Munich, 1985), 188.

14. Adolf Hitler, *Mein Kampf*, translated by Ralph Mannheim (Boston, 1971), 412.

15. Michael H. Kater, *The Nazi Party: A Social Profile of Members and Leaders 1919–1945* (Oxford, 1983), 139–48.

16. Michael Burleigh and Wolfgang Wippermann, *The Racial State: Germany 1933–1945* (Cambridge, 1991), 204–5; Detlev Peukert, "Youth in the Third Reich," in Richard Bessel, ed., *Life in the Third Reich* (Oxford, 1987), 27.

17. J. Noakes and G. Pridham, eds., *Nazism 1919–1945*, vol. 2, *State, Economy, and Society 1933–1939* (Exeter, U.K., 1984), 421.

18. Adolf Klein, *Köln im Dritten Reich: Stadtgeschichte der Jahre 1933–1945* (Cologne, 1983), 168.

19. Peukert, "Youth in the Third Reich," 27.

20. Ute Frevert, *Women in German History: From Bourgeois Emancipation to Sexual Liberation*, translated by Stuart McKinnon-Evans (New York, 1989), 244.

21. Ibid., 242.

22. Richard Grunberger, *A Social History of the Third Reich* (1971; London, 1987), 347.

23. Ibid., 355.

24. See, for example, Klein, *Köln im Dritten Reich*, 176, and Wilfried Breyvogel, "Resistenz, Widersinn, und Opposition: Jugendwiderstand im Nationalsozialismus," in Wilfried Breyvogel, ed., *Piraten, Swings, und Junge Garde: Jugendwiderstand im Nationalsozialismus* (Bonn, 1991), 9–16, esp. 10–11.

25. Grunberger, *A Social History of the Third Reich*, 347. Grunberger states that even though 17.5 percent of all recorded crimes in 1943 were attributable to youth, this was a considerably lower figure than the comparable one for 1917, when youth accounted for 27 percent of all crimes.

26. For assessments of public opinion in the Third Reich, see Ian Kershaw, *Popular Opinion and Political Dissent in the Third Reich: Bavaria 1933–1945* (Oxford, 1983); Ian Kershaw, *The "Hitler Myth": Image and Reality in the Third Reich* (Oxford, 1987); Peukert, *Inside Nazi Germany;* and Marlis Steinert, *Hit-*

ler's War and the Germans: Public Mood and Attitude During the Second World War, translated by T. E. J. de Witt (Athens, Ohio, 1977).

27. Peukert, *Inside Nazi Germany,* 152–53.

28. For a critical assessment of the Cologne Edelweiss Pirates, see Bernd-A. Rusinek, *Gesellschaft in der Katastrophe: Terror, Illegalität, Widerstand— Köln 1944–1945* (Essen, 1989). For assessments of youthful opposition in many other localities, see Breyvogel, *Piraten, Swings, und Junge Garde;* and Arno Klönne, "Jugendprotest und Jugendopposition: Von der HJ-Erziehung zum Cliquenwesen der Kriegszeit," in Martin Broszat et al., *Bayern in der NS-Zeit,* vol. 4, *Herrschaft und Gesellschaft im Konflikt* (Munich, 1981), 527–620.

29. Barbara Schellenberger, "Katholischer Jugendwiderstand," in Schmädeke and Steinbach, *Der Widerstand gegen den Nationalsozialismus,* 314. See also her book *Katholische Jugend und Drittes Reich: Eine Geschichte des katholischen Jungmännerverbandes 1933–1939 unter besonderer Berücksichtigung der Rheinprovinz* (Mainz, 1975).

30. Klein, *Köln im Dritten Reich,* 171.

31. For examples in the Cologne area, see ibid., 171–72, and Schellenberger, "Katholischer Widerstand," 315–18.

32. Schellenberger, "Katholischer Widerstand," 320.

33. Klein, *Köln im Dritten Reich,* 171.

34. Ibid., 172.

35. Quoted in Schellenberger, "Katholischer Jugendwiderstand," 321.

36. Klein, *Köln im Dritten Reich,* 172.

37. HStADK, Rep. 112/9225.

38. Ibid.

39. Ibid.

40. See the excellent discussion of these groups in the Rhine-Ruhr area in Alfons Kenkmann, "Navajos, Kittelbach- und Edelweisspiraten: Jugendliche Dissidenten im 'Dritten Reich,'" in Breyvogel, *Piraten, Swings, und Junge Garde,* 138–58.

41. HStAD, RW58/29356. The German names of the songs they had sung were "Jenseits des Tales," "Wenn wir streiten," "Wer schleicht dort im finsteren Walde," and "In einem polen Städtchen."

42. In an interview on February 10, 1993, a Cologne artist named Raffael B., who had been a member of one of these youth groups in Cologne known as the Navajos, described the dress (long white stockings, short shorts with zippers on both sides, and so on) and the activities (such as singing and touring) of Cologne

Navajos in considerable detail. He also related that he and some other members of his small band were arrested in the summer of 1938 while they were on a bicycle tour and that he had spent three days in a basement cell in Cologne Gestapo headquarters before his father was allowed to take him home. In his interview, it became clear that Raffael B. had not considered himself an opponent of the regime, even though he was not an ardent Nazi either. Just as he presents himself today, he simply was mildly nonconformist. During the war he served his country honorably as a member of a flak battalion in northern Norway. After the war he became a well-respected local artist known in part for his depictions of Cologne's *Karneval* and other aspects of Cologne life. Always somewhat independent of spirit but no real radical, he now believes that the Cologne Edelweiss Pirates were "largely criminals" and that there was "too little freedom in those days, but perhaps too much today."

43. Kenkmann, "Navajos, Kittelbach- und Edelweisspiraten," 142.

44. Ibid., 141. See also Arno Klönne, *Jugend im Dritten Reich: Die Hitler Jugend und ihre Gegner* (Düsseldorf, 1982).

45. Peukert, "Youth in the Third Reich," 16.

46. Kenkmann, "Navajos, Kittelbach- und Edelweisspiraten," 138–39.

47. For a mostly positive assessment of the actions and intentions of the Edelweiss Pirates, see Matthias von Hellfeld, *Edelweisspiraten in Köln: Jugendrebellion gegen das 3. Reich: Das Beispiel Köln-Ehrenfeld* (Cologne, 1983); Detlev J. K. Peukert, *Die Edelweisspiraten: Protestbewegung jugendlicher Arbeiter im Dritten Reich: Eine Dokumentation* (Cologne, 1983); and Peukert, *Inside Nazi Germany*, 154–65. For a harsher assessment, see Rusinek, *Gesellschaft in der Katastrophe*.

48. Kenkmann, "Navajos, Kittelbach- und Edelweisspiraten," 154.

49. Michael Kater, *Different Drummers: Jazz in the Culture of Nazi Germany* (New York, 1992), 103. See also Rainer Pohl, "'Schräge Vögel, mausert euch!' Von Renitenz, Übermut, und Verfolgung: Hamburger Swings und Pariser Zazous," in Breyvogel, *Piraten, Swings, und Junge Garde*, 241–70; Peukert, "Youth in the Third Reich," 37–40; and Peukert, *Inside Nazi Germany*, 166–69.

50. Kater, *Different Drummers*, 103–9.

51. Ibid., 104.

52. The first large roundup of swing youth took place in Hamburg in October 1940. See Pohl, "Schräge Vögel, mausert euch!," 252.

53. Quoted in ibid., 243.

54. Peukert, *Inside Nazi Germany*, 202.

55. These are phrases used by the Nazi Party newspaper *Völkischer Beobachter* in a denunciation of swing and Benny Goodman that it published on June 29, 1944, cited in ibid., 201.

56. The text of this interview with Helmut Goldschmidt is published in Barbara Becker-Jákli, ed., *Ich habe Köln doch so geliebt: Lebensgeschichten jüdischer Kölnerinnen und Kölner* (Cologne, 1993), 136. In an interview I conducted with him in his home in Cologne on July 11, 1997, he provided even more details about his past and present enthusiasm for swing music.

57. See, for example, Grunberger, *A Social History of the Third Reich*, 151–52.

58. In September 1942, the Krefeld Gestapo arrested a twenty-two-year-old girl of mixed parentage named änne Hermes after it had been reported to the Gestapo by a fifteen-year-old neighboring girl that she had gone out in public without wearing her Jewish star. According to a letter in her file from Commandant Höss of Auschwitz, she died on May 5, 1943. HStAD, RW58/21813 and RW58/29343.

59. Reported in the *Kölnische Rundschau*, July 7, 1954.

60. See, for example, George L. Mosse's chapter on fascism and sexuality in his *Nationalism and Sexuality: Respectability and Abnormal Sexuality in Modern Europe* (New York, 1985), 153–80.

61. See, for example, the autobiography of Pierre Seel, an Alsatian homosexual who spent months in a concentration camp and then joined the German army. Pierre Seel, *I, Pierre Seel, Deported Homosexual: A Memoir of Nazi Terror*, translated by Joachim Neugroschel (New York, 1995).

62. According to official statistics compiled by the *Statistischen Reichsamt* and published in the *Statistisches Jahrbuch für das Deutsche Reich* (Berlin, 1937), 593, only four women were convicted under paragraph 175 of the German criminal code in 1934 and six women in 1936. On the situation of lesbian women in Nazi Germany, see Claudia Schoppmann, "Zur Situation lesbischer Frauen in der NS-Zeit," in Günter Grau, ed., *Homosexualität in der NS-Zeit: Dokumente einer Diskriminierung und Verfolgung* (Frankfurt am Main, 1993), 35–42; and Claudia Schoppmann, *Nationalsozialistische Sexualpolitik und weibliche Homosexualität* (Pfaffenweiler, 1991).

63. Burleigh and Wippermann, *The Racial State*, 190.

64. *Statistisches Jahrbuch für das Deutsche Reich* (Berlin, 1937), 592; and ibid. (1938), 610.

65. Harry Oosterhuis, "Medicine, Male Bonding, and Homosexuality in Nazi Germany," *Journal of Contemporary History* 32 (1997): 189.

66. For estimates on the number of homosexuals who were interned in concentration camps and their death rate in these camps, see ibid., 188; Burleigh and Wippermann, *The Racial State*, 196–97; Richard Plant, *The Pink Triangle: The Nazi War Against Homosexuals* (New York, 1986), 180; Rüdiger Lautmann, ed., *Seminar: Gesellschaft und Homosexualität* (Frankfurt, 1977), 351.

67. Mosse, *Nationalism and Sexuality*, 158.

68. Oosterhuis, "Medicine, Male Bonding, and Homosexuality in Nazi Germany," 189. Oosterhuis's assessment finds support in an essay by Burkhard Jellonnek, "Staatspolizeiliche Fahndungs-und Ermittlungsmethoden gegen Homosexuelle: Regionale Differenzen und Gemeinsamkeiten," in Gerhard Paul and Klaus-Michael Mallmann, eds., *Die Gestapo: Mythos und Realität* (Darmstadt, 1995), 343–56.

69. Ibid., 188.

70. As prime examples, Oosterhuis cites Burleigh and Wippermann, *The Racial State*; Robert H. Proctor, *Racial Hygiene: Medicine Under the Nazis* (Cambridge, Mass., 1988); and Robert J. Lifton, *The Nazi Doctors: Medical Killing and the Psychology of Genocide* (New York, 1986).

71. Oosterhuis, "Medicine, Male Bonding, and Homosexuality in Nazi Germany," 191.

72. On this institute's treatment of homosexuals, see Geoffrey Cocks, *Psychotherapy in the Third Reich: The Göring Institute* (New York, 1985), esp. 202–16.

73. See, for example, the autobiography of Pierre Seel, *I, Pierre Seel, Deported Homosexual*.

74. For the dental technician's case, see HStAD, RW58/62605 and RW58/36005. For the traveling salesman's case, see HStAD, RW58/2448.

75. There were on average two persons per case in the random sample of sixteen cases. The largest case involved seven persons who were accused of homosexual activity, another had three, and the remaining six cases had only one each.

76. See, for example, HStAD, RW58/62752.

77. See, for example, HStAD, RW58/62605.

78. HStAD, RW58/63516 and RW58/35377.

79. Ibid.

80. HStAD, RW58/23922.

81. Ibid.

82. Ibid.

83. HStAD, RW58/24269.

84. HStADK, Rep. 112/10776. The statement about her penchant for making denunciations was made by the man she accused, Josef P., in the course of the investigation in the case she started against him.

85. That this often happened is clear from many cases in the files. On the Nazi Party's handling of denunciations, see Gisela Diewald-Kerkmann, *Politische Denunziation im NS-Regime;* and John Connelly, "The Uses of *Volksgemeinschaft:* Letters to the NSDAP Kreisleitung Eisenach, 1939–1940," in *Journal of Modern History* 68 (1996): 899–930.

86. HStADK, Rep. 112/10739 and Rep. 112/15295.

87. HStADK, Rep. 112/11449.

88. Ibid.

89. Ibid.

90. Ibid.

91. On the Nazis' persecution of "asocials," see, for example, Burleigh and Wipperman, *The Racial State,* 167–82. On the Nazis' treatment of those who displayed friendship toward Jews, see Sarah Gordon, *Germans and the "Jewish Question"* (Princeton, N.J., 1984); and Robert Gellately, *The Gestapo and German Society: Enforcing Racial Policy* (Oxford, 1990), esp. 160–84.

CHAPTER EIGHT:
NAZI TERROR AND "ORDINARY" GERMANS: THE WAR YEARS

1. The standard account of the Gleiwitz raid credits the SS major (*Sturmbannführer*) Naujocks with having led it. After the war, Naujocks became a businessman in Hamburg and sold a story to the press that he had started World War II. See, for example, William L. Shirer, *The Rise and Fall of the Third Reich: A History of Nazi Germany* (New York, 1960), 519–20; and Louis L. Snyder, *Encyclopedia of the Third Reich* (1976; New York, 1989), 116, 245. But in the investigation of Schäfer for his role in the deportation and murder of the Cologne Jews, it was revealed that he claimed to have been the man who in fact had led the raid. HStADK, Rep. 231/447, Bl. 14–15. Schäfer's role in the raid also received considerable play in the newspapers. See, for example, the article in the *Kölner Stadtanzeiger* on October 7, 1952, entitled "Kölner Schwurgericht: Aktion Auerhahn' eröffnete den Krieg 1939." See also "6000 Frauen und Kinder Vergast," *Westdeutsche Neue Presse,* October 7, 1952.

2. On the progression of the war, see Gerhard L. Weinberg, *A World at Arms:*

A Global History of World War II (Cambridge, 1994). On the mood of the German people at the beginning of the war, see Ian Kershaw, *The "Hitler Myth": Image and Reality in the Third Reich* (Oxford, 1987), 151–52, 165.

3. Howard K. Smith, *Last Train from Berlin* (New York, 1942), 116–17.

4. Ibid., 118ff.

5. Gerhard Weinberg contends that German rations were the best available to any of the major belligerents until the last months of the war. *A World at Arms,* 470. For conditions in Cologne, see Adolf Klein, *Köln im Dritten Reich: Stadtgeschichte der Jahre 1933–1945* (Cologne, 1983), 250.

6. Weinberg, *A World At Arms,* 473.

7. Whether Galen's sermon led Hitler to call a halt to the euthanasia program on August 24, 1941, is still a matter of debate. Michael Burleigh and Wolfgang Wippermann argue, for example, that the program was probably stopped because it had already reached its original target figure. *The Racial State: Germany 1933–1945* (Cambridge, 1991), 153.

8. Klein, *Köln im Dritten Reich,* 256.

9. Kershaw, *The "Hitler Myth,"* 187; and Ian Kershaw, *Popular Opinion and Political Dissent in the Third Reich: Bavaria 1933–1945* (Oxford, 1983), 309–10.

10. Kershaw, *The "Hitler Myth,"* 187, 192.

11. A janitor informed the Munich Gestapo that he had caught the Scholls in the act of placing flyers in a stairway and in the corridors of a Munich University building on February 18, 1943. On February 22, the Scholls and another man named Christian Probst were tried hastily by the People's Court under the leadership of Roland Freisler, who had come specially from Berlin. All three were beheaded a few hours after the trial ended. A second trial against fourteen other members of the White Rose group began on April 19, 1943; Alexander Schmorell, Willi Graf, and Professor Kurt Huber were sentenced to death, and all but one of the other defendants received either jail or prison terms lasting from six months to ten years. In a third trial, which began on July 13, 1943, an additional conspirator received a six-month jail sentence and three others were acquitted. These trials did smash the core of the White Rose group in Munich, but they did not bring an end to the group's influence. Some students continued to disseminate the White Rose's flyers in Munich and other localities, the RAF dropped thousands of the flyers across Germany from the air, Thomas Mann and others broadcast speeches on BBC in July 1943 about the White Rose group, and the resistance group known as the National Committee "Free Ger-

many" distributed flyers about them at the front. On the White Rose group, see Inge Scholl, *Die Weisse Rose* (Frankfurt, 1982); Christian Petry, *Studenten aufs Schafott: Die Weisse Rose und ihr Scheitern* (Munich, 1968); and Michael Schneider and Winfried Süss, *Keine Volksgenossen* (Munich, 1993).

12. For recent works on the July plot, see, for example, Peter Hoffmann, *Stauffenberg: A Family History, 1905–1944* (Cambridge, 1995); and Joachim C. Fest, *Plotting Hitler's Death: The Story of the German Resistance*, translated by Bruce Little (New York, 1996).

13. On Freisler and the People's Court, see, for example, H. W. Koch, *In the Name of the Volk: Political Justice in Hitler's Germany* (London, 1989); Klaus Marxen, *Das Volk und sein Gerichtshof: Eine Studie zum nationalsozialistischen Volksgerichtshof* (Frankfurt am Main, 1994); and Edmund Lauf, *Der Volksgerichtshof und sein Beobachter: Bedingungen und Funktionen der Gerichtsberichterstattung im Nationalsozialismus* (Opladen, 1994).

14. For useful summaries of and literature on these and other resistance groups, see Wolfgang Benz and Walter H. Pehle, eds., *Encyclopedia of German Resistance to the Nazi Movement*, translated by Lance W. Garmer (New York, 1997).

15. Weinberg, *A World at Arms*, 483.

16. On the Allied bombing, see, for example, Alan J. Levine, *The Strategic Bombing of Germany, 1940–1945* (Westport, Conn., 1992); and Hans Rumpf, *The Bombing of Germany*, translated by Edward Fitzgerald (New York, 1962).

17. Reinhard Feinendegen and Dieter Pützhofen, eds., *22. Juni 1943 als Krefeld brannte: Augenzeugenberichte von der Bombennacht* (Krefeld, 1993), 17. See also the similar assessment by Bernhard Schmidt and Fritz Burger of the effect of the bombing on the neighboring city of Moers in *Tatort Moers: Widerstand und Nationalsozialismus im südlichen Altkreis Moers* (Moers, 1995), 391. These authors argue that the leaflets dropped by RAF bombers urging the civilian population to turn against Hitler also had little effect.

18. For eyewitness accounts of the bombing in Cologne, for example, see Heinz Decker et al., eds., *Alltagsgeschichte im Agnesviertel: Die Kriegszeit 1939–1945* (Cologne, 1989).

19. Klein, *Köln im Dritten Reich*, 253.

20. Quoted in Robert Frohn, *Köln 1945–1981: Vom Trümmerhaufen zur Millionenstadt* (Cologne, 1982), 25; also cited in Klein, *Köln im Dritten Reich*, 260.

21. Klein, *Köln im Dritten Reich*, 280.

22. For an intriguing comparison of how Germans and Japanese remember the war, see Ian Buruma, *The Wages of Guilt: Memories of War in Germany and Japan* (New York, 1994). For an excellent comparison of the different ways that East and West Germans have dealt with the Nazi past, see Jeffrey Herf, *Divided Memory: The Nazi Past in the Two Germanys* (Cambridge, Mass., 1997).

23. On foreign workers in Nazi Germany, see Ulrich Herbert, *Fremdarbeiter im Dritten Reich: Politik und Praxis des "Ausländer-Einsatzes" in der deutschen Kriegswirtschaft des Dritten Reiches* (Berlin, 1985); and Edward L. Homze, *Foreign Labor in Nazi Germany* (Princeton, N.J., 1967).

24. See the discussion of the size of the Gestapo in Cologne and in other cities in chapter 2.

25. For disturbing studies detailing the role of ordinary Germans in the murder of the Jews, see, for example, Christopher R. Browning, *Ordinary Men: Reserve Police Battalion 101 and the Final Solution in Poland* (New York, 1992); Daniel Jonah Goldhagen, *Hitler's Willing Executioners: Ordinary Germans and the Holocaust* (New York, 1996); and Raul Hilberg, *Perpetrators, Victims, Bystanders: The Jewish Catastrophe 1933–1945* (New York, 1992).

26. The local Nazi Party newspaper, *Westdeutscher Beobachter*, which was the leading Nazi propaganda organ in the area, carried the story at the greatest length, but the once highly respected and still less biased *Kölnische Zeitung* also reported the execution in some detail. Other descriptions of this case are found in Hans Wüllenweber, *Sondergerichte im Dritten Reich: Vergessene Verbrechen der Justiz* (Frankfurt am Main, 1990), 17; and in Ralph Angermund, *Deutsche Richterschaft 1919–1945: Krisenerfahrung, Illusion, politische Rechtsprechung* (Frankfurt am Main, 1990), 213.

27. Angermund, *Deutsche Richterschaft*, 213.

28. In the entire month of June 1942, for example, the Cologne edition of the Nazi newspaper *Westdeutscher Beobachter* carried articles on a total of twenty people (fifteen men and five women) convicted of criminal activity. All of the cases involved either plundering or theft. Only three, including Paula W.'s case, ended with the death penalty. One of the stories involved a forty-four-year-old married woman named Maria H. from the working-class section of Cologne-Ehrenfeld who was also caught plundering after the bombing attack of May 31, 1942. Unlike Paula W., however, she received only a four-year prison sentence.

29. The "Klingelpütz Gefangenenbücher" (register of prisoners) also shows that two additional Cologne women were found hanged in their cell, both in March 1942. HStADK, Rep. 300, nos. 1–15. From these records, one can deter-

mine that in addition to the five women from Cologne who were executed in Klingelpütz, women from Bonn, Krefeld, Duisburg, Düsseldorf, Essen, Arnsberg, Dortmund, and other localities, including one from Berlin, were also executed in Klingelpütz prison. One cannot be fully certain that the register of prisoners in Klingelpütz included all of the women who were executed in Cologne during these years. For example, at least one other woman, a woman of Jewish background, is known to have been put to death by a lethal injection in a kind of concentration camp that was erected in the Cologne conference hall in the Deutz section of the city. But the register of prisoners does seem to be rather complete until the very last months of the war, and it is certainly more complete than the "Verzeichnis über Hinrichtungen 1941–1944" (catalog of executions, 1941–1944) found in the same archive, which lists only a total of thirteen executed women in Klingelpütz prison. HStADK, Rep. 132/715.

30. Angermund, *Deutsche Richterschaft*, 213.

31. Quoted in Klein, *Köln im Dritten Reich*, 264.

32. For examples of these complaints made by the Reich Justice Ministry to Cologne justice officials in the first years of the war, see HStADK, Rep. 11/1812, "Zu milde Urteile," and HStADK, Rep. 11/1661, "Kriege gegen Deutschland."

33. Angermund, *Deutsche Richterschaft*, 201.

34. HStADK, Rep. 11/1161, Bl. 83.

35. Ibid., Bl. 102.

36. Ibid., Bl. 109.

37. Ibid.

38. Angermund, *Deutsche Richterschaft*, 206–7, 228–29.

39. A computer analysis of a random sample of 51 prewar and 49 wartime cases prosecuted by the Cologne Special Court that led to convictions shows that, between 1933 and 1939, the average length of time from the day a case was opened against a defendant to the day a verdict was reached by the court was 3.4 months. Between 1940 and 1945, the average case took 6.2 months to resolve. Judgments in the war years, however, were measurably harsher. In the prewar years, the median sentence for a person convicted by the Cologne Special Court was imprisonment for six months. During the war, the median sentence of a convicted defendant rose to eighteen months.

40. Richard J. Evans, *Rituals of Retribution: Capital Punishment in Germany 1600–1987* (Oxford, 1996), 689.

41. Ibid., 689–90.

42. Angermund, *Deutsche Richterschaft*, 206; Lothar Gruchmann, *Justiz im Dritten Reich: Anpassung und Unterwerfung in der ära Gürtner* (Munich, 1988), 252.

43. Wolfgang Idel, *Die Sondergerichte in politischen Strafsachen* (Schramberg, 1935), 36; quoted in Ingo Müller, *Hitler's Justice: The Courts of the Third Reich*, translated by Deborah Lucas Schneider (Cambridge, Mass., 1991), 142.

44. Müller, *Hitler's Justice*, 143.

45. Evans, *Rituals of Retribution*, 693.

46. Ibid., 729.

47. Angermund, *Deutsche Richterschaft*, 216–17.

48. See Heinz Wagner, "Die Polizei im Faschismus," in Udo Reifner and B. R. Sonnen, eds., *Strafjustiz und Polizei im Dritten Reich* (Frankfurt am Main, 1984), 161–72, esp. 167ff.

49. HStADK, Rep. 11/1661, Bl. 102.

50. Ibid.

51. Only 40 out of a random sample of 368 non-Jewish defendants with no prior criminal record were convicted between 1933 and 1945 by the Cologne Special Court. Of those who were convicted, 60 percent were sent to jail (usually for periods of less than one year), 20 percent were sent to prison (for periods of one year or more), and 18 percent received fines. One additional person was sent to a mental institution.

52. In a random sample of every eighth Krefeld Gestapo case file, the percentage of non-Jewish defendants with a criminal record rose from 22 percent in the prewar period to 30 percent during the war years. Although these records do not always indicate what ultimately happened to the defendants whose cases were referred to the courts, those with a prior criminal record appear to have received prison sentences that lasted on average for about a year while those with no prior record received an average sentence that called for a period of confinement lasting from a few weeks to a few months.

53. Angermund, *Deutsche Richterschaft*, 212.

54. See, for example, Reinhard Mann, *Protest und Kontrolle im Dritten Reich: Nationalsozialistische Herrschaft im Alltg einer rheinischen Grossstadt* (Frankfurt am Main, 1987), 261–66; Klaus-Michael Mallmann and Gerhard Paul, *Herrschaft und Alltag: Ein Industrierevier im Dritten Reich* (Bonn, 1991), 346–52; and Ana Perez Belmonte, "'Schwarzhören' im II. Weltkrieg: Die Ahndung von 'Rundfunkverbrechen' im Sondergerichtsbezirk Essen 1939–1945" (M. A. thesis, University of Cologne, 1997).

55. An average worker earned 100 to 200 marks per month. According to Klein, a large set in Cologne cost about 70 marks and a small set cost about 35 marks. *Köln im Dritten Reich,* 247. Elsewhere the price was similar. It should be noted, however, that most German households could afford an even better radio than the inexpensively priced people's radio. According to figures provided by Ansgar Dillar, people's radios accounted for only 39 percent of the 18.2 million radio sets in operation in Germany in 1943. On the price, power, and volume of radios in Nazi Germany, see his article "Der Volksempfänger: Propaganda- und Wirtschaftsfaktor," *Studienkreis Rundfunk und Geschichte* 9 (1983): 140–57.

56. On the nature and content of these broadcasts, see Conrad Pütter, *Rundfunk gegen das "Dritte Reich": Ein Handbuch* (Munich, 1986); and BBC External Services, *"Hier ist England—Live aus London": Das Deutsche Programm der British Broadcasting Corporation 1938–1988* (London, 1988).

57. Konrad Adenauer, *Konrad Adenauer: Memoirs 1945–1953,* translated by Beate Ruhm von Oppen (Chicago, 1966), 18.

58. Smith, *Last Train from Berlin,* 109.

59. Ibid., 110.

60. BBC External Services, *"Hier ist England—Live aus London,"* 7, 10.

61. As discussed in chapter 7, 53 percent of the respondents to our survey of elderly Cologne residents answered that they had listened to BBC broadcasts during the war, and 51 percent of the respondents to a U.S. Army survey taken just after the war in other localities said they had listened to such broadcasts. Hence, if about 50 percent of Germans had listened to these broadcasts during the war, the BBC had perhaps as many as twenty to thirty million German listeners.

62. HStADK, Rep. 112/6215. According to official statistics, Bayenthal had 13,173 inhabitants in January 1941, and 13,002 inhabitants in January 1942. For these statistics, see HStADK, Rep. 23/272.

63. In my random sample of every eighth Krefeld Gestapo case file, I uncovered a total of four cases of this offense that were not already listed under the heading of *Rundfunkverbrechen* in the archival card file. Multiplying this figure by eight and adding the result to the sixteen cases listed in the archival card file yields a total of forty-eight cases of this offense.

64. An analysis of the gender background of all 310 Cologne Special Court cases involving this offense shows that 70 percent of the defendants were male and 30 percent were female.

65. From 1942 to 1945, the yearly number of cases was 46, 30, 35, and 4, respectively.

66. Interview with Adam G., a former soldier who often listened to BBC on the eastern front, Krefeld, June 14, 1995. Interview with Alfred E., a former Eberswalde policeman and guard in Dachau concentration camp who regularly listened to BBC in his home, Cologne, June 17, 1995.

67. In her study of sixty-four people investigated by the Essen Gestapo for the crime of listening to foreign-radio broadcasts, Ana Perez Belmonte found that the Gestapo sent only two of them to a concentration camp; both had a prior criminal record, and one had also been a former Communist Party member. "'Schwarzhören' im II: Weltkrieg," 49.

68. HStAD, RW58/11707.

69. Two of the cases are from the Krefeld Gestapo case files: HStAD, RW58/48526 and RW58/4257; RW58/2018 and RW58/59973. The other is from the Cologne Special Court files: HStADK, Rep. 112/18332.

70. HStADK, Rep. 112/18332.

71. Ibid.

72. Ibid.

73. HStADK, Rep. 112/13663.

74. HStADK, Rep. 112/12215.

75. HStADK, Rep. 112/12214.

76. Ibid.

77. On the People's Court treatment of *Wehrkraftzersetzung*, see, for example, Koch, *In the Name of the Volk*, esp. 235. On the military courts, see Manfred Messerschmidt and Fritz Wüllner, *Die Wehrmachtsjustiz im Dienste des Nationalsozialismus* (Baden-Baden, 1987). See also Mallmann and Paul, *Herrschaft und Alltag*, 381–83.

78. Cited in Müller, *Hitler's Justice*, 146.

79. Ibid.

80. Koch, *In the Name of the Volk*, 235.

81. Müller, *Hitler's Justice*, 145.

82. Messerschmidt and Wüllner argue that about 700 German soldiers were condemned to death for this offense each month in the last quarter of 1944. *Die Wehrmachtsjustiz im Dienste des Nationalsozialismus*, 132.

83. HStAD, RW58/6323.

84. HStAD, RW58/26359.

85. Ibid. After the defeat of Poland, nearly 11,000 Polish soldiers, including

8,300 officers, could not be accounted for and seemed to have disappeared mysteriously. In February 1943, in the Katyn forest near Smolensk, a German communications regiment uncovered the graves of 4,800 Polish soldiers who, the German government claimed, had been killed by the Russians in the spring of 1940. At the Nuremberg Trials after the war, the Russians disputed this. The tribunal decided to side with the Germans, however, since the Polish soldiers had not written any letters after April 1940, when the Russians still controlled the territory. See Joseph Persico, *Nuremberg: Infamy on Trial* (New York, 1994), 359.

86. The court was the Gericht der Feldkommandantur (V) 244. The number the court assigned to the case was STLNr 73/44.

87. See, for example, Kershaw, *Popular Opinion and Political Dissent in the Third Reich*, 224–77.

88. For a discussion of some of our survey results dealing with the German population's knowledge of the mass murder of the Jews, see Eric A. Johnson and Karl-Heinz Reuband, "Die populäre Einschätzung der Gestapo: Wie allgegenwärtig war sie wirklich?," in Gerhard Paul and Klaus-Michael Mallmann, eds., *Die Gestapo: Mythos und Realität* (Darmstadt, 1995), 428–30.

89. See, for example, HStAD, RW58/29078, RW58/29078, and RW58/62370.

90. HStAD, RW58/65449.

91. Bernward Dörner, who has also researched the Gestapo's treatment of *Heimtücke* offenses in Krefeld, reminds us, however, of the trauma and hardships many people continued to face after their cases had been dismissed: "The dismissal of investigations did not mean the end of the terror. The accused persons [usually] had to sign a declaration that warned them that they would be threatened with 'state police measures' if they were accused again in a new case. . . . In numerous cases the accused persons lost their job or had to give up their business." "Gestapo und 'Heimtücke': Zur Praxis der Geheimen Staatspolizei bei der Verfolgung von Verstössen gegen das 'Heimtücke-Gesetz,'" in Paul and Mallmann, *Die Gestapo: Mythos und Realität*, 325–42, esp. 341–42.

92. HStADK, Rep. 112/8237.

93. Ibid.

94. On the internal situation in Germany near the end of the war, see, for example, Rolf-Dieter Müller and Gerd R. Ueberschär, *Kriegsende 1945: Die Zerstörung des Deutschen Reiches* (Frankfurt am Main, 1994).

95. For a moving portrait of the terrifying experiences of one man who was caught in the clutches of the Cologne Gestapo in the last year of the war, see

Leo Schwering, *In den Klauen der Gestapo: Tagebuchaufzeichnungen der Ja-hre 1944–1945* (Cologne, 1988).

96. Thousands of these people were incarcerated in "protective custody," and large numbers were foreigners. Unfortunately, prison statistics for the city of Cologne are available for only some of the years of the Third Reich. But, for example, according to those that exist for 1934, some 18,203 people (15,740 men and 2,463 women) spent some period of confinement in Klingelpütz in that year alone. "Gefängnisstatistik Köln," HStADK, Rep. 321/190–91. It is also uncertain how many people were executed in Klingelpütz. The estimate of 1,000–1,500 executions comes from a volume on resistance and persecution in Cologne that accompanied an exhibit at the Cologne's historical archive in 1974. See Historisches Archiv der Stadt Köln, *Widerstand und Verfolgung in Köln 1933–1945* (Cologne, 1981), 367. For an analysis of the male and female inmates in Klingelpütz prison, see my article "German Women and Nazi Jus-tice: Their Role in the Process from Denunciation to Death," *Historical Social Research/Historische Sozialforschung,* 20 (1995): 59–62.

97. Klingelpütz prison served as the place of execution for the Special Courts of Cologne, Dortmund, Düsseldorf, Essen, Hagen, Duisburg, Aachen, Wup-pertal, Koblenz, and Münster. Records detailing the numbers of people exe-cuted in Klingelpütz are missing for most of the period, but the records that do exist for the period between February 1941 and March 1944 show that at least 529 men and 22 women were executed during this period, which, except for the last year of the war, was certainly the heaviest execution period. HStADK, Rep. 132/715, "Verzeichnis über Hinrichtungen 1941–1944." The women have al-ready been discussed in this chapter. Of the men who were executed in Klingel-pütz between February 1941 and March 1944, 38 were born in Cologne, 5 in Aachen, 2 in Bonn, 4 in Dühren, 2 in Brühl, and none in Bergheim. Many of the executed men were foreigners: 23 were born in Paris, 4 in Brussels, and nu-merous others in Ukraine and Russia.

98. Barbara Becker-Jákli, *Ich habe Köln doch so geliebt: Lebensgeschichten jüdischer Kölnerinnen und Kölner* (Köln, 1993), 141–42. Goldschmidt's ac-count of his experience in Klingelpütz was similar to that of another young Jewish man named Heinrich Becker who was also confined in Klingelpütz in 1943, though about six months later than Goldschmidt. Ibid., 223–24.

99. There are several large files on this trial. Unfortunately, it was only possi-ble to read three of them; the others seem to still be with the Bundeskrimina-lamt, which is using them for an ongoing investigation. The ones I have read

are entitled "Rechtswidrige Tötung von Stapo Häftlingen in Klingelpütz,"
HStADK, Rep. 248/265–66, and "Gestapoflügel in Klingelpütz," HStADK,
Rep. 231/95. The ones that are still with the Bundeskriminalamt are Rep. 248/
334–344.

100. These were the reasons given by the state prosecuting attorney's office
for the dismissal of the case. HStAD, Rep. 248/266, Bl. 351–64.

101. HStAD, Rep. 248/265, Bl. 21.

102. HStADK, Rep. 231/95, Bl. 67.

103. HStADK, Rep. 248/265, Bl. 21 and Bl. 166, and Rep. 231/95, Bl. 52.

104. HStADK, Rep. 231/95, Bl. 68.

105. HStADK, Rep. 248/266, Bl. 278ff.

106. HStADK, Rep. 248/266, Bl. 230.

107. HStADK, Rep. 248/265, Bl. 24.

108. HStADK, Rep. 248/265, Bl. 170e. In testimony during the 1947 denazification trial of the Krefeld Gestapo officer Alfred Effenberg, the Association of
Victims of Nazi Persecution (VVN) related that the U.S. Army had also discovered the bodies of several victims buried in the courtyard of the former Gestapo
headquarters in Krefeld. BAK, Z 42 IV/4222 (Alfred Effenberg, Spruchgericht
Bielefeld), Bl. 28.

CHAPTER NINE: A SUMMATION

1. Robert Gellately, for example, who has done more than perhaps anyone to
bring attention to the importance of political denunciations in Nazi Germany,
has recently begun to question whether Nazi Germany was a police state at all:
"These findings about the role of denunciations in the everyday operation of
the police, and my characterization of the Nazi police as generally reactive and
greatly reliant upon help from the outside, does put into further question at
least some of our understandings of the very notion of a 'police state' and all
that concept implies." "Denunciation in Twentieth-Century Germany: Aspects
of Self-Policing in the Third Reich and the German Democratic Republic,"
Journal of Modern History 68 (1996): 942. Elsewhere Gellately has recently
referred to Nazi Germany as "a radical version of a self-policing society." "Denunciations and Nazi Germany: New Insights and Methodological Problems,"
Historical Social Research/Historische Sozialforschung 22 (1997): 230. Several other scholars also now argue that the Gestapo was primarily a "reactive"
organ. See, for example, Gisela Diewald-Kerkmann, *Politische Denunziation*

im NS-Regime oder "die kleine Macht der Volksgenossen" (Bonn, 1995); and Klaus-Michael Mallmann and Gerhard Paul, "Allwissend, allmächtig, allgegenwärtig?: Gestapo, Gesellschaft, und Widerstand," *Zeitschrift für Zeitgeschichte* 41 (1993): 992.

2. On these issues, see, for example, Michael Burleigh, *Death and Deliverance: Euthanasia in Nazi Germany c. 1900–1945* (New York, 1994); Henry Friedlander, *The Origins of Nazi Genocide: From Euthanasia to the Final Solution* (Chapel Hill, 1995); Gisela Bock, *Zwangssterilisation im Nationalsozialismus: Studien zur Rassenpolitik und Frauenpolitik* (Opladen, 1986); Claudia Koonz, *Mothers in the Fatherland: Women, the Family, and Nazi Politics* (New York, 1987); Atina Grossmann, *Reforming Sex: The German Movement for Birth Control and Abortion Reform* (New York, 1995); Michael Burleigh and Wolfgang Wippermann, *The Racial State: Germany 1933–1945* (New York, 1991); Eric A. Johnson, "German Women and Nazi Justice: Their Role in the Process from Denunciation to Death," *Historical Social Research/Historische Sozialforschung* 20 (1995): 33–69; and Eric A. Johnson, "Gender, Race, and the Gestapo," *Historical Social Research/Historische Sozialforschung* 22 (1997): 240–53.

3. As already mentioned in the discussion in chapter 7 of our survey of the elderly Cologne population, 65 percent of Protestants against only 51 percent of Protestants in Cologne responded that they had believed in National Socialism during the Third Reich.

4. Gellately's first major work on the subject was *The Gestapo and German Society: Enforcing Racial Policy 1933–1945* (Oxford, 1990). For citations of some of his other recent studies of denunciation, and for Diewald-Kerkmann's recent book on the subject, see note 1. For studies of denunciation in a comparative perspective, see Robert Gellately and Sheila Fitzpatrick, eds., *Accusatory Practices: Denunciation in Modern European History, 1989–1989* (Chicago, 1997).

5. Diewald-Kerkmann, *Politische Denunziation*, 9.

6. To this point, no one, to my knowledge, has systematically investigated denunciations of targeted groups like Communists, Socialists, Jehovah's Witnesses, recalcitrant priests and ministers, and other serious resisters. Of those who have done the most important work on denunciations, Robert Gellately focused originally on cases of *Rassenschande* and "friendship with Jews" in his pioneering book on the Gestapo, *The Gestapo and German Society*. More recently, he has extended his work on denunciations to include analyses of the

persecution of Polish workers and people who listened to foreign-radio broad-casts. For some of his new findings, see his article "Denunciation in Twentieth-Century Germany," esp. 935–39. Another leading figure in the study of the Gestapo, Gerhard Paul, has also recently analyzed denunciations in cases of listening to foreign-radio broadcasts in *Die Gestapo in Schleswig-Holstein* (Hamburg, 1996). The pioneer in the systematic study of denunciations in Nazi Germany, Reinhard Mann, did not study denunciations of Communists, Jews, or religious sects in his study of Düsseldorf Gestapo cases. See his *Protest und Kontrolle im Dritten Reich: Nationalsozialistische Herrschaft im Alltag einer rheinischen Grossstadt* (Frankfurt am Main, 1987). Diewald-Kerkmann's im-portant study of political denunciations to Nazi Party authorities in Lippe, *Poli-tische Denunziation im NS-Regime*, also does not directly analyze denuncia-tions of members of religious sects, Communists, Socialists, priests, and other serious opponents of the Nazi regime.

7. If one simply subtracts Jews and foreigners from the random sample of Kref-eld Gestapo case files, one finds that 97 cases were begun by voluntary denunci-ations, against 211 cases that the Gestapo initiated on the basis of other types of information it received. When one compares the cases initiated by civilian denunciations against the rest, one finds several clear indications that the for-mer were of much less consequence. Those whose cases did not begin with a denunciation, for example, were more than twice as likely to be taken into pro-tective custody (33 percent versus 14 percent) or sent to a concentration camp (4 percent versus 2 percent), and almost three times as likely to have been arrested before appearing at Gestapo headquarters (71 percent versus 26 percent) than those whose cases began with a denunciation. Furthermore, although this is a subjective measure based on an interpretation of the gravity of the acts that the defendants were accused of committing, serious and direct protest or criticism of the regime was the charge in the case of 29 percent of those in the former group, but in only 4 percent of those in the latter group.

8. This conclusion is supported by the results of the survey of the elderly Co-logne population that Karl-Heinz Reuband and I conducted. In that survey, only a similarly small fraction of the respondents reported that they had ever been the victim of a denunciation in Nazi Germany. It also finds support in Mil-ton Mayer, *They Thought They Were Free: The Germans 1933–1945* (Chicago, 1955), 188. In a discussion between Mayer and a German teacher in a town in the province of Hesse in the early 1950s, the teacher told Mayer that there had been thirty-five teachers in his school during the Nazi years and that all but five

joined the Nazi Party. But of the thirty-five teachers, the man explained to Mayer, "only four, well, five, were fully convinced Nazis." And of these people, "only one was a real fanatic, who might denounce a colleague to the authorities."

9. Timothy Garton Ash, "The Romeo File," *New Yorker,* April 28 and May 5, 1997, 165. Some estimates of the number of *Stasi* informers in the GDR are much higher. In a recent article, Robert Gellately cites a former *Stasi* member's statement that in the 1980s one in every eight persons in the GDR worked for the *Stasi* and about one-third of the population had worked for the *Stasi* at one time or another. "Denunciations in Twentieth-Century Germany," 955. For a lengthier analysis of East German informers, see Hanjörg Geiger, *Die Inoffi-ziellen Mitarbeiter: Stand der gegenwärtigen Erkenntnisse* (Berlin, 1993).

10. Peter Wyden, *Stella* (New York, 1992).

11. Richard Grunberger, *A Social History of the Third Reich* (1971; London, 1974), 153. For other studies of female denunciations that are also based on a case studies approach, see Inge Marssolek, *Die Denunziatin: Helene Schwärzel 1944–1947* (Bremen, 1993); and Helga Schubert, *Judasfrauen: Zehn Fallg-eschichten weiblicher Denunziation im Dritten Reich* (Frankfurt am Main, 1990).

12. Diewald-Kerkmann, *Politische Denunziation im NS-Regime,* 131–36. Klaus Marxen, *Das Volk und sein Gerichtshof: Eine Studie zum nationalsozia-listischen Volksgerichtshof* (Frankfurt am Main, 1994), 71.

13. Grunberger again provides several examples of German youths, with the encouragement of the Hitler Youth organization, denouncing their parents and teachers. *A Social History of the Third Reich,* 151–52.

14. Of the 1,132 randomly selected cases, only six involved teachers accused of illegal behavior. Two were Krefeld Jewish teachers found in the sample of Kref-eld Gestapo case files; the other four were non-Jewish teachers found in the sample of Cologne Special Court case files. The only one of these teachers who was denounced by a pupil was discussed in chapter 6. HStADK, Rep. 112/11381. It involved a Catholic priest and teacher in a seminary in Bad Godesberg who was denounced in 1934 by a former pupil for attempting to stir up revolu-tionary agitation among the seminarians. The case was dismissed four years later when the priest's pupil decided to take back his accusation and after the priest had already left the country for fear of arrest. The cases of the other three teachers in the Cologne Special Court case files also ended in dismissals. See HStADK, Rep. 112/14520, Rep. 112/4078, and Rep. 112/6232. The two Jewish

teachers in Krefeld, however, met a worse fate. The first of these cases began on April 11, 1933, when the superintendent of schools in Krefeld ordered a background check on a twenty-eight-year-old teacher named Walter K. who was suspected of being a Communist. Walter K. fled to Paris before he could be caught. See HStAD, RW58/54083. The other case began in July 1941 and involved a case of alleged political libel, started by a denunciation made by a city inspector against a forty-seven-year-old teacher named Josef D. who taught at the Jewish *Volkshochschule* in Krefeld. Although the Gestapo decided to issue only a warning in Josef D.'s case at the time, on April 21, 1942, he and his family were "evacuated to the east." See HStAD, RW58/59311.

15. On the Nazi vote, see especially Thomas Childers, *The Nazi Voter: The Social Foundations of Fascism in Germany, 1919–1933* (Chapel Hill, N. C., 1983); Richard Hamilton, *Who Voted for Hitler?* (Princeton, N.J., 1982); and Jürgen W. Falter, *Hitlers Wähler* (Munich, 1991). On Nazi Party membership, see Michael H. Kater, *The Nazi Party: A Social Profile of Members and Leaders* (Cambridge, Mass., 1983); and William Brustein, *The Logic of Evil: The Social Origins of the Nazi Party, 1925–1933* (New Haven, Conn., 1996).

CHAPTER TEN:
PERSECUTION AND DEPORTATION, 1939–1942

1. See, for example, Bernard Wasserstein, *Britain and the Jews of Europe, 1939–1945* (Oxford, 1979); David S. Wyman, *The Abandonment of the Jews: America and the Holocaust, 1941–1945* (New York, 1984); David S. Wyman, "Why Auschwitz Wasn't Bombed," in Yisrael Gutman and Michael Berenbaum, eds., *Anatomy of the Auschwitz Death Camp* (Bloomington, Ind., 1994), 569–87; and Deborah E. Lipstadt, *Beyond Belief: The American Press and the Coming of the Holocaust 1933–1945* (New York, 1986).

2. Christopher R. Browning, *Ordinary Men: Reserve Police Battalion 101 and the Final Solution in Poland* (New York, 1992); Daniel Jonah Goldhagen, *Hitler's Willing Executioners: Ordinary Germans and the Holocaust* (New York, 1996).

3. Browning, *Ordinary Men*, 170.

4. Ibid., 184.

5. Goldhagen, *Hitler's Willing Executioners*, 14, 455 (Goldhagen's italics).

6. Walter Laqueur, *The Terrible Secret: An Investigation into the Suppression of Information About Hitler's "Final Solution"* (London, 1980).

7. Interview with Helene S. and her husband, Cologne, February 3, 1994. Whereas Helene S. had answered on a written questionnaire in the fall of 1993 that she had heard about the mass murder of the Jews before the end of the war, she was not given the chance to confirm this to me when I interviewed her because her husband interrupted our discussion with the statement attributed to him in the text.

8. Marion A. Kaplan, *Between Dignity and Despair: Jewish Life in the Third Reich* (New York, 1998), 15.

9. Adolf Klein, *Köln im Dritten Reich: Stadtgeschichte der Jahre 1933–1945* (Cologne, 1983), 242.

10. There is considerable debate about when the decision was reached to set the Holocaust in motion. On this debate, see, for example, Christopher R. Browning, "Beyond 'Intentionalism' and 'Functionalism': The Decision for the Final Solution Reconsidered," in *The Path to Genocide: Essays on Launching the Final Solution* (New York, 1992), 86–121.

11. Joachim Remak, ed., *The Nazi Years: A Documentary History* (Englewood Cliffs, N.J., 1969), 145.

12. Marion Kaplan finds that 229 anti-Jewish decrees were passed by "various government organs" between *Kristallnacht* and September 1, 1939, after which time 525 decrees were passed that "tormented Jews between the outbreak of war and the 'Final Solution.'" *Between Dignity and Despair*, 150. See also Konrad Kwiet, "Nach dem Pogrom: Stufen der Ausgrenzung," in Wolfgang Benz, ed., *Die Juden in Deutschland 1933–1945: Leben unter nationalsozialistischer Herrschaft* (Munich, 1988), 545–659.

13. Benz, "Jüdische Bevölkerungsstatistik," in Benz, *Die Juden in Deutschland,* 738.

14. Ibid., 733. Kaplan cites one estimate that there were no more than 14,500 Jews left in Germany in July 1944 even though the deportation and murder of the Jews continued into the spring of 1945. *Between Dignity and Despair*, 193.

15. Her testimony is in Barbara Becker-Jákli, ed., *Ich habe Köln doch so geliebt: Lebensgeschichten jüdischer Kölnerinnen und Kölner* (Cologne, 1993), 111–13.

16. Bernhard Schmidt and Fritz Burger, *Tatort Moers: Widerstand und Nationalsozialismus im südlichen Altkreis Moers* (Moers, 1995), 356.

17. Kaplan, *Between Dignity and Despair*, 146–63.

18. Cited in ibid., 158. For other reactions and for the regulations about the star, see Kwiet, "Nach dem Pogrom," 614–33.

19. Victor Klemperer, *Ich will Zeugnis ablegen bis zum letzten: Tagebücher 1933–1941* (Berlin, 1995), 669, 671.

20. Becker-Jákli, *Ich habe Köln doch so geliebt*, 111.

21. HStADK, RW8/9.

22. Most of the details of this case are also reported by Dieter Hangebruch in his "Emigriert—Deportiert: Das Schicksal der Juden in Krefeld zwischen 1933–1945," *Krefelder Studien* 2 (1980): 234. For a discussion of other Jews' experiences during bombing raids, see Kaplan, *Between Dignity and Despair*, 160–61.

23. During the war years, 66 percent (nineteen out of twenty-nine) of the cases of alleged illegal activity involving so-called full Jews investigated by the Krefeld Gestapo did not result from civilian denunciations and were thus initiated by either the Gestapo itself or other Nazi officials.

24. HStAD, RW 58/35173.

25. HStAD, RW58/35180.

26. In the appendix to his study of the fate of Krefeld Jews, "Emigriert—Deportiert," Dieter Hangebruch notes that Frau P. died in 1939. It is noted in her case file that she was ill at the time of her interrogation, but no specifics about her illness are provided.

27. HStAD, RW58/42306.

28. Dieter Hangebruch calculates that by 1941, 48 percent of Krefeld's Jews had left the city. He also explains that most of the Jews who emigrated were "as a rule in their young and middle years," and that wealthy Jews were more apt to have emigrated than poor Jews. "Emigriert—Deportiert," 197.

29. HStAD, RW58/4439.

30. Michael Zimmermann, "Die Gestapo und die regionale Organisation der Judendeportation: Das Beispiel der Stapo-Leitstelle Düsseldorf," in Gerhard Paul and Klaus-Michael Mallmann, eds., *Die Gestapo: Mythos und Realität* (Darmstadt, 1995), 358.

31. HStAD, RW58/26125.

32. See, for example, HStAD, RW58/29938.

33. Hangebruch, "Emigriert—Deportiert," 244.

34. Raul Hilberg, *The Destruction of the European Jews* (New York, 1961), 299–300. On the Cologne deportations, see Horst Matzerath, "Der Weg der Kölner Juden in den Holocaust: Versuch einer Rekonstruction," in Horst Matzerath, ed., *Die jüdischer Opfer des Nationalsozialismus aus Köln: Gedenkbuch* (Cologne, 1995), 530–53.

35. In October 1941, there were roughly 73,000 Jews in Berlin—about 40 per-

cent of all Jews left in Germany. Wolfgang Benz, "Überleben im Untergrund 1943–1945," in Benz, *Die Juden in Deutschland,* 660–700, esp. 684.

36. HStADK, Rep. 231/447–519.

37. The judgment in the trial is found in HStADK, Rep. 231/519, Bl. 4–33.

38. Hilberg, *The Destruction of the European Jews,* 299.

39. The indictment, found in HStADK, Rep. 231/517, Bl. 31–102, was filed on December 11, 1952. The quoted passage is on Bl. 75.

40. HStADK, Rep. 231/512. In his testimony of May 13, 1952, Löffler stated: "As the [Jewish] desk head, I personally had nothing to do with the evacuations. The actual evacuation itself and indeed the number of people to be evacuated was ordered by decree from the Reich Central Security Office (RSHA). The compilation of the list for the transports, that is, the task of naming the people, lay with the Association of German Jews. For the city district of Cologne, the Cologne Jewish Community under the leadership of the Jewish Community secretary Bähr and later Bernhard were responsible. The Jewish Community secretary then informed the Jews who were to be evacuated what luggage they could take with them and when and where they had to report. The way it went was the following: The RSHA sent an order about the number of Jews to be evacuated to the responsible Gestapo post and also to the Association of German Jews in Berlin. The latter then notified the local Jewish Community in question about the number and age of the Jews to be evacuated. The date of the evacuation was specified in the order sent by the RSHA. The selection of the Jews to be evacuated lay not with the Gestapo post, rather with the Jewish Community. Neither the [Jewish] desk head nor the head of the Gestapo post had any influence in determining which particular Jews were to be evacuated."

41. Hangebruch, "Emigriert—Deportiert," 237. Additional proof of this comes from a letter written by a Jewish man from Krefeld named Max S. on July 20, 1954, which Schulenburg used to support his case for regaining his full police pension. In this letter, Max S. credited Schulenburg with saving his daughter's life by taking her name off the list of the Krefeld Jews to be deported to Theresienstadt in the fall of 1944. HStAD, NW130/310, Bl. 13.

42. For the role that the Jewish community in Budapest played in the deportation of the Hungarian Jews, for example, see the Israeli journalist and historian Tom Segev's discussion of the great stir that the Rudolf Kastner trial caused in Israel in the 1950s. *The Seventh Million: The Israelis and the Holocaust,* translated by Haim Watzman (New York, 1993), 255–310. In my interview with a Holocaust survivor named Herbert K., who was the son of the former head of

Nuremberg's Jewish community, he told me that his father was often in daily contact with the head of the Nuremberg Gestapo's Jewish desk as they worked out the details of the deportations of Jews from Nuremberg. Interview with Herbert K., Saddlebrook, N.J., July 28, 1995.

43. HStADK, 231/517, Bl. 75.

44. Ibid., Bl. 78.

45. Zimmermann, "Die Gestapo und die regionale Organisation der Judendeportationen," 364.

46. HStADK, Rep. 231/517, Bl. 79.

47. Ibid., Bl. 80–82.

48. Ibid., Bl. 83.

49. Ibid., Bl. 83–84.

50. A copy of this letter was sent to me by Bernard K.'s son, Herbert K., who himself is a concentration camp survivor.

51. Hangebruch, "Emigriert—Deportiert," 236–52; Zimmermann, "Die Gestapo und die regionale Organisation der Judendeportationen."

52. Hangebruch, "Emigriert—Deportiert," 249.

53. Schmidt and Burger, *Tatort Moers,* 363.

54. Michael Zimmermann explains that even the Gestapo found the connection between the deportations and the slaughterhouse embarrassing and therefore decided to change the name of the depot from whence the Jews of the Düsseldorf area were deported from "Schlachthof (slaughterhouse) in Düsseldorf-Derendorf" to "Gebäude (building) in Düsseldorf-Derendorf, Rathausstrasse 23/25." "Die Gestapo und die regionale Organisation der Judendeportationen," 366.

55. Hangebruch, "Emigriert—Deportiert," 244.

56. Ibid., 244–47.

57. Ibid., 248–49.

58. Zimmermann, "Die Gestapo und die regionale Organisation der Judendeportation," 358, 365.

59. Ibid., 371.

60. Ibid., 370–71.

CHAPTER ELEVEN: MURDER ONE BY ONE, 1943–1945

1. As Raul Hilberg has written: "With the gradual disappearance of more than a quarter-million Jews in the mysterious 'East,' a wave of rumors drifted back

to Germany. The rumors were connected and combined with earlier reports of mobile killing operations in Russia, and as the flow seeped into every town and every social quarter, the Gestapo felt itself surrounded by whispers." *The Destruction of the European Jews* (New York, 1961), 299.

2. Daniel Jonah Goldhagen, *Hitler's Willing Executioners: Ordinary Germans and the Holocaust* (New York, 1996). See ch. 1, n. 38.

3. HStAD, RW58/869, RW58/53199, RW58/34515, and RW58/46518.

4. See the Krefeld and Düsseldorf Gestapo case files of Oskar H., HStAD, RW58/58325 and RW58/62562.

5. Hangebruch records that Hedwig Mahler probably died in 1943 and that she was officially declared deceased on December 31, 1945. See the appendix to his "Emigriert—Deportiert: Das Schicksal der Juden in Krefeld zwischen 1933 und 1945," *Krefelder Studien* 2 (1980). On the deportations of Jews from the Netherlands, see Bob Moore, *Victims and Survivors: The Nazi Persecution of the Jews in the Netherlands 1940–1945* (London, 1997), 91–115.

6. The translation of Goebbels's remarks is from Joachim Remak, ed., *The Nazi Years: A Documentary History* (Englewood Cliffs, N.J., 1969), 157. For the original German text of Goebbels's article "Die Juden sind schuld," see Hans Dieter Müller, *Facsimile Querschnitt durch das Reich* (Munich, 1964), 98–101.

7. Arnold Paucker, *Standhalten und Widerstehen: Der Widerstand deutscher und österreichischer Juden gegen die Nationalsozialistische Diktatur* (Essen, 1995), cited in Marion Kaplan, *Between Dignity and Despair: Jewish Life in Nazi Germany* (New York, 1998), 214. The Krefeld Gestapo case files support Paucker's assertion, especially in regard to Jewish protest during the war. Whereas only 10 percent of the Krefeld Gestapo's cases started against non-Jews involved some kind of protest against the regime, and only 2 percent had to do with what might be considered serious protest, 18 percent of the wartime cases of Krefeld Jews investigated for wrongdoing involved protest against the regime, and 10 percent involved serious protest.

8. Victor Klemperer, *Ich will Zeugnis ablegen bis zum letzten: Tagebücher 1933–1945*, 2 vols. (Berlin, 1995).

9. Kaplan estimates that between 3,000 and 5,000 Jews in Germany came out of hiding after the war. *Between Dignity and Despair*, 288. Hannah Arendt's *Eichmann in Jerusalem: A Report on the Banality of Evil* (New York, 1963) caused a great stir when it was published, especially because of her argument about Jewish passivity and compliance during the Holocaust. For examples of the criticism that was lodged against her, see Marie Syrkin, "Hannah Arendt:

The Clothes of an Empress," *Dissent* 10 (1963): 345–52; John Gross, "Arendt on Eichmann," *Encounter* (November 1963): 65–74; Bruno Bettelheim, "Eichmann; the System; the Victims," *New Republic* (June 1963): 23–33; and Norman Podhoretz, "Hannah Arendt on Eichmann: A Study in the Perversity of Brilliance," *Commentary* (September 1963): 201–8.

10. Nathan Stoltzfus, *Resistance of the Heart: Intermarriage and the Rosenstrasse Protest in Nazi Germany* (New York, 1996), 192–208.

11. Kaplan, *Between Dignity and Despair*, 78.

12. An official governmental report on deportation statistics listed 51,327 Jews still in Germany as of January 1, 1943. Hilberg, *The Destruction of the European Jews*, 299.

13. Wolfgang Benz, "Überleben im Untergrund 1943–1945," in Wolfgang Benz, ed., *Die Juden in Deutschland 1933–1945: Leben unter nationalsozialistischer Herrschaft* (Munich, 1988), 684, 690. This figure did not include the approximately 5,000 Jews who had gone into hiding.

14. On these categories and the restrictions that applied to them, see Stoltzfus, *Resistance of the Heart*, 70–71; Kaplan, *Between Dignity and Despair*, 77–93, 148–50; Benz, "Überleben im Untergrund," 686–87; and Raul Hilberg, *Perpetrators, Victims, Bystanders: The Jewish Catastrophe 1933–1945* (New York, 1992), 131–32, 152–53.

15. Stoltzfus, *Resistance of the Heart*, 71.

16. See, for example, Victor Klemperer's diary entry of February 27, 1943, on the eve of the "Final Roundup" of Jews in Berlin. Klemperer discusses rumors that all Jews would soon be deported and his fears that Jews like himself in mixed marriages would no longer be spared. *Ich will Zeugnis ablegen bis zum letzten*, 2:334–36.

17. HStAD, RW58/26145 and RW58/65190.

18. HStAD, RW58/18674.

19. Stoltzfus, *Resistance of the Heart*, 203.

20. Ibid., 203–8.

21. Kaplan explains that most of these Jews were deported to Theresienstadt and not to death camps. *Between Dignity and Despair*, 190. On Berlin razzias, see Stoltzfus, *Resistance of the Heart*, 182–85.

22. HStAD, RW58/30180 and RW58/37672.

23. See, for example, the Krefeld and Düsseldorf Gestapo case files of änne H., HStAD, RW58/21813 and RW58/29393.

24. HStAD, RW58/37672, Bl. 30.

25. See Saul Friedländer's discussion of laws and decrees passed in 1938 to allow divorce on racial grounds and especially to encourage Aryan women to leave their husbands. Saul Friedländer, *Nazi Germany and the Jews*, vol. 1, *The Years of Persecution, 1933–1939* (New York, 1997), 290. On the pressure to divorce during the war years, see Ursula Büttner, *Die Not der Juden teilen: Christlich-jüdische Familien im Dritten Reich* (Hamburg, 1988), 56ff.

26. Kaplan, *Between Dignity and Despair*, 89. Büttner, *Die Not der Juden teilen*, 57.

27. In September 1944, only 230 out of 13,217 registered Jews in Germany did not live in mixed marriages. Stoltzfus, *Resistance of the Heart*, xxvii.

28. Ibid., 333.

29. Ibid., xxvi.

30. Ibid., 106–7, 125–26. Klemperer comments on these issues on almost a daily basis in his diary during the war years, *Ich will Zeugnis ablegen bis zum letzten*.

31. See, for example, Klemperer's comments in his diary on February 15, 1942, ibid., 23.

32. Stoltzfus, *Resistance of the Heart*, 209–77; Gernot Jochheim, ed., *Frauenprotest in der Rosenstrasse: "Gebt uns unsere Männer wieder"* (Berlin, 1993).

33. Jews from many other cities were also included in the roundup, but in Dresden, for example, Jews from mixed marriages were not deported, despite a flurry of rumors that they would be. On February 27, 1943, Victor Klemperer wrote in his diary: "It is now seven o'clock so I have been saved." In his entry on the next day, he wrote that all Jews who were not *Mischlinge* or in mixed marriages were to be evacuated. In his entry of March 4, he explains that 290 Dresden Jews had been deported and that that left only three Jews in the city who were not either *Mischlinge* or Jews in mixed marriages. Klemperer also notes that Jews from Erfurt and Halle had accompanied Dresden Jews on the transports to the east. *Ich will Zeugnis ablegen bis zum letzten*, 2:336–37ff. There apparently was not, however, a roundup of Jews in either Cologne or Krefeld at this time. For Cologne, see Horst Matzerath, "Der Weg der Kölner Juden in den Holocaust: Versuch einer Rekonstruktion," in Horst Matzerath, ed., *Die jüdischen Opfer des Nationalsozialismus aus Köln: Gedenkbuch* (Cologne, 1995), 543. For Krefeld, see Hangebruch, "Emigriert—Deportiert," 244–48.

34. Stoltzfus, *Resistance of the Heart*, 243.

35. Ibid., 245.

36. HStAD, RW58/29393 and RW58/21813.

37. According to a telegram from Commandant Hoess to the Düsseldorf Gestapo, a Krefeld *Geltungsjude* in his midthirties named Michael C. died of an "ulcer" in an Auschwitz concentration camp hospital at 9:40 A.M. on February 14, 1943. Michael C. had been sentenced in June 1939 to a two-year prison sentence for the crime of race defilement. After he completed his sentence, the officers Weber and Jung of the Krefeld Gestapo recommended that he be sent to a concentration camp. In the spring of 1941, he was put in Buchenwald. A year and a half later, he was transferred to Auschwitz, where he died four months later. HStAD, RW58/54900. See also HStAD, RW58/9233, in which the "-German-blooded" wife of a forty-eight-year-old Jewish man named Leopold C. from Duisburg was notified that her husband had died of "colitis" on February 4, 1943, after spending only five days in Auschwitz. Also mentioned in this case file is a forty-year-old Jewish woman from Krefeld named Marta B., who had accompanied Leopold C. to Auschwitz after both of them and four other remaining Jews in Anrath prison outside Krefeld were summarily declared to be "asocials" and transferred to Auschwitz. According to the information in another Krefeld Gestapo case file (HStAD, RW58/15819), her half-Jewish, seventeen-year-old daughter (whose Aryan father was away at the front) was informed by the Krefeld Gestapo that her mother had died in Auschwitz because of "heart and circulatory weakness" on February 10, 1943.

38. A copy of the letter is in Schulenburg's *Innenministerium* file, HStAD, NW130/130.

39. Stoltzfus, *Resistance of the Heart*, 204.

40. See, for example, the case of a partially Jewish man from Krefeld in his early twenties who was sent to Theresienstadt concentration camp in June 1943. After a family quarrel, his non-Jewish brother-in-law appears to have denounced him to the Gestapo for not wearing his Star of David in public. HStAD, RW58/55235 and RW58/53206.

41. Max Israel L., a fifty-five-year-old Jewish man with a non-Jewish wife, was arrested while playing poker in a local bar in Krefeld by the Kripo in July 1944. After spending two months in protective custody in Krefeld, the Gestapo had him sent to Auschwitz in September 1944. HStAD, RW58/66092.

42. A letter of January 5, 1943, from the Düsseldorf Gestapo headquarters to the Gestapo outpost in Krefeld ordered that all prisoners in Anrath prison near Krefeld who were considered "asocials" were to be sent to a concentration camp,

either to Auschwitz if they were Jewish or to Mauthausen if they were not. Two of the seven Jewish "asocials" who were slated to be transferred to Auschwitz, Marta B. and Siegfried A., were residents of the city of Krefeld who had been serving sentences for minor property offenses. Marta B. died two weeks after she arrived in Auschwitz. Siegfried A., however, had already died in Anrath prison on November 26, 1942. HStAD, RW58/9233 and RW58/15819.

43. In the *Mischlinge* cases, three were started by civilian denunciations, and one began with an anonymous denunciation that probably came from a civilian. Two of the other three cases were started by the Gestapo itself, and the final case was initiated by another Nazi official. In addition to the two cases started by civilian denunciations in the intermarried cases (of which one was made anonymously), one was initiated by the police, two by other Nazi officials, and the last two by the Gestapo itself.

44. HStAD, RW58/29938. For other details in the case, see Hangebruch, "Emigriert—Deportiert," 235–36.

CHAPTER TWELVE: MASS MURDER, MASS SILENCE

1. Hans Mommsen, "The Reaction of the German Population to the Anti-Jewish Persecution and the Holocaust," in Peter Hayes, ed., *Lessons and Legacies: The Meaning of the Holocaust in a Changing World* (Evanston, Ill., 1990), 142. See also, for example, Jörg Wollenberg, ed., *"Niemand war dabei und keiner hat's gewusst": Die deutsche Öffentlichkeit und die Judenverfolgung 1933–1945* (Munich, 1989); and Hanno Loewy, ed., *Holocaust: Die Grenzen des Verstehens* (Hamburg, 1992).

2. Walter Laqueur, *The Terrible Secret: An Investigation into the Suppression of Information About Hitler's "Final Solution"* (London, 1980); David Bankier, *The Germans and the Final Solution: Public Opinion Under Nazism* (London, 1992). Perhaps the best other comprehensive treatment of the question of what Germans knew about the Holocaust is Volker Ullrich, "'Wir haben nichts gewusst': Ein deutsches Trauma," *1999* 4 (1991): 11–46. See also Michael R. Marrus, *The Holocaust in History* (London, 1987), esp. 157–64; Lutz Niethammer, "Juden und Russen im Gedächtnis der Deutschen," in Walter H. Pehle, ed., *Der historische Ort des Nationalsozialismus* (Frankfurt am Main, 1990), 114–34; Hans Mommsen, "Was haben die Deutschen vom Völkermord an den Juden gewusst?," in Walter H. Pehle, ed., *Der Judenpogrom 1938: Von der "Reichkris-*

tallnacht" zum Völkermord (Frankfurt am Main, 1988), 176–200; and Walter Kempowski, *Haben Sie davon gewusst?: Deutsche Antworten* (Hamburg, 1979).

3. Bankier, *The Germans and the Final Solution,* 103; Laqueur, *The Terrible Secret,* 31–32.

4. For examples of these letters, see Ortwin Buchbender and Reinhold Sterz, eds., *Das andere Gesicht des Krieges: Deutsche Feldpostbriefe 1939–1945* (Munich, 1982), 168–73; Ullrich, "Wir haben nichts gewusst," 22–24, 35–38; and Klaus Latzel, *Deutsche Soldaten—nationalsozialisticher Krieg?: Kriegserlebnis—Kriegserfahrung 1939–1945* (Paderborn, 1998), 201–6.

5. On the censorship of soldiers' letters, see Latzel, *Deutsche Soldaten,* 25–31; and Buchbender and Sterz, *Das andere Gesicht des Krieges,* 13–25.

6. Laqueur, *The Terrible Secret,* 19–20.

7. Christopher R. Browning, *Ordinary Men: Reserve Police Battalion 1010 and the Final Solution in Poland* (New York, 1992); Daniel Jonah Goldhagen, *Hitler's Willing Executioners: Ordinary Germans and the Holocaust* (New York, 1996).

8. Heiner Lichtenstein, *Himmlers grüne Helfer: Die Schutz- und Ordnungspolizei im "Dritten Reich"* (Cologne, 1990), esp. 41–47.

9. Debórah Dwork and Robert Jan van Pelt, *Auschwitz: 1270 to the Present* (New York, 1996); Schmuel Krakowski, "The Satellite Camps," in Yisrael Gutman and Michael Berenbaum, eds., *Anatomy of the Auschwitz Death Camp* (Bloomington, Ind., 1994), 50–60."

10. Laqueur, *The Terrible Secret,* 23–24.

11. Krakowski, "The Satellite Camps," 53. On IG Farben, for example, see Peter Hayes, *Industry and Ideology: IG Farben in the Nazi Era* (New York, 1987).

12. Bankier, *The Germans and the Final Solution,* 113–14. See also Laqueur, *The Terrible Secret,* 28.

13. Bankier, *The Germans and the Final Solution,* 114.

14. In his recent and detailed analysis of the letters of Germans soldiers, Klaus Latzel argues that it is unclear how many and how often soldiers on the front wrote letters home about the murder of the Jews. In his opinion, all one can say for certain about such letters is that they reveal that German soldiers could have known about Jewish executions, did know about them, and had taken part in them. *Deutsche Soldaten,* 204–5.

15. Bankier, *The Germans and the Final Solution,* 115.

16. Victor Klemperer, *Ich will Zeugnis ablegen bis zum letzten: Tagebücher*

1933–1941, 1942–1945, 2 vols. (Berlin, 1995). The English-language translation of the first volume has just been published, and a translation of the second volume will appear soon. Victor Klemperer, *I Will Bear Witness: A Diary of the Nazi Years, 1933–1941,* translated by Martin Chalmers (New York, 1998). For an excellent review article on the Klemperer diaries, see Gordon A. Craig, "Destiny in Any Case," *New York Review of Books,* December 3, 1998, 4–6.

17. See, for example, Klemperer's entries in *Ich will Zeugnis ablegen bis zum letzten* for November 28 and 30, 1941; April 5 and 20, July 24, September 8, October 27, and November 29, 1942; and February 28, 1943.

18. Ibid., November 2 and December 29, 1942.

19. Ibid., March 16, July 4, August 29, November 29, 1942; February 27, 1943.

20. Ibid., July 4, September 8 and 21, October 2, 1942; February 27, 1943.

21. Ibid., 2:224–27.

22. Ibid., 2:238.

23. Ibid., 1:686.

24. Ibid., 1:689.

25. Ibid., 2:47.

26. Ibid., 2:154.

27. Ibid., entry of November 29, 1942 (284).

28. Ibid., entry of January 14, 1943 (312).

29. Ibid., 2:335.

30. Bankier does, however, discuss some of the BBC broadcasts about the Holocaust that Nazi *Funk-Abhör Berichte* (Reports on foreign radio broadcasts) commented on. *The Germans and the Final Solution,* 113.

31. Bernard Wasserstein, *Britain and the Jews of Europe 1939–1945* (Oxford, 1979) 297.

32. British Broadcasting Corporation, Written Archives Centre, Reading, England (henceforward BBC/WAC), E2/131/8, European news directives, file VIII, November-December 1942 (emphasis in the original).

33. Ibid., December 27, 1942.

34. On broadcasting hours and times, see BBC External Services, *"Hier ist England—Live aus London": Das deutsche Program der British Broadcasting Corporation 1938–1988* (London, 1988), 7. The European news directives of the BBC in the summer and fall of 1941 carry several references to BBC reporting on Jewish massacres. One example came on November 13, 1941, when the head of the BBC's foreign broadcasting, Noel F. Newsome, wrote: "There seems little doubt that the story of the Odessa massacre of Jews is true, and it

NOTES

should be given wide publicity as an example of bestial barbarism under German inspiration without parallel in modern history." BBC/WAC, E2/131/2. See also, for example, the European news directives of September 21 and 24, 1941, E2/131/1."

35. See, for example, Uwe Naumann, ed., *Bruno Adler: Frau Wernicke: Kommentare einer "Volksjenossin"* (Mannheim, 1990).

36. See Fraser's discussion of propaganda efforts, both the BBC's and his own, in his book *Propaganda* (London, 1957), esp. 87–106.

37. On December 18, 1942, the program *England diese Woche* (England This Week), for example, communicated the following message to its German audience about Jewish massacres in Poland: "The extermination of the Jews in that country was planned and is now being carried out ruthlessly. Men, women, and children are being killed—through normal murder, through poison gas, or on the railway; in the most severe winter weather and without food and drink they are being carted off to still unknown destinations, and on the long journey dead children are simply thrown out of the wagons along the line." Among the many special feature broadcasts that appeared later in the war to deal with the Holocaust are the Frau Wernicke program on October 2, 1943, "Frau Wernicke über Evakuierung," and the Lindley Fraser program of October, 19, 1944, entitled "More Polish Atrocities." The transcript of the Frau Wernicke program has been reprinted in Naumann, *Bruno Adler*, 129–32. The Fraser program is found in BBC/WAC, Lindley Fraser: Talks and Features, Sonderbericht—Miscellaneous, 1944.

38. BBC/WAC, "*Kurt and Willi* on the Persecution of the Jews," German Features, December 29, 1942.

39. BBC/WAC, German Features, December 24 and 27, 1942.

40. Ullrich, "Wir haben nichts gewusst," 12. Ullrich takes this from Margaret Bourke-White, *Deutschland—April 1945: "Dear Fatherland Rest Quietly"* (Munich, 1979), 90.

41. For a comparison of how East and West Germany have remembered the Nazi past, see Jeffrey Herf, *Divided Memory: The Nazi Past in the Two Germanys* (Cambridge, Mass., 1997).

42. For a broader discussion of the results of this survey than are presented in this chapter, see Eric A. Johnson and Karl-Heinz Reuband, "Die populäre Einschätzung der Gestapo: Wie allgegenwärtig war sie wirklich?," in Gerhard Paul and Klaus-Michael Mallmann, eds., *Die Gestapo: Mythos und Realität* (Darmstadt, 1995), 417–36.

43. Thirty-four percent of those who had not believed in National Socialism responded that they had either known or heard about the mass murder of the Jews prior to the end of the war; only 13 percent of those who had believed in National Socialism gave this response.

44. Thirty-one percent of the survey participants who were born before 1915 responded that they had either known or heard about the mass murder. This compares with only 18 percent of those born after 1923 who responded that they had known or heard about it.

45. Fifty percent of those with a university education responded that they had known or heard about the mass murder, but only 19 percent of those with only a primary school education answered in this manner.

46. Thus, if one adds those who responded that they had surmised that the Holocaust was taking place to those who responded that they had either known or heard about it, one finds that 31 percent of Catholics, 29 percent of Protestants, 31 percent of women, and 31 percent of men responded that they had had some level of awareness about the mass murder of the Jews during the war.

47. Twenty-nine percent of the survey participants who had lived in Cologne during the Nazi period responded that they had had some level of awareness about the mass murder of the Jews, against 34 percent of the participants who moved to Cologne after 1945.

48. Reuband and I have now mailed our surveys to more than 5,000 residents of Cologne, Krefeld, and Dresden and to an additional 1,000 former German Jews now spread out around the world. Detailed results of these surveys and discussions of the follow-up interviews will be published in a book provisionally titled *Life and Death in the Third Reich: Germans and Jews Remember*.

49. Interview with Helene S., Cologne, February 3, 1994.

50. Interview with Anna-Maria S., Cologne, January 20, 1994.

51. Interview with Dr. Hiltrud K., Cologne, January 24, 1994.

52. Hirt and his experiments are discussed in Raul Hilberg, *The Destruction of the European Jews* (New York, 1961), 608–9.

53. Interviews with Dr. Winfried S., Cologne, January 14, 1994; interview with Arthur V., Cologne, January 20, 1994.

54. Interview with E. W., Cologne, October 13, 1994.

55. Interviews with Alfred E., Cologne, June 17, 1995, and January 8, 1996.

56. Transcripts of these and the other interviews that Karl-Heinz Reuband and I have conducted and other materials from our surveys will be stored at the Zentralarchiv für empirische Sozialforschung of the University of Cologne.

57. Ullrich, "Wir haben nichts gewusst—Ein deutsches Trauma," 18.

58. In a brief and highly personal essay on how memories and revelations about the past constantly change over time, the prominent German historian Reinhart Koselleck writes that the news of a large massacre of Jews in September 1941 spread "like wildfire" to him and other soldiers on the front beyond Kiev. He did not learn until after the war, he has explained to me in a private conversation, that this was the Babi Yar massacre that took the lives of 35,000 Jews. What he remembers hearing at the time was that about 10,000 Jews had been killed near a quarry outside Kiev. Despite his knowledge of this massacre, however, he says that it was not until May 1945 that he heard about the gassings in Auschwitz. Interned there for two to three months as a Soviet prisoner of war and informed about the gassings by his captors, he first believed he had been told a "Soviet propaganda lie." "Vielerlei Abschied vom Krieg," in Brigitte Sauzay, Heinz Ludwig Arnold, and Rudolf von Thadden, eds., *Vom Vergessen vom Gedenken: Erinnerungen und Erwartungen in Europa zum 8. Mai 1945* (Göttingen, 1999), 19–25.

CHAPTER THIRTEEN: CHRISTMAS PRESENTS FOR THE GESTAPO

1. On the prosecution of Nazi war criminals, see Adalbert Rückerl, *The Investigation of Nazi Crimes, 1945–1978: A Documentation*, translated by Derek Rutter (Hamden, Conn., 1980); Adalbert Rückerl, *NS-Verbrechen vor Gericht: Versuch einer Vergangenheitsbewältigung* (Heidelberg, 1982); Jörg Friedrich, *Die kalte Amnestie: NS-Täter in der Bundesrepublik* (Frankfurt am Main, 1984); Jürgen Weber and Peter Steinbach, eds., *Vergangenheitsbewältigung durch Strafverfahren?: NS-Prozesse in der Bundesrepublik Deutschland* (Munich, 1984).

2. Bundesarchiv Koblenz (hereafter BAK), Z 42 II/2520, Bl. 7.x.

3. Ibid., Bl. 8. This becomes clear in a character reference Diefenbach wrote for Löffler on February 11, 1947. See Löffler's *Spruchkammerverfahren* file.

4. Ibid.

5. Ibid., Bl. 9. Encke enjoyed a reputation in postwar Cologne as one of the few Protestant clergymen from that city to have opposed the Nazi regime—if only mildly, by his own admission—and he was known to have worked closely with Konrad Adenauer on rebuilding the Cologne school system. He also worked with Cologne's Jewish community on many issues after the war. During the Nazi years, he had been a pastor in Cologne-Niehl and served as a leading inter-

mediary between the Confessing Church and the Jewish community in the Rhineland. Konrad Adenauer, *Erinnerungen 1945–1953* (Stuttgart, 1965), 28; Adolf Klein, *Köln im Dritten Reich: Stadtgeschichte der Jahre 1933–1945* (Cologne, 1983), 195; Willehad Paul Eckert, "Christen—Juden—Deutsche: Zum Dialog in Köln 1958–1978," in Günther B. Ginzel and Sonja Güntner, *"Zuhause in Köln": Jüdisches Leben 1945 bis heute* (Cologne, 1998), 181–82; Monika Grübel, "Jüdisches Leben in Köln 1945 bis 1949," in Ginzel and Güntner, *"Zuhause in Köln,"* 51; Hermann-Josef Arentz, "Die Anfänge der Christlich-Demokratischen Union in Köln," in Otto Dann, ed., *Köln nach dem Nationalsozialismus: Der Beginn des gesellschaftlichen und politischen Lebens in den Jahren 1945–1946* (Wuppertal, 1981), 130.

6. Ibid., Bl. 10.

7. Ibid., Bl. 11.

8. Ibid., Bl. 19.

9. HStADK, *Personalakten Sammelbestand,* BR PE/49505, Bl. 4.

10. Löwenstein, whose family owned a large Cologne textile firm, was the son of a former head of the Jewish community in nearby Solingen. Soon after the U.S. Army took over Cologne in March 1945, the Americans named Löwenstein "the provisional head of the Cologne Jewish community." Günther B. Ginzel, "Phasen der Etablierung einer Jüdischen Gemeinde in der Kölner Trümmerlandschaft 1945–1949," in Jutta Bohnke-Kollwitz et al., eds., *Köln und das rheinische Judentum: Festschrift Germania Judaica 1959–1984* (Cologne, 1984), 445–61, esp. 446ff; Monika Grübel, "Nach der Katastrophe: Jüdisches Leben in Köln 1945 bis 1949," in Ginzel and Günter, *Jüdisches Leben,* 43, 46; Klaus Heugel, "Danach: Die Stadt Köln und die jüdische Bevölkerung seit 1945," in Ginzel and Günter, *Jüdisches Leben,* 198.

11. BAK, Z 42 II/2520, Bl. 25–28.

12. On the functioning of these courts in the British occupational zone, see Wolfgang Krüger, *Entnazifiziert!: Zur Praxis der politischen Säuberung in Nordrhein-Westfalen* (Wuppertal, 1982), esp. 72–77. On these courts in the American occupational zone, see Lütz Niethammer, *Die Mitläuferfabrik: Die Entnazifizierung am Beispiel Bayerns* (Berlin, 1982), 538–652. There were six of these courts in the British occupational zone; all were located near large internment camps. The punishments these courts meted out ranged from fines to imprisonment of up to ten years. In general, three types of defendants came before these courts: leading Nazi Party officials, Gestapo and SD officers, and members of the SS.

13. BAK, Z 42 II/2520, Bl. 28.

14. Ibid., Bl. 26.

15. Ibid., Bl. 44.

16. Ibid., Bl. 26.

17. Ibid., Bl. 27.

18. For a similar description of *Persilscheine*, see Mary Fulbrook, *The Divided Nation: A History of Germany 1918–1990* (New York, 1992), 148. For more detailed discussions of who wrote and received *Persilscheine*, see Niethammer, *Die Mitläuferfabrik*, 613–17; and Krüger, *Entnazifiziert!*, 108–14.

19. See, for example, Krüger, *Entnazifiziert!*, 109.

20. These *Persilscheine* appeared above all in crimes-against-humanity trials, in denazification records, and in Interior Ministry records. Three members of the Krefeld Gestapo serve as examples. In his crimes-against-humanity trial in October 1949 (HStADK, Rep. 8/6), Alfred Effenberg produced twenty-one character references. Among the more significant people who supported him in this way were the head of the Catholic Church in Krefeld, a former mayor of the city of Mönchengladbach, the mayor of a small town near Krefeld, and two retired policemen. The denazification records of Karl Schmitz (HStAD, NW1010/12909), who had been second in command of the Krefeld Gestapo and the head of the notorious "special treatment" section, reveal that he received positive character references from two members of the SPD, a man whose daughter was married to a man of mixed Jewish background, and several others. According to the Interior Ministry file of Johann Krülls (HStAD, NW130/243), who had been active in combating Communist and other left-wing threats to the Nazi regime, he received *Persilscheine* from a Catholic priest, a leading police official, a medical doctor, and many others.

21. See his Interior Ministry file, NW130/293.

22. Schulenburg's *Persilscheine* are found in his two denazification files (HStAD, NW 1037 BI 18164; NW1023/6433) and in his Interior Ministry file (HStAD, NW130/310).

23. HStAD, NW 1023/6433, Bl. 29–30.

24. Ibid., Bl. 4. It should also be mentioned that this was not the first *Persilschein* Schulenburg received from a head of the local Protestant Church in Krefeld. On March 1, 1947, an earlier presiding president of the presbytery in Krefeld wrote: "He always treated me in a very obliging manner and never placed any difficulties or unpleasantness in my way. I had the impression that he did not want to hinder the work of the church." Ibid., Bl. 31.

25. HStAD, NW1037 BI 18164, Bl. 67ff.

26. Ibid. For the *Persilscheine* of Krefeld's *Bundestagsabgeordneter* and for several others, see Schulenburg's Interior Ministry file, HStAD, NW130/310.

27. HStAD, NW130/310, Bl. 12–13. For the relevant Gestapo files pertaining to the case of the young woman who was sent to Auschwitz and the mother who was spared, see HStAD, NW58/21813 and NW58/29393.

28. HStAD, RW58/55235 and RW58/53206. Telephone interview with Werner H., June 5, 1996.

29. For an excellent treatment of the Kastner affair, see Tom Segev, *The Seventh Million: The Israelis and the Holocaust,* translated by Haim Watzman (New York, 1993), esp. 255–310.

30. Ibid., 257–58.

31. HStADK, Rep. 231/512.

32. In his own statement of August 18, 1948, about his life and career, dictated to a court stenographer and signed in the presence of the prosecuting attorney in his denazification court case, Löffler stated: "At the end of September 1942, I was detached to the BdS in Brussels." BAK, Z 42 II/2520, Bl. 15.

33. HStADK, Rep. 231/512.

34. HStADK, Rep. 231/513, Bl. 208ff.

35. Hans Encke, the head of Cologne's Protestant Church after the war who wrote letters on Karl Löffler's behalf, also publicly acknowledged his guilt for remaining silent about the Nazis' persecution of Jews and others. In a speech given at a meeting of the Cologne district synod of the Protestant Church on January 26, 1946, Encke said: "It is a matter of grave seriousness for me when I here say for myself: Mea culpa, mea maxima culpa! Because I know that I have remained silent when I needed to speak out in the face of the injustice committed by our people against Jews and Russians and Poles and even our own brothers. We remained silent in the Confessional Church because we were faint hearted." Eckert, "Christen—Juden—Deutsche," 181.

36. In addition to the fact that these clergymen wrote such letters in the first place, it is also somewhat curious that some of them wrote letters for other Gestapo officers as well, as did, for example, the head of Krefeld's Catholic Church, Dr. Gregor Schwamborn, who wrote letters for Alfred Effenberg, Richard Schulenburg, and possibly other Gestapo officers in Krefeld. It is also somewhat suspicious that the clergymen who wrote for Löffler and Schulenburg continued to write letters for them well into the middle and late 1950s, and perhaps later. Dean Diefenbach of Cologne's Catholic Church and Superintendent

Encke of Cologne's Protestant Church wrote letters in early 1947 for Löffler during his denazification process and in October 1956 when he was trying to regain his full pension. These letters are in Löffler's police personnel file, HStADK, BR PE/49505; his denazification court proceedings, BAK, Z 42 II/2520; and his Interior Ministry file, HStAD, NW 130/252. Likewise, Dr. Schwamborn, the head of Krefeld's Catholic Church, and the head of Krefeld's Protestant Church (President of the Presbytery), Friedrich Neuhaus, wrote letters on Schulenburg's behalf in early 1947 during his denazification process and in 1955 during his attempt to recover his full pension. Also another clergyman, Paul Engels, who became President of the Presbytery of Krefeld's Protestant Church after the war, wrote on several occasions for Schulenburg as late as the mid-1950s. These clergymen's letters are in Schulenburg's denazification records, HStAD, NW1023/6433, NW1037 BI 18164; and in his Interior Ministry file, HStAD, NW130/310.

37. The judgment of Bernhard Schmidt and Fritz Burger, the authors of an in-depth study of the small city of Moers near Krefeld, could be applied almost everywhere in Germany: "The murder of forced laborers, Jews of the city, and resistance fighters—all remained unatoned for." *Tatort Moers: Widerstand und Nationalsozialismus im südlichen Altkreis Moers* (Moers, 1995), 420. On the prosecution of Nazi war criminals in Cologne, see Heiner Lichtenstein, "Verdunklungsgefahr!: Die Kölner Justiz und die Verfolgung der NS-Verbrechen," in Horst Matzerath, Harald Buhlan, and Barbara Becker-Jákli, *Versteckte Vergangenheit: Über den Umgang mit der NS-Zeit in Köln* (Cologne, 1994), 233–41.

38. Eva Maria Martinsdorf, "Von den Schwierigkeiten, die Gegenwart von ihrer Vergangenheit zu 'säubern': Entnazifizierung in Köln," in Matzerath, Buhlan, and Becker-Jákli, *Versteckte Vergangenheit*, 125–62, esp. 145.

39. Schmidt and Burger, *Tatort Moers*, 419. In Moers not one single resident was put into either of these categories. Lütz Niethammer has demonstrated that things were not much different in the American occupation zone. *Die Mitläuferfabrik*, 540–50.

40. In the end, therefore, the only punishment suffered by both Löffler and Schulenburg was a temporary loss in their retirement pensions, although Löffler also spent a period of time after the war in a British internment camp. On December 9, 1948, the Benefeld denazification court found Löffler guilty of illegal activity during his years in the Gestapo and sentenced him to pay a fine of 2,500 marks. But the court also ruled that he did not have to pay this fine

because, in the court's opinion, it had already been covered by his two years and ten months as a British prisoner. A copy of the court's judgment is found in BAK, Z 42 II/2520, Bl. 53–56. For documentation on both men's attempts to revise their denazification status and regain their pensions, see their denazification, personnel, and Interior Ministry files (see note 36).

41. On the fate of Gestapo officers in postwar Germany, see Gerhard Paul, "Zwischen Selbstmord, Illegalität, und neuer Karriere: Ehemalige Gestapo-Bedienstete im Nachkriegsdeutschland," in Gerhard Paul and Klaus-Michael Mallmann, eds., *Die Gestapo: Mythos und Realität* (Darmstadt, 1995), 529–55; In *The Gestapo and German Society: Enforcing Racial Policy 1933–1945* (Oxford, 1990), Robert Gellately, who focuses especially on the Gestapo in Würzburg, states that most members of the Würzburg Gestapo "were able to exonerate themselves. Gestapo members charged with participation in the deportations of Jews from Germany got off because it could not be proven that they knew what went on in the extermination camps in Poland" (262). Detailed evidence that this dubious excuse was also used throughout Germany in the late 1960s and early 1970s to suspend investigations of the involvement of Gestapo officers in the murder of the Jews is found at the Zentrale Stelle für Landesjustizverwaltungen in Ludwigsburg, 415 AR 846/64 (2 volumes).

42. Hannah Arendt, *Eichmann in Jerusalem: A Report on the Banality of Evil* (1963; New York, 1994).

43. This is not to argue that most Gestapo officers were either social misfits or obvious psychopaths, and one must concede that in many ways most Gestapo officers seemed quite normal. For important discussions of the nature and backgrounds of Gestapo officers that point more toward their normality than toward their abnormality, see Gerhard Paul, "Ganz normaler Akademiker: Eine Fallstudie zur regionalen staatspolizeilichen Funktionselite," in Paul and Mallmann, *Die Gestapo*, 236–54; and George C. Browder, *Hitler's Enforcers: The Gestapo and the SS Security Service in the Nazi Revolution* (New York, 1996).

44. Christopher R. Browning, *Ordinary Men: Reserve Police Battalion 101 and the Final Solution in Poland* (New York, 1992); Daniel Jonah Goldhagen, *Hitler's Willing Executioners: Ordinary Germans and the Holocaust* (New York, 1996).

45. For some of their best-known work on the issue of denunciations, see Gisela Diewald-Kerkmann, *Politische Denunziation im NS-Regime oder die kleine Macht der "Volksgenossen"* (Bonn, 1995); Gellately, *The Gestapo and German Society*; and Reinhard Mann, *Protest und Kontrolle im Dritten Reich:*

Nationalsozialistische Herrschaft im Alltag einer rheinischen Grossstadt (Frankfurt am Main, 1987).

46. Victor Klemperer, *Ich will Zeugnis ablegen bis zum letzten: Tagebücher 1933–1945*, 2 vols. (Berlin, 1995).

47. For a provocative treatment of the burden that National Socialism has placed on Germans and German society and of how Germans and German society have dealt with Nazi crimes, see Ralph Giordano, *Die zweite Schuld oder von der Last Deutscher zu sein* (Hamburg, 1987).

48. Interview with Alfred E., Cologne, June 17, 1995.

BIBLIOGRAPHY

ARCHIVAL SOURCES

Only the most essential file groups are mentioned. Full citations are found in the notes to the text.

Leo Baeck Institute, New York

Berlin Document Center: Partei Kanzlei Korrespondenz (PKK), Rasse- und Siedlungs-Hauptamt-SS (RuSHA), and SS Offizier Personalakten (SSO)

British Broadcasting Corporation Written Archives Centre, Reading, England: BBC/WAC (German Features; Lindley Fraser: Talks and Features) and BBC/WAC, E2/131 (European news directives)

Bundesarchiv Koblenz: Z 42 IV (*Spruchgericht Bielefeld*) and Z 42 II (*Spruchgericht Benefeld-Bomütz*)

Evangelisches Gemeindearchiv, Cologne

Hessisches Hauptstaatsarchiv, Wiesbaden

Historisches Archiv der Stadt, Köln

Kölnisches Stadtmuseum

National Archives, Washington, D.C. (microfilm copies of former Berlin Document Center records)

Norddeutsche Provinz SJ Archiv, Cologne: Nachlass Josef Spieker

Nordrhein-Westfälisches Hauptstaatsarchiv Düsseldorf-Kaiserswerth, Schloss Kalkum: BR PE (*Personalakten Sammelbestand*), Rep. 8 (*Verbrechen gegen die Menschlichkeit*), Rep. 10 (*Verbrechen gegen die Menschlichkeit*), Rep. 11/1812 (*Zu milde Urteile*), Rep. 11/1661 (*Kriege gegen Deutschland*), Rep. 23 (population statistics), Rep. 112 (*Sondergericht Köln*), Rep. 132/715 (*Verzeichnis über Hinrichtungen 1941–1944*), Rep. 231/95 (*Gestapoflügel in Klingelpütz*), Rep. 231/447–519 (Schäfer trial), Rep. 248/265–66 (*Rechtswidrige Tötung von Stapo Häftlingen in Klingelpütz*), Rep. 300/1–15 (*Klingelpütz Gefangenenbücher*), and Rep. 321/190–91 (*Gefängnisstatistik Köln*)

Nordrhein-Westfälisches Hauptstaatsarchiv Düsseldorf-Mauerstrasse: NW130

(*Innenministerium*), NW1000 (*Entnazifizierung*), NW1010 (*Entnazifizie-rung*), NW1023 (*Entnazifizierung*), NW1037-BI (*Entnazifizierung*), NW1049 (*Entnazifizierung*), RW34 (*Stapostelle Köln*), RW36 (*Stapostelle Düsseldorf, Aussenstellen*), RW58 (*Gestapo-Personalakten*)

NS-Dokumentationszentrum Köln

R. K. Paters Jezuïeten Berchmanianum, Nijmegen

Rheinisches Amt für Denkmalpflege, Cologne

Rheinisches Bildarchiv, Cologne

Sächsisches Hauptstaatsarchiv, Dresden

Stadtarchiv, Cologne: *Westdeutscher Beobachter, Kölnische Zeitung, Kölner Stadt-Anzeiger*

Stadtarchiv, Krefeld: Film B58; Mitglieder-Liste der NSDAP in Krefeld, Mel-dewesen Kartei, *Rheinische Post, Westdeutsche Neue Presse, Westdeutsche Zeitung,* Photograph Archive

Zentrale Stelle für Landesjustizverwaltungen, Ludwigsburg: 414 AR 345/71 (*Angehörige der Stapoleitstelle Düsseldorf*), 415 AR 846/64 (*Evakuierung v. Juden*), 107 AR-Z 571/67

INTERVIEWS

Only those interviews mentioned in the text or the notes are listed.

Raffael B., Cologne, February 10, 1993

Aurel Billstein, Krefeld, January 30, 1995

Wolf Bleiweiss, New York, July 27, 1995

Alfred E., Cologne, June 17, 1995

Adam G., Krefeld, June 14, 1995

Helmut Goldschmidt, Cologne, July 11, 1997

Werner H. (Chile), June 5, 1996 (by telephone)

Herbert K., Saddlebrook, New Jersey, July 28, 1995

Hiltrud K., Cologne, January 24, 1994

Lore M., Krefeld, January 31, 1995

Karl Muschkattblatt (Chicago), April 12, 1996 (by telephone)

Anna-Maria S., Cologne, January 20, 1994

Helene S., Cologne, February 3, 1994

Max S., Cologne, March 1995

Winfried S., Cologne, January 14, 1994
Artur V., Cologne, January 20, 1994
E. W., Cologne, October 13, 1994

Private Collections and Written Communications with the Author
Otto B.
Kurt Gimnicher
Herbert K.
Max Rein
John Rosing
Helma T.

NEWSPAPERS

Bonner Rundschau
Kölner Stadt-Anzeiger
Kölnische Rundschau
Kölnische Volkszeitung
Kölnische Zeitung
Rheinische Post
Völkischer Beobachter
Westdeutscher Beobachter
Westdeutsche Neue Presse
Westdeutsche Zeitung

SECONDARY AND PRINTED SOURCES

Abel, K. D. *Die Presselenkung im NS-Staat.* Munich, 1968.
Adam, Uwe. *Judenpolitik im Dritten Reich.* Düsseldorf, 1972.
Adenauer, Konrad. *Konrad Adenauer: Memoirs 1945–1953.* Translated by Beate Ruhm von Oppen. Chicago, 1966.
Adler, H. G. *Der verwaltete Mensch: Studien zur Deportation der Juden aus Deutschland.* Tübingen, 1974.
Angermund, Ralph. *Deutsche Richterschaft 1919–1945: Krisenerfahrung, Illusion, politische Rechtsprechung.* Frankfurt am Main, 1990.
Arendt, Hannah. *The Origins of Totalitarianism.* New York, 1951.

——. *Eichmann in Jerusalem: A Report on the Banality of Evil*. 1963; New York, 1994.

Arentz, Hermann-Josef. "Die Anfänge der Christlich-Demokratischen Union in Köln." In *Köln nach dem Nationalsozialismus: Der Beginn des gesellschaftlichen und politischen Lebens in den Jahren 1945–1946*, edited by Otto Dann, 117–38 (Wuppertal, 1981).

Aronson, Schlomo. *Reinhard Heydrich und die Frühgeschichte von Gestapo und SD*. Stuttgart, 1971.

Asaria, Zvi, ed. *Die Juden in Köln: Von den ältesten Zeiten bis zur Gegenwart*. Cologne, 1959.

Aschheim, Steven E. *Culture and Catastrophe: German and Jewish Confrontations with National Socialism and Other Crises*. New York, 1996.

Ash, Timothy Garton. "The Romeo File." *New Yorker*, April 28 and May 5, 1997, 162–71.

Bankier, David. *The Germans and the Final Solution: Public Opinion Under Nazism*. Oxford, 1992.

Barkai, Avraham. *From Boycott to Annihilation: The Economic Struggle of German Jews, 1933–1943*. Translated by William Templer. 1987; Hanover, N. H., 1989.

Bartov, Omer. *Hitler's Army: Soldiers, Nazis, and War in the Third Reich*. New York, 1992.

——. *Murder in Our Midst: The Holocaust, Industrial Killing, and Representation*. Oxford, 1996.

Bästlein, Klaus, Helge Grabitz, and Wolfgang Scheffler, eds. *"Für Führer, Volk, und Vaterland . . . ": Hamburger Justiz im Nationalsozialismus*. Hamburg, 1992.

Bauer, Fritz, et al., eds. *Justiz und NS-Verbrechen: Sammlung deutscher Strafurteile wegen nationalsozialistischer Tötungsverbrechen 1945–1966*. Vol. 22. Amsterdam, 1981.

BBC External Services. *"Hier ist England—Live aus London": Das Deutsche Programm der British Broadcasting Corporation 1938–1988*. London, 1988.

Becker-Jákli, Barbara, ed. *Ich habe Köln doch so geliebt: Lebensgeschichten jüdischer Kölnerinnen und Kölner*. Cologne, 1983.

Belmonte, Ana Perez. "'Schwarzhören' im II. Weltkrieg: Die Ahndung von 'Rundfunkverbrechen' im Sondergerichtsbezirk Essen 1939–1945." M. A. thesis, University of Cologne, 1997.

Benz, Wolfgang, ed. *Die Juden in Deutschland 1933–1945: Leben unter nationalsozialistischer Herrschaft.* Munich, 1988.

——. "Überleben im Untergrund 1943–1945." In *Die Juden in Deutschland 1933–1945: Leben unter nationalsozialistischer Herrschaft,* edited by Wolfgang Benz, 660–700 (Munich, 1988).

Benz, Wolfgang, and Walter H. Pehle, eds. *Encyclopedia of German Resistance to the Nazi Movement.* Translated by Lance W. Garmer. New York, 1997.

Bergen, Doris L. *Twisted Cross: The German Christian Movement in the Third Reich.* Chapel Hill, N. C., 1996.

Besier, Gerhard. "Ansätze zum politischen Widerstand in der Bekennenden Kirche: Zur gegenwärtigen Forschungslage." In *Der Widerstand gegen den Nationalsozialismus: Die deutsche Gesellschaft und der Widerstand gegen Hitler,* edited by Jürgen Schmädeke and Peter Steinbach, 265–80 (Munich, 1985).

Bessel, Richard. *Political Violence and the Rise of Nazism: The Stormtroopers in Eastern Germany, 1925–1934.* New Haven, Conn., 1984.

——. ed. *Life in the Third Reich.* Oxford, 1987.

Best, Werner. *Die deutsche Polizei.* Darmstadt, 1941.

Bethge, Eberhard. "Zwischen Bekenntnis und Widerstand: Erfahrungen in der Altpreussischen Union." In *Der Widerstand gegen den Nationalsozialismus: Die deutsche Gesellschaft und der Widerstand gegen Hitler,* edited by Jürgen Schmädeke and Peter Steinbach, 281–94 (Munich, 1985).

Bettelheim, Bruno. *The Informed Heart: Autonomy in a Mass Age.* New York, 1960.

——. "Eichmann; the System; the Victims." *New Republic* (June 1963): 23–33.

Billstein, Aurel. *Christliche Gegnerschaft am Niederrhein 1933–1945 im Bereich der ehemaligen Gestapo-Aussendienststelle Krefeld.* Viersen, 1987.

——. *Fremdarbeiter in unserer Stadt 1939–1945: Kriegsgefangene und deportierte "fremdvölkische Arbeitskräfte" am Beispiel Krefeld.* Frankfurt am Main, 1980.

——. *Geheime Staatspolizei Aussendienststelle Krefeld: Alltägliche Wirklichkeit im Nationalsozialismus.* Krefeld, n.d.

Billstein, Reinhold, ed. *Das andere Köln: Demokratische Tradition seit der Französischen Revolution.* Cologne, 1979.

Bock, Gisela. *Zwangsterilisation im Nationalsozialismus: Studien zur Rassenpolitik und Frauenpolitik.* Opladen, 1986.

Bohnke-Kollwitz, Jutta, et al., eds. *Köln und das rheinische Judentum: Festschrift Germania Judaica 1959–1984.* Cologne, 1984.

Botz, Gerhard, ed. *Der Ort Mauthausen in der Geschichte.* Frankfurt am Main, forthcoming.

Bourke-White, Margaret. *"Dear Fatherland Rest Quietly": A Report on the Collapse of Hitler's "Thousand Years."* New York, 1946.

———. *Deutschland—April 1945: "Dear Fatherland Rest Quietly."* Munich, 1979.

Bracher, Karl Dietrich. *The German Dictatorship: The Origins, Structure, and Effects of National Socialism.* Translated by Jean Steinberg. 1969; New York, 1970.

Brather, Hans-Stephan. "Aktenvernichtungen durch deutsche Dienststellen beim Zusammenbruch des Faschismus." *Archivmitteilungen* 8 (1958): 115–17.

Braun, Gerhard. "Köln in den Jahren 1945 und 1946: Die Rahmenbedingungen des gesellschaftlichen Lebens." In *Köln nach dem Nationalsozialismus: Der Beginn des gesellschaftlichen und politischen Lebens in den Jahren 1945–1946,* edited by Otto Dann, 35–72 (Wuppertal, 1981).

Brenner, Michael. *After the Holocaust: Rebuilding Jewish Lives in Postwar Germany.* Translated by Barbara Harshav. Princeton, N.J., 1997.

Breyvogel, Wilfried, ed. *Piraten, Swings, und Junge Garde: Jugendwiderstand im Nationalsozialismus.* Bonn, 1991.

———. "Resistenz, Widersinn, und Opposition: Jugendwiderstand im Nationalsozialismus." In *Piraten, Swings, und Junge Garde: Jugendwiderstand im Nationalsozialismus,* edited by Wilfried Breyvogel, 9–16 (Bonn, 1991).

Briggs, Asa. *The History of Broadcasting in the United Kingdom.* Vol. 3, *The War of Words.* London, 1970.

Broszat, Martin. *The Hitler State: The Foundation and Development of the Internal Structure of the Third Reich.* Translated by John W. Hiden. 1969; New York, 1981.

———. "Resistenz und Widerstand: Eine Zwischenbilanz des Forschungsprojektes." In *Bayern in der NS Zeit,* edited by Martin Broszat et al., 4:691–709 (Munich, 1977–83).

Broszat, Martin, et al., eds. *Bayern in der NS Zeit.* 6 vols. Munich, 1977–83.

Browder, George C. *Foundations of the Nazi Police State: The Formation of Sipo and SD.* Lexington, Ky., 1990.

———. *Hitler's Enforcers: The Gestapo and the SS Security Service in the Nazi Revolution.* New York, 1996.

Browning, Christopher R. *Ordinary Men: Reserve Police Battalion 101 and the Final Solution in Poland.* New York, 1992.

———. *The Path to Genocide: Essays on Launching of Final Solution.* Cambridge, 1992.

Brustein, William. *The Logic of Evil: The Social Origins of the Nazi Party, 1925–1933.* New Haven, Conn., 1996.

Buchbender, Ortwin, and Reinhold Sterz, eds. *Das andere Gesicht des Krieges: Deutsche Feldpostbriefe 1939–1945.* Munich, 1982.

Buchheim, Hans. "Die SS-das Herrschaftsinstrument." In *Das andere Gesicht des Krieges: Deutsche Feldpostbriefe 1939–1945,* edited by Ortwin Buchbender and Reinhold Sterz, 15–212 (Munich, 1982).

———. "Befehl und Gehorsam." In Buchheim, Hans, et al. *Anatomie des SS-Staates,* 15–212 (Munich, 1967).

Burleigh, Michael. *Death and Deliverance: Euthanasia in Nazi Germany c. 1900–1945.* New York, 1994.

Burleigh, Michael, and Wolfgang Wippermann. *The Racial State: Germany 1933–1945.* Cambridge, 1991.

Buruma, Ian. *The Wages of Guilt: Memories of War in Germany and Japan.* New York, 1994.

Büttner, Ursula. *Die Not der Juden teilen: Christlich-jüdische Familien im Dritten Reich.* Hamburg, 1988.

Calic, Edouard. *Reinhard Heydrich: The Chilling Story of the Man Who Masterminded the Nazi Death Camps.* Translated by Lowell Blair. New York, 1982.

Cassirer, Henry R. *Seeds in the Winds of Change: Through Education and Communication.* Norfolk, U. K., 1989.

Chernow, Ron. *The Warburgs.* New York, 1993.

Childers, Thomas. *The Nazi Voter: The Social Foundations of Fascism in Germany, 1919–1933.* Chapel Hill, N. C., 1983.

Cocks, Geoffrey. *Psychotherapy in the Third Reich: The Göring Institute.* New York, 1985.

Connelly, John. "The Uses of *Volksgemeinschaft:* Letters to the NSDAP Kreisleitung Eisenach, 1939–1940." *Journal of Modern History* 68 (1996): 899–930.

Conway, J. S. *The Nazi Persecution of the Churches 1933–1945.* New York, 1968.

Craig, Gordon A. *The Germans.* New York, 1982.

———. "Destiny in Any Case." *New York Review of Books,* December 3, 1998, 4–6.

Crankshaw, Edward. *Gestapo: Instrument of Tyranny.* London, 1956.

Dahrendorf, Ralf. *Society and Democracy in Germany.* 1965; Garden City, N.Y., 1967.

Dann, Otto, ed. *Köln nach dem Nationalsozialismus: Der Beginn des gesellschaftlichen und politischen Lebens in den Jahren 1945–1946.* Wuppertal, 1981.

Decker, Heinz, et al., eds. *Alltagsgeschichte im Agnesviertel: Die Kriegszeit 1939–1945.* Cologne, 1989.

Delarue, Jacques. *The Gestapo: A History of Horror.* Translated by Mervyn Savill. 1962; New York, 1987.

Denzler, Georg. *Widerstand oder Anpassung?: Katholische Kirche und Drittes Reich.* Munich, 1984.

Diels, Rudolf. *Lucifer ante portas.* Stuttgart, 1950.

Diewald-Kerkmann, Gisela. "Denunziatentum und Gestapo: Die Freiwilligen 'Helfer' aus der Bevölkerung." In *Die Gestapo: Mythos und Realität,* edited by Gerhard Paul and Klaus-Michael Mallmann, 288–305 (Darmstadt, 1995).

———. *Politische Denunziation im NS-Regime oder die kleine Macht der "Volksgenossen."* Bonn, 1995.

Dillar, Ansgar. "Der Volksempfänger: Propaganda- und Wirtschaftsfaktor." *Studienkreis Rundfunk und Geschichte* 9 (1983): 140–57.

Dillman, Don. *Mail and Telephone Surveys: The Total Design Method.* New York, 1978.

Dördelmann, Katrin. *Die Macht der Worte: Denunziationen im nationalsozialistischen Köln.* Cologne, 1997.

Dörner, Bernward. "Gestapo und 'Heimtücke': Zur Praxis der Geheimen Staatspolizei bei der Verfolgung von Verstössen gegen das 'Heimtücke-Gesetz.' " In *Die Gestapo: Mythos und Realität,* edited by Gerhard Paul and Klaus-Michael Mallmann, 325–42. (Darmstadt, 1995).

Drobisch, Klaus, and Günther Wieland. "Die Judenreferate des Geheimen Staatspolizeiamtes und des Sicherheitsdienstes der SS 1933 bis 1939." *Jahrbuch für Antisemitismusforschung* (1992): 230–54.

———. *System der NS-Konzentrationslager 1933–1939.* Berlin, 1993.

Duhnke, Horst. *Die KPD von 1933 bis 1945*. Cologne, 1972.

Dwork, Debórah, and Robert Jan van Pelt. *Auschwitz: 1270 to the Present*. New York, 1996.

Eckert, Brita. *Die jüdische Emigration aus Deutschland 1933–1941: Die Geschichte einer Austreibung*. Frankfurt am Main, 1995.

Eckert, Willehad Paul. "Christen—Juden—Deutsche: Zum Dialog in Köln 1958–1978." In *"Zuhause in Köln": Jüdisches Leben 1945 bis heute*, edited by Günther B. Ginzel and Sonja Güntner, 180–97 (Cologne, 1998).

Evans, Richard J. *In Hitler's Shadow: West German Historians and the Attempt to Escape from the Nazi Past*. London, 1989.

———. *Rituals of Retribution: Capital Punishment in Germany 1600–1987*. Oxford, 1996.

Falter, Jürgen W. *Hitlers Wähler*. Munich, 1991.

Faust, Anselm. *Die "Kristallnacht" im Rheinland: Dokumente zum Judenpogrom im November 1938*. Düsseldorf, 1987.

Feinendegen, Reinhard, and Dieter Pützhofen, eds. *22. Juni 1943 als Krefeld brannte: Augenzeugenberichte von der Bombennacht*. Krefeld, 1993.

Fest, Joachim C. *The Face of the Third Reich: Portraits of the Nazi Leadership*. Translated by Michael Bullock. New York, 1970.

———. *Plotting Hitler's Death: The Story of the German Resistance*. Translated by Bruce Little. New York, 1996.

Finkelstein, Norman G., and Ruth Bettina Birn. *A Nation on Trial: The Goldhagen Thesis and Historical Truth*. New York, 1998.

Fischer, Conan. *Stormtroopers: A Social, Economic, and Ideological Analysis, 1929–1935*. London, 1983.

Fitzpatrick, Sheila, and Robert Gellately, eds. *Accusatory Practices: Denunciation in Modern European History, 1789–1989*. Chicago, 1997.

Fraser, Lindley. *Propaganda*. London, 1957.

Frevert, Ute. *Women in German History: From Bourgeois Emancipation to Sexual Liberation*. Translated by Stuart McKinnon-Evans. New York, 1988.

Friedlander, Henry. *The Origins of Nazi Genocide: From Euthanasia to the Final Solution*. Chapel Hill, N. C., 1995.

Friedländer, Saul. *Nazi Germany and the Jews*. Vol. 1, *The Years of Persecution, 1933–1939*. New York, 1997.

———, ed. *Probing the Limits of Representation: Nazism and the "Final Solution."* Cambridge, Mass., 1992.

Friedrich, Jörg. *Die kalte Amnestie: NS-Täter in der Bundesrepublik.* Frankfurt am Main, 1984.

Frohn, Robert. *Köln 1945–1981: Von Trümmerhaufen zur Millionenstadt.* Cologne, 1982.

Fulbrook, Mary. *The Divided Nation: A History of Germany 1918–1990.* New York, 1992.

Funk, Albrecht. *Polizei und Rechtsstaat: Die Entwicklung des staatlichen Gewaltmonopols in Preussen, 1848–1914.* Frankfurt am Main, 1986.

Garbe, Detlev. *Zwischen Widerstand und Martyrium: Die Zeugen Jehovahs im "Dritten Reich."* Munich, 1994.

Geiger, Hanjörg. *Die Inoffiziellen Mitarbeiter: Stand der gegenwärtigen Erkenntnisse.* Berlin, 1993.

Gellately, Robert. *The Gestapo and German Society: Enforcing Racial Policy 1933–1945.* Oxford, 1990.

———. "Situating the 'SS-State' in a Social-Historical Context: Recent Histories of the SS, the Police, and the Courts in the Third Reich." *Journal of Modern History* 64 (1992): 338–65.

———. "Allwissend und allgegenwärtig?: Entstehung, Funktion, und Wandel des Gestapo-Mythos." In *Die Gestapo: Mythos und Realität,* edited by Gerhard Paul and Klaus-Michael Mallmann, 47–70 (Darmstadt, 1995).

———. "Denunciations in Twentieth-Century Germany: Aspects of Self-Policing in the Third Reich and the German Democratic Republic." *Journal of Modern History* 68 (1996): 931–67.

———. "Denunciations and Nazi Germany: New Insights and Methodological Problems," *Historical Social Research-Historische Sozialforschung* 22 (1997): 228–39.

Gellately, Robert, and Sheila Fitzpatrick, eds. *Accusatory Practices: Denunciations in Modern European History, 1789–1989.* Chicago, 1997.

Gernot, Jochheim. *Frauenprotest in der Rosenstrasse: "Gebt uns unsere Männer wieder."* Berlin, 1993.

Gilbert, G. M. *Nuremberg Diary.* 1947; New York, 1995.

Giles, Geoffrey J. *Students and National Socialism in Germany.* Princeton, N.J., 1985.

Gimnicher, Kurt. "Prelude to Freedom: An Autobiography." Unpublished manuscript, n.d.

Ginzel, Günther B. "Phasen der Etablierung einer Jüdischen Gemeinde in der

Kölner Trümmerlandschaft 1945–1949." In *Köln und das rheinische Judentum: Festschrift Germania Judaica 1959–1984*, edited by Jutta Bohnke-Kollwitz et al., 445–61 (Cologne, 1984).

Ginzel, Günther B., and Sonja Güntner, eds. *"Zuhause in Köln": Jüdisches Leben 1945 bis heute*. Cologne, 1998.

Giordano, Ralph. *Die zweite Schuld oder von der Last Deutscher zu sein*. Hamburg, 1987.

Gisevius, Hans Bernd. *To the Bitter End*. Translated by Richard and Clara Winston. London, 1948.

Goldhagen, Daniel Jonah. *Hitler's Willing Executioners: Ordinary Germans and the Holocaust*. New York, 1996.

Gordon, Sarah. *Hitler, Germans, and the "Jewish Question."* Princeton, N.J., 1984.

Graf, Christoph. *Politische Polizei zwischen Demokratie und Diktatur: Die Entwicklung der preussischen Politischen Polizei vom Staatsschutzorgan der Weimarer Republik zum Geheimen Staatspolizeiamt des Dritten Reiches*. Berlin, 1983.

Grau, Günter, ed. *Homosexualität in der NS-Zeit: Dokumente einer Diskriminierung und Verfolgung*. Frankfurt am Main, 1993.

Gross, John. "Arendt on Eichmann." *Encounter* (November 1963): 65–74.

Grossmann, Atina. *Reforming Sex: The German Movement for Birth Control and Abortion Reform*. New York, 1995.

Grübel, Monika. "Nach der Katastrophe: Jüdisches Leben in Köln 1945 bis 1949." In *"Zuhause in Köln": Jüdisches Leben 1945 bis heute*, edited by Günther B. Ginzel and Sonja Güntner, 42–55 (Cologne, 1998).

Gruchmann, Lothar. *Justiz im Dritten Reich: Anpassung und Unterwerfung in der ära Gürtner*. Munich, 1988.

Grunberger, Richard. *A Social History of the Third Reich*. New York, 1974.

Gutman, Yisrael, and Michael Berenbaum, eds. *Anatomy of the Auschwitz Death Camp*. Bloomington, Ind., 1994.

Hale, Oran J. *The Captive Press in the Third Reich*. Princeton, N.J., 1964.

Hamburg Institut für Sozialforschung. *Vernichtungskrieg: Verbrechen der Wehrmacht 1941 bis 1944*. Hamburg, 1996.

Hamilton, Richard. *Who Voted for Hitler?* Princeton, N.J., 1982.

Hangebruch, Dieter. "Emigriert—Deportiert: Das Schicksal der Juden in Krefeld zwischen 1933 und 1945." *Krefelder Studien* 2 (1980): 137–412.

Harris, James F. *The People Speak!: Anti-Semitism and Emancipation in Nineteenth-Century Bavaria*. Ann Arbor, Mich., 1994.

Hayes, Peter. *Industry and Ideology: IG Farben in the Nazi Era*. New York, 1987.

———, ed. *Lessons and Legacies: The Meaning of the Holocaust in a Changing World*. Evanston, Ill., 1990.

Hehl, Ulrich von. *Katholische Kirche und Nationalsozialismus im Erzbistum Köln 1933–1945*. Mainz, 1977.

———. *Priester unter Hitlers Terror: Eine biographische und statistische Erhebung*. Mainz, 1984.

Heil, Johannes, and Rainer Erb, eds. *Geschichtswissenschaft und Öffentlichkeit: Der Streit um Daniel J. Goldhagen*. Frankfurt am Main, 1998.

Hellfeld, Matthias von. *Edelweisspiraten in Köln: Jugendrebellion gegen das 3. Reich: Das Beispiel Köln-Ehrenfeld*. Cologne, 1981.

Helmreich, Ernst Christian. *The German Churches Under Hitler: Background, Struggle, and Epilogue*. Detroit, 1979.

Herbert, Ulrich. *Fremdarbeiter im Dritten Reich: Politik und Praxis des "Ausländer-Einsatzes" in der deutschen Kriegswirtschaft des Dritten Reiches*. Berlin, 1985.

———. *Best: Biographische Studien über Radikalismus, Weltanschauung, und Vernunft 1903–1989*. Bonn, 1996.

Herf, Jeffrey. *Divided Memory: The Nazi Past in the Two Germanys*. Cambridge, Mass., 1997.

Hetzer, Gerhard. "Ernste Bibelforscher in Augsburg." In *Bayern in der NS Zeit*, 6 vols., edited by Martin Broszat et al., 4:621–43 (Munich, 1977–83).

Heugel, Klaus. "Danach: Die Stadt Köln und die jüdische Bevölkerung seit 1945." In *"Zuhause in Köln": Jüdisches Leben 1945 bis heute*, edited by Günther B. Ginzel and Sonja Güntner, 198–203 (Cologne, 1998).

Hilberg, Raul. *The Destruction of the European Jews*. New York, 1961.

———. *Perpetrators, Victims, Bystanders: The Jewish Catastrophe 1933–1945*. New York, 1992.

Hinze, Sibylle. "Vom Schutzmann zum Schreibtischmörder: Die Staatspolizeistelle Potsdam." In *Die Gestapo: Mythos und Realität*, edited by Gerhard Paul and Klaus-Michael Mallmann, 118–32 (Darmstadt, 1995).

Historisches Archiv der Stadt Köln. *Widerstand und Verfolgung in Köln 1933–1945*. Cologne, 1974.

Hitler, Adolf. *Mein Kampf.* Translated by Ralph Mannheim. 1927; Boston, 1971.

Hockerts, H. G. *Die Sittlichkeitsprozesse gegen katholische Ordensangehörige und Priester 1936–1937.* Mainz, 1971.

Hoegner, Wilhelm. *Der Schwierige Aussenseiter.* Munich, 1963.

Hoffmann, Peter. *The History of the German Resistance.* Cambridge, Mass., 1977.

———. *Stauffenberg: A Family History, 1905–1944.* London, 1995.

Homze, Edward L. *Foreign Labor in Nazi Germany.* Princeton, N.J., 1967.

Huiskes, Manfred. "Die Staatspolizeistelle Köln im EL-DE-Haus." In *Die Wandinschriften des Kölner Gestapo-Gefängnisses im EL-DE-Haus 1943–1945.* Cologne, 1983.

Hürten, Heinz. *Deutsche Katholiken 1918–1945.* Paderborn, 1992.

Hüttenberger, Peter. "Heimtückefälle vor dem Sondergericht München 1933–1939." In *Bayern in der NS Zeit,* 6 vols., edited by Martin Broszat et al., 4:435–526 (Munich, 1977–83).

Idel, Wolfgang. *Die Sondergerichte in politischen Strafsachen.* Schramberg, 1935.

Jellonnek, Burkhard. "Staatspolizeiliche Fahndungs-und Ermittlungsmethoden gegen Homosexuelle: Regionale Differenzen und Gemeinsamkeiten." In *Die Gestapo: Mythos und Realität,* edited by Gerhard Paul and Klaus-Michael Mallmann, 343–56 (Darmstadt, 1995).

Johnson, Eric A. "German Women and Nazi Justice: Their Role in the Process from Denunciation to Death." *Historical Social Research/Historische Sozialforschung* 20 (1995): 33–69.

———. *Urbanization and Crime: Germany 1871–1914.* New York, 1995.

———. "Gender, Race, and the Gestapo." *Historical Social Research/Historische Sozialforschung* 22 (1997): 240–53.

Johnson, Eric A., and Karl-Heinz Reuband. "Die populäre Einschätzung der Gestapo: Wie allgegenwärtig war sie wirklich?" In *Die Gestapo: Mythos und Realität,* edited by Gerhard Paul and Klaus-Michael Mallmann, 417–36 (Darmstadt, 1995).

Jung, Werner. "Von der Trümmerlandschaft zur modernen Metropole: Köln 1945 bis 1998." In *Zuhause in Köln": Jüdisches Leben 1945 bis heute,* edited by Günther B. Ginzel and Sonja Güntner, 17–39 (Cologne, 1998).

Kahler, Erich. "The Jews and the Germans." In *Studies of the Leo Baeck Institute,* edited by Max Kreutzberger, 17–43 (New York, 1967).

Kaplan, Marion A. *Between Dignity and Despair: Jewish Life in the Third Reich.* New York, 1998.

Kater, Michael H. "Die Ernsten Bibelforscher im Dritten Reich." *Vierteljahrshefte für Zeitgeschichte* 17 (1969): 181–218.

———. *The Nazi Party: A Social Profile of Members and Leaders, 1919–1945.* Oxford, 1983.

———. *Different Drummers: Jazz in the Culture of Nazi Germany.* New York, 1992.

Katz, Jacob. *From Prejudice to Destruction: Anti-Semitism, 1700–1933.* Cambridge, Mass., 1980.

Kempner, Benedicta Maria. *Priester vor Hitlers Tribunalen.* Munich, 1966.

Kempowski, Walter. *Haben Sie davon gewusst?: Deutsche Antworten.* Hamburg, 1979.

Kenkmann, Alfons. "Navajos, Kittelbach- und Edelweisspiraten: Jugendliche Dissidenten im 'Dritten Reich.' " In *Piraten, Swings, und Junge Garde: Jugendwiderstand im Nationalsozialismus,* edited by Wilfried Breyvogel, 138–58 (Bonn, 1991).

Kershaw, Ian. *Popular Opinion and Political Dissent in the Third Reich: Bavaria 1933–1945.* Oxford, 1983.

———. *The Hitler Myth: Image and Reality in the Third Reich.* Oxford, 1987.

King, Christine Elizabeth. *The Nazi State and the New Religions: Five Case Studies in Non-Conformity.* New York, 1982.

Klee, Ernst. *"Die SA Jesu Christi": Die Kirche im Banne Hitlers.* Frankfurt am Main, 1989.

Klein, Adolf. "Hundert Jahre Akten—Hundert Jahre Fakten: Das Landgericht Köln ab 1879." In *Justitia Coloniensis: Amtsgericht und Landgericht Köln erzählen ihre Geschichte(n),* edited by Adolf Klein and Günter Rennen, (Cologne, 1981).

———. *Köln im Dritten Reich: Stadtgeschichte der Jahre 1933–1945.* Cologne, 1983.

Klemperer, Victor. *Ich will Zeugnis ablegen bis zum letzten: Tagebücher,* vol. 1, *1933–1941,* vol. 2, *1942–1945.* Berlin, 1995.

———. *I Will Bear Witness: A Diary of the Nazi Years, 1933–1941.* Translated by Martin Chalmers. New York, 1998.

Klönne, Arno. *Jugend im Dritten Reich: Die Hitler Jugend und ihre Gegner.* Düsseldorf, 1982.

———. "Jugendprotest und Jugendopposition: Von der HJ-Erziehung zum

Cliquenwesen der Kriegszeit." In *Bayern in der NS Zeit*, 6 vols., edited by Martin Broszat et al., 4:527–620 (Munich, 1977–83).

——. "Bündische Jugend, Nationalsozialismus, und NS-Staat." In *Der Widerstand gegen den Nationalsozialismus: Die deutsche Gesellschaft und der Widerstand gegen Hitler*, edited by Jürgen Schmädeke and Peter Steinbach, 182–89 (Munich, 1985).

Koch, H. W. *In the Name of the Volk: Political Justice in Hitler's Germany*. London, 1989.

Kogon, Eugon. *Der SS-Staat: Das System der deutschen Konzentrationslager*. Munich, 1946.

Koonz, Claudia. *Mothers in the Fatherland: Women, the Family, and Nazi Politics*. London, 1988.

Koselleck, Reinhart. "Vielerlei Abschied vom Krieg." In *Vom Vergessen vom Gedenken: Erinnerungen und Erwartungen in Europa zum 8. Mai 1945*, edited by Brigitte Sausay, Heinz Ludwig Arnold, and Rudolf von Thadden, 19–25 (Göttingen, 1999).

——. "Recollections of the Third Reich: An Interview with Reinhart Koselleck." *NIAS Newsletter* 22 (1999): 5–16.

Krakowski, Schmuel. "The Satellite Camps." In *Anatomy of the Auschwitz Death Camp*, edited by Yisrael Gutman and Michael Berenbaum, 50–60 (Bloomington, Ind., 1994).

Krausnick, Helmut. *Hitlers Einsatzgruppen: Die Truppe des Weltanschauungskrieges 1938–1942*. 1981; Frankfurt am Main, 1998.

Krüger, Wolfgang. *Entnazifiziert!: Zur Praxis der politischen Säuberung in Nordrhein-Westfalen*. Wuppertal, 1982.

Kwiet, Konrad. "Nach dem Pogrom: Stufen der Ausgrenzung." In *Die Juden in Deutschland 1933–1945: Leben unter nationalsozialistischer Herrschaft*, edited by Wolfgang Benz, 545–659 (Munich, 1988).

Kwiet, Konrad, and Helmut Eschwege. *Selbstbehauptung und Widerstand: Deutsche Juden im Kampf um Existenz und Menschenwürde 1933–1945*. Hamburg, 1984.

Lapomard, Vincent A. *The Jesuits and the Third Reich*. Lewiston, N.Y., 1989.

Laqueur, Walter. *The Terrible Secret: An Investigation into the Suppression of Information About Hitler's "Final Solution."* London, 1980.

Laska, Vera, ed. *Women in the Resistance and in the Holocaust: The Voices of Eyewitnesses*. Westport, Conn., 1983.

Lassen, Hans-Christen. "Der Kampf gegen Homosexualität, Abtreibung, und

'Rassenschande': Sexualdelikte vor Gericht in Hamburg 1933–1939." In
*"Für Führer, Volk und Vaterland ": Hamburger Justiz im Nationalsozialis-
mus,* edited by Klaus Bästlein, Helge Grabitz, and Wolfgang Scheffler, 216–
89 (Hamburg, 1992).

Latzel, Klaus. *Deutsche Soldaten–nationalsozialistischer Krieg?: Kriegser-
lebnis-Kriegserfahrung 1939–1945.* Paderborn, 1998.

Lauf, Edmund. *Der Volksgerichtshof und sein Beobachter: Bedingungen und
Funktionen der Gerichtsberichterstattung im Nationalsozialismus.* Opladen, 1994.

Lautmann, Rüdiger, ed. *Seminar: Gesellschaft und Homosexualität.* Frankfurt, 1977.

Levine, Alan J. *The Strategic Bombing of Germany, 1940–1945.* Westport,
Conn., 1992.

Lewy, Guenter. *The Catholic Church and Nazi Germany.* New York, 1964.

Lichtenstein, Heiner. *Himmlers grüne Helfer: Die Schutz- und Ordnungspolizei im "Dritten Reich."* Cologne, 1990.

Lifton, Robert J. *The Nazi Doctors: Medical Killing and the Psychology of
Genocide.* New York, 1986.

Lipstadt, Deborah E. *Beyond Belief: The American Press and the Coming of the
Holocaust 1933–1945.* New York, 1986.

Loewy, Hanno, ed. *Holocaust: Die Grenzen des Verstehens.* Hamburg, 1992.

Lucassen, Leo. *Die Geschichte eines polizeilichen Ordnungsbegriffes in
Deutschland 1700–1945.* Cologne, 1996.

Lukacs, John. *The Hitler of History.* New York, 1997.

Maier, Charles S. *The Unmasterable Past: History, Holocaust, and German
National Identity.* Cambridge, Mass., 1988.

Mallmann, Klaus-Michael. "Die V-Leute der Gestapo: Umrisse einer kollektiven Biographie." In *Die Gestapo: Mythos und Realität,* edited by Gerhard
Paul and Klaus-Michael Mallmann, 268–87 (Darmstadt, 1995).

Mallmann, Klaus-Michael, and Gerhard Paul. *Herrschaft und Alltag: Eine Industrierevier im Dritten Reich.* Bonn, 1991.

———. "Allwissend, allmächtig, allgegenwärtig?: Gestapo, Gesellschaft, und
Widerstand." *Zeitschrift für Geschichtswissenschaft* 41 (1993): 984–99.

———, eds. *Die Gestapo: Mythos und Realität.* Darmstadt, 1995.

Mann, Reinhard. *Protest und Kontrolle im Dritten Reich: Nationalsozialistische Herrschaft im Alltag einer rheinischen Grossstadt.* Frankfurt am
Main, 1987.

Marrus, Michael R. *The Holocaust in History*. London, 1987.

Marssolek, Inge. *Die Denunziantin: Helene Schwärzel 1944–1947*. Bremen, 1993.

Marssolek, Inge, and Rene Ott. *Bremen im Dritten Reich: Anpassung-Widerstand-Verfolgung*. Bremen, 1986.

Martinsdorf, Eva Maria. "Von den Schwierigkeiten, die Gegenwart von ihrer Vergangenheit zu 'säubern': Entnazifizierung in Köln." In *Versteckte Vergangenheit: Über den Umgang mit der NS-Zeit in Köln*, edited by Horst Matzerath, Harald Buhlan, and Barbara Becker-Jákli, 125–62 (Cologne, 1994).

Marxen, Klaus. *Das Volk und sein Gerichtshof: Eine Studie zum nationalsozialistischen Volksgerichtshof*. Frankfurt am Main, 1994.

Matzerath, Horst. "Der Weg der Kölner Juden in den Holocaust: Versuch einer Rekonstruktion." In *Die jüdischen Opfer des Nationalsozialismus aus Köln: Gedenkbuch*, 530–53 (Cologne, 1995).

Matzerath, Horst, et al., eds. *Versteckte Vergangenheit: Über den Umgang mit der NS-Zeit in Köln*. Cologne, 1994.

Mayer, Milton. *They Thought They Were Free: The Germans 1933–1945*. Chicago, 1955.

McKale, Donald M. *The Nazi Party Courts: Hitler's Management of Conflict in His Movement, 1921–1945*. Lawrence, Kan., 1974.

Meershoek, Guus. *Dienaren van het gezag: De Amsterdamse politie tijdens de bezetting*. Amsterdam, 1999.

Meier, Kurt. *Kreuz und Hakenkreuz: Die evangelische Kirche im Dritten Reich*. Munich, 1992.

Merkl, Peter. *The Making of a Stormtrooper*. Princeton, N.J., 1980.

Messerschmidt, Manfred, and Fritz Wüllner. *Die Wehrmachtsjustiz im Dienste des Nationalsozialismus*. Baden-Baden, 1987.

Mommsen, Hans. "Was haben die Deutschen vom Völkermord an den Juden gewusst?" In *Der Judenpogrom 1938: Von der "Reichkristallnacht" zum Völkermord*, edited by Walter H. Pehle, 176–200 (Frankfurt am Main, 1988).

———. "The Reaction of the German Population to the Anti-Jewish Persecution and the Holocaust." In *Lessons and Legacies: The Meaning of the Holocaust in a Changing World*, edited by Peter Hayes, 141–54 (Evanston, Ill., 1990).

Moore, Bob. *Victims and Survivors: The Nazi Persecution of the Jews in the Netherlands 1940–1945*. London, 1997.

Mosse, George L. *Germans and Jews: The Right, the Left, and the Search for a "Third Force" in Pre-Nazi Germany.* New York, 1970.

———. *Nationalism and Sexuality: Respectability and Abnormal Sexuality in Modern Europe.* New York, 1985.

Mühlen, Patrik von zur. "Die SPD zwischen Anpassung und Widerstand." In *Der Widerstand gegen den Nationalsozialismus: Die deutsche Gesellschaft und der Widerstand gegen Hitler,* edited by Jürgen Schmädeke and Peter Steinbach, 86–98 (Munich, 1985).

Müller, Hans Dieter. *Facsimile Querschnitt durch Das Reich.* Munich, 1964.

Müller, Ingo. *Hitler's Justice: The Courts of the Third Reich.* Translated by Deborah Lucas Schneider. 1987; Cambridge, Mass., 1991.

Müller, Rolf-Dieter, and Gerd R. Ueberschär. *Kriegsende 1945: Die Zerstörung des Deutschen Reiches.* Frankfurt am Main, 1994.

Naumann, Uwe, ed. *Bruno Adler: Frau Wernicke: Kommentare einer "Volksjenossin."* Mannheim, 1990.

Niethammer, Lutz. *Entnazifizierung in Bayern: Säuberung und Rehabilitierung unter amerikanischer Besatzung.* Frankfurt am Main, 1972.

———. *Die Mitläuferfabrik: Die Entnazifizierung am Beispiel Bayerns.* Berlin, 1982.

———. *"Die Jahre weiss man nicht, wo man die heute hinsetzen soll": Faschismus-Erfahrungen im Ruhrgebiet.* Berlin, 1983.

———. "Juden und Russen im Gedächtnis der Deutschen." In *Der historischer Ort des Nationalsozialismus,* edited by Walter H. Pehle, 114–34 (Frankfurt am Main, 1990).

Noakes, J., and G. Pridham, eds. *Nazism 1919–1945: A Documentary Reader.* Vol. 1, *The Rise to Power 1919–1934.* Exeter, U.K., 1983.

———, eds. *Nazism 1919–1945: A Documentary Reader.* Vol. 2, *State, Economy, and Society 1933–1939.* Exeter, U.K., 1984.

Norden, Günter van. "Zwischen Kooperation und Teilwiderstand: Die Rolle der Kirchen und Konfessionen—Ein Überblick über Forschungspositionen." In *Der Widerstand gegen den Nationalsozialismus: Die deutsche Gesellschaft und der Widerstand gegen Hitler,* edited by Jürgen Schmädeke and Peter Steinbach, 227–39 (Munich, 1985).

Oosterhuis, Harry. "Medicine, Male Bonding, and Homosexuality in Nazi Germany." *Journal of Contemporary History* 32 (1997): 187–205.

Padover, Saul. *Experiment in Germany: The Story of an American Intelligence Officer.* New York, 1946.

Paucker, Arnold. *Standhalten und Widerstehen: Der Widerstand deutscher und österreichischer Juden gegen die Nationalsozialistische Diktatur.* Essen, 1995.

Paul, Gerhard. "Kontinuität und Radikalisierung: Die Staatspolizeistelle Würzburg." In *Die Gestapo: Mythos und Realität,* edited by Gerhard Paul and Klaus-Michael Mallmann, 161–99 (Darmstadt, 1995).

———. "Ganz normale Akademiker: Eine Fallstudie zur regionalen staatspolizeilichen Funktionselite." In *Die Gestapo: Mythos und Realität,* edited by Gerhard Paul and Klaus-Michael Mallmann, 236–54 (Darmstadt, 1995).

———. "Zwischen Selbstmord, Illegalität, und neuer Karriere: Ehemalige Gestapo-Bedienstete im Nachkriegsdeutschland." In *Die Gestapo: Mythos und Realität,* edited by Gerhard Paul and Klaus-Michael Mallmann, 529–55 (Darmstadt, 1995).

———. *Die Gestapo in Schleswig-Holstein.* Hamburg, 1996.

Paul, Gerhard, and Klaus-Michael Mallmann. *Milieus und Widerstand: Eine Verhaltensgeschichte der Gesellschaft im Nationalsozialismus.* Bonn, 1995.

———, eds. *Die Gestapo: Mythos und Realität.* Darmstadt, 1995.

Paul, Gerhard, and Alexander Primavesi. "Die Verfolgung der 'Fremdvölkischen': Das Beispiel der Staatspolizeistelle Dortmund." In *Die Gestapo: Mythos und Realität,* edited by Gerhard Paul and Klaus-Michael Mallmann, 388–401 (Darmstadt, 1995).

Pehle, Walter H., ed. *Der Judenpogrom 1938: Von der "Reichskristallnacht" zum Völkermord.* Frankfurt am Main, 1988.

———, ed. *Der historische Ort des Nationalsozialismus.* Frankfurt am Main, 1990.

Persico, Joseph. *Nuremberg: Infamy on Trial.* New York, 1994.

Peterson, Edward N. *The American Occupation of Germany: Retreat to Victory.* Detroit, 1978.

Petry, Christian. *Studenten aufs Schafott: Die Weisse Rose und ihr Scheitern.* Munich, 1968.

Peukert, Detlev J. K. *Ruhrarbeiter gegen den Faschismus: Dokumentation über den Widerstand im Ruhrgebiet 1933–1945.* Frankfurt am Main, 1976.

———. *Die Edelweisspiraten: Protestbewegungen jugendlicher Arbeiter im Dritten Reich: Eine Dokumentation.* Cologne, 1980.

———. *Die KPD im Widerstand: Verfolgung und Untergrundarbeit an Rhein und Ruhr 1933–1945.* Wuppertal, 1980.

——. *Inside Nazi Germany: Conformity, Opposition, and Racism in Everyday Life.* Translated by Richard Deveson. London, 1987.

——. "Youth in the Third Reich." In *Life in the Third Reich,* edited by Richard Bessel, 25–40 (Oxford, 1987).

Plant, Richard. *The Pink Triangle: The Nazi War Against Homosexuals.* New York, 1986.

Podhoretz, Norman. "Hannah Arendt on Eichmann: A Study in the Perversity of Brilliance." *Commentary* (September 1963): 201–8.

Pohl, Rainer. "'Schräge Vögel, mausert euch!' Von Renitenz, Übermut, und Verfolgung: Hamburger Swings und Pariser Zazous." In *Piraten, Swings, und Junge Garde: Jugendwiderstand im Nationalsozialismus,* edited by Wilfried Breyvogel, 241–70 (Bonn, 1991).

Proctor, Richard H. *Racial Hygiene: Medicine under the Nazis.* Cambridge, Mass., 1988.

Pütter, Conrad. *Rundfunk gegen das "Dritte Reich": Ein Handbuch.* Munich, 1986.

Rauschning, Hermann. *The Voices of Destruction.* New York, 1940.

Read, Anthony, and David Fischer. *Kristallnacht: The Nazi Night of Terror.* New York, 1989.

Reifner, Udo, and B. R. Sonnen, eds. *Strafjustiz und Polizei im Dritten Reich.* Frankfurt am Main, 1984.

Reinke, Herbert, ed. *"Nur für die Sicherheit da?": Zur Geschichte der Polizei im 19. und 20. Jahrhundert.* Frankfurt am Main, 1993.

Reitlinger, Gerald. *The SS: Alibi of a Nation 1922–1945.* (1956; Englewood Cliffs, N.J., 1981.

Remak, Joachim, ed. *The Nazi Years: A Documentary History.* Englewood Cliffs, N.J., 1969.

Reuband, Karl-Heinz. "Survey Methods as a Monitoring Instrument." In *Illegal Drug Use: Research Methods for Hidden Populations,* edited by H. S. L. Garritsen et al., 22–27 (Utrecht, 1993).

Robinsohn, Hans. *Justiz als politische Verfolgung: Die Rechtsprechung in "Rassenschandefällen" beim Landgericht Hamburg 1936–1943.* Stuttgart, 1977.

Rückerl, Adalbert. *Die Strafverfolgung von NS-Verbrechen 1945–1978: Eine Dokumentation.* Heidelberg, 1979.

Rückerl, Adalbert. *The Investigation of Nazi Crimes, 1945–1978: A Documentation.* Translated by Derek Rutter. Hamden, Conn., 1980.

———. *NS-Verbrechen vor Gericht: Versuch einer Vergangenheitsbewältigung.* Heidelberg, 1982.

Rumpf, Hans. *The Bombing of Germany.* Translated by Edward Fitzgerald. New York, 1962.

Rusinek, Bernd-A. *Gesellschaft in der Katastrophe: Terror, Illegalität, Widerstand—Köln 1944–1945.* Essen, 1989.

———. " 'Wat denkste, wat mir objerümt han': Massenmord und Spurenbeseitigung am Beispiel der Staatspolizeistelle Köln 1944–1945." In *Die Gestapo: Mythos und Realität,* edited by Gerhard Paul and Klaus-Michael Mallmann, 402–16 (Darmstadt, 1995).

Salomon, Ernst von. *Der Fragebogen.* Hamburg, 1951.

Schellenberger, Barbara. *Katholische Jugend und Drittes Reich: Eine Geschichte des katholischen Jungmännerverbandes 1933–1939 unter besonderer Berücksichtigung der Rheinprovinz.* Mainz, 1975.

———. "Katholischer Jugendwiderstand." In *Der Widerstand gegen den Nationalsozialismus: Die deutsche Gesellschaft und der Widerstand gegen Hitler,* edited by Jürgen Schmädeke and Peter Steinbach, 314–26 (Munich, 1985).

Schmädeke, Jürgen, and Peter Steinbach, eds. *Der Widerstand gegen den Nationalsozialismus: Die deutsche Gesellschaft und der Widerstand gegen Hitler.* Munich, 1985.

Schmid, Hans-Dieter. " 'Anständige Beamte' und 'üble Schläger': Die Staatspolizeistelle Hannover." In *Die Gestapo: Mythos und Realität,* edited by Gerhard Paul and Klaus-Michael Mallmann, 133–60 (Darmstadt, 1995).

———. *Gestapo Leipzig: Politische Abteilung des Polizeipräsidiums und Staatspolizeistelle Leipzig 1933–1945.* Leipzig, 1997.

Schmidt, Bernhard, and Fritz Burger. *Tatort Moers: Widerstand und Nationalsozialismus im südlichen Altkreis Moers.* Moers, 1995.

Schnabel, Raimund. *Die Frommen in der Hölle: Geistliche in Dachau.* Frankfurt am Main, 1966.

Schneider, Michael, and Winfried Süss. *Keine Volksgenossen.* Munich, 1993.

Scholl, Inge. *Die Weisse Rose.* Frankfurt, 1982.

Schoppmann, Claudia. *Nationalsozialistische Sexualpolitik und weibliche Homosexualität.* Pfaffenweiler, 1991.

———. "Zur Situation lesbischer Frauen in der NS-Zeit." In *Homosexualität in der NS-Zeit: Dokumente einer Diskriminierung und Verfolgung,* edited by Günter Grau, 35–42 (Frankfurt am Main, 1993).

Schubert, Helga. *Judasfrauen: Zehn Fallgeschichten weiblicher Denunziation im Dritten Reich.* Frankfurt am Main, 1990.

Schwering, Leo. *In den Klauen der Gestapo: Tagebuchaufzeichnungen der Jahre 1944–1945.* Cologne, 1988.

Seel, Pierre. *I, Pierre Seel, Deported Homosexual: A Memoir of Nazi Terror.* Translated by Joachim Neugroschel. New York, 1995.

Segev, Tom. *The Seventh Million: The Israelis and the Holocaust.* Translated by Haim Watzman. New York, 1993.

Shirer, William L. *The Rise and Fall of the Third Reich: A History of Nazi Germany.* New York, 1960.

Siedler Verlag. *Briefe an Goldhagen.* Berlin, 1998.

Smith, Howard K. *Last Train from Berlin.* New York, 1942.

Snyder, Louis L. *Hitler's Third Reich: A Documentary History.* Chicago, 1981.

——. *Encyclopedia of the Third Reich.* 1976; New York, 1989.

Speer, Albert. *Inside the Third Reich.* Translated by Richard and Clara Winston. New York, 1970.

Spieker, Josef. *Mein Kampf gegen Unrecht in Staat und Gesellschaft: Erinnerungern eines Kölner Jesuiten.* Cologne, 1971.

Spielvogel, Jackson. *Hitler and Nazi Germany: A History.* 2d ed. Englewood Cliffs, N.J., 1992.

Stadt Bergheim. *Kreisstadt Bergheim: Zahlen, Daten, Fakten.* Bergheim, n.d.

Stadt Krefeld. *Krefelder Juden in Amerika: Dokumentation eines Briefwechsels.* Vol. 1. Krefeld, 1984.

——. *Vor dem Besuch in Krefeld—29. Juni bis 7. Juli 1987: Briefe ehemaliger Krefelder Juden an Schüler des Gymnasiums am Moltkeplatz.* Vol. 2. Krefeld, n.d.

——. *Ehemalige Krefelder Juden berichten über ihre Erlebnisse in der sogenannten Reichskristallnacht.* Vol. 3. Krefeld, 1988.

——. *Ehemalige Krefelder Juden im Gespräch mit Krefelder Schülern 1987.* Vol. 4. Krefeld, 1988.

Statistisches Jahrbuch Deutscher Gemeinden. 1972.

Statistisches Jahrbuch für das Deutsche Reich. 1937.

Steinbach, Peter. *Nationalsozialistische Gewaltverbrechen: Die Diskussion in der deutschen Öffentlichkeit nach 1945.* Berlin, 1981.

Steinert, Marlis G. *Hitler's War and the Germans: Public Mood and Attitude During the Second World War.* Translated by T. E. J. de Witt. Athens, Ohio, 1977.

Stephenson, Jill. *Women in Nazi Society.* London, 1975.

———. *The Nazi Organisation of Women.* London, 1981.

Stern, Frank. "Wolfsschanze versus Auschwitz: Widerstand als deutsches Alibi?" *Zeitschrift für Geschichtswissenschaft* 42 (1994): 645–50.

Stolleis, Michael. *The Law Under the Swastika: Studies on Legal History in Nazi Germany.* Translated by Thomas Dunlap. Chicago, 1998.

Stoltzfus, Nathan. *Resistance of the Heart: Intermarriage and the Rosenstrasse Protest in Nazi Germany.* New York, 1996.

Strauss, Herbert A. "Jewish Emigration from Germany: Nazi Policies and Jewish Responses." *Yearbook of the Leo Baeck Institute* 25 and 26 (1980 and 1981).

Strohm, Christoph. "Der Widerstandskreis um Dietrich Bonhoeffer und Hans von Dohnanyi: Seine Voraussetzungen zur Zeit der Machtergreifung." In *Der Widerstand gegen den Nationalsozialismus: Die deutsche Gesellschaft und der Widerstand gegen Hitler,* edited by Jürgen Schmädeke and Peter Steinbach, 295–313 (Munich, 1985).

Syrkin, Marie. "Hannah Arendt: The Clothes of an Empress." *Dissent* 10 (1963): 345–52.

Szepansky, Gerda. *Frauen leisten Widerstand 1933–1945: Lebensgeschichten nach Interviews und Dokumenten.* Frankfurt am Main, 1983.

Tappe, Rudolf, and Manfred Tietz, eds. *Tatort Duisburg 1933–1945: Widerstand und Verfolgung im Nationalsozialismus.* 2 vols. Essen, 1989, 1993.

Tenfelde, Klaus. "Proletarische Provinz: Radikalisierung und Widerstand in Penzberg/Oberbayern 1900 bis 1945." In *Bayern in der NS Zeit,* 6 vols., edited by Martin Broszat et al., 4:1–382 (Munich, 1977–83).

Tent, James F. *Mission on the Rhine: Reeducation and Denazification in American-Occupied Germany.* Chicago, 1982.

Thalmann, Rita, and Emmanuel Feinermann. *Die Kristallnacht.* Frankfurt am Main, 1988.

Tuchel, Johannes, and Reinold Schattenfroh. *Zentrale des Terrors: Prinz-Albrecht-Strasse 8; Das Hauptquartier der Gestapo.* Berlin, 1987.

Ullrich, Volker. "'Wir haben nichts gewusst': Ein deutsches Trauma." *1999* 4 (1991): 11–46.

Vogt, Hans, and Herbert Brenne. *Krefeld im Luftkrieg 1939–1945.* Bonn, 1986.

Vollnhals, Clemens. *Evangelische Kirche und Entnazifizierung 1945–1949: Die Last der nationalsozialistischen Vergangenheit.* Munich, 1989.

Wagner, Heinz. "Die Polizei im Faschismus." In *Strafjustiz und Polizei im Drit-*

ten Reich, edited by Udo Reifner and B. R. Sonnen, (Frankfurt am Main, 1984).

Wasserstein, Bernard. *Britain and the Jews of Europe, 1939–1945.* Oxford, 1979.

Weber, Herman. "Die Ambivalenz der kommunistischen Widerstandsstrategie bis zur 'Brüsseler' Parteikonferenz." In *Der Widerstand gegen den Nationalsozialismus: Die deutsche Gesellschaft und der Widerstand gegen Hitler*, edited by Jürgen Schmädeke and Peter Steinbach, 73–85 (Munich, 1985).

Weber, Jürgen, and Peter Steinbach, eds. *Vergangenheitsbewältigung durch Strafverfahren?: NS-Prozesse in der Bundesrepublik Deutschland.* Munich, 1984.

Wechsberg, Joseph, ed. *The Murderers Among Us: The Simon Wiesenthal Memoirs.* New York, 1967.

Weinberg, Gerhard L. *A World at Arms: A Global History of World War II.* Cambridge, 1994.

Welch, David. *The Third Reich: Politics and Propaganda.* London, 1993.

Werle, Gerhard, and Thomas Wandres. *Auschwitz vor Gericht: Völkermord und bundesdeutsche Strafjustiz.* Munich, 1995.

Wetzel, Juliane. "Auswanderung aus Deutschland." In *Die Juden in Deutschland 1933–1945: Leben unter nationalsozialistischer Herrschaft*, edited by Wolfgang Benz, 413–98 (Munich, 1988).

Weyrauch, Walter Otto. *Gestapo V-Leute: Tatsachen und Theorie des Geheimdienstes.* Frankfurt am Main, 1989.

Wiener, Ralph. *Gefährliches Lachen: Schwarzer Humor im Dritten Reich.* Hamburg, 1994.

Wollenberg, Jörg, ed. *"Niemand war dabei und keiner hat's gewusst": Die deutsche Öffentlichkeit und die Judenverfolgung 1933–1945.* Munich, 1989.

Wüllenweber, Hans. *Sondergerichte im Dritten Reich: Vergessene Verbrechen der Justiz.* Frankfurt am Main, 1990.

Wyden, Peter. *Stella.* New York, 1992.

Wyman, David S. *The Abandonment of the Jews: America and the Holocaust, 1941–1945.* New York, 1984.

——. "Why Auschwitz Wasn't Bombed." In *Anatomy of the Auschwitz Death Camp*, edited by Yisrael Gutman and Michael Berenbaum, 569–87 (Bloomington, Ind., 1994).

Zillmer, Eric A., et al. *The Quest for the Nazi Personality: A Psychological Investigation of Nazi War Criminals.* Hillsdale, N.J., 1995.

Zimmermann, Michael. "Die Gestapo und die regionale Organisation der Judendeportation: Das Beispiel der Stapo-Leitstelle Düsseldorf." In *Die Gestapo: Mythos und Realität,* edited by Gerhard Paul and Klaus-Michael Mallmann, 357–72 (Darmstadt, 1995).

Zipfels, Friedrich. *Kirchenkampf in Deutschland.* Berlin, 1965.

INDEX